Kate McKean

Manual of social science

Being a condensation of the Principles of Social science

Kate McKean

Manual of social science
Being a condensation of the Principles of Social science

ISBN/EAN: 9783742802231

Manufactured in Europe, USA, Canada, Australia, Japa

Cover: Foto ©Suzi / pixelio.de

Manufactured and distributed by brebook publishing software
(www.brebook.com)

Kate McKean

Manual of social science

MANUAL

OF

SOCIAL SCIENCE;

BEING A CONDENSATION OF THE

"PRINCIPLES OF SOCIAL SCIENCE"

OF

H. C. CAREY, LL.D.,

BY

KATE McKEAN.

"The universe is a harmonious whole, the soul of which is God. Himself the perfection of harmony, He has impressed upon every soul, as His image, its own especial harmony. Numbers, figures, the stars, all nature indeed, harmonize with the mysteries of religion."—KEPLER.

PHILADELPHIA:
HENRY CAREY BAIRD,
INDUSTRIAL PUBLISHER, 406 WALNUT ST.
1871

[illegible], STEREOTYPER.
COLLINS, PRINTER.

PREFACE.

WHY do misery and crime exist? Why, when so large a portion of the earth is yet unoccupied, are human beings suffering for food, and crowded together in unwholesome dens, to the sacrifice of comfort, decency, and health? Why does one nation export food of which its own members are in need, while another sends its manufactures throughout the world although hundreds of thousands at home are scarcely clothed? Why are nations or individuals seen elbowing each other, so to speak, for room to live? Why are we called to witness everywhere an uneasy jealousy among communities, each watching with an unfriendly eye the expansion of the other—the strong ever encroaching on the rights of the weak? Why should the chief of European nations wage a ceaseless "warfare"* against the industry and prosperity of the world at large? In short, what is the cause of the measureless woe that exists in this fair world which its Creator pronounced to be "very good"?

Who that has ever reflected on human affairs has not asked himself these questions, has not at some period of his life sought to solve these problems? It is not, however, in this hitherto favored land that such subjects press with their full weight on heart and mind, adding a heavy item to individual cares and troubles: it is in Europe, especially in the British Isles,—that portion of the earth in which man's power over nature seems to be most complete,—that the immense mass of human suffering, the breadth and depth of which no imagination can measure, most bewilders the understanding while sickening the very soul.

Is there, then, no law regulating human affairs? When every portion of this vast universe is ordered by unerring

* See Parliamentary Report on the Iron Manufacture, page 199.

wisdom, are the concerns of God's highest work alone left to the blindest chance? Is there any principle, broad, simple, comprehensive, which can account for all this confusion, and reconcile these contradictions? If so, where is it to be found, to whom has it been revealed? While Physical Science has had its Newton, Physiology its Harvey, Philosophical Anatomy its Geoffroy Saint Hilaire, Palæontology its Cuvier, Chemistry its Lavoisier—has the Newton of Social Science not yet appeared?*

An answer to this question will be vainly sought in European literature. The greatest of English economists, Adam Smith, while setting forth much of valuable truth, failed to reach the fundamental principle, and erred on many important points. England, however, has since his day far retrograded both in theory and practice; and in the monstrous doctrines of the Ricardo-Malthusian school, which attribute human suffering to error of an all-wise Creator, has initiated that which she herself so fitly terms "the dismal science," the "philosophy of despair;" while her literature for well nigh half a century bears constant witness to the existence of a need which it cannot supply, each writer testifying of evils the cause and remedy of which none appear to see. Nor have the writers of the continent been more successful, none of them having attained to any really fundamental truth.

The editor of the following volume having, like so many others, long vainly sought light on this most interesting subject, first found it in the "Past, Present, and Future" of H. C. Carey. The principles there contained are enlarged, expanded, and corrected by the test of subsequent events in his "Principles of Social Science;" a work which, it is believed, no one capable of understanding it can carefully study without feeling that the Newton of Social Science has indeed appeared.

It may, however, be asked:—If this be so, if the truth on this highest of sciences has indeed been discovered, how is

* See *Histoire Naturelle Générale*, by Isidore Geoffroy Saint Hilaire, vol. I. p. 234.

it that mankind have not hailed it with a burst of enthusiastic welcome? that when it has been now for seven years before the world, it is as yet so little known? What, however, is the reception ever accorded to a great and fundamental truth? Is it not, that it is at first simply neglected because unrecognized? A few earnest minds, indeed, perceive and embrace it heartily; but the majority brush past it, so to speak, unconscious of its presence. When by degrees it makes way and gains for itself a hearing, it is met by a storm of opposition. Some minds simply dislike what is new; others hate to be disturbed in their ordinary modes of thought; the self-love of some is wounded by finding that they know nearly nothing of what has been their life-long study, and they are unwilling to submit to become learners where they have so long been teachers; while others again find their interests or their influence imperilled by the new idea. In the darker ages of the world's history, persecution, imprisonment, or death, was commonly the reward of the discoverer; now it is simply opposition or misrepresentation, when not even calumny. When at length its opposers are unable to resist the evidence presented of its truth, they next turn round and say:—Well, granted that it is so, this is not new; it is to be found in the pages of such or such an author, ancient or modern. And true it is, that those who now in the full light of a truth look back to earlier ages to search for it, will often detect its first faint glimmerings in the works of those who were themselves utterly unconscious of the scope of the idea that had for a moment flashed across their minds, as quickly disappearing, and leaving the darkness as complete as it had been before.* At length, however, the time arrives when the new truth finds its place in the intelligence of the age: it is discussed in philosophical works, set forth in elementary treatises, and finally is adopted as the basis of public instruction. Does its discoverer at length meet with the honor due? Rarely even then. Few know the source whence the idea had been derived. Ask them and they will answer: "I never thought otherwise; I

* See *Life, Labors, and Scientific Doctrines of Etienne Geoffroy Saint Hilaire*, p. 280.

learned the theory at college; or I derived it from such or such a work."

It is under the impression that the most certain mode of spreading a knowledge of truths which lie at the root of all national progress, is by making them a part of the instruction of the young, that the editor has ventured, encouraged by the approbation of the author, to undertake a work more suited to a masculine than to a feminine intellect. This *Manual of Social Science*, it will be perceived, is little more than a selection from the great work above referred to the words of which have been as far as possible preserved, although the vast variety of facts and illustrations which give to it such a living interest have necessarily been sacrificed to brevity. The object in view will account for the free use of italics, which, though perhaps an offence against taste, every experienced teacher knows to be useful in awakening the attention and understanding of the youthful student.

In the years that have now elapsed since Mr. Carey's work was written, and since his first volume was given to the world, there have been many changes, and most especially in the facts presented by these United States, but the editor has deemed it best to give them here as they had been there presented, believing that the careful student may find in them the causes of those greater changes which are now in course of progress.

That this volume may be of some use in impressing upon the rising generation that the true principles of Social Science are in perfect accordance with the great precepts of Christianity, and may thus help to hasten the reign of universal peace and justice upon earth, is the earnest wish and prayer of the Editor,

KATE McKEAN.

CUMBERLAND, MD.,
August 20*th*, 1864.

NOTE.

Believing that many of her readers might be pleased to study the gradual development of the many new ideas presented in this work, the editor gives the following extract from Mr. Carey's preface :

"Of the principles here enunciated, some now [1857] make their appearance for the first time ; whereas, others were first published twenty years ago.* Since then, the latter have reappeared in another work, by a distinguished French economist,† which—its circulation having been extensive—has been read by thousands who have never seen the volumes in which the same ideas had previously been published. Finding here a repetition of what they had read elsewhere, and given without acknowledgment, those persons would, most naturally, be disposed to suspect the present author of having wrongfully appropriated the property of another ; when, in point of fact, he was himself the real owner. This would be an unpleasant state of things ; and, as the only mode by which it can be avoided, he deems it well to make, on this occasion, a brief statement of the order of discovery of the various new ideas contained in the following pages.

The theory of value, as now given, was first published in 1837. Being very simple, it was very comprehensive, embracing every commodity, or thing, in reference to which the idea of value could exist—whether land, labor, or their products. This was one step towards establishing the universality of natural laws, the value of land having been ascribed by all previous economists to causes widely different from those which gave value to its products.‡

* CAREY : *Principles of Political Economy.* Phila., 1837-1840.

† BASTIAT : *Harmonies Economiques.* Paris, 1850.

‡ "Carey, and after him Bastiat, have introduced a formula *à posteriori*, that I believe destined to be universally adopted ; and it is greatly to be regretted that the latter should have limited himself to occasional indications of it, instead of giving to it the importance so justly given by the former. In estimating the equilibrium between the cost to one's self and the utility to others, a thousand circumstances may intervene ; and it is desirable to know if there be not among men a law, a principle of universal application. Supply and demand, rarity, abundance, etc., are all insufficient, and liable to perpetual exceptions. Carey has remarked, and with great sagacity, that this law is the labor saved, *the cost of reproduction*—an idea that is, as I think, most felicitous. It appears to me that there cannot arise a case in which a man shall deter

Consequent upon this was the discovery of a general law of distribution, embracing all the products of labor, whether that applied to cultivation or conversion—to change of place or form. According to the theories then most generally received, the profit of one was always attended with loss to another, rents rising as labor became less productive, and profits advancing as wages retrograded—a doctrine that, if true, tended to the production of universal discord; and that, too, as the natural consequence of a great law instituted by the Deity for man's government.

Directly the reverse of this, however, was the law that was then published, and now is reproduced, proving, as it did, that both capitalist and laborer profited by every measure tending to render labor more, while losing by every one that tended to render it less, productive—and thus establishing a perfect harmony of interests.

Thoroughly persuaded of the truth of the laws then presented for consideration, the author felt not less certain that the really fundamental law remained yet to be discovered; and that, until it could be brought to light, many of the phenomena of society must continue unexplained. In what direction, however, to seek it, he could not tell. He had already satisfied himself that the theory presented for consideration by Mr. Ricardo—not being universally true—had no claim to be so considered; but it was not until ten years later that he was led to remark the fact, that it was universally false. The real law, as he then saw, was directly the reverse of that propounded by that gentleman, the work of cultivation having, and that invariably, been commenced on the poorer soils, and having passed to the richer ones as wealth had grown and population had increased. Here was the great fundamental truth, of which he before had thought, and the one, too, that was needed for the perfect demonstra-

mine to make an exchange, in which this law will not be found to apply. I will not give a quantity of labor or pains, unless offered in exchange an utility equivalent; and I will not regard it as equivalent, unless I see that it will come to me at less cost of labor than would be necessary for its reproduction. I regard this formula as most felicitous; because, while on one side it retains the idea of cost, which is constantly referred to in the mind, on the other it avoids the absurdity to which we are led by the theory, which pretends to see everywhere a value equivalent to the cost of production; and, finally, it shows more perfectly the essential justice that governs us in our exchanges."—FERRARA: *Biblioteca dell' Economista*, vol. xii. p. 117.

tion of the truth of those he previously had published. Here, too, was further proof of the universality of natural laws, the course of man, in reference to the earth itself, being thus found to have been the same that we see it to have been, in reference to all the instruments into which he fashions the several parts of the great machine. Always commencing with the poorest axes, he proceeds onward to those of steel: always commencing with the poorer soils, he proceeds onward to those richer ones which yield the largest return to labor, the increase of numbers being thus proved to be essential to increase in the supply of food. Here was a harmony of interests directly opposed to the discords taught by Mr. Malthus.

This great law was first announced now ten years since.* While engaged in its demonstration, the author found himself constantly impelled to the use of physical facts in illustration of social phenomena, and hence was led to remark the close affinity of physical and social laws. Reflecting upon this, he soon was brought to the expression of the belief, that closer examination would lead to the development of the great fact, that there existed but a single system of laws—those instituted for the government of matter in the form of clay and sand, proving to be the same by which that matter was governed when it took the form of man, or of communities of men.

In the work then published, the discoveries of modern science, proving the indestructibility of matter, were, for the first time, rendered available to social science—the difference between agriculture and all other of the pursuits of man having been there exhibited in the fact, that the farmer was always employed in *making* a machine, whose powers increased from year to year; whereas, the shipmaster and the wagoner were always *using* machines, whose powers as regularly diminished. The whole business of the former, as there was shown, consisted in making and improving soils, his powers of improvement growing with the growth of wealth and population. To fully develop the law of the perpetuity of matter in its bearing upon the law of population was, however, reserved for the author's friend, Mr. E. Peshine Smith, numerous extracts from whose excellent little Manual will be found in the present volume.

The great and really fundamental law of the science—the

* *The Past, the Present, and the Future.* Philad., 1848.

one required for the demonstration of the identity of physical and social laws—still however remained to be discovered; but it is now, as the author thinks, given in the second chapter of the present volume. In the third will be found the law developed by Mr. Smith. The fourth gives that of the occupation of the earth, as published ten years since—those of value and distribution, published ten years earlier, following, in chapters five and six. The order here required for their proper exhibition is thus, as the reader sees, precisely the inverse one of their discovery, thus proving the truth of the idea, that first principles are always last to be discovered.

CONTENTS.

CHAPTER I.—OF SCIENCE.

PAGE

§ 1. Bacon's distributions and partitions of the tree of knowledge. Roots and branches of the tree ... 23

§ 2. Method of discovery the same in all departments of knowledge. British economists recognize not the real man of society, but the artificial man of their own system. All sciences and their methods embraced in Sociology. Analysis leads to synthesis. Science one and indivisible. The economical relations of man require mathematical formulæ to render them into systematic truths. The monetary laws undetermined. Terms of the theorists insufficient and equivocal ... 27

§ 3. Social Science, the constituent and concrete of all others, waits upon their development for its own. Its impediments. The metaphysical method is replaced by the methodical study of man. Physical and social laws indivisible in the study of society, and all the phenomena of the subject constituting but a single science ... 33

CHAPTER II.—OF MAN—THE SUBJECT OF SOCIAL SCIENCE.

§ 1. Association essential to the existence of man. As the planets gravitate to each other, man tends towards his fellow-man. Local centres balance and distribute the masses in order and harmony. Centralizing and decentralizing analogous, and alike necessary, among planets and societies. Illustrative history of the nations. Freedom of association maintained by the balancing attractions. The welfare of the individual, and of the aggregate, dependent upon their freedom ... 37

§ 2. Individuality of man proportioned to the diversity of his endowments and activities. Free association develops individuality. Variety in unity, and peace in diversity. The balance of worlds, and of societies, maintained by counter-balance ... 40

§ 3. Responsibility of man measured by his individuality. Historic illustrations. Association, individuality, and responsibility, grow and decline together ... 43

§ 4. Man a being of growth and progress. Progress is motion requiring attraction, depending upon reciprocal action, and implying individuality and association. Progress is in the ratio of these conditions. The laws of being the same in matter, man, and communities. Definition of Social Science ... 46

CHAPTER III.—OF INCREASE IN THE NUMBERS OF MANKIND.

§ 1. Quantity of matter not susceptible of increase. Susceptible of being changed in place and in form. Constantly taking new and higher forms—passing from the inorganic to the organic, and ending in man. Man's power limited to the direction of the natural forces. Law of endless circulation ... 48

§ 2. Preparation of the earth for the reception of man ... 50

§ 3. Man, in common with other animals, a consumer of food. His mission, on this earth, so to direct the natural forces, as to cause the soil to yield larger supplies of the commodities required for his use. Conditions upon which, alone, those supplies can be augmented ... 51

§ 4. Law of the relative increase in the numbers of Mankind, and in the supply of food ... 55

§ 5. Malthusian law of population. Teaches, that while the tendency of matter to assume the lowest forms, augments in an arithmetical ratio only, when it seeks to attain the highest form, that tendency is found existing in a geometrical one ... 66

CHAPTER IV.—OF THE OCCUPATION OF THE EARTH.

§ 1. Limited power of man, in the hunter and the shepherd state. Movements of the isolated settler. Commences always with the poorer soils. With increase of numbers he acquires increase of force, and is enabled to command the services of the richer

PAGE

soils—thence obtaining larger supplies of food. Gradual passage from being the slave of nature, towards becoming nature's master 56

§ 2. Mr. Ricardo's theory. Based upon the assumption of a fact that never has existed. The law, as proved by observation, directly the reverse of the theory by him propounded 63

§ 3. Course of settlement in the United States 66

§ 4. Course of settlement in Mexico, the West Indies, and South America 69

§ 5. Course of settlement in Great Britain 71

§ 6. Course of settlement in France, Belgium, and Holland 72

§ 7. Course of settlement in the Scandinavian Peninsula, Russia, Germany, Italy, the islands of the Mediterranean, Greece, and Egypt 73

§ 8. Course of settlement in India. Mr. Ricardo's theory that of depopulation and growing weakness; whereas, the real law is that of growing association, and augmenting power 74

CHAPTER V.—OF THE OCCUPATION OF THE EARTH—CONTINUED.

§ 1. Decrease of numbers compels the abandonment of the richer soils, and drives man back to the poorer ones. Causes of the decline of population. The supply of food diminishes in a ratio greater than that of man 77

§ 2. Real facts directly the reverse of those supposed by Mr. Ricardo. Progress of depopulation in Asia, Africa, and various parts of Europe 79

§ 3. Exhaustion of the soil, and progress of depopulation in the United States. With every step in that direction, man loses value, and nature acquires power at his expense 80

CHAPTER VI.—OF VALUE.

§ 1. Origin of the idea of Value. Measure of value. Limited by the cost of reproduction 83

§ 2. Idea of comparison inseparably connected with that of value. Commodities and things decline in value as the power of association and combination becomes more and more complete. Man grows in value as that of commodities declines 84

§ 3. Diminution in the proportions charged for the use of commodities and things, a necessary consequence of diminution in the cost of reproduction. Definition of value 86

§ 4. What are the things to which we attach the idea of value? Why are they valued? How much is their value? 87

§ 5. Erroneous view of Bastiat in relation to the idea of value. Its adoption as the foundation of a new politico-economical school 89

§ 6. Inconsistencies of Adam Smith and other economists, in reference to the cause of value. Phenomena in relation to value as exhibited in Great Britain, the United States, and other countries 90

§ 7. Law of distribution. Its universal application 94

§ 8. All values merely the measure of the resistance offered by nature to the possession of the things desired 94

§ 9. All matter susceptible of being rendered useful to man. That it may become so, he must have power for its direction. Utility the measure of the power of man over nature. Value, that of nature's power over man 96

CHAPTER VII.—OF WEALTH.

§ 1. In what does wealth consist? Commodities, or things, not wealth to those who have not the knowledge how to use them. First steps towards the acquisition of wealth always the most costly and the least productive. Definition of wealth 98

§ 2. Combination of action essential to the growth of wealth. The less the machinery of exchange required, the greater the power of accumulation. Wealth grows with the decline in the value of commodities, or things, required for man's uses and purposes 100

§ 3. Of positive and relative wealth. Man's progress in the ratio of the decline in the value of commodities, and the growth in his own 102

§ 4. Material character of the modern political economy. Holds that no values are to be regarded as wealth, but those which take a material form. All employments regarded as unproductive that do not result in the production of commodities or things 103

§ 5. Definition of wealth now given, in full accordance with its general signification of happiness, prosperity, and power. Grows with the growth of the power of man to associate with his fellow-man 104

PAGE

CHAPTER VIII.—OF THE FORMATION OF SOCIETY.

§ 1. In what society consists. The words society and commerce but different modes of expressing the same idea. That there may be commerce, there must be differences. Combinations in society subject to the law of definite proportions 106

§ 2. Every act of association an act of motion. Laws of motion those which govern the societary movement. All progress in the direct ratio of the substitution of continued for intermitted motion. No continuity of motion, and no power where there exist no differences. The more numerous the latter, the more rapid is the societary movement, and the greater the tendency towards acceleration. The more rapid the motion, the greater is the tendency towards diminution in the value of commodities, and increase in that of man 107

§ 3. Causes of disturbance tending to arrest of the societary motion. In the hunter state brute force constitutes man's only wealth. Trade commences with the traffic in bones, muscles, and blood—the trade in man 110

§ 4. Trade and commerce usually regarded as convertible terms, yet wholly different—the latter being the object sought to be accomplished, and the former only the instrument used for its accomplishment. Commerce grows with decline in the power of the trader. War and trade regard man as the instrument to be used; whereas, commerce regards trade as the instrument to be used by man 113

§ 5. Development of the pursuits of man the same as that of science—the passage being from the abstract to the more concrete. War and trade the most abstract, and therefore first developed 116

§ 6. Labors required for effecting changes of place, next in the order of development. Diminish in their proportions, as population and wealth increase 118

§ 7. Labors required for effecting mechanical and chemical changes of form. Require a higher degree of knowledge 118

§ 8. Vital changes in the forms of matter. Agriculture the great pursuit of man. Requires a large amount of knowledge, and therefore late in its development 119

§ 9. Commerce last in the order. Grows with the growth of the power of association 120

§ 10. The more perfect the power of association, the more does society tend to take a natural form, and the greater its tendency to durability 120

§ 11. Natural history of commerce. Subjects, order, succession, and co-ordination, of the classes of producers, transporters, and consumers of industrial products, classified and illustrated. The analogies of natural law universal 121

§ 12. Erroneous idea that societies tend, naturally, to pass through various forms, ending always in death. No reason why any society should fail to become more prosperous from age to age 123

§ 13. Theory of Mr. Ricardo leads to results directly the reverse of this—proving that man must become more and more the slave of nature, and of his fellow-men 124

CHAPTER IX.—OF APPROPRIATION.

§ 1. War and trade the characteristics of the early periods of society. Necessity for the services of the warrior and the trader diminishes with the growth of wealth and population 126

§ 2. Close connection between war and trade visible in every page of history. Their centralizing tendencies. Their power diminishes with the growth of commerce 127

§ 3. Social phenomena exhibited in the history of Attica 128

§ 4. Social phenomena exhibited in the history of Sparta 130

§ 5. Social phenomena exhibited in the history of Carthage 130

§ 6. Social phenomena exhibited in the history of Rome 131

§ 7. Social phenomena exhibited in the history of Venice, Pisa, and Genoa 131

§ 8. Social phenomena exhibited in the history of Holland 132

§ 9. Social phenomena exhibited in the history of Portugal 132

§ 10. Social phenomena exhibited in the history of Spain 132

§ 11. Social phenomena exhibited in the history of France 134

§ 12. The higher the organization of society, the greater is its vigor, and the better its prospect of life. The more numerous the differences, the higher is the organization, and the greater the commerce. Increase in the proportions of soldiers and traders leads towards centralization, and moral, physical, and political death 137

§ 13. Modern political economists teach the reverse of this. Errors resulting from using the same words, to express ideas that are wholly different 139

CHAPTER X.—OF CHANGES OF MATTER IN PLACE.

PAGE

§ 1. Difficulty, in the early period of society, of effecting changes in the place of matter. The necessity for so doing the chief obstacle to commerce. Decline in the proportion of the society required for effecting such changes. Accompanied by rapid growth of commerce, and corresponding growth of power to obtain better means of transportation........ 137

§ 2. The more perfect the commerce among men the greater the tendency towards removal of the remaining obstacles to association. Man's progress, in whatsoever direction, one of constant acceleration........ 138

§ 3. The first and heaviest tax to be paid by land and labor that of transportation. The farmer, near to market, always making a machine: the one distant therefrom always destroying one........ 139

§ 4. Manure, the commodity most needed by man, and the one that least bears transportation. The less the quantity of labor given to effecting changes of place, the greater that which may be given to production. Power to maintain commerce grows with this change of proportions........ 140

§ 5. Freedom grows with the growth of the power of association. That power grows with every diminution of the necessity for effecting changes of place........ 142

CHAPTER XI.—OF CHANGES OF MATTER IN PLACE—CONTINUED.

§ 1. Colonial Policies of Greece, Spain, and France. That of Britain the first in which we meet with prohibition of association among the colonists. Object of the prohibition, that of producing a necessity for effecting changes in the place of matter. The policy barbaric in its tendencies, and hence it is, that it has given rise to the theory of over-population........ 143

§ 2. British policy looks to the dispersion of man, and to increase in the proportion of society engaged in trade and transportation. Views of Adam Smith in opposition to this system........ 145

§ 3. British colonial system, as exhibited in the West India Islands........ 146

§ 4. Theory of over-population an effort to account for facts artificially produced, by aid of supposed natural laws........ 151

CHAPTER XII.—OF CHANGES OF MATTER IN PLACE—CONTINUED.

§ 1. Phenomena of society, as presented in the history of Portugal........ 152

§ 2. Phenomena of society, as presented in the history of the Turkish Empire........ 153

§ 3. Phenomena of society, as presented in the history of Ireland........ 156

§ 4. Real causes of the decay of Ireland........ 159

CHAPTER XIII.—OF CHANGES OF MATTER IN PLACE—CONTINUED.

§ 1. Local action, and local combination, conspicuous throughout the history of Hindostan. Their disappearance under the British rule........ 163

§ 2. Commerce sacrificed at the shrine of trade. Annihilation of Indian manufactures. Its ruinous effects........ 166

§ 3. Waste of capital, and destruction of the power of accumulation........ 167

§ 4. Diminution in the security of person and property correspondent with the extension of British rule, and with the growing centralization........ 168

§ 5. Trivial value of private rights in the land of India. India a paying country under its native princes. Its steady deterioration under the system which looks to increasing the necessity for the trader and transporter's services........ 169

§ 6. Review of the phenomena observed in the four great communities, above referred to. Differing in all other respects, they are alike in the fact, that they have been deprived of all power to diversify their employments, and have thus been forced to increase their dependence on the transporter and the trader........ 170

§ 7. Destructive effects of a growing necessity for the services of the trader. British policy looks solely to the increase of trade. Constant waste of capital in all the countries subject to the system........ 172

§ 8. Origin of the idea of over-population........ 173

CHAPTER XIV.—OF CHANGES OF MATTER IN FORM.

I.—*Of Chemical and Mechanical Changes.*

§ 1. For effecting changes in the forms of matter, a knowledge of the properties of

PAGE

matter is required. The work of conversion more concrete and special than that of transportation; and, therefore, later in its development. Instruments required for obtaining power to command the services of the natural forces. That power constitutes wealth. Conversion diminishes the labor required for transportation, while increasing that which may be given to production. Economy of human effort resulting from increased facility of conversion 176

§ 2. Societary motion tends to increase in a geometrical ratio, when permitted to proceed onward and undisturbed. Efforts to obtain a monopoly of the control of the natural forces required in the work of conversion 177

§ 3. Rude character of English commerce at the opening of the fourteenth century. Phenomena then presented precisely similar to those exhibited in the agricultural communities of the present day 178

§ 4. Change of policy under Edward III., and its effects. Adoption of the protective policy under Charles II. 179

§ 5. Effects of dependence upon the distant market, as shown in England in the early portion of the eighteenth century. Changes in the condition of the people consequent upon diminution of that dependence 181

§ 6. Monopolistic character of the British system. Nothing comparable with it, in its power for evil, ever before devised 182

§ 7. Power for evil when wrongly directed, exists, everywhere, in the ratio of that for good when guided in the right direction. British system looks to diminishing the tax of transportation for the British people, but increasing it for the other nations of the world 183

CHAPTER XV.—OF CHEMICAL AND MECHANICAL CHANGES IN THE FORM OF MATTER—CONTINUED.

§ 1. Errors of the British system obvious to Adam Smith. His caution to his countrymen in regard to the dangers necessarily incident to an exclusive dependence upon trade. His advice neglected, and hence the growth of pauperism and the origination of the theory of over-population 186

§ 2. Warlike and monopolistic character of the system 188

§ 3. By destroying among other people the power to sell their labor it destroys competition for the purchase of British labor. Teaching, that to enable capital to obtain a fair remuneration labor must be kept down, it tends to the production of slavery everywhere 189

§ 4. Approximation in the prices of raw materials and finished commodities the one essential characteristic of civilization. British system looks to the prevention of that approximation. Its tendency towards reduction of other communities to a state of barbarism 192

§ 5. Stoppage of the circulation a necessary consequence of the predominance of the British system. Disappearance of the small proprietors of England. Condition of the agricultural laborer 193

§ 6. The higher the organization the more perfect the power of self-government. That power diminishing among the people, and in the government, of England. Gulf dividing the higher and lower classes a constantly widening one 195

§ 7. Necessity for careful study of the system under which originated the theory of over-population. Inevitable tendency of the Ricardo-Malthusian doctrine that of making slavery the ultimate condition of the laborer. The system of the British school a retrograde one. Had its origin in a retrograde policy. Sees in man a mere instrument to be used by trade 197

CHAPTER XVI.—OF CHANGES OF MATTER IN FORM.

II.—*Of Vital Changes.*

§ 1. Irregularity in the demand for the powers of the early settler, and consequent waste of force. Economy of force resulting from increased ability to command the services of nature. The more perfect the power of association, the greater is the economy of human force 199

§ 2. The greater that economy the larger is the proportion of the labor employed that may be given to the development of the powers of the earth, and towards the creation of a scientific agriculture. Difficulty of combination among a purely agricultural people. Slavery of the laborer its necessary consequence 201

§ 3. The farmer near to market always making a machine; the one distant from it, always destroying one. With the one, labor and its products are daily more and more economized. With the other, the waste increases from day to day—man's progress, in whatever direction, being one of constant acceleration. Population makes the land come from the rich soils, while depopulation drives them back to the poor ones 201

PAGE

§ 4. Gambling character of the labors of the field where the market is distant. Diminution of risk resulting from the approximation of the consumer and the producer. The labor given to the work of conversion so much saved that would otherwise be wasted. Social phenomena observed in Ireland, India, and other countries, in which the consumer and producer are becoming more widely separated........ 202

§ 5. British system looks to the separation of the consumers and producers of the world—to the consequent destruction of agriculture—and to the elevation of trade at the expense of commerce. Hence it is, that it has given rise to the theory of over-population. Resistance thereto, by all the advancing communities of the world........ 204

CHAPTER XVII.—OF VITAL CHANGES IN THE FORMS OF MATTER—CONTINUED.

§ 1. Constant alliance between war and trade, as exhibited in the history of France. Poverty and dishonesty of its sovereigns........ 206

§ 2. Uniform tendency of its policy, prior to the days of Colbert, towards giving to trade the mastery over commerce. Tendency of his measures, that of increasing the rapidity of the societary movement........ 207

§ 3. Warlike policy of Louis XIV., and consequent necessity for abandonment of Colbert's system. Expulsion of the Huguenots, and annihilation of manufactures. Consequent unproductiveness of agriculture, and wretchedness of the people........ 208

§ 4. Colbert's policy maintained by Turgot. Abandoned by the negotiators of the Eden Treaty. Consequent annihilation of commerce. Poverty of the people leads to revolution. Colbert's system re-established. Extraordinary growth in the quantity and value of the products of French agriculture........ 209

§ 5. Changes in the distribution of labor's products resulting from increase in the power of association and combination, and in the quantity of commodities produced. Great increase in the value of land, resulting from diminution of the tax of transportation........ 211

§ 6. France a country of "contrasts"—its social system tending towards decentralization, while its political one tends, more and more, towards centralization. Colbert's policy in strict accordance with the doctrines of Adam Smith. Causes of poverty among the French people........ 216

CHAPTER XVIII.—OF VITAL CHANGES IN THE FORMS OF MATTER—CONTINUED.

§ 1. Wide difference between the French and British systems—the former looking to the approximation of the producer and consumer, and the latter to their separation... 219

§ 2. Consequences of this exhibit themselves in the great increase in the value of French land, as compared with that of the United Kingdom. Comparative growth of French and British agriculture........ 220

§ 3. French land being more divided, the small proprietor profits by increase in the prices of his products and his land. British tenants ruined by decline in the price of food........ 221

§ 4. French policy looks to making manufactures subsidiary to agriculture—facilitating the export of the products of the soil of France. Consequent increase of French commerce........ 222

§ 5. British policy makes agriculture subsidiary to manufactures. Trade, therefore, replaces the former British commerce........ 223

§ 6. British system taxes the agricultural communities of the world for its maintenance. That of France looks to their emancipation from taxation........ 224

§ 7. Solidarity of interests among the land-owners and laborers of the world at large. Deterioration of the condition of the farm-laborers of England. Centralization, over-population, and physical and mental decline travel hand in hand together........ 225

CHAPTER XIX.—OF VITAL CHANGES IN THE FORMS OF MATTER—CONTINUED.

§ 1. Agricultural distress throughout the world, consequent upon the return of peace in 1815. Cause thereof, to be found in the decline of manufactures, and in the separation of the consumer from the producer, in all the countries of the world, outside of Britain. General adoption of measures looking to counteraction of the British policy 229

§ 2. Few natural advantages of Denmark. Following in the lead of France, her policy looks, however, to the approximation of the consumer and the producer, and the relief of her farmers from the tax of transportation. Consequent prosperity of her people. Steady enlargement of the agricultural base of society. Constant increase in the power of association and combination—in the development of individuality—and in the power of further progress........ 231

§ 3. Decline of Spanish manufactures, diminution in the power of association, and

PAGE

decay of agriculture, consequent upon the expulsion of the Moors, and the acquisition of distant colonies. Loss of those colonies followed by the adoption of a system tending to promote the growth of commerce, and diminish the trader's power. Great increase in the value of land, and in the freedom of man.......... 229

CHAPTER XX.—OF VITAL CHANGES IN THE FORMS OF MATTER—CONTINUED.

§ 1. The German manufacturing system due to the revocation of the Edict of Nantes. Its gradual development down to the close of the war in 1815. Its decline, under the free-trade system which followed the peace. First Prussian tariff having for its object the diversification of the employments of the people.......... 236

§ 2. Gradual formation of the *Zoll-Verein*, or Customs Union. Great increase of foreign and domestic commerce consequent upon the adoption of measures tending to the emancipation of German land from the oppressive tax of transportation. Protection having cheapened finished commodities, Germany now exports them. Having raised the prices of raw materials, they are now imported.......... 239

§ 3. Growing division of the land, accompanied by an enlargement of the proportions borne by the agricultural class to the mass of which society is composed. Increased respect for the rights of property, consequent upon its more general diffusion among the people. Steady increase in the freedom of man, and in the strength of the State. 240

§ 4. Rude character of Russian agriculture half a century since. Growth of manufactures under the Continental system of Napoleon. Their disappearance under the free trade system. Re-adoption of the policy of Colbert, and its effects. Great increase in the quantity and value of agricultural products since the re-adoption of protection 241

§ 5. Increase in the competition for the purchase of the laborer's services and growing freedom of man.......... 243

§ 6. Obstacles standing in the way of the creation of a scientific agriculture. Communism and its effects.......... 244

§ 7. Growing individuality among the people, with corresponding growth of strength in the State.......... 245

§ 8. Sweden, like Russia, follows in the lead of France—maintaining the policy of Colbert, to the exclusion of that advocated by the economists of Britain. Its effects, as exhibited in bringing the consumer and producer into close proximity to each other. Comparative movement of the population, and of the supply of food.......... 246

§ 9. Division of land and increase of its value—resulting from its emancipation from the tax of transportation. Intellectual development, consequent upon the creation of local centres of activity.......... 247

§ 10. Social decentralization gradually correcting the errors of political centralization 249

§ 11. Differing in race, habits, manners, and religion, France and Germany, Spain and Denmark, Sweden and Russia, are agreed in nothing, except in the maintenance of a policy which looks to the promotion of association, the extension of commerce, and the emancipation of the land from the tax of transportation, in accordance with the ideas of Adam Smith. In all of them agriculture steadily advances, the land becomes more divided, and men become more free. Agreeing in nothing else, Portugal and Turkey, Ireland and India, unite in the maintenance of the policy advocated by the Ricardo-Malthusian school. In all of them agriculture declines, the land becomes consolidated, and the freedom of man has almost wholly passed away.......... 249

CHAPTER XXI.—OF VITAL CHANGES IN THE FORMS OF MATTER—CONTINUED.

§ 1. The American Union a country of contrasts—its social system tending towards centralization and slavery, while its political one is based upon the idea of decentralization and freedom. Natural tendency towards association and combination. Counteracted by a national policy tending towards dispersion.......... 252

§ 2. Early tendencies towards the adoption of the system which looked towards bringing together the producer and the consumer. Variable character of American policy since the close of the great European war.......... 256

§ 3. Policy of Colbert and Cromwell adopted in regard to shipping. Freedom of trade obtained by means of protective measures.......... 258

§ 4. American policy, generally, in full accordance with the doctrines of the British school. Consequent decline in the prices of the rude products of the farm. The man who must go to any market, must pay the tax of transportation. Heavy taxation of American farmers.......... 265

§ 5. Civilization grows in the direct ratio of the removal of obstacles standing between the producers and the consumers.......... 269

§ 6. The planter steadily giving more of his raw materials, and receiving less in exchange for them. Consequent exhaustion of the soil, and weakness of the State.......... 272

§ 7. Barbarism grows, everywhere, in the direct ratio of the export of the rude products of the soil, and consequent decline in the powers of the land.......... 274

CHAPTER XXII.—OF VITAL CHANGES IN THE FORMS OF MATTER—CONTINUED.

PAGE

§ 1. Wealth consists in the power to command the services of nature. Great increase of British wealth, resulting from the command of steam. Extraordinary amount of undeveloped power in the United States. Combination of action required for its development. National policy adverse to association and combination...... 266

§ 2. Waste of power resulting from the exhaustion of the soil, and consequent dispersion of men. Gradual consolidation of the land...... 267

§ 3. Trader's power steadily increases, while that of the farmer and planter as steadily declines. Consequent instability and irregularity of the societary movement. Trader profits by instability. Remarkable steadiness and regularity of the societary movement in all those periods in which the protective policy has been maintained.... 268

§ 4. Growing commerce enables the farmer to pass from the cultivation of the poorer to the richer soils. American policy restricts him to the former. Growing commerce tends to increase the power of labor over capital. American policy gives to capital greater power over labor. Growing commerce tends towards peace, and an economical administration of the affairs of government. American policy looks to extension of the trader's power at the expense of commerce. Increasing tendency towards war and waste. Growing commerce tends towards development of the latent powers of earth and man. American policy tends towards exhaustion of the one and enslavement of the other...... 269

§ 5. Speculative and gambling spirit engendered by a growing dependence upon the trader and transporter. Decline in the feeling of responsibility resulting from irregularity in the societary movement. Political and judicial corruption resulting from the growth of centralisation...... 271

§ 6. The higher the societary organisation the more rapid is the movement and the more instant the exhibition of the effects of a sound, or unsound, course of policy. Frequency and rapidity of changes in these United States...... 273

§ 7. Phenomena of declining civilisation now (1858) exhibited throughout the Union 275

§ 8. Human progress manifests itself in decline in the trader's power, and the attendant creation of a scientific agriculture. Opposite tendency of the American policy, and consequent decline of civilisation...... 276

§ 9. As agriculture becomes a science the land becomes more productive, and its products tend to rise in price. Consequent double profit to the farmer. As raw materials rise in price finished products fall, with further profit to the farmer. Man and land at one end of the scale of prices, and the more highly finished products at the other. The more rapid the societary circulation the greater is their tendency towards approximation. Agricultural improvement waits upon, and never precedes, industrial development...... 277

§ 10. As raw materials and finished products approximate in price, commerce grows, with constant increase in the steadiness of the societary movement. As they become more widely separated, trade acquires power, and the movement becomes, from year to year, more fitful and irregular. With the one, the real MAN becomes daily more developed. With the other, man becomes from day to day more thoroughly enslaved 279

CHAPTER XXIII.—OF THE INSTRUMENT OF ASSOCIATION.

I.—Of Money and Price.

§ 1. Difficulty, in the early periods of society, of making exchanges of service. General adoption of some certain commodity as a standard for the comparison of values. Recommendations, for this purpose, of the precious metals...... 280

§ 2. Facility of association and combination resulting from the use of money. Of all the machinery in use among men it is the one which most economises human effort. To the social body it is what atmospheric air is to the physical one—both supplying the machinery of circulation...... 281

§ 3. Definition of price. Prices of raw materials rise as we approach the centres of civilisation, while those of finished commodities as regularly decline. Double loss to the farmer who is distant from market, resulting from the low prices of the one, and the high prices of the other. The more highly finished a commodity, the greater is its tendency to fall of price...... 281

§ 4. Land and labor, the ultimate raw material of all commodities, rise in price, as men are more enabled to associate, and combine their efforts. Money the great instrument furnished by Providence for facilitating association and combination. The more perfect the supply the more, the greater is the tendency towards freedom...... 28[illegible]

CHAPTER XXIV.—OF THE INSTRUMENT OF ASSOCIATION—CONTINUED.

II.—Of the Supply of Money.

§ 1. Commodities tend to leave those places at which they have the least utility and

PAGE

greatest value, and to seek those at which their value is least and their utility greatest. The raw material of money flows, therefore, from those places at which food and wool are cheap and cloth and iron dear, towards those at which the former are dear and the latter cheap 289

§ 2. Flowing always towards those countries in which raw materials and finished commodities approximate most in price, the power to command their services is proof conclusive of advancing civilization 290

§ 3. Central and Northern Europe now becoming the great reservoirs of those metals. The more the rude products of their soil rise in price the greater must be the tendency of gold and silver in that direction. Raw materials tend to leave the countries in which employments are not diversified, and to go to those in which diversification most exists. The precious metals follow in their train 291

§ 4. Results of American experience. Excess export of those metals in all the free trade periods, and excess import of them in all the protected ones. Stoppage of the societary circulation in the former, and increased rapidity of movement in the latter. General tendency of American policy that of reducing the prices of rude products and increasing those of finished commodities 293

§ 5. Money, the indispensable instrument of society. Of all the instruments in use among men, the one that performs the largest amount of service in proportion to its cost. Economists assert that the only effect of an influx of the precious metals is that of rendering a country a good place to sell in, but a bad one in which to buy. That theory contradicted by all the facts of history, the direct tendency of such influx having, and that invariably, been that of reducing the prices of the finished commodities required by the producers of gold and silver. With every step in this direction agriculture tends to become a science, and the supply of food becomes more abundant 294

§ 6. The use of circulating notes tends to diminish the value of the precious metals, while increasing their utility. All commodities going to those places at which their utility is greatest, the use of such notes should promote the influx of those metals. Error of Great Britain and the United States in seeking to promote that influx by means of a war against circulating notes 298

CHAPTER XXV.—OF THE INSTRUMENT OF ASSOCIATION—CONTINUED.

III.—*Of the Charge for the Use of Money.*

§ 1. The charge for the use of land, houses, ships, and all other commodities and things, declines with every diminution in the cost of reproduction. So, too, with money, the rate of interest tending downwards, as man acquires greater power for the direction of the natural forces—that power constituting wealth. Interest, therefore, tends to fall in all those countries which follow in the lead of Colbert and of France, while rising in all those that follow in the lead of England. Phenomena presented for consideration by the United States 300

§ 2. Money is capital, but capital is not necessarily money. Interest paid for the use of money alone. Various modes in which compensation is made for the use of capital in its various forms. Error of distinguished economists in supposing that interest is paid for the use of capital in other forms than that of money. Tendency of interest to fall as the societary motion becomes more rapid 301

§ 3. The utility of money increases as its circulation becomes more rapid. Its value increases as its movement becomes retarded 302

§ 4. Increase in the supply of money tends to promote equality among men. Phenomena observed in India, France, and Holland 304

§ 5. Communities increase in strength as the rate of interest declines—raw products then rising, and finished commodities falling, and thus presenting evidence of advancing civilization. Teachings of economists generally in regard to money directly opposed to the lessons taught by the common sense of mankind. Gold and silver properly denominated the precious metals—being, of all commodities, those which most contribute to the development of individuality, and to the promotion of the power of association 306

CHAPTER XXVI.—OF THE INSTRUMENT OF ASSOCIATION—CONTINUED.

IV.—*Of the Trade in Money.*

§ 1. The precious metals the only commodities of universal acceptance, being the indispensable instruments of commerce 308

§ 2. Proportion borne by money to the amount of commerce increases in declining countries and decreases in advancing ones 310

PAGE

§ 3. Centralization, retarding the societary motion, increases that proportion. Decentralization diminishes it. Man then becomes more valuable and more free.... 310

§ 4. Money being the one indispensable instrument of society, governments have always assumed to control its management, as supplying the most productive of all the machinery of taxation. Falsification of money by European sovereigns.... 310

§ 5. Banks established with a view to the emancipation of the currency from the control of governments. Deposit banks of Italy, Germany, and Holland. Institution of banks of discount.... 312

§ 6. Enlargement of the operations of discount banks.... 313

§ 7. Banks of circulation commence with the Bank of England.... 314

§ 8. How the expansions and contractions of banks affect the societary movement.... 316

§ 9. Great power of banks for good or evil. Banking monopolies, like those of France and England, give to a few individuals a power over the societary movement compared with which that exercised by the sovereigns of old sinks into insignificance.... 317

CHAPTER XXVII.—OF THE INSTRUMENT OF ASSOCIATION—CONTINUED.

V.—*Of Banking in England.*

§ 1. Great power exercised by the Bank of England.... 319

§ 2. No banking business in England at the date of the Restoration. Under Charles II. jewellers become bankers. Consequent increase in the utility of money. Establishment of the Bank of England.... 320

§ 3. Movements of the bank from 1797 to 1815.... 322

§ 4. Changes therein, subsequent to the close of the war. Resumption of specie payments. Productive of wide-spread ruin. Producing classes impoverished, while the merely consuming ones are enriched.... 323

§ 5. Effect of these measures that of giving to the moneyed capitalist increased command over land and labor, always an evidence of declining civilization.... 324

§ 6. Constant succession of expansions, contractions, and financial crises, each in succession tending to increase the power of money over land-owner and laborer.... 325

§ 7. Bank Act of Sir Robert Peel. Its object, that of producing steadiness in the monetary movement. Its effect, that of increasing the power of the bank to control the societary movement. Its total failure.... 326

§ 8. Cause of its failure to be found in the fact that it sought to regulate the currency in use, leaving wholly out of view the action of the bank in affecting the currency seeking to be employed.... 327

§ 9. Currency in use almost a constant quantity. Essential error of the Bank Act. Under it monetary changes become more frequent and more severe.... 329

CHAPTER XXVIII.—OF THE INSTRUMENT OF ASSOCIATION—CONTINUED.

VI.—*Of Banking in France.*

§ 1. Taxation of the French people by means of regulation of the currency.... 331

§ 2. Private banks established at the close of the Revolution. Consolidated in the Bank of France. Monopoly powers of that institution. Directly interested in producing changes in the currency.... 333

§ 3. Steadiness in the amount of currency in use. Financial crises have their origin in changes in the amount of currency unemployed.... 334

§ 4. These changes due to the irregularity in the movements of the one great bank. Their result seen in the augmentation of its dividends.... 334

§ 5. Political and monetary centralization tends to enfeeble the societary action and to diminish the amount of commerce. Counteracted, in some degree, by the maintenance of a policy having for its object the emancipation of the land from the tax of transportation.... 336

CHAPTER XXIX.—OF THE INSTRUMENT OF ASSOCIATION—CONTINUED.

VII.—*Of Banking in the United States.*

§ 1. Gradual development of the American banking system. How it stood at the close of the half century which followed the Revolution. Its progress since that time. Large proportion borne by capital to the amount of investments.... 337

§ 2. Steadiness in the action of banks is in the direct ratio of their dependence upon the power of affording means of circulation, and in the inverse ratio of their depend-

PAGE

[illegible] as deposits. American banks possess more of the elements of stability than those of France and England 339

§ 3. Small proportion borne by the currency to production when compared with either of the above-named countries 340

§ 4. Superior economy of the American system 341

§ 5. Steadiness in its own value the great desideratum in a currency. Tendencies of the American system in that direction 342

§ 6. Trivial amount of losses by American banks under the system of local action prior to 1837. Heavy losses of the people of England from the failures of private banks 344

§ 7. Growth of centralization in the last twenty years, and consequent diminution in the steadiness of the currency. Maintenance of a sound and stable currency incompatible with the existence of an unfavorable balance of trade. That balance unfavorable in relation to all purely agricultural countries 345

§ 8. Instability of American policy. Periods of protection and free trade alternating with each other. Prosperity the invariable attendant of the former, and bankruptcy of the people and the State that of the latter 347

§ 9. The money-shop, or bank, one of the most necessary portions of the societary machinery. More than any other, the American banking system tends to promote the habit of association, the development of individuality, and the growth of wealth 349

CHAPTER XXX.—OF THE INSTRUMENT OF ASSOCIATION—CONTINUED.

VIII.—*Of Hume, Smith, and other Writers on Money.*

§ 1. Theories of Mr. Hume in regard to money. Directly opposed to all the facts of history 353

§ 2. His failure to observe, that while increase in the supply of money raises the prices of raw materials, it reduces those of finished products. Throughout inconsistent with himself. Accuracy of his views when asserting that no country need fear an unfavorable balance of trade that "preserved with care its people and its manufactures" 354

§ 3. General accordance of the views of Hume and Adam Smith. Inconsistencies of the latter. A medium of circulation the one great need of society. Hence the desire of all communities to establish in their favor a balance of trade. Inconsistencies of the opponents of this idea 356

§ 4. Doctrines of the Ricardo-Malthusian school in regard to money. Mr. J. S. Mill. His views in regard to the inefficiency of money. Failure of the British economists to appreciate the services of the precious metals 358

§ 5. M. Bastiat. Correspondence of his views with those of Hume and Smith. His doctrines being received as true, there can be no harmony of international interests 360

§ 6. M. Chevalier holds that money is indispensable to man, and yet, that disadvantage may result from increase in its supply. The precious metals, the great instruments furnished by the Creator for the production of societary motion. The more rapid that motion, the greater must be, everywhere, the power of the individual to obtain supplies of food, and of the community to command the services of those metals 361

CHAPTER XXXI.—OF PRODUCTION AND CONSUMPTION.

§ 1. Man the ultimate object of all production. Production consists in the direction of natural forces to human service. Every act of consumption an act of production. Demand the cause of supply 364

§ 2. Labor-power the most perishable of all commodities. Perishes, unless the demand follows instantly upon its production. Waste of labor one of the conditions of early society and scattered population. Errors of Mr. Malthus and his disciples 365

§ 3. Wages and productive power of England at various periods 366

§ 4. The more continuous and steady the societary motion the more instant the demand for, and the economy of, labor. That continuity the test of real civilization. Diversity of employments indispensable to its existence. Waste of power in, and consequent poverty of, all purely agricultural countries 369

§ 5. Errors of modern economists in regard to productive and unproductive labor. All labor productive which tends to enable man more thoroughly to direct the forces of nature to his service, wealth consisting in the existence of that power of direction. The greater the power of man over nature the more rapid the progress of accumulation 371

CHAPTER XXXII.—OF ACCUMULATION.

§ 1. Power of accumulation exists in the ratio of the rapidity of the circulation.

PAGE

Capital the instrument by means of which man is enabled to direct the natural forces to his service. Power of association grows as he obtains increased command over the instrument ... 374

§ 2. Movable capital declines in its proportions as compared with that which is fixed, that decline being an evidence of advancing civilization. Centralisation produces the reverse effect. Increase of movable capital in all the present free-trade countries ... 374

§ 3. Errors of modern economists in regarding saving as the cause of the growth of capital ... 376

§ 4. That growth due to the economy of human effort. That economy a consequence of diversification of employments, and consequent combination of action ... 377

§ 5. Errors of Adam Smith in regard to the origin of capital ... 378

§ 6. Chief difficulty of social science. Summary of definitions thus far given in the present work ... 380

CHAPTER XXXIII.—OF CIRCULATION.

§ 1. Little circulation of either land or man, in the early stages of society. Large proportion then borne by movable to fixed capital ... 381

§ 2. Circulation increases in its rapidity in the direct ratio of the tendency of capital to become fixed and immovable ... 382

§ 3. The more rapid the circulation the greater the tendency towards the creation of local centres, towards the development of individuality, and towards having society assume its natural form ... 383

§ 4. Circulation becomes more rapid as employments become diversified, and land becomes divided. Social phenomena exhibited by France ... 384

§ 5. Tendency of British policy to promote increase in the proportions of movable capital at the expense of that which is fixed. Consequent stagnation of circulation in all the countries subject to it ... 386

§ 6. Circulation becomes more rapid in the ratio of the tendency towards approximation in the prices of rude products and finished commodities ... 387

§ 7. Tendencies of the British colonial system to produce stoppage of the circulation. Its effects, as exhibited in the past and present of these United States ... 388

§ 8. The more rapid the circulation the more equitable the distribution. Identity of the physical and social laws ... 389

CHAPTER XXXIV.—OF DISTRIBUTION.

I.—Of Wages, Profits, and Interest.

§ 1. Of wages, profits, and interest. Large proportion, in the early stages of society, assigned to capital ... 392

§ 2. Capitalist's proportion diminishes as the cost of reproduction declines ... 393

§ 3. General law of distribution. Laborer's share increases in both its proportion and amount. That of the capitalist increases in amount, while diminishing in its proportion. Tendency of this law to produce equality in the condition of mankind. Its harmony and beauty ... 394

§ 4. Universal application of the law that is here propounded ... 395

§ 5. Labor's proportion increases as the prices of rude products and those of finished commodities tend to approximate to each other. That tendency found in all the countries in which employments become more diversified. The reverse of this found in all the countries that adopt the doctrines of the British school ... 396

§ 6. Erroneous views of Adam Smith in regard to the natural law regulating the charge for the use of money. Absence of consistency in the doctrines of the Ricardo-Malthusian school. The value of man rises as the rate of profit, interest, and rent, declines ... 397

CHAPTER XXXV.—OF DISTRIBUTION—CONTINUED.

II.—Of the Rent of Land.

§ 1. Of the rent of land. Large proportion of the landlord in the days of early cultivation. That proportion diminishes as labor becomes more productive, but the amount of rent increases. The laborer's share increases with large increase in its amount, both thus profiting by increase in the power to command the services of nature 400

§ 2. Ricardo's theory of rent. Teaches the reverse of this, the landlord's proportion increasing as agricultural labor becomes less productive ... 401

PAGE

§ 3. That theory based upon the false assumption that cultivation commences on the rich soils, and that labor becomes less productive as men increase in number and in power..... 403

§ 4. No such rent as that indicated by Ricardo has ever been, or ever can be paid..... 405

§ 5. The ultimate slavery of man the natural tendency of the Ricardo-Malthusian theory, rent rising as labor becomes less productive..... 406

§ 6. Simplicity and universal truth of natural laws. Complexity and error of the Ricardo theory..... 406

§ 7. Growth of rent supposed by Mr. Ricardo to be retarded by improvements in cultivation. Interests of the landlord supposed to be promoted by diminution in the supply of food, and increasing poverty of the laborer..... 408

§ 8. The Ricardo theory one of universal discords. Harmony and beauty of the real laws..... 409

§ 9. The more rapid the circulation, the greater the tendency towards equality and freedom among the people, and strength in the State..... 410

§ 10. War among nations, and discord among individuals, grow with the growth of monopoly of the land. That monopoly a necessary consequence of the British policy. With every stage of its progress the more must the people suffer in the distribution between themselves and the State..... 411

CHAPTER XXXVI.—OF DISTRIBUTION—CONTINUED.

III.—*The People and the State*

§ 1. Of the distribution between the people and the State. Small security obtained at the cost of heavy contributions in the early stages of society. As employments become diversified security increases and is obtained at diminished cost..... 413

§ 2. Necessity for indirect taxation in the early period. Diminishes as fixed property increases in the proportions borne by it to that which is movable..... 414

§ 3. Commerce tends to become more free as the proportion of movable to fixed property declines..... 416

§ 4. Tendency towards increase of indirect taxation an evidence of declining civilization. Phenomena presented for consideration by Greece and Rome. Indirect taxation of Holland, Turkey, and other countries that are becoming more subject to the domination of the trader..... 417

§ 5. Substitution of indirect for direct taxation in Great Britain. Taxation of India and Carolina. The real payers of British taxes the land and labor of the various countries which furnish the raw materials consumed in British workshops..... 418

§ 6. Revenue system of the United States. The countries in which direct taxation tends to supersede those which are indirect, are those which have protected themselves against the British system..... 420

§ 7. The more direct the taxation the less will be its proportion to production..... 421

§ 8. The more rapid the circulation the less the power for interference with commerce, and the greater the tendency towards improvement in the condition of man. Why not, then, at once abolish all indirect taxation? Because the power of direct taxation—being an evidence of that high civilization which is marked by the near approach of the prices of rude products and finished commodities—cannot be exercised in any country that has not prepared for it by placing consumers and producers in close proximity to each other..... 422

§ 9. The more perfect the power to apply directly to the land and labor of the country, the greater the competition for the purchase of both, and the greater the strength of the State..... 424

CHAPTER XXXVII.—OF COMPETITION.

§ 1. In the absence of competition for the purchase of labor-power, the laborer becomes enslaved. That power the only commodity that cannot be preserved, even for an instant, beyond the moment of its production..... 426

§ 2. The more the competition for the purchase of labor the more rapid the circulation, the larger the production, and the greater the power of accumulation..... 427

§ 3. Competition for the purchase of labor tends toward freedom. The trader desires to produce competition for its sale..... 427

§ 4. Trading centralization seeks to produce competition for the sale of raw materials and labor. Therefore adverse to the growth of value in land or man..... 428

§ 5. Effect of trading centralization upon the condition of the British people..... 429

§ 6. Trading centralization deteriorates the condition of the laborers of the world. Necessity for resistance thereto..... 431

PAGE

§ 7. Competition for the control of nature's services raises the value of both land and man ... 423

§ 8. Competition for the purchase of labor tends to strengthen custom into law, in favor of the laborer. Competition for its sale tends to the annihilation of customary rights in favor of the capitalist. Where this last is found, the societary circulation becomes more sluggish, with constant growth of the disease of over-population ... 428

CHAPTER XXXVIII.—OF POPULATION.

§ 1. That the earth may be subdued, man must multiply and increase. Fecundity and development in the inverse ratio of each other. Man should therefore increase but very slowly. However long the period of duplication, if the procreative tendency is a fixed and positive quantity, the time must arrive when there will be but standing-room for the population. Can the Creator have subjected man to laws, in virtue of which he must become the slave of nature and of his fellow-man? ... 436

§ 2. Physical science testifies that order, harmony, and reciprocal adjustment, reign throughout all the realms it has yet explored. Modern economists have mistaken facts for laws. Laws are rules, permanent, uniform, and universal in their action. Theory of Mr. Malthus deficient in all these characteristics. The procreative function, in common with all others, placed under the law of circumstances and conditions. Are war and pestilence required for correcting errors of the Creator, or has the Creator so adjusted the procreative tendency as to provide the means of correcting human error? 438

§ 3. Power of progress in the ratio of the perfection of organization. Man, the being most susceptible of change—passing from the mere animal and becoming the real MAN, responsible to his family, his fellow-men, and his Creator. Responsibility grows with the growing power of association, and with division of the land ... 442

§ 4. Growth of population modified by the development of that feeling of responsibility which comes with the ownership of land ... 444

§ 5. Recklessness and poverty consequent upon absence of diversity in the modes of employment and consolidation of the land. Adaptability of the procreative power to the circumstances in which a community is placed ... 445

§ 6. Consolidation of the land, and the disease of over-population, necessary consequences of a policy which looks to the cheapening of labor, and of the rude products of the earth. British system tends to the production of these effects. Its results, as exhibited in the condition of the English people ... 448

§ 7. Pioneer life favorable to increase of numbers. Effects of American policy as exhibited in the duration of life ... 456

§ 8. Reproductive function not a constant quantity. General predominance of the nutritive and sexual functions. Antagonism of the animal propensities and higher sentiments. Fertility of the drudges of an imperfect civilisation. Infertility of the higher tribes. Activity of the intellect checks procreation. Cerebral and generative powers of man mature together. Fecundity in the inverse ratio of organization. A self-acting law of population secures harmony in the growth of numbers and of food 461

CHAPTER XXXIX.—OF FOOD AND POPULATION.

§ 1. Population makes the food come from the rich soils of the earth, depopulation driving men back to the poorer ones. Increased regularity in the supply of food consequent upon the increased demands of a population that is growing in numbers and in power. Diminution in the waste of human force that attends increase in the supply of food ... 466

§ 2. Substitution of vegetable for animal food. Causes the action of man upon nature to become more direct, thereby diminishing friction and increasing power ... 468

§ 3. The mineral world co-operates in diminishing man's dependence on the animal one. Diminution in the demand upon man's physical powers, and in the quantity of food required to supply the daily waste ... 469

§ 4. Tendency of the lower animals to disappear. Consequent diminution in the supply of carbonic acid. Increased demand for supplies of that acid which attends the extension of cultivation. Consequent necessity for increase in the number of men. Wonderful beauty of all natural arrangements ... 469

§ 5. That man may profit by these arrangements he is required to conform to that law of nature which demands that the consumer and producer take their places by each other. Population pressing upon subsistence in all communities by which it is violated ... 471

§ 6. Destructive effects of British policy in causing the exhaustion of the countries that follow in the lead of her economists. Tendency in all of them towards centralization, slavery, and death ... 476

PAGE

§ 7. Simplicity and beauty of the laws which regulate the demand for food, and its supply. Perfect harmony, throughout nature, in the adaptation of means to ends ... 463

CHAPTER XL.—OF COLONIZATION.

§ 1. Early colonization. Nature goes on adding perfection to perfection, from the poles to the tropics. Richer soils of the world as yet unoccupied, nature being there all-powerful. With the growth of wealth and population man is enabled to turn against her such of her forces as he has mastered—passing steadily from triumph to triumph and subjugating more fertile soils ... 466

§ 2. Manufactures always precede, and never follow, the creation of a real agriculture. The country that exports its soil in the form of rude products, must end in the export of men. Trading centralization tends to annihilation of local centres, exhaustion of the soil, and destruction of the value of land and man. Errors of Ricardo-Malthusian teachers. Declining power of association throughout the American Union ... 469

§ 3. Error in one community tends to the production of error in all. British warfare on the manufactures of other nations tends to the production of slavery abroad and at home ... 473

§ 4. Tendency towards over-population in the direct ratio of the separation of the prices of raw materials and finished commodities. Countries which follow in the lead of England are those which furnish the facts required for demonstrating the truth of Malthusian doctrines ... 474

CHAPTER XLI.—OF THE MALTHUSIAN THEORY.

§ 1. Constant tendency, according to Mr. Malthus, in all animated life, to increase beyond the nourishment prepared for it. Facts, however, prove that supply is everywhere, a consequence of demand, the quantity of food prepared for beings of every kind being practically unlimited. Laws of nature vindicate the ways of God to man ... 477

§ 2. Misery and vice attributed to deficiency in the powers of the earth to furnish food to increasing numbers. Facts of history prove the difficulty to lie with man himself, and not in errors of the Creator ... 480

§ 3. Mr. Malthus gives facts, and calls them science. Science demands principles, asking, Why it is that such things are? Failure of Mr. Malthus to establish "the one great cause" of the various facts observed. His *Principle of Population* a mere form of words, indicating the existence of an altogether imaginary fact ... 481

§ 4. Responsibility grows with the growth of the gifts of God to man. Poor laborer the slave of circumstances, yet held responsible for his acts. Tendency of the Malthusian doctrine to shift responsibility from the rich and strong to the poor, the weak, and the uninstructed ... 485

CHAPTER XLII.—OF COMMERCE.

I.—Of the Relations of the Sexes.

§ 1. Relations of the sexes. Woman a slave to man, in the early stages of society. Her condition improves as wealth and population grow, and as the real MAN is more developed. The more rapid the societary circulation, and the greater the tendency towards the creation of a scientific agriculture, the more does the sex tend towards occupying its true position ... 487

§ 2. Condition of woman in Central and Northern Europe. Woman rises in the scale as land becomes divided, and man becomes more free ... 488

§ 3. Saxon women sold to slavery. General improvement in the condition of the women of England. Loss of the rights of property secured to them by the early English law. Deterioration of the condition of the sex, in all the countries that follow in the train of England ... 490

§ 4. How the condition of English women is affected by trading centralization. Growing competition for the sale of female labor. Consequent low wages, and necessary resorting to prostitution. Protection tends to produce competition for its purchase, thereby benefiting the sex throughout the world ... 492

§ 5. Extraordinary contrasts presented by the condition of the sex in the several portions of the American Union. Theory of the government favorable to the creation of local centres, and to the elevation of the sex. Its practice, tending towards centralization, adverse thereto, and hence the rapid growth of female crime and prostitution 496

CHAPTER XLIII.—OF COMMERCE—CONTINUED.

II.—*Of the Relations of the Family.*

PAGE

§ 1. Relations of the Family. Weakness of the Family ties, in the early stages of society. Responsibility, in both parent and child, grows with division of the land, and with the approximation of consumers to producers 496

§ 2. Education in Central and Northern Europe. Growing feeling of responsibility for proper training of youth, as manifested in all those countries in which employments are becoming more diversified 497

§ 3. Reverse of this exhibited in those which follow in the train of England—employments there becoming less diversified. Condition of English children. Absence of provision for general education. Child-murder. Children regarded as mere instruments to be used by trade. Consequent necessity for a theory of over-population 499

§ 4. Extraordinary contrasts here again presented by the American Union. That education given in the school may prove useful, it is needed that there be demand for the faculties there developed. That there may be such demand, it is required that there be diversity in the modes of employment. That the latter may exist, there is needed an exercise of the power of the State 502

CHAPTER XLIV.—OF COMMERCE—CONTINUED.

III.—*Of the Commerce of the State.*

§ 1. Commerce of the State. Solidarity of the human race. Two-fold nature of man. Correspondence between the structure and functions of the individual man and the aggregate man denominated Society. Co-ordinating office of the brain. Its power limited by the necessary liberty of the individual organs. Various degrees of subordination of the parts. Necessity for exercise of the power of co-ordination grows in individuals and societies as the organization becomes more complete. Local centres of the physical and social systems. Power and duties of the brain. Order and liberty combined and secured. Graduated and federated system of government in the human body analogous to the political organization of that social one which constitutes these United States 505

§ 2. Social science here branches into political economy—the one treating of natural laws, and the other of the measures required for enabling those laws to have full effect. Relation of science and art as exhibited by M. Comte. Necessity for exercise of the power of co-ordination. The more perfect the co-ordination the more complete the development of all the parts, and the more harmonious the action of the whole. Tendency to the creation of local centres. The more perfect the balance of opposing forces, the greater the tendency towards human freedom. Duty of the co-ordinating power limited to the removal of obstacles to association 508

§ 3. Colbert and his policy. His full appreciation of the necessity for the exercise, by the State, of a power of co-ordination. Hume, on the necessity for preserving with care the manufactures of a nation. Adam Smith no advocate of the indiscriminate adoption of the system of *laisser faire*. Say, Rossi, Mill, and others, on the duties of a government, in reference to diversification of employments. M. Chevalier holds that, within certain limits governments are but performing a positive duty when they favor the taking possession of all the branches of industry whose acquisition is authorized by the nature of things. Holds that French agriculture has ceased to be unprotected. Inaccuracy of the view thus presented. Heavy taxation of transportation paid by American farmers, and comparative exemption of those of France. Freedom of trade enjoyed by the latter, as compared with the restrictions on the former. Necessity for exercise of the co-ordinating power grows with the growth of wealth and numbers. The more perfect the power of association within the State, the greater the power of its people to contribute to the commerce of the world 511

CHAPTER XLV.—OF COMMERCE—CONTINUED.

IV.—*Of the Commerce of the World.*

§ 1. Commerce of the World. In societies, as in the individual man, the power to maintain commerce is in the ratio of development—that becoming more complete as the power of co-ordination is more discreetly exercised 517

§ 2. Organized bodies grow from within. Brute matter increases only by aggregation. The more perfect the development of human faculties, the higher the societary organization, and the more complete the self-dependence 518

§ 3. Power for maintaining exterior commerce grows as the community becomes more self-dependent 519

PAGE

§ 4. Limited internal commerce of the States of the American Union. Slow growth of the power to maintain foreign commerce 519

§ 5. Ultimate object of all production found in the real MAN. The higher his development, the greater the tendency towards the substitution of the commerce of taste and intellect, for that which requires for its maintenance mere brute force. Peace and harmony come with the proper exercise of the power of co-ordination. Subordination of all the parts becomes more complete as the societary organization becomes more perfect 520

CHAPTER XLVI.—OF THE SOCIETARY ORGANIZATION.

§ 1. Throughout nature, dissimilarity of the parts is evidence of the perfection of the whole, the highest organization presenting the most numerous differences. The higher the organization, the more complete the subordination of the parts. The more perfect the subordination, the more harmonious and beautiful the interdependence of the parts. The more complete that interdependence the greater the individuality of the whole, and the more perfect the power of self-direction 522

§ 2. Throughout the physical and social world, harmony of movement—interdependence—a result of that local attraction which preserves a perfect independence. Subordination grows with the growth of the power of self-direction and protection. Harmony a result of the equal action of opposing forces. Its growth in all those countries in which the co-ordinating action is in accordance with the principles of social science 524

CHAPTER XLVII.—OF SOCIAL SCIENCE.

§ 1. Identity of the physical and social laws. Harmony the universal result of the unrestrained operation of natural laws. Identity of individual and national interests throughout the world 526

§ 2. Agriculture the last developed of the pursuits of man. The laborer in the field the last that is emancipated. Minute machinery, by means of which nature performs her greatest operations, the last that is observed. Advantages of peace and harmony, last to meet their full appreciation. Science the interpreter of nature. Having recorded her processes it accepts them as true. Social Science treats of the laws in virtue of which man is enabled to obtain power over nature and over himself. Careful study of those laws would enable all, from the farmer and the laborer to the sovereign and the statesman, to see that advantage would result from full obedience to the great precept which requires that men should do by others as they would that others should do by them 528

SOCIAL SCIENCE.

CHAPTER I.

OF SCIENCE.

§ 1. Bacon's distributions and partitions of the tree of knowledge. Roots and branches of the tree.

§ 2. Method of discovery the same in all departments of knowledge. British economists recognize not the real man of society, but the artificial man of their own system. All sciences and their methods embraced in Sociology. Analysis leads to synthesis. Science one and indivisible. The economical relations of man require mathematical formulæ to render them into systematic truths. The societary laws undetermined. Terms of the theorists insufficient and equivocal

§ 3. Social science, the constituent and concrete of all others, waits upon their development for its own. Its impediments. The metaphysical must be replaced by the methodical study of man. Physical and social laws indivisible in the study of society, and all the phenomena of the subject constituting but a single science.

§ 1. "The distributions and partitions of knowledge," says Lord Bacon, "are not like several lines that meet in one angle, and *touch but in a point;* but are like branches of a tree that meet in a stem, which hath a dimension and quantity of entireness and continuance before it comes to discontinuance and break itself into arms and boughs; therefore," as he continues, "it is good before we enter into the former distribution, to create and constitute one universal science by the name of Philosophia Prima, or Summary Philosophy, as the main or common way, before we come where the ways part and divide themselves."

Concerned as he was with the order and division of the sciences, and pledged as he was in the introduction to his work to furnish it, he failed to do so, as a consequence of which his editor submitted a study in its stead.

The several *branches* of natural science are commonly spoken of, but the figure has a larger parallelism with the subject, a tree having not only branches but also roots. These latter are properly under-ground branches, constituting the structural support and furnishing the vital subsistence of the tree, which grows from its roots and with them. Its stem, branches, flowers, and fruits, being converted aliment supplied by and through the roots, the allusions of the figure here given are in good keeping with the natural history of the subject intended to be illustrated.

The central or taproot, as the reader sees, represents MATTER, with its essential properties of inertia, impenetrability, divisibility, and attraction. The lateral ones stand, on one side, for mechanical and chemical forces, and on the other, for vegetable and animal ones, and from these substantive roots of being rises the stem man, so composed as to his natural constitution. The soul, being the occult life of the structure, is incapable of representation, though manifested by its proper evidence in the flowers and fruits, the emotions and thoughts of his faculties.

We have now the stem—the man—"having dimension and quantity of entireness and continuance before it came to discontinue and break itself," branching off into his diverse activities. These branches are his functions, ramifying into all their specific differences of application. The first branch on the material side is Physics, which ramifies itself into natural philosophy and chemistry—masses and atoms; and the shoots from these are mechanics and chemical dynamics; the one being the action of masses and the other that of atoms.

The main branch on the vital side of the tree, rising a little above Physics, must necessarily be Organology, branching first into the science of vegetable beings, Phytology, and sending off the shoot, Vegetable Physiology; and second, into that of animal beings, Zoology, leading to Biology, or the science of life.

Following the stem in the natural order of rank and successive development it is seen next giving off Social Science, which divides itself into Jurisprudence and Political Economy, while on the corresponding side the main branch, Psychology, ramifies itself into Ethics and Theology, the tree finally topping out with Intuition as the material branch and Inspiration as the vital one. These highest and last named, are rightly the source of the other science or sciences to which Bacon alludes as standing above Metaphysics, when he says that, "as for the vertical point, the summary law of nature, we know not whether man's inquiry can attain unto it;" that is, so as to order and methodize its teachings.

In this scheme of the sciences of things, there is no place for either Logic or Mathematics, the respective regulative sciences of mind and matter. Neither of these belongs to

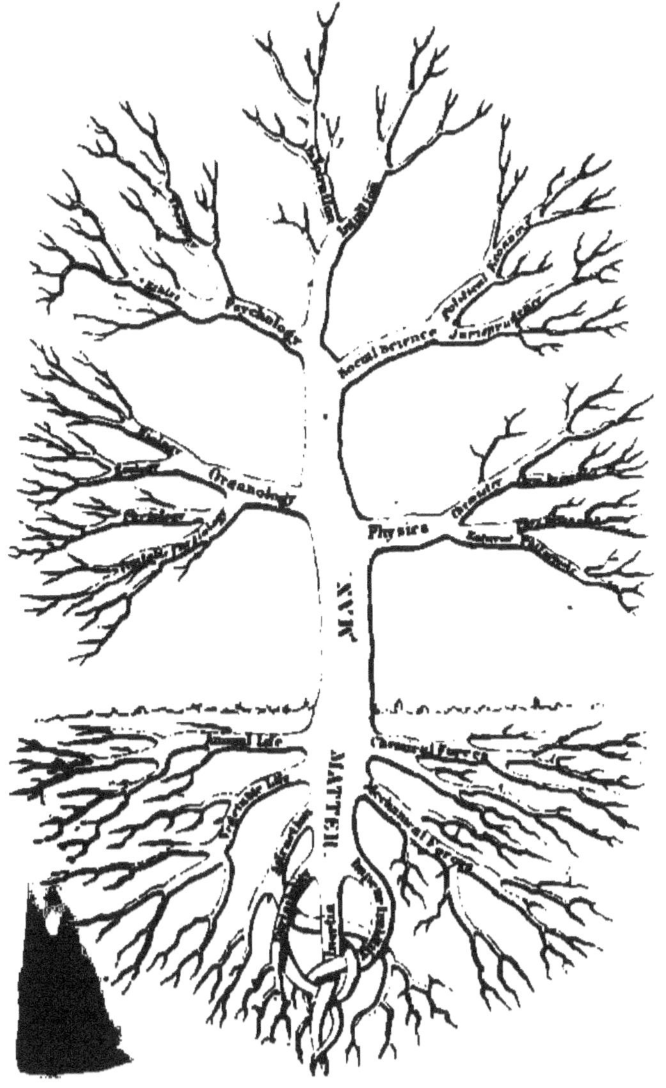
Psychology
Social Science
Jurisprudence
Organology
Physics
Chemistry
MAN
Animal Life
Vegetable Life
Chemical Forces
Mechanical Forces
MATTER

Natural History, being both alike mere instruments to be used in the study of nature.*

Historically, the top branches of the tree of knowledge, as of all other trees, are first produced, and the branches next below are soon put forth, but mature later, the instincts of religion and reason appearing in their vigor in the childhood of the race. Social science, necessarily, and metaphysics, spontaneously, present themselves as early as societies take form, and speculation is awakened; and they bring forth quickly the flowers and fruits of music, poetry, the fine arts, logic, mathematics, and those generalities of speculative truth which are the products of imagination and reflection. The correspondence between the figure chosen and the facts to be illustrated would seem to be complete.

In time, the branches nearer to the earth, more material in their substance and more dependent upon observation, obtain development in their larger diversity of use. The sciences of substance, of natural objects, grow and ramify themselves almost indefinitely, physical philosophy and organology, in their dependencies, shooting out in every direction of observation and experiment, at first overshadowed by the speculative branches above them, but always vivified by them; while in their turn repaying this service by affording substantive strength and corrective modification as they grow into maturity.

Such is the history of science, and such the illustration of its orderly division, succession, and co-ordination; it represents the compound nature of man, the sources of his powers and the order of their development.

§ 2. Seeking now to understand the history of man in past ages, or in distant lands, we must commence by studying him in the present, and having mastered him in the past and present, we may then be enabled to predict the future. To do this, it is required that we do with society as does the chemist with the piece of granite, resolving it into its several parts and studying each part separately, ascertaining how it would act were it left to itself, and comparing what *would be* its independent action with that we see *to be* its societary action; and then by help of the same law of which the mathematician, the physicist, the chemist, and the physiologist, avail them-

* Science asks the questions, What? and Why? Those asked by Mathematics are, How much? and Where?

selves—that of the composition of forces—we may arrive at the law of the effect.

That law requires that we study *all* the causes tending to produce a given effect. That effect is MAN—the man of the past and the present; and the social philosopher who excludes from consideration his feelings and affections, and the intellect with which he has been endowed, makes precisely the same mistake that would be made by the physical one who should look exclusively to gravitation, forgetting heat; and should thence conclude that at no distant day the whole material of which the earth is composed would become a solid mass, plants, animals and men having disappeared. Such is the error of modern economists, and its effects are seen in the fact that they present for our consideration a mere brute animal, to find a name for which they desecrate the word "man," recognized by Adam Smith as expressing the idea of a being made in the likeness of its Creator.

It was well asked by Goethe—"*What is all intercourse with nature, if by the analytical method we merely occupy ourselves with individual material parts, and do not feel the breath of the spirit* which prescribes to every part its direction, and orders or sanctions every deviation by means of an inherent law?" And what, we may ask, is the value of an analytical process that selects only the "material parts" of man—those which are common to himself and the beast—and excludes those common to the angels and himself? Such is the tendency of Ricardo-Malthusianism, which not only does not "feel the breath of the spirit" but even ignores the existence of the spirit itself, and is therefore found defining what it is pleased to call the natural rate of wages, as being "that price which is necessary to enable the laborers, one with another, to subsist and perpetuate their race, without either increase or diminution"*—that is to say, such price as will enable some to grow rich and increase their race, while others perish of hunger, thirst, and exposure. Such are the teachings of a system that has fairly earned the title of the "dismal science"—that one the study of which led M. Sismondi to the inquiry—"What, then, is wealth every thing, and is man absolutely nothing?" In the eyes of most modern teachers he *is* nothing, and can be nothing, because they take no note of the qualities by which he is distinguished from the brute, and are therefore led to regard him as being a

* Ricardo.

mere instrument to be used by capital to enable its owner to obtain compensation for its use. "Some economists," said a distinguished French economist, shocked at the material character of the so-called science, "speak as if they believed that men were made for products, not products for men;"* and at that conclusion must all arrive who commence by the method of analysis, and close with exclusion of all the higher and distinctive qualities of man.

Does this method, however, supersede entirely the *à priori* one? Because we pursue the method of analysis, are we necessarily precluded from that of synthesis? By no means. The one, however, is the indispensable preparation for the other. It was by careful observation of particular facts that Le Verrier was led to the grand generalization that a new and unobserved planet was bound to exist, and in a certain part of the heavens, and there it was almost at once discovered. To careful analyses it was due that Davy was led to the announcement of the great fact that all earths have metallic bases—one of the grandest generalizations on record, and one whose truth is being every day more and more established. The two methods were well described by Goethe, when he said that synthesis and analysis were "the systole and diastole of human thought," and that they were to him "like a second breathing process—never separated, ever pulsating." "The vice of the *à priori* method," says the writer from whom this passage is taken, "when it wanders from the right path, is *not* that it *goes before* the facts, and anticipates the tardy conclusions of experience, but that it rests contented with its own verdicts, or seeking only a partial, hasty confrontation with facts—what Bacon calls '*notiones* temerè à rebus abstractas.'" †

Science being one and indivisible the method of study must in like manner be one. That this is so with regard to all the departments of knowledge that underlie social science, physics, chemistry, and physiology, cannot now be doubted, yet it is but recently that there has been reason to believe in any such connection. With each new discovery the approximation becomes more close, and with each we see how intimately are the facts of all the earlier and more abstract departments of knowledge connected with the progress of man toward that state of high development for which he

* Droz. *Economie Politique.*

† *Westminster Review*, Oct 1852: Article, *Goethe as a Man of Science.*

seems to have been intended. From hour to hour, as he acquires further control over the various forces existing in nature, he is enabled to live in closer connection with his fellow-man, to obtain larger supplies of food and clothing, to improve his own modes of thought and action, and to furnish better instruction to the generation destined to succeed him. The knowledge that leads to such results is but the foundation upon which we are required to build when undertaking to construct that higher department denominated Social Science, and the instrument that has been so successfully used in laying the foundation cannot but be found equally useful in the construction of the building itself.

Mathematics must be used in social science, as it is now in every other branch of inquiry, and the more the former is used the more the latter takes the form of real science, and the more intimate are shown to be its relations with other departments of knowledge. The Malthusian law was the first instance of its application, and had it proved a true one it would have given a precision to political economy of which before it had been utterly incapable, making the progress of man directly dependent upon the presence or absence of certain powers in the soil on which he lived. So, too, with Mr. Ricardo's celebrated theory of rent, by which was established what he deemed to be the natural division of the products of labor. The method of both these great laws was right, and the fact of their having adopted it has properly placed their authors in the front rank of economists, and has given to their works an amount of influence never before exercised by any writers on economical science. That they fell into the error above described of "seeking only a partial, hasty confrontation with facts," and, therefore, furnished the world with theories directly the reverse of true, does not prevent us from seeing of what infinite advantage to the progress of science it would have been to have had the facts brought under these relations, if true, nor of how great importance it must be to have the real facts brought under such relations wherever possible.

Let us, for example, take the following proposition:—

In the early period of society, when land is abundant and people are few in number, labor is unproductive, and of the small product, the land-owner or other capitalist takes a large *proportion*, leaving to the laborer a small one. The larger proportion yields, however, but a small amount, and both laborer and capitalist are poor—the former so poor that he is everywhere seen to have been a slave to the latter. Population and wealth, however, increasing, and labor becoming more productive, the land-owner's share diminishes in its *proportion*, but increases in its *amount*. The laborer's share increases not only in its amount, but also in its proportion, and the more rapid the increase in the productiveness of his labor, the greater is the *proportion* of the augmented quantity retained by him; and thus, while the interests of both are in perfect harmony with each other, there is a constant tendency towards the establishment of an equality of condition—the slave of the early period becoming the free man of the latter one.

Admitting this to be true—and if so, it establishes directly the reverse of what was propounded by Messrs. Malthus and Ricardo—we have here the distinct expression of a mathematical relation between the concomitant variations of power of man and matter—of the man representing only his own faculties, and of the man representing the accumulated results of human faculties upon matter and its forces. The problem of social science, and the one attempted to be solved by those writers, is, what are the relations of man and the outside material world. They change as we see, men becoming in some countries from year to year more and more the masters, and in others, the slaves of nature. In what manner is it that changes in one tend to produce further changes in itself, or to effect changes in the other? To this question we need a mathematical answer, and until it shall be furnished—as it is believed to be in the above very simple proposition—political economy can bear only the same relation to social science that the observations of the Chaldean shepherds bear to modern astronomy.

Social science can scarcely be said yet to have existence. That it might exist, it was required first to obtain the physical, chemical, and physiological knowledge required for enabling us to observe how it is that man is enabled to obtain command over the various forces provided for his use, and to pass from being the slave to becoming the master of nature. "Man," says Goethe, "only knows himself in as far as he knows external nature," and it was needed that the more abstract and general departments of knowledge should acquire a state of high development before we could advantageously enter upon the study of the highly concrete and special, and infinitely variable, science of the laws by which man is governed in his relations with the external world, and with his fellow-man. Chemistry and physiology are both, however, of recent date. A century since, men knew nothing of the composition of the air they breathed, and it is within that period that Haller laid the foundation of the physiological science that now exists. In this state of things there could be but little progress towards understanding how far it was in the power of man to compel the earth to yield the supplies required for a steadily increasing population; and without that knowledge there could be no such thing as social science.

Science requires laws, and laws are but universal truths—truths to which no exceptions can be found. Those obtained, harmony and order take the place of chaos, and we are led to recognize effects as having been the natural results of certain definite causes, and to look for the reappearance of similar effects when like causes shall again occur, as did the first man when he had definitely connected the presence and absence of light with the rising and setting of the sun.

Where, however, is there in social science a proposition whose truth is universally admitted? There is not even a single one. A century since, the strength of a nation was regarded as tending to increase with augmentation of its numbers, but now we are taught that such increase brings with it weakness instead of strength. From year to year we have new theories of the laws of population, and new modifications of the old one; and the question of the laws governing the distribution of the proceeds of labor is now discussed as vigorously as it was fifty years since. Of the disciples of Messieurs Malthus and Ricardo no two are quite agreed as to what it was that their masters really meant to teach. The strongest advocates for the removal of all restrictions on trade in cloth are found among the fiercest opponents of freedom in the trade in money; and among the most enthusiastic friends of competition for the sale of merchandise, are to be found the most decided opponents of competition for the purchase of the laborer's time and talents. Teachers who rejoice in every thing tending to increase the prices of cloth and iron, as leading to improvement in the condition of man, are found among the foremost of those who deprecate advance in the price of the laborer's services, as tending to diminution of power for the maintenance of trade. All is therefore confusion, and nothing is settled, no approach having yet been made even to an understanding as to the meaning of the various terms in common use. "The great defect of Adam Smith, and of our economists in general," says Archbishop Whately, "is the want of definitions," and in proof of this he gives his readers the numerous and widely different ones furnished by the most distinguished teachers in relation to the highly important terms, Value, Wealth, Labor, Capital, Rents, Wages, and Profits, and shows that, for want of clear conceptions, the same word is used by the same writer at one time in a manner totally inconsistent with that in which he uses it at another. To that list he might, as he most truly says, add many others "which are often used without any more explanation, or any more suspicion of their requiring it, than the words 'triangle, or 'twenty'"—and as a consequence of this it is that, as will be hereafter shown, words of the highest importance are used by distinguished writers as being entirely synonymous, when really expressing not only different, but directly opposite ideas.

§ 3. Of all the departments of knowledge, Social Science is the most concrete and special, the most dependent on the earlier and more abstract departments of science, the one in which the facts are most difficult of collection and analysis, and therefore the last to obtain development. Of all, too, it is the only one that affects the interests of men, their feelings, passions, prejudices, and therefore the one in which it is most difficult to find men collating facts with the sole view to deduce from them the knowledge they are calculated to afford. Treating, as it does, of the relations between man and man, it has everywhere to meet the objection of those who seek the enjoyment of power and privilege at the cost of their fellow-men. The sovereign holds in small respect the science that would teach his subjects to doubt the propriety of his exercise of power by the grace of God. The soldier cannot believe in one that looks to the annihilation of his trade, nor can the monopolist readily be made to believe in the advantages of competition. The politician lives by managing the affairs of others, and he has small desire to see the people taught the proper management of their own concerns. All these men profit by teaching falsehood, and therefore frown upon those who would desire to teach the truth. The landlord believes in one doctrine and his tenant in another, while the payer of wages looks at all questions from a point of sight directly the opposite of the one occupied by him to whom the wages are paid.

We here meet a difficulty with which, as has been already said, no other science has had to contend. Astronomy has wrought its way to its present prodigious height with but temporary opposition from the schools, because no one was personally interested in continuing to teach the revolution of the sun around the earth. For a time the teachers, secular and spiritual, were disposed to deny the movement of the latter, but the fact was proved, and opposition ceased Such, too, was the case when geology began to teach that the earth had had a longer existence than previously had been believed. The schools that represented by-gone days did then as they had done in the days of Copernicus and Galileo, denouncing as heretics all who doubted the accuracy of the received chronology, but short as is the time that has since elapsed the opposition has already disappeared. Franklin, Dalton, Wollaston, and Berzelius prosecuted their inquiries without fear of opposition, for their discoveries were unlikely to affect injuriously the pockets of land-owners, merchants, or politicians. Social science is, however, still to a great extent in the hands of the schoolmen, backed everywhere by those who profit by the ignorance and the weakness of the people.

The occupants of academic chairs in Austria may not teach what is unfavorable to the divine rights of kings, or favorable to increase of popular rights. The doctrines of the schools of France vary from time to time as despotism yields to the people, or the people yield to it. The landed aristocracy of England were gratified when Mr. Malthus satisfied it that the poverty and misery of the people resulted necessarily from a great law emanating from an all-wise and all-benevolent Creator; and the manufacturing one is equally so when it sees, as it thinks, the fact established that the general interests of the country are to be promoted by measures looking to the production of an abundant supply of cheap, or badly paid, labor.

The system of these United States being based upon the idea of an entire political equality, we might, perhaps, be warranted in looking to our teachers for something different, even if not better, but if we should do so we should, in general, be disappointed. With few and slight exceptions, our professors teach the same that is taught abroad by men who live by inculcating the divine rights of kings; and they teach self-government by the aid of books from which their pupils learn that the greater the tendency towards equality the greater is the hatred among the several classes of which society is composed. Social science, as taught in some of the colleges of this country and of Europe, is now on a level with the chemical science of a century since; and there it will remain so long as its teachers shall continue to look inwards to their own minds and *invent* theories, instead of looking outwards to the great laboratory of the world for the collection of facts with a view to the *discovery* of laws. In default of such laws, they are constantly repeating phrases that have no real meaning, and that tend, as Goethe most truly says, to "ossify the organs of intelligence," of both the teacher and his pupil.

The state in which it now exists is what M. Comte is accustomed to denominate the metaphysical one,* and there it must remain until its teachers shall waken to the fact, that there is but one system of laws for the government of all matter, whether existing in the form of a piece of coal, a tree, a horse, or a man, and but one mode of study for all departments of it.

The laws of physical science are equally those of social science, and in every effort to discover the former we are but paving the way for the discovery of the latter. "The entire succession of men," says Pascal, "through the whole course of ages, must be regarded as one man, always living, and incessantly learning;" and among the men who have most largely contributed towards the foundation of a true social science are to be ranked the eminent teachers to whose labors we have been so much indebted for the wonderful development of physical, chemical, and physiological science in the last and present centuries.

The later man is, therefore, the one possessing the most of that knowledge of the societary action required for comprehending the causes of the various effects recorded in the pages of history, and for predicting those which must result in future from causes now existing. The early man possessed little of science but the instrument (mathematics) required for its acquisition, and what of it he did acquire was purely physical in its character and most limited in its extent. The

* The true method of science consists in proceeding from the near to the distant, from the simple to the compound, from the known to the unknown, from the parts to the whole. This is called the Analytical or Mathematical method. The reverse is that called the Metaphysical; and this it is that has hitherto been pursued in social science.

present one is in possession not only of physical science to an extent that is wonderful compared with what existed a century since, but to this he has added the chemical and physiological sciences then scarcely known, and has proved that the laws of the former and more abstract are equally those of the latter more concrete and special ones. If, then, there is truth in the suggestion of Pascal that we are to consider the endless succession of men as one man, may it not be that the laws of all the earlier and more abstract departments of science will be found to be equally true in reference to that highly concrete and special one which embraces the relations of man in society, and that, therefore, all science will prove to be but one, its parts differing as do the colors of the spectrum, but producing, as does the sun's ray, undecomposed, one white and bright light? To show that such is certainly the case is the object of the present work.

Turning again to the figure, the reader will remark that the branch of science of which it is proposed now to treat, finds its place between those of material and mental life, organology and psychology, and that it is through it that both must look for their development. That the mind may be active and vigorous, the body must be properly cared for. Social Science looks to the care of both. It is the science of the relations of man with the physical world over which it is given to him to rule, and with that social one in which it is given to him to perform a part. Upon the nature of those relations depends the stimulation into activity of those qualities which constitute the real MAN—those by which he stands distinguished from other animals. What they are it is proposed now to show.

CHAPTER II.

OF MAN—THE SUBJECT OF SOCIAL SCIENCE.

§ 1. Association essential to the existence of man. As the planets gravitate to each other, Man tends towards his fellow-man. Local centres balance and distribute the masses in order and harmony. Centralization and decentralization analogous, and alike necessary, among planets and societies. Illustrative history of the nations. Freedom of association maintained by the balancing attractions. The welfare of the individual, and of the aggregate, dependent upon their freedom.

§ 2. Individuality of man proportioned to the diversity of his endowments and activities. Free association develops individuality. Variety in unity, and peace in diversity. The balance of worlds, and of societies, maintained by counter-balance.

§ 3. Responsibility of man measured by his individuality. Historic illustrations. Association, individuality, and responsibility, grow and decline together.

§ 4. Man a being of growth and progress. Progress is motion requiring attraction, depending upon reciprocal action, and implying individuality and association.—Progress is in the ratio of these conditions. The laws of being the same in matter, man, and communities. Definition of social science.

§ 1. MAN, the molecule of society, is the subject of Social Science. Like all other animals, he requires food and sleep; but his greatest need is that of ASSOCIATION with his fellow-men. Born the most helpless of animals, he requires the largest care in infancy. Capable of acquiring the highest degree of knowledge, he is yet destitute of the instinct of the bee, the beaver, and other animals. Dependent for all his knowledge on the experience of himself or others, he needs *language* for the interchange of thought; and there can be no language without *association*. Isolate him, and he loses the power of speech, and with it the reasoning faculty: restore him to society, and with the return of speech he becomes again the reasoning man.

We have here the great law of MOLECULAR GRAVITATION as the indispensable condition of the existence of the being known as man. The particles of matter have each an independent existence, the atom of oxygen, or the grain of sand being perfect in itself. The tree produces the same fruits when standing alone, as do those which remain in their native groves; and each dog, cat, or rabbit, possesses all its powers in a state of entire isolation. Such not being the case with man, he tends of necessity to gravitate towards his fellow-man. Of all animals he is the most gregarious; and the greater the number collected in a given space, the greater is the attractive force that is there exerted, as was shown in the cities of the ancient world,—Nineveh and Babylon, Athens and Rome; and as is now shown in Paris and London, New York and Philadelphia. Gravitation is here, as everywhere, in the *direct* ratio of the mass, and the *inverse* one of the distance.

Why then do not all men tend to come together on a single spot? Because of that same simple and universal law which maintains the beautiful order of the solar system, COUNTER-ATTRACTION. Each of the great bodies of which the universe is composed, has its own centre of attraction, which holds its parts together. Were those centres annihilated, all would crumble at once to ruin. In like manner, we see everywhere throughout the world, local centres of attraction exercising an amount of influence that is in near proportion to their size, and to the mental development of their population.

London and Paris may be regarded as the rival suns of Europe; and but *for* the counter-attraction of local centres, like Vienna and Berlin, Florence, Brussels, and other cities, Europe would present one great centralized system, whose population was tending always towards them, there to make their exchanges, and thence to receive their laws. So, too, is it in these United States. The tendency is strong towards New York, despite the attractions of local centres such as Philadelphia, Washington, Cincinnati, and New Orleans, and the capitals of the several States. Were we to obliterate these local centres, and place in New York a strong centralized government, like those of England, France, and Russia, that city would soon far exceed the present size of London. The local governments would fall to pieces, and voluntary association would speedily be replaced by the forced association of masters and dependents. Every village requiring to have a road, bridge, or bank, would be forced to apply at the great city, paying innumerable officers, as is now the case in France, before obtaining the desired permission. Every community suffering from any oppression would find its voice drowned by those who profited by the abuse, as is the case with complaints to Parliament from Ireland or India. Instead of obtaining the required laws without cost from the little capital, they would be compelled to employ agents, who, as is now the case in England, would accumulate fortunes at their expense. Much of this is already seen at Washington, but very trivial is it compared with what it would be were all the business transacted by State Legislatures and County Boards, brought before Congress, as it now is before the British Parliament.

The centralizing tendency of the State Capital is, in its turn, neutralized by the attraction of the various county-seats. Obliterate these, and the State Capital would grow rapidly, while local associations would be in a great degree annihilated.

Further, whatever tends to the production of *local* employment for time and talent, gives value to land, promotes its division, and enables parents and children to remain in closer connection with each other. On the contrary, whatever diminishes *local* employment, tends to the consolidation of land, the breaking up of families, the increase of absenteeism, and the building up of great cities at the expense of the country at large.

History furnishes evidence that the tendency to association, without which the human animal cannot become the true MAN, has everywhere grown with the growth of local centres of attraction, and declined with their decline. Such centres existed in nearly all the Grecian Islands, while Laconia and Attica, Bœotia, Argos, and other States, possessed each its own. Local association there existed to an extent till then unequalled in the world, yet the tendency towards general association was shown in the establishment of the Olympic and other games, which drew together the distinguished men of Greece, as well as those of Italy and Asia. The Amphictyonic League gave further evidence of the tendency to *general* as a consequence of *local* association; but, unhappily, the attractive power of this central sun was insufficient for maintaining order among the planets, which, as a consequence, frequently shot madly from their spheres, and jostled one another.

Destroy local centres, and centralize power in the hands of the general government, and there will be diminution in the power of *voluntary* association for the purposes of peace, and a tendency towards *involuntary* association for the purposes of war. Destroy the central government, and conflicts amongst the States become inevitable. The people of Greece had all this yet to learn; and their frequent wars at length resulted in the establishment of a highly centralized government, controlling the funds contributed by subject cities, whose people, having lost the power of defending their own rights, had to seek justice at the hands of Athens. To that city resorted all who sought power or profit, all who were unable to obtain a living at home, and all who preferred plunder to labor; until at length, as voluntary association disappeared, Attica became to a great extent the property of a single individual, surrounded by slaves, and all the States of Greece became involved in one common ruin.

So was it, too, in early Italy, which possessed numerous cities, each the centre of a district in which local association existed in a high degree. In time, however, as Rome, perpetually disturbing her weaker neighbors, grew by help of plunder, power became centralized within her walls, her people became more and more dependent on the public treasury, and voluntary association gradually disappeared—all Italy presenting thenceforward the spectacle of great landlords occupying palaces and surrounded by troops of slaves.

Looking next to modern Italy, we see Milan, Genoa, Venice, Florence, Rome, and other cities, each a local centre such as had once existed among the Greeks. For want, however, of a sun with attractive force sufficient for the maintenance of harmony, they were perpetually at war among themselves, thereby enabling Austria and France to become masters of the peninsula, after which the habit of voluntary association wholly disappeared.

India had once numerous centres of attraction. Besides its various capitals, each village was a self-governing community, in which the power of association existed to an extent unknown elsewhere; but with the centralization of power in Calcutta it has almost entirely disappeared.

Spain once had numerous local centres. Association existed to a great extent, not only amongst the enlightened Moors, but also amongst those of the Christian faith. The discovery of the New World, of which the government became the absentee landlord, unduly increasing the central power, local activity and association declined, and weakness and depopulation were the necessary consequences.

Germany is the home of European decentralization, of jealousy of central power, and of zeal for local rights. Local association having steadily grown, it has been followed up, in our own day, by the formation of the Zollverein, or Customs Union, one of the most important events in modern European history. Germany, however, like Greece, wanting the central sun round which the numerous planets might peacefully revolve, has been retarded in civilization by the interference of foreign powers, who have stirred up internal discord. Strong for defence, she has been weak for offence, and has shown no such tendency towards wars for conquest as has been exhibited by her highly centralized neighbor, France. Though abounding in local centres of attraction, she has had no great central city to direct the modes of thought; and to this it is due, that Germany is now rapidly taking the position of the great intellectual centre of Europe, and even of the world.

Amongst the states of Germany, Prussia is pre-eminent for a policy tending to the maintenance of local centres. All the ancient divisions, from the communes to the provinces, have been preserved, and their rights respected, in consequence of which the people advance rapidly in freedom as the state advances in power. Under the lead of Prussia, Northern Germany has been brought under a great federal system which places internal commerce on a footing very similar to that of these United States.

No state in Europe has, more than Switzerland, exhibited a tendency to decentralization, and to that peaceful association within which gives strength for resistance to attacks from without.

In France, the revolution of 1789 annihilated the local governments and thus increased centralization, the consequences of which are seen in a perpetual succession of wars and revolutions. Much was done towards decentralization when the lands of the Church, and of absentee nobles, were divided amongst the people, and to this it is partly due that France has grown in strength, notwithstanding the extraordinary centralization of her system.

Belgium and Holland present remarkable instances of the tendency of local action to produce habits of association. In both, the towns were numerous; and the effect of combined action is seen in the wonderful productiveness of what was originally one of the poorest of European countries.

In no part of Europe was the division of land so complete as in Norway, even before the Norman Conquest of England. The tendency of local attraction to produce habits of association was shown in the development of a popular literature which diffused a common intelligence throughout all parts of the social body. The skill exhibited in working iron, and the great diversification of employments, furnish striking evidence of the existence of the habit of combination at that early period. The same habit still exists, giving to this little people a force of resistance to centralization that has recently been exhibited in a manner scarcely paralleled in history.

The attraction of local centres in the British Islands, formerly so great, has long steadily diminished. Edinburgh, once the metropolis of a kingdom, has become a mere provincial city; while Dublin, once the seat of an independent Parliament, has so declined, that were it not the place where a representative of majesty holds his occasional levees, it would scarcely now be heard of. London and Liverpool, Manchester and Birmingham, have grown rapidly; but with these exceptions, the population was stationary in the decade ending with 1851. Everywhere is seen a steady tendency towards centralization, with decrease of local attraction, increase of absenteeism, and decline in the power of voluntary association,—the latter strikingly shown in the emigration of the few past years. With every step in that direction is seen an increase in the necessity for involuntary association, manifested by an increase in fleets and armies, and in the amount of contributions required for their support.

The Northern States of the Union present such a combination of the centralizing and decentralizing forces as has not been elsewhere equalled; and there we find, in the highest degree, the tendency to local action for the erection of schools, the making of roads, and for every other imaginable purpose. In the Southern States the reverse of this is seen; masters owning men who may not even sell their labor, or exchange its products. This is centralization; and hence it is that we here see so great a tendency to disturbance of the power of association elsewhere. All the wars of the Union have here had their origin.

Barbarism is the necessary consequence of the absence of ASSOCIATION. Deprived of this, Man, losing his distinctive qualities, ceases to be the subject of Social Science.

§ 2. The next distinctive quality of man is INDIVIDUALITY. Each animal is the type of all his species; but in man we find differences of tastes, feelings, and capacities almost as numerous as are those of the human countenance. That these differences may be developed he needs association with his fellows; and their highest development is found in towns and cities, where there is the greatest variety of employment, and therefore the greatest power of association.

"The more imperfect a being," says Goethe, "the more do its parts resemble each other, and the more do the parts resemble the whole. The more perfect a being, the more dissimilar are the parts. In the former case, the parts are more or less a repetition of the whole; in the latter, they are totally unlike the whole. The more the parts resemble each other, the less is the subordination of one to the other, subordination of parts indicating a high grade of organization."

This is as true of societies as it is of plants and animals. The more imperfect they are, the less is the variety of employments and the smaller the development of intellect, and the more do the parts resemble each other, as is seen in all purely agricultural countries. The greater the variety of employments, the greater the demand for intellectual effort, the more dissimilar become the parts, and the more perfect becomes the whole; as is seen by comparing a purely agricultural district with one in which agriculture, manufactures, and commerce are happily combined. *Difference* is essential *to association.* The farmer does not need to associate with his brother farmer, but with the carpenter, the blacksmith, and the miller; as does the miller with the mason and the farmer. In every society there exists a vast amount of intellectual power that is wasted for want of the demand afforded by variety in the demands for human service. Life being a "mutual exchange of relations," where difference does not exist, exchanges cannot take place; and the development of individuality has ever been in the ratio of the power of man to combine with his fellow-men.

That power, as we have seen, *has always existed in the ratio of the equal action of the centralizing and decentralizing forces.* Its existence was manifested in the highest degree in Greece just prior to the invasion of Xerxes, and then and there we find the greatest development of intellectual power. To the men produced in that period the age of Pericles owes its illustration. The destruction of Athens by the Persian armies brought with it the conversion of the citizens into soldiers, with increase of centralization, and decline in the power of voluntary association and of individuality; until at length, the free citizen having disappeared, the slave alone is found cultivating the lands of Attica. So, likewise, was it in Italy, the highest individuality having existed when the Campagna was filled with cities. Following the decline of these, the great city grew, filled with paupers, the capital of a land tilled by slaves. So, now, throughout the East, society is divided into two great parts: the men who toil, and those who live on the product of their toil. As between these there can be no *association*, the chain of society wants the connecting links, and there is none of that *motion* among the parts needed for developing the power of each and all.

The numerous Italian towns of the Middle Ages were remarkable for the *motion* by means of which individuality is developed. So, likewise, in Belgium and in Spain prior to the centralization which followed the expulsion of the Moors, and the discovery of the gold and silver deposits of the Western Continent. Such, too, was the case in each of the several parts of the United Kingdom. Ireland, at the close of the last century, gave to the world such men as Burke, Flood, Grattan, Sheridan, and Wellington; but, centralization having greatly grown, individuality has passed away. Scotland, too, a century since, possessed a body of men as distinguished as any in Europe; but her local institutions have since decayed, and we are now told that she has "few individual thinkers," the mind of the whole country being "cast in the mould of English universities," a state of things "unfavorable to originality and power of thought."

In England the progress of centralization has caused an increase of pauperism, and a decline of individuality; the small proprietors having given way to the farmer with his hired laborers, and the great manufacturer surrounded by his hosts of operatives. London grows enormously at the expense of the country at large; and thus does centralization produce the disease of over-population; a disease which is, as we are told, to be cured by a colonization tending still farther to diminish the power of association.

In France, in the days of Louis XIV., nearly the whole land was in the hands of a few great proprietors and dignitaries of the Church, who were mere dependents on the sovereign will. The right to labor was a privilege exercised at the pleasure of the monarch; and men were forbidden on pain of death to worship God according to their consciences.

In the Northern States of the American Union, centralization being very limited, and association free, individuality exists to a degree unknown elsewhere; the feeling that every man can rise if he will, furnishing the strongest inducement to strive for the attainment of knowledge. In the Southern States association can take place only through the master, so that there is little individuality.

The more perfectly the local attraction counterbalances that of the centre—the more society tends to conform to the laws that govern our system of worlds—the more harmonious must be the action of all the parts, and the greater the tendency towards voluntary association, towards the development of individual powers, and towards the maintenance of peace at home and abroad.

§ 3. The next quality which distinguishes man from the animals, is RESPONSIBILITY for his actions, before his Creator and his fellow-men.

The slave is not responsible; he but obeys his master. The soldier is not responsible for the murders he commits; he is but an instrument in the hands of his superior officer, who in turn but obeys the orders of the State. The pauper is not responsible, though often held to be so by his neighbor men. The savage slays his fellow-men, and exhibits their scalps as evidence of his cunning or his courage. The soldier boasts of his prowess, and gladly enumerates those who have fallen by his sword. The warlike nation prides itself on the glory acquired at the cost of thousands of lives, and decorates its galleries with pictures plundered from their rightful owners, while generals and admirals live in affluence on their portion of the plunder. With growing individuality men learn to call such acts by their only true and proper names—robbery and murder.

The Spartans permitted no responsibility of parents for their children; and they sought to prevent the growth of wealth, while surrounding themselves with slaves to whom all individual will was utterly denied. In Attica, on the contrary, though slaves were numerous, labor was held in much higher honor, and diversity of employment caused great demand for intellectual effort. As a consequence of this the rights of parents were respected, while those of the children were fully cared for by the laws of Solon.

In the East, and in Africa, where individuality has no existence, parents kill their children, and children expose their aged and helpless parents. In highly centralized France, foundling hospitals abound; and it is but recently that any effort has been made to diffuse education among the masses of the people. With the growth of centralization in England, child-murder has taken the place occupied by the foundling hospitals in France.* Little provision has been

* It was declared by the coroner of Leeds, and assented to as probable by the surgeon, that there were, as near as could be calculated, about three hundred children put to death yearly in Leeds alone, that were not registered by the law. In other words, three hundred infants were murdered to avoid the consequences of their living; and these murders, as the coroner said, are never detected. —*Leader*.

made for the proper education of the people, and the feeling of responsibility declines with the decline of individuality that has attended the consolidation of the land, and the substitution of day laborers for small proprietors.

In decentralized Germany there is a steady increase in the provision for education. It is in the Northern States of the American Union, however, that we find the strongest feeling of responsibility in this regard. The system of universal education commenced in Massachusetts by the early settlers, has made its way through New England, New York, Pennsylvania, and all the Western States; aided in these latter by grants of land from the general government expressly devoted to this object. New York, unaided, exhibits in her public schools, 900,000 students, with school libraries containing now 2,000,000 of volumes. The public schools of Pennsylvania contain 650,000 students, while the young State of Wisconsin, in this respect, rivals her elder sisters.

In no part of the world is education the object of so much attention as in the Northern States, whereas in the highly centralized South all instruction of the laboring class is by law prohibited. As a consequence, schools of any kind are few, and the proportion of uninstructed among even the white population is extremely great.

RESPONSIBILITY, INDIVIDUALITY, and ASSOCIATION thus grow together; and they everywhere advance in proportion as the social government approaches to the system which maintains the wonderful harmony of the heavens.

§ 4. Lastly, man is distinguished by his CAPACITY FOR PROGRESS. The hare, the ox, and the camel, are now what they were in the days of Homer—man alone recording his experience and profiting by that of his predecessors. That there may be progress, there must be *motion;* which is itself the result of the incessant decomposition and recomposition of matter. To have motion there must be *heat. Vital heat* results from chemical action, the fuel being food. *Social heat* results from the *combination produced by difference.* The more rapid the consumption of food, either material or intellectual, the greater will be the heat resulting, and the more rapid the increase of power to replace the food consumed.

The laws here given are those which govern matter in all its forms, whether that of coal, iron, stones, clay, corn, oxen or men. If true of communities they must be equally so of each and every one of its members; as are those relating to the atmosphere at large in reference to the countless atoms of which it is composed.*

Social Science treating of man in his efforts for the maintenance and improvement of his condition, it may be now defined as being:—*The Science of the laws which govern man in his efforts to secure for himself the highest* INDIVIDUALITY, *and the greatest power of* ASSOCIATION *with his fellow-men.*

* "To Nature nothing can be added; from Nature nothing can be taken away; the sum of her energies is constant, and the utmost man can do in the pursuit of physical truth, or in the applications of physical knowledge, is to shift the constituents of the never-varying total, and out of one of them to form another. The law of conservation rigidly excludes both creation and annihilation. Waves may change to ripples, and ripples to waves,—magnitude may be substituted for number, and number for magnitude,—asteroids may aggregate to suns, suns may resolve themselves into floræ and faunæ, and floræ and faunæ melt in air,—the flux of power is eternally the same. It rolls in music through the ages, and all terrestrial energy,—the manifestations of life, as well as the display of phenomena, are but the modulations of its rhythm."—Tindall. *Heat considered as a Mode of Motion.*

The following account of an experiment made before the Royal Institution of London exhibits the manner in which heat is generated by means of motion:

"An instrument was exhibited by means of which the temperature of a small quantity of water contained in a shallow circular case, provided with vanes in its top and bottom, and violently agitated by a circular disc provided with similar vanes, and made to turn rapidly round, could easily be raised in temperature several degrees in a few minutes by the power of a man, and by means of which steam-power applied to turn the disc had raised the temperature of the water by thirty degrees in half an hour. The bearings of the shaft, to the end of which the disc was attached, were entirely external; so that there was no friction of solids under the water, and no way of accounting for the heat developed except by the friction in the fluid itself. It was pointed out that the heat thus obtained is not *produced from a source*, but is *generated;* and that what is called into existence by the work of a man's arm cannot be matter."—*Annual of Scientific Discovery*, 1853, p. 183

CHAPTER III.

OF INCREASE IN THE NUMBERS OF MANKIND.

§ 1. Quantity of matter not susceptible of increase. Susceptible of being changed in place and in form. Constantly taking new and higher forms—passing from the inorganic to the organic, and ending in man. Man's power limited to the direction of the natural forces. Law of endless circulation.

§ 2. Preparation of the earth for the reception of man.

§ 3. Man, in common with other animals, a consumer of food. His mission, on this earth, so to direct the natural forces, as to cause the soil to yield larger supplies of the commodities required for his use. Conditions upon which, alone, those supplies can be augmented.

§ 4. Law of the relative increase in the numbers of Mankind, and in the supply of food.

§ 5. Malthusian law of population. Teaches, that while the tendency of matter to assume the lowest forms, augments in an arithmetical ratio only, when it seeks to attain the highest form, that tendency is found existing in a geometrical one.

§ 1. That the power of association may increase, population must increase in density. That it has done so is shown in the fact, that the population of France has doubled since the beginning of the last century, and that of Great Britain during the present one; while the numbers of New York and Massachusetts, which sixty years since were but 700,000, have now arrived at more than 4,000,000.

As, however, the quantity of matter cannot increase, the changes thus indicated tend to prove that portions of it must have assumed higher forms, passing from the simple ones of granite, clay, shale, or sand, to the complex ones of the bones, muscles, or brains of men.

With this increase in the number of persons needing to be fed, there has been required a corresponding one in the quantity of animal and vegetable food; and, that this might be furnished, it has been necessary that other portions of the rocks, or of the clays and sands resulting from their decomposition, should take upon themselves the forms of wheat and rye, of oats and grass, while others still have passed into the forms of sheep and calves, hogs and oxen. That this change must have taken place is obvious from the fact, that large as has been the increase in the number to be fed, the facility of obtaining food is greater now than at any former period. What, however, has been the agency of man in bringing about these results? Let us inquire.

Force is compounded of matter and motion. Man can

neither create nor destroy matter, but he can change it in its place and in its form. He cannot alter the existing quantity of force, but he can affect its distribution and its mode of manifestation. His power resembles that of the wire which connects the extremities of the magnetic apparatus, and thus produces development of latent forces. Every such development causes matter to assume a different form. In the propelling of a steamboat, coal and water are decomposed; and with every motion of the human body, the brain and muscles, in the giving and the executing of a command, lose a portion of their substance, which must be replaced by fresh supplies of fuel in the form of food. Matter is thus in perpetual circulation, and the more rapid the *motion*, the greater is the *force* produced.

This circulation has endured from all time, but with every step in the progress of the earth towards its present condition, there has been an increase in the machinery of decomposition and recomposition, with a steady tendency towards development of the forces which are always latent in matter, waiting until man shall come to set them free. Geologists inform us that in the Silurian period the animal and vegetable life was uniform in character, and lowest in development. Later, during the period of the coal formation, vegetation abounded, but still of the most monotonous character, the plants exhibiting that absence of true flowers which marks the lowest stages of vegetable life.

What was the object of all this vegetation? To produce decomposition, and set free the latent forces of nature. In the stomach of plants are digested the inorganic elements supplied by the soil and the air. The constituents of all are: carbon, nitrogen, hydrogen, and oxygen, the four principal elements of the organic creation; sulphur, phosphorus, chlorine, lime, potassium, sodium, iron, and a few other inorganic substances. These pass into the frame of vegetables; the vegetables are consumed by animals, man in his turn supporting life by means of the consumption of both. Organic bodies are subject to a constant process of renovation, while inorganic are fixed in their composition. Man can, to some small extent, put together and fashion inert bodies, but the lowest form of life, whether vegetable or animal, is wholly beyond his reach.

Vegetables alone can assimilate and organize inorganic matter. The vegetable life must therefore precede the animal life, which latter needs organic matter for its support.

5

Some animals prey upon other and inferior animals, while themselves furnishing food for beings more highly organized. Again, vegetables *eliminate* oxygen, and exhale it into the air. Animals, on the contrary, *absorb* oxygen, which combines with certain parts of the body, burning the combustible substances, and thus generating animal heat. Combining with the carbon of the food, it produces carbonic acid gas; which, being thrown out of the lungs, is absorbed by the leaves of plants; the carbon separated becomes a part of their frame, while the oxygen is restored to the atmosphere.

Thus animals and vegetables are mutually dependent on each other for existence, their elements being interchanged through the medium of the atmosphere, "the grand receptacle from which all things spring, and to which they all return."

§ 2. Development, beginning in the stomach of vegetables, is continued in that of animals until the earth becomes fitted for the purposes of man, the only being gifted with power to become the lord of nature, while all others remain her slaves.

Looking now over the earth, we see the same forces everywhere in action, producing new combinations for the support of vegetable life, and thus preparing the land, as a residence, at first for the lower animals, but ultimately, for man.

The amount of heat by which the sea water is raised in the form of vapor, is estimated as being equal to the power of sixteen billions of horses. This vapor, condensing, descends in rain, carrying down to the valleys large quantities of soil resulting from decomposition of the rocks. Here again we find *difference* producing *combination* and *motion*. The greater the variety of the particles the richer is the soil produced, as is seen in the deltas of such rivers as the Mississippi, the Ganges, and the Indus.

Vast quantities of this earth pass into the ocean, to be taken up by the myriads of its inhabitants. The minute coral insect raises massive walls of limestone, in which two-fifths of their weight of carbon are chained down and fast imprisoned. New supplies thereof are, however, furnished by the escape of carbonic acid gas from innumerable fissures in the earth's surface, such as the *Grotto del Cane*, or the fatal "Valley of Death," the wonder of the isle of Java. Thus carbonic acid, like watery vapor, is continually circulating, from the atmosphere, through the plant and the animal, and back again to the air, assuming on the way the various forms of life. The coral rocks on emerging from the water, become covered with loose materials from debris that is wafted along the surface by tides and currents. The cocoanut, thus brought, nourished by the organic remains of the insect builders, takes root there, and furnishes food and a scanty clothing to the first inhabitants. Next, the rocks become disintegrated, while the earlier vegetable matter decays; and the two combining furnish a richer soil, upon which vegetation of a higher order takes its place, and in turn prepares the soil for still higher forms of life.

The leaf of the living plant sucks in carbonic acid from the air, but gives off the oxygen contained in this gas, retaining the carbon alone. The roots drink in water from the soil; and out of carbon and water thus obtained, the plant forms starch, sugar or fat, and other substances. The animal introduces this starch, sugar or fat, into its stomach, and draws in oxygen from the atmosphere by its lungs; with these materials it undoes the labors of the living plant, delivering back again from the lungs and the skin both the starch and the oxygen in the form of carbonic acid and water. The process is clearly represented in the following scheme:—

	Takes in	Produces
The Plant	*Carbonic acid* by its leaves; *Water* by its roots.	*Oxygen* from its leaves; *Starch, etc.,* in its solid substance.
The Animal	*Starch* and *fat* in the stomach; *Oxygen* into the lungs.	*Carbonic acid* and *water* from the skin and the lungs.

The circle thus begins with taking in carbonic acid and water, and ends with the delivery of the same substances.

§ 3. In the early period of society the changes of form are very slow indeed. In the days of the Plantagenets, the yield of an acre was but six or eight bushels of wheat. Step by step, however, as man obtained the command of the various forces provided for his use, he obtained thirty, forty, or fifty bushels, and of other produce almost as many tons.

Without vital heat that command could not be obtained, and without fuel there could be no such heat That fuel, as we see, is food, without which there can be no vital action, and thus it is that we reach the point at which man and animals stand on a level with each other. In common with them all he eats, drinks, and sleeps, and in common with them all he must have supplies of food.

The earth is a vast magazine of latent power. Loosening

the soil to admit the action of the sun and rain, man places in it a seed which sprouts, grows by aid of the earth and atmosphere, and yields the corn required for his support. In this, he does no more than does he who feeds the locomotive, placing matter in a situation to be decomposed, and thus fitting its atoms for entering into other combinations. *Combination is motion*, and *motion gives force*. He ploughs deeper, digs drains to enable the water to escape, and precisely as he thus facilitates the motion of matter, is he rewarded by larger returns to his exertions. With the increased control over the natural forces thus obtained, he obtains a larger quantity of food from a given surface, and is thus steadily enabled to live more and more in connection with his fellow-man. Association bringing into activity other forces, he now turns to use the limestone, coal, and iron ore, the decomposition of which supplies materials for organic life. The motion thus begun continues, these substances rarely again returning to their original state.

Where vegetation exists without animal life, the mineral matter furnished by the soil returns directly to it by the process of decay. Not so, however, where vegetable produce is consumed by animals. Being then digested, it is conveyed to the different parts of the body, the saline matter to the blood and tissues, and the phosphate of lime chiefly to the bones, composing nearly half their weight.

These changes are represented as follows:

Taken in by		Produced
The Plant	Phosphoric acid, lime, common and other salts from the soil.	Perfect substance of plants.
The Animal	a. Parts of plants. b. The bone and tissues, with oxygen from the lungs.	Perfect bone, blood, and tissues. Phosphates and other salts in the excretions.
The Soil	Excretions of animals, dead animals and plants.	Phosphoric acid, lime, etc.

Plants and animals thus return their materials to mother earth, and *it is upon this condition alone that motion can be increased, or even maintained*. Our great mother, the Earth, *gives* nothing, but she is willing to *lend* every thing; and the larger the demand made upon her, the larger will be the supply, provided that man recollect that he is but a borrower from a great bank in which punctuality of re-payment is as much required as in the banks of America, France or England.

That this condition may be complied with, there must be association, and *difference* is indispensable to association whether in the social or the material world. The farmer or sugar planter does not need to associate with his brother farmer or planter, nor the wool-grower with him who has wool to sell; but they each and all find it advantageous to exchange the produce of their labor with the carpenter, the blacksmith, the mason, the miner, the furnace-man, the spinner, the weaver and the printer, as all these require to purchase food and the materials of clothing, and to pay for them with their services, or the commodities they have produced. Where the producer and consumer are placed side by side there is rapid motion of the products of labor, with increased power to repay to mother earth what she has lent, and to establish a credit with her for larger loans in future. Where, on the contrary, there are only farmers or planters, and where consequently there is but little societary motion, the powers of the earth diminish, and the producer and consumer become more widely separated, with heavy diminution of both heat and force. This is seen in all purely agricultural countries. Virginia and the Carolinas have been steadily engaged in exhausting the elements of fertility in the soil, because of the absence of consumers, and the necessity for dependence on distant markets; and such, to a great extent, is the case throughout our Southern States. The farmer who commences on rich prairie land, obtains at first forty or fifty bushels to the acre; but the quantity declines from year to year, and finally falls to twenty, or often even less. A century since, the farmers of New York were reported as obtaining generally twenty-four bushels of wheat per acre, but the average now is little more than twelve, while that of the rich State of Ohio has fallen yet lower. The power of the soil to yield food being the measure of the power of men to live together, with each stage of its decline the ability to associate diminishes; as is shown in the remarkable emigration now going on from Ohio, the settlement of which is yet so recent—from Georgia, with a population of 1,000,000, and a territory capable of supporting half the people of the Union—and from Alabama, which but forty years ago was a wilderness occupied chiefly by a few straggling Indians. *The consumer must take his place beside the producer in order to enable man to comply with the condition on which he obtains loans from the great bank of mother earth—the simple condition that when he shall have done with the capital furnished to him he shall return it to the place whence it had been taken.*

Wherever this condition is complied with we see a steady increase in the motion of the matter destined to furnish man with food, and an equally steady increase in the number of persons requiring to be supplied, with a constant improvement in the quantity and quality of the food to be divided among the claimants. In the days of the Plantagenets, when the population of England little exceeded 2,000,000, an acre yielded but six bushels of wheat, and famines were frequent. Now, we see 18,000,000 occupying the same surface, and obtaining greatly increased quantities of very superior food.

So, likewise, has it been in France. In 1760 the population was 21,000,000, and the produce of grain 94,500,000 hectolitres; whereas, in 1840, the former had risen to 34,000,000, and the latter to 182,516,000, giving to each and every person twenty per cent. more in quantity, with great improvement in the quality of the grain; and yet the surface cultivated had scarcely at all increased. Within this period the potato culture has been introduced, and green crops now furnish supplies of food two-thirds as great as the whole quantity produced less than a century since. The total product has trebled, while the numbers to be fed have increased but sixty per cent. A constantly growing diversity of employment now enables the French peasant to pay his debts to mother earth, returning to her the manure yielded by his crops; whereas, when manufactures scarcely existed, famines were so numerous and severe, as sometimes to sweep off a large proportion of the widely scattered population.

So, too, is it in Belgium, Germany, and every other country in which diversity of employment facilitates association; while the reverse is seen in all those purely agricultural countries which are steadily exhausting their soil, and diminishing the power of association, as in Virginia and Carolina on one side of the ocean, Portugal and Turkey on the other.

In proportion as increased motion leads to increased power of association, man is enabled to call to his aid other forces to be employed in grinding his grain and transporting its product to market; in converting his trees into planks and preparing them for houses; and, finally, in carrying his messages with such rapidity that time and space seem almost annihilated. At each successive stage of progress in this direction, he finds himself enabled more and more to devote his time and mind to the production of the grain to be ground, the trees to be sawed, and the wool to be spun; and thus to make provision for increased association with his fellow-men, each step being but the preparation for a new and greater one.

§ 4. The law of the relative increase in the numbers of mankind, and in the supply of food and other commodities required for their support may now be found in the following propositions:

Motion gives force, and the more rapid the motion the greater is the force obtained.

With motion matter takes on itself new and higher forms, passing from the simple ones of the inorganic world and through those more complex of the vegetable world to the highly complicated forms of animal life, and ending in man.

The more rapid the motion the greater is the tendency to changes of form, to increase of force, and to increase of the power at the command of man.

The more simple the forms in which matter exists, the less is the power of resistance to gravitation, the greater the tendency to centralization, the less the motion, and the less the force.

The more complex the form the greater becomes the power of resistance to gravitation, the greater the tendency to decentralization, the greater the motion, and the greater the force.

With every increase of power on the one hand there is diminished resistance on the other. The more motion produced the greater must, therefore, be the tendency to further increase of motion and of force.

The most complex and highly organized form in which matter exists is that of man; and here alone do we find the capacity for direction required for producing increase of motion and of force.

Wherever the greatest number of men exist we should therefore find the greatest tendency to the decentralization of matter, to increase of motion, to further changes of form, and to the higher development commencing in the vegetable world and ending in the increased production of men.

With every increase in the extent to which matter has assumed the form of man, there should, consequently, be an increase of his power to control and direct the forces provided for his use; with constantly accelerated motion, and constantly accelerated changes of form, and constant increase in his power to command the food and clothing needed for his support.

In the material world, motion among the atoms of matter is a consequence of physical heat. Greatest at the equator, it diminishes until, as we approach the poles, we reach the region of centralization and physical death.

In the moral world it is a consequence of social heat; and motion, as has been already shown, consists in "an exchange of relations" resulting from the existence of those differences that develop social life. It is greatest in those communities in which agriculture, manufactures, and commerce are happily combined, and in which, consequently, society has the highest organization. It diminishes as we approach the declining despotisms of the East, the regions of centralization and social death. It increases as we pass from the purely agricultural States of the South towards the regions of more diversified industry in those of the North and East, and there, accordingly, do we find decentralization, life, and force.

Centralization, slavery, and death, travel hand in hand together in both the material and the moral world.

§ 5. The view here presented differs totally from that commonly received, and known as the Malthusian law of population, which may thus be given:

Population tends to increase in a *geometrical* ratio, while the supplies of food increase in an *arithmetical* one only. The former is, therefore, perpetually outstripping the latter, and hence arises the disease of over-population, with its accompaniments, poverty, wretchedness and death; a disease requiring for its remedy, wars, pestilences and famines on the one hand, or on the other, the exercise of that "moral restraint" which shall induce men and women to refrain from matrimony, and thus avoid the dangers resulting from addition to the numbers requiring to be fed. Reduced to distinct propositions, the theory is as follows:

1. Matter tends to take upon itself higher forms, passing from the simple ones of inorganic life to those more beautiful of the vegetable and animal life, and finally terminating in man.

2. This tendency exists in a slight degree in the lower forms of life, matter tending to take on itself the forms of potatoes and turnips, herrings and oysters, in an arithmetical ratio only.

3. When, however, we reach the highest form of which matter is capable, we find the tendency to assume it existing in a geometrical ratio; as a consequence of which, while man

tends to increase as 1, 2, 4, 8, 16, 32, potatoes and turnips, herrings and oysters, increase only as 1, 2, 3, 4; causing the highest form perpetually to outstrip the lower, and producing the disease of over-population.

Were this asserted of any thing else than man, it would be deemed in the highest degree absurd; and it would be asked, why a general law should here be set aside. Everywhere else, increase in number is in the *inverse* ratio of development. Thousands of billions of coral insects are needed to build up islands for men and animals that count by thousands or by millions. Of the *clio borealis*, thousands furnish but one mouthful for the mighty whale. The progeny of a single pair of carp would in three years amount to thousands of billions; that of a pair of rabbits would in twenty years count by millions; whereas that of a pair of elephants would not number dozens. When, however, we reach the highest form, we hear of a new law, in virtue of which man increases in a geometrical ratio, while increase of the commodities required for his use is limited to the arithmetical one.

Endowed with faculties that can be developed solely by association with his kind, made in the image of his Creator, and gifted with the power to distinguish right from wrong, man is thus required to choose between starvation on the one hand, or, on the other, abstinence from that association which tends, in accordance with the divine command, to promote increase of numbers. Such is the generally received doctrine of modern political economy, and, strange as it appears, no proposition has ever yet exercised more influence on the fortunes of the human race. That it should so have done has partly resulted from the fact that it has been propped up by another, in virtue of which man is supposed to have commenced the work of cultivation on the rich soils which would give large returns to his labors, and to have been compelled, with the growth of population, to resort to poorer ones, with constant decline in the reward of his toil,—a theory that, if true, would establish the correctness of the Malthusian law of population. What are its claims to being received as true, will now be shown.

CHAPTER IV.

OF THE OCCUPATION OF THE EARTH.

§ 1. Limited power of man, in the hunter and the shepherd state. Movements of the isolated settler. Commences always with the poorer soils. With increase of numbers, he acquires increase of force, and is enabled to command the services of the richer soils—thence obtaining larger supplies of food. Gradual passage from being the slave of nature, towards becoming nature's master.

§ 2. Mr. Ricardo's theory. Based upon the assumption of a fact that never has existed. The law, as proved by observation, directly the reverse of the theory by him propounded.

§ 3. Course of settlement in the United States.

§ 4. Course of settlement in Mexico, the West Indies, and South America.

§ 5. Course of settlement in Great Britain.

§ 6. Course of settlement in France, Belgium, and Holland.

§ 7. Course of settlement in the Scandinavian Peninsula, Russia, Germany, Italy, the islands of the Mediterranean, Greece, and Egypt.

§ 8. Course of settlement in India. Mr. Ricardo's theory that of depopulation and growing weakness; whereas, the real law is that of growing association, and augmenting power.

§ 1. Man has everywhere commenced his career as a hunter, subsisting on the spoils of the chase and dependent entirely on the voluntary contributions of the earth, having been thus the slave of nature. In time, he is seen in the shepherd state, deriving food and clothing from the animals which he has subjected to his power.

In neither of those states can there exist more than the very slightest power of association. In the first, eight hundred acres of land are required for producing no more food than half an acre can be made to do with proper cultivation. In the second, the land and the flocks being in common, any failure in the supply of food compels the whole tribe to migrate, he who should refuse to do so running the risk of being butchered by other roving tribes. In this stage of society man is thus not only the slave of nature, but also of his fellow-man.

Absence of power in the minority to act independently, is, as we here see, a necessary consequence of that inability to command the natural forces used in the producing of food which we see so plainly testified by the imperfection of savage implements. Let the reader walk into the nearest museum, and he will see with astonishment the rude nature of the industrial machinery that, of necessity, was made to suffice for the wants of long series of generations.

For the purpose of studying the course of man in his efforts to subjugate the various natural forces, and thus to compel them to contribute to the supply of his wants, let us now take a suppositious case. Let us imagine a settler and his descendants placed on an island, and then trace their operations through any period of time, years or centuries; and having thus ascertained what *would be* their course if undisturbed, we shall be prepared to examine the causes which so generally have made their careers so widely different.

The first cultivator, the Robinson Crusoe of his day, provided, however, with a wife, has neither axe nor spade. He works alone. Population being small, he can freely select the land best suited to his purpose. The rich soils around are, however, covered with immense trees that he cannot fell, or they are swamps that he cannot drain; and there being no free circulation of air, the impurity of the atmosphere threatens loss of health if not even of life; while the luxuriant vegetation would again cover the patch he had cleared before he could reduce it to cultivation. He is forced, therefore, to commence on the poor soil of the hill slope, bare of trees, and upon which water cannot stand. Here, drilling a few holes with a stick, he drops the grain which, in due season, yields him a return of twice his seed; and pounding this between stones, he makes a sort of bread. While the earth thus labors for him, he has been trapping birds or rabbits, and gathering fruits. His condition is thus improved.

Sharpening a stone for a hatchet, he destroys the trees by the laborious operation of girdling; but, at length, finding a copper ore, he succeeds in burning it, and thus obtains a better axe with far less labor. Fashioning a rude spade, too, he penetrates to a deeper and better soil; and his seed, being better protected both from drought and frost, the produce is thrice increased. He finds a soil which yields him tin, and this mixed with his copper gives him brass; by aid of which he now proceeds more rapidly. While penetrating more deeply into the land first occupied, he is enabled to clear some portion of the richer soils around, undeterred by the fear that the shrubs exterminated may be almost at once replaced. His children, too, having grown, can now render him assistance, and he thus adds to the power already obtained over various natural forces, that which results from *association* and *combination* with his fellow-men. Next, burning a piece of the iron soil around, he obtains a real spade and axe, rude indeed, but much superior to those he had yet possessed. Removing, with the help of his grown-up sons, the light pine of the steep hill-side, he thus extends his cultivable ground; while his spade enables him to penetrate still further beneath the surface, and to mix the sand with the underlying clay, obtaining thus a more productive soil. The aid of his sons and grandsons now enables him to attempt operations which had been impracticable to himself alone; and each of the largely increased family now obtains much more food in return to far less severe exertion.

Increased *power of association* now brings with it *division of employment*, one portion of the little community performing the labors of the field, while another develops the surrounding mineral wealth. They invent a hoe, by means of which the children are enabled to keep the ground free from weeds. Extending their operations down towards the lower grounds, they burn the brush to let the air circulate, and now girdle the larger trees. Having tamed the ox, they next invent a rude plough, and attaching him to it with a piece of twisted hide, they find themselves enabled to improve and extend their cultivation. The community grows, and with it wealth that exhibits itself in the forms of improved machinery and larger supplies of food and clothing. The dwelling, too, is better. At first it was but a hole in the ground; subsequently it was composed of such decayed logs as the first settler could succeed in placing one upon the other. Windows and chimneys being unknown, he had been forced to live in smoke, if he would not perish of cold; and if the severity of the weather obliged him to close his door, he was not only stifled, but passed his days in utter darkness His time, during a large portion of the year, was thus made unproductive, while his life was liable to be shortened by reason of foul air within, or severe cold without, his miserable hut. Now, however, the increase of population and wealth, resulting from the cultivation of better soils, and from his increased mastery of the great natural forces having increased the power of association, they are enabled to fell the heavy oak and pine, and construct better and more healthy dwellings. Employment becoming more diversified, and individuality become more and more developed, a part of the increasing population is now employed in the field, while another prepares the skins for clothing, and a third fashions implements with which to aid the others in their labors. The supply of food increases, and now, relieved from all fear of famine, they find a surplus to be stored away as provision against failure of future crops.

As cultivation extends downward towards the richer soils of the river bottom, the community are now enabled to engage in the work of drainage, and thus to obtain more copious harvests. Enclosing a meadow for the use of the oxen, they now obtain with diminished labor, larger supplies of meat, milk, butter, and hides. To the flesh of the hog, which lived on mast, they now add beef, and perhaps mutton, the lands first cultivated being abandoned to the sheep.

Numerous generations having now passed away, the younger ones, profiting by the wealth already accumulated, apply their labor with constantly increasing advantage, obtaining as constantly increasing returns to less severe exertion. Calling new powers to their aid, the water, and even the air, is made to work, windmills grinding the grain, and sawmills cutting the timber. The little furnace now appears, charcoal being applied to the reduction of iron ore, and the labor of a single day becomes more productive than that of many weeks had been before. Population spreads along the hill side and down the slope, becoming more and more dense at the seat of the original settlement; and with every step we find increasing tendency to combination of action for the production of food, the manufacture of clothing, the construction of houses, and the preparation of machinery for aiding in all such operations. Marshes are drained, and roads are made between the old settlement and the newer ones that have sprung up around it, thus facilitating exchanges of corn or wool for improved spades or ploughs, for cloths or blankets.

As population increases, with still further development of wealth and power, leisure is acquired for reflection on the experience of themselves and their predecessors, and mind becomes more and more stimulated to action. All being better fed, clothed, and housed, all are incited to new exertions, while with the power of working in or out of doors, according to the season, they can apply their labor with greater steadiness. Thus far, they have found it difficult to gather their crops in season. Harvest time being short, the whole strength of the community has been insufficient to prevent much of the grain from perishing on the ground. Labor has been superabundant during the rest of the year, while the harvest produced a demand that could not be supplied. The reaping-hook and the scythe now, however, take the place of the hand, and the cradle and horse-rake follow, all tending to facilitate accumulation, and increase the power of applying labor to new soils which require embankment as well as drainage. The clay is found to be underlaid with lime, which latter needs to be decomposed, a work that is much facilitated by the road, the horse, and the wagon, which enable the former to procure supplies of the carbon-yielding soil, called coal. Burning the lime and mixing it with clay, he now obtains a soil yielding larger crops with constant diminution in the severity of exertion. Population and wealth farther increasing, the steam-engine assists the work of drainage, while the railroad facilitates transportation of the produce to its market. The cattle being now fattened at home, a large portion of the produce of the rich meadow is converted into manure to be applied to the poorer soils, and he obtains from the market their refuse in the form of bones to be applied to maintaining the powers of his land. Passing thus, at every step, from the poorer to the better soils, the rapidly increasing population obtain from the same surface a constantly increasing supply of the necessaries of life, with constant increase of power to live in connection with each other. The *desire* for association grows with the *power* to satisfy it, labor becomes more productive, and the facilities for commerce increase, with constant tendency toward harmony, peace, and security at home and abroad, and constant increase of numbers, prosperity, wealth and happiness.

Such has been the history of man wherever wealth and population have been permitted to increase. Everywhere he is seen to have commenced poor and helpless, and consequently the slave of nature. Everywhere, as numbers have increased, he is seen to have become, from year to year, and from century to century, more and more her master, every step in that direction being marked by rapid development of *individuality*, increased power of *association*, increased sense of *responsibility*, and increased power of *progress*.

That such has been the case with all nations, and in all parts of the earth, is so obvious that it would seem almost unnecessary to offer any proof of the fact, nor could it be so but that it has been asserted that the course of things had been directly the reverse—that man had always commenced the work of cultivation on the rich soils of the earth, and that then food had been abundant—but that, as population has increased, his successors had found themselves forced to resort to inferior ones, yielding steadily less and less in return to labor; with constant tendency to over-population, poverty, wretchedness, and death. Were this really so, there could be no such thing as universality in the natural laws to which man is subjected, for in regard to all other descriptions of matter, we see him uniformly commencing with the inferior, and passing, as wealth and population grow, to the superior, with constantly increasing return to labor. He is seen to have commenced with the axe of stone, and to have passed through those of copper, bronze, and iron, until he has finally arrived at those of steel; to have passed from the spindle and distaff to the spinning-jenny and the power-loom; from the canoe to the ship; from transportation on the backs of men to that in railroad cars; from rude hieroglyphics painted on skins to the printed book; and from the wild society of the savage tribe where might makes right, to the organized community in which the rights of those who are weak in numbers, or in muscular power, are respected. Having studied these facts, and having satisfied ourselves that such had been his course in reference to all things other than the land required for cultivation, we should be disposed to believe that it must there also prove to have been the case, and that the theory referred to, that of Mr. Ricardo—by virtue of which man is rendered more and more the slave of nature as wealth and population grow—must be untrue.

§ 2. Nearly half a century since Mr. Ricardo published his theory of the nature and causes of RENT;* and during

* The theory is thus stated by its author:—
On the first settling of a country in which there is an abundance of rich and fertile land, a very small portion of which is required to be cultivated for the support of the actual population, or indeed can be cultivated with the capital which the population can command, there will be no rent; for no one would pay for the use of land when there was an abundant quantity not yet appropriated, and therefore at the disposal of whomsoever might choose to cultivate it. . . . . . . If all land had the same properties, if it were boundless in quantity and uniform in quality, no charge could be made for its use, unless where it possessed peculiar advantages of situation. It is only, then, because land is not unlimited in quantity and uniform in quality, and because, in the progress of population, land of an inferior quality or less advantageously situated is called into cultivation, that rent is ever paid for the use of it. When, in the progress of society, land of the second degree of fertility is taken into cultivation rent immediately commences on that of the first quality; and the amount of rent will depend on the difference in the quality of these two portions of land. . . . . . . When land of the third quality is taken into cultivation, rent immediately commences on the second; and it is regulated, as before, by the difference in their productive powers. At the same time,

nearly all that time it has been received by most of the economists of Europe and America, as being so unquestionable, that doubt of its truth could proceed only from incapacity for its comprehension. Attributing the poverty existing in the world to a law emanating from an all-wise and all-beneficent Creator, it relieved the governing classes from all responsibility for the wretchedness by which they were surrounded, and was therefore at once adopted. Since then it has been the doctrine of a large portion of the schools of this country and of Europe, although no two of its teachers have ever yet quite agreed as to what it was that their master had meant to teach. The student, finding an almost universal disagreement amongst them, turns in despair to Mr. Ricardo himself; but only to discover in his celebrated chapter on rent, such contradictions and complications as were scarcely ever before found in the same number of lines, and such as leave him at no loss to account for the variety of doctrines taught by his disciples.

Looking around, he sees that all the recognized laws of nature are characterized by the most perfect simplicity, and the greatest breadth of application. The simplicity of Kepler's law of "equal areas in equal times" is perfect. Its truth, consequently, is universal; and all to whom it is explained feel not only that it *is* true, but that it must continue to be so in relation to all the planets that hereafter may be discovered. A child may understand it; it needs neither commentary nor modification, therein differing greatly from that which is under consideration, and which cannot certainly be charged with either simplicity or universality.

At first sight, however, it seems very simple. Rent is said to be paid for land of the first quality, yielding a hundred quarters in return to a given quantity of labor, when the increase of population renders it necessary to cultivate land of the second quality, yielding but ninety quarters in return

the rent of the first quality will rise, for that must always be above the rent of the second, by the difference of the produce which they yield with a given quantity of capital and labor.

The most fertile and most favorably situated land will be first cultivated, and the exchangeable value of its produce will be adjusted in the same manner as the exchangeable value of all other commodities, by the total quantity of labor necessary in various forms from first to last, to produce it and bring it to market. When land of inferior quality is taken into cultivation, the exchangeable value of raw produce will rise, because more labor is required to produce it.—*Ricardo's Political Economy*, chap. ii.

to the same amount of effort; and the sum of the rent then paid for number one is equal to the *difference* between their respective products. Every man who hears this proposition, sees around him land that pays rent, and sees, too, that that which yields forty bushels to the acre pays more than that which yields but thirty, the difference being nearly equal to the difference of product. He becomes at once a disciple of Mr. Ricardo, admitting that prices are paid for the use of land because soils differ in their qualities; when he would regard it as absurd to assert that prices are paid for oxen because one ox is heavier than another, or that rents are paid for houses because some will accommodate twenty persons, and others only ten or twelve.

The whole system is based upon the assumed fact, that in the beginning of cultivation, when population is small and land abundant, the richest soils alone are cultivated. This fact exists, or it does not. If it has no existence, the system falls to the ground. That it has none, and never had, it is now proposed to show.

The picture drawn by Mr. Ricardo differs totally from that we have above presented for the reader's consideration. The former, placing the settler on the most fertile lands, requires that his children and children's children in succession, should find themselves driven, by sad necessity, to occupy the poorer soils; thus becoming, from generation to generation, more and more the slaves of nature. The latter, placing the early settler on the poorer soils, exhibits his successors exercising constantly increasing power to pass to the cultivation of the richer soils; thus becoming, from generation to generation, more the masters of nature, compelling her to do their work, and pressing onward from triumph to triumph, with constant increase in the power of association, in the development of individuality, in the feeling of responsibility, and in the power of further progress. Which of these pictures is the true one, is to be settled by the determination of the fact, what it is that men in times past have done, and what it is they are now doing, in regard to the occupation of the earth. If it can be shown that, in every country and at every age, the order of events has been in direct opposition to what it is supposed by Mr. Ricardo to have been, then must his theory be abandoned as wholly destitute of foundation. That it has been so will now be shown by a brief examination of facts presented by the history of the world, commencing with these United States. Their settlement having been recent, and being, indeed, still in progress, the settler's course can be traced more readily than would be possible in any of the older countries of Europe.

§ 3. The first settlers of English race established themselves on the barren soil of Massachusetts, founding the colony of Plymouth. The continent was before them, but they had to take what, with their small means, they could obtain. Other settlements were formed at Newport and New Haven, and thence they may be traced, following the course of the rivers, but taking in all cases the higher lands and leaving the clearing of timber and the draining of swamps to their successors. The richest soils of New England remain even yet uncultivated, while of those in cultivation the most productive are those reclaimed within the last half century.

In New York the process has been the same. The unproductive soil of Manhattan Island, and the higher lands of the opposite shore, claimed early attention, while richer and lower lands, close at hand, remain even yet uncultivated. We trace the population along the Hudson to the Valley of the Mohawk, where they established themselves near the head of the stream on lands requiring but little of either clearing or drainage. Geneva, and other towns and villages now seen in the rich western lands of the State, scarcely existed sixty years since; while the high lands bordering on Pennsylvania were early settled—those on Coshocton Creek having been described as very valuable because of "their total exemption from all periodical disorders, particularly fever and ague."

In New Jersey we see the Quakers occupying the high lands towards the heads of rivers, or selecting along the Delaware the light soils that bear the pine, while avoiding the heavier ones on the opposite shore of Pennsylvania, and neglecting altogether rich lands that still remain covered with the finest timber. Passing through sandy districts of the State we find hundred of little clearings long since abandoned, attesting the character of the land that men cultivate when population is small, and land is most abundant.

On the sandy soil of Delaware, the Swedes settled Lewistown and Christiana; and in the now decaying little towns of Elkton and Charlestown, near the head of the Chesapeake Bay, we find evidence of the poverty of the soils first occupied, when fine meadow lands, now the richest farms in the State, were wholly worthless.

Penn follows the Swedes, first selecting the high lands on

the Delaware, about twelve miles north of the site of his future city, but afterwards taking the tongue of land near the confluence of that river and the Schuylkill. Thence we find population extending northwest along the ridge running north and between the river, where miles of early settlements still remain. On the maps of a somewhat later period, the fertile lands near the river, almost to the head of tide water, are shown as held in large tracts and yet uncleared, while the higher ones are divided into numerous little farms. Further on, cultivation almost leaves the river bank, but at a distance from it we find farms that have now been cultivated for more than a hundred years. The old road, made to suit the early settlers, is seen winding about, as if in search of hills to cross; while the new roads keep near the stream, on the low lands which have but recently been subjected to cultivation. Crossing the mountains, we see, near their tops, the habitations of early settlers, who selected the land of the pine, whose knots afforded a substitute for candles they were too poor to purchase. Beyond, we find in the valley of the Susquehanna, meadow lands, still uncleared, and covered with heavy timber. Everywhere, we find cultivation to have commenced on the hill sides, and gradually to have descended, the valleys becoming more cleared of timber, and meadows and cattle appearing, the most certain signs of increasing wealth and population. Passing west, at the foot of the Muncy hills, we find fine limestone land whose food-producing qualities not being obvious to the early settlers, whole tracts of it were exchanged for a jug of whiskey, or a dollar. Taking a bird's eye view of the country, we trace the course of every little stream by the timber standing on its banks, conspicuous among the cleared, but elevated, lands that are everywhere around. Crossing the ridge of the Alleghany to the head-waters of the Ohio, we see a scattered population occupying the higher lands; but as we descend the river the lower ones become cleared, until at length we find ourselves at Pittsburg, in the midst of a dense population actively employed in bringing into connection the coal, the limestone, and the iron ore, with a view to preparation of the machinery required for enabling the farmer to plough more deeply, and to drain the fertile lands of the river bottoms.

The early settlers of the West uniformly selected the higher lands, avoiding the valleys of streams on account of the fevers which even now sweep off so many emigrants. Seeking a dry place for his dwelling, the settler always selected the ridges, which afforded also a facility for getting speedily some small crop, the same reason which prevented him from attempting artificial drainage in reference to his house, operating with equal force in regard to the land required for cultivation.

In Wisconsin, the traveler finds the first white settler placed on the highest land, known by the title of "The Blue Mound;" and he follows the early roads along the ridges upon which are found the villages of the primitive settlers, occasionally crossing a "wet prairie," the richest land of the State, and always the terror of the early emigrant.

Arrived at the confluence of the Ohio and the Mississippi, we find only the poor wood-cutter, who risks his health while providing wood for the numerous steamers which pass the place. For hundreds of miles we pass through fertile land clothed with the heaviest timber, that is yet of no value for cultivation, because the air around is filled with gases that are destructive of both life and health.

Descending further, we meet population and wealth ascending the Mississippi, from the shores of the Gulf of Mexico. Embankments, or *levées*, keep out the river, and the finest plantations are seen on land corresponding with the uncultivated region left behind, while to seek the habitations of the early settlers we must leave the river bank and ascend the hills. If, instead of descending the Mississippi, we ascend the Missouri, the Kentucky, the Tennessee, or the Red River, we find, invariably, that the more dense the population, and the greater the mass of wealth, the more are the rich soils cultivated; that as population diminishes with our approach to these head-waters, and land becomes more abundant, cultivation recedes from the river bank, and the undrained meadow and timber lands become more abundant—the scattered inhabitants obtaining from the superficial soils a scanty return to labor, with little power to command the necessaries and comforts of life.

In Texas, we see the town of Austin, the seat of the first American settlement, to have been placed high up on the Colorado, while millions of acres of the finest lands were passed over as incapable of paying the cost of simple appropriation. In the Spanish colony of Bexar, we see further illustration of the same universal fact, that colonization tends always toward the head-waters of the rivers.

So, too, in the Southern Atlantic States. The richest lands of North Carolina still remain undrained, while men waste labor on those which yield but three to five bushels of wheat per acre. South Carolina, Georgia, Alabama, and Florida, have millions of acres of the finest lands unoccupied and waiting the growth of population to yield immense returns to labor.

The facts are everywhere the same: for the same reason that the settler builds himself a log-house, to provide shelter till he can have one of stone, he begins cultivation where he can raise some small crop. Wherever settlements have been attempted on rich lands they have either failed, or their progress has been very slow indeed. We see this in the repeated failures of the French colonies of Louisiana and Cayenne, compared with the steady growth of those formed in the region of the St. Lawrence; and in the slow progress of the colonies planted on the rich lands of Virginia and Carolina, as compared with that of those begun on the sterile New England soils. The former can not compensate men working for themselves, and hence it is that we find the richer colonists purchasing negroes and compelling them to perform the work, while the free laborer seeks the light sandy lands of North Carolina. No man, left to himself, will begin the work of cultivation on the rich soils, because it is from them that the return is then the least; and it is upon them that the condition of the laborer is worst, when the work is undertaken in advance of the habit of association that comes with the growth of wealth and population. The settler on the high lands obtained, at least, food; had he attempted to drain the rich soils of the Dismal Swamp he would have starved, as did the men who sought to occupy the fertile island of Roanoke.

§ 4. Crossing the Rio Grande, into Mexico, the reader will find further illustration of the universality of this law of occupation. Near the mouth of the river, but at some distance from its bank, is Matamoras, a city of recent date. Following the river through rich lands in a state of nature, he reaches the mouth of the San Juan, ascending which he finds himself in a rather populous country, with Monterey for its capital. Northward, on the high land of Chihuahua, he sees cultivation keeping way from the river banks; while westward from Monterey, through Saltillo, his road lies over sandy plains, which yet are occupied. Arriving in Potosi, he finds himself in a country without rivers, in which failure of the periodical rains is followed by famine and death; yet downwards towards the coast, he sees a magnificent country, watered by numerous rivers, in which cotton and indigo grow spontaneously, and which could supply the world with sugar; but there he sees no sign of population. The land is uncleared, for those who should undertake the work, with the present means of the country, would either starve, or perish by reason of the fevers that there so much prevail.

Passing on, he sees Zacatecas, high and dry like Potosi, yet cultivated. Tlascala, once the seat of a wealthy people, occupies the high lands whence descend little streams flowing to both the Atlantic and the Pacific Oceans. The valley of Mexico, in the time of Cortez, supported forty cities; but population has declined, and the remaining people have retired to the high lands around to cultivate the poorer soils from which the single city that yet remains derives its supplies of food. Fertile land is superabundant, but the people fly from it, whereas, according to Mr. Ricardo, it should be the first appropriated.

Passing southward, the fertile lands of Tabasco are seen almost unoccupied; but in Yucatan, a region in which water is a luxury, we find a prosperous population, near neighbors to the better soils of Honduras, still a wilderness, affording subsistence to but a few miserable logwood and mahogany cutters.

In the Caribbean Sea we find the little rocky islands of Monserrat, Nevis, St. Lucia, St. Vincent, and others, cultivated throughout, while the rich soil of Trinidad remains almost in a state of nature, and the fertile Porto Rico is but now beginning to be subjected to cultivation.

Looking now southward, we see, in Costa Rica, and in Nicaragua, lands of incomparable fertility totally unoccupied, while Indian villages abound on the mountain slopes.

Farther south, are seen the cities of Santa Fé de Bogota and Quito, centres of population, where men cluster together on high and dry lands while the valley of the Orinoco remains unoccupied; the same facts being here exhibited which, on a smaller scale, have been shown to exist in Pennsylvania. The only civilized people of the days of Pizarro, occupied Peru, the rapid course of whose little streams prevented the formation of marshes where decaying vegetable matter might give richness to the soil.

On the east is Brazil, watered by the largest rivers in the world, and capable of yielding in untold abundance all the products of the tropics, and with the precious metals lying near the surface, but yet a wilderness. Having no elevated table lands, it affords no eligible site for European colonists. On the steep slope of Chili, we find a people advancing in population and wealth, while the fertile valley of the La Plata is plunged in barbarism.

§ 5. Crossing the ocean, and landing in the south of England, the traveler finds himself in a country where the streams are short and the valleys limited; and, consequently, fitted for early cultivation. There, Cæsar found the only people of the island who had made any progress in the art of tillage, the more inland tribes living on the spoils of the chase, or on the milk yielded by their flocks. In the barren Cornwall he sees marks of cultivation of great and unknown antiquity; and in a part thereof now seldom visited, are found the ruins of Tintagel, the castle in which King Arthur held his court. He finds the seats of early cultivation in the sites of rotten boroughs, or in those parts of the kingdom where men who can neither read nor write still live in mud-built cottages, and receive but six or eight shillings for a week of labor. He sees the palace of the Norman kings at Winchester, and not in the valley of the Thames; while in South Lancashire, with its rich fields of waving grain, he finds the country whose morasses had nearly swallowed up the army of the conquering Norman on his return from devastating the North, and which daunted the antiquary, Camden, so late as the age of James I. Asking for the lands most recently reduced to cultivation he will be shown the fens of Lincoln and Cambridgeshire, now yielding the best crops of England, but which were valueless until the steam-engine had been brought to aid the labors of the agriculturist.

To find the seats of the earliest cultivation in Scotland, he must visit remote districts, now abandoned to a few black cattle; while the newest soils are found in the Lothians, or on the banks of the Tweed, but recently inhabited by barbarians whose chief pleasure was found in plundering expeditions into England—the forests and swamps of the days of Mary and Elizabeth, presenting the finest farms of Scotland. We find the poorest people in the Western Isles, or in the Orkneys, once deemed so valuable as to be received by the King of Norway in pledge for the payment of a sum of money far greater than would now purchase the fee simple of the land.

§ 6. In France, in the days of Cæsar, we see the most powerful tribes seated on the flanks of the Alps, and the centres of trade in the rich cities of Bibracte, Vienne, and Noviodunum, while the now fertile Belgica presented but a single place of note, and that at the passage of the Somme, where now stands Amiens. Amongst the Alps themselves, the Helvetii had a dozen cities and near four hundred villages. Seeking the cities of the days of Philip Augustus, Chalons, St. Quentin, Soissons, Rheims, Troyes, Nancy, Orleans, Bourges, Dijon, Vienne, Nismes, Toulouse, or Cahors, the last once the centre of the banking operations of France, we find them far towards the heads of the streams on which they stand, or on the high ground between the rivers. The centres of power at a later period are found in the wild Brittany, where wolves even yet abound; in Dijon, on the flank of the Alps: in Auvergne, but recently "a secret and safe asylum of crime;" in the Limousin, which gave to the Church so many popes that the Limousin cardinals almost dictated the proceedings of the Conclave; or on the slopes of the Cevennes, where literature and art flourished when the richer soils, vast tracts of which even yet remain undrained, were wholly waste.

In Belgium we find the poor Luxemburg and Limburg to have been cultivated from a remote period, while the fertile Flanders remained until the seventh century an impenetrable desert. Even till the thirteenth century, the forest of Soignies covered the site of Brussels, and the fertile Brabant was almost uncultivated; while in the now almost abandoned *Campine* of Antwerp were found the ancient cities of Gheel and Heerenthal, and the castle of Westerloo, one of the oldest in Belgium, whose ditches even yet supply their visitors with implements of war dating back to the days of the Romans. In the time of Cæsar, Maestricht was only known as the place of passage of the Maes, as the Broecksel of a later period, now Brussels, was but the passage of the Senne.

In Holland, we see a miserable people, living on islands of sand and subsisting chiefly on fish, whose poverty exempted them from the grinding taxation of Rome. Slowly they increased in numbers and in wealth. Chief among the provinces was the narrow and barren Hauptland, which gave its name to the entire region. Unable to obtain food by means of agriculture, the Dutch sought it in the direction of manufactures and trade; but with the growth of population and wealth came the clearing of woods and draining of marshes, and we see them then becoming the richest nation of Europe.

§ 7. Further north, we find a people whose ancestors, passing from the neighborhood of the Don through the rich plains of Northern Germany, selected the barren mountains of Scandinavia as the land best suited to their then condition. Everywhere throughout this country the marks of early cultivation are found on high and poor lands long since abandoned. To such an extent is this the case, that it has afforded countenance to the belief that this must have been the seat of the great "Northern Hive" by which Southern Europe was supposed to have been overrun. The facts, however, are only a repetition of those described in regard to North and South America, England, Scotland, France, and Belgium, and which recur again in Russia, where, as an English traveler says, "we see the poorest soil selected for cultivation, while the richest remains neglected in its close vicinity."

Germany, in the country watered by the Danube and its tributaries, exhibits a population abounding at the heads of streams, but diminishing as we descend that great river, until reaching the richest lands we find them to be entirely unoccupied. In Hungary, "the Puzta," the cradle of Hungarian nationality, presents to view a wide plain consisting of wave-like sand hills; while beyond the Theiss rich lands abound, destitute of human life.

In Italy, a numerous population occupied the highlands of Cisalpine Gaul, when the rich soils of Venetia were yet unoccupied. Southward, along the flanks of the Appenines, we find a gradually increasing population, and towns whose age may almost be inferred from their situation. The Samnite hills were peopled, Etruria occupied, and Veii and Alba built, before Romulus gathered together his adventurers on the banks of the Tiber.

In Greece, we meet the same universal fact. On the hills of Arcadia were settlements which long preceded those of the lands of Elis watered by the Alpheus; and the meagre soil of Attica was early occupied, while the fat Bœotia followed slowly in the rear. On the hill-tops, in various quarters, the sites of deserted cities presented, in the historical times of Greece, evidences of long previous occupation. On the short slope of eastern Argolis, early abandoned, are found the ruins of the palace of Agamemnon; and north of the Gulf of Corinth, we see the Phocians, Locrians, and Ætolians clustered on the high and poor lands, while the rich plains of Thessaly and Thrace were destitute of population.

The mountainous Crete, likewise, was occupied from a period when the Delta of the Nile was a wilderness. Ascending that river, cultivation becomes at each step more ancient, until we reach Thebes, the first great city of Egypt. With the growth of population and wealth, Memphis became the capital, the Delta not being reclaimed until a still later period.

Along the north of Africa, the most civilized portion of the people are seen clustering on the slopes of Mount Atlas; and farther south, the capital of Abyssinia is found at an elevation of eight thousand feet above the sea, while lands of the greatest fertility remain entirely uncultivated.

§ 8. In the Pacific Ocean we find innumerable islands whose lower lands are unoccupied, their richness rendering them fatal to life; while population clusters round the hills. The valleys of Australia are inhabited by tribes the lowest of the human race; while on the little high-pointed islands around are found a superior race, with houses, cultivation and manufactures. In the dominions of the king of Candy, in Ceylon, the people show the same aversion to the low and rich lands as is felt by those of Mexico and Java. Entering India by Cape Comorin, and following the range of high lands, we find the cities of Seringapatam, Poonah, and Ahmedmugger, while below, near the coast, are the recent European cities of Madras, Calcutta and Bombay. The Indus rolls its course through hundreds of miles almost without a settlement on its banks; while on the higher country, right and left, exists a numerous population. The rich Delta of the Ganges is unoccupied, but far towards the head of the river we meet Delhi, the capital of India while the government yet remained in the hands of native sovereigns. Here, as everywhere, man avoids the rich soils that need drainage, and raises his food on the higher lands which drain themselves; and here, as always when the superficial soil alone is cultivated, the return to labor is small; and hence it is that we find the Hindoo working for a rupee or two per month, sufficient only to give him a handful of rice per day, and to purchase a rag of cotton cloth with which to shield his nakedness. The most fertile soils exist in unlimited quantity close to that which the laborer scratches with a stick for want of a spade, gathering his harvest with his hands for want of a reaping-hook, and carrying home on his shoulders the miserable crop for want of a horse and cart.

Passing northward, by Caboul and Affghanistan, leaving to the left Persia, whose dry and barren soil has been for ages cultivated, we find even amongst the Himalayas, the villages placed on slopes which yield but scanty crops of millet, maize, and buckwheat. Here we have the cradle of the human race, and may trace hence the course of successive tribes passing toward more productive soils; sometimes stopping to cultivate such hilly lands as can be made to yield a small supply of food; then crossing the sea to place themselves on little peaked islands like those of the Ægean, so early cultivated. Some of these tribes reach the Mediterranean, where civilization is first found, and soonest lost under succeeding waves of emigration: others, passing farther west, enter Italy, France, and Spain, while still others reach the British Isles. After a few centuries of rest, we find them crossing the Atlantic, and ascending the slope of the Alleghany, preparatory to the ascent and passage of the great range which divides the waters of the Pacific from those of the Atlantic. In all cases we see the pioneers seizing on the clear dry land of the steep hill-side, thence, as population increases, descending towards the rich lands of the river bottom, or penetrating to the lower soils, combining the upper clay or sand with the lower marl or lime, and thus compounding a soil capable of yielding large returns to labor. Everywhere, with increased power of union, man exercises increased power over land. Everywhere, as new soils are brought into activity, we find more rapid increase of population, producing increased tendency to combination of exertion, by the help of which the powers of men are often fifty-fold increased, enabling them to provide better for their immediate wants, while accumulating the machinery needed for bringing to light the vast treasures of nature. Everywhere, we find that with increasing population the supply of food becomes more abundant and regular, clothing and shelter are obtained with greater ease, famine and pestilence tend to pass away, health becomes more general, life more prolonged, and man more happy and more free.

In regard to all human wants, except the single one of food, such is admitted to be the case. It is seen that with the growth of population and wealth men obtain water, iron, coal, and clothing, and the use of houses, ships, and roads in return for diminished labor. It is not doubted that the gigantic works by means of which rivers are carried through our cities enable men to obtain water at smaller cost than when each man took a bucket and helped himself on the river bank. It is seen that the shaft which it took years to sink, supplies fuel at far less cost of labor than was required when the settler carried home scraps of half-decomposed timber, for want of an axe with which to cut the already fallen log; that the grist mill does the work of thousands of human arms; and that the gigantic factory supplies cloth more cheaply than the little loom:—but it is denied that such is the case in reference to the supply of food. In regard to every thing else, man begins with the worst machinery, and proceeds upward to the best; but in regard to land, and that alone, he begins, according to Mr. Ricardo, with the best and proceeds downward towards the worst; and with every stage of his progress finds a decreasing return to labor, threatening starvation, and admonishing him against raising children to aid him in his age, lest they should, like the people of India, or of the Pacific Isles, bury him alive or expose him on the river bank, that they may divide among themselves his modicum of food.

How far this is so the reader will now determine for himself. All the other laws of nature are universally true; and he may now agree with us that there is but *one* law for food, light, clothing, and fuel—that man, in all cases, commences with poor machinery and proceeds onward to the better, being thus enabled with the growth of wealth, population, and the power of association, to obtain with constantly diminishing labor an increased supply of all the necessaries, conveniences, comforts, and luxuries of life.

CHAPTER V.

OF THE OCCUPATION OF THE EARTH—CONTINUED.

§ 1. Decrease of numbers compels the abandonment of the richer soils, and drives man back to the poorer ones. Causes of the decline of population. The supply of food diminishes in a ratio greater than that of man.

§ 2. Real facts directly the reverse of those supposed by Mr. Ricardo. Progress of depopulation in Asia, Africa, and various parts of Europe.

§ 3. Exhaustion of the soil, and progress of depopulation in the United States. With every step in that direction man loses value, and nature acquires power at his expense.

§ 1. Population and wealth tend to increase, and cultivation tends toward the more fertile soils, when man is allowed to obey those instincts which prompt him to seek association with his fellow-man; while as combination declines, the fertile soils are everywhere abandoned.

When men are poor, they must select such soils as they *can*, not such as they *would*, cultivate. Though settled on the same mountain range, the absence of roads prevents them from associating for self-defence. The little tribe embraces some who would prefer to live by the labor of others rather than by their own; and half a dozen men, with a daring leader at their head, can rob in succession all the members of the little community, and thus enable themselves to pass their own time in idleness and dissipation. Assisted by the spoil their chief augments his little army, and increases the number of his subjects. As the society increases, he is led, however, to commute with them for a share of their produce, which he calls rent, tax, or *taille*. Population and wealth grow but slowly, because of the large proportion which the consumers bear to the producers.

By slow degrees, however, they are enabled to occupy better lands, thus lessening the distance between themselves and the neighboring settlement, where rules another little sovereign. Each chief now desires to tax the subjects of his neighbor, and war ensues, the object of both being plunder, but disguised under the name of "glory." Each invades the domain of the other, endeavoring to weaken his opponent by murdering his rent-payers, burning their houses, and wasting their little farms, while manifesting, perhaps, the utmost courtesy to the chief himself. The richer lands are abandoned, and their drains fill up; while the tenants are compelled to seek for food on the poor soil of the hills to which they have fled for safety. At the end of a year or two, peace is made, and the work of clearing is recommenced, but under the most disadvantageous circumstances of diminished wealth and population. After a few years of peace, cultivation regains the point it had before attained. New wars, however, ensue, to decide which of the chiefs shall collect the whole of the (so-called) rent. After great waste of life and property, one of them being slain, the other falls his heir, having thus acquired both plunder and glory. He now obtains a title, becoming a little king. Similar operations being performed elsewhere, such kings become numerous; and as each covets the dominions of his neighbors, new wars are made, attended always with the same result—the people flying to the hills for safety, the best lands being abandoned, food becoming scarce, and famine and pestilence sweeping off those who had escaped the invading force.

Small kings now become great ones, surrounded by lesser chiefs, who glory in the number of their murders, and the amount of their plunder. Counts, earls, marquises, and dukes, appear upon the stage, heirs of the power and the *rights* of early robber chiefs. Population and wealth diminish, and the love of *title* grows with the growth of barbarism. Wars are now made on a larger scale, and greater "glory" is acquired. In distant and fertile lands, occupied by a numerous population, are wealthy cities, whose people, unused to arms, may be robbed with impunity—always an important consideration to those with whom the pursuit of glory is a trade. Provinces are laid waste, and the population exterminated; or if a few escape, they fly to the mountains, there to perish for want of food. Peace follows, after years of destruction, but the rich lands are overgrown; the spades and axes, the cattle and sheep, are gone; the houses are destroyed; their owners have ceased to exist; and a long peace is required to regain the period from which cultivation had been driven. Population grows again slowly, and wealth but little more rapidly, for ceaseless wars have impaired the disposition and respect for honest industry; while the necessity for beginning once more on the poor soils adds to the distaste for labor. Swords and muskets are now held to be more honorable implements than spades and pickaxes; and the habit of union for any honest purpose being almost extinct, thousands are always ready for plundering expeditions. War thus feeds itself by producing poverty, depopulation, and the abandonment of the fertile soils; while peace also feeds itself by increasing the number of men and the habit of association, because of the constantly increasing power to draw supplies of food from the surface already occupied, as the almost boundless powers of the earth are developed in the progress of population and of wealth.

§ 2. The views above given are not in accordance with the doctrines of Mr. Ricardo, yet history furnishes everywhere ample evidence of their truth. In India, we see the rich soil relapsing into jungle, while its late occupant starves among the hills. In hither Asia, the fertile country washed by the Tigris and Euphrates, which once maintained the most powerful communities of the world, is now so utterly abandoned, that Mr. Layard had to seek the hills when he sought to find a people at home. Farther west are the high lands of Armenia, still so well occupied as to support a city like Erzeroum; while around the ancient Sinope nothing is to be seen but forests of gigantic timber. Near Constantinople, we find the great valley of Buyukdéré, once known as the "fair land," totally abandoned, while the city is supplied with food from hills forty or fifty miles distant; and this is but a picture in miniature of the whole of the great Turkish Empire. The rich lands of the Lower Danube, once the busy theatre of Roman industry, furnish now but a miserable subsistence to a few Servian swineherds and Wallachian peasants. In the Ionian islands, the richest lands, once highly cultivated, are almost abandoned; and must continue so to be until that habit of association which alone enables man to subjugate nature shall once more arise amongst their inhabitants.

In Africa, with the decline of population, we see the fertile soils of the Delta abandoned and the canals filled up; while in the Roman Province we find the rich lands of the Metidja, of Bona, and others, almost abandoned—the yet remaining population clustering on the slopes of the Atlas. In Italy, the once smiling lands of Latium and the Campagna now afford but a miserable subsistence to men whose number scarcely exceeds that of the cities which once flourished there. More north, we see the rich lands of the Siennese Republic to have been in cultivation till the sixteenth century, when the ferocious Marignan drove to the hills the remnant of the population that had escaped the sword, and changed the flourishing farms into a pestilential desert.

In France, in the days of the English wars, the richer country was constantly ravaged by fierce bands—the wild

Breton, the ferocious Gascon, and the mercenary Swiss, driving its cultivators to seek refuge even in the savage Brittany itself. *La Beauce*, one of the most fertile provinces, became again a forest; while from Picardy to the Rhine not a house unprotected by city walls, was left to stand. In later times, Lorraine was reduced to a desert. Throughout France, we witness the effects of perpetual war in the concentration of the agricultural population in villages, causing them to waste half their time in transferring themselves, their rude implements, and their products, to and from the lands they cultivate; whereas the same labor bestowed on the land itself, would reduce to cultivation the richer soils that remain even yet unoccupied.

§ 3. Crossing the Atlantic, we find further evidence of the fact, that as population brings the food from the rich soils, so depopulation drives men back to the poor ones. The valley of Mexico, which, in the days of Cortez, afforded food for a numerous people, is now desolate, its canals choked up, and its cultivation abandoned; while strings of mules carry provisions to the city from a distance of fifty miles.

In these United States, Virginia once stood at the head of the Union; but the policy she has so uniformly advocated having tended to the exhaustion and abandonment of her soil, the consequence is seen in the increasing unhealthiness of the parts first occupied, the lower counties bordering on the rivers of the Chesapeake. "The entire country," says a recent writer, "is full of the ruins of gentlemen's mansions, some of them palatial in size, and noble old churches, whose solid walls were built of imported bricks. The splendor which once filled the counties of Lower Virginia, has departed. And why? Because the abandoned country has become again miasmatic."

This miasmatic region covers all the sea-coast of Virginia, North and South Carolina, Georgia, Florida, Alabama, Mississippi, and Louisiana, except occasionally an isolated spot; and extends inland from ten to a hundred miles In the vicinity of Charleston, it is death to sleep a single night outside the city; and even riding across the infected district by night, on the railroad, has, as we are assured, caused all the passengers to vomit like a sea-sick company on shipboard.

As a consequence of this, Virginia and Carolina have steadily declined in their position in the Union; and must continue so to do until increase in the power of association shall enable them to cultivate their richest lands. In Jamaica, the same fact is found—a recent return of property showing that sugar and coffee estates, embracing an area of more than 400,000 acres, have been abandoned.

Whenever *population* and *wealth*, and the consequent *power of combination*, are permitted to *increase*, there arises a tendency towards the abandonment of the *poor* lands first cultivated, as is proved by the experience of England, Scotland, Sweden, and some of our Northern States. Whenever, on the contrary, these *decline*, it is the rich soils that are abandoned, men flying to the poor ones to obtain the means of subsistence. With every step in the former direction, there is an increase in the value of man, and a decline in that of all the commodities required for his use, accompanied by a growing facility of accumulation; whereas, with every movement in the latter one, he becomes more and more the slave of his fellow-man, with constant increase in the value of commodities, and as constant decline in his own.

CHAPTER VI.

OF VALUE.

§ 1. Origin of the idea of Value. Measure of value. Limited by the cost of reproduction.

§ 2. Idea of comparison inseparably connected with that of value. Commodities and things decline in value as the power of association and combination becomes more and more complete. Man grows in value as that of commodities declines.

§ 3. Diminution in the proportions charged for the use of commodities and things, a necessary consequence of diminution in the cost of reproduction. Definition of value.

§ 4. What are the things to which we attach the idea of value? Why are they valued? How much is their value?

§ 5. Erroneous view of Bastiat in relation to the idea of value. Its adoption as the foundation of a new politico-economical school.

§ 6. Inconsistencies of Adam Smith and other economists, in reference to the cause of value. Phenomena in relation to value in land exhibited in Great Britain, the United States, and other countries.

§ 7. Law of distribution. Its universal application.

§ 8. All values merely the measure of the resistance offered by nature to the possession of the things desired.

§ 9. All matter susceptible of being rendered useful to man. That it may become so, he must have power for its direction. Utility the measure of the power of man over nature. Value, that of nature's power over man

§ 1. WITH the growth of numbers, and of the power of association, man is everywhere seen to become more and more the master of nature; and possessed of numerous objects to which he attaches the idea of VALUE. Why he does so, and how he measures value, we may now examine.

Our Crusoe, on his island, was surrounded by fruits and flowers, birds and beasts, nearly all of which were beyond the reach of his unassisted forces. The hare could escape him by means of superior speed; the bird could soar on high, or the fish descend into the ocean depths; while he was dying of hunger in sight of all these materials of food. The tree would furnish him with a house, had he only an axe and a saw; but for want of these he is compelled to dwell in a cave of the earth. Working at first with his hands alone, he is forced to depend on the fruits spontaneously yielded by the soil. Later, having formed a bow, or fashioned a canoe, he obtains a little animal food, to which, because of the difficulty of obtaining it, he attaches high importance, and here it is that we find the origin of the idea of VALUE, which is simply *our estimate of the resistance to be overcome before we can enter upon the possession of the thing desired.* That resistance diminishes with every increase in the power of man to command the always gratuitous services of nature;

and hence we see in advancing communities a steady increase in the value of labor as measured by commodities, and decline in that of commodities when measured by labor.

At first, vegetable food could be obtained with less exertion than animal food; but now possessed of the bow, meat can be obtained more readily than fruit. Relative values change at once, birds and rabbits falling as compared with fruits. Fish are still unattainable, and he would give, perhaps, half a dozen rabbits for a single perch. Converting a bone into a hook, he next obtains fish at less cost than any other kind of food. At once, the former declines as compared with the latter; but man rises in value as compared with all, because of the new command he has acquired over the forces of nature. Obtaining food, now, at the cost of only half his time, he can apply the remainder to the making of clothing, the enlargement of his habitation, and the improvement of all his instruments.

With every step, his first machinery declines in value, because of the diminished *cost of reproduction*. In the outset, he could with difficulty obtain a cord with which to make a bow; but now the bow enables him to obtain birds and rabbits that furnish him with cords; and thus the bow itself causes a depreciation of its own value. So is it everywhere —coal aiding us in obtaining supplies of iron ore, which diminish the value of iron; and iron enabling us to obtain larger supplies of coal, with constant decline in the value of fuel, and increase in that of man.

Passing along the coast in his canoe, Crusoe finds another person similarly situated, except that in some directions he has acquired more, in others less, power over nature. The latter has no boat, but his arrows are better, enabling him to kill more birds in a day than the former could do in a week. The value of these is, therefore, less in his eyes, while that of fish is greater. Here we have the circumstances preliminary to the establishment of a system of exchanges. The one could obtain more meat in a day, by the indirect process of catching fish to be exchanged with his neighbor, than he could in a week with his inefficient bow and arrows, while the other could obtain more fish by devoting a day to the shooting of birds than he would in a month while deprived of the hook and line; and both see that by means of exchange labor may be made more productive. Each, however, seeks to obtain day's labor for day's labor. The one has fish of various kinds, and he values each in proportion to the difficulty of obtaining it, regarding perhaps a single rock-fish as the equivalent of half a dozen perch. The other has animal food of various kinds, and he, in like manner, regards a turkey as the equivalent of half a dozen rabbits. Value in exchange is, thus, determined by the same rules that governed each when working by himself. Both now profit by combining their efforts to improve their condition, each being able to devote himself with less interruption to the pursuit for which he is most fitted; and the returns to labor increase as *individuality* becomes more and more developed. Had our islander, instead of a neighbor, been so fortunate as to obtain a wife, a similar system of exchange would have been established. He would follow the chase, while she would cook the meat and convert the skins into clothing. He would raise the flax, and she would convert it into cloth. The family increasing, one would till the earth, a second furnish animal food, and a third manage the household, manufacture clothing, or prepare food. Here would be a system of exchanges as complete, so far as it went, as that of the largest city.

§ 2. The idea of *comparison* is inseparably connected with that of *value:* we compare the commodities produced with the labor of body or mind given for them. In exchanging, the most obvious mode is to give labor for labor; and each watches carefully that he does not give more effort than is given in return.

Our colonists having now succeeded in making a rude axe of flint, there is an immediate change in the value of the houses, boats, or fuel, previously produced, because they can now be reproduced with diminished labor; but the value of fish or rabbits remains unchanged. If now, one has fish to part with, while another has a surplus of fuel, the latter must give twice as much as before, because with the aid of the axe he can reproduce that quantity with half the labor. The *cost of production* has now ceased to be the measure of value, the *cost of reproduction* having fallen in consequence of improvement in the means of applying human power. The more slowly such improvements are made, the more steady is the value of property as compared with labor; the more rapidly they are made, the more rapid is the growth of the power of accumulation, and the decline of value in all existing machinery as compared with labor.

Suppose now a vessel to arrive, the master of which needs

fruit, fish or meat, in exchange for which he offers axes, or muskets. Our colonists, valuing their commodities by the effort required for their production, will not give five days' labor in venison if they can obtain what they require in exchange for potatoes that have cost only that of four.

In precisely the same manner will they estimate the value of the commodities offered to them in exchange. If it had cost them the labor of six months to make a rude axe, and if they could now obtain a good one at the same cost, it would be more advantageous to do so than to employ their time in producing another similar to that which they already have. As, however, they could not themselves make a musket of any kind, they would be willing to give for it the provisions accumulated in a year.

Let us here suppose each supplied with an axe and a musket, and examine the effect. Both possessing the same machinery, their labor will be of equal value, and the produce of a day of one will still exchange for that of a day of the other. The house that had cost the labor of a year, could now be built in a month, but is so inferior to those that can be constructed with the aid of the new axe, that it is abandoned. The first axe in like manner declines in value. The increase of capital has caused a diminution in the value of all that had been accumulated before the ship's arrival; while that of labor, as compared with houses, has risen, two months now providing shelter superior to what had at first been obtained in twelve. The value of provisions likewise falls, a week's labor of a man armed with a musket producing more venison than that of months without its aid.

A man can draw 200 pounds four miles in an hour, and a horse, at the same rate, 1800; therefore, in mere brute force, nine men equal only a single horse. Mastering the latter by means of his intelligence, and availing himself of his strength, a man can move ten times the previous weight. Discovering the wonderful power of steam, he now, with the help of half a dozen men to furnish fuel, controls a power equal to hundreds of horses, or thousands of men. The force by which this is accomplished is in THE MAN; and as this force is brought to bear upon matter, his labor becomes more productive, with constant increase in his power of future progress. The master of the vessel obtained for an axe, produced by a mechanic in a single day, provisions that had required months for their collection—and why? Because the labors of the mechanic had been aided by intelligence, whereas the poor and lonely settlers had been almost entirely dependant on that quality in which they were excelled by the horse and many other animals—mere brute force.

So is it throughout the world. The savage gives skins, the product of months of exertion, for a few beads, a knife, a musket, and a little powder. The people of Poland give wheat produced by the labor of months for clothing produced by that of a few days, assisted by capital in the form of machinery, and the intellect required for guiding it. The people of India give a year's labor for as much clothing as is given in these United States for that of a month. The mechanic earns as much in one week as the mere laborer does in two.

In order that quantity of labor may be a measure of value, there must be equal power to command the services of nature. The product of two carpenters in New York will not vary much from that of two tailors or shoemakers. The time of a laborer in Boston is nearly equal in value to that of another in Cincinnati or St. Louis; but it will not be given for that of a laborer in Paris or Havre, because the latter is not aided by machinery to the same extent. The value of labor varies slightly in different parts of France, England, or India; but the variation is trifling compared with that which exists between any part of India, and any portion of these United States. Here we find the same effect at the same time, but at different places, that has before been shown to be produced at the same place, but at different times. Labor grows in value with the substitution of *mental* for *muscular* force—of the peculiar qualities of *man* for those which he possesses in common with the animals; and in precisely the same ratio do all commodities decline in value.

§ 3. Diminution in the value of capital is attended by diminution in the *proportion* of labor given for its use by those who, unable to purchase, desire to hire it. Had the first axe been the exclusive property of one of our colonists, he would have demanded more than half of the wood that could be cut, in return for its mere use. The axe, however, great as was its cost, could do but little work; and large as was the *proportion* of its product that he could demand, the *quantity* he would receive would still be very small. His neighbor, on the other hand, would find it to his advantage to give three-fourths of the product for the use of the axe; as with it he could fell more trees in a day, than without it in a month. The arrival of the ship having given them better axes at a smaller cost, the one would not give, nor could the other demand so large a proportion as before. When A possessed the only house in the settlement, he could have demanded for its use a much larger number of days' labor than B would give, when with his axe he could construct a similar one in a month. In the fourteenth century, when a week's labor would command only 7½d. in silver, the owner of a pound of that metal could demand as compensation for its use a much larger proportion than now, when the laborer can obtain that quantity in little more than a fortnight. Every improvement by which production is aided, is attended not only by a reduction in the value of all previously existing machinery; but also, by a diminution in the proportion of the product of labor that can be demanded in return for the use of it.

Value is the measure of the resistance to be overcome in obtaining those commodities required for our purposes—of the power of nature over man. The great object of MAN, in this world, is to acquire dominion over NATURE, compelling her to do his work; and with every step in that direction labor becomes less severe, while its reward increases. With each, the accumulations of the past become less valuable, having less power over labor. With each, the power of association grows, with increase in the development of the faculties of the individual man, and equally constant increase in the power of further progress; and thus, while combination of action enables man to overcome the resistance of nature, each successive triumph is attended by increased facility for further combinations, to be followed by new and greater triumphs.

§ 4. The reader who desires now to verify the correctness of the view here presented to him, may do so without leaving his room. Let him look around, and see *what* are the things to which he attaches the idea of value. He finds that amongst them is *not* included the air without which he could not live. Reading by day, he attaches no value to light; nor if in summer, to heat. If he reads by night, he attaches value to the gas that affords him light; and if it is winter, to the fuel by whose combustion he is warmed. *Why?* Because the former is supplied gratuitously by nature, when and where it is needed; whereas, labor is required to obtain the latter. Coal is supplied by nature gratuitously, but effort is required to place it where it is to be consumed. To prepare candles also requires a certain amount of labor; and we value the coal and the candle because of the necessity for overcoming the obstacles to the gratification of our desires.

Asking himself next, *how much* value he attaches to each object, he finds that it is limited to the cost of reproduction, and that the longer the time which has elapsed since it was made, the greater has been the decline in its value. That of the pen just now produced is unchanged; while the chair or table, ten years old, has fallen below its original value, because of improvement in the machinery by which it may be reproduced. The book which he reads has perhaps declined still more. A copy of the Bible, of Milton, or of Shakespeare, can now be obtained by the labor of a single day of a skilled workman, better in quality than could, half a century since, have been obtained in return for that of a week; the necessary consequence of which has been a decline in the value of all existing copies, whether in private libraries or in the hands of book-sellers—*the cost of reproduction being the limit which value cannot exceed.**

§ 5. The most recent theory on this subject is that of M. Bastiat, who, in his *Harmonies Economiques*, tells his readers that "it is exchange that gives existence to value," this latter idea having made its first appearance on the first occasion on which, when one man had said to another do this for me and I will do that for you, the two had arrived at an agreement as to the conditions of the exchange. His definition of value is, that it is the relation between the service to be rendered and that which is to be received in return.

To this it may be objected, that Crusoe, when alone on his island, attached to the poorest instruments a value greatly exceeding that which he attached to those better ones that he was enabled to obtain after the arrival of Friday permitted him to enter upon the exchange of service. All experience proves that the more perfect the power of combination, and the greater the facility of exchange, the more rapid is the tendency towards diminution in the value of commodities, and towards increase in the value of man. Were the theory

* It may be asked, Why then should a very rare copy of an ancient work sell for many times its original price? Value is limited to the cost of reproduction; and where an object cannot be reproduced, its value has no limit but the fancy of those who desire to possess it.

now under consideration a true one, directly the reverse of this would be the case.

Exchanges establish measures of value suited to the places and times at which they are made, but they have no more to do with the creation of the idea of value than has the yard stick with the origination of the idea of length. The perception of distance leads to a comparison of distances, and ultimately to the construction of instruments by means of which they may be measured. In like manner, the perception of value leads to a comparison of values, and finally to those exchanges which demand an adjustment of the relations of the things to be exchanged.

Commenting upon this remarkable error of so eminent an economist, Professor Ferrara, of Turin, tells his readers, that "the judgment which in the social state expresses itself in the exchange of money against a hat or a coat—that one which prompts us to say that a crown is worth as much as a cap—is precisely similar to that of the isolated savage who decides within himself, that his only money, that is, the effort required for mounting a tree, is worth as much, or more, than the fruit it will enable him to secure." That such is certainly the case, no one who reflects at all upon the subject can, even for a moment, hesitate to admit.

That M. Bastiat should so far have erred is certainly extraordinary, but still more so is it, that another and very voluminous writer should be now engaged in building up a new system of political economy based upon this error alone, proclaiming it aloud as having made "the greatest revolution that has been effected in any science since the days of Galileo."* In his view, "value requires the concurrence of two minds," although Crusoe is seen to have given the continued labor of many months to the effort to construct a poor canoe. In strict accordance with that idea he assures his readers, that it is "demand alone that gives value to production;" and yet, history abounds with evidences of the fact that it is demand that stimulates supply, and thus diminishes the value of things while augmenting that of man. The present annual demand of Britain for coal requires for its satisfaction little less than 100,000,000 tons, and yet, the value of fuel as compared with labor is not one-fourth as great as it was when the demand of all Europe was less than a single million.

* Macleod. *Dictionary of Political Economy*, article *Bastiat*.

§ 6. "Labor," says Adam Smith, "was the first price, the original purchase-money, paid for all things, and it constitutes the ultimate and real standard by which their values can be estimated and compared." In another place, however, he tells his readers that the price paid for the use of land "is not at all proportioned to what the landlord may have laid out upon its improvement," "but to what the farmer can afford to give," and "is naturally a monopoly price." We have here a cause of value in land additional to the labor expended for its benefit; and thus does he establish a law for it entirely different from that propounded as the cause of value "in all things."

Mr. McCulloch informs us that "labor is the only source of wealth," and that "none of the spontaneous productions of nature have any *value*, except what they owe to the labor required for their appropriation." Nevertheless, he thus continues: "The natural forces may be engrossed by some individuals who may exact a price for their services. But does that show that these services cost the engrossers any thing? If A has a waterfall on his estate, he may probably get a rent for it. It is plain, however, that the work performed by it is as gratuitous as that performed by the wind acting on the blades of a windmill. The only difference is, that all have it in their power to avail themselves of the services of the wind, and no one can intercept the bounty of nature, or exact a price for that which she freely bestows; whereas A, having acquired a command over the waterfall, has it in his power to prevent its being used, or to sell its services."

We have here the same contradiction already seen in the *Wealth of Nations*. Labor is, we are told, the only cause of value; yet the chief item among the values of the world is in the hands of those who "intercept the bounty of nature, and exact a price for that which she freely bestows"—and they are enabled to demand that price because, "having acquired a command over certain natural forces, they can prevent them from being used by any who are unwilling to pay for their services." There are thus, according to both these authorities, two causes of value—labor and monopoly; the first standing alone as regards all "the spontaneous productions of nature;" and the two being combined in reference to *land*, the great source of all production.

In like manner, Mr. Ricardo assures his readers that the price paid for the use of land is to be divided into two portions: first, that which may be demanded in return for the labor which has been "employed in ameliorating the quality of the land, and in erecting such buildings as are necessary to secure and preserve the produce;" secondly, "that which is paid to the landlord for the use of the original and indestructible powers of the soil."

Mr. J. B. Say informs us that: "The earth is not the only material agent with productive power; but it is the only one, or nearly so, which can be appropriated. The water of rivers and of the sea, which supplies us with fish, gives motion to our mills, and supports our vessels, has productive power. The wind gives force, and the sun heat, but happily no man can say, 'The wind and sun belong to me, and I will be paid for their services.'"

Mr. Senior, on the contrary, insists that air and sunshine, the waters of the river and the sea, "the land and all its attributes," are susceptible of appropriation. In order, in his view, that a commodity may have value, it must be useful, susceptible of appropriation, and, of course, transferable, and limited in supply; all of which qualities are, as he supposes, possessed by land, the owners of which are therefore enabled to charge monopoly prices for its use.

Mr. Mill says, that the rent of land is a "price paid for a natural agency;" that no such price is paid in manufactures; that "the reason why the use of land bears a price is simply the limitation of its quantity;" and that, "if air, heat, electricity, chemical agencies, and the other powers of nature employed by manufacturers were sparingly supplied, and could, like land, be engrossed and appropriated, a rent would be exacted for them also." Here again we have a monopoly value *additional* to the price which is paid for the labor bestowed on the land.

The reader has seen that of those portions of the earth which man converts into bows, canoes, ships, houses, books, or steam-engines, the value is determined by the cost of *reproduction;* that, in all advancing communities, this is less than the cost of *production;* and that the decline is always most rapid when population and the power of association increase most rapidly. When, however, we look to those portions of it which he cultivates, we find, according to all these writers, an opposite law—the value of land being equal to the cost of producing it in its existing form, *plus* the value of a monopoly power increasing with the growth of numbers, and most rapidly when the growth of population and of the power of association is most rapid.

To admit this, would be to deny the *universality* of the laws that govern matter, and to assert that the great Architect of the universe had given us a system in the working of which there was no harmony whatsoever. To determine whether this be so or not, let us examine the facts of the case, as exhibited in the value of land compared with the labor that would now be required to reproduce it in its existing form.

Twenty years since, the annual value of the land and mines of Great Britain, including the share of the Church, was estimated by Sir Robert Peel at £47,800,000, which, at twenty-five years purchase, would give a principal of nearly £1,200,000,000. Estimating the wages of laborers, miners, mechanics, and those by whom their labors are directed, at £50 per annum, the land would thus represent the labor of 24,000,000 of men for one year, or of one million for twenty-four years.

Let us now suppose the island reduced to the state in which it was found by Cæsar, covered with forests, and abounding in heaths, swamps, and sandy wastes; then estimate the labor that would be required to place it in its present position: with its lands cleared, enclosed, and drained; with its turnpikes and railroads, its churches, school-houses, colleges, court-houses, market-houses, furnaces and forges; its coal, iron, and copper mines; and the tens of thousands of other improvements needed for bringing into activity the powers of nature; and it will be found that it would require the labor of millions of men for centuries, even though provided with all the best machinery of modern times.

The value of the farms of New York, under the last census, was $554,000,000. Adding the value of roads, buildings, etc., we shall probably obtain double that amount, or the equivalent of the labor of 1,000,000 of men working 300 days in the year for four years, at a dollar a day. Were the land restored to its condition in the days of Hendrick Hudson, and given to an association of the greatest capitalists in Europe, with a bonus equal to its present value, their private fortunes and the bonus would be exhausted before one-fifth of the existing improvements had been accomplished.

The farming land of Pennsylvania was returned at $403,000,000. Doubling this to obtain the value of real estate and its improvements, we have $806,000,000, equivalent to the labor of 670,000 men for five years, not one-tenth of what would be required to reproduce the State in its present condition, were it restored to that in which it stood at the date of the arrival of the Swedes, who commenced the work of settlement.

William Penn followed, profiting by what they had done. When he had received a grant of all that now constitutes Pennsylvania, and westward to the Pacific Ocean, it was supposed he had obtained a princely estate. He invested his capital in the transport of settlers, and devoted his attention to the new colony; but, after years of turmoil and vexation, found himself so much embarrassed, that in 1708 he mortgaged the whole for £6600, to pay the debts incurred in settling the province. He had received the grant in payment of a debt amounting, with interest, to £29,200, and his expenditure, interest included, was £52,373; while the whole amount received in twenty years was but £19,460, leaving him *minus* £62,113. Some years later the government agreed to give him for the whole £12,000; but a fit of apoplexy carried him off before the completion of the agreement. At his death, he left his Irish estates to his favorite child as the most valuable part of his property, the value of the American portion being far less than it had cost. The Duke of York, in like manner, obtained a grant of New Jersey, but many years afterwards it was offered for sale at £5000 less than had been expended on the province.

It would be easy to multiply proofs of the fact, that property in land obeys the same law as all other property; and that this applies to cities as well as to land. London, Paris, New York, and New Orleans, in spite of their advantages of situation, would exchange but for a small portion of the labor that would be required for their reproduction were their sites restored to their original condition.

Every one knows that farms sell for little more than the value of the *improvements;* and yet the heaviest of these are omitted: nothing being put down for clearing and draining the land, for the roads made and the court-house built with the taxes paid; for the church and school-house built by subscription; or for a thousand other advantages that give value to the property. Were these calculated, it would be found that the selling price is cost, *minus* a large difference.

With every step in the progress of man towards obtaining dominion over the forces of nature, there is a diminution of the cost of producing the things required for his use; with constant increase in the value of labor as compared with them. That this is as true in regard to land as it is to axes or engines, wheat or cotton-cloth, is proved by the fact that it may everywhere be purchased at less than the cost of production.

§ 7. It may, however, be said: Here are two fields, on which equal labor has been bestowed, one of which will command twice the cost, and sell for twice the price, of the other. If value results exclusively from labor, why is the owner of the one so much richer than is he that owns the other?

In reply it is easy to show that similar facts exist in relation to things whose value is admitted by all to be due exclusively to labor. The glass-blower produces various qualities of glass from the same material; some of it almost worthless, while a part is of the highest value; yet the labor employed on all has been equally great. All has still the same limit of value—the *cost of reproduction*. The resistance offered by nature to the production of that of the first quality being great, it is equal in value to a large amount of labor; whereas, the resistance to the production of that of the lowest quality is small, and it exchanges for a small amount of labor.

A farmer raises a hundred horses, expending upon each a similar quantity of food and labor. Arrived at maturity, they exhibit a variety of qualities, and their values are likewise different. Nevertheless, all those values are but the reward of labor and skill applied to the production of horses of certain qualities. From year to year the farmer learns to diminish the resistance at first experienced, and is enabled to obtain a larger proportion of that description of animals which commands the highest price.

Jenny Lind could get a thousand dollars for singing a single evening; while young women who sing in the chorus receive less than a single dollar. Were some enterprising Barnum now to determine on raising up a new Jenny Lind, he would find it necessary to make the experiment on some hundreds, or even thousands, of individuals. After enormous outlay, if he produced one prodigy who could earn as much as that famous songstress, he would also have on hand a number inferior to her; and a still larger number of chorus-singers whose earnings would not repay the cost of their maintenance and education; not to speak of those who had died, or had altogether failed.

Why is Jenny Lind so highly valued? Because of the obstacles to be overcome before an equal voice can be reproduced. So is it with all things whatsoever. To what extent are they valued? To that of the cost of reproduction, and no more. So is it with land; the present value of which represents but a very small portion of its cost.

§ 8. A century since, nature's power over man was strikingly exhibited in the difficulty attendant upon effecting changes of place. Later still, the obstacles to emigration from the banks of the Danube to those of the Rhine were little less than those which stand now between the shores of Europe and those of the Mississippi. Man's power has thus greatly grown, and with that growth there comes a tendency towards diminution in the value of German land. That land, nevertheless, has risen rapidly in price. Why? Because of a simultaneous great development of domestic commerce, making demand for labor and its products that had before been wasted. The attractive and counter-attractive forces are here in vigorous action, and the consequent growth of human power now manifests itself in a steady increase of the laborer's *proportion* of a constantly increasing product. Nature's power, here represented by the land-owner, steadily declines; that decline, however, being accompanied by a constant growth in the *quantity* of products assigned to him.

The *money* value of land tends, therefore, steadily to rise, and must continue to do so as man becomes more and more nature's master. Man himself rises in the scale as compared with all, and must continue so to do as land is made more productive, and its products are more fully utilized.

The limit of nature's power is found in the *cost of reproduction*. With the growth of human power that tends steadily to fall, to the apparent injury of the land-owner. Nevertheless, so perfect is the harmony of all real interests that his wealth as steadily increases; that increase coming to him as a necessary consequence of the pursuit of a policy tending to the perfect emancipation of the laborer.

§ 9. Man is surrounded by various natural forces susceptible of being *utilized*. The coal that lies thousands of feet below the surface, is as capable of being useful to him as that which now burns in the grate; and the ore remaining in the mine, as that converted into stoves or railroad bars. To render them useful requires in most cases a great amount of physical and intellectual effort; and it is because of the necessity for this effort that man attaches the idea of value to the things obtained.

Being in some cases supplied in unlimited abundance —as for example the air—they are wholly without value. In others—as in the case of water and electricity—they are furnished in the form in which they are to be used; but when they need a change of place, they have a value equal to the effort required for effecting it. In a more numerous class of cases they require changes both of place and form, and have then a much higher value because of the increased resistance to be overcome.

That man may be enabled to effect these changes, he must first utilize those faculties by which he is distinguished from the brute, and for this, *association* is indispensable. Had Bacon, Newton, Leibnitz, or Des Cartes, been placed alone on an island, though their capacity for being useful to their fellow-men would have been just the same, it would have lain dormant and without utility. Being, however, enabled to associate with other men, like and unlike themselves, their various idiosyncrasies, or utilities, became developed.

If we desire proof that "knowledge is power," we have only to observe the weakness of various communities occupying the richest soils, which remain unimproved for want of that combination so indispensable to the development of the intellectual faculties; and on the other hand, the strength of others occupying almost the least fertile lands. Few countries have a poorer soil for cultivation than our Eastern States; they have little coal, and little metallic wealth; yet New England occupies a high place among the communities of the earth, because amongst her people the habit of association exists to an extraordinary degree, with a corresponding mental activity. In Brazil, we see a picture directly the reverse, nature there furnishing a rich soil, abounding in valuable minerals which remain almost useless for want of that activity of mind which results from the association of man with his fellow-men.

The capability of being useful to man exists in all matter; but in a state of isolation he cannot acquire the force necessary for utilizing it. Place him in the midst of a large community where employment is infinitely diversified, and his faculties become developed. With individuality comes the power of association, accompanied with that activity of mind which gives power over nature. A century since, he was surrounded by electricity, but had not the knowledge required for making it serve his purposes. Franklin made one step by identifying lightning with it; but since then Arago, Ampère, Biot, Henry, Morse, and many others, have increased the knowledge of its qualities required for controlling its movements. Thus, instead of looking upon lightning and the aurora as mere objects of wonder, we now regard them as manifestations of a great force that can be made to carry our messages, plate our forks, and propel our ships.

UTILITY *is the measure of man's power over nature.* VALUE, *the measure of nature's power over man.* The former *grows*, the latter *declines* with the power of combination among men. Moving thus in opposite directions, they exist always in the inverse ratio of each other.

The waste of food resulting from the various processes to which corn is subjected, with a view to improvement in the appearance of the bread made from it, is estimated at one-fourth of the whole quantity—and this, upon the twenty millions of quarters required for Great Britain, is equal to five millions. Were all this economized the utility of corn would be greatly increased—but the corresponding increase in the facility with which food could be obtained, would be attended with large decline of value; and so is it, as we see, with all other commodities and things. The man who has to descend a hill to the distant spring, pays largely in labor for a supply of water for his family; but when he has sunk a well, he obtains a supply quadrupled in quantity in return to a twentieth part of the muscular effort. The utility having increased, the exchangeable value has greatly diminished. Next, he places a pump in the well, and here we find a similar effect produced. Again, with the growth of population and wealth, we find him associating with his neighbors to give utility to great rivers, by directing them through streets and houses; and now he is supplied so cheaply that the smallest coin in circulation pays for more than his predecessors could obtain at the cost of a whole day's labor—as a consequence of which his family consumes more in a day than had before, of necessity, sufficed for a month; and has its benefits almost free of charge.

The utility of matter increasing with the growth of the power of association and combination among men, every step in that direction is accompanied by a decline in the value of commodities required for their use, and an increase in the facility with which wealth may be accumulated.

CHAPTER VII.

OF WEALTH.

§ 1. In what does wealth consist? Commodities, or things, not wealth to those who have not the knowledge how to use them. First steps towards the acquisition of wealth always the most costly and the least productive. Definition of wealth.

§ 2. Combination of action essential to the growth of wealth. The less the machinery of exchange required, the greater the power of accumulation. Wealth grows with the decline in the value of commodities, or things, required for man's uses and purposes.

§ 3. Of positive and relative wealth. Man's progress in the ratio of the decline in the value of commodities, and the growth in his own.

§ 4. Material character of the modern political economy. Holds that no values are to be regarded as wealth, but those which take a material form. All employments regarded as unproductive, that do not result in the production of commodities, or things.

§ 5. Definition of wealth now given, in full accordance with its general signification of happiness, prosperity, and power. Grows with the growth of the power of man to associate with his fellow-man.

§ 1. WHEN Crusoe had made a bow he had acquired *wealth*. In what did it consist? In the *power* he had thus obtained for substituting the elasticity of the wood and the tenacity of the cord for the muscular effort by means of which alone he had hitherto secured supplies of food. Having made a canoe, his wealth was again increased, because he could command the gratuitous services of water; and having erected a pole in his canoe, and placed on it a skin by way of a sail, he could command the service of the wind with still further augmentation of his wealth.

Suppose, however, that instead of making a bow or a canoe, he had found one, but without the knowledge how to use it, would his wealth have been increased? Certainly not. Wealth does not consist in the mere possession of the instrument, unconnected with the skill required for its direction. The mills and furnaces of the Union would not add to the wealth of the savages of the Rocky Mountains; nor would all our books do so to the man who could not read.

The people of England were for a thousand years in possession of boundless supplies of that fuel a bushel of which can raise 200,000 pounds a foot in a minute, thus doing the work of hundreds of men; yet, in the absence of the knowledge how to utilize its powers, it was not wealth. So, too, with the anthracite coal of Pennsylvania. That fuel was capable of doing a greater amount of work than any other; but *for that very reason*, greater knowledge was needed for the development of its latent powers. The greater the amount of utility latent in any commodity, the greater is always the resistance to be overcome in subjecting it to the control of man.

The earth is a great machine given to man to be fashioned to his purposes. The more he fashions it the better it maintains him, because each step is but preparatory to a new and more productive one, requiring less effort and yielding larger return thereto. The labor of clearing is great, yet the return is small, the earth being covered with stumps, and filled with roots. Each year, as the latter decay, the soil becomes enriched, while the labor of ploughing is much diminished. The owner has done nothing but crop the ground, nature having done the rest; and the aid thus granted him now yields far more food than had been at first obtained in return to all the labor given to clearing the land. The surplus, too, has furnished manure with which to enrich the poorer lands; giving him a daily increasing power over the various treasures of the earth.

In every operation by means of which man subjects the earth to his control, the first step is invariably the most costly, and the least productive. The drain beginning near the stream where the labor is heaviest, frees from water but little land. Further distant, the same quantity of labor, profiting by what has been already done, frees thrice the extent; and now the most perfect system of drainage may be established with less labor than had been at first required for one of the most imperfect kind. To bring lime into connection with the clay on fifty acres, is less laborious than the clearing of a single one had been; yet the process doubles the return. The man who needs a little fuel, spends much labor in opening a vein of coal. The enlargement of this, by which he is enabled to use a wagon, requires comparatively little effort, but it gives him a return that is vastly greater. The first railroad runs by towns occupied by a few hundred thousand persons. Little branches, costing far less labor, bring into connection with it thrice the population.

All labor given to fashioning the great machine is thus but the prelude to its further application with increased returns. The man who cultivated the thin soils was happy to obtain a hundred bushels as compensation for his year's work; but with the descent of himself and his neighbors towards the more fertile soils, wages have risen, and two hundred bushels may be now expected. His farm will yield a thousand bushels; but it requires the labor of four men who must have two hundred each, and the surplus is no more. At twenty years' purchase, this surplus gives a capital of four thousand bushels, or the equivalent of twenty years' wages; whereas, it may have cost, in the labor of himself, his sons, and assistants, the equivalent of a hundred years of labor. It has, however, fed and clothed them while they worked; and has been brought to its present value by insensible contributions made from year to year.

It is now worth four thousand bushels, because its owner has for years taken from it a thousand bushels annually; but when it had lain for centuries accumulating fertility, it was scarcely worth acceptance. Such is the case with the earth everywhere. When the coal mines of England were untouched, they had no money value. It is now almost countless; yet the land contains supplies for thousands of years. Iron ore lands, a century since, being in low esteem, leases upon it were granted at almost nominal rents. Now, although great quantities have been removed, such leases are deemed equivalent to the possession of the largest fortunes.

The rich lands above described, the coal, the lime, and the ore, always possessed the power to be useful to man; yet they were not wealth, because he had not the knowledge needed for compelling them to labor in his service. Their utility was latent, waiting the action of the human mind for its development.

WEALTH *consists in the power to command the ever gratuitous services of nature.* The greater the *power* of association, the more diversified are the demands upon the human intellect; and the greater, as we have seen, must be the development of the peculiar faculties of each member of the society; and the greater the *capacity* for association. With the latter comes increase of man's power over nature and over himself; and the more perfect his capacity for self-government, the more rapid must be the societary motion, the greater the tendency toward further progress, and the more rapid the growth of wealth.

§ 2. In the early periods of society, when men cultivate the poor soils, there can be little association or combination of action. Population increasing, roads are made and richer soils cultivated. The store and the mill coming nearer, the settler, having no longer to carry his products many miles in search of shoes or flour, has more leisure for the preparation of his machine, and the returns to labor are increased

More people now obtaining food from the same surface, new places of exchange appear. The wool being converted into cloth on the spot, he exchanges directly with the clothier. The saw-mill being at hand, he exchanges with the miller. The tanner gives him leather for his hides, and the paper-maker exchanges paper for his rags. His *power to command* the machinery of exchange is constantly augmenting; whereas, his *necessity for its use* is constantly decreasing, there being, with each successive year, a greater tendency towards having the consumer and the producer take their places by each other's side.

The loss from the use of the machinery of exchange is in the ratio of the bulk of the article to be exchanged. Food stands first; fuel next; building-stone, third; iron, fourth; cotton, fifth; and so on,—diminishing until we come to laces and nutmegs. The raw material being that in the formation of which the earth has most co-operated, the nearer the place of exchange can be brought to that of production, the less must be the loss in the process; according to the well-known law of physical science, that whatever diminishes the quantity of machinery required, diminishes friction and increases power.

The man who raises food on his own land, is building up a machine for giving larger supplies in the future. His neighbor, to whom it may be *given*, on condition of sitting still, loses a year's work on his machine, and has only gained the pleasure of idling away his time. If he has employed himself and his horses for as much time as would have been required for raising it, he has wasted labor and manure. As nobody, however, gives, it is obvious that the man who has a farm, and obtains his food elsewhere, must pay both for raising and transporting it; and though he may have obtained as good wages in some other pursuit, his farm, instead of being improved by a year's cultivation, is deteriorated by a year's neglect; and he is a poorer man than if he had raised his own supplies of food.

The article of next greatest bulk is fuel. While warming his house, he is clearing his land. He would lose by sitting idle, if his neighbor brought him his fuel; still more if he hauled it; for he would be wearing his wagon and losing manure. Were he to hire himself and his wagon to another for the same quantity of fuel that he could have cut on his own property, he would lose, for his farm would be uncleared. So likewise, in taking the stone for his house from his own fields, he gains doubly, for his house is built, and his land is cleared.

With every improvement in the machinery of exchange, there is a diminution in the proportion which that machinery bears to the mass of the commodities exchanged. The man who formerly sent to market his half-fed cattle, with horses and men to drive them, and food for their consumption on the road, now fattens them on the ground, and sends them by railroad ready for the slaughter-house—keeping his men and horses at home to fence and drain; and employing the refuse of his hay and oats in fertilizing his farm. His production doubling, he accumulates rapidly, while the people around him have more food and clothing. He needs laborers in the field, and these require shoes, coats, and houses. The shoemaker and carpenter now join the community, eating the food on the spot where it had been produced. The consumption of flour increasing, the miller comes to eat his share while preparing that of others, and the labor of exchanging is again diminished, leaving more to be given to the land. The lime being now turned up, *tons* of turnips are obtained from the same surface that before gave *bushels* of rye. The woollen-mill coming next, and the wool no longer employing wagons and horses, these are turned to transporting coal or iron ore. Production again increasing, the new wealth takes the form of a cotton-mill; and with every step the farmer finds thus new demands on the great machine he has constructed, with increase in his power to improve it. He now obtains large supplies of beef and mutton, wheat, butter, eggs, poultry, cheese, and other commodities for which the climate is suited; and all from the same land which at first had scarcely afforded the rye required for the support of life.

We have here the establishment of a local attraction tending to neutralize that central one of the great city; and where such local centres most exist, there will be always found the greatest development of individuality, and the most rapid progress in wealth and power. The more nearly the societary action approximates to that established throughout the great system of which our planet forms a part, the more perfect will be the harmony; and the more rapidly will man move towards his true position, that of a being of power.

§ 3. We are accustomed to measure the wealth of individuals or communities, by the *value* of the property they hold;

whereas wealth grows, as we have seen, with the decline of values. This may seem to be in opposition to the general idea of wealth, but the opposition is only apparent and not real. The *positive* wealth of an individual is to be measured by the power he exercises; but his *relative* wealth, by the amount of effort required of others before they can acquire similar power. A man, owning a house that affords him shelter, and a farm that yields him food and clothing, has positive wealth. If asked to fix a price at which he would part with them, he would estimate the amount of effort that would be required of others before they could acquire similar power, and find therein the measure of his wealth as compared with that of others. His positive wealth consists in his power over nature; his relative wealth is the measure of his power as compared with that of his fellow-men.

Improvements, however, taking place in the mode of making bricks and clearing lands, he finds forthwith a diminution of his *comparative*, but not of his *positive* wealth, for his house shelters, and his farm feeds him, as before. The decline in the former is a consequence of increase in the wealth and power of the whole community; and that decline becomes more rapid as improvements multiply, because each successive step is attended by diminution in the obstacles offered by nature to the production of houses and farms, and increase in the number produced, with steady improvement in the condition of the community at large.

Wealth existing in the ratio of the power to command the services of nature, the greater that power the less will be the value of commodities, and the greater the quantity that may be obtained in return to any given amount of labor. With every step in this direction, there will be a diminution in the *proportion* borne by the time required for producing the necessaries of life, to that which may be given to the preparation of machinery for obtaining further control over nature; or, to the purposes of education, recreation, or enjoyment. The progress of man is, therefore, in the ratio of the decline in the value of commodities, and of the increase in his own.

§ 4. Modern political economy, having made for itself a being which it denominated man, from whose composition it excluded all those parts of the ordinary man that are common to him and the angels, retaining carefully all those common to him and the beasts of the forest, has been forced to exclude from its definition of wealth all that pertains to the feelings, the affections, and the intellect. Its teachers are, therefore, driven to the necessity of treating as unproductive, all employments of mind or of time that do not take a material form. Magistrates, and men of letters, teachers, men of science, artists, and others—the Humboldts and the Thierrys, the Savignys and the Kents, the Aragos and the Davys, the Canovas and the Davids, are regarded as unproductive, except so far as they produce *things;* that is, they are considered unproductive in so far as they act directly upon mankind; and yet productive when considered in their consequences, that is to say in regard to the abilities, the faculties, and the values—the knowledge, the skill, the virtue,—which they diffuse among men.

By the definition of wealth above given, this inconsistency is avoided, and the word brought back to its original signification of general happiness, prosperity, and power; not the power of man over his fellow-man, but over himself, his faculties, and the wonderful forces provided for his use.

§ 5. Adam Smith was no advocate of centralization. He believed in a policy tending to the creation of local centres of action, and not in that one which looked to prevent association by compelling all the farmers of the world to resort to a single and distant market when they desired to convert their food and wool into cloth. Such, however, was the policy of Britain; and therefore did it become necessary for Mr. Malthus to prove that the pauperism which was the necessary consequence of centralization, had its origin in a great natural law which forbade that the quantity of food should keep pace with the demands of an increasing population. Next came Mr. Ricardo, to whom the world is indebted for the idea that cultivation had always commenced on the rich soils of the earth, and that the men then flying to the colonies were going from the poor soils to the rich ones; when directly the reverse had always been the case. His doctrine, and that of his followers, is therefore that of dispersion, centralization, and large cities; whereas that of Dr. Smith looked towards association, towards local self-government, and towards countries abounding in towns and villages, in which should be performed the various exchanges of the surrounding territory.

The whole tendency of modern political economists has been in a direction opposite to that indicated by the author of the Wealth of Nations as the true one; and therefore it has been, that their science has become limited to the single idea, how it is that material wealth may be increased —leaving altogether out of view the consideration of the morality, the intelligence, or the happiness, of the communities they desired to teach. Hence it is that it has gradually taken so repulsive a form, and that one among its most eminent teachers—Mr. Senior—has found himself called upon to say to his readers, that the political economist is required to look solely to the growth of wealth, and to the measures by which it may be promoted; allowing "neither sympathy with indigence, nor disgust at profusion and avarice, neither reverence for existing institutions, nor detestation of existing abuses, neither love of popularity, nor of paradox, nor of system, to deter him from stating what he believes to be the facts, or from drawing from those facts what he believes to be the legitimate conclusions."

Happily, true science makes no such demands upon its teachers. The more they study it, the more must they become satisfied that the "indigence" they see around them is the result of human, not of divine, laws; the greater must be their "detestation of existing abuses" tending to perpetuate poverty and wretchedness; and the stronger their determination honestly to labor for their extirpation.

Wealth grows with the power of man to satisfy the greatest want of his nature, the desire for association with his fellow-man. The more rapid its growth, the greater is the tendency towards the disappearance of "indigence" on the one hand, and of "profusion and avarice" on the other; towards the development of individuality and of the feeling of responsibility towards both God and man; and towards having society assume that form which is most calculated for facilitating the progress of the latter towards the high position for which he was at first intended, that of master and director of the great forces of nature.

CHAPTER VIII.

OF THE FORMATION OF SOCIETY.

§ 1. In what society consists. The words society and commerce but different modes of expressing the same idea. That there may be commerce, there must be differences. Combinations in society subject to the law of definite proportions.

§ 2. Every act of association an act of motion. Laws of motion those which govern the societary movement. All progress in the direct ratio of the substitution of continued for intermitted motion. No continuity of motion, and no power where there exist no differences. The more numerous the latter, the more rapid is the societary movement, and the greater the tendency towards acceleration. The more rapid the motion, the greater is the tendency towards diminution in the value of commodities, and increase in that of man.

§ 3. Causes of disturbance, tending to arrest of the societary motion. In the hunter state, brute force constitutes man's only wealth. Trade commences with the traffic in bones, muscles, and blood—the trade in man.

§ 4. Trade and commerce usually regarded as convertible terms, yet wholly different—the latter being the object sought to be accomplished, and the former only the instrument used for its accomplishment. Commerce grows with decline in the power of the trader. War and trade regard man as the instrument to be used; whereas, commerce regards trade as the instrument to be used by man.

§ 5. Development of the pursuits of man the same as that of science—the passage being from the abstract to the more concrete. War and trade the most abstract, and therefore first developed.

§ 6. Labors required for effecting changes of place, next in the order of development. Diminish in their proportions, as population and wealth increase.

§ 7. Labors required for effecting mechanical and chemical changes of form. Require a higher degree of knowledge.

§ 8. Vital changes in the forms of matter. Agriculture the great pursuit of man. Requires a large amount of knowledge, and therefore late in its development.

§ 9. Commerce last in the order. Grows with the growth of the power of association.

§ 10. The more perfect the power of association, the more does society tend to take a natural form, and the greater its tendency to durability.

§ 11. Natural history of commerce. Subjects, order, succession, and co-ordination, of the classes of producers, transporters, and consumers of industrial products, classified and illustrated. The analogies of natural law universal.

§ 12. Erroneous idea that societies tend, naturally, to pass through various forms, ending always in death. No reason why any society should fail to become more prosperous from age to age.

§ 13. Theory of Mr. Ricardo leads to results directly the reverse of this—proving that man must become more and more the slave of nature, and of his fellow-men.

§ 1. Crusoe was obliged to work alone. When he had been joined by Friday, society commenced; but in what did it consist? In the existence of another person on his island? Certainly not. Had Friday refrained from talking to him and from exchanging services with him, there would still have been no society. It was the exchange of services which produced society; or in other words, association. Every act of association being an act of commerce, the terms society and commerce are but different modes of expressing the same idea.

That commerce may exist, there must be *difference*. Had

Crusoe and Friday been limited to the exercise of any one and the same faculty, there could have been no more association between them than between two particles of oxygen or hydrogen. Bringing these two elements together, combination takes place; and so it is with man. Society consists in combinations resulting from the existence of differences. Among purely agricultural communities association scarcely exists; whereas, it is found in a high degree where the farmer, the lawyer, the merchant, the carpenter, the blacksmith, the mason, the miller, the spinner, the weaver, the builder, the smelter of ore, the refiner of iron, and the maker of engines, have been brought together.

So, too, is it in the inorganic world; the power of combination growing with the increase of differences, but always in accordance with the law of *definite proportions*. A thousand atoms of oxygen placed in a receiver, will remain motionless; but introduce a single atom of carbon, and excite their affinities, and motion will be produced, a portion of the former combining with the latter, and producing carbonic acid. The remainder of the oxygen will continue motionless. If, however, successive atoms of hydrogen, nitrogen, and carbon, be introduced, new combinations will be formed, until motion will have been produced throughout the whole, but always in obedience to a certain well-ascertained law of proportions.

So is it with Society, the tendency to motion being in the direct ratio of the harmony of the *proportions* of the parts. Inorganic bodies, however, have always, and in all places, the same power of combination. Not so with man. Being capable of progress, the power of combination, with him, grows with the successive development of his faculties; and should increase from year to year as society attains more and more to those *proportions* which are necessary for taking up each and every faculty of the individual man. Association increases with the increase of differences, and diminishes with their diminution, until at length motion ceases to exist; as has been the case in all countries which have declined in wealth and population.

§ 2. In the inorganic world, every combination is an act of motion. So it is in the social one, every act of association being an act of motion, ideas being communicated, services rendered, and commodities exchanged. All force results from motion. What, then, are its laws?

A body moved by a single force proceeds always in the same direction until stopped by a counteracting one. The latter, we know, is found in gravitation, and so long as the force exercised by man is so counteracted, his motions are liable to constant intermission. In the early period of society he obtains power to grind his grain by raising and dropping a stone; he moves through the water by help of an oar; or he knocks an animal on the head by means of a club—all these operations being the applications of a single force, and all of them, consequently, intermittent motions, requiring a constant repetition of that same force. There is thus a constant waste of power, while the motion produced is small.

For this reason it is, that he constantly endeavors to obtain a continuous motion; and this he does by imitating the mechanism that governs the motions of the heavenly bodies. In rolling a ball, a hogshead, or a bale of cotton, he brings gravitation to his aid. To move bodies which cannot be rolled, he constructs an instrument—a wheel—that will revolve on its own axis, as does the earth, and between two such machines he places the body required to be moved. To conquer the resistance of friction, he lays down an iron rail, and thus obtains continuous action with high velocity.

Examining the progress of man towards obtaining power over nature, we find it to be in the direct ratio of the substitution of continuous for intermitted action. From the sharpened shell of Crusoe, he passes to the knife, the saw, the cross-cut saw, and finally to the circular one; obtaining thus from the same muscular effort results many thousands of times increased.

In the process of drainage, the farmer seeks only the establishment of continuity of motion. Knowing that stagnant water is destructive of vegetable life, he digs canals, lays pipes, and cuts away the trees to admit the sun; and having thus enabled motion to take place, he obtains crops thrice increased in quantity.

Everywhere in nature, whether in the circuit necessary to develop electricity, the motion of the winds, the formation of the dew, or the circulation of the blood, we find force applied by means of continuous motion; and the more rapid the motion the greater is the force exerted.

In the movements of the isolated settler there can be none of the continuity needed for the attainment of force. Dependent for food on his powers of *appropriation*, he wanders over extensive surfaces, often in danger of death from famine.

Even when successful, he is compelled to intermit his efforts, and to give much of his time to the work of effecting the *change of place* required for bringing his food, his miserable habitation, and himself together. He must be, in turn, cook and tailor, mason and carpenter. Deprived of artificial light, his nights are wholly useless; while the power to apply his days productively is dependent on the chances of the weather.

Discovering, however, that he has a neighbor, exchanges arise between them, but, being at a distance from each other, an effort is needed for bringing their commodities together. Difficulties, too, exist in settling the terms of trade. The fisherman has taken many fish, but now the hunter, having chanced to obtain a supply, needs only fruit, of which the fisherman has none to give. The absence of *difference* is here a bar to association; and this difficulty is seen to exist in every community in which there is no *diversity of employment*. The farmer or planter has no need to exchange with his brother farmer or planter, nor the shoemaker with the shoemaker; and to the absence of that variety which is necessary for the production of unity it is due, that in the infancy of society there are so many obstacles in the way of commerce as to render the trader, who assists in their removal, the most important member of the community.

As wealth and population grow, there is an increase in the societary motion, the husband exchanging services with the wife, the parents with the children, and the children with each other. Other families are seen around, each revolving on its own axis, while the community of which they form a part, is steadily revolving around a common centre—a system corresponding with that which maintains the wonderful order of the universe being thus gradually established.

With each step gained, we find a tendency to increased velocity; and as to man has been granted the capacity for further progress, such must necessarily be the case. To the first little society, the making of a footpath required great exertion; but now, with the growth of numbers and of wealth, it constructs turn-pike roads and railroads, each of these in succession, although so greatly more efficient, being accomplished with diminished effort. We have here the accelerated motion witnessed when a body falls to the earth. In the first second it may fall but a single foot, but at the end of ten seconds, it has fallen 100 feet; at the end of the second ten, 400,—of the third, 900,—of the fourth, 1,600,—of the fifth,

2,500,—and so on until at the end of a thousand seconds, it has fallen a million of feet. Had it been stopped at the end of each foot, and required to take a new departure, it would have fallen but 1000 feet. Thus is it with society. At first there is little motion; but as association grows, the power of further advance increases at a constantly accelerating rate. The improvements of the last ten years have been greater than those of the preceding thirty; the latter had exceeded those of the century which had preceded; and in that century man had obtained more power over nature than in the long period that had elapsed since the days of Alfred and of Charlemagne.

In order that there may be continuous societary motion, there must be security of person and property; but when men are widely scattered, this can have no existence. The only law then prevailing being that of force, the strong man tramples on and plunders those who are weak; sometimes seizing on land, and compelling them to work it for his profit; at others, placing himself across the road and forbidding all intercourse except on terms settled by himself; or lastly, dispossessing them of houses, farms and implements, and perhaps selling husbands and wives, parents and children, into slavery, as further addition to the spoils of "glorious war." In all these cases there is, as the reader will observe, a retardation of motion, at the cost of those who live by labor, for the benefit of those who live by appropriating to themselves the produce of the labor of others.

Whatever promotes *motion* in society, diminishes the value of commodities, and *increases that of man*. Whatever retards the societary movement, and prevents the power of association, prevents also the decline of values, retards the growth of wealth, arrests the development of individuality, and *diminishes the value of man.*

§ 3. Our colonists have hitherto been presented as the heads of the only two families on the island, enjoying security of person and property; and, therefore, enabled to pass steadily onward towards increased wealth, prosperity, and happiness. Such, however, has never yet been seen to be the case: always and everywhere there have existed causes of disturbance, the action of which we shall here examine.

Let us now add to the occupants of the island a third, remarkable for the strength of his arm, able to dictate to his neighbors and willing to live at their expense rather than work himself. Placing himself between them, he says to A, the possessor of the canoe: "Bring your fish to me; it will give you less trouble than to carry them across the island, and I will arrange the terms of exchange between you and my neighbor B." To the latter he says: "Bring me your birds, rabbits and squirrels, and I will negotiate the terms on which you shall have fish from A."

To this they might object, that they were perfectly competent to manage their own exchanges, and that they would thus save the cost of an agent; and were they united they might effectually resist him in his efforts to live at their expense. As any such combination, however, would baffle him, he stirs up strife, knowing well that the wider apart he can keep them the more they must be dependent on his will, and the larger the *proportion* of their property which he can appropriate to himself.

Their families, however, increasing, it occurs to some of them that their situation might be improved by measures that would enable them to work together. Although A has only a bow, his son might procure a canoe, and thus be enabled to exchange fish for meat without the necessity for passing across the island This, however, does not suit the purposes of the trader, nor will he permit it to be done. Already enriched by the product of his neighbors' labor, he can now pay for help to be used in maintaining his authority; and amongst their children he knows of some who would live by the labor of others rather than by their own. Poor and dissolute, they are ready to sell their services to an employer who will enable them to eat, drink, and make merry; and now the hired ruffian appears upon the stage.

Larger revenues being now needed, new efforts are required for preventing association at home, or exchange abroad, without contribution to the trader's treasury. With every step in this direction there is a diminution of ability to construct machinery by the help of which to obtain power over nature, an increase in the value of commodities consequent on the increase in the difficulty of obtaining them, a decline in the value of man, and a retardation of his progress towards wealth, prosperity, and happiness. How far this view is in accordance with the facts of history, we may now examine.

In the absence of power to command the services of nature that marks the origin of society, man is dependent almost entirely on his physical powers for the necessaries of life; and these powers varying in different persons, there is great inequality in the conditions of their existence. Children and women are the slaves of husbands and parents; while those who from either age or disease are incapacitated for labor are generally permitted to perish for want of food.

In the hunter state, where man merely appropriates the spontaneous gifts of nature, his only wealth consists in mere brute force. Compelled to severe exercise in search of food, and deficient in the clothing requisite for the maintenance of animal heat, he needs large supplies of food to repair the waste—the hunters and trappers of the West being allowed as much as even eight pounds of meat a day.

To furnish the mere hunter with as much food as could be obtained from half an acre under cultivation, it requires, as we are told, no less than 800 acres of land. Famines being consequently frequent, men are forced to have recourse to the most nauseous food; hence we find eaters of earth and eaters of men, both belonging to that stage of society in which, men being few, they may, according to Mr. Ricardo, select at will from the rich soils which then so much abound.

Game becoming yearly more scarce, famines become more frequent and severe, and this necessitates change of place. That in its turn brings with it a necessity for dispossessing the fortunate owners of places where food can be more readily obtained. Deficiency of power over nature thus compels man everywhere to become the robber of his fellow-man. The history of the world, throughout, shows us the people of the high and poor lands—the early Germans, the Swiss, the Highlanders, and the people of Central Asia—plundering those whose peaceful habits had enabled them to accumulate wealth and to cultivate the more productive soils.

In this early period, we see the strong men everywhere to have appropriated large bodies of land; while men, women, and children have been converted into property, reduced to slavery, and forced to work for masters who performed the part of traders—standing between those who produced and those who desired to consume, taking the entire product of the labor of the first, and giving to the last only what was absolutely necessary for the support of life. The whole business of the great proprietor consisting in the prevention of any combination of effort amongst his slaves, the more perfectly that object is attained, the larger is the *proportion* of the products retained by him, and the smaller that divided among those who labor for their production, and those who need to have them for their consumption.

Trade thus commences with the traffic in bone and muscle, *the trade in man*. The warrior buys his commodities in the cheapest of all markets—burning villages at dead of night, and carrying off their poor inhabitants. Retaining for himself as many as he pleases, he sells the rest to other traders, who, having bought in the cheapest market, now carry their property elsewhere, seeking to sell it in the dearest.

At this period of society men are always found among the highlands of the interior, or on small rocky islands, like those of the Egean Sea. There being no roads, the little communication that exists is maintained by boats, for the management of which these islanders are early fitted; and here it is that trade is first developed. There being, however, equal facility for robbing and murdering the people of the coast, piracy and trade go hand in hand together. In time, however, as population increases, it is found more profitable to establish places at which exchanges must be made, and where contributions may more advantageously be levied on the exchangers: thus we see great cities arising on the sites of Tyre, Corinth, Palmyra, Venice, Genoa, and others, whose growth was due exclusively to trade.

§ 4. The first necessity of man, as has been seen, is combination, or association, with his fellow-man, without which he is not the being to which we attach the idea of man. The warrior opposes obstacles to commerce by preventing all intercourse except that which passes through himself. The landed proprietor and slave-owner is the middle-man—the trader—who regulates the exchanges made by the people owned by him, with other persons, the property of his neighbors. The trader in merchandise opposes obstacles to all commerce carried on without his aid, desiring to have a monopoly, in order that the producer of food may obtain but little cloth, and the maker of cloth but little food,—his essential principle being that of buying at the lowest price, and selling at the highest.

The words Commerce and Trade are commonly regarded as convertible terms, yet are the ideas they express most widely different. *All* men desire to combine *with* each other, to exchange services and ideas—and thus to maintain COMMERCE. *Some* men seek to perform exchanges *for* others, and thus to maintain TRADE.

Commerce is *the object* everywhere sought to be accomplished. Traffic is *the instrument* used by commerce for its accomplishment, and the greater the necessity for the instrument, the less is the power of those who need to use it. The *nearer* the producer and consumer, the less is the necessity for the trader's services, and *the greater is the power to maintain commerce*. The *more distant* they are, the greater is the trader's power and the need of his services, but the weaker become the producers and consumers, and *the smaller is the commerce.*

The value of all commodities being the measure of the obstacles to their attainment, it must increase with every increase of these latter. The necessity for the trader's services being an obstacle in the way of commerce, every diminution of it tends to diminish the value of things, while increasing that of men. The tendency in that direction grows with the growth of wealth and population, commerce thus growing with the increase of its power over the *instrument* known as trade, precisely as we see in reference to roads, wagons, ships, and other instruments. The men who trade desire to prevent association and thus preclude the maintenance of commerce, and the more perfectly their object is accomplished, the larger is the *proportion* which they retain of the commodities which pass through their hands, and the smaller the proportion divided among those who labor to produce, and those who need to consume.

In illustration of this we may take the post-office, an admirable machine for maintaining commerce in words and ideas, but quite useless to those who live in close proximity to each other. Separate these, and the machine becomes a necessity, with diminution of commerce. Bring them together again and the necessity disappears, with great increase of commerce, half an hour's conversation accomplishing more than can be done by half a year of correspondence. In the early periods of society the trade in letters was a monopoly of governments, which dictated the terms on which commerce might be maintained; but with the progress of population, the people of various countries have been enabled to diminish the power of the trader, and commerce has therefore very largely grown. Even now, the intercourse between America and Continental Europe is heavily taxed by Great Britain, which permits no letter to pass over its limited territory but at a cost nearly equal to that of transporting it across the Atlantic Ocean.

Ships are not commerce, nor are wagons, sailors, letter-carriers, brokers, or commission merchants. The necessity for using them is an obstacle to commerce which adds largely to the value of the commodities that are exchanged. That this is felt by all is proved by the fact, that every measure tending to the diversification of employment, or the improvement of communication, and consequently to the reduction of the power of the trader and transporter, is hailed as tending to improvement in the condition of each and every other portion of society. The laborer rejoices when the erection of a furnace or the construction of a road brings to his door the demand for his services. The farmer rejoices in the opening of a market close at hand, giving him consumers for his food. His land rejoices in the home consumption of its products, for its owner is thereby enabled to return to it, in the form of manure, the refuse of its products. The planter rejoices in the erection of a mill which gives him a market for his cotton and his food. The parent rejoices when a market for the labor of his sons and daughters enables them to obtain readily the needed supplies of food and clothing. Every one rejoices in the growth of a home market, for commerce then increases surely and with great rapidity. Every one mourns the diminution of the home market, for commerce then becomes languid, land and labor diminish in value, consumption and production diminish, and laborer and land-owner become poor together.

Trade tending towards centralization, every stage of advance in its power over producers and consumers is an approach to slavery and death. Commerce, on the contrary, tending towards the establishment of local centres of action, every movement in that direction is an approach to freedom and to further increase of activity and life.

The movements of trade being, like those of war, greatly dependent on the will of individuals, are necessarily very spasmodic. Traders, collected in great cities, find it easy to combine together for depressing the prices of commodities they desire to obtain, and raising those of the things they hold, thus taxing both consumers and producers. Commerce, on the contrary, tends to produce that steadiness and regularity without which there can be no more durability in the societary machinery than there can be in that of the ill-constructed watch, or engine.

War and trade regard man as an instrument to be used, whereas commerce regards trade as the instrument to be used by man; and therefore it is that man declines when the power of the warrior and trader grows, and rises when it declines.

It is a well-known physical law, that with every diminution in the machinery required for producing a given effect, there is a diminution of friction, and a consequent increase of power. The friction of commerce results from the necessity for the services of the trader, his ships, and his wagons. As that necessity has diminished, there has been everywhere observed a constantly accelerated tendency towards continuous motion among the various portions of society, with rapid increase of individuality, and of the power of further progress. What is the process by means of which society is formed we may now examine.

§ 5. In science, as the reader has already seen, it is the most abstract and general that is first developed, the concrete and special following slowly in the rear. So is it too with the pursuits of man. To rob and murder our fellowmen, to seek glory by the destruction of towns, requires no scientific knowledge; whereas agriculture calls for the aid of science. Trade, too, demands but little intellect. The postman cares not whether the letter he delivers carries news of births or deaths, of war or peace. To the dealer in cotton or sugar it matters little whether his commodities grow in the valleys or on the hills. To the slave-dealer, needing, as he does, only to know whether, having bought it cheaply he can sell it dearly, it is immaterial whether the chattel be male or female, parent or child. Trade is to commerce what mathematics are to science. Both are *instruments* to be used for the accomplishment of a purpose.

The abstract mathematics deal simply with number and form; whereas chemistry looks to the decomposition, and physiology to the recomposition, of bodies. Trade deals with bodies to be moved or exchanged; whereas, commerce looks to the decomposition and recomposition of the various societary forces resulting from the habit of association.

In the early periods of society robbery and murder were deified under the names of Odin or of Mars. Alexander and Cæsar, Tamerlane and Nadir Shah, Wallenstein and Napoleon, were great because of the number of murders they had perpetrated, and of cities they had ruined. The "merchant princes" of Venice and Genoa were great because of large fortunes they had realized from dealing in slaves and other merchandise, doing nothing themselves but stand between the people who produced and those who consumed—thus adding largely to the value of the commodities that passed through their hands, at the cost of all who were forced to contribute to the growth of their already enormous wealth.

In this condition of society, the only qualities that command respect are brute force and craft—the one represented by Ajax, the other by the wise Ulysses. The morals of war and trade are the same. The warrior glories in deceiving his antagonist; while the trader purchases respect by a large fortune acquired, perhaps, by selling to the poor African guns that explode at the first attempt to fire them, or cloth that falls to pieces on being washed. In both, the end is held to sanctify the means, the only test of right being found in success or failure. The pre-eminence of soldiers and traders may, therefore, be regarded as conclusive proof of barbaric tendencies.

The mercenary soldier, obeying orders, is so far from holding himself responsible to God or man that he glories in the extent of his robberies, and the number of his murders. The savage adorns his person with the scalps of his enemies, while the more civilized murderer adds a ribbon to the decoration of his coat; but both are savages alike. The sailor is among the most brutalized of human beings, being bound, like the soldier, to obey orders, under penalty of application of the lash. The human machines used by war and trade are the only ones, except the negro slave, who are now liable to be flogged.

The soldier desires labor to be cheap that recruits may readily be obtained; the great land-owner, that he may retain a larger proportion of the proceeds of his land; and the trader, that he may dictate the terms on which he will buy as well as sell.

The object of all being the same, that of obtaining power over their fellow-men, it affords no cause for surprise that we find the soldier and the trader uniformly helping each other. The bankers of Rome were as ready to furnish aid to Cæsar, Pompey, and Augustus, as are now those of London, Paris, or Vienna, to grant it to the Emperors of France, Austria, and Russia; and as indifferent to the end for whose attainment it is to be applied. War and trade thus travel together, as is shown by the history of the world; the only difference between wars for conquest, and those for the maintenance of the monopolies of trade, being that the virulence of the latter is by very much the greater. The conqueror is sometimes moved by a desire to improve the condition of his fellow-men; but the trader has no other idea than that of buying in the cheapest market and selling in the dearest, cheapening merchandise even to the extent of starving the producers, and raising his prices, even to that of starving the consumers.

§ 6. Closely connected with the movements of the trader are the labors given to effecting *changes of place*. In the early periods these are nearly limited to changing the places of the men held as slaves; as is now the case in many parts of Africa, and to some extent in our Southern States. By degrees the camel-driver, the wagoner, and the sailor, appear upon the scene, constituting an important portion of society because of the great effort required for moving a little merchandise. Here, again, we see that the earliest in development is that which makes least demand for knowledge. The wagoner cares not whether he carries cotton, rum, or prayer-books; nor the sailor whether he brings gunpowder to the African, or clothing to the people of the Sandwich Isles. With the growth of population and of the habit of association, the necessity for transportation declines, while the facilities for it increase, the turnpike road and the railroad replacing the Indian path as the ship had done with the canoe; and with every step in this direction there is a diminution in the *proportion* of the population required to be so employed, and an increase in the proportion of the muscular and mental power that can be applied to increasing the quantity of things that may be carried.

§ 7. Next in order come *mechanical and chemical changes of matter in form*, more concrete and special, and requiring a much higher degree of knowledge.

A branch torn from a tree sufficed Cain for the murder of Abel; but it would have required some knowledge of the nature of the wood to make a bow or a canoe. The stone may be used as a weapon of defence, but it requires some knowledge to discover that it contains iron; and still more, to convert that iron into spades.

With this knowledge comes man's power over matter,—in other words, his wealth; and with every increase of power he is more and more enabled to associate with his fellow-men for the protection of the rights of person and of property. Motion now becomes more rapid and continuous, and society tends to take upon itself a more natural form, the *proportion* of those who live by appropriation declining, with increase in the *proportion* of those who live by the exertion of their physical and intellectual faculties. Right tends now to triumph over might, with diminution in the proportion of labor required for self-defence, and increase in the proportion that may be devoted to obtaining power over nature; and with every step in this direction the appreciation of the responsibility which attends the exercise of power tends steadily to increase.

§ 8. Following the above in the order of development come the labors given to effecting *vital changes in the forms of matter*, attended with an augmentation in the quantity of things to be converted, transported, or exchanged.

The labor of the miller makes no change in the quantity of food, nor that of the spinner in the quantity of cotton, but to those of the farmer we owe an increase in the quantity of both.

That power is limited to the earth alone. Man cannot, with all his science, fashion the elements by which he is surrounded into a grain of corn or a lock of wool. A part of his labor being given to fashioning the great machine itself, produces changes that are permanent. The limestone once reduced to lime, passes into the food of men and animals and ever after takes part in the same round with the clay with which it had been combined; and the iron, rusting, passes into the soil to take its part with the lime and clay in the production of further supplies of food.

The first poor cultivator obtains for his year's wages a hundred bushels, the pounding of which between two stones requires much labor, and yet is most imperfectly done. Were there a mill at hand, he would have better flour, and be able to bestow almost his whole time upon his land. He pulls up his grain: had he a scythe, he would have more time for the preparation of the great machine that alone can furnish grain. He loses his axe, and many days of travel are required before he can obtain another. His land loses the time and the manure which would have been saved had the axe-maker been near at hand. The advantage derived from the mill and the scythe consists simply in economizing labor, so as to enable him to devote his time to the great machine of production; and such is the case with all the machinery of preparation and exchange. The plough enabling him to do as much in one day as with a spade he could do in many, he has more time to give to drainage,

The steam-engine draining as much as without it would require thousands of days of labor, he has more leisure to marl, or lime, his land. Spades, ploughs, and engines, disappear in the act of being used; the earth alone is the great labor-savings' bank, and the value of other things to man is in the direct ratio of their power to aid him in increasing his deposits in that only bank whose dividends are ever increasing, while its capital is ever augmenting in its amount. That it may continue for ever so to do, all that it asks is, that motion may be maintained by returning to it the refuse of its produce, the manure; and for this it is needed that the producer and consumer take their places by each other's side.

The great pursuit of man is agriculture. It is the science that requires the greatest variety of knowledge, and is therefore the latest in development. It is, indeed, but now becoming a science, and that by aid of geological, chemical, and physiological knowledge, most of which is the result of the labors of the present day. It is the latest, too, because the most liable to be interfered with by the soldier and the trader, and therefore most requiring the establishment of that habit of order, and of respect for the rights of person and property, which always result from the growth of commerce.

§ 9. Last in order of development comes *commerce*. Every act of association being an act of commerce, the latter increases as men are enabled to obtain larger supplies of food from smaller surfaces. While they cultivate the poor soils alone, and are forced to remain apart, commerce scarcely exists; but when, with the progress of population, they are enabled to cultivate the rich soils, they have leisure for that improvement of their minds which, in turn, enables them to improve their modes of cultivation; while diversity of employment brings with it the power of association and the development of individuality, with greater feeling of responsibility, and constant acceleration in the rate of progress.

§ 10. The human frame is composed of portions acting independently, yet in perfect harmony with each other. Each changes its constituent parts from day to day, the machine remaining still the same; and the more rapid the assimilation of the food administered, the more healthful is the action of the whole, and the greater the tendency to stability and permanence. So, too, is it with the societary machine, its tendency to steadiness and durability being in

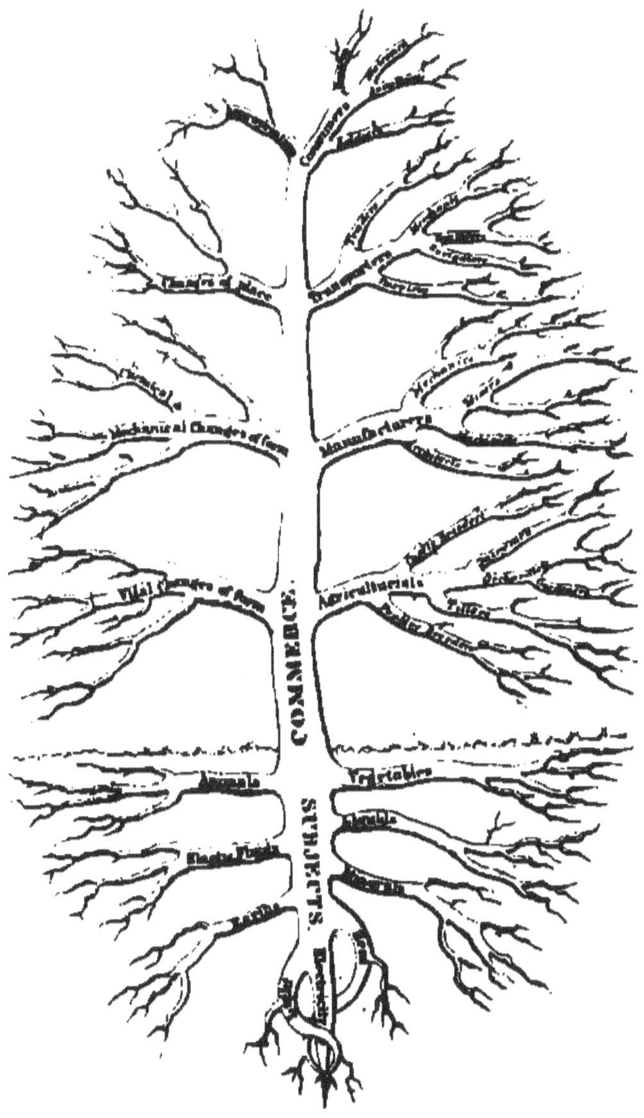

Changes of place
Transporters
Mechanical Changes of form
Manufacturers
Mechanics
Vital Changes of form
Agriculturists
Tillers
COMMERCE.
Animals
Vegetables
Elastic Fluids
Minerals
Earths
SUBJECTS
Electricity

the direct ratio of the rapidity of motion among its various parts, or the activity of commerce.

The more natural the form, the more stable is the building. Discharge a load of earth, and it will assume nearly the form of a pyramid; and with every increase in the quantity of matter the base is seen to widen as the apex increases in its height. The Andes have endured forever because they have the most natural of forms, that of a cone. How durable is that form is shown by the pyramids of Egypt, remaining after thousands of years almost as perfect as when they first were built. In the vegetable world we see that the tendency to durability is in the ratio of the depth and spread of the root, as compared with the height of the stem. The tree grown in a forest runs up in search of light and air, but having very little root it has little durability; while those which have abundant light and air stand for centuries, as is the case with so many of the oaks of England.

The greater the power of association, the more regular and rapid is the motion, the more perfect the development of the faculties, and the greater the tendency to sink deep the foundations of society by developing the wondrous treasures of the earth. The more the various forces of water-power, of coal, iron, lead, and other minerals, are utilized, the greater is the tendency to the formation of local centres neutralizing the attraction of the capital; with steady tendency towards decline of centralization, and with constant diminution in the *proportion* borne by soldiers, politicians, traders, and all others who live by appropriation, to the mass of which society is composed—society itself gradually assuming that form which most combines beauty, strength, and durability, that of a cone or pyramid.

§ 11. A tree conforming in its structure to the conditions above described, let us take advantage of it to illustrate the subject. Let the stem be commerce, and the roots its subjects. In the earliest, or hunter, state, the business of man is simple appropriation,—fruits and wild animals being his prey. In this stage there is neither trade, manufactures, nor agriculture; and the young plant, in parallel circumstances, shows but the topmost branches, and the slightly produced topmost roots.

In the second era, property being somewhat recognized, trade arises, founded on it. Change of place being then effected by the rudest methods of transportation, the water and air—root-branches—are the natural forces then used, the canoe and the sail-boat utilizing the rivers and the winds. Thus the sailor and the merchant, the land-carrier with his camel, ox, or horse, and perhaps his wagon, constitute important portions of the societary system of this period.

Next come manufactures, corresponding with the roots that are third in order, for among the earliest subjects that mark this epoch are the minerals and earths that are essential both as materials and implements. The precious metals, like wild fruits and animals found ready at once for use, are early employed for ornament; but iron, the great civilizer, and coal, the great agent in its conversion, are among the latest triumphs of man over the mighty forces of nature.

To the branch, manufactures, therefore, the metals and earths—root-branches—correspond in necessary relation, and in the date of their development. This being the stage of scientific progress, we see that, just as the cultivator of the rich soils returns to the poor ones with augmented means for developing their latent powers—so the science of the later period searches out the hidden elements of the vegetable and animal kingdoms, and the properties of liquid and elastic fluids, and places them under the control of man, thus adding largely to his force, and diminishing the resistance to further efforts. The water now yields steam; the air is resolved into gases which furnish light and heat; while the animal and vegetable worlds now yield, not merely food and medicines, but acids, alkalies, oils, gums, resins, drugs, dyes, perfumes, hair, silk, wool, cotton, and leather, furnishing the conveniences and luxuries of life in a thousand forms.

Last comes agriculture, embracing all the discoveries of the earlier ages. Appropriating the ready-formed elements of nature, it commands the aid of trade and transportation, while seizing on the chemical and mechanical forces furnished by the age of manufactures—thus covering all the progress of ages that had preceded.

The secondary branches mark the successive production of the agencies of the several classes: thus, in the topmost branch, the hunter is followed by the soldier, the statesman, and the annuitant, all non-producers, growing from the same stem with the growth of civilization, but diminishing in their *proportion* as society becomes more developed. In the infant state, this top branch constituted the whole tree.

The next branch, transportation, bears carriers and traders; and with the growth of science, engineers; but their *propor-*

tion to the mass of society declines as the powers of man become more developed.

The third, consisting of chemical and mechanical changes of form, branches into mechanics, architects, miners, machinists, etc., and greatly overbalances the classes that live by appropriation, trade, and transportation.

Lastly, we have agriculturists, branching into cattle-breeders, dairymen, gardeners, tillers, etc., to fulfil the grand underlying function of producers for all other laborers in the work of social commerce.

The reader must carry with him, in the theory of the parallels here attempted, the recollection that the *figure* herewith presented is capable of no more than contemporaneous presentment of the social distribution of the various functions. The topmost branches are, in point of fact, the last produced by its growth; and the earliest are resolved, by change of form and increase of substance, into the lowest boughs of the perfected tree; but the identity of the boughs is, in fact, as much lost in the limbs of the tree, as in the successive functionaries of the social state—the hunters of a race growing, through their descendants, into transporters, manufacturers, and scientific cultivators of the soil, successively, and by the process of civilizing development. The native Briton —having passed, by the process of generation and regeneration, successively into every form of man—now appears in the aristocracy of England; but his correspondent, in Australia, is still a hunter and a savage. The rudest savage was, in his day, the topmost branch of the shrub, living upon plunder; and not producing by his labor. The soldier of our own day is, like him, a privileged spoliator; while the politician lives by tribute, and the state annuitant derives his whole support from contributions levied upon all the classes who contribute to the growth of commerce.

In relative position, therefore, the top branch is still in place; and throughout all changes in the general system, it always has occupied, and always must occupy, a position corresponding to the relation borne by the appropriators of the race to the social toilers.

§ 12. We have here observed that great mathematical law which requires that when several forces unite to produce any given result, each should be separately examined. It is known that man tends to increase in numbers, and in power over nature; yet is it seen that there are communities in which numbers and wealth decrease, lands once populous having been entirely abandoned, or being now occupied by but a few miserable and wretched individuals. Hence it has been hastily concluded, that it is the natural tendency of human society to pass through various forms of existence, ending in physical and moral death. This, however, is not the case. Where societies do not become more prosperous from year to year, it is a consequence of disturbing causes, each of which must be separately studied, with a view to ascertain how far it has tended to produce the state of things which is observed.

Having now completed the study of the physiology of society, we shall in our next chapter turn to its pathology, with a view to ascertain the causes of decline and death.

§ 13. The theory of Mr. Ricardo in regard to the occupation of the earth, leads to results directly the reverse of those we have described. Commencing cultivation on the richest soils, always the valleys, as men become more numerous they must disperse themselves, climbing the hills, or seeking elsewhere valleys as yet unappropriated. Dispersion, bringing with it an increased necessity for the services of the soldier, the sailor, and the trader, produces a constant increase in the importance of the classes that live by appropriation. Centralization grows as association declines, and men become from year to year more the slaves of nature and of their fellow-men; and this, as we are told, in virtue of a great law instituted by the Creator for the government of mankind.

Were this so, society would assume the form of an inverted pyramid, every increase in numbers and wealth being marked by an increasing instability and corresponding decline in the condition of men. "Order," however, being "Heaven's first law," the mere fact that this one would be productive of such disorder would seem to be sufficient reason for instantly rejecting it. So, too, with that of Mr. Malthus, which leads inevitably to the subjection of the many to the will of the few, to centralization and slavery. No such law can possibly exist. The Creator established none in virtue of which matter must take upon itself the highest form, that of man, in a ratio more rapid than those lower ones of potatoes or turnips, herrings or oysters, required for his sustenance. The great Architect of the universe was no blunderer, such as modern political economy would make Him. All-wise, He has not established different sets of laws for the govern ment of the same matter. All-just, He was incapable of instituting any that would justify tyranny and oppression. All-merciful, He could make none that would afford a warrant for want of mercy among men towards their fellow-men, such as is now daily exhibited in books of high authority.*

Speaking of the Ricardo theory, an eminent writer assures his readers that this "general law of agricultural industry is the most important proposition in political economy;" and that "were the law different nearly all the phenomena of the production and consumption of wealth would be other than they are." Rather, other than they have been described by political economists to be, but *not other than they really are.* The law *is* different, and produces totally different results. The supposititious one leads to the glorification of *trade*, of all the pursuits of man the one that tends least to the development of intellect, and most towards hardening of the heart to the sufferings of his fellow-men; while the real one finds its highest point in the development of that *commerce* of man with his fellow-man which tends most to his advancement as a moral and intellectual being, and most to the establishment of the feeling of responsibility to his Creator for the use he makes of the faculties with which he has been endowed, and the wealth he is permitted to obtain. The one is unchristian in all its parts; while the other is in every line in strict accordance with the great law of Christianity teaching that we should do to others as we would they should do unto us, and with the feeling that prompts the prayer—

"That mercy I to others show
That mercy show to me."

* Labor is, as we are told by English economists, "a commodity;" and if men will, by marrying, indulge the natural desire which prompts them to seek association with their kind, and will bring up children "to an overstocked and expiring trade," it is for them to take the consequences; and "*if we stand between the error and its consequences, we stand between the evil and its cure*—if we intercept the penalty, (where it does not amount to positive death,) we perpetuate the sin." (Edinburgh Review, October, 1849. The italics are those of the reviewer.) It would be difficult to find stronger evidence of the tendency of an unsound political economy to crush out all Christian feeling, than is contained in the above passage.

CHAPTER IX.

OF APPROPRIATION.

§ 1. War and trade the characteristics of the early periods of society. Necessity for the services of the warrior and the trader diminishes with the growth of wealth and population.
§ 2. Close connection between war and trade visible in every page of history. Their centralising tendencies. Their power diminishes with the growth of commerce.
§ 3. Social phenomena exhibited in the history of Attica.
§ 4. Social phenomena exhibited in the history of Sparta.
§ 5. Social phenomena exhibited in the history of Carthage.
§ 6. Social phenomena exhibited in the history of Rome.
§ 7. Social phenomena exhibited in the history of Venice, Pisa, and Genoa.
§ 8. Social phenomena exhibited in the history of Holland.
§ 9. Social phenomena exhibited in the history of Portugal.
§ 10. Social phenomena exhibited in the history of Spain.
§ 11. Social phenomena exhibited in the history of France.
§ 12. The higher the organization of society, the greater is its vigor, and the better its prospect of life. The more numerous the differences, the higher is the organization, and the greater the commerce. Increase in the proportions of soldiers and traders tends towards centralization, and moral, physical, and political death.
§ 13. Modern political economists teach the reverse of this. Errors resulting from using the same words, to express ideas that are wholly different.

§ 1. WAR and TRADE being, as has been shown, the characteristics of the early periods of society, their close connection is shown at almost every step of societary life that has thus far been recorded. History, indeed, may with perfect truth be said to be little else than a record of the efforts of the few to tax the many, and of the many to escape taxation.

The Ishmaelites, whose hand was against every man, while every man's hand was against them, were extensive dealers in slaves and other merchandise. The Phoenicians, free-booters at one time, traders at another, were always ready for any measures tending towards enabling them to maintain the monopolies of trade they had established. Homer presents Menelaus boasting of the plunder he had acquired by means of piracy, and the wise Ulysses as feeling his honor untouched by the inquiry whether he came as trader or as pirate. The Norwegian sea-kings are seen alternately engaged in "gathering property," as robbery was then naively termed, or in trading from one kingdom to another, both pursuits being held in equally high esteem. The same connection is seen in the histories of Hawkins, Drake, and Cavendish; in those of the African slave trade, and the West

Indian Buccaneers; in the French and English wars on this continent, in the West Indies, and in India; in the closing of the Scheldt; in the wars of Spain and England; in the paper blockades of the wars of the French Revolution; in the occupation of Gibraltar as a smuggling depot; in the late wars in India, especially the last with Burmah, begun about a trader's claim of a few hundred pounds; in the opium war in China; in the manner in which Indian wars are gotten up in this country; in our own recent warlike demonstration against Japan, made with a view to compel that country to accept the blessings that were to follow in the wake of trade, and which now exhibit themselves in the forms of civil and foreign wars; in the proceedings of France in the Sandwich and Marquesas Islands; and last, though not least, in the application of British capital and British skill to the fitting out of pirate ships, to be manned by British seamen, and employed in driving from the ocean the stars and stripes under which the people of these United States have thus far so successfully competed with those of Britain for the carrying trade of the world at large.

War and trade tend towards centralization. The support of soldiers and sailors produces a necessity for taxation, the proceeds of which must seek a central point before they can be distributed, and the distribution collects together hosts of men anxious to secure their share of plunder, as was the case in Athens and in Rome, and as it now is in Paris, London, New York, and Washington. Under their reign, the city becomes from year to year a better place for trading in merchandise or in principles, while rapidly increasing centralization destroys the attraction of local centres.

The greater the power of association, and the more perfect the development of the individual powers of each member of society, the more do warriors, politicians, and traders, tend to occupy their proper place, that of *instruments to be used by society;* and the greater the durability of the society, as well as its power to repel invasions of its rights. Whatever diminishes the power of association tends to *make society the instruments of these men;* centralization, slavery, and death always traveling hand in hand together.

The policy of Athens, Rome, and other communities, having tended in this latter direction, a state of things was brought about which gave rise to the idea that societies, like trees and men, had their various stages of growth and decline, ending naturally in death. To determine how far this is so, we may now briefly examine the course of action of some of the leading communities of the world.

§ 3. The people of Attica, at an early period divided into small communities, became united under Theseus, with Athens for their capital. The Bœotians, in like manner, associated themselves with Thebes, and the little States of Phocis followed their example; while the tendency to general combination is seen in the institution of the Amphyctionic league and the Olympic and other games.

For a long period the history of Athens is almost a blank, because of its peaceful progress. Peace brought with it such a steady growth, that long prior to the days of Solon mechanics and artisans constituted an affluent and intelligent body, while throughout the State labor and skill were given to developing the various treasures of the earth; and the habit of association thus produced developed that individuality to which Athens has since stood indebted for the prominent place she has occupied in the pages of history.

Under the legislation of Solon, the whole body of citizens had the right of voting in the popular assemblies, but all were not equally eligible to office. All, however, were not equally taxed for the maintenance of government, the heaviest contributions having been required from the first class, eligible to the highest offices, and their amount diminishing downwards till they disappeared at the fourth, which was exempt from taxation as it was excluded from the magistracy; and here we find the most equal apportionment of rights and duties exhibited in the history of the world. Elsewhere, the few have taxed the many for their support, while monopolizing the offices; while here, the few who had a right to claim the offices paid the taxes.

Towards the close of the century succeeding this organization, we find Attica divided into a hundred townships, each having its own local assembly and magistracy; a system more perfectly in accordance with the laws of the universe than any the world had seen before the settlement of the provinces now constituting these United States.

With the Persian invasion there came, however, a total change. The country had been wasted and population had diminished; and henceforth we see the Athenians passing from the condition of a peaceful democracy in which every man was engaged at home in combining his efforts with those of his fellow-citizens, to that of a warlike aristocracy, engaged in preventing association abroad, and using their power so to do as a means of self-enrichment. Having accumulated fortunes by extortion, Themistocles and Cimon could secure the services of thousands of poor dependants. Poverty producing a thirst for plunder, it was easy to fill the army and man the ships which were employed in subjecting states and cities hitherto regarded as equals and allies. Athens having now become mistress of the seas, "upon her will," said Xenophon, "depended the exportation of the surplus produce of all nations;" and to enable her to exercise that will, we see her compelling the allies to compound for personal service by money payments, by help of which nearly the whole of the Athenian people were maintained in the public service. War having become her trade her armies are now largely increased, and for their maintenance and support she first seizes on the public treasury, then requires the allies to pay to her taxes on all the goods exported or imported. Next, declaring herself the court of final resort in all criminal, and nearly all civil, cases, her people become converted into judges, ready to sell their awards to the highest bidder, and States are now obliged to purchase protection by means of agents employed to distribute bribes among the citizens.

The many become impoverished, while the few are thus enriched. Temples are erected, and theatres maintained at the public cost. The right thus to live by the labors of others being, however, regarded as a privilege to be limited to the few, and inquiry being made into the right of citizenship, no less than five thousand persons are rejected, and sold as slaves. With every increase of splendor we find an increase of indigence, and a necessity for exporting men to distant colonies, there to exercise over previous settlers the same power which the rich now exercise at home. The people, all fully occupied in the management of public affairs, are paid out of the public purse; and so great has become the general poverty that an obolus (about three cents) is regarded as compensation for a day's service in the courts.

Tyranny and rapacity next give rise to the Peloponnesian war, at the close of which Attica passes under the dominion of the Thirty Tyrants. Taxation grows, industry declines, and man becomes (to use a modern phrase) superabundant. Licentiousness becoming universal, military command is sought as the only road to fortune. New oppressions producing the Social War, towns are everywhere plundered, and thus on and on may we trace the people of Attica exhausting themselves in the effort to impede the movement of others, until they become mere instruments in the hands of Macedonian monarchs. Thence we find them passing under the sway of Roman proconsuls, and Herodes Atticus becoming almost sole owner of a land which, in happier days, had given support and prosperity to hundreds of thousands of industrious and prosperous freemen.

§ 4. The institutions of Sparta having been based upon the idea of preventing voluntary association, she never passed beyond the cultivation of the poorer soils. Man was there regarded but as an instrument, forming a part of an imaginary being called The State, to whom all his feelings and affections must be sacrificed. The *home* had no existence, for not only were parents deprived of the society of their children, and of all control over their education, but they themselves might not even eat in private. Her people could neither buy nor sell, nor profit in any manner of the services of the precious metals. They might not study the sciences, and from music, as well as from all theatrical amusements, they were entirely debarred. The system thus preventing the development of individual faculties, wealth could not grow, nor could the people advance beyond the rudest pursuits, those looking to the appropriation of the property of others; and therefore it was, that while always engaged in war, they were ever ready to sell themselves to the highest bidder. Poor and rapacious, perfidious and tyrannical, Sparta exhibits in her history but a picture of growing inequality and constantly retarded motion, until her soil passes into the hands of a few proprietors; and she leaves, as her sole bequest to posterity, the record of her avarice and her crimes.

§ 5. The history of Carthage is little more than the record of wars made for the purpose of securing the monopoly of trade. Her colonies being allowed no communication with the world except through the ships and merchants of the mother country, the system under which they suffered was supported by their contributions. Monopolies filled the treasury, and the disposal of the revenue gave power to a trading aristocracy ever ready to subsidize barbarian armies. The city grew in splendor, but the day of trial showed that the foundation of the social edifice was weak and rotten, and Carthage then passed from existence, thus supplying further proof of the truth that "they who live by the sword must die by the sword."

§ 6. In the days of Numa and of Servius the Campagna of Rome was filled with cities, each constituting a local centre to the people of the surrounding country. From the days of the Tarquins, however, we find a change; and henceforward we see her energies to have been devoted to appropriating the property of her neighbors, and centralizing power within the Roman walls. The city grew in splendor; but the condition of the people declined, until at length we find them reduced to pauperism and dependent on daily distributions of bread, the contributions of distant provinces taxed for their support; and thus is Roman history but a repetition, on a grander scale, of that of Athens. Palaces multiply, but the land that formerly supported thousands of small proprietors is abandoned, or is tilled by slaves. *Panem et circenses*, free bread and free exhibitions of gladiatorial shows, now constitute the sole bill of rights of the degraded populace. Depopulation and poverty spread from Italy to the utmost bounds of the empire; which at length passes away, after having existed almost a thousand years, a model of rapacity and fraud, and having scarcely produced a dozen men whose names have descended to posterity with untarnished fame.

Traders, gladiators, and buffoons were classed together by the Romans, yet their history is but a record of traders' operations. For centuries we see a perpetual war between plebeian debtors and their patrician creditors, proprietors of private dungeons. Later, we find the knights acting as middlemen, purchasing the right of taxation, paying to the receiver the smallest sum and collecting from the tax-payer the largest one. Scipio plundered the public treasury, and when asked for his accounts adjourned the meeting to the temple, there to return thanks to the gods for victories by which he had been enriched. Verres, in Sicily, and Fonteius, in Gaul, were but traders. Brutus lent money at 4 per cent. per month; and all dealt in slaves, whom they treated in a manner that was worthy only of barbarians.

§ 7. Venetian history presents to view a perpetual series of wars for trade, accompanied by increasing centralization of power—the government, originally democratic, becoming from age to age more aristocratic, until it centred in the Council of Ten, whose spies penetrated every house, and whose tortures could reach every individual however located. Taxing her colonies so as to produce constant attempts at revolution, requiring great fleets and armies for their suppression, her whole history is one of increasing monopoly of trade and centralization of power, as a consequence of which she struck no roots into the earth; and when the day of trial came, she fell, almost without a blow.

The histories of Genoa and Pisa are likewise but a succession of wars for the monopoly of trade; and the power thus acquired proved as fleeting as had been that of Athens.

§ 8. The early history of Holland exhibits a people among whom the habit of association and the development of individuality grew with great rapidity; but her later one is distinguished among those of modern Europe for the desire to monopolize trade, for the resistance it provoked from France and England, for the wars thereby brought about, and for the exhaustion thus produced. The land that once gave to the world such men as Erasmus, Spinoza, John de Witt, and William of Orange, now exercises not the smallest influence in the world of literature or science, and but little even in that of trade.

§ 9. In the history of Portugal we have striking evidence of the weakness of communities dependent chiefly upon trade. The close of the fifteenth century witnessed the passage of the Cape of Good Hope, and the establishment of Portuguese power in India, where wars were fomented in the hope of thereby promoting trade. Lisbon growing by the help of these monopolies, rose to a high place among European cities; but here, as elsewhere, the strength of the community declined as the capital grew in splendor, and before the lapse of another century Portugal became a province of Spain.

§ 10. In Spain we see anarchy attaining the highest point shortly previous to the discovery of this western continent in 1492. The country was filled with castles, mere dens of robbers, from which the nobles sallied forth to plunder travelers, whose spoil they disposed of publicly in the cities, while its late owners were sold to the Moors for slaves. Rival nobles carried on private wars even in the cities, attacking churches, and burning dwellings by thousands. Instead of five royal mints, there were a hundred and fifty private ones, and the coin became so debased that the common articles of life were more than sixfold enhanced in price. Famine and pestilence were frequent, and the people were reduced to a state of poverty and wretchedness.

With the union of Castile and Aragon under Ferdinand and Isabella, we see a change; castles being everywhere destroyed, the country cleared of the banditti, and security of person and property established. Turning their attention to the revival of commerce, the sovereigns now remove internal restrictions, construct roads, bridges, quays and lighthouses, deepen harbors, and invite foreigners to the Spanish ports. Coinage is once again limited to the royal mints, numerous monopolies are abolished, and the *alcavala*, a tax on exchanges, previously arbitrary, is now limited to ten per cent.

The habit of association growing rapidly, the mercantile marine, at the close of the century, amounted to a thousand vessels. The woollen and silk fabrics of Toledo employed a thousand workmen; Segovia manufactured fine cloths; Grenada and Valencia produced silks and velvets; Valladolid became distinguished for its cutlery and plate, while the manufactures of Barcelona rivalled those of Venice. The fair of Medina del Campo became the great mart for the exchanges of the peninsula, and the quays of Seville were thronged with merchants from the remotest parts of Europe. The impulse thus given awakening mind, ancient seminaries were remodelled and new ones created, all swarming with disciples and employing more printing-presses than existed at a very recent date.

Union at home, however, gave power to sovereigns who, most unhappily, desired to use it for the destruction of association abroad, and for centralizing in their own hands the modes of action and thought of all their subjects. Millions of the most industrious people in the kingdom were expelled for difference of belief, and thus was the societary motion seriously arrested. That, in turn, facilitated the gathering together of armies to be employed in Italy and the Netherlands, Peru and Mexico; until in the effort to destroy self-government abroad, Spain lost all individuality at home. Mistress of the Indies, and yet unable to preserve her own Gibraltar, she has for a century been forced to see it held for the sole purpose of enabling foreigners to set at naught her laws. In every page of her history we find further confirmation of the lesson: That if we desire to command respect for our own rights, we must respect those of our neighbors.

§ 11. For more than a thousand years France has been engaged in the effort to destroy the power of association among the various nations of the world; as is shown in the histories of the Netherlands and Germany, Spain and Italy, India and Egypt. Her study has been to increase the machinery of trade, and destroy the power to maintain commerce. Swords have abounded, while spades were rare; ships of war have been numerous, while roads were bad, and canals unknown. Camps have grown as villages decayed, and gentlemen have become numerous as ploughmen have disappeared.

Pepin and Charlemagne sought glory in Italy and Germany, leaving to their successors a kingdom incapable of defence against a few Norman pirates, and whose kings were unable to repress the robber chiefs by whom they were surrounded. The social system relapsed into a state of anarchy to which historians have given the pompous title of "The Feudal System."

Population and wealth grew, however, slowly, and with them came a gradual approach towards the re-establishment of a central power, round which society might regularly revolve; but accompanied, as in Spain, by a desire to use the power thus acquired in preventing any development of societary motion abroad. Louis IX. squandered the wealth of his kingdom in the East: his successors invaded the territories of their neighbors in the West, plundering their towns and murdering the inhabitants. This constant pursuit of glory, however, causing weakness at home, English armies repeated on the soil of France the scenes of devastation the latter had herself enacted abroad, occupying her capital, and dictating laws to her people.

Under Louis XI. we witness a near approach towards the re-organization of society, followed, however, by repeated invasions of the neighboring countries, and ending in the state of chaos exhibited in the closing reigns of the House of Valois, when foreign armies invaded France and the kingly power almost entirely disappeared.

Once again society revived under Henry IV., but accompanied, as before, by the desire to injure the communities around. Centralization grew with the growth of armies, and the exhaustion of the people increased with the splendor of the throne; but here again we see weakness accompanying splendor, the closing years of Louis XIV. being embittered by the necessity of begging a peace the terms of which were to be dictated by Marlborough and Prince Eugene.

The wars of Louis XV. and XVI. paved the way for the Revolution; when the descendant of the founder of Versailles was seen paying forfeit with his head for the previous splendor of the throne. Order once more established, we see the whole energies of the country turned to the destruction of association among the nations of Europe. Again were Spain and Italy, the Netherlands and Germany, desolated by invading armies; and again did France exhibit a corresponding weakness at home, her capital being occupied by foreign armies, and her throne filled by direction of foreign sovereigns.

Order again restored, we see France for twenty years engaged in destroying life and property in Northern Africa. Louis Philippe thus centralized power in Paris, while destroying it in the provinces; and when the day of trial came, he, too, fell, and without a blow. Again, we see the present emperor engaged in the work of centralization, diminishing the power of association at home, and seeking to do the same abroad; and enlarging fleets and armies, while denying to the people the right to discuss his measures. Such being the case it may well be doubted if the dynasty he desires to establish can be permanently maintained.

In no country has the connection between war and trade been more fully exhibited. Its sovereigns have always been traders, buying the precious metals at low prices, and selling them at high ones, until the pound of silver degenerated to the *franc;* selling offices to their subjects to divide with them the taxation of the people; and selling to that people the privilege to employ themselves in the useful pursuits of life.

§ 12. Resistance to gravitation, whether in the vegetable or animal world, is in the direct ratio of organization. So is it with human societies; their chance of life increasing as they become more highly organized.

Every increase in the *proportion* of society engaged in war and trade tends towards centralization and slavery, it being the result of declining individuality, and diminished power of voluntary association. Every diminution of that proportion tends towards decentralization, life, and freedom, it being a consequence of higher development of individuality, increased power of association, and greater perfection of the societary organization.

The power of association is in the ratio of the observance of that great law of Christianity which teaches respect for the rights of our fellow-men; and as strength grows with the growth of association, it follows that the nation which would increase in strength should carry into the management of public affairs the same system of morals recognized as binding on individual men.

§ 13. The Ricardo-Malthusian doctrine having been invented to account by means of laws instituted by the Creator for the existence of social disease, it is not surprising that modern political economy looks upon the soldier and the trader in a different light from that in which they have been here presented. M. Bastiat informs us that it is one of the errors of modern socialism to class amongst the parasitic races, the middlemen, such as the broker and the merchant; who, as creators of value, ought, he thinks, to rank with agriculturists and manufacturers. Now, it is quite true that the middleman is "a creator of values;" but it is for that reason that men always rejoice in finding themselves enabled to dispense with his services. Value being the measure of nature's power over man, whatever increases it diminishes the value of man. The trader is *a necessity, not a power;* and the more that men come together to arrange their affairs for themselves, thus dispensing with brokers, traders, policemen, soldiers and magistrates, the greater must be the strength and durability of the societary organization.

The word *commerce* is constantly used to express ideas that are totally different. The man who makes shoes for a thousand people, each of whom comes to him to be fitted, pays neither porters nor commission merchants. His neighbor, whose customers are distant, pays a porter to carry them to the trader, and then pays the trader for finding persons to buy them. Here are three distinct operations: that of the *trader*, who simply arranges the terms of exchange, appropriating part of the proceeds as compensation for his services; that of the *porter*, who effects *changes of place*, and must likewise be paid out of the proceeds; and that of the shoemaker, who effects *changes of form*, and whose reward depends entirely on the quantity remaining after the others have been paid. All these operations it is the habit to include under the general head of commerce; whereas, the real parties to the commerce are only the man who makes the shoes and those who wear them. The others are useful in so far as they are necessary; but whatever diminishes the need of their services is as much a gain to man, as is improvement in machinery of any other description whatsoever.

CHAPTER X.

OF CHANGES OF MATTER IN PLACE.

§ 1. Difficulty, in the early period of society, of effecting changes in the place of matter. The necessity for so doing, the chief obstacle to commerce. Decline in the proportion of the society required for effecting such changes. Accompanied by rapid growth of commerce, and corresponding growth of power to obtain better means of transportation.

§ 2. The more perfect the commerce among men, the greater the tendency towards removal of the remaining obstacles to association. Man's progress, in whatsoever direction, one of constant acceleration.

§ 3. The first and heaviest tax to be paid by land and labor that of transportation. The farmer, near to market, always making a machine: the one distant therefrom always destroying one.

§ 4. Manure, the commodity most needed by man, and the one that least bears transportation. The less the quantity of labor given to effecting changes of place, the greater that which may be given to production. Power to maintain commerce grows with this change of proportions.

§ 5. Freedom grows with the growth of the power of association. That power grows with every diminution of the necessity for effecting changes of place.

§ 1. The first poor colonist, unable to raise logs with which to build a house, is forced to seek shelter in a cave. Compelled to wander far in quest of food, he is often obliged to waste it for want of means of transport. As his sons grow up, however, they combine their exertions and make instruments by help of which they bring together logs, and build themselves a hut. Again, they construct other instruments by aid of which they obtain more food from smaller surfaces, and thus lessen the labor required for effecting *changes of place*.

The life of man is a contest with nature. His prime necessity is that of association with his fellow-man. The first settler, forced to cultivate the poor soils which yield but little food, must, of necessity, remain apart from other men. With increase of numbers he cultivates the richer soils, with constant increase in his powers of combination with others like himself. From a creature of necessity he thus passes into a being of power, from year to year more able to maintain commerce with distant men, while less dependent on that commerce for the conveniences, comforts, and luxuries of life. The powers of nature become embodied in THE MAN, whose value grows as that of all commodities declines.

The solitary settler of the West, though provided with axe and spade, with difficulty constructs the poorest hut. A neighbor arrives, possessing a horse and cart; and now a better dwelling can be built with half the labor that had been at first required. Others coming, a third is still more readily completed. The new-comers having brought with them ploughs and hoes, better soils can now be cultivated, with large increase in the return to labor.

The Indian path becomes a road, and a store is soon established. The settlement grows into a little town; and with each addition to its numbers the farmer finds a new consumer for his products, and a new producer ready to supply his wants, the blacksmith and the shoemaker coming to eat on the spot the corn he has hitherto carried to the distant market.

The little community has thus far occupied only the higher lands. Roads being now made through the bottom lands, richer soils are brought into cultivation, and the new wealth takes the form of a bridge, which enables them to exchange services with another small community on the opposite bank of the little stream. Employments become more diversified as exchanges increase; the societies grow in strength, and forests are cleared, giving to cultivation the richest soils, with increasing returns to labor less severe, and corresponding facility of combination for every useful purpose.

We here witness a constantly accelerating motion of society and an increase of commerce resulting from a diminution in the labor required for effecting changes of place. *The power to maintain commerce grows thus with every diminution of the necessity for trade and transportation.*

§ 2. In the early stages of society the obstacles to intercourse are almost insuperable; hence we see, even now, that while the value of commodities at the place of consumption is, in many cases, so great as to put them out of the reach of any but the wealthy, it is so small at the place of production as to keep the producer in a state of poverty and slavery. The sugar producer of Brazil cannot obtain clothing, while the cloth producer of England cannot obtain sufficient sugar for his family and himself. Both would have sufficient food and clothing could the one obtain all the cloth given for his sugar, the other all the sugar given for his cloth. It is because so large a portion is absorbed on its way from one to the other that both are so much enslaved.

Thirty years since, the price of wheat in Ohio was less than one-third of what it would sell for on the Atlantic coast, the difference being then absorbed in the passage from the producer to the consumer. But recently, corn abounded in Castile while Andalusia looked to America for food. Food is wasted in one part of India, while men perish of famine in another. So it is everywhere, in default of that diversity of employment which makes a market on the land for all its products. In purely agricultural countries the crops are almost altogether absorbed in the cost of transportation, because of the exceeding distance of the consumer from the producer. Hence it is that slavery, or serfage, still prevails in those communities in which employments are not diversified.

§ 8. The first and heaviest tax to be paid by land and labor is that of *transportation*. It increases in *geometrical* proportion as the distance from market increases *arithmetically;* so that corn which would produce at market $25 per ton, is worth nothing at a distance of only 120 miles, if carried on the ordinary wagon road, the cost of transportation being equal to the selling price. By railroad, the cost is about one-tenth of this, or $2 50, leaving nine-tenths as the amount of tax saved by the construction of the road. Taking the product of an acre at an average of only a ton, the saving is equal to interest, at six per cent. on $375 an acre. If the product of an acre of wheat be twenty bushels, the saving is equal to the interest on $200; but if we take the more bulky products,—hay, potatoes, and turnips,—it amounts to thrice that sum. Hence it is, that an acre of land near London sells for thousands of dollars, while one of equal quality in Iowa or Wisconsin may be purchased for little more than a single dollar. The owner of the first can take from it several crops in the year, returning a quantity of manure equal to all he had extracted, and thus improving his land from year to year. He is *making* a food-producing machine; whereas, his western competitor, forced to lose the manure, is *destroying* one. Having no transportation to pay, the former can raise those things of which the earth yields largely,—as potatoes and turnips,—or those whose delicate character forbids that they should be carried to distant markets; and thus the power of combination with his fellow-men enables him to obtain large reward for service. The latter, being heavily taxed for transportation, cannot raise turnips, potatoes, or hay, of which the earth yields by tons, because they would be absorbed on the way to market. He may raise wheat, of which the earth yields by bushels; or cotton, of which it yields by pounds; but if he raises even Indian corn, he must manufacture it into pork before it will bear the cost of transportation. Much of his land lies fallow, while the cost of maintaining the fences and roads is as great as if it were producing crops. A great part, too, of his time and that of his horses, is unemployed, while they must still be fed. His harvests, too, may fail. The farmer near London is in the condition of an underwriter, who has a thousand risks, some of which are maturing every day; whereas the distant one is like a man who has risked his whole fortune on a single ship. When close to her destined port, she may strike on a rock, and be lost, her owner thus being ruined. So a farmer who has risked his all on a single crop, may see it destroyed by blight or mildew almost at harvest time.

But still more important is the difference in the power of maintaining the productiveness of the land. The farmer distant from market is always selling the soil that constitutes his capital; whereas, the one near London not only returns to it the refuse of its own products, but adds thereto the manure resulting from the consumption of those products of other lands which are consumed by the millions of his own immediate neighborhood.

§ 4. Of all the things needed for the purposes of man, the one that least bears transportation is manure; and yet, this is of all the most important. Each crop withdraws from the earth certain elements; and if these are not replaced, that crop must soon cease to be produced. When cattle are fed upon the land, their excrements restore much of the material of which the soil is robbed by the plants they eat. If, however, their products be sent to distant markets, the pasture must eventually become exhausted. The grass lands of Cheshire, which had been impoverished by the exportation of butter and cheese produced upon them, were restored by the application of ground bones from the battle-fields of the continent, containing, like the milk, phosphate of lime. Different crops take very different substances, but each deprives the land of some ingredient, which must be restored, or its fertility must be diminished. The value of the manure applied to the soil of Great Britain in 1850, was £103,369,139 —$500,000,000—a sum much exceeding the entire value of the British foreign trade. The sewer-water of towns contains the refuse of the food of their inhabitants in a state of dilution, highly favorable to the increase of fertility. "From every town of a thousand inhabitants," says Professor Johnston, "is carried annually into the sea, manure equal to 270 tons of grain," worth $13,000. The drainage of a part of the city of Edinburgh has been made to overflow a tract of flat land, which is thus rendered so productive as to be sometimes mown seven times in a season. A German agriculturist has thus calculated the distance at which the farmer can afford to bring manure from town: the quantity which would be worth $5 40 in the suburbs, is worth $4 20 if carried a single German mile—(4.6 English miles)—$3 50 if the distance be two—if three, $1 90—if four, 83 cents. At the distance of 4½ German, or 22 English miles, he can pay nothing for it, the cost of transportation being fully equal to its value.

We see thus that the vicinity of the consumer is indispensable for enabling the producer to raise crops of which the earth makes large returns. At a distance from the consumer, two causes contract his power: the cost of transporting the crop to market, and the difficulty of bringing back the manure. This is a fact fatal to the theory of Mr. Malthus, showing, as it does, that density of population is necessary to the production of abundant supplies of food.

The sum of these taxes is immense, yet are they but a portion of those to which the Western farmer is subjected. The man who *must* go to any market, *must pay the cost of getting there, let it take what form it may;* and among the charges are those of marine* and fire insurance, always estimated in fixing the prices of his products. All the losses from the numerous fires occurring in great commercial cities, are payable out of the commodities furnished by the farmer, and not by those who stand between him and his consumers.

Every act of association is an act of commerce. In order that commerce may increase, it is *indispensable* that man be enabled to pay the debt which he contracts towards mother earth when taking from the soil the elements of those commodities required for his support. *It is the condition upon which alone progress can be made.* When that is not done, motion in the earth diminishes, men separate more widely from each other, the power of association declines, land becomes valueless, the *proportion* of the labors of the com-

* From a return in the British House of Commons, it appears that from January 1857, to December 1860, there happened at sea upwards of 12,000 casualties.

munity required to be given to the work of transportation steadily increase, man sinks into a state of poverty, becoming daily more and more the slave of his fellow-man.

§ 5. Freedom grows with the growth of the power of association and combination. The obstacle to association is that resulting from distance between men and their fellow-men. That diminishes as men are enabled to obtain instruments by help of which to command the services of nature, and to develop the treasures of the earth. With every new development, they are enabled to command the aid of better machinery to be used in the work of transportation, while steadily diminishing the necessity for transportation—with constant increase in the power of combination, and in the growth of freedom.

Such are not the doctrines of modern political economy; which is based upon the idea of the "constantly increasing sterility of the soil;" and which sees the evidence of national prosperity in tables of imports and exports, in an increased demand for ships, and a growing necessity for the trader's services. Now, as a century since, when the idea was denounced by Adam Smith, "England's treasure" is sought in the foreign trade; and the "home trade" which *he* thought the most important of all, is considered as entirely subsidiary thereto. How the idea of over population has sprung from this essential error, the reader may judge after having accompanied us in an examination of the British colonial system, which it is proposed now to make.

CHAPTER XI.

OF CHANGES OF MATTER IN PLACE—CONTINUED.

§ 1. Colonial Policies of Greece, Spain, and France. That of Britain the first in which we meet with prohibition of association among the colonists. Object of the prohibition, that of producing a necessity for effecting changes in the place of matter. The policy barbaric in its tendencies, and hence it is, that it has given rise to the theory of over-population.

§ 2. British policy looks to the dispersion of man, and to increase in the proportion of society engaged in trade and transportation. Views of Adam Smith in opposition to this system.

§ 3. British colonial system, as exhibited in the West India Islands.

§ 4. Theory of over-population an effort to account for facts artificially produced, by aid of supposed natural laws.

§ 1. The States to whose policy reference has thus far been made, placed restrictions on the communication of their colonies with each other, and with other nations, without attempting to restrict them in regard to their internal commerce. The early Grecian colonies were free to make their exchanges where they would—at home, or abroad. Carthaginian colonists might change the forms of their various products to fit them for consumption; but if they wished to send them abroad, they were required to pass them through the port of Carthage. Spain and Portugal denied to the Indies the right to trade with England or with Holland, except through the ports of Seville or of Lisbon; but they never interfered with the domestic employments of the Hindoo people. France sought to establish colonies in both the East and in the West, but she never prevented her colonists from refining their own sugar, or making their own cloth. Far otherwise has it been with the great colonial system of modern times, to which the reader's attention now is asked.

In the colonial system of England we meet, for the first time, with *prohibitions of that association of man with his fellow-man which leads to the development of the individual faculties;* and with regulations intended to perpetuate the difficulties resulting from the necessity for effecting *changes in the place* of matter.

Nearly two centuries have elapsed since the merchants of London prayed their government to use its best efforts "to discourage the woollen manufacture in Ireland," in order thereby to diminish the habit of combined action then rapidly growing up in that country, and to prevent the consumption of Irish wool until it should have passed through English looms. Instead of converting it into cloth at home, the Irish were required to send it abroad in its rudest state, and receive it back in its most finished one. Already interdicted from all direct intercourse with foreigners, they were to be now restricted in their commerce among themselves.

Trade thus becoming paramount, wars were now waged for the purpose of obtaining colonies; or, according to Adam Smith, of "raising up colonies of customers;" for which purpose it was required that all attempts at local association should be discouraged among the colonists as effectually as had been the case in Ireland.

That they were so, is seen in the fact, that the first attempt at manufacture in the American colonies was followed by interference on the part of the British Legislature. In 1710 the House of Commons declared that "the erecting of manufactories in the colonies tended to lessen their dependence on Great Britain;" and the Board of Trade was ordered to report upon the subject. In 1732, the exportation of hats from province to province was prohibited, and the number of hatters' apprentices limited. In 1750, the erection of any mill or engine for splitting or rolling iron was prohibited; but pig iron might be imported into England duty free, thence to be returned in a finished form. Later, Lord Chatham declared that he would not allow the colonists to make for themselves so much as even a single hobnail.

In 1765, the exportation of artisans from Britain was prohibited under a heavy penalty; in 1781, that of utensils required for the manufacture of wool or silk was likewise prohibited; and in 1782, the prohibition was extended to artificers in printing calicoes, muslins, cottons, or linens, or in making implements used in their manufacture. In 1785, the prohibition was extended to tools used in the iron and steel manufactures, and to the workmen so employed; while in 1799 it was so extended as to embrace even colliers.

Great Britain thus aimed at preventing the people of her colonies, and of independent nations, from obtaining the machinery required for enabling them to combine their efforts for the purpose of obtaining cloth and iron; and thus compelling them to bring to her their raw materials, that she might convert them into the commodities required for consumption, to be then in part returned to the producers, burdened with heavy charges for transportation and conversion. The soil of the latter was thus to be impoverished, while that of the former was being enriched.

The centralization sought to be established by Athens or Rome, Carthage or Venice, was to the last degree unimportant, compared with that aimed at by the system above described. They prohibited merely the commerce with distant men; but here it was *home commerce*, the power of association, that was sought to be annihilated. For the accomplishment of this, no effort was omitted. Prohibition of manufactures on the one hand, and bounties on the import of raw materials on the other, were resorted to, to prevent the colonists from preparing commodities for their own consumption. The great object of the system was that of maintaining in its most bulky form the commodity to be transported; and the more perfectly that idea could be carried out the smaller would be the quantity of cloth obtainable by the man who produced the sugar, and of sugar obtainable by the man who produced the cloth; but the more the trader and the transporter would be enriched at the cost of producers and consumers, both abroad and at home.

§ 2. The one great need of man is that of combination with his fellow-men; and the one great obstacle to its accomplishment is, as the reader has already seen, the absence of those differences which result from diversity of employments, and fit him for association. The object that, by means of the laws above referred to, was sought to be obtained, was the prevention of the existence of those differences, and the perpetuation of a state of society in which the people of other lands should continue mere tillers of the earth, compelled to constant exhaustion of the soil, by reason of the necessity for sending to the distant workshop their commodities in the rudest forms; and to constant exhaustion of themselves, consequent upon the enormous transportation to which they were thus subjected. This, in its turn, involved dispersion, constantly increasing by reason of the perpetually increasing necessity for resorting to new and more distant soils; with constant increase in the *proportion* of the labor of the community required to be given to the works of trade and transportation, and diminution in the *proportion* that could be given to producing commodities to be transported or exchanged. It was, in effect, *the sacrifice of commerce at the shrine of trade*, and tended, *necessarily*, to the enslavement of man in all the communities in which it could be enforced.

The plain good sense of Adam Smith enabled him clearly to comprehend the error of a system which found in exports and imports the only index to prosperity; and also, fully to understand the enormous waste of labor resulting from its posing upon communities a necessity for exporting wool corn, cotton, and other products of the earth, in their rudest shape, to be returned again in the form of cloth. He was no believer in centralization of any kind. Least of all did he believe in that which looked to compelling all the farmers and planters to go to a single market, and to augmenting the necessity for dependence on wagons and ships, while increasing the profits of trade, and the *proportion* of every population required to be employed in the work of effecting changes of place. On the contrary, having full and entire faith in the system of local centres by help of which, as he so clearly saw, commerce had been everywhere so much developed, that was the system to whose advantages he desired to call the attention of his countrymen. From that hour to the present, however, they have pursued the system that he denounced, all their efforts having been directed towards producing the effect of continuing at its highest point the tax of transportation; and here it is, perhaps, that we may find the cause of the idea of over-population.

§ 3. Manufactures of every kind were prohibited in the British West Indies, the inhabitants not having been permitted even to refine their own sugar. There was no employment for women and children but in the labors of the field. All were required to remain producers of raw materials, having no commerce among themselves except through the intervention of a people thousands of miles distant, who so used their power as not only to prohibit manufactures, but to prevent diversification of employment even in agriculture itself. In Jamaica, indigo had been tried; but so large a portion of the price for which it could be sold in England was found to be absorbed by ship-owners, brokers, and the government, that its culture had been abandoned. Coffee was introduced, and as it grows on higher and more salubrious lands, its culture would have been of great advantage to the community; but here again so small a part of the price was allowed to come to the producer, that it would have been abandoned had not government reduced its claims to a shilling a pound; but even this proved so burthensome as soon to limit production almost entirely to the sugar-cane.

All direct commerce with foreign nations was likewise prohibited, except the slave trade with Africa, which was carried on so extensively that most of the demand for Spanish colonies was supplied from British islands. In 1775 the colonial legislature, desirous to prevent the excessive importation of negroes, imposed a duty of £2 per head; but the home government disallowed this law, on the petition of English merchants. The value of the annual export of sugar, duty free, was then stated to be £1,699,421; but so large a portion of the product was absorbed by freight, insurance, and commission, that the net proceeds of 775 sugar estates were only £726,992, or less than £1000 each. Add to the value above given the share of the government (12s. 3d. per cwt.), and the further charges before the sugar reached the consumer, and it will be seen that the producer received but a fourth of the price at which his produce sold. The planter was, therefore, little more than an overseer of slaves, whom he worked for the benefit of his British masters, and not for his own. Placed between the slave, whom he must support, on the one hand, and the merchants and government on the other, he could take for himself only what was left; and when the crop proved large, and prices fell, he found himself a ruined man. In twenty years 177 estates were sold by the sheriff, and no less than 55 wholly abandoned. It is easy now to understand the cause of the extraordinary waste of life in the British islands. The planter, unable to accumulate machinery with which to work his land, had to depend on mere brute force; and it was easier to buy this ready made on the coast of Africa, than to raise it on his own plantation. Hence, a constant supply of negroes was required, of whom little more than one in three was represented on the day of emancipation.*

The planter himself was nearly as much a slave as his negro. Ever in debt, his property was in the hands of middlemen, representing English factors, who accumulated fortunes at his expense. In the days of Adam Smith, such persons, 193 in number, held in charge 606 establishments, yielding sugar and rum to the value of £4,000,000, on which they were entitled to six per cent. We have here a state of things similar to that existing in Ireland, where absentees' estates are managed by middlemen, who, having no interest

* The total number imported into the British Islands in the West Indies cannot have been less than 1,700,000, yet the number emancipated was but 660,000. The number imported into the United States cannot have exceeded half a million: they are now upwards of 4,000,000.

in the land or in the virtual slaves upon it, are anxious only to take from both all that can be taken, giving back as little as possible to either. In both Ireland and the Indies, centralization, absenteeism, and slavery, have walked hand in hand, as they did in the days of the Scipios and the Cæsars.

Why, however, did not the land-owners remain upon their estates? Because the policy that limited the whole population to the culture of sugar, prevented the growth of any middle class to form the population of towns in which the planter might find a society that might make him regard the island as his home. In the French islands all was different. The French government not having sought to prevent the growth of commerce, towns had sprung up, and men of all classes had made the islands *their homes;* whereas the English colonists looked only to realizing fortunes, and then returning to England to spend them. In the French islands were to be found shops of every kind, where clothing, books, jewellery, etc., might be obtained; while in the others, those who had purchases to make, were obliged to import themselves directly from England. In the one there was commerce, society; in the other, only trade; and of all this, absenteeism, with its frightful evils, was a necessary consequence.

As no towns could arise under such a system, there could be no schools; and even the resident planter must send his children to England to be educated, there most naturally to contract a dislike for colonial life. With inexhaustible supplies of timber, Jamaica possessed, so late as ten years since, not even a single saw-mill. Of the amount paid by the British people, thirty years since, for the products of its 320,000 black laborers, the home government took no less than $18,000,000, or almost $60 per head; and this for merely superintending the exchanges.

Under such a system, waste of life was inevitable; and therefore do we see hundreds of thousands of men to have been imported who have perished, leaving behind no traces of their existence. On whom must rest the responsibility for so hideous a state of things? Not, surely, upon the planter, for he exercised no volition whatsoever. He might not employ his surplus power in refining his own sugar, nor could he introduce into the island either a spindle or a loom. He could neither mine coal nor smelt his copper ore Unable to repay his borrowings from mother earth, the loans he could obtain from her diminished steadily in quantity; and small even as they were, they were absorbed by the exchangers and the government. Mere instrument in their hands, as he was, for the destruction of negro morals, intellect, and life, it is on them, and not on him, must now rest the responsibility for the fact, that of all the slaves imported into the island, not more than two-fifths were represented on the day of emancipation.

Nevertheless, he it was that was regarded as the tyrant; and the public opinion of that very community which had absorbed so large a portion of the products of negro labor, drove the government to the measure of releasing the slave, appropriating a certain amount of the ransom to the payment, first, of the mortgage debts due in England—leaving the owner in many cases, without a shilling for carrying on the work of his plantation. The consequence has been seen in the extensive abandonment of land, any quantity of which, prepared for cultivation, and of the best quality, might be bought at $5 per acre; and in the fact, that after centuries of connection with a community that boasts the perfection of its machinery, there was recently not even a tolerable axe to be found upon the island.

"A piece of fine cloth," says Adam Smith, "which weighs only eighty pounds, contains in it the price, not only of eighty pounds of wool, but sometimes of several thousand weight of corn, the maintenance of the different working people, and their immediate employers;" and it is the wool and the corn that travel cheaply in the form of cloth. The corn, however, though eaten, is not destroyed; going back in the form of manure, it enriches the land, which thus produces larger crops, enabling the farmer to make a constantly increasing demand for the services of the artisan. The reward of human effort growing with the growth of value in land, all become rich and free together; and thus it is that the interests of all the members of a community are so closely connected with the adoption of a policy looking to increase in the amount of domestic commerce, and in the price of land.*

* "They," the workmen, "work up the materials of manufacture which the land produces, and exchange their finished work, or, what is the same thing, the price of it, for more materials and provisions. *They give a new value to the surplus part of the rude produce, by saving the expense of carrying it to the water-side or to some distant market:* and they furnish the cultivators with something in exchange for it, that is either useful or agreeable to them, upon easier terms than they could have obtained it before. The cultivators get a better price for their surplus produce, and can purchase

The colonial policy above described, looking, as it did, to results directly the reverse of this, forbade association, and thereby limited the whole population to a single pursuit. It forbade the immigration of artisans, the growth of towns, or the establishment of schools, and thus forbade the growth of intellect. It impoverished the land and its owners, exterminated the slave, and weakened the community, making it a mere instrument in the hands of those who effected or superintended the exchanges, the class that in all ages has thriven at the cost of the farmers of the world.

In this state of things the master was required to accept a fixed sum of money, and release his slave from the performance of the work to which he had been accustomed. Unfortunately, the system pursued had prevented that improvement of taste and feeling in the latter which could have led him to desire any thing beyond the merest necessaries of existence. Towns not having grown, he had not been accustomed even to see the commodities by which his fellow-laborers in the French islands were tempted to exertion. Schools not having existed even for the whites, he had himself acquired no wish for books, or for instruction for his children. His wife, having been always limited to field labor, had acquired no taste for dress. When, therefore, he was suddenly emancipated from control, he gratified the only desire that had been developed in him, the love of perfect idleness, to be indulged to the extent consistent with obtaining the trivial quality of food and clothing needed for the support of life.

cheaper other conveniences which they have occasion for. They are thus both encouraged and enabled to increase this surplus produce by a further improvement and better cultivation of the land; and as the fertility of the land has given birth to the manufacture, so the progress of the manufacture reacts upon the land, and increases still further its fertility. The manufacturers first supply the neighborhood, and afterwards, as their work improves and refines, more distant markets. *For, though neither the rude produce, nor even the coarse manufacture, could, without the greatest difficulty, support the expense of a considerable land carriage, the refined and improved manufacture easily may. In a small bulk it frequently contains the price of a great quantity of the raw produce. A piece of fine cloth, for example, which weighs only eighty pounds, contains in it the price, not only of eighty pounds of wool, but sometimes of several thousand weight of corn, the maintenance of the different working people, and of their immediate employers.* The corn which could with difficulty have been carried abroad in its own shape, is in this manner virtually exported in that of the complete manufacture *and may easily be sent to the remotest corners of the world.*"—Adam Smith. *Wealth of Nations.*

§ 4. The power to command the services of nature grows with the growth of association, and for this it is necessary that constantly increasing numbers may be enabled to obtain supplies of food from any given space. Modern political economy, however, teaches directly the reverse of this, assuring us that as numbers increase, there arises a necessity for resorting to inferior soils, with constantly increasing difficulty of obtaining food; and that hence arises the disease of over-population. That theory, as the reader has seen, had its origin in England, and was simply an attempt to explain unnatural phenomena, the work of man, by help of imaginary natural laws attributed to man's Creator.

In a state of barbarism, population is always superabundant; as civilization grows, larger numbers obtain more food in return to diminished labor. The more rapid is the growth of this power over nature, the less is the *proportion* of labor required for the work of transportation; and the more completely is it proved that food tends to increase more rapidly than population.

The system above described, based on the idea of preventing local association, increased the *proportion* of the labor required for transportation; while by preventing the development of the human faculties, it reduced the subject of its operations nearly to the condition of a mere brute beast. Hence it has been that the world has been called upon to witness the extermination of the vast body of people imported into the British West Indies, the pauperization of the people of England, and the invention of a system of political economy that ignores the distinctive qualities of man, retaining only those he has in common with the horse and the ox.

The idea of over-population having originated in England, it is needed that we examine the history of those communities subject to the British system, with a view to ascertain if it be really a law of nature, or only a natural consequence of the policy that looked to the separation of the artisan and the agriculturist, and to the creation of a single workshop for the world. Portugal, Turkey, Ireland, and India, having been the countries most subjected to it, will now be examined, in order to ascertain how far the phenomena there observed correspond with those above exhibited as having occurred in the island of Jamaica.

CHAPTER XII.

OF CHANGES OF MATTER IN PLACE—CONTINUED.

§ 1. THE splendor of PORTUGAL, in the sixteenth century, resulting from her exercise throughout the East of the power of appropriation, had, as has ever been the case, been attended with growing weakness; and the close of that century saw her reduced to the condition of a Spanish province. Having recovered her independence, the close of the seventeenth century exhibits her engaged in a vigorous effort for securing it by means of the establishment among her people of the habit of association needed for the extension of their domestic commerce. Long celebrated for her wool, she had lacked the means of converting it into cloth. Now, however, she imported foreign artisans, by whose help the woollen manufacture soon grew so rapidly as to supply the home demand; thus lessening her dependence on the chances of trade abroad, while greatly promoting commerce.

In 1703 was signed with England the famous Methuen Treaty, by which, in return for favors accorded to her wines, she renounced the idea of creating a home demand for either her wool or her food. At once her markets were inundated with British goods, her manufactures were ruined, and the precious metals disappeared.

Thus reconverted into a purely agricultural country, exhaustion of the soil followed as a necessary consequence, attended by a decline in the numbers of her people so great and so continuous, that they now number but three millions, the decrease of the last century having been no less than 700,000. The consequences exhibit themselves in the facts, that in a country which in the days of the Cæsars was already well supplied with roads, the mails are now carried on horseback at the rate of three miles an hour, and that the only mode of conveying goods from one port to another is in bullock-carts; or for light goods, on mules, or on the backs of *gallegos;* the value of man being there so small that he is regarded as little better than a beast of burden. "It is surprising," says a recent traveler, "how ignorant the Portuguese are of every kind of handicraft. They seem to disdain improvement, and are so inferior to the rest of Europe as to form a sort of disgraceful wonder in the middle of the twelfth century."

The system thus described has now endured for a century and a half, during which the power to command the services of nature has been constantly declining; and with the decay of commerce at home, the power to maintain it abroad has so far diminished, that Portugal has ceased to enter into the consideration of those who at the commencement of the last century so anxiously sought her trade. Such is the condition of that naturally rich land after long subjection to the policy of the country in which originated the theory of over-population.

§ 2. No portion of the Eastern hemisphere possesses greater natural advantages than that constituting the TURKISH EMPIRE in Europe and Asia. Wool and silk, corn, oil, and tobacco, might be produced in unlimited quantities, while Thessaly and Macedonia, long celebrated for cotton, could yield enough to clothe the whole of Europe. Coal and iron ore abound, while in some places the hills are almost masses of carbonate of copper. Nature has done every thing for that country; yet the Turkish rayah is little better than a slave, and the government is compelled to submit in all things to the dictation of other States. Why it is so, we may now inquire.

Two centuries since, the trade with Turkey was the most important portion of that maintained by Western Europe; and Turkish merchants were amongst the wealthiest of those who frequented the markets of the West. A little later, the government bound itself by a treaty with France and England to charge no higher duty on their imports than three per cent.; and as their vessels were to be exempted from all port charges, the system thus established was, practically, one of the most absolute freedom of trade.

For more than a century, however, Turkey could still compete, to some extent, with the nations of the West. "Ambelakain," says M. de Beaujour, "supplied industrious Germany, not because of the perfection of its jennies, but because of the industry of its spindles and the perfection of its colors."

Revenue from customs having no existence, the government had, from the date of the treaty, been dependent on poll, house, and land taxes. Trade had been freed from all let or hindrance, but, as a consequence, commerce at home became shackled by constantly increasing interferences. The system of local centres, nevertheless, continued in existence until the close of the last century, and the country remained both rich and strong. Great Britain, however, had even then invented machinery for spinning cotton, and by prohibiting its export, as well as that of the artisans who could elsewhere have made it, had, to the best of her ability, provided that all the cotton of the world should be brought to her looms, to be by them converted into cloth. The consequence was, that of 600 looms at Scutari in 1812, but 40 remained in 1821; and of 2000 weaving establishments at Tournovo in 1812, but 200 remained in 1830. Since then, the cotton manufacture has, it is believed, entirely disappeared.

For a time, cotton went abroad, to be returned in the form of yarn, traveling thousands of miles in search of the little spindle; but even this trade has passed away, and with it the power to obtain any reasonable reward for labor. In 1832, women's wages were but four cents a day; men employed in gathering mulberry leaves, and attending silk-works, could earn but five cents; while at Salonica, the shipping port of Thessaly, men could be hired at fifty cents a week. Commerce had ceased to exist, and the value of man, as well as the utility of the earth, had almost disappeared; while the value of commodities had become so great as to cause men, women and children, to perish for want of food.

While manufactures existed, agriculture flourished, because, the market being at hand, the tax of transportation was moderate. Roads and bridges could then be kept in order; but as manufactures declined, and it became more necessary to carry the bulky products of the earth to distant markets, the *need of roads* increased, but *the power to maintain them* declined, always a result of the sacrifice of commerce at the shrine of trade. "The increased expense of transport," says a recent traveler, "enabled a few capitalists to monopolize the whole export trade; in consequence of which the ruin of the landed proprietors and agriculturists soon commenced, and families were impoverished as villages disappeared; while in many extensive districts the whole rural population abandoned the cultivation of their native soil to emigrate to the nearest cities."

Depopulation and poverty having always followed increase in the power of the trader, it is not surprising that travelers should exhibit the nation as passing steadily towards ruin, and the people as becoming more enslaved, the inevitable result of that policy which excludes the mechanic, and thus prevents the development of individuality. At the date above referred to (1850), not only had the silk manufacture disappeared, but even the filatures for preparing the raw silk had ceased to operate. The silk cultivators had become entirely dependent on a foreign market, in which there then existed one of those "crises" by means of which the agricultural dependents of Great Britain are so often ruined. On one occasion, during Mr. Macfarlane's travels, there came a report that silk had risen in England, producing a momentary stir and animation, "that," as he says, "flattered his national vanity to think that an electric touch, parting from London, the mighty heart of commerce, should thus be felt, in a few days, in a place so distant." Such is trading centralization! It renders the agriculturists of the world mere slaves, dependent for food and clothing upon the will of a few people, proprietors of a small amount of machinery at "the mighty heart of commerce."

The silk that is made, badly prepared because of the difficulty of obtaining good machinery, is now required to go to England in its rudest state, there to be fitted for being sent to Persia; and thus does commerce with foreign nations become more impeded with every diminution in the power to maintain commerce at home.

Not only is the foreigner free to introduce his wares, but he may, on payment of a duty of two per cent , peddle them throughout the empire until he finds a market. Traveling by caravan, he is lodged without expense; while the store-keeper is subjected to both rent and taxes, and is unable to contend with him. As a consequence of this entire freedom of trade, the poor cultivator finds himself deprived of all power to exchange his scanty products for the commodities he needs, except on the arrival of a caravan which is far more likely to absorb the little money in circulation than any of the more bulky products of the earth.

As usual in purely agricultural countries, the whole body of cultivators is hopelessly in debt, and the money-lender fleeces all As a necessary consequence, real estate is almost wholly valueless—square miles of the richest land, near to Constantinople, being purchasable at less than thousands of dollars. Domestic commerce having scarcely an existence, it follows here, as everywhere else, that foreign commerce is insignificant. But recently, the exports amounted only to $33,000,000, while those from Great Britain to Turkey were but $11,000,000; and much of even this small quantity was sent there only on its way to other more Eastern markets.

In the real and permanent interests of nations there is no discord. *Whatever permanently benefits one tends equally to do so by all others;* and the day may perhaps come when it will be admitted among nations as among individuals, that an enlightened self-interest dictates the observance of that golden rule of Christianity which teaches that we should do unto others as we would they should do unto us.

But a century since, Turkey, Portugal, and the West India Islands, were the best of England's customers. What are they now? The constant cause of British wars and expenditure, poor in themselves while despised by others, and most especially so by Britain herself. Compelled to the pursuance of a policy that has destroyed commerce at home, they have become mere instruments in the hands of foreign traders, and have ceased to command respect among the communities of the world.

§ 3. At the date of the Revolution of 1688, the woollen manufacture was advancing rapidly in Ireland; but the government of William and Mary, in reply to an application of the London merchants, pledged itself to "discountenance" that manufacture, so as to compel the transmission of wool to England, while its export to foreign countries was entirely prohibited.

Irish ships were next deprived of all participation in the benefits of the navigation laws, as well as excluded from the fisheries. Sugar could be imported only through England; and as no drawback was allowed on its exportation to Ireland, the latter was thus taxed for the support of the foreign government as well as for that of her own. All colonial produce was required to be carried first to England; and when reshipped to Ireland, it must be in English ships, manned by English seamen, and owned by English merchants, thus increasing to the utmost the tax for transportation, while denying to Ireland any share in the expenditure of the public revenue so collected. While thus depriving the people of the power of combination, every inducement was held out to them to confine themselves to the production of materials for English manufactures; wool, flax, and hemp having been admitted free of duty. Men, women, and children were regarded as mere instruments to be used by trade, and, as in Jamaica, to be deprived of all employment but in the labors of the field.

Pending the war of the American Revolution, however, freedom of commerce being claimed for Ireland and under circumstances that compelled compliance with the demand, changes were gradually made, until, at length, in 1783, her legislative independence was fully admitted. First among the measures then adopted was the imposition of duties on various articles of foreign manufacture, with the avowed intention of enabling the Irish people to employ their labor in converting their corn and wool into cloth, in accordance with the teachings of Adam Smith. Thenceforward, commerce made rapid progress, attended with such development of mind, that the great demand for books warranted the reproduction of all the principal English law-reports of the day, and very many of the earlier ones, as well as the principal novels, travels, and miscellaneous works. More books were then published in Dublin by a single house, than are now, probably, required to supply the greatly increased population of the entire kingdom.

With 1801, however, centralization being then fully re-established, there came a change. By the Act of Union, the copyright laws were extended to Ireland, and at once disappeared the large and growing manufacture of books. The patent laws were also extended to that country; and while England had the home, the foreign, and the Irish market open to her, the Irish manufacturers had to contend for existence on their own soil, and under every possible disadvantage. As a consequence, Irish manufactures disappeared as the act of Union gradually took effect. By its provisions, the duties established by the Irish Parliament with a view to aid the farmers in bringing the artisan into close proximity to themselves, were to be diminished until free trade should be arrived at; or, in other words, Manchester and Birmingham were to have a monopoly of supplying Ireland with both iron and cloth. The duty on English woollens was to continue twenty years. Those on English calicoes and muslins were to continue till 1808; then, gradually diminishing, were to cease in 1821. Those on cotton yarn were to cease in 1810. The effect of this exhibited itself in the facts, that in 1840 the woollen manufacturers of Dublin had declined from 91 to 12; the hands employed from 4918 to 602; and, that the wool-combers and carpet manufacturers had almost disappeared. Such, too, was the case in Cork, Kilkenny, Wicklow, and all other of the numerous seats of manufacture.

Deprived thus of all employment other than agriculture, the people had but the choice between the occupation of *land at any rent on the one hand, or starvation on the other.* The landlord having the power to dictate his own terms, enormous rents, low wages, the re-letting of land by intermediate oppressors at five times its value, and the misery consequent on this, led to a succession of outrages, followed by Insurrection Acts and Coercion Acts; when the real remedy was to be found in the adoption of a system that might enable them to combine their efforts, and thus to maintain the commerce that was then being sacrificed at the shrine of trade.

English writers assure us that Ireland has always been deficient in the capital required for manufactures; but such must always be the case in purely agricultural countries. No such deficiency was felt in the period which immediately preceded the Act of Union, because commerce was then steadily growing, and was producing a demand for all the physical and intellectual force of the community. After that time commerce declined, till it died away; and then there was wasted, *in each and every year*, an amount of capital *adequate, if properly applied, to the creation of all the cotton and woollen machinery existing in England.* In this enforced waste of capital may be found the true cause of the decline and fall of the Irish nation.

As commerce declined, the middlemen accumulated fortunes which they *could* not invest in machinery, and *would* not apply to the improvement of the land, but which might be sent to England; and thus were cheap labor and cheap capital forced to contribute to the building up of "the great works of Britain." Further, it was provided by law, that, whenever the poor people of a neighborhood contributed even to a saving fund, it might not be so applied as to furnish local employment, but should be sent abroad to be invested in the British funds.

The raw products of the soil, consumed abroad, returned nothing to the land, which thus became impoverished. The

Irish people were thus selling their soil to pay for cotton and woollen goods that they should have manufactured for themselves; for coal and iron which abounded at home; and for a small quantity of tea, sugar, and other foreign commodities; while the amount paid in rent to absentees, and in interest on mortgages, was estimated at more than thirty millions of dollars. The inducements to remain at home diminishing, those who could live without labor fled to England, Italy, or France. Those who desired to work, and felt qualified for something beyond manual labor, fled to England or America, and thus was the unfortunate country depleted of every thing which could render it a home, while those who could not fly were "starving by millions" and happy when a full-grown man could find employment at sixpence a day, without allowance for clothing, lodging, or even for food!

The advocates of the system which seeks to convert all the world outside of England into one great farm, accounted for the existence of such a state of things by the fact that population was too numerous for the land: and yet *a third of the surface, including the richest lands in the kingdom, was lying waste.* The one thing needed to render that population prosperous and happy was *employment*, giving the power to maintain domestic commerce; but this could have no existence under the system which in so brief a period had caused the annihilation of the cotton manufacture of India, notwithstanding the advantage of having the cotton on the spot, free from all cost for carriage.

Bad, however, as was this state of things, worse was then at hand. Poverty compelling the wretched people to fly in thousands across the Channel, a cry arose that the laborers of England were likely to be swamped by starving Irishmen; to provide against which it was needed that Irish landlords should be made to support their own poor, as they were by Act of Parliament forthwith compelled to do; although for half a century previously England had rung with denunciations of the poor-law system. Then arose, of course, an increased desire to rid the country of people who, unable to sell their labor, could pay no rent; and from that time to the present, Ireland has presented, in the destruction of houses and the expulsion of their inhabitants, the most shocking scenes—scenes more worthy of the most uncivilized part of Africa than of an integral portion of the British Empire.

Thus far, Irish agriculture had been protected in the English market as some small compensation for the sacrifice of the domestic one; but even that trivial boon was now to be withdrawn. The people of Ireland, like those of Jamaica, having become poor, their trade had ceased to be of value, though but seventy years before they had been England's most valued customers. The system having exhausted all the countries subjected to it, India, Portugal, Turkey, the West Indies, and Ireland herself, it had become necessary to seek markets in those which had to a greater or less extent placed the consumer beside the producer, France, Belgium, Germany, Russia, and America; and the same system was offered them by which Ireland had been exhausted. The farmers everywhere were invited to impoverish their soil by sending its products to England to be consumed; and the corn laws were repealed to enable them to compete with the Irishman, who was thus deprived of the English market, as he had by the Act of Union, been deprived of his own. The cup of misery was now full. The price of food fell, and the laborer was ruined, for his whole product could scarcely pay his rent. The landlord was ruined, for while unable to collect rents, he was heavily taxed to support his own impoverished tenants. His land was encumbered with mortgages and settlements, on which he could no longer pay the interest. And now the British people resorted to the revolutionary measure of creating a special court for the sale of encumbered property, and the distribution of its proceeds, thus bringing on the impoverished landholder the same fate that had already befallen his poor tenant.

The great object to be accomplished by means of this measure of spoliation was, as we were assured, the introduction of that British population and British capital which were needed for giving new life to Irish industry and agriculture. How it has operated, and is operating, is exhibited in the following figures, representing the movement of the few past years:

	1857	1863
Number of acres under cereal crops	2,183,354	2,408,762
" horses	600,601	619,173
" cattle	3,618,544	3,138,275
" sheep	3,448,676	3,303,291
" pigs	1,262,152	1,064,502

Such being the facts, it can afford to the reader little cause for surprise to know that the tendency towards emigration is a constantly increasing one.

§ 4. The *Times*, and other English journals, declared that "*for a whole generation man had been a drug, and population* a *nuisance*," and rejoiced at the gradual disappearance of the native population, finding "in the abstraction of the Celtic race at the rate of a quarter of a million a year, a surer remedy for the inveterate Irish disease than any human wit could ever have imagined."

That "disease" is simply the absence of all demand for labor, resulting from the unhappy determination of the people of England to destroy the power of association throughout the world. The nation which begins by exporting raw products must end by exporting men; as is shown by the fact that in the decade ending in 1851, the population of Ireland had decreased but little less than two millions. To what causes is this to be attributed? Not to any deficiency of land, for nearly one-third, including millions of acres of the richest soils remain in a state of nature. Not to any inferiority of the soil, which is confessedly among the richest in the empire. Not to a deficiency of mineral wealth, for coal, iron, and other metals abound. Not to any deficiency of physical qualities in the Irishman, it being an established fact that he is capable of performing more labor than the Englishman, the Frenchman, or the Belgian. Not to any deficiency of intellectual ability, Ireland having given to England her most distinguished soldiers and statesmen, and having throughout the world furnished evidence that the Irishman is capable of the highest intellectual attainments. In spite of all these advantages, he is, at home, a slave to the severest taskmasters, and in a condition of poverty such as exhibits itself in no other part of the civilized world. No choice being left him but between expatriation and starvation, he abandons the home of his fathers to seek elsewhere that subsistence which Ireland can no longer afford him. The state of things there existing is often charged to the account of the potato, which, as Mr. McCulloch informs his readers, has lowered the standard of living, and tended to the multiplication of population. "The peasantry of Ireland," he says, "live in miserable mud cabins, without either a window or a chimney, or any thing that can be called furniture;" hence it is, as he says, they work for low wages. We have here effect substituted for cause. The absence of demand for labor causes wages to be so low, that the laborer can obtain nothing but mud cabins and potatoes; and this is caused by that trading centralization which looks to destroying the power of association and preventing that diversity of employment to which, alone, can we look for maintenance of the powers of the land, or for advance in wealth, civilization and power.

It is singular that modern political economy should have so entirely overlooked the great fact, *that man is a mere borrower from the earth, and that when he does not pay his debts, she does as do all other creditors, expelling him from his holding.* England makes of her soil a reservoir for the refuse yielded by the raw commodities of almost half the world, thus obtaining manure that has been valued at $500,000,000, or five times more than the value of the cotton crop of America; yet so important is that commodity that she imports in a single year more than 200,000 tons of guano, at a cost of more than $10,000,000. Nevertheless, her writers teach other nations, that the true way to become rich is to exhaust their land by exporting its products in their rudest state; and then, when Irishmen follow the soil that has been sent to England, the world is assured that "the unexampled misery of the Irish people is owing to the excessive augmentation of their numbers;" and that "nothing can be more futile than to expect any real or lasting amendment in their situation until an effectual check has been given to the progress of population." "How," asks the Times, "are they to be fed and employed?" "That," as it continues, "is the question which still baffles an age that can transmit a message round the world in a moment of time, and point out the locality of a planet never yet seen."

It is, nevertheless, a question readily answered. *Let them have commerce*, let them be emancipated from the dominion of trade, and they will find at once a demand for their powers, whether mental or physical. What Ireland needs is, that societary motion and that power of combination which result from diversity of employments. Let her have them, and she will cease to export food, while her people perish of famine. Give her them, and her land, ceasing to be impoverished by the exportation of its most valuable elements, will both "feed and employ her people;" and the doctrine of over-population will then cease to find support in the harrowing details of Irish history. In none other can there be found such proof conclusive of the fact, that the raising of raw produce for the supply of foreign markets is an employment fit only for the slave and the barbarian.

CHAPTER XIII.

OF CHANGES OF MATTER IN PLACE—CONTINUED.

§ 1. Local action, and local combination, conspicuous throughout the history of Hindostan. Their disappearance under the British rule.

§ 2. Commerce sacrificed at the shrine of trade. Annihilation of Indian manufactures. Its ruinous effects.

§ 3. Waste of capital, and destruction of the power of accumulation.

§ 4. Diminution in the security of person and property correspondent with the extension of British rule, and with the growing centralization.

§ 5. Trivial value of private rights in the land of India. India a paying country under its native princes. Its steady deterioration under the system which looks to increasing the necessity for the trader and transporter's services.

§ 6. Review of the phenomena observed in the four great communities, above referred to. Differing in all other respects, they are alike in the fact, that they have been deprived of all power to diversify their employments, and have thus been forced to increase their dependence on the transporter and the trader.

§ 7. Destructive effects of a growing necessity for the services of the trader. British policy looks solely to the increase of trade. Constant waste of capital in all the countries subject to the system.

§ 8. Origin of the idea of over-population.

§ 1. In no part of the world has there been seen a greater tendency to voluntary association than once existed in Hindostan. In none did the smaller communities exercise to a greater extent the power of self-government. Each village had its distinct organization, under which the natives lived from the earliest times down to a recent date. Revolutions might occur and dynasties might succeed each other, but so long as his own little society remained undisturbed the simple Hindoo gave himself no concern about what might happen in the distant capital.

The Mahometan conquest left these simple institutions untouched. Each Hindoo village had its distinct municipality; and over a certain number of villages was a hereditary chief and accountant, both possessing great local authority, and certain territorial estates. The Mahometans early saw the policy of not disturbing an institution so complete; and they availed themselves of the local influence of these officers to reconcile their subjects to their rule.

Local action and combination everywhere exhibit themselves throughout the history of India. Rulers being numerous, taxation was heavy; but, the taxes being locally expended, nothing went from off the land. Manufactures, too, were widely spread, employing the labor not required in agriculture. On the coast of Coromandel and in the province of Bengal, sixty years since, it would have been difficult to find a village in which every man, woman, and child, was not employed in making a piece of cloth. Its progress included no less than a description of the lives of half the people of Hindostan. Bengal was celebrated for fine muslins, and the Coromandel Coast for chintzes and calicoes, while Western India produced coarse goods of every kind. Though over-taxed, and often plundered by invading armies, the country continued both rich and prosperous.

The battle of Plassey having established British power in India centralization thenceforward grew rapidly, and the country became filled with adventurers, men whose sole object was the accumulation of fortune by any means, however foul; as is well known to all familiar with the indignant denunciations of Burke.* England was thus enriched as India became impoverished.

Step by step the British power was extended, and everywhere was adopted the Hindoo principle that the sovereign, as proprietor of the soil, was entitled to half of the gross produce. The land tax, now called rent, had formerly been limited to a thirteenth, then raised to a sixth; but in the reign of Akbar (sixteenth century) it was fixed at one-third, numerous other taxes having been then abolished. With the decline of the empire, the local sovereigns had not only increased it, but had revived taxes that had been discontinued, while instituting others, all of which were now continued under the British rule. Further, having a monopoly of trade, the company could dictate the prices of all that it sold, as well as of all that it bought, another most oppressive tax imposed for the benefit of absentee landlords.†

* "The country was laid waste with fire and sword; and that land distinguished above most others by the cheerful face of fraternal government and protected labor, the chosen seat of cultivation and plenty, is now almost throughout a dreary desert covered with rushes and briers, and with jungles full of wild beasts." . . . . . "That universal, systematic breach of treaties, which had made British faith proverbial in the East!"—*Speech on Fox's East India Bill.*

† "The misgovernment of the English was carried to a point such as seemed hardly compatible with the existence of society. They forced the natives to buy dear and sell cheap. They insulted with impunity the tribunals, the police, and the fiscal authorities of the country. Enormous fortunes were thus rapidly accumulated at Calcutta, while 30,000,000 of human beings were reduced to the extremity of wretchedness. They had been accustomed to live under tyranny, but never under tyranny like this." . . . . "Under their old masters, they had at least one resource; when the evil became

Exhaustion being the natural consequence of centralization, the ability to pay taxes diminished, and a sort of landed aristocracy, responsible to the government for their payment, was now created in the Zemindars. From mere officers of the crown these become now great landed proprietors, masters of a host of poor tenants, who hold their land at will and are liable to torture if they fail to pay. Thus do we find the middleman system of Ireland and of the Western Indies, transplanted to those of the East.

The Zemindars, however, unable to collect the taxes, were in their turn sold out and ruined. That system having failed, it was next determined to arrest the extension of the permanent settlement, and arrange with each little ryot, or cultivator, to the entire exclusion of the village authorities. How this has operated is thus described by Mr. Fullerton, a member of the Madras Council:—

"Imagine the revenue leviable through the agency of one hundred thousand revenue officers, collected or remitted at their discretion, according to the occupant's means of paying, whether from the produce of his land or his separate property; and in order to encourage every man to act as a spy on his neighbor, and report his means of paying, that he may save himself from all extra demand; imagine all the cultivators of a village liable at all times to a separate demand, in order to make up the failure of one or more individuals of the parish. Imagine collectors to every county, acting under the orders of a board, on the avowed principle of destroying all competition for labor by a general equalization of assessment, seizing and sending back all runaways to each other. Lastly, imagine the collector the sole magistrate or justice of peace of the county, through the medium of whom alone any complaint of personal grievance suffered by the subject can reach the superior court. Imagine, at the same time, every subordinate officer employed in the collection of the land revenue to be a police officer, vested with the power to fine, confine, put in the stocks, and flog any inhabitant within his range, on any charge, without oath of the accuser or sworn recorded evidence of the case."

insupportable, the people rose and pulled down the goverment. But the English government was not to be shaken off. That government, oppressive as the most oppressive form of barbarian despotism, was strong with all the strength of civilization. It resembled the government of evil genii rather than the government of human tyrants."—*Macaulay*.

Under such a system there could be no circulation, no commerce, and without that there could be neither force nor progress. In some districts the share of the government was no less than sixty or seventy per cent., heaped on which were taxes on every description of machinery in use, requiring interferences of the most inquisitorial kind, and forbidding all improvement. In settling the taxes paid by looms, the weaver was required to report the number of his children, and what assistance they rendered him; and the more they all exerted themselves the higher became the contribution. The oil-mill, the potter's kiln, the goldsmith's tools, the sawyer's saw, the blacksmith's anvil, the carpenter's tools, the cotton-beater's bow, the weaver's loom, and the fisherman's boat—all were taxed. No machinery of any description was allowed to escape; and large allowances were made to informers to induce those who did not desire to work to become spies on those who did; *and this system is, or was quite recently, still in force.*

Further taxes were collected, at local custom-houses, on exchanges between the several parts of the country, while monopolies of salt, opium, and tobacco, were created for the benefit of the public revenue. The manufacture of salt was prohibited; and even its collection along the sea-shore, where nature freely furnishes it, was punishable by fine and imprisonment. Even the quantity collected by the Company's officers was limited to that required for supplying the demand at monopoly price, the rest being regularly destroyed, lest the poor ryot should obtain at diminished cost what was needed to render palatable the rice which constituted almost his only food.

Under the native princes, the produce of taxation was locally expended; but under the centralization system it is required to go constantly abroad, the real weight of taxation being thus almost indefinitely increased by the consequent destruction of the power of combination. In this manner is *commerce* sacrificed to *trade.*

§ 2. Cotton abounded, and half a century since native labor not only supplied the home demand but produced a hundred millions of pounds of cloth per annum for export to distant countries. Exchange was so much in favor of India, that a rupee, now worth but 44 cents, was then worth no less than 64. The company had a monopoly of collecting taxes, but in return it preserved to the people the control of their domestic market. Such protection was required, because, while England prohibited the export of a single collier who might instruct the people in mining coal, of a steam-engine or a mechanic who could make one, of a power-loom, or of an artisan who could give to the poor Hindoo instruction in the use of such machines—and thus systematically prevented them from acquiring control over the great forces of nature—she at the same time imposed heavy duties on the produce of Indian looms received in Britain.

Later, however, the trade to India was thrown open, *the restrictions on the export of machinery and artisans being still maintained in full force;* and thus were the poor and ignorant people of that country suddenly exposed to competition with a community possessed of implements greatly more effective than their own. Twenty years still later we find a whole year to have passed without the export of a single piece of cloth; and thus did commerce perish under the oppressive demands of trade!

When the export of machinery from Britain was prohibited, it was done with a view to compel all the wool and cotton of the world to come thither to be spun and woven, thus depriving all other nations of the power to apply their labor except in raising the raw materials required for keeping in operation the one great "workshop of the world." Its effects in India exhibit themselves in a ruin and distress to which, said Sir Robert Peel, "no parallel can be found in the annals of commerce." Great seats of manufacture have wholly disappeared, the flourishing city of Dacca, once containing 90,000 houses, being now but a mass of ruins, overgrown with jungle. For the accomplishment of this work of destruction, the *children* of Lancashire, according to the same authority, were employed fifteen and seventeen hours per day, during the week, and on Sunday morning, from six to twelve, in cleaning the machinery. In Coventry ninety-six hours a week was the time usually required; and of those employed, many obtained but 2s. 9d. (66 cents) as the wages of a week. The object to be accomplished was that of underworking the poor Hindoo, and driving him from the market of the world, and from his own; and the means employed was that of cheapening labor, the laborer being, according to modern doctrines, little more than a mere instrument to be used by trade.

§ 3. The poor ryot pays fifteen or twenty pence for the

British cloth made from a pound of cotton that had yielded him but a penny; and all this difference is paid for the service of others, while he himself is unemployed. "Half the human time and energy of India," we are told by Mr. Chapman, in his *Cotton and Commerce of India*, "runs to waste." He might, however, have gone much further than this. Where there is no commerce, and where, consequently, men are forced to depend on distant trade, *nine-tenths* of the power of a community runs to waste. In India *capital is wasted weekly to an amount greater than the annual value of the goods imported.* The works constructed in former times for the purposes of irrigation, have gone to ruin, and the richest lands have been abandoned. In the valley of the Ganges not one-third of the cultivable lands, according to Mr. Chapman, is under cultivation; and, as he says elsewhere, over all India one-half is waste. In the Madras presidency not one-fifth is cultivated, yet are severe famines facts of frequent occurrence. Look where we may in that magnificent country, we see evidence of declining individuality and diminished power of combination, accompanied by increasing centralization, and *centralization, slavery, and death, always travel hand in hand together.*

§ 4. The tendency towards civilization having been, in all ages, in the ratio of the development of individual faculty, and the system now before us looking to the reverse of this, we might reasonably expect here to find society moving in the direction of growing barbarism. Accordingly, we find a marked increase of crime of every kind in passing from the newly acquired to the older of the company's possessions. Robbery, perjury, and forgery, abound in Bengal and Madras; while in the Punjaub, they are infrequent, and, as Mr Campbell, in his *Modern India and its Government*, informs us, "an oath is astonishingly binding. The longer we possess a province," he says, "the more common and general does perjury become;" while Col. Sleeman, another high authority, assures us, "that the hill tribes are remarkable for their strict veracity." In the newly acquired provinces, too, the people read and write with facility; whereas, from the older ones education has disappeared. As regards intemperance, Mr. Campbell finds himself obliged to state that "it increases where our rule and system have been long established;" and Captain Westmacott tells his readers that "in places the longest under our rule, there is the largest amount of depravity and crime."

§ 5. The gross land revenue obtained from a country that is, naturally, one of the richest of the world, and with an area of 300,000,000 acres, is $72,000,000. In no case does the land subject to taxation seem to be worth more than four years' purchase; while over a large portion of the country it appears to be wholly destitute of exchangable value. There being, however, some lands tax free, it is possible that the whole may be worth, on an average, four years' purchase, giving $288,000,000 as the money value of all the rights in land acquired by the people of India in the thousands of years it has been under cultivation. The few people of the little and sandy State of New Jersey, with its area of 6900 square miles, have acquired rights in the land valued at $150,000,000; while the little island on which stands the city of New York, would sell for almost twice as much as all the proprietary rights to land in India, with its hundreds of millions of acres, and its 150,000,000 of inhabitants!

"Under its native princes," says Mr. Campbell, "India was a paying country." Under absentee rule it has ceased to pay, because, the power of combination having been annihilated, the internal commerce declines steadily, while the external, until the recent stoppage of the supply of cotton caused an increased demand for the produce of India with large increase of prices, has amounted to but fifty cents a head. Centralization has grown daily, and every stage of its growth has been marked by an increasing inability to meet taxation; and the wider the extension of the system, the greater has been the difficulty of collecting revenue sufficient for keeping in motion the machine of government. This it has been that has forced the representatives of British power and civilization into becoming traders in that pernicious drug, opium, by means of which the Chinese people are taxed, annually, to the extent of nearly twenty millions of dollars, and not less than half a million of human lives. "The immolations of an Indian Juggernaut," says a recent writer, "dwindle into insignificance before it;" and yet, for the maintenance of this trade it has been that the towns and cities of China have been sacked, and their people ruined, even when not exterminated. Trade and war have gone hand in hand from the beginning of the world, and all their triumphs have been obtained at the expense of commerce.

Nowhere in the world have they traveled so thoroughly together, as in India under the British domination, and nowhere, consequently, could we more reasonably have looked for such a rebellion as that which recently has occurred, attended, as it has been, with barbarities, on both sides, such as find no parallel in modern European or American history. Studying the facts here presented for examination by this magnificent country, we are forcibly reminded of the bitter and prophetic denunciation of the system contained in the following lines by one of the most distinguished of British poets:

> "'Foes of mankind!' her guardian spirits say,—
> 'Revolving ages bring the bitter day,
> When heaven's unerring aim shall fall on you,
> And blood for blood these Indian plains bedew!'"—CAMPBELL.

The history of the world is little more than a record of the efforts of the few who were strong to restrain the growth of the power of association, to prevent the organization of society, to interfere with the maintenance of commerce, and to retard the acquisition of that power over nature which constitutes wealth; and thus to enslave the many who were weak. Its every page presents evidence of the fleeting character of all prosperity obtained by aid of measures violative of that great and fundamental law of Christianity which requires us to respect the rights of our neighbor as we would have our own respected; but in none is found a more instructive lesson than that which records the annihilation of commerce in India, and the growth of that pauperism in England which gave rise to the doctrine of over-population. Both waxed together, and together both must wane—the measures required for the relief of the Hindoo being precisely those required for the extirpation of pauperism among the Britons.

§ 6. The reader has now had placed before him a picture of the movements of four considerable nations, and of one assemblage of nations, the whole comprising more than a fifth of the population of the globe. All of these have been subjected to that system of policy which looks to the prevention of combination, and to the maintenance at its highest point that most oppressive of all taxes, *the tax of transportation*. In all, nature is daily obtaining greater power over man; in all, wealth diminishes, with constant decrease in the value of man, who becomes from year to year more the slave of his fellow-man.

It may however be said, that the people of India are indolent; that the Turks are Mohammedans and fatalists; that the Portuguese and Irish nations have a religious faith adverse to the development of mind; that the laborers of Jamaica are but little removed from barbarism; and, that in facts like these may be found the causes of the growing weakness of the several communities whose situation is above described. The people of the Turkish Empire had, however, precisely the same modes of thought a century since that they have now; yet the commerce with them was accounted the most valuable portion of that of Western Europe. The faith of the enlightened Moors of Spain was the same as that of the men of the shores of the Hellespont, and we know well that it there presented no obstacle to the progress of civilization. The Portuguese are no more Catholic than were those of their predecessors who made the Methuen treaty, and whose commerce was then deemed by Englishmen to be of such high importance. They, as well as the Irish people, hold the same faith with those of France, among whom agriculture and manufactures are now advancing with such rapidity. The negroes imported into Jamaica were no more barbarian than those brought to Virginia and Carolina; yet, while each of these latter is represented by seven of his descendants, the British Islands present but two for every five received. Differing in religious faith, color, race, and climate, these communities are alike in one respect; that they have been deprived of the power so to diversify employment as to be enabled to develop the various faculties of their members, and thus to fit them for that association and combination without which man can obtain no power to command the great forces of nature. Limited entirely to the pursuits of the field, they have been compelled to export their produce in its rudest state; thus exhausting the soil, and diminishing the return to human effort. Under such circumstances commerce would necessarily decline, and the power of the trader and transporter increase, while the cultivator would more and more become a mere instrument to be used by those who live by the exercise of their powers of appropriation. That he does so become in all these countries is most certain; and that such are the inevitable consequences of a policy which looks to the prevention of combination, and of the development of the latent powers of man, cannot admit of a moment's doubt. In each and every of them we find evidence of the great truth, that the raising of raw products for distant markets is the proper work of the slave and the barbarian, and that the policy which looks to the production of that effect is unworthy of a community that claims a place among the Christian communities of the world. In attributing to it, then, the existing state of things, we obtain one great and uniform cause for one great and uniform effect—a policy tending to the production of barbarism, leading to famines and pestilences, ending in decay and death, and thus giving color to the theory of over-population.

§ 7. That man may acquire power over nature, it is *indispensable* that the market for his labor and his products be near at hand. When it is distant, however perfect may be the means of transportation, the manure cannot be returned to the land, nor can its powers be maintained. The facilities of transportation throughout Ireland have been greatly increased in the half century that has just elapsed; but with every stage of that improvement famines and pestilences have increased in number and in force, the completion of an extensive system of railroads having at length been signalized by one of such severity as entirely to distance all that had preceded it. With each such stage the soil was still more rapidly impoverished, the laborers more and more fled from their homes, and intellect more tended to disappear.

Railroads are now being made *for*, and not *by*, the people of India. This is done, avowedly, for the further promotion of the export of the raw produce of the soil, and the effect must inevitably be the same as that observed in Ireland. The little that remains of Indian manufactures must disappear, and cotton must be more and more required to find its way from the producer in the heart of India to the consumer of his immediate neighborhood, by the circuitous route of Calcutta and Manchester. The more railroads made the smaller will be the domestic demand for labor; and the greater will be the tendency of the men to abandon their wives and children and fly to the sugar plantations of the Mauritius in search of food.

An enlightened self-interest teaches that all men profit by the improvement of their neighbors; and it should induce the stronger of the communities of the world to protect and strengthen the weaker. Such, however, has never been the policy of nations, and for the reason, that they have been, to so great an extent, in the hands of the class that lives by appropriation, the soldier, the slave-owner, the trader, and the politician. To this it is due that even these United

States have shown so great a disposition to oppress their weaker neighbors, the Mexicans on the one hand, and the poor remnant of the Indian tribes on the other. By no people of the world, however, has this course been so uniformly pursued, as by that of England, the only one whose policy has looked wholly to the advancement of the trader's interest; and the only one that now recognizes, as its cardinal principle, the trader's motto: "Buy in the cheapest market, and sell in the dearest." Prohibiting association where it did not yet exist, and annihilating it where it did, the results are seen in the reduction of the people subject to its sway to the dead level of mere tillers of the earth, with rapid progress towards decay and barbarism. Such are the consequences that must result in the existing state of national immorality, from perfect freedom of intercourse between a strong and well developed community on the one side, and a weak and imperfect one on the other.

§ 8. The steam-engine digests fuel and power is produced. Man digests fuel in the form of food, by the help of which he obtains power to labor with his mind or his body, or with both together. Alike in the fact that they both digest capital in one form, and reproduce it in another, they differ in one important respect, namely: that while the iron locomotive *can* exist without food, man *cannot*. The railroad manager avoids the consumption of fuel when he does not need the services of the engine, knowing it to be a *waste of capital*. The manager of the human machine *must* burn fuel even when there is no demand for power; and therefore it is that in countries in which there is no diversity of employment muscular force and mental energy go to waste, while the powers of the soil decline from year to year because of the constant withdrawal of the constituent elements of food and clothing—a course of proceeding to which nature has affixed the penalties of poverty, slavery, famine, and death. The British system, looking as it does to the limitation of the people of the world to a single and diminutive workshop, tends to the production of these effects, and hence it has been that British economists have been led to find in a theory of over population an explanation of the fact that growing pauperism had been the steady attendant upon an increase of power to command the forces of nature.

CHAPTER XIV.

OF CHANGES OF MATTER IN FORM.

1.—*Of Chemical and Mechanical Changes.*

§ 1. For effecting changes in the forms of matter, a knowledge of the properties of matter is required. The work of conversion more concrete and special than that of transportation; and, therefore, later in its development. Instruments required for obtaining power to command the services of the natural forces. That power constitutes wealth. Conversion diminishes the labor required for transportation, while increasing that which may be given to production. Economy of human effort resulting from increased facility of conversion.

§ 2. Societary motion tends to increase in a geometrical ratio, when permitted to proceed onward and undisturbed. Efforts to obtain a monopoly of the control of the natural forces required in the work of conversion.

§ 3. Rude character of English commerce at the opening of the fourteenth century. Phenomena then presented, precisely similar to those exhibited in the agricultural communities of the present day.

§ 4. Change of policy under Edward III., and its effects. Adoption of the protective policy under Charles II.

§ 5. Effects of dependence upon the distant market, as shown in England, in the early portion of the eighteenth century. Changes in the condition of the people consequent upon diminution of that dependence.

§ 6. Monopolistic character of the British system. Nothing comparable with it, in its power for evil, ever before devised.

§ 7. Power for evil when wrongly directed, exists, everywhere, in the ratio of that for good when guided in the right direction. British system looks to diminishing the tax of transportation for the British people, but increasing it for the other nations of the world.

§ 1. To transport the sticks of wood by means of which our colonist might, in some degree, shelter himself from the weather, required the exertion of brute force alone; but before he could succeed in converting any one of them into a bow it was needed that he should make himself acquainted with certain properties of matter known to us as tenacity and elasticity. For the effectuation of changes of form there was required, therefore, a knowledge of the *qualities* of the things to be converted; whereas, for effecting changes of place, he needed only to know their *number*, *magnitude*, or *weight*. Thus, the work of *conversion*, more concrete and special, followed in order of development the more abstract one of transportation.

Few things are yielded by the earth in the precise form in which they are fitted for serving the purposes of man. He may eat apples, dates, or figs, as they come from the tree; but the potato must be cooked, the grain crushed, and the flour baked, before they can be consumed. He may wrap the skin around his shoulders; but before he can convert the wool into a proper garment, he must make himself familiar with the properties by which it is distinguished. The foliage may shield him from the sun, but to obtain proper shelter from the weather he must learn to fell the tree, and to convert it into logs, or planks.

Of all the wonderful provisions of nature, there is probably none more beautiful than that which is here observed. The necessity for changing the form of nature's products before they can be fitted for man's consumption, constitutes an obstacle to be surmounted; and one that does not exist in relation to birds, beasts, or fishes, to all of which food is furnished in the precise form in which it may be consumed. The clothing, too, of the lower animals is similarly supplied by nature, whereas man must change the form of the flax, the silk, or the wool, before it can be made to serve his purposes. In the necessity for exertion thus imposed upon him, we find the greatest stimulus to activity of mind, leading to the development of individuality, and fitting him for association with his fellow-men. Had food and clothing been supplied to him in their perfect form, his faculties would everywhere have remained as much inert as are now those of the inhabitants of the Pacific Islands, whole families of whom are supplied with food from a single bread-fruit-tree, while clothing is superseded by a constant summer's sun. Nature giving these unasked, there is little inducement for the exercise of those faculties by which man is distinguished from the brute—faculties by means of which he was eventually to be enabled to obey the command which requires of him that he should "Replenish the earth and subdue it."

Power to direct the forces of nature constitutes wealth. The greater the wealth, the smaller is the *proportion* of human labor required for effecting chemical or mechanical changes in the form of matter, and the larger is the proportion thereof that may be given to the accomplishment of those *vital* changes by means of which there is obtained an increase in the quantity of things to be converted. The mill, the spinning-jenny, and the power-loom, by diminishing the labor required for effecting changes in the forms of grain and wool, set free a large amount of labor that may be given to augmenting the supply of both. The steam-engines of Great Britain are estimated as being capable of doing the work of 600,000,000 of men, while the planing-machines of these United States, driven by steam, are estimated as being equal to the labor of several millions. Here is great economy of human effort, but to this must yet be added the further saving resulting from the transportation of finished as compared with unfinished products.

With every approach towards increased facility in the work of conversion near at home, there is witnessed a great increase in the economy of human effort resulting from increased economy of the gifts of nature. The poor savage of the West spends days and nights roaming over the prairies in search of food, and is yet obliged to waste the larger portion of the products of the chase; while the early settler destroys the tree and sells its ashes to distant men who gladly pay for them, with all the enormous cost of transportation added to their original price. As wealth and population grow, the stem is made to yield planks for houses and mills; the bark to help in fitting skins for being converted into shoes; and the branches to furnish the pegs with which those shoes are made. The rags of a poor and scattered settlement are wasted, but as numbers increase mills appear, and these rags become converted into paper. The little and lonely furnace of the West wastes half the power afforded by its fuel; but the great one of the East applies its heat to drive the engine, and its gas to heat the blast. In the hands of the chemist, clay becomes alumina, and promises soon to furnish a cheap and perfect substitute for the expensive silver. Horse-shoe nails dropped in the streets during the daily traffic, reappear in the shape of swords and guns. The clippings of the traveling-tinker are mixed with the parings of the horses' hoofs, or the cast-off woollen garments of the poorest laborer, and soon afterward, in the form of dyes of the brightest hue, grace the dress of courtly dames. The main ingredient of the ink with which we write may have been part of the hoop of an old beer-barrel. The bones of dead animals yield the chief constituent of lucifer matches.

The pound of flax, having passed through the hands of the lace-maker, exchanges for more than its weight in gold. The leaves of the fir and the pine, in Silesia, become blankets. The scraps of leather become glue, and the hair that is cut from the human head may be exchanged for gloves and ribbons; and thus it is that as men are more and more enabled to associate, and to combine their efforts, each and every particle of matter is more and more *utilized*, with constant decline in the value of commodities required for their use, and constant increase in the value of man himself.

§ 2. As population increased, men were enabled more and more to combine together for obtaining power to direct the natural forces; obtaining, too, at every step, increased command over themselves—building towns, or local centres, in which the artisan and the trader could associate for self-defence. The more they could associate, the more was individuality developed; and therefore has it been that freedom grew so rapidly in the towns and cities of Greece and Italy, France and Germany, the Netherlands and Britain.

Power has thus everywhere resulted from association; but it has almost universally been accompanied by a selfish desire for securing a monopoly of its exercise. The Phœnicians carefully guarded the secret of their dyes, and the Venetians were so jealous of their secrets that they, by prohibiting emigration, reduced their artisans to a condition approaching that of slavery. The Flemings having succeeded in establishing among themselves the diversity of employments required for developing intellectual force, exercised for a long time the power of association to an extent then unparalleled in Northern or Central Europe. Here, too, however, the spirit of monopoly made its appearance, bringing with it regulations tending to give the trader advantages over both the domestic artisan and the foreign producer of raw materials, thereby causing emigration of the one, and a war of tariffs on the part of the other; and in due season Flemish power followed in the wake of that of Carthage and of Tyre. The Dutch, profiting of the difficulties of their immediate neighbors, became the most extensive manufacturers in Europe; but they, in their turn, while greatly enlarging their dominion, gave to various bodies monopoly powers, having for their object the prevention of intercourse between important portions of the world except by means of their own ships, ports, seamen, and merchants. The oppressive character of this system forced both France and England to measures of resistance, exhibited in the Navigation Act of Cromwell, and the tonnage duties and tariff of Colbert; and the power of Holland began from that period to pass away, as that of Venice and Genoa had already done. In all these cases the object in view had been that of preventing circulation abroad, with a view to an increase of the societary motion at home, and to foster centralization by compelling commerce to pay extra taxes in the form of transportation; and in all, the results had been failure and decline, even where the system had not led to absolute ruin.

Among nations, as among individuals, selfishness generally defeats itself. All the communities above referred to sought to obtain power, not by commerce *with* others based upon a great commerce among themselves, but by carrying on trade *for* them, thereby enriching themselves at others' cost. Trade had built up among the Flemings large fortunes, the possession of which but stimulated the appetite for further acquisition, while giving greater power for controlling the movements of other nations. To that end, they sought monopoly both at home and abroad; but the end proved widely different from their expectations, their measures producing resistance both abroad and at home. Workmen, flying to England, found in Edward III. a monarch fully sensible of the advantages which must result from enabling the farmer and the artisan to take their places by each other's side, and one, too, both able and willing to give them complete protection. Not only were franchises granted to them, but all restrictions upon domestic commerce, so far as related to the making of cloth, were at once repealed; while by an Act of Parliament of 1337, the export of wool and the import of cloth were both prohibited. The effects of these measures we may now consider.

§ 3. At the opening of the fourteenth century the commerce of England was such as indicated a very rude condition of its people, wool, hides, and tin, being the chief articles of export, and cloth, of import. The custom of foreign nations for raw materials was sought by means of grants of privileges to their merchants, while oppressive export duties threw upon the land-owner and his tenants the burden of the support of government. Sent abroad in their rudest state, their products returned in the form of cloth, admitted on payment of a nominal duty of one per cent. Raw products were consequently cheap, while finished commodities were very dear.

Commerce at home was impeded by numberless restrictions, while the domestic market was freely opened to Flemish and other manufacturers who were unsparing in their efforts to monopolize, on one side of the channel, the purchase of the raw material, and on the other, the conversion of it, and thus to maintain the largest difference between the prices of the wool they bought and the cloth they had to sell.

The power of association scarcely existed then in England, diversity of employment being but little known. Consequently, though wool was low in price, all articles of food were greatly lower, their bulk being much too great to admit of their exportation to distant countries, and there being no market for them at home. Wool, representing food that had undergone a single process of manufacture, commanded a price twenty times as great as did the food itself. The cost of transportation, therefore, being so much less, it could travel to a distance, whereas corn was often wasted in one part of the kingdom, while famine prevailed in others; and therefore was it that sheep and hogs constituted almost the entire capital of those who professed to farm the land.

The facts here observed are precisely similar to those occurring in all the purely agricultural countries of the present hour. The cotton of India can be sent to a distance, because, like the English wool, it is the representative of food that has undergone a single change. The food of India cannot travel even from one part of the country to another; and therefore is it that famines prevail in one district while rice is wasted in another. The Russian wheat can with difficulty go abroad, but the wool can readily be sent. The corn of Illinois and Iowa is to so great an extent absorbed by the transporter, that the farmer desires to subject it to the first rude process of manufacture by passing it through the stomach of the hog, and carrying it to market in the form of pork. That of Virginia is passed through the stomachs of negro men and women, and taken to market in the form of slaves. That of Carolina, after being digested by slaves, is taken to England in the form of cotton. The necessity for effecting changes of place was then, as it is now, the great obstacle to improvement; and as that diminishes with the bulk of the commodities to be transported, it is not surprising that we find the English people taking the first step in the career of which the advantage was afterwards so clearly exhibited by Adam Smith, when showing how great was the weight of corn and wool contained in a piece of cloth, and how readily when they had assumed that form the two could be sent together throughout the world.

§ 4. Prohibition of the export of wool and of the import of cloth was a measure of resistance to the monopoly of the Flemish manufacturers, and it tended greatly to the promotion of the domestic commerce. It went, however, too far. The difficulty of English corn and wool-growers consisted in the absence of competition for the purchase of their commodities; and a remedy therefor was to be found in the creation of a domestic market, while leaving untouched the export of raw material required for the supply of distant countries.

What was required was the imposition of such a duty on foreign cloth as would have made it the interest of the weaver to come to the producer and there to consume his corn while converting his wool. The nation, however, being poor, and the ability to purchase foreign merchandise being small, while the king's necessities were great, the latter needed to retain all possible sources of revenue, chief among which was that resulting from the export of wool. The prohibition of that trade throwing it chiefly into his own hands, he profited largely by it. Direct commerce was, however, in some degree established between the producer of wool and corn, and the consumer of cloth; and from that time there was a steady increase in the power of association, manifested by the growth of towns, the enfranchisement of serfs, and the growing power of the Commons to direct the movements of the ship of state. Magna Charta secured the privileges of the aristocracy; but the statute of 1347 laid the foundation of the liberties of the people by providing for the diversity of their employments and the development of individual faculties; as a consequence of which, the change of system was followed by a rapid increase of both individual and national power.

For centuries, nevertheless, England continued to import cloth, iron, and other manufactured goods, and to export raw produce, remaining, therefore, poor and weak when compared with other communities across the channel, in which employments were more diversified; and hence it is that we find the Dutch of that period almost monopolizing the management of England's commerce with the outer world. The period of the Protectorate, however, brought with it a successful effort, by means of navigation laws, at establishing direct commerce with foreign nations, and thus laying the foundation of Britain's present power on the ocean. Still later was a similar effort made to promote commerce at home by the adoption of measures by aid of which to *bring machinery and skill to the raw materials*, and thus remove the necessity for sending abroad the bulky corn and wool. Andrew Yarranton is said to have been the first to suggest, in his very remarkable little work entitled *England's Improvement by Sea and Land*, published in 1677, the measures that have since led to the manufacturing greatness of England. The nation profited of his advice, and from that time the English statute-book became more and more filled with laws having for their object the bringing together of the farmer and the artisan, with a view to the production of association and combination, and thus diminishing the necessity for exhausting the land by the exportation of its products in their rudest state.

§ 5. The insular position of England had given her security from the devastations of war to an extent unknown in any other part of Europe; and thus was she prepared for the adoption of a system which should promote combination. Its growth, however, was the work of time: for centuries the current of raw materials had set towards the continent, and to change it required serious effort. Before this could be accomplished the English farmer had, in the gradual decline in the price of wheat from 43s. 6d. per quarter, before the peace of Utrecht, in 1713, to 21s. 3d. in the decade ending in 1755, full experience of the loss resulting from a dependence on distant markets. The product slightly exceeding the consumption, a small portion needed to go abroad; and that *the price obtained for the surplus fixes the price for the whole crop* is well known to all who study the course of trade. A deficiency to the extent of even a hundred thousand bushels raises the price of all to the level of that at which that small supply may be brought from the distant market; while an excess to that extent reduces the whole to the level of the price at which this trivial quantity must be sold. The total product of wheat at that time must have been more than 40,000,000 of bushels; and as that grain then entered little into consumption compared with what it since has done, it is perhaps fair to place the whole production of food at the equivalent of 100,000,000 of bushels. Of this, about four per cent. constituted the surplus thrown on the markets of the world, depressing the prices there, and in a corresponding degree depressing those obtained for all that was consumed at home; to the injury of the land and labor of the kingdom, of both the farmer and the artisan, and of all but those who were dependent on fixed incomes for their support.

The population was at that period but 6,000,000, of whom the land-owners, then numbering nearly 200,000, and their families, must have been about one-sixth part. Add to these the laborers in husbandry, and we have a very large proportion of the community directly dependent upon the success of agriculture. In their prosperity the mechanic was largely interested, their power to purchase the results of his skill and labor being wholly dependent upon their ability to sell the produce of their own. What England then needed was direct commerce between the producer and consumer at home; in default of which the farmer found himself compelled to accept 21s. 2d. per quarter for his wheat, and corresponding prices for all other descriptions of food, while exporting but four millions of quarters, and importing, in the forms of cloth and iron, perhaps thrice as much.

Progress was, however, being made. With the middle of the century it was discovered that iron could be smelted by the help of mineral coal; and thenceforward changes tending to the diversification of pursuits became numerous and rapid. The power of steam was discovered and applied, and the spinning-jenny was invented. These and other improvements in the processes of manufacture gave life and activity to the domestic market, and freed the farmer from dependence on the distant one, as a consequence of which the price of wheat had more than doubled in 1775; and so remained for twenty years, with an increase in the total return to agricultural labor that could have been but little short of $100,000,000.

§ 6. So far as protection had been resorted to with a view to enable the farmers to call to their aid the foreign skill and machinery required for fitting their products for consumption, it was certainly right. It relieved them from the tax of transportation, promoted the diversification of employment and the development of intellect, and tended to give to society that form in which strength and beauty are most combined; and therefore was it that the years immediately preceding the French Revolution exhibited so great a tendency towards such a reform in Parliament as should give a fairer representation of the various portions into which society had become divided.

Had that been the limit of the movement—had the policy of England looked solely to the emancipation of *her own* people from dependence on the casualties of distant markets—had her statesmen been governed by that great fundamental law of Christianity which requires of us to respect the rights of others as carefully as we desire that they should respect our own—all would have been well; and the doctrines of over population, of the necessity for "a cheap and abundant supply of labor," of the expediency of expelling a kindred nation with a view to supply its place by "one more docile and more serviceable" that could "submit to a master"—the doctrines, in short, of modern political economy—would have remained to this hour unheard of.

Unfortunately, there has always and everywhere existed a disposition to monopolize the knowledge by means of which progress has been attained; and the more free the people who have desired the monopoly the more unscrupulous are certain to have been the means employed for securing it. It is, therefore, no matter of surprise, that to the freest people of Europe we owe the invention of the oppressive and exhausting system described in former chapters.

Nothing comparable with it in its power of evil has ever been devised. Invasion of armies is attended with waste of property, destruction of life, and suspension of commerce; but with the return of peace men can again combine their efforts, and in a few years all is again nearly as it had been before. Such, however, is not the case with the substitution of trade for commerce. Under it the power of association dies away, intellect declines in its development, and man gradually loses all the power over nature which he before had gained. The one is a sudden shock from which, with care, the patient may recover; whereas, the other consists in opening the veins and permitting the life's blood slowly to ebb away, rendering recovery from day to day more difficult, and closing at length in material and moral death. No country in Europe has suffered so much from the evils of war as Belgium, yet has it always ranked among the most prosperous of them all. Of all, the only ones that have for centuries been unprofaned by a hostile foot are the British Islands, yet there it was that the Malthusian theory was invented, and in one of them is found the great treasury of facts by which it is supported. France has suffered heavily from war, yet she advances in wealth and power because she promotes *commerce*. Portugal, except in the closing years of the wars of the French Revolution, has long been almost exempt from war, yet she declines in strength because wholly subject to the exhaustive influences of *trade*.

§ 7. The more rapid the circulation in a community the greater is the power at its command; but whether or not mankind shall profit by this power, is wholly dependent upon the spirit in which it is exercised. Wrongly guided, its capacity for evil is as great as it is for good; and thus the grievousness of the tyranny has everywhere been in the direct ratio of the freedom of the people by whom the power was exercised. A people tyrant is a hydra-headed monster, compared with which an aristocratic one is harmless.

The English system looked to diminishing the bulk of *their own products;* but it also sought to prevent any such diminution in that of *the products of other countries.* Directed to the extension of commerce at home, it was directed also to the annihilation of commerce among the people of other communities; and there it was, as has been already said, that it went far beyond any other that had been before devised. Irish cloths had been celebrated in the days when England exported all her wool, and imported all her cloth; yet we find the latter availing herself of all the power at her command to suppress the Irish manufacture, and compel the wool of Ireland to pass through the mills of England before the Irish people themselves could use it. Had she simply prohibited the manufacture, leaving the wool-growers to seek a market where they would, she would thus have greatly augmented the cost of transportation while diminishing the power of association and promoting the exhaustion of the land; but to this was added a prohibition of commerce with the world except through English ports; and such was the policy afterwards adopted towards all the British colonies.

Having thus acquired wealth and power, Britain next sought to carry out this policy in reference to independent nations, and hence the passage of various laws, from 1765 to 1799, prohibiting the export of either machinery or artisans, which laws were maintained in force until 1825. Their object was that of compelling all the rude produce of the earth to come to England, there to be subjected to the processes required for fitting it for consumption. Thence it might go abroad, to be exchanged for sugar, tea, or coffee; but even those articles were, as far as possible, required to pass through English ports, and by means of English ships. British policy looked thus to making every country outside of England a purely agricultural one; but, were all the communities of the world reduced to that condition, each and every of them, and each and every of its parts, would be compelled to produce all the commodities required for consumption, as of commerce there could be little or none, abroad or at home. To enable distant commerce to exist, the bulk of commodities must be reduced, and in the effort to accomplish that object diversity of employment is necessarily produced. That diversity having arisen in England, all her efforts were now given to preventing its appearance in any other part of the world, and thus to establish the entire supremacy of the trader and transporter over the producer.

So oppressive a system as this had never before been imagined. It sought everywhere to cause the bulky wool and cotton to travel thousands of miles in quest of the little spindle and loom, thus maintaining the size of all commodities at the largest, and contracting to the smallest the aperture through which they were required to pass, as here is represented:—

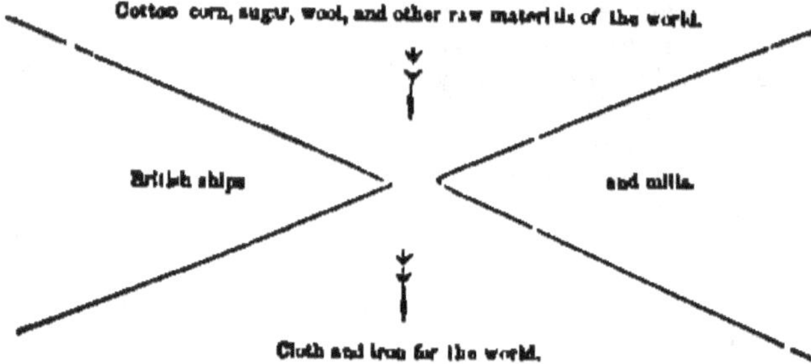

The quantity being great and the aperture narrow it followed that the friction was immense, and that the greater part of the produce disappeared under the process to which it was thus subjected. The larger the crop the higher were freights, and the larger the charges for storage and insurance, but *the smaller became the prices.* As a consequence of this most unnatural process farmers and planters were forced to deprecate the extension of production, for to them it was fraught with ruin. Small crops, giving low freights and charges, and high prices in the distant market, were profitable, whereas, large ones were injurious to all engaged in the culture of the earth.

Until now, increase of population had been looked upon as an element of strength; but as the British system came fairly into operation the modes of thought were changed, and growth of numbers came to be held an evidence of weakness rather than of strength. How far an unsound and unjust system of policy tended to produce this change of doctrine, will be examined in another chapter.

CHAPTER XV.

OF CHEMICAL AND MECHANICAL CHANGES IN THE FORM OF MATTER—CONTINUED.

§ 1. Errors of the British system obvious to Adam Smith. His caution to his countrymen in regard to the dangers necessarily incident to an exclusive dependence upon trade. His advice neglected, and hence the growth of pauperism and the origination of the theory of over-population.

§ 2. Warlike and monopolistic character of the system.

§ 3. By destroying among other people the power to sell their labor it destroys competition for the purchase of British labor. Teaching, that to enable capital to obtain a fair remuneration labor must be kept down, it tends to the production of slavery everywhere.

§ 4. Approximation in the prices of raw materials and finished commodities the one essential characteristic of civilization. British system looks to the prevention of that approximation. Its tendency towards reduction of other communities to a state of barbarism.

§ 5. Stoppage of the circulation a necessary consequence of the predominance of the British system. Disappearance of the small proprietors of England. Condition of the agricultural laborer.

§ 6. The higher the organization the more perfect the power of self-government. That power diminishing among the people, and in the government, of England. Gulf dividing the higher and lower classes a constantly widening one.

§ 7. Necessity for careful study of the system under which originated the theory of over-population. Inevitable tendency of the Ricardo-Malthusian doctrine that of making slavery the ultimate condition of the laborer. The system of the British school a retrograde one. Had its origin in a retrograde policy. Sees in man a mere instrument to be used by trade.

§ 1. The *Wealth of Nations* was first published in 1776; and its essential object was that of enforcing upon the author's countrymen the great truth, that *trade and manufactures were useful only so far as they contributed to the development of the treasures of the earth, and to the promotion of commerce.* Adam Smith saw that the colonial system, looking exclusively to trade, tended unnaturally to increase the *proportion* of the British population employed in the work of exchange and transportation, thereby raising up "a nation of mere shopkeepers," and forcing industry to run principally in one great channel, instead of in a number of smaller ones; and he warned his countrymen of the dangers they thus incurred. Great, however, as were, even then, those dangers, England was but entering on the effort to reduce the world at large under the system so long imposed upon her colonial dependents. The interdiction of the emigration of artisans dated then back but a single decade, and the battle of Plassy, by which the British power in India was established, was then not twenty years old. Five years later came the prohibition of the export of silk and woollen machinery; and before the close of the century the policy had been perfected by the extension of this prohibition to all other descriptions of machinery, as well as to artisans by whom it might be made and to colliers.

Prior to 1791, the price of wheat having more than doubled as a consequence of the creation of a great domestic market, there had gradually arisen an import of foreign food for the prevention of which the agricultural interest procured, in that year, the passage of a law limiting the price at which it might be entered. During all this time the policy denounced by Dr. Smith had been still more fully carried out. English armies had been steadily engaged in India in extending trade at the expense of commerce. Trade had stirred up strife between the mother country and her American colonies, and thus produced the war of 1776. The class living by traffic and transportation had constantly increased in numbers and in power, but it was reserved for the war of 1793—a war largely due to the thirst for "ships, colonies, and commerce" —to see it attain its full dimensions. Taxation grew with great rapidity, and with it the splendor of bankers' and traders' fortunes. The price of food advanced while that of labor remained stationary, and the effects of this soon exhibited themselves in the rapid growth of the almshouse population.

Pauperism prevailed to an extent before unknown; and then it was that Mr. Malthus furnished the world with those "*Principles of Population*," by help of which his readers might, as they were assured, understand the causes of "the poverty and misery observable among the lower classes of the people in every nation," and of "the repeated failures in the efforts of the higher classes to relieve them." Dr. Smith had seen that the policy based upon cheap labor and cheap raw materials was the work of those "higher classes;" and *upon them* he had urged the abandonment of a system which, as he so clearly saw, tended towards the pauperism and enslavement of those who labored. Mr. Malthus, on the contrary, found the cause in a great law of God, by means of which he relieved those classes from all responsibility for that poverty, and enabled them to close their purses, and even their hearts, against the commonest dictates of charity, comforting themselves with the reflection that if they should in any manner "stand between the error and its consequences," or "intercept the penalty" affixed to the procreation of their species by those who had not accumulated the means of support for children—*which penalty was poverty, wretchedness, and death*—they would but "perpetuate the sin" and thereby become themselves participants in the crime! This theory was precisely what was needed to prevent the adoption of any of the remedial measures proposed by Adam Smith, proving, as it professed to do, that pauperism existed in obedience to the laws of God, and that therefore the rich might safely and conscientiously "eat, drink, and be merry" though surrounded by poverty, wretchedness, disease, and death!

§ 2. The system which looked to foreign trade being more extensively carried out with each successive year, peace rarely existed throughout the British Empire. The war then existing was followed by one with these United States; since which there have been wars for the annexation of Scinde and Affghanistan, of Ava and the Punjaub—for the maintenance of the opium trade—for the extension of power in South Africa—for the development of new avenues for trade throughout the Turkish Empire, and others still,—all having for their essential object the cheapening of the raw products of the earth, and of the labors of the man by whom it is tilled.

For the attainment of that end the union with Ireland was perfected, and her manufactures annihilated. With that end in view the people of India were required to receive the cotton goods of England duty free, while prevented from procuring more efficient machinery from abroad, and taxed to an unheard of extent for the use of that which they already possessed. For this, Gibraltar has been, and yet is, maintained as a smuggling depot against Spain, while other colonies have been used for smuggling goods into various countries of Europe and America, the smuggler having come to be regarded as "the great reformer of the age." For this, have been formed combinations among the masters to keep down the price of labor at home, and to discourage the growth of manufactures in all the other countries of the world. That all these are really acts of war, is shown in the following extract from an official document first published in 1854, by order of the British House of Commons:—

"The laboring classes generally, in the manufacturing districts of this country, especially in the iron and coal districts, are very little aware of the extent to which they are often indebted for being employed at all to the immense *losses* which their employers voluntarily incur in bad times in order *to destroy foreign competition, and to gain and keep possession of foreign markets*. Authentic instances are well known of employers having in such times carried on their works at a loss amounting in the aggregate to three or four hundred thousand pounds in the course of three or four years. If the efforts of those who encourage the combinations to restrict the amount of labor and to produce strikes were to be successful for any length of time, the great accumulations of capital could no longer be made *which enable a few of the most wealthy capitalists to overwhelm all foreign competition in times of great depression*, and thus to clear the way for the *whole trade* to step in when prices revive, and to carry on the business before *foreign* capital can again accumulate to such an extent as to be able to establish competition in prices with any chance of success. *The large capitals of this country are the great instruments of warfare* (if the expression may be allowed) *against the competing capital of foreign countries*, and are *the most* essential instruments now remaining by which our manufacturing supremacy can be maintained; the other elements, cheap labor, abundance of raw materials, means of communication, and skilled labor, being rapidly in process of being analized."

The system here described is very properly characterized as a "warfare," and for what purpose, and against whom is it waged? It is a war to compel the people of all other lands to confine themselves to agriculture, to prevent the diversification of employment in other countries, to retard the development of intellect, to palsy every movement elsewhere looking to the utilization of the mineral treasures of the earth, to diminish the demand for labor, and to produce pauperism both at home and abroad.

§ 3. It is said that this system is beneficial to the people of England. Were this so, it would establish the lamentable fact that nations *could*, in accordance with a divine law, thrive by the perpetration of injustice. Happily no such law exists. Nations can permanently prosper only by means of obedience to the golden rule of Christianity; and when they fail to yield it, Nemesis never fails to claim her rights. That she has so done on this occasion, and that the pauperism of England is due to failure in this respect the reader may perhaps be satisfied after a brief examination of the effects of the system upon the condition of the English laborer.

The manufactures of Ireland declined from the date of the Union in 1801, and the Irish people were forced to seek employment in the field. Production being thus increased while the home consumption was being diminished, the exports of wheat rose in thirty years from 300,000 quarters to 2,500,000, with a fall of price from 80s. to 52s. This reduction might seem to have been an advantage, but unfortunately, it was accompanied by still greater cheapness of human power. Millions of the Irish people being totally idle, Great Britain was, says a British journal, "flooded with crowds of half-clad Celts, reducing the standard of living" among English laborers. Labor, therefore, fell more rapidly than food, and one-ninth of the total population of England was reduced to pauperism—the poor tax rising in thirty years from twenty-five to forty-five millions of dollars, the price of wheat at the same time falling no less than forty per cent. Food was low, but wages were so very low, that the laborer could not purchase. Labor was low, but food was so cheap that the farmer was unable to pay wages and rent. Manufactures, too, suffered, for the decline of wages in other pursuits was accompanied by a diminution in the power to purchase cloth. All thus suffered alike. The destruction in Ireland of the home market for food and labor, consequent upon the annihilation of Irish commerce, had produced the same effect in England. Did the great manufacturer profit? On the contrary, his market in England had been lessened, while that of Ireland had almost totally failed; and thus had a nation been almost annihilated with no profit to those who had done the work, but with the most serious loss to all, resulting from the fact that the standard of living and of morals had been greatly reduced; that the disease of over-population had more widely spread; and that the gulf dividing the higher and lower classes of English society had greatly widened.

It might, however, be supposed that the other markets which had been acquired were of a character to make some amends for these losses by English land and labor. That we may determine that question, we now turn to the trade with the hundred millions of India. The export of cotton yarn and cloth to that country, at the breaking out of the cotton rebellion of our Southern States scarcely exceeded 70,000,000 of pounds, while the import of India cotton was little more than 80,000,000, and yet this constituted almost the only item of the trade with that country that was of any essential importance. The quantity of cotton then converted into cloth in the little town of Lowell, with its 13,000 operatives, having been 40,000,000 pounds, it followed that two such little places could perform all the labor required for the trade for which England had been indebted to the destruction of the vast cotton manufacture and the great domestic commerce of India, a measure that, according to Sir Robert Peel himself, had been productive of an amount of misery and destitution wholly "unparalleled in the history of commerce."

For its accomplishment it had been needed that English children of the most tender age should be kept employed for twelve or fourteen hours a day, and spend the Sunday morning in cleaning the machinery, and that men, women, and children should be brutified by poverty to an extent scarcely possible to be conceived. For the present maintenance of the system it is required, as has been recently shown in a debate in the House of Commons, that men, women, and children work from sixteen to twenty hours per day in bleaching establishments maintained at so high a heat that the laborers' feet are blistered, and in which destruction of life is so certain, and so rapid, that they are commonly known by the style and title of "wasting shops."

The student of Indian history is shocked when he reads the account of the invasion of Nadir Shah, closing with the plunder of Delhi, and the massacre of 100,000 of its inhabitants; and yet how utterly insignificant was the loss thus caused compared with that resulting from the destruction of a manufacture that but half a century since gave employment to the people of whole provinces, one, the account of whose progress included "no less than a description of the lives of half the inhabitants of Hindostan!" How utterly insignificant is it when compared with the daily and hourly waste of capital now resulting from the total absence of all demand for physical or mental capacity, with the decline and death of commerce, the ruin of Dacca and other flourishing cities, the abandonment of rich lands, the exhaustion of the soil, the resolution of society into a body of grasping money-lenders on the one hand and wretched cultivators on the other, and the inauguration of famine and pestilence as the chronic diseases of a people inferior to none in moral and intellectual qualities, and embracing a tenth of the population of the globe. The booty obtained on that occasion was estimated at five hundred millions of dollars, but how infinitely greater is the annual tax imposed on the people of Hindostan by a system that forbids the development of human faculties, and the existence of that commerce to which alone they might look for the power of accumulation. Greatly superior as is the loss inflicted, as greatly inferior is the gain to those by whom the loss has been caused. The Shah did obtain an enormous amount of plunder; but the English people have gained nothing but the privilege of employing themselves as transporters, spinners, and weavers of a trivial quantity of cotton; a privilege obtained at the cost of the rights of a hundred millions of people abroad, and of the establishment at home of the doctrine that "to enable capital to obtain a fair remuneration, the price of labor must be kept down," in other words, *that men must be enslaved.*

Turning to Portugal, to the West Indies, and to Turkey, we see everywhere the same result, the power to purchase the products of English labor having perished with the power to sell their own. All of these countries are paralyzed; and Britain now presents to view the extraordinary spectacle of a nation possessing more than any other the power to render service to mankind, yet surrounded by colonies and allies, all of whom, with the exception of the gold-producing Australia, are passing slowly, but certainly, towards entire inanition; while she is exhausting her energies in the ceaseless effort to extend throughout the world the system by means of which they have been ruined.

§ 4. *Approximation in the prices of the raw material and the finished commodity is the one essential characteristic of civilization*, it being the manifestation of a diminution of the obstacles standing in the way of association. As the mill comes nearer to the farm, the price of wheat approaches nearer to that of flour. As the processes of tanning are improved, the price of leather declines, with increase in that of hides. Rags increase in price while paper declines; raw silk advances, while silk goods tend steadily downward. Look where we may we see that under a natural system the rude products of the earth tend to increase in their power to command the precious metals in exchange, while finished commodities tend as steadily to decline in price, thus enabling all, whether producers of corn or gold, of wool or silver, to profit by, and rejoice in, the constantly increasing power of their fellow-men to command the services of nature. Among communities, as among individuals, *the harmony of all real and permanent interests is perfect.*

The British system looks, however, in a direction directly

opposite to this, being based upon the idea of cheapening all the raw materials of manufacture, labor included. From 1830 to 1835 the average export of American cotton was 320,000,000 pounds, worth about $35,000,000, and capable of commanding in Liverpool 18,500,000 pieces of cloth, or about 1,100,000 tons of iron. In 1845 and 1846, the average price being 6¼ cents, a similar quantity would yield but $20,000,000. But the prices of cloth and iron had risen, so that for the same quantity of cotton the planter could have but 12,500,000 pieces of cloth.

In the first period, the planter had thirty-four per cent. of his cotton returned to him in the form of cloth; but in the second, only twenty-four per cent. The lower the price of cloth, and the higher that of food and cotton, the greater must be the tendency toward freedom. The higher that of cloth and the lower those of food and cotton, the greater must be the tendency toward slavery. The British system tends to cheapen the raw materials of cloth and to enhance the difficulty of obtaining cloth itself; and thus does it look in a direction precisely opposite to that of advancing civilization; and hence it is that it has furnished the idea of over-population, an idea inseparably connected with that of the ultimate enslavement of man. Hence, too, it has been that under the system so generally pursued throughout these United States—a system which, in opposition to the teachings of Adam Smith, has looked to separating the producer and the consumer, with further widening of the differences between raw products and finished merchandise—the slave power has, until now, so steadily grown in strength.

§ 5. Stoppage of circulation, as fatal to the social as it is to the physical body, is the natural tendency of the prevalence of the British system. Therefore it has been that Portugal and Ireland have so steadily declined, and therefore it is, that the advance of British pauperism keeps steady pace with the decline in the home demand for the labor power of Ireland and India, and of all other countries subjected to the British power.

Most unwilling to admit, or even to see, these facts, the advocates of the cheap labor system insisted upon charging the growing pauperism to the account of the corn-law system. The land-owners believing, with Adam Smith, that "if the whole produce of America" in food were forced into the English market, it would be "a great discouragement to agriculture," had endeavored to shield themselves against the operation of the mercantile system by the passage of laws to prevent the importation of food except under certain circumstances; and to those laws was now ascribed the existing wretchedness, the people being assured that their repeal would be followed by an increased demand for labor, and low prices for food.

The laws were repealed, but the effect proved to be directly the reverse: circulation diminished still more rapidly, and the rural population fled the kingdom in increased numbers; while of those who remained, Mr. Cobden now says, that "never within the recollection of living man was the farm laborer's condition so bad as at present"—that he does not know "a Protestant country in which the masses of the people are so illiterate"—that "the condition of the English peasantry has no parallel on the face of the earth"—and that there is no other in which it is "so entirely divorced from the land." In the days of Adam Smith, the land-owners of England were about 200,000; now they but little exceed 30,000. Such has been the result of the steady maintenance of the system so vehemently denounced by him—a system whose tendency has been that of sacrificing the domestic commerce at the shrine of foreign trade.

With the growth of *association*, the power of the middleman decreases, while that of the laborer rises; with constant tendency towards *equality* in the conditions of men. With the growth of *trade*, inequality steadily increases, the laborer losing power over himself, while the trader acquires it.

"The manufacturing districts," says a recent writer, "present the peculiar spectacle of a small and very wealthy class standing apart on a great height, far above the level of the rest of the population. The connection between the two has never yet had time to become clothed with the soft and warm interlacement of affectionate moral association." "The work carried on by the two parties is essentially one of co-operation; but their moral attitude toward each other is much more one of hostility than of friendship." Another writer informs us that "mutual defiance is the common attitude of employer and employed, especially in Scotland, where the feeling of personal independence is stronger and keener than in England." The gulf dividing the higher and lower classes of society is an ever-widening one, the immense fortunes acquired by bankers and traders being in the direct ratio of the poverty of the working classes. "The peasant," says Mr. Kay, "knows that he must die in the same position in which he was born." After careful examination of the condition of the people of Continental Europe, he assures his readers that the peasantry of England "are more ignorant, more demoralized, less capable of helping themselves, and more pauperized, than those of any other country of Europe, if we except Russia, Turkey, South Italy, and some parts of the Austrian Empire."

Under such circumstances the middle class tends to pass away, and its condition is well expressed by the term now so frequently used, "the uneasy class." There is a perpetual strife for life, each man "endeavoring to snatch the bread from his neighbor's mouth." The atmosphere of England is one of gloom. Every one is anxious about the future, for himself or his children, and this is a necessary consequence of the system that looks to increasing the difficulties standing in the way of commerce.

§ 6 The higher the organization the more perfect is the development of the various faculties, and the more complete the power of self-government—and this is as true of societies as of individuals. The more perfect the power of association, and the more complete the development of the various faculties of its members, the more entire is its power to control its own action; and the less is it liable to outside influence. In England, as we see, centralization constantly increases as the power of local self-government tends to disappear. Hence we remark a growing weakness, indicated by an increased necessity for modifying her policy in obedience to the dictates of other nations. The change in the navigation laws was forced upon her by the resistance of the United States, and that of Prussia and other powers. So, too, with regard to protection. For seventy years, down to 1819, the duties on foreign manufactures had been steadily increased. In that and the five following years, several nations of Europe adopted measures of resistance, while in the last of them was passed the first American tariff based on the idea of bringing nearer the farmer and the artisan, and thus approximating the prices of raw materials and finished goods. To this was due the change of measures commenced by Mr. Huskisson in 1825, a change, however, looking steadily towards the cheapening of all raw materials of manufacture, whether corn, cotton, or labor. The successful resistance of Russia, the formation of the German Zollverein, and the

American tariff of 1842, were the causes of the total change of policy that occurred in 1846. So, likewise, with the sugar duties. The emancipated negroes of Jamaica had been assured of protection against slave-grown sugar, yet Brazil compelled a violation of the well-understood agreement.

These changes are said, however, to have been made in deference to the advancing spirit of the age. Were this so, a similar spirit might be expected in other directions. Nothing can be more unjust than the tax imposed on all the correspondence between America and Continental Europe, yet it is persisted in, in spite of all remonstrances. The people of the West India Islands have for years petitioned in vain for such an alteration in the duties as would enable them to refine their own sugar. The British colonies of the continent and the islands recently desired to establish between themselves perfect reciprocity, abolishing all duties upon their respective productions; and in so doing only sought to carry into full effect the views so strenuously urged upon the government of the United States in regard to the—so-called—Reciprocity Treaty, then just made with Canada. Upon submitting the question, however, to the home government, the answer was that "it would be inconsistent with the imperial policy of free trade!"

The Spanish people find themselves greatly aggrieved by the use of Gibraltar as a smuggling depot, yet is there no change made in that respect, although when the place was ceded, it was a part of the treaty stipulations that it never should be used for such a purpose. Spanish commerce is thus sacrificed to the promotion of British trade. The people of China being forced, in spite of the opposition of their government, to receive from fifteen to twenty millions of dollars' worth of opium annually, the result is seen in growing intemperance and an enormous waste of life; yet Hong Kong is retained as a necessary appendage to the Indian Empire, because "expediency" justifies the carrying out of measures utterly unjustifiable on the ground of "right." Such being the course of proceeding toward the weaker communities of the earth, the adoption of any other toward the stronger ones can be attributed only to a diminution of power to pursue that which has so long been practised.

Action and reaction are equal and opposite, the ball that stops another in its motion being retarded, if not arrested, in its own. So is it with communities, commerce at home suffering from every injury they inflict upon commerce abroad

The real interests of all are to be promoted by every measure that tends to increase the power of association in the bosom of every other; thereby increasing the value of man, diminishing the value of the commodities required for his use, facilitating the development of intellect, and thus enabling men more and more to combine their efforts for obtaining that power over nature which constitutes wealth; and therefore is it that an enlightened self-interest would prompt each and all to carry into the management of public affairs the same spirit that should animate every Christian in his dealings with his fellow-men.*

§ 7. The theory of over-population having originated in England, as also the supporting one of Mr. Ricardo in relation to the occupation of the earth, it has been right to study carefully the English system, to ascertain how far its peculiar policy has tended to produce such serious error on the part of her economists. If the doctrines of the English school are right, then the all-wise Creator has made a serious blunder; having established slavery as the ultimate condition of a vast majority of the human race. If, on the contrary, they are wrong, then is freedom the ultimate lot of man; and then are there found throughout the natural laws regulating the social system, the same order, beauty, and harmony of arrangement which we see prevailing everywhere else throughout the organic and inorganic world. *One of these things is absolutely and universally true, the other is absolutely and universally false.*

Modern political economy, so justly named "the dismal science," arose out of this attempt to account for facts exhibited throughout the British Empire. Retrograde throughout, it requires that we should wholly ignore the existence of an all-wise and benevolent Deity, and put our trust in a Being by whom have been instituted great natural laws in virtue of which men shall necessarily and "regularly die of want."

Retrograde throughout, it teaches:—

That, in the early stages of society, as the first miserable tools are obtained by means of which to work, men are

* The hesitating and unsteady policy of Britain in reference to American difficulties of the three past years, and more recently in regard to those of Denmark and Germany, may here be cited in proof of the great truth that the power of self-direction declines with every increase in the necessity for dependence upon trade and transportation.

enabled to compel the earth to yield *larger* rewards to labor; but that, as soon as they "have applied themselves to cultivation with any energy, and have brought to it any tolerable tools," a new law supervenes, in virtue of which the return to labor becomes yearly *smaller* than before:

That, although progress toward civilization has everywhere been marked by an increase in the power of man over matter, there exist "fixed and permanent causes" why matter must everywhere, and under all circumstances, obtain greater power over man:

That, though the value of man has everywhere increased as the value of the commodities required for his use has diminished, yet the true road to progress is to be found in the direction of increased use for ships and wagons, because this causes the greatest *increase* in the value of those commodities:

That, although men have everywhere become more free as employments have become more diversified, the true road to progress lies in the division of nations into agricultural and manufacturing ones, the single workshop being thousands of miles distant from the places at which the materials are produced:

That, although man has always thriven in the precise ratio in which the price of the raw material has approximated to that of the commodity manufactured therefrom, his further progress is to be increased by the adoption of a policy looking to cheapening the raw materials and increasing the quantity thereof required to be given for the finished article:

That, although man has always acquired value with the growth of commerce, and with decline in the necessity for trade and transportation,—yet his condition must be improved by establishing the supremacy of trade:

That, although progress has always been marked by increase in the power of labor over capital,—yet it is now required that "labor should be abundant and cheap" in order that it may be kept "sufficiently under the control of capital."

Such being the tendency of all its teachings, it is no matter of surprise that modern English political economy sees in man only an instrument to be used by trade; that it repudiates all the distinctive qualities of man, and limits itself to those that he holds in common with the beast of burden or of prey; and that it denies that the Creator meant that every man should have his place at the great table which he had spread for all his children.

CHAPTER XVI.

OF CHANGES OF MATTER IN FORM.

II.—*Of Vital Changes.*

§ 1. Irregularity in the demand for the powers of the early settler, and consequent waste of force. Economy of force resulting from increased ability to command the services of nature. The more perfect the power of association, the greater is the economy of human force.

§ 2. The greater that economy the larger is the proportion of the labor employed that may be given to the development of the powers of the earth, and towards the creation of a scientific agriculture. Difficulty of combination among a purely agricultural people. Slavery of the laborer its necessary consequence.

§ 3. The farmer near to market always making a machine; the one distant from it, always destroying one. With the one, labor and its products are daily more and more economised. With the other, the waste increases from day to day—man's progress, in whatever direction, being one of constant acceleration. (Population makes the food come from the rich soils, while depopulation drives them back to the poor ones.)

§ 4. Gambling character of the labors of the field where the market is distant. Diminution of risk resulting from the approximation of the consumer and the producer. The labor given to the work of conversion so much saved that would otherwise be wasted. Social phenomena observed in Ireland, India, and other countries, in which the consumer and producer are becoming more widely separated.

§ 5. British system looks to the separation of the consumers and producers of the world—to the consequent destruction of agriculture—and to the elevation of trade at the expense of commerce. Hence it is, that it has given rise to the theory of over-population. Resistance thereto, by all the advancing communities of the world.

§ 1. THE early settler—the Crusoe of our island—dependent on his hands alone, is forced to exhaust his powers in traveling over extensive surfaces in quest of game; and it is only occasionally that he has the opportunity of applying his labors even to the simple work of appropriation. In time, however, having made a bow and arrows and thus secured the aid of certain of the natural forces, he obtains larger and more regular supplies of food; and in return to a diminished *proportion* of his time and labor. His powers being thus economized, he is enabled to apply a larger proportion to the augmentation of his capital—to increasing his supplies of arrows—to the making of a boat—or to the construction of a hut. Each and every of these changes being attended by further diminution in the effort required for effecting changes of place, while increasing that which may be given to other employments, there is thus produced a continuity in the demand for the force resulting from the consumption of food; with consequent economy of power, greatly facilitating the further accumulation of capital.

The cost to a community of maintaining a man in a state of perfect efficiency for mental and physical effort is the same, precisely, whether his powers be wasted or reproductively applied. He must eat, be clothed, and be protected from the weather; and must therefore consume a quantity of capital, which is thus withdrawn from the common stock. Although withdrawn and consumed it is not, however, destroyed; it reappears in a higher form, the food having become MAN, the being made in the likeness of his Creator, and capable of directing the forces of nature for the accomplishment of his purposes. The community thus becomes from hour to hour more wealthy than before; provided always, that the capital, thus reproduced, be so directed that its consumption shall be in itself an act of further reproduction. The power of man to change the forms of matter so as to fit it to serve his purposes, greatly exceeds the demand of the animal man for food and clothing; and all the difference between the quantity of things consumed and the quantity produced, is so much added to the general wealth. Each of its individuals, therefore, is capable of adding largely to the common stock; and whether he shall do so or not, is dependent altogether on the existence of a prompt demand on the spot for the services he is prepared to render. *Labor-power is, of all commodities, the most difficult to be transferred, and the most perishable; for, if not put to use on the instant of its production it is lost forever.* Where there is a regular demand for it communities rapidly increase in wealth and power, but where there is not, they decline with even more rapidity.

Commerce, association, and society being, as the reader has already seen, but different modes of expressing the same idea—and all the power of man for controlling the forces of nature being consequent on the existence of the power of combination—it follows, necessarily, that the more perfect the commerce the more rapid will be the circulation; the more *instant* will be the demand for human force; the greater will be the returns to labor; and the larger will be the *proportion* borne by the things produced to the things consumed. To the economy of power it is due that associated men so rapidly accumulate capital by means of which they obtain increased command over the great natural forces, and are enabled to march steadily onward from triumph to triumph—each successive one being greater than that by which it had been preceded. Their pace is a constantly accelerated one; whereas, that of the savage, daily more and more obliged to waste his capital, is a constantly retarded one; and therefore it is, that while the former become from day to day more and more masters over nature and over themselves, the latter finds himself becoming constantly more and more the slave of nature and of his fellow-men.

§ 2. With every increase in the rapidity of the societary motion there is an augmentation of the force at its command, enabling it to devote a *larger proportion of a constantly increasing quantity to* the development of the resources of the earth. The more the motion becomes accelerated, the less is the amount of those disturbing forces which tend to lessen the powers of the land and of the man who tills it; and therefore is it that agriculture becomes a science, and that the cultivator, the man to whose labors we are indebted for all that we eat and wear, becomes more free as employments become more diversified. Whenever, on the contrary, manufactures decline and the miner and the artisan become more widely separated from the farmer and the planter, the separation is followed by a rapid diminution in the quantity of physical and mental effort that can be given to the cultivation of the earth, and agriculture, ceasing to be a science, passes into the hands of men who from year to year become more and more enslaved.

The mechanic, having skilled labor to sell, obtains high wages; whereas, the man who tills the earth has unskilled labor to dispose of, and is everywhere almost, even when not quite, a slave; and yet the pursuit which requires the highest degree of knowledge, and which pays best for it, is agriculture. The reason for this is found in the fact that in almost all countries the policy generally pursued has favored the establishment of centralization, and the consolidation of power in great trading cities, while it has been adverse to the creation of those local centres required for the maintenance of domestic commerce.

§ 3. The skilled agriculturist is perpetually *making a machine*, utilizing material heretofore unavailable for human purposes. He is perpetually increasing the return to his labor; and the more he takes from his land the larger is the quantity of manure he can return to it, *provided the market be near at hand.*

With every stage of progress in this direction, the various

utilities of the raw materials of the neighborhood become more and more developed. The new mill requires granite, and the houses for the workmen require bricks and lumber; and now the rock of the mountain side, the clay of the river bottoms, and the timber with which they have so long been covered, grow rapidly in man's esteem. The granite dust is useful in the garden, enabling the cultivator to furnish cabbages, beans, peas, and smaller fruits for the supply of workmen in the neighboring mill. The glass works need sand, and the glass-makers require peaches and apples; and the more numerous the men who make the glass, the greater is the facility for returning the manure to the land, and increasing the crops of corn. On one hand there is a demand for potash, on another for madder. The woollen manufacturer asks for teazles, and the maker of brooms urges an extension of the culture of broom corn. The basket-makers and the gunpowder manufacturers claim the produce of the willows; and thus does the farmer find that diversity of employment among those around him produces diversity in the demands for his physical and intellectual powers, and for the use of his various soils at the various seasons of the year, with constant increase in the powers and in the price of his labor and his land.

Directly the reverse of all this is the case as the consumer is more removed from the producer, and as the power of association declines. The madder, the teazle, the broom corn, and the osier, cease to be required; and the granite, the sand, and the clay, are left where nature had placed them. The societary motion, or commerce, declines; and with that decline we witness a stoppage in the motion of matter, with constantly increasing waste of the powers of man, and of the machine given by the Creator for his use. His time is wasted, because he has no choice in the employment of his land. He *must* raise wheat, cotton, or sugar, or some other commodity of which the yield is small, and which can, therefore, bear the cost of carriage to the distant market. He neglects his fruit trees, and his potatoes are given to the hogs. He wastes his rags and straw, because there is no paper-mill at hand. His cotton-seed wastes upon the ground, or he destroys the fibre of the flax that he may sell the seed.* Not only

* "It is certainly a curious contrast, that on the one side British India is exporting £300,000 worth of flaxseed, and throwing away £300,000 of fibre; and on the other, Ireland is raising to the value of £2,000,000 of flax-fibre, and rotting in the steep-pools £500,000 of seed! It is Russia alone that has been benefiting by the igno-

does he sell his wheat in a distant market, and thus impoverish his land, but he does the same with the very bones of the animal fattened with his corn.* The yield, therefore, regularly decreases in quantity, with constant increase in the risk of danger from the changes of the weather, because of the necessity for dependence on a single crop; and with equally constant diminution in the powers of the man who cultivates it, until at length he finds himself a slave, not only to nature, but to those of his fellow-men whose physical powers are greater than his own. That it is population which makes food come from the rich soils, and enables men to grow in wealth, is a truth the evidence of which may be found in every page of history; and equally true is it, that in order to the cultivation of those soils, there must be that development of the latent powers of man which can be found only in those communities in which employments are much diversified.

§ 4. Steadiness and regularity in the returns to agricultural labor grow with increase in the variety of commodities to the production of which the land may be devoted. Disease, too, tends to disappear as population grows, and a market is created on, or near, the land. The poor laborer of Ireland sees his crop of potatoes perish of rot, consequent on the unceasing exhaustion of the soil; and the agriculturist of Portugal witnesses the destruction of his hopes by the constant recurrence of the vine disease; while the American farmer is perpetually visited by blight resulting from the necessity for constantly withdrawing from the soil the material required for enabling it fully to supply the ever-recurring crop of wheat. The man who has a market at his door finds both blight and insects vanish from his land; and is further enabled from year to year more fully to profit by the discoveries of scientific men, and by their aid to free himself from disturbing causes that hitherto have brought loss to

rance of the Hindoo ryot, and the prejudices and carelessness of the Irish farmer. Not a particle of the valuable plant is allowed by her nobles to go to waste. She sells us to the value of £3,000,000 of fibre and £900,000 of seed each year, and does not even take our manufactures in return."—*Belfast Mercury*.

* "Not a month passes that there is not in the harbor of New York or Boston a ship loading with bones for England; the result is seen in the decrease of American wheat from thirty to twelve bushels per acre, and the increase of English from eleven to forty three."—*Agriculturist*.

himself or others, thus making his pursuit so nearly certain in its results as to add largely to the value of his labor and his land.

Not only is all the labor given to manufacture so much saved that would otherwise be wasted, but by means of that economy, and by that alone, it is, that we are enabled to increase the quantity of mental and physical effort given to agriculture. Such being the case, we can have no difficulty in understanding the cause of weakness in all purely agricultural communities; nor why it is, that famines, pestilences, and death, follow so rapidly in the train of a system like that of Britain, which looks to having but a single workshop for the world.

Of the combined physical and mental power of Ireland, nine-tenths are waste. Taking its population of twenty years since, male and female, capable of doing a full day's work, at three-fifths of the whole, or 5,000,000, the waste would be equal to that of 4,500,000 persons; whereas, the whole number of persons engaged in Great Britain in mining coal and ore, and in every branch of the iron and cloth manufacture, was but 1,333,000. In India we find the same state of things in reference to a population of more than a hundred millions; and looking throughout the world we find hundreds of other millions similarly situated.

The direct tendency of the system under which such effects have been produced, is that of causing enormous waste of capital and thus annihilating demand for human service. Of all that have ever been devised it is the one most destructive of morals, intellect, and life; and hence it is that we see whole communities subject to it gradually disappearing from existence, and likely before the lapse of another century to have left behind them scarcely any evidence that the lands they had occupied had ever been the homes of civilized men.

§ 5. The views now presented may be reduced to the following propositions:

I. That, in the early periods of society, when population is small and land abounds, the *proportion* of human effort required for obtaining the absolute necessaries of life is great, but the *quantity* actually given thereto is small, the mass of the labor power produced being wasted in the effort to effect changes in the place, or in the form, of the commodities yielded by the earth; as a consequence of which, man perishes for want of food.

II. That, with the growth of population and of wealth, the power of association increases, with constant increase in the ability productively to apply the force derived from the consumption of food, and constant diminution in the *proportion* of that force required for effecting changes of place, or mechanical and chemical changes of form.

III. That the total quantity applied being a steadily increasing one, with constant diminution in the *proportion* thus required, there remains a constantly increasing proportion of a regularly increasing quantity to be given to augmenting the mass of commodities needed for man's use, and susceptible of being changed in place or form; and that with every step in this direction larger supplies of food and of all other commodities are obtained in return for diminished quantities of physical or intellectual effort.

IV. That with every stage of progress individuality becomes more and more developed, with constant increase in the tendency towards association and combination, increase in the love of harmony and peace, and increase in the tendency towards the creation of local centres of attraction, neutralizing the centralization of trading and political capitals.

V. That as the powers of the earth are more and more developed, the commodities required for the purposes of man steadily decline in value, while man himself becomes more valuable, more happy, and more free.

VI. That while such is the natural course of events, directly the reverse is observed in all the countries subject to the British policy—individuality there everywhere declining, the power of association diminishing, and the warlike tendency as steadily increasing; with constant increase in the value of commodities and decline in that of man, who becomes from year to year more and more enslaved.

The tendencies of the system being thus opposed to the satisfaction of man's first and greatest need, there can now be little difficulty in understanding why it is that it has given birth to the Ricardo-Malthusian theory; nor why it is that, in the leading countries of the civilized world, it has provoked resistance.

CHAPTER XVII.

OF VITAL CHANGES IN THE FORMS OF MATTER—CONTINUED.

§ 1. Constant alliance between war and trade, as exhibited in the history of France. Poverty and dishonesty of its sovereigns.

§ 2. Uniform tendency of its policy, prior to the days of Colbert, towards giving to trade the mastery over commerce. Tendency of his measures, that of increasing the rapidity of the societary movement.

§ 3. Warlike policy of Louis XIV., and consequent necessity for abandonment of Colbert's system. Expulsion of the Huguenots, and annihilation of manufactures. Consequent unproductiveness of agriculture, and wretchedness of the people.

§ 4. Colbert's policy maintained by Turgot. Abandoned by the negotiators of the Eden Treaty. Consequent annihilation of commerce. Poverty of the people leads to revolution. Colbert's system re-established. Extraordinary growth in the quantity and value of the products of French agriculture.

§ 5. Changes in the distribution of labor's products resulting from increase in the power of association and combination, and in the quantity of commodities produced. Great increase in the value of land, resulting from diminution of the tax of transportation.

§ 6. France a country of "contrasts"—its social system tending towards decentralization, while its political one tends, more and more, towards centralization. Colbert's policy in strict accordance with the doctrines of Adam Smith. Causes of poverty among the French people.

§ 1. Of all the European communities, there is none in which war and trade have been in more close and constant alliance than has been the case in France; or in which the effects of that alliance in preventing the development of the treasures of the earth, have been more fully manifested. Abroad, from the days of Charlemagne to those of Waterloo, she has constantly been engaged in arresting the societary motion among her neighbors, wasting in the effort the powers, physical and mental, of her own population. At home, her people have been deprived of the right to determine for whom, or at what wages, they would labor, while liable to be taxed at the pleasure of the sovereign. Always poor, her rulers have with one hand farmed to others the privilege of taxing their subjects; while with the other, they have granted in exchange for money, exemptions from contribution. At one time they have sold titles carrying with them such exemptions; at another, they have annulled all such grants. Henry IV. made such sales in 1593, recalled them without repayment in 1598, and resold them in 1606. Louis XIII. continued to sell them until 1638; then, in 1640, annulled the grants of all the previous thirty years. Louis XIV. resold, in 1661, privileges that had been annulled in 1640, and three years later reannulled all those which had been granted since 1634.

Still worse than this has been their conduct in reference to the important question of the currency. Philip the Fair changed the weight of the coin more than a hundred times during his reign, and as often as thirteen times in a single year. His successors followed his example, buying gold and silver at low prices and selling them at high ones; and thus affording proof of the fact that dishonesty and meanness are the almost inseparable companions of arbitrary power.

Under John (1356), interior custom-houses were established, at which were collected, on all merchandise passing from province to province, the same duties as upon similar commodities coming from distant countries, peculiar privileges being at the same time granted to foreign traders engaged in exchanging their wares against the rude products of the soil. Commerce being thus sacrificed at the shrine of trade there prevailed throughout the kingdom, during several centuries, the most entire ignorance of the simplest mechanic arts; while in the Netherlands and Germany, Italy and Spain, art and science were making rapid progress.

Directly the reverse was then the policy of England. While John was extending the dominion of trade, Edward III. was inviting Flemish artisans into England and thus enlarging domestic commerce, while limiting the powers of the foreigners by whom English products had been till then monopolized. The same difference exhibits itself in the measures of their successors, and as a consequence the records of the House of Valois close, in 1589, with a state of society in which the laborer was enslaved, and brute force constituted the only law; while the contemporary English history presents to us a community advancing steadily towards freedom—one that was even then preparing to give to the world the Hampdens and the Pyms, the Winthrops and the Williamses, the men who at home set limits to the power of the crown, and those who abroad laid the foundation of the great republic of modern times. In the one, we find the States-general declining steadily in its influence; whereas in the other we mark a gradual growth in the power of Parliament to control the affairs of state.*

§ 2. The example of the sovereign was followed in every

* The last assembly of the States-General, prior to that which, in 1789, ushered in the Revolution, was in 1605, when the popular branch of the English Parliament was rapidly acquiring the power so strongly manifested in the reign of Charles I.

quarter of the kingdom; offices were bought and sold; local taxes were innumerable; and manufacturers surrounded themselves with regulations looking to the prevention of domestic competition for the purchase of raw materials, or for the sale of manufactures. Commerce having almost perished, the nation presented to view little more than two great classes, one of which lived and labored in wretchedness even when its members failed to perish of famine and pestilence, while the other revelled in barbaric luxury. In no part of Europe was the magnificence of the few so great, or the misery of the many so complete; and at no period was the contrast more perfect than when, in 1661, Colbert was called to the financial management of the kingdom.

The system of internal intercourse then existing greatly resembled that of Germany at the opening of the present century, custom-houses on the borders of the provinces obstructing the passage of men and things throughout the State. These Colbert transferred, as far as was then possible, to the frontiers, thus establishing freedom of circulation throughout the kingdom. He next sought to improve the means of transportation; and the canals of Orleans, Briare, and Languedoc, still attest the importance of his efforts. Further, desiring to re-establish the various industries that had so nearly perished during previous centuries, he imposed heavy duties on foreign manufactures, while exerting himself to naturalize both the raw materials of manufacture and the skill required for their conversion into finished products. Throughout the reign of Louis XIV. political centralization tended constantly to increase, but the system of his great minister looked to social and commercial decentralization; and to his measures it is largely due that agriculture, manufactures, and commerce, have made the extraordinary progress since exhibited.*

§ 3. Repeating, however, the error of the early English Parliaments, Colbert prohibited the export of raw produce. He sought to aid the agricultural interest by bringing the artisan nearer to the farmer, and thus relieving the land from the tax of transportation; but by interdicting the farmer from going with his products to the distant market he established

* "Louis XIV might with truth and justice say that, in giving him Colbert, God had done much for the prosperity and glory of his reign. . France might add, that she owes to his wise counsels the wonderful development of her industry."—*Thierry.*

a monopoly in favor of the domestic artisan. Time and further experience would have corrected this had peace been maintained, but such proved not to be the case. Scarcely had his system begun to operate when his master commenced the movement against the Protestants, which terminated, in 1685, in the Revocation of the Edict of Nantes. Two millions of the most intellectual, best instructed, and essentially manufacturing part of the people were, by that act, exposed to persecutions of every kind, resulting in the death of half a million of persons; while at least an equal number, escaping into England, Holland, and Germany, carried with them their skill and intelligence, as well as the secrets of their various manufactures. When we add, that Louis was incessantly engaged in wars demanding enormous sacrifices, and closing invariably with treaties requiring the abandonment of the protection to manufactures which Colbert had established,* it is no matter of surprise that at his death the condition of the people should have been miserable to a degree of which we can scarcely now form an idea; nor, that the reign of his successor should have been marked by an almost total absence of commerce, and a universal depression of the agricultural interest, consequent on the almost entire annihilation of the manufacturing one.

§ 4. A century after Colbert we find Turgot, animated by the same views, laboring to free land and labor from the monopolies that still retarded the growth of commerce. The period during which he occupied the post of Comptroller-General of the Finances exhibits a constant series of edicts looking to the abolition of exclusive privileges, and the emancipation of labor from the control of corporations that stood between the producer and the consumer. His administration endured but three years; and with its close disappeared all hope of a peaceful solution of the financial difficulties of the government, or of the peaceful removal of the burdens under which the people had so long suffered. Theoretically, Turgot was opposed to the idea of granting protection to the farmer in the effort to bring the consumer to his side; but he never interfered with the protective system he had found established. His incapable successors, however, negotiated, in

* Nimeguen, in 1679; Ryswick, 1697; and Utrecht in 1713; all of which contained provisions setting aside Colbert's tariff of 1667; and one of which went so far as to limit the power of the king to grant protection to his subjects.

1786, a treaty with England under which the towns and cities of France were so flooded with English merchandise that before the lapse of even the second year the varied industry that had been so carefully built up had almost ceased to exist. Workmen were discharged, agriculture suffered, and commerce perished. The distress was universal, paralyzing the government, and forcing it into the initial measure of the Revolution—the calling together of the Notables in 1788.

All that Turgot had vainly claimed in behalf of the people was now taken by them; the privileges of corporations were swept away, the property of the nobility and the church confiscated, and peer and peasant declared equal before the law. Commerce was in a great measure freed from the restrictions by which its course had been impeded; the right to labor ceased to be a privilege; the soil became the subject of purchase and sale; and the laborer could bestow his labor on a piece of land, confident that the benefit would accrue to himself and to his heirs. These decentralizing measures, however, were accompanied with the highly centralizing ones of the abolition of local governments, the annihilation of ancient boundaries, and the division of the country into departments, all tending to diminish that feeling of local pride which so much contributes to the activity of social life. Provision was thus made for the future diminution of social centralization, but political centralization was at once and largely increased; and hence it is, that France has not yet been able to obtain a stable government.

Amid this war of elements the system of Colbert, so far as it had established direct intercourse between producers and consumers, stood unharmed, the retrograde step of those who had negotiated the treaty of '86 having speedily been retraced, and protection re-established. The war that followed, producing a necessity for looking homeward for supplies of cloth and iron, tended in the same direction. Such, too, was the tendency of the Continental system of Napoleon; and therefore was it that the return of peace found the people and the government prepared to act together in carrying out, and even strengthening, the measures of resistance to trading centralization begun, a century and a half before, by the illustrious minister of Louis XIV. How far these measures have tended to the advancement of agriculture is seen in the fact that during a period of twenty-seven years, from 1813 to 1840, the annual average increase in the money value of the products of the farm was no less than 20,000,000 of dollars, the return to the labor employed in cultivation having almost doubled, although the population had increased but twenty-five per cent.

Nor is it the money value alone of the produce that has thus increased. The cereal products doubled in quantity in the period from 1760 to 1840; and the potato culture, which has been introduced within that time, now yields 96,000,000 of hectolitres, while the crops of garden vegetables have wonderfully increased. Of sugar from the beet-root, a manufacture introduced by Napoleon, the yield now amounts to 200,000,000 of pounds, while the amount of silk cocoons produced, which in 1812 scarcely exceeded 10,000,000 of pounds, had risen to more than 50,000,000.

France had then nearly 40,000,000 of sheep against 20,000,000 in 1789; but the improvement in quality had been far greater than in quantity, the demand from the woollen manufacture having offered a large bounty upon the devotion of time, mind, and means, to the improvement of the race.

Cloth has declined in price, while wool and corn have risen, the prices of the raw material and the finished commodity thus steadily approximating, always a sign of advancing civilization; and the consequence is seen in the fact that the average money value of land has more than trebled. Much of this augmented value results from the great increase in the yield, especially of those products that, because of their bulk, will not bear transportation. A further, and very large, portion of it is consequent on the increased utility of many portions of the product, resulting from the proximity of the market. Thus, the straw alone is valued at $150,000,000, being as much as the product of the whole cotton crop of these United States, which occupies so nearly exclusively the land of no less than ten of our States, and furnishes almost the whole employment of so many millions of our people.

§ 5. The general effect of the changes above described is found in the following brief summary of the contents of an extended article communicated by M. de Jonnès to the *Annuaire de l'Economie Politique et Statistique*, for 1851, for which we are indebted to the excellent little *Manual of Political Economy*, of Mr. E. Peshine Smith.

"The inquiry extends back to the period of Louis XIV., embracing the experience of one hundred and fifty years, divided, for the purposes of comparison, into five periods. The facts, as condensed in a tabular form, are as follows :—

"The first table contains a statement of the aggregate expenditure, at different periods, for the cultivation of the soil of France (excluding the value of the seed), in millions of francs—of the proportion which the sum total of wages bore to the whole value of the product of the soil—and of the amount of such expenditure per head to the actual population of the kingdom at each epoch, as follows :—

Epoch.	Cost of cultivation. *Francs.*	Proportion to the entire product. *Per cent.*	To each inhabitant. *Francs.*
1700, Louis XIV	458,000,000	35	24
1760, Louis XV	442,000,000	37	21
1788, Louis XVI	725,000,000	43	30
1813, The Empire	1,827,000,000	60	61
1840, Louis Philippe	3,016,000,000	60	90

"The following statement gives the division of wages among the agricultural families of the kingdom at the same period, upon the estimate that they averaged four and a half persons to a family, giving the annual wages of each family, and the amount per day for each of its members :—

	Number of agricultural families.	Annual wages. *Francs.*	Daily wages of each. *Francs.*	*Centimes.**	*Sous*
1700	3,350,000	135	0	37	or 7½
1760	3,500,000	126	0	35	" 7
1788	4,000,000	161	0	45	" 9
1813	4,000,000	400	1	10	" 22
1840	6,000,000	500	1	37	" 27

"M. de Jonnès compares these prices of labor with those of wheat, for the purpose of seeing how far they would go in the respective periods towards supplying the prime necessities of life. He reckons that thirteen and a half hectolitres (the hectolitre is $2\frac{85}{100}$ bushels) of wheat has been about the quantity of grain needed for the consumption of a family—needed more during the earlier than the latter periods, because its want is now, in a great degree, obviated by a variety of garden vegetables formerly unknown or very little cultivated. He constructs a table giving the mean price of wheat, deduced from an average of the market for long series of years, under each reign, as follows :—

"* The *centime* is the hundredth part of a franc, or about one-fifth of a cent: the *sou* is five centimes, or about one cent."

			Mean price per hectolitre. Francs.	Centimes.
Under Louis XIV.,	average of 72 years	...	18	85
" Louis XV.,	" 60 "	...	13	05
" Louis XVI.,	" 16 "	...	16	00
" The Empire,	" 10 "	...	21	00
" Constitutional Monarchy,	" 10 "	...	19	03

"The result of a comparison of the annual earnings of a family of agricultural laborers, with the cost of thirteen and a half hectolitres of wheat required for their annual consumption, is given in the following table:—

Period.	Wages. Francs.	Cost of 13½ hectolitres. Francs.		Francs.
1	135	254;	deficit,	119
2	126	176;	"	50
3	161	216;	"	55
4	400	283;	excess,	117
5	500	259;	"	244

"During the reign of the *Grand Monarque*, the rural population of France wanted bread half of the time. Under the sway of Louis XV., it had bread two days out of three. Sufficient progress had been made under Louis XVI. to give it bread three-fourths of the year; while, under the Empire and the rule of the Citizen King, wages were sufficient to supply the laborer with bread through the year, and leave a surplus towards procuring other food and clothing. Doubtless, the laboring classes at the earliest period obtained food enough, such as it was, to support animal life, and made shift to get some clothing also. But their bread was made of the inferior grains, chestnuts, and even worse materials. De Jonnès quotes the Marquis d'Argenson, one of the ministers of Louis XV., as saying, in 1739, 'At the moment when I write, in the month of February, in the midst of peace, with appearances promising a harvest, if not abundant at least passable, men die around us like flies, and are reduced by poverty to eat grass.' He ascribes their condition to excessive taxation, declaring that the kingdom was treated like an enemy's country laid under military contribution. The Duke of Orleans, to bring the condition of his people to the knowledge of the sovereign, finally carried a loaf of *fern* bread to the meeting of the king's council, and at the opening of the session laid it before his Majesty, saying, 'See, Sire, what your subjects live upon.' This may be regarded as an exceptional case; but a very small portion even of well-read men, at the present day, have any adequate impression of the wretchedness of the food upon which the mass of the people of Europe fed a century and a half ago, and which even now makes the subsistence of a large portion of them.* De Jonnès says of his countrymen, in the year of grace 1850, 'A large part of the population of our rural districts continue, from habit and from necessity, to feed upon a detestable bread, an indigestible mixture of rye, barley, bran, beans, and potatoes, which is neither leavened nor cooked sufficiently;' and Blanqui, who, under a commission of the Institute, has for two years past been journeying through the provinces to examine into and report upon their condition, declares that they alone who have seen it, can conceive the degree in which the clothing, furniture, and food of the rural population are slender and sorry. An official report for 1845, of the number of houses in France subject to the *door-and-window tax*, shows that there are, in all, 7,519,310 houses—of which 500,000 have only one aperture, 2,000,000 with only two, and 1,500,000 with from four to five. Two-sevenths only of the whole have six or more openings. Thus are the French people lodged.

"Recurring now to the tables for the purpose for which they were adduced, we see that they prove a great advance, both in the absolute amount of wages, and in the *proportion* which they bear to the entire product, and to the share of the capitalist. The proportion to the entire product has almost doubled in one hundred and fifty years, having risen from 35 per cent. to 60. As between the laborers and the capitalists, it was, in 1700, 35 per cent. to the former, and 65 to the latter. It is now 60 per cent. to the former, and 40 to the latter, who, instead of getting two-thirds of the product—twice as much as the laborers—now get but two-fifths, leaving the laborers three-fifths, or 50 per cent. more than the capitalists. But, although the latter get a diminished proportion, the increased efficiency of labor and capital has so much increased the crop, that this diminished proportion yields an amount not only absolutely greater, but greater relatively to the increased population. This is readily shown by a few figures, deduced from the tables of M. Jonnès.

"* According to a Report of the Central Agricultural Congress, at Paris, published in the *Journal des Debats*, March 30, 1847, it appears that in 1760 only 7,000,000 of the French people lived on wheat and corn; while, in 1843, 20,000,000 lived on wheat and corn, and the remainder were much better nourished than in the former period."

Taking for comparison the two extremes, we find the following results:—

	Total population.	Agricultural population.	Paid to agricul. laborers. Francs.	Total product. Francs.	Leaving for rest of population. Francs.
1700,	19,500,000	15,000,000	458,000,000	1,308,000,000	850,000,000
1840,	36,000,000	27,000,000	3,016,000,000	6,025,000,000	2,009,000,000

"From this it appears that, notwithstanding the laborers are so much better paid—three and two-thirds times more than in 1700—(or, rather, *because* they are so much better paid,) the remainder, left to be divided among the capitalists and non-agricultural classes, is larger than before, and they fare better also. The entire population of France lacks three millions of having doubled, while the crop has nearly quadrupled; so that, on an equal distribution, there is now twice as much for each mouth as in 1700. But, looking to the actual distribution, now and then, we see that while the non-agricultural population has increased 100 per cent., the surplus left, after paying the agricultural laborers their increased wages and enlarged proportion, has increased 127 per cent. This is the state of the case, the comparison being made in money. If it is desired to estimate it in food, we have the necessary elements of calculation, when we know that the mean price of wheat at the first epoch was 18 francs 85 centimes per hectolitre, while at the latter it was 19 francs 3 centimes—a difference of less than two cents a bushel. If it should be objected that these figures do not show how much goes to the landlord in his quality of owner of the soil, and how much to the man who advances capital in the shape of seed, tools, etc., for its cultivation, the answer is, that the *proportion* of the crop which pays both is less than formerly: if the landlord took the whole, it would be a less share than both obtained in 1700; and if he now gets nothing in his quality of proprietor of land, leaving the whole to remunerate himself or third persons for the use of capital other than land, it is less in ratio than he originally received for the use of the land and all the other capital employed in tilling it.

"The operation of the law is indicated by a comparison of different portions of France. 'It is,' says Passy, 'a country of contrasts. There are departments which seem to have made no agricultural progress for a century; there are others whose agriculture is not behind that of the most advanced countries of Europe. In the departments most backward, the expenses of cultivation do not exceed an average of

30 francs to the hectare ($2\frac{47}{100}$ acres), and the gross revenue is about 70 francs. In the advanced departments, on the contrary, the expenditure amounts to 200 francs and over to the hectare; and at this cost a gross product is realized of at least 320 francs, leaving the farmers, as well to pay the rent as for their own profits, about 120 francs. In the latter, the excess of the produce above the cost of production is three times that of the former; but it requires nearly *seven* times the amount of advances of capital."* The capitalists, who obtain for rent and profits four-sevenths of the value of the crop, have but one-third the *amount* received by those whose proportion is but three-eighths. The remaining five-eighths, which the latter expend in the wages of laborers and the improvement of the soil, is five times as much in amount as is furnished for those objects in the poorer departments. Decreasing proportion for the capitalists, with increasing quantity, is thus exhibited, as well by the comparison between different districts of the same country, as by that of the country at large in different stages of its progress. The converse of the proposition must clearly hold in respect to the wages of labor; and, after better wages have been provided for the existing laborers, there is still three times the amount to be added to the capital of the advanced departments, and to furnish wages for new laborers in the advanced departments, that the more backward could supply. Instead of population encroaching upon the limits of subsistence, those limits recede before the advance of population."

§ 6. The more perfectly a community *finishes* the raw products of its soil, so as to fit them for consumption, the larger will be the quantity of physical and mental power productively employed, and the larger will be the *proportion* of that *increased quantity* given to the work of augmenting the produce demanding to be finished. *The labor given to the work of conversion is all of it economized;* not only so, but the relief thus obtained from the necessity for transportation enables the cultivator so to vary his demands upon the soil as largely to increase his crops. Further, he is enabled to return to the soil the manure from the neighboring town, thus increasing the powers of his land. Food therefore becomes more abundant as the farmer and the artisan are more and more enabled to take their places by each other's side.

* *Dictionnaire de l'Economie Politique*, vol. I. p. 38; article, *Agriculture*.

Directly the reverse of all this is what is taught in that economical school which sees the perfection of social arrangement in having a single workshop for the world, and confining all other communities to the mere tillage of the earth. The consequences of this latter system are seen in Ireland, Turkey, and other countries heretofore referred to, all of them being in a gradual course of decay and dissolution; whereas, when we turn to France, whose policy is, and so long has been, entirely opposed to the teachings of the English school, we find abundant evidence of the proposition:—That a nation which desires that the supply of the raw products of the earth may be abundant, must make demand for them by means of bringing their consumers as near as possible to the producers, and thus *diminishing the tax of transportation.*

That the raising of raw produce for consumption in distant markets was the proper work of the barbarian and the slave, was a truth clearly obvious to the observant eyes of Adam Smith. So, too, was it with the great statesman to whom France has been so much indebted for the great progress she since has made. Great as it has been, however, her people, as a rule, are still poor, and her productive powers are small when compared with her vast advantages. For the maintenance of a vast naval and military establishment, there are required enormous contributions in money; and yet, oppressive as they are, they are less injurious than the withdrawal, annually, from the labors of the field and the workshop, of so large a portion of the younger population, and this at the precise period when their habits for life are to be determined.

This, however, is but one of the many of the restraints by which commerce is impeded, centralization being universal, and producing everywhere a waste of physical and mental faculty. As nothing can be done without the intervention of the government, far more power is wasted daily than is profitably applied; and to this it is due that agriculture has not as yet made the progress that could have been desired.

CHAPTER XVIII.

OF VITAL CHANGES IN THE FORMS OF MATTER—CONTINUED.

§ 1. Wide difference between the French and British systems—the former looking to the approximation of the producer and consumer, and the latter to their separation.

§ 2. Consequences of this exhibit themselves in the great increase in the value of French land, as compared with that of the United Kingdom. Comparative growth of French and British agriculture.

§ 3. French land being more divided, the small proprietor profits by increase in the prices of his products and his land. British tenants ruined by decline in the price of food.

§ 4. French policy looks to making manufactures subsidiary to agriculture—facilitating the export of the products of the soil of France. Consequent increase of French commerce.

§ 5. British policy makes agriculture subsidiary to manufactures. Trade, therefore, replaces the former British commerce.

§ 6. British system taxes the agricultural communities of the world for its maintenance. That of France looks to their emancipation from taxation.

§ 7. Solidarity of interests among the land-owners and laborers of the world at large. Deterioration of the condition of the farm-laborers of England. Centralization, over-population, and physical and mental decline travel hand in hand together.

§ 1. Two systems are now before the world,—one, whose objects are to be promoted by increasing competition for the *sale* of all the raw materials of manufacture, labor included; and another, which looks to increasing competition *for their purchase*.

The first tends towards increasing the necessity for the machinery of transportation, and thus augmenting the influence of *trade*. The second would promote the growth of the associative power and thus diminish the necessity for such machinery, while enlarging the field of *commerce*.

The first looks to widening the space by which the producer and the consumer are separated; the second looks to its contraction.

The one would increase the difference between the prices of raw materials and finished commodities; the other would secure their more close approximation.

The one looks to adding to the value of commodities and thus diminishing that of man; the other, to diminishing the value of things, and increasing that of the men who need to use them.

The one looks to increasing the proportion of mental and physical power given to trade and transportation, and thus diminishing that which might be applied to production; the other, to an increase in the proportion given to production, and a diminution in that applied to effecting changes in the places of the things produced.

Leader in the advocacy of the first has been, and is, Great Britain. Leader in the establishment of the second, and most consistent in its maintenance, is France; and thus, after striving for so many ages to injure each other by means of warlike operations, are those two nations now engaged in a peaceful contest for the leadership of the world; but, peaceful as it is, it is destined to exercise an amount of influence compared with which that resulting from the movement of fleets and armies in the past will prove to have been utterly insignificant.

For centuries, both have been almost unceasingly engaged in war, but widely different have been the objects aimed at; France having sought for glory and dominion, while England has looked with a single eye to the supremacy of trade. Equally different have been their respective policies:—France having imitated Rome, who, universal plunderer that she was, left the local arrangements of her provinces untouched; while Great Britain has imitated Holland, in seeking to monopolize the machinery of trade and transportation, and thereby to compel the whole people of the world to make their exchanges in her single and distant market. The policy of the one has been that of the soldier; the other, that of the trader, founded on the single idea of "buying in the cheapest market and selling in the dearest."

France permitted her colonists to refine their own sugar, and to make their own cloth. England, on the contrary, desiring that the "mischievous practice" might be prevented, inserted in her grants of land clauses declaring the same to be void should the grantee "apply himself to the making of woollen, or such like manufactures." Looking towards the enlargement of commerce, France, under the lead of Turgot, abolished the monopolies of earlier times; while at the same moment the Parliament of England, looking always toward trade, was adding, year after year, to the restrictions upon the movements of her artisans, and thus seeking to create a monopoly to be held against the world. By an examination of the results we may perhaps judge which must ultimately remain conqueror; merely reminding the reader that the question is one of *progress, not of actual condition*. In both there is much of poverty and wretchedness; in both, centralization is great. What, however, we need to know is, whether they are advancing or declining, and what is the rate at which they move. If one can be shown to be steadily gaining on the other, then we may feel assured that, however backward it may appear, to it must ultimately be adjudged the prize of victory.

§ 2. The essential characteristic of advancing civilization is *an approximation of the prices of raw materials to that of the finished commodities into which they are converted.* With every step in this direction the land, the source from which we derive the corn, cotton, sugar, and ore, tends to acquire a *higher money value*, being more freed from the tax of transportation.

Forty years since, the total product of agricultural labor in France was but 3,333,000,000 of francs; of which, according to M. de Jonnès, the portion representing the value of the land was 45 per cent., or 1,500,000,000. In 1840 the product was about 6,000,000,000, and it now exceeds 8,000,000,000, of which the land may claim a third, or little less than 3,000,000,000. Estimating these quantities at twenty-five years' purchase, we obtain as the money value of the soil of France—

1815	37,500,000,000 francs.
1840	50,000,000,000 "
1856	70,000,000,000 "

In less than half a century the price has almost doubled.

Crossing the channel, we meet a picture widely different. Forty years since the annual value of the land of the United Kingdom, exclusive of metals, mines, fisheries, etc, was as follows:—

England and Wales	£34,330,462
Scotland	3,804,221
Ireland	12,715,778

Thirty years later that of England had slightly increased, the assessment of 1843 having been £37,412,000; and at the same amount it was estimated by Mr. Caird, the highest authority in regard to British agriculture, in 1857. That of Ireland, however, had so greatly fallen, that the total scarcely exceeded that of 1815; while, as we have seen, that of France had nearly doubled.

The total quantity of food produced in Great Britain has largely increased, but the prices have fallen; as here presented in the case of wheat

1800 to 1809	£4 2 2	1830 to 1839	£2 16 5
1820 " 1829	2 18 5	1840 " 1849	2 15 11

The following are the prices, per hectolitre, in France, for nearly the same period:—

1805 to 1814	21.09 francs.	1831 to 1840	19.03 francs.
1815 " 1830	20.62 "	1840 " 1849	21.60 "

In the one we have a production that *does not* keep pace with the growth of population, yet the price has greatly fallen: while in the other, we have a production that outstrips the growth of numbers, yet the price in the closing period is higher than in those by which it had been preceded.

§ 3. In France, land being much divided, the occupants were generally its owners; and every increase in the price of land and of its products accrued to the advantage of the cultivator, who was thus enabled to improve his own methods while becoming a better customer to his neighbors.

In England, lands were generally held under leases requiring large money payments, failing to make which, tenants were liable to be expelled, leaving to landlords all the advantage resulting from the expenditure the former had incurred. The heavy fall of prices rendering it impossible that he should pay such rents, the consequences are seen in such facts as the following, furnished by Mr. Caird:—

"Seven of these first-class farms, all contiguous, and the very pick of the country, tell the following tale:—The first, after having been held seven years, was given up, and relet, at a reduction of 20 per cent. The second, the tenant having become bankrupt, was let to a new tenant at a reduction. The third was given up, and relet at a reduction of about 22 per cent. The fourth, the tenant having failed, was let to a new tenant at a reduction of 13 per cent. The fifth, the tenant having also failed, has been relet to a new one. The sixth has been also relet at a reduction of 20 per cent. The seventh has been given up, and is now offered at a reduction of 20 per cent."

The small proprietors had disappeared, and their places had been taken by the tenant and the hired laborer.* The tenants in their turn were being ruined, and thus did the

* "Instead of several millions of our people having a share or direct interest in the soil of this country, as would have been the case had small properties and the cottage system continued until now,—the number of proprietors is dwindling down to a handful, and the tenants, owing to the enlargement of farms, are undergoing a corresponding diminution."—*Blackwood's Magazine*, December, 1855

system tend to the annihilation of all those classes which before had stood between the great land-owner and the mere farm-laborer. The whole British system is based upon the idea that the prosperity of man is to be promoted by cheapening the raw products of the earth; and yet all experience teaches, that *where they are cheapest the cultivator is the most enslaved.*

§ 4. As a general rule, France feeds herself. In 1847 her imports were adequate to the supply of 2,700,000 persons. In 1832 and 1846 she imported half that quantity. In 19 out of 33 years her imports were insignificant.

The annual average of her exports in the ten years ending 1836, but little exceeded 500,000,000 francs. In 1852 the amount was 1,250,000,000, being an increase of 150 per cent; and yet nearly the whole amount of labor thus exported *directly represented food produced on the soil of France.*

In 1854, the value of the cotton fabrics exported was 60,000,000 francs, while the weight was but 16,000,000 pounds, so that the raw cotton which had passed into the manufacturer's hands at, probably, ten cents, had attained a value eight times greater. The total weight of textile fabrics exported in that year was under 16,000 tons, which could be carried in thirty ships of moderate size; while in that small bulk was contained probably not less than sixty millions of dollars' worth of French food, so condensed (according to the ideas of Adam Smith) as to enable it to travel freely to the remotest corners of the world.

The tendency of French policy is that of making manufactures subsidiary to agriculture, combining a small amount of foreign raw materials with a large quantity of those produced at home, and thus enabling her farmers to maintain commerce with distant countries. Scarcely any thing passes out until it has attained a form so high as to cause the skill and taste which represent her own food, to bear a very large proportion to the value of the raw material employed. Her exports of raw produce are insignificant; and even of wine the amount sent abroad little exceeds that of the years preceding the Revolution, the average from 1844 to 1846 having been but 1,401,800 hectolitres, against 1,247,700 from 1787 to 1789.

The total value of French exports in 1854 was $280,000,000, of which the foreign raw materials could scarcely have exceeded a fifth; leaving above $220,000,000 as the value of domestic products furnished to the world.

§ 5. In 1815 the declared value of British manufactures exported was £51,632,791, while the import of wool, cotton, silk, and flax amounted to 155,747,000 pounds weight. If to the cotton, wool, silk, and flax re-exported, we add the dyeing materials, etc , used in their manufacture, we obtain of foreign commodities re-exported 12 or 13 millions, leaving nearly 40 millions as the actual value of British produce exported: which, divided among the people, would give about £2 per head.

The producer of food and the sheep farmer were both then profiting by the export trade. If the cotton and silk that went abroad were foreign, the corn and wool embodied in the cloth were principally of domestic origin.

In 1851 the exports were £68,492,599, nearly the whole increase being found in four branches of manufacture, the materials of which were wholly drawn from abroad.

The reader must bear in mind that those who furnish the food, clothing, and lodging, do, in fact, furnish the labor. A steam-engine is an instrument by means of which the force *yielded by the consumption of fuel* is made to serve the purpose of man. So is it with men. Their daily power to labor results from their daily consumption of food; and therefore *those who supply the food and clothing really supply the power*. Let us now inquire how many of the people of England are fed by the agricultural nations of the earth, and how many of the former work for these latter.

The foreign food imported in 1851 would, if divided among four millions of people, give much more than the average consumption of the men, women, and children employed in the British workshops, and it may therefore fairly be assumed that the world furnishes four millions of her laborers with food and clothing, and with shelter, too, the greater part of the timber there consumed being drawn from abroad. To this may be further added all the tea, coffee, cocoa, sugar, lemons, oranges, figs, raisins, spices, and tobacco consumed by the 28,000,000 of the population of the United Kingdom.

Of raw materials, foreign nations supply all the silk, cotton, oil, saltpetre, and dye-stuffs. Of hides, wool, flax, hemp, and various other articles, they not only furnish all that is re-exported in the shape of manufactures, but as much more as is adequate to meet the demands of a large portion, if not the whole, of the four millions above referred to, who may therefore be considered as being fed, lodged, clothed, and supplied to the English people by the other communities of the world

§ 6. In 1841 the number of persons employed in the—

Cotton, hose, wool, lace, worsted, silk, flax, and linen manufactures, was	800,246
In the mines	193,825
In the working of metals and making of instruments	303,368
Making a great total of	1,297,439
The number employed in 1851 may perhaps have been	1,500,000

If so, it follows that the world, in addition to nearly all the raw materials, furnishes the labor of nearly three times as many persons as are employed in all these great branches of industry.

Of this million and a half, but a small proportion is employed in working for the foreigners who supply this food and these raw materials. Of the commodities exported, nearly all are of the coarser kinds, requiring little skill or taste. Thus, out of an export of £87,000,000 in 1854, there was of

Metals in their rudest state	£15,000,000	Earthenware, alkali, beer and ale, butter, candles, cordage, fish, salt, wool	£6,000,000
Coals	1,500,000	Cotton cloth, averaging 7 cts. per yard	24,000,000
Yarns	10,000,000		
Linen averaging 16 cts.	4,000,000		

Except machinery and mill-work amounting to £2,000,000, and hardware and cutlery £4,000,000, there is scarcely any thing in the list of English exports requiring either skill or taste. It may therefore well be doubted if more than one-fifth of the labor given to manufactures is applied to the production of the things exported, but to avoid the possibility of error, we may assume it at one-third. The account between England and the world at large would then stand as follows:—

Dr.	Cr.
To the labor of four millions of persons employed in Great Britain, fed, clothed, and lodged by other nations.	By the labor of half a million of men, women, and children, employed in the lowest order of the labors of conversion.
To the tea, sugar, coffee, tobacco, fruits, and other commodities consumed by twenty-eight millions of persons.	
To the cotton, flax, hemp, silk, lumber, and other raw materials required for domestic consumption and for exportation.	By a small portion of the raw material employed.

The change above exhibited in the movements of these two great communities is the most remarkable on record, to have been accomplished in so short a time. Forty years since

Great Britain carried on a great commerce *with* the world, giving corn, wool, etc., in the shape of cloth and iron, in exchange for tea, sugar, coffee, etc. Now, that commerce has wholly disappeared, having given place to a trade carried on *for* the world, in which she takes in corn, wool, sugar, coffee, and cotton, and turns them out again in the forms of cloth, yarn, and iron. The reverse is what we find in the movement of France. Forty years since the commerce of that country with foreign nations was but $100,000,000; now, it amounts to thrice that sum, still retaining nearly its original character, France being dependent on foreign raw materials for little more than is required for so compressing the bulky food so as to enable it cheaply to go abroad.

Forty years since, Great Britain fed herself, and had nearly two hundred millions of dollars' worth of *things* produced from her own soil, to give to the world in exchange for the commodities she required for her own consumption. Now, with millions of people whom she cannot feed, she has, in point of fact, *nothing* of her own to give in exchange for the enormous quantity of foreign products consumed at home. She has become a mere trader in the productions of other lands, changing their form by aid of the labor furnished by the people of those lands, and living entirely on the taxation thus imposed upon the world.

§ 7. It can not be too steadily borne in mind that *there is a perfect solidarity of interest, of prosperity or adversity, among all the agriculturists of the world.* That all communities prosper by the prosperity of all others, and that all suffer from injury received by others, is a truth that will, at some day, come to be admitted; and then the farmers and planters everywhere will be found combining together to compel the maintenance, in the conduct of public affairs, of a sound morality looking to the advancement of the interests of commerce, and to their own emancipation from the most oppressive of all tyrannies, that of trade.

That large quantities of produce are received in England, and that very little is given in return, is a fact that does not admit of a doubt; and it is one the conviction of whose existence must sooner or later force itself upon the agricultural communities of the world. Were these latter now to arrive at the conclusion that they might as well mine and smelt their own ore, twist and weave their own cotton, and make their own earthenware; and were they to say to the people engaged in doing this work for them in England:—"Come among us and mine ore, make iron, spin thread, and weave cloth"—thus having the work performed at home, the effect would be, that instead of feeding several millions of foreigners, they would have but half a million of their own people to feed; and that, instead of giving such prodigious masses of cotton, sugar, coffee, tea, lumber, dye-stuffs, and other raw products, in exchange for a little coarse cloth, and a very little iron, they would have nearly the whole of that immense quantity to apply to the purchase of improved machinery, or to that of the comforts and luxuries of life. What, however, would be the condition of the people of England? Where would be the commodities to pay for the supplies which they would still need? Nowhere! for Great Britain has now nothing of her own to sell. All her accumulations, and the major part of the supplies required for her own people, and for the support of government, are derived from *profits*—from buying cotton, wool, corn, and other raw products, at low prices and selling them as cloth and iron, at high ones; and from the moment those profits ceased to be made, she would cease to have the power to feed or clothe her people *without a total change of system.*

Such a change would look to elevating the workman, instead of depressing him, to developing his faculties instead of crushing them, to making him a MAN instead of a mere machine. Such a change, however, would require time, the tendency of the system for so long a period having been towards the brutification of the laborer, and towards reducing him to a condition near akin to slavery.*

* Half a century since, Mr. Southey, after describing the state of things in Birmingham and Manchester, resulting from the effort to underwork the world, told his countrymen that—"The poor must be kept poor, or such a state of things could not continue; there must be laws to regulate their wages, not by the value of their work, but by the pleasure of their masters; laws to prevent their removal from one place to another within the kingdom, and to prohibit their emigration. They would not," he continues, "be crowded in hot task-houses by day, and herded together in damp cellars by night; they would not toil in unwholesome employments from sunrise until sunset whole days and quarters, for with twelve hours' labor the avidity of trade is not satisfied; they would not sweat night and day, keeping up this *lues perennis* of the Devil, before furnaces which are never suffered to cool, and breathing in vapors which inevitably produce disease and death;—the poor would never do these things unless they were miserably poor, unless they were in that state of abject poverty which precludes

In all countries and in all ages, centralization, over-population, and physical and mental decline have traveled hand in hand; and therefore it is that no permanent prosperity has ever yet resulted from the attempt to establish the supremacy of trade. In none has that attempt been made more continuously and consistently than in England; and therefore is it that all the phenomena she now presents are those of a system that is to be maintained so long as, and no longer than, the agricultural communities of this world shall show themselves willing to submit to it.

The days of Pericles were those of Athens' greatest splendor; but that splendor was only the forerunner of decline, and of moral and political death; the little landed proprietors having even then diminished in number; land having become more and more monopolized; and men having come to be regarded as little else than mere machines. The most splendid days of Rome were those of the Antonines; but even then she tottered to her fall, so near at hand. As had been before the case in Athens, the base of the societary structure had gradually narrowed, the free laborer having disappeared from the soil, and the land itself having become vested in

instruction, and by destroying all hope for the future, reduces man, like the brutes, to seek for nothing beyond the gratification of present wants."—*Espriella's Letters*, Letter xxxvii.

"The whole mass of human life, as seen in England at the present day, presents violent extremes of condition, huge mountains of wealth and luxury, contrasted with awful depths of poverty and wretchedness; but in respect of mental ability, we find immense flats of uniformity, dead levels of respectable talent, with scarcely any such thing as originality, freshness, or high creative genius in any department of literature, art, science, or even trade."—Johnson, *England as it is*, vol. i. p. 217.

No system has ever been devised so destructive of human happiness and morals as that denounced by Dr. Smith, and justly described in the following passages from a speech made some years since on the occasion of an election at Bradford, in Yorkshire:—

"That system is based on foreign competition. Now I assert, that under the *buy-cheap-and-sell-dear principle, brought to bear on foreign competition, the ruin of the working and small trading classes must go on.* Why? Labor is the creator of all wealth. A man must work before a grain is grown, or a yard woven. But there is no self-employment for the working-man in this country. Labor is a hired commodity, a thing in the market that is bought and sold; consequently, as labor creates all wealth, labor is the first thing bought.—'Buy cheap! buy cheap!' Labor is bought in the cheapest market. But now comes the next: 'Sell dear! sell dear!' Sell what? *Labor's produce.* To whom? To the foreigner—ay! *and to the laborer himself;* for labor, not being self-employed, the laborer is *not* the

absentee proprietors.* Like causes produce like effects, and the historian of future times may find that the period of England's greatest splendor had been the period in which property in land had become the privilege of the few—that in which the free laborer was gradually disappearing from

partaker of the first-fruits of his toil. 'Buy cheap, sell dear!' How do you like it? Buy the working-man's labor cheaply, and sell back to that very working-man the produce of his own labor dear! The principle of inherent loss is in the bargain. The employer buys the labor cheap—he sells, and on the sale he must make a profit; he sells to the working-man himself; and thus every bargain between employer and employed is a deliberate cheat on the part of the employer. Thus labor has to sink through eternal loss, that capital may rise through lasting fraud. But the system stops not here. *This is brought to bear on foreign competition—which means, that we must ruin the trade of other countries, as we have ruined the labor of our own.* How does it work? The high-taxed country has to undersell the low-taxed. *Competition abroad is constantly increasing, consequently cheapness must increase also.* Therefore, wages in England must keep constantly falling. And how do they effect the fall? By *surplus labor.* How do they obtain the surplus labor? By monopoly of the land, which drives more hands than are wanted into the factory. By monopoly of machinery, which drives those hands into the street; by woman-labor, which drives the man from the shuttle; by child-labor, which drives the woman from the loom. Then planting their foot upon that living base of surplus, they press its aching heart beneath their heel, and cry—'Starvation! Who'll work? A half loaf is better than no bread at all!'—and the writhing mass grasps greedily at their terms. Such is the system for the working-man. But, electors, how does it operate on you? how does it affect the home trade, the shopkeeper, poor rate, and taxation? *For every increase of competition abroad, there must be an increase of cheapness at home.* Every increase of cheapness of labor is based on an increase of labor surplus, and this surplus is obtained by an increase of machinery. I repeat, how does this operate on you? The Manchester liberal on my left establishes a new patent, and throws three hundred men as a surplus in the streets. Shopkeepers! three hundred customers less! Rate-payers! three hundred paupers more! But, mark me! the evil stops not here. *These three hundred men operate first to bring down the wages of those who remain at work in their trade.* The employer says:—'Now I reduce your wages.' The men demur. Then he adds:—'Do you see those three hundred men who have just walked out? *You may change places if you like;* they are sighing to come in on any terms, for they're starving.' The men feel it, and are crushed. Ah, you Manchester Liberal! Pharisee of politics! Those men are listening—have I got you now? But the evil stops not yet. *Those men, driven from their own trade, seek employment in others, when they swell the surplus, and bring wages down.*"

* "The Scotch miners' strike, the most extensive and bitterly contested which has ever been known in the west of Scotland, may be

the soil—that in which the Ricardo-Malthusian doctrine had been invented—and that in which man was becoming, from day to day, more and more a mere instrument to be used by trade.*

held to have terminated. When it was at its height, about six weeks since, at least 40,000 men were engaged in it, remaining in a state of voluntary idleness. It is calculated that the sacrifice in wages alone amounted to more than £500,000; but to this must be added the loss of masters' profits, and the dislocation of business endured by all who depend on the coal and iron-mining trades. The men have returned to their work in a very gloomy mood, and under a burning sense of injustice."—*London Paper*, June 11, 1856.

* "While bread and meat are rising in price, man is growing cheaper. The reason we shall be told, why man is so cheap, and woman too, is that 'the supply exceeds the demand;' but this is really nonsense." . . . . "The true reason why men are so cheap, is that the whole system of our laws and government rests upon the principle, that we should have a reverent care of the material productions, and leave the men to take care of themselves." . . . . "It is not the dress-maker we consider, but the dress; it is not the butcher whose well-being we care for, but the meat; it is not the grocer whose moral and physical condition is the object, but the grocery; it is not the baker or the bread-eater whose sole satisfaction we seek, but the bread. Nor is it even these goods for the sake of their utility to man, it is the goods as salable commodities alone. The bread may be adulterated, so that it passes and gets the price of a loaf; it is the same with the butcher's meat, it may rot; with the gown, it may be of counterfeit stuff. But it is the *trade* in the gown, the meat, the grocery, the bread, etc., that is the object of existence; and it is the trade to which our law-makers look, not the tradesman, the working-man, or the consumer."—*Leader*, July 12, 1856.

"I remembered that Adam Smith and Gibbon had told us that there would never again be a destruction of civilization by barbarians; the flood, they said, would no more return to cover the earth. And they seemed to reason justly, for they compared the immense strength of the civilized part of the world with the weakness of that part which remained savage, and asked from whence were to come those Huns and Vandals that were again to destroy civilization? Alas! it did not occur to them that in the very heart of great capitals, in the very neighborhood of splendid palaces, and churches, and theatres, and libraries, and museums, vice, ignorance, and misery might produce a race of Huns fiercer than those who marched under Attila, and Vandals more bent on destruction than those who followed Genseric."—*Macaulay*.

CHAPTER XIX.

OF VITAL CHANGES IN THE FORMS OF MATTER—CONTINUED.

1. Agricultural distress throughout the world, consequent upon the return of peace in 1815. Cause thereof to be found in the decline of manufactures, and in the separation of the consumer from the producer, in all the countries of the world, outside of Britain. General adoption of measures looking to counteraction of the British policy.

§ 2. Few natural advantages of Denmark. Following in the lead of France, her policy looks, however, to the approximation of the consumer and the producer, and the relief of her farmers from the tax of transportation. Consequent prosperity of her people. Steady enlargement of the agricultural base of society. Constant increase in the power of association and combination—in the development of individuality—and in the power of further progress.

§ 3. Decline of Spanish manufactures, diminution in the power of association, and decay of agriculture, consequent upon the expulsion of the Moors, and the acquisition of distant colonies. Loss of those colonies followed by the adoption of a system tending to promote the growth of commerce, and diminish the traders' power. Great increase in the value of land, and in the freedom of man.

§ 1. The peace which in 1815 closed the wars of the French Revolution, was hailed as the precursor of universal prosperity, but in its place it brought universal ruin. The mills and furnaces of America, as well as those of Continental Europe, were closed, because of the inability of farmers to purchase cloth or iron; and farmers were ruined because of the inability of artisans to purchase food. Under the Continental system manufactures had grown up in Germany, Russia, and other countries, while measures of non-intercourse with Great Britain, and the war of 1812, had produced the same effect in these United States. With the peace those manufactures disappeared, and the farmer ceased to be able to make exchanges except through the medium of foreign mills and furnaces. The man who *must* go to market, *must pay the cost of getting there*, let that cost take what form it may; and from the moment the mills of Germany were closed, and her farmers compelled to seek abroad a market for any portion of their products, however small, *the price obtained for that small quantity determined that of the greatly larger one consumed at home.* The more that needs to go abroad the greater is the decline in the central market, the larger become the sacrifices of the farmer, and the more perfect his dependence on foreign masters. With the disappearance of manufactures throughout the countries we have named, the less became the power at home to pay for food, the greater the proportion of the crop pressing upon a dim-

lucrative foreign market, and the more decided and universal the decline in the prices of all raw materials, land and labor included. With each succeeding day the laborer became more dependent upon his employer, and thus was furnished proof conclusive of the truth of the idea that the raising of raw materials for foreign markets is the proper work of the slave and the barbarian, and of them alone. The trader, however, profited, because there was increased demand for his services. The ship-owner profited, because it made a demand for ships. The government-officer profited, because he had more food for less money. The annuitant profited, because his five per cent. purchased more food and cloth than ten had done before. The land-owner suffered, for he received but little rent; and the workman suffered, for he could not sell his labor.

This state of affairs, which made of peace a greater calamity than war had been, led to the almost simultaneous adoption, both in Europe and America, of measures looking to an increase of the power of association, the policy that had been seen to be so successfully pursued by both France and England. The movement in Germany which led in 1835 to the German Customs-Union, or Zoll-Verein, commenced in 1820, Russia and these United States following in 1824. Since then the relative positions of France and England have greatly changed; the former having steadily adhered to the policy which seeks the extension of commerce; while the latter has directed all her energies to the consolidation of the trader's power. Thus far the latter has found no imitators but in these United States; Denmark and Spain, Russia, Sweden, and Germany, having continued to follow in the lead of France. What have been the results will now be shown.

§ 2. Compared with Ireland, India, or Turkey, Denmark is a poor country. "She has," says one of the most enlightened of British travelers, "no metals or minerals, no fire power, or water-power;" nor "any products or capabilities for becoming a manufacturing country for supplying foreign consumers." Having no harbors on the North Sea, her navigation is confined to the Baltic; and "her commerce is naturally limited to the home consumption of the necessaries and luxuries of civilized life which the export of her corn and other agricultural products enables her to import." "She stands alone, in her corner of the world, exchanging her loaf of bread which she can spare, for articles which she cannot provide for herself; but still providing for herself every thing she can by her own industry."

That industry is protected by heavy import duties imposed avowedly for the purpose of protecting commerce by bringing together the producer and the consumer. "The greater part of their clothing," says Mr. Laing, "linen, mixed linen and cotton, and woollen cloth, is home-made. The flax and wool are grown and manufactured on the peasant's farm; the spinning and weaving done in the house; the bleaching, dyeing, and frilling done at home or in the village."

The manufacture of clothing finds employment for almost the whole female population of the country, and for a considerable portion of the males during the winter months, and thus gives value to labor and skill that would otherwise be wasted. Under a different system, the money price of clothing would be less; but what would become of this labor-power? What would be *its* money value? Capital must be consumed in its production, and if, when produced, it be not put to use, that capital must be wasted, as we see to be the case in Ireland.

The whole Danish system tends to the local employment of labor and capital, and therefore to the growth of wealth, the division of land, and the improvement of agriculture. As a consequence, there is a large and constantly increasing proportion of the real estate held in small farms. In the duchies of Holstein and Schleswig, with a population of 662,500 souls, there are no less than 125,150 small proprietors of a class "corresponding to the small freeholders of the north of England." The poorest laboring householder has a garden, some land, and a cow, while the larger farmers "attend the English cattle-shows, are educated men, acquainted with every agricultural improvement, and have meetings and cattle-shows of their own, and publish the transactions and essays of the members. They use guano, and all the animal and chemical manures, have introduced tile-draining, machinery for making pipes and tiles, and are no strangers to irrigation on their old grass meadows." The house accommodation is good, the country people being "well lodged in buildings the materials of whose walls are brick, and the floors of wood." Every parish has its schoolmaster, as well as minister; and the teachers are "men of much higher education than their Scotch brethren." Education, literature, and literary tastes, being universally diffused, libraries, museums, and newspapers are found in all the large towns, while in "every little one, the traveler finds educational institutions and indications of intellectual development, such as the taste for reading, music, theatrical representations, which he cannot but admit surpass what he finds in England among the same classes."

The Danish system looks to the development of individuality; and therefore is it that even in the poorest houses the windows "rarely want a bit of ornamental drapery, and are always decked with flowers and plants in pots," the whole people "having a passion for flowers," and having "leisure to be happy, amused, and educated."

The material and intellectual condition of this people is declared by Mr. Laing to be higher than that of any other in Europe; while Mr. Kay places the people of England among the most ignorant and most helpless. "The houseless are unknown," and employment is fixed and stationary, because there is no foreign trade "to occasion great and sudden activity and expansion in manufactures, and equally sudden stagnation and relapse," such as periodically occur in all countries whose policy looks to increasing the dependence on machinery of transportation and of trade.

§ 3. In no part of Europe did there exist, a few centuries since, so great a diversification of employments as in the South of Spain; in none was commerce so great. With a constant succession of wars there came a change; the enlightened and industrious Moors were expelled, and centralization of the power of directing thought and action was established, at the moment when the discoveries in the East and West gave power to the crown to direct the forces of the nation to wars of conquest. But here, as everywhere else, centralization has gone hand in hand with poverty and weakness. Before that period the kingdom contained thirty millions of people, whereas it has now but half that number; and the population of its largest cities now numbers not more than one-fourth to one-eighth what it once had been. In 1778 there were counted 1511 abandoned villages. The great middle class of artisans had died out, and land had become more and more consolidated in the hands of the nobles and the Church. Commerce had been destroyed, and the necessity for the transporter's services had greatly grown. Raw materials of every kind, in their passage from the place of production to that of consumption, were burthened with heavy imposts. The whole system tended effectually to prevent the artisan from taking his place beside the grower of food and wool; hence the depopulation and weakness of a country that had been once so powerful.

Fortunately for Spain, the day arrived when she was to lose her colonies, and be compelled to look at home for revenue. From that day to the present, her course, though slow, has been steadily onward, each year having brought with it increased diversity of employment, and greater power of association and combination. Among the earliest measures looking to the emancipation of France and Germany, was the removal of restrictions upon the commerce in land, the great instrument of production; and so has it been in Spain. Forty years since but twenty millions of acres were owned by the men employed in cultivation, while twice that quantity was held by the nobles and the Church. The property of the latter having since been sold, the number of small proprietors has more than doubled.

A further step toward freedom was found in the abolition of taxes by which the internal commerce had been impeded, and most especially those on the transport of raw materials, and in the substitution of a land tax payable alike by the great and the small proprietor. As a consequence of all this, and of the maintenance of efficient protection against foreign interference, the cotton, woollen, silk, linen, and iron manufactures have since advanced with great rapidity. With growing proximity of the market, likewise, agriculture is becoming more a science. Thirty years since, the value of its products was but 232,000,000 of reals; whereas it is now more than thrice that sum. The means of transportation were then so bad that men might die of famine in Andalusia, while grain was wasting on the fields of Castile. Even yet, prices are extremely different in the several parts of the kingdom; but with the construction of railroads and the rapid development of internal commerce the modes of communication have been so much improved as closely to approximate the prices paid by the consumer and those received by the producer.

With increased power of association there is a steady improvement in the provision for mental culture. Half a century since the number of students at all the educational establishments was but 30,000. Now, the number in the public schools alone, for which there is a large annual appropriation, is as 1 to 15 of the total population.

The effect of the changes above described is seen in a great increase of the value of land. The church property that has been sold has commanded an average of nearly double the price at which it was officially assessed; and we need desire no better evidence of progress than thus is furnished.

The progress of Spain has been already great, but it is slower than it should be, because both France and England are engaged in the effort to prevent the growth of manufactures in the Peninsula, believing, apparently, that their own increase in wealth and power is dependent on the extent to which they can impoverish their neighbors. At an expense ten times exceeding the profit on the trade with Spain England retains Gibraltar, to be used, in defiance of treaty stipulations, as a smuggling depot; and her economists discern much advantage in the existing relations with Portugal, because of the facilities thus afforded for sending woollens and cottons "by contraband into Spain." In trade and war the end is held to sanctify the means; and as the British policy looks only to the extension of trade, it is natural that British teachers should have arrived at the conclusion that the smuggler is "the great reformer of the age," and that their government should afford every facility for the violation of the laws of all countries that seek, by means of protection, to promote the growth of foreign and domestic commerce.

A more short-sighted policy than that of both those nations towards Spain cannot be imagined. By keeping her poor, they destroy her productive power, and prevent her from obtaining the ability to purchase the products of the land and labor of their people. The total amount of their joint sales to her scarcely exceeds, as we believe, the sum annually expended in the effort to prevent her from manufacturing for herself. Rich in ores, and abounding in fertile land that is poorly, even where at all, cultivated, were she permitted to carry into full effect a policy looking to the development of her mineral resources—to the utilization of the products of her soil that now are wasted—to the husbanding of the powers of her people—and to the enlargement of domestic commerce—she would, in a few years, be enabled to purchase from abroad twice as much, and thus aid in the improvement of the condition of the people of both France and England—while relieving both from the heavy expense to which, in the effort to govern her, they now subject themselves. Common sense, common honesty, and true policy, travel always together whether in private or in public life; and where they are most combined, population tends most rapidly to increase, with constant decline in the dread of over-population.

CHAPTER XX.

OF VITAL CHANGES IN THE FORMS OF MATTER—CONTINUED.

§ 1. The German manufacturing system due to the revocation of the Edict of Nantes. Its gradual development down to the close of the war in 1815. Its decline, under the free trade system which followed the peace. First Prussian tariff having for its object the diversification of the employments of the people.

§ 2. Gradual formation of the *Zoll-Verein*, or Customs Union. Great increase of foreign and domestic commerce consequent upon the adoption of measures tending to the emancipation of German land from the oppressive tax of transportation. Protection having cheapened finished commodities, Germany now exports them. Having raised the prices of raw materials, they are now imported.

§ 3. Growing division of the land, accompanied by an enlargement of the proportions borne by the agricultural class to the mass of which society is composed. Increased respect for the rights of property, consequent upon its more general diffusion among the people. Steady increase in the freedom of man, and in the strength of the State.

§ 4. Rude character of Russian agriculture half a century since. Growth of manufactures under the Continental system of Napoleon. Their disappearance under the free trade system. Re-adoption of the policy of Colbert, and its effects. Great increase in the quantity and value of agricultural products since the re-adoption of protection.

§ 5. Increase in the competition for the purchase of the laborer's services and growing freedom of man.

§ 6. Obstacles standing in the way of the creation of a scientific agriculture. Communism and its effects.

§ 7. Growing individuality among the people, with corresponding growth of strength in the State.

§ 8. Sweden, like Russia, follows in the lead of France—maintaining the policy of Colbert, to the exclusion of that advocated by the economists of Britain. Its effects, as exhibited in bringing the consumer and producer into close proximity to each other. Comparative movement of the population, and of the supply of food.

§ 9. Division of land and increase of its value—resulting from its emancipation from the tax of transportation. Intellectual development, consequent upon the creation of local centres of activity.

§ 10. Social decentralization gradually correcting the errors of political centralization.

§ 11. Differing in race, habits, manners, and religion, France and Germany, Spain and Denmark, Sweden and Russia, are agreed in nothing, except in the maintenance of a policy which looks to the promotion of association, the extension of commerce, and the emancipation of the land from the tax of transportation, in accordance with the ideas of Adam Smith. In all of them agriculture steadily advances, the land becomes more divided, and men become more free. Agreeing in nothing else, Portugal and Turkey, Ireland and India, unite in the maintenance of the policy advocated by the Ricardo-Malthusian school. In all of them agriculture declines, the land becomes consolidated, and the freedom of man has almost wholly passed away.

"GERMANY," says Professor List, the man to whose patriotic labors the existence of the *Zoll-Verein*, or Customs Union, is due,—"Germany owes her first progress in manufactures to the revocation of the Edict of Nantes, and to the numerous refugees who brought with them the manufactures of woollens, silks, glass, china, gloves, jewellery, and many other articles."

The first public steps for the encouragement of German manufactures were taken by Austria and Prussia; in the former, under Charles VI. and Maria Theresa, but more especially under Joseph II. Austria had previously suffered much from the expulsion of the Protestants, her most industrious inhabitants; nevertheless, by the aid of protective duties, improvements in the rearing of sheep, construction of roads, etc., the industrial arts made remarkable progress even under the reign of Maria Theresa; and still greater under that of Joseph II., in spite of the precipitation with which that monarch urged on measures of reform for which the country was not yet prepared.

Prussia had suffered much from the Thirty Years' War; her cloth manufacture had been almost annihilated, and the larger part of the manufacturers had transferred themselves to Saxony. At the Revocation of the Edict of Nantes, however, a great number of the fugitives, encouraged by the Great Elector, settled in Prussia, and introduced many new branches of industry. Succeeding rulers, especially Frederick II., promoted agriculture, and stimulated home manufactures, by means of a revenue system the provisions of which were of a highly protective character.

The Continental system of Napoleon, however, constitutes the great era in the history of German as well as of French industry; for under it commenced the forward progress of every kind of manufacture, with corresponding increase in the attention to the breeding of sheep, the production of wool, and the development of domestic commerce. "On the return of peace, however," continues List, the English, who had greatly improved their machinery, renewed their rivalry; and general ruin and distress ensued, especially in the country of the Lower Rhine, which after being for some years attached to France, now lost her markets. At length, in 1818, the cry of distress could no longer be unheeded, and now a Prussian tariff gave the protection needed against that inundation of English goods by means of which Great Britain sought to stifle in the cradle the industry of other nations.* Very moderate in its duties, this tariff had the merit of being *specific*, and not *ad valorem*, thus not only preventing frauds and smuggling, but also encouraging the production of those articles of coarse manufacture the quantity and bulk of which

* It was at this period that Mr., now Lord, Brougham, declared in his seat in the House of Commons, that "England could afford to bear some loss on the export of her goods, *for the purpose of destroying foreign manufactures in the cradle;*" and that the well-known liberal, Mr. Hume, also expressed the desire that "*the manufactures of the Continent might be strangled in the cradle.*"

gives them their great importance. This measure, however, was a heavy blow to the smaller States of Germany, already excluded from the markets of Austria, France, and England, many of which, too, were enclosed within the Prussian limits.

§ 2. Germany was, at that date, entirely disunited, each State having its local custom-houses. In 1819, however, Prussia effected an arrangement with Mecklenburg, Saxe-Weimar, and other States, in virtue of which her tariff became the general one, and the internal custom-houses disappeared. Prussia continued her efforts for inducing other States to join in a general system, but for some time without effect; the opposition being headed by Hanover, then entirely under British influence, by Saxony, and by Hesse. At length, however, in 1831, Hesse joined the Prussian league, and from that day the German Union dates its existence.

Thus was accomplished the most important European movement of the present century. By means of it Northern Germany has become one great society, with entire freedom of circulation, its several States retaining their perfect individuality, governing themselves in their own manner, and possessing all the local centres of activity that had before existed. The effect is shown by the following facts:—

In 1825 Germany *exported* to England alone 28,000,000 pounds of wool, mostly paid for by the return of the same wool in the form of cloth. In 1851 the net quantity *imported* into Germany was 25,000,000, and the quantity of cloth *exported*, was 12,000,000. Not less, thus, than 50,000,000 pounds has been added to the domestic consumption, a consequence of that approximation of the prices of raw materials and of finished merchandize by means of which the producer of food and of wool had become enabled to consume a much larger quantity of the commodities produced. The import of cotton, and cotton twist had, in the meantime, so largely grown, that the export of cotton cloth, more than ten years since, amounted to 159,241 cwts., leaving for domestic consumption, 1,200,000 cwts., and proving that while cloth had become cheap, the power of consumption among the agricultural population had greatly grown.

Thirty years since, Germany supplied the world with rags, and imported most of the paper for which she could make demand. Since then, the net *import* of rags has exceeded 40,000,000 pounds, while the *export* of paper has become very large. The prices of the two had greatly approximated, causing a home consumption that absorbed not merely the largely increased quantity of rags produced at home, but, in addition, more than thirty millions of pounds of those obtained from abroad.

In 1830 the total quantity of coal mined was but 8,200,000 *tonnes*, of 391 lbs. each. In 1854 it amounted to 46,000,000. In 1834 there were made 76,000 tons of bar iron. In 1850 the quantity had risen to 200,000, and that of pig iron to 600,000 tons. In 1849, not a furnace was to be seen in the neighborhood of Minden, Westphalia; "now," says a recent traveler, "they stand like towers about the broad plain." Of the numerous copper-mines of Prussia, a large proportion have been opened within the last few years. Every mine, mill, and furnace, aids in the improvement of the roads, the utilization of the powers of nature, and the development of individual faculties; thus increasing the value of man while diminishing that of all the commodities required for his use.

The value of the cotton and woollen goods exported in 1851 was $25,000,000, the chief part of which consisted of the food that had been combined with the wool in the process of converting it into cloth. As a consequence of this, the necessity for seeking abroad a market for food had so greatly diminished, that the *net* export from the country which thirty years since was regarded as the great granary of Europe, had fallen to 10,000,000 bushels.

Prussia has now a mile of railroad for every five square miles of surface; and local combination, as evidenced by the formation of joint stock companies for mining coal, making cloth, constructing roads, building steamers, or granting security against loss by fire, is increasing with a rapidity that is scarcely anywhere else exceeded. With every step in that direction local centres spring up, the demand for labor grows, and the farmer finds the market brought nearer to his door, with constantly increasing power to command the use of improved machinery—*the societary motion, whatsoever its direction, being one of constant acceleration.*

The facts above given prove conclusively—

I. That the prices of raw products have tended upwards, to the benefit of German farmers, and to that of the agricultural interest of the world at large:

II. That the prices of all manufactured commodities have tended downward, enabling the farmer to profit doubly: first, by obtaining more of the precious metals for his corn;

second, by obtaining more cloth for any given quantity of those metals:

III. That the reduction in the cost of conversion has been so great as to enable the German people largely to supply the world with food and wool in the form of cloth; and thus to aid the farmers everywhere in obtaining supplies of clothing:

IV. That the improved condition of German farmers has enabled them greatly to increase their demands upon the tropical countries for cotton, coffee, rice, and other rude products of the earth:

V. That under the system of Colbert, now adopted in that country, commerce grows steadily, with corresponding decline in the trader's power:

VI. That with the increase of commerce there has been a rapid increase of individuality in the great community that has now been formed, manifested by a steady and regular increase of public and private revenue.

These results correspond precisely, as the reader will perceive, with those obtained in France, Spain, and Denmark; while they are directly the reverse of those observed in Ireland and India, Turkey and Portugal, all of which latter are subjected to the British system.

§ 3. In no country has there been a more rapid increase than is here observed in the diversification of employment. Everywhere men are beginning to combine the labors of the workshop with those of the field and garden; thus benefiting their health by out-door labor, and adding to their comfort by the power of raising their own milk and vegetables; while the farmer, being enabled to raise a succession of crops, is placed more beyond the reach of those accidents by which those who are dependent on a single crop are so often ruined. Under these circumstances, every kind of soil is utilized, and agriculture becomes a science. "Everywhere," says an eminent agricultural writer, "there is a singular and increasing interest in the breeding of cattle," while "almost universal progress has been made in the cultivation of the soil."

The land is being more and more divided, and is highest in price where small properties are most numerous. "People of all classes," says Mr. Kay, in his excellent volumes on *the Social Condition of the people of England and the Continent*, "are able to become proprietors. Shopkeepers and the laborers of the towns purchase gardens outside the town, where they and their families work in the fine evenings, in raising vegetables and fruits for their households; farmers purchase the land they used formerly to rent; and the peasants purchase farms of their own." The possession of property produces here, as everywhere, respect for the rights of property. "All the poor have friends or relations who are proprietors," and each feels that he may some day become so himself. All are, consequently, "immediately interested in the preservation of property, and in watching over the rights and interests of their neighbors."

As employments become diversified, man becomes more and more free. Eighty years since, the Elector of Hesse sold large numbers of his poor subjects to England to aid her in establishing unlimited control over these her American colonies. The German people generally were then enslaved, badly fed, clothed, and lodged, and ruled by petty tyrants. The language of the higher classes was French, German having been then considered as fit only for the poor serf. German literature was then but struggling into existence. Little was known of the mechanic arts, and the machinery used in agriculture was of the very rudest kind. Even later, a *quasi* slave trade furnished cargoes to most of the vessels that passed between America and the German cities. Men, women, and children, were then brought out and sold for terms of years, and many of the most respectable people of the Middle States are descended from those "indented" German servants. Now, Germany stands first in Europe in point of intellectual development, and is advancing in the physical and moral condition of her people with a rapidity exceeding that of any other portion of the Eastern hemisphere.

§ 4. With an immense territory and a scattered population, Russia was, half a century since, an almost purely agricultural country, in which man was the slave of his fellow-man. Manufactures having been then almost unknown, caravans laden with the products of British and other foreign workshops, traversed the interior and supplied even the distant tribes of Asia. Even so late as 1825 the country was compelled to look abroad for the cloth required for army purposes.

Russian produce having then to seek the markets of the world in its rudest form, burdened with enormous charges for transportation, there was little power for maintaining foreign commerce, and the imports, small as they were, consisted chiefly in articles of luxury demanded by the masters of the serfs.

The Continental system gave to manufactures a temporary impulse, but with the close of the war there came a fearful change in the opposite direction. The Emperor Alexander having taken his lessons in political economy from a thorough believer in the omnipotence of trade, determined to carry into practical effect the lessons he had learned, and the results speedily exhibited themselves in the fact, that British goods flowed in, Russian gold flowed out, the currency became largely depreciated, the government was paralyzed, and the manufacturers were ruined.

The year 1824 witnessed the inauguration of a new system, looking to increase in the power of association throughout the empire, and harmonizing with the system pursued by France. Commerce and manufactures began again to grow, and with such rapidity that, ten years later, Russian cloth was sent to the Asiatic fairs. Since then, Central Asia has been chiefly supplied by the products of Russian looms, while even in Affghanistan and China they have been rapidly supplanting British cloths, although the latter have had great advantage in point of transportation.

From that time until quite recently the protective policy has been steadily maintained, and its effects in economizing human power have exhibited themselves in the constantly improving condition of the people; as shown by the following facts derived chiefly from the work of M. Tegoborski on the productive forces of the Empire, published a few years since.

The value in money of the agricultural produce was then $1,600,000,000. This, however, gives but a small idea of the quantity, which is treble that of France, although the distance of the market causes the total price to be somewhat less. The quantity of cereals produced was given at 1,600,000,000 of bushels. Prices, too, had risen with remarkable steadiness, while the export of wheat had averaged but 15,000,000 bushels, or *less than one per cent. of the total cereal product.* What becomes of all the vast amount of food produced? It is consumed by the people who make cloth, build houses and factories, mine gold, iron ore, and coal, build ships, and perform the various services incident to an extensive domestic commerce. The number of persons more or less employed in the flax and hemp manufactures alone was then estimated at 5,000,000, and the consumption of linen cloth at 550,000,000 yards, or 9 yards per head of the population. This branch of manufacture was found everywhere, and "had its seat in the humblest cabins." The consumption of wool was about 100,000,000 pounds, or 1¾ pounds per head, and made demand for a large amount of labor to be employed in its conversion into cloth.

The first cotton mill was then but little more than twenty years old, yet were there then no less than 495 factories, employing 112,427 operatives. The peasants received the yarn from the contractors, and occupied themselves in weaving during the winter. Much cotton velvet was manufactured for China, such as had formerly been supplied from English looms. In five years—from 1846 to 1850—the importation of raw cotton had doubled, while that of yarn, for which the country had been entirely dependent upon Britain, had much diminished. The production of iron had steadily increased, while that of gold and silver had risen to more than $20,000,000.

Throughout Russia, the tendency to local activity and combination is very great indeed. In some parts of the country all are potters; in another, all are rope and harness-makers. On one estate, all are makers of candles; on another, of felt hats; on a third, they are smiths, employed chiefly in making axes. The families of a district unite in a sort of joint-stock company, selling the product of their labor and dividing among themselves the proceeds.

Nor is it in the coarser manufactures, alone, that Russia is successful. The ingenuity and skill of her workmen are becoming conspicuous in all departments of industry, as was proved but a few years since on the occasion of the Great Exhibition in the English Crystal Palace. The labor thus given is, all of it, *power economized that would otherwise be wasted.* As that economy grows, men become more free, while communities increase in power.

§ 5. Resistance to the system which looks to cheapening labor and raw materials, is everywhere attended by increase in the freedom of the laborer. So has it been in Russia; the great proprietors having permitted their serfs, on payment of a small annual rent, to sell their own labor at its market price. This was a preparation for the emancipation that has been since effected.

In that direction, however, had tended every measure of the government. In 1827, the serf had been declared an integral part of the soil, and thus had been abolished the trade in human flesh. Shortly after, a great bank had been established for making loans to the great land-owners on conditions which had tended to make the crown proprietor; and the serfs, in becoming crown peasants, became tax-payers, free to employ, at their pleasure, both their land and labor. Next, to the serf had been secured the right of possessing property, of entering into contracts, and of testifying in a court of justice. As yet, he could not buy his own freedom, but he became free by the purchase of the soil to which he was attached, and the hope to accomplish this stimulated his industry, formed him to habits of frugality and sobriety, and thus made preparation for his ultimate entire freedom.

§ 6. The reader must bear in mind that the subject under consideration is the question of *progress, not of actual condition*. Russia still labors under immense difficulties, resulting from the almost universal existence of the *communal* system. Everywhere throughout the empire land remains undivided, being held in common and distributed annually among the members of the commune. As under such circumstances there can be no permanent property in land, there are few inducements to devote labor to the making of any permanent improvements upon it. Agriculture, therefore, makes but little progress, trade and manufactures withdrawing labor from it. Whatever may be the accumulations resulting from trade, they remain the private property of the individual, and at his death he may bequeath them to his wife and children; whereas, however great may be the money value added to the land, that value becomes the property of the community, no part of it remaining with the family of the man by whose labors the improvements have been made.

Communism is everywhere the same, whether we meet with it in Russia or in France, in the customs of a people, or amongst teachers who fail to see that the power of association grows with the development of individuality, and seek to promote the growth of the former by the destruction of the latter. As now presented in the books of communistic teachers, it can be regarded only as a project for reducing man to a state of barbarism, and hence it is that all efforts at its introduction among civilized men have, thus far, so signally failed.

Such are some of the obstacles standing in the way of

scientific agriculture. They are great, but great as they are, they are much exceeded in amount by those resulting from the want that still exists, of the proper diversification of employments, without which association and combination cannot take place. Throughout large portions of the empire, the farmer cannot, in any manner, vary the objects of his cultivation. He *must* confine himself to those commodities alone which will bear transportation; and he cannot raise potatoes, turnips, hay, or any other of the bulky articles which require to be consumed at home. He *must* exhaust his land, and his crops *must* therefore diminish, with constant increase in the liability to disease, by which they are so often swept away—reducing his family and himself to poverty, if not starvation. He *must* confine himself to the cultivation of the poorer soils, so large a portion of the crop being consumed in the work of transportation that he is unable to obtain machinery by help of which to clear and drain the rich ones. He thus becomes from year to year more and more the slave of nature, and, as a consequence, more and more dependent upon the chances of trade, and slave to his fellow-man. If the crops of Western Europe prove large, he finds himself to be nearly ruined. Therefore is he forced to pray for droughts and frosts, and other causes of damage to his fellow-men; and all because of his inability to determine for himself how to employ his labor and his land. Commerce would give him that power, and enable him to rejoice in the prosperity of other nations; but commerce now grows nowhere in the absence of the system inaugurated by that first of modern statesmen, Colbert.

The differences of price in the various parts of the empire are enormous—rye being in one place worth less than 1 rouble per tchetwert, while in another it sells at more than 11, and wheat varying between 2 and 13 roubles. Such is the taxation resulting from a necessity for dependence on distant markets.

§ 7. The system of centralization sought to be established by the British people requires cheap labor at home and abroad, and tends everywhere to its production. The less the domestic commerce, the greater is the dependence of other nations on the people who have ships and wagons; and the less is their power to develop the resources of their land, or to increase the quantity of raw materials requiring to be transported. This, of course, leads to efforts at stimulation of the various communities of the world into competition with each other for the sale of raw products in the distant market, to their own great injury, but to the present, though only temporary, benefit of the distant trader; who thus kills the goose that he may obtain the golden eggs. The more wool that can be obtained from Australia, the greater must be the decline in price of that of Russia; the more cotton and hemp that can be obtained from India, the lower must be the prices of Russian hemp and American cotton; and the greater must be the dependence of the agriculturists of both upon the chances and changes of the distant market, and upon the combinations that there so readily are formed. Hence it is that we witness among the purely agricultural communities of the world so entire an absence of the power of self-government—so great an inability to make the roads that are so much required—and so complete a dependence upon the distant trader for all the machinery of trade and transportation.

Individuality, whether in men or nations, grows with the growth of commerce. By aid of efficient protection it grew rapidly in Russia; and hence it has been, that she has, in the last decade, exhibited a power of resistance to assaults from without that would not have been possible had the free-trade policy been maintained, and had she continued to follow in the lead of England. That such would have been the case, is clearly shown by Mr. Cobden, who furnishes the most conclusive argument in favor of French and Russian policy, when telling his readers that "to have cut off the people of the Russian Empire," in the period from 1815 to 1824, "from all commerce with foreign countries, would have been to doom a portion of its people to nakedness." The system subsequently adopted tended towards decentralization, individuality, life, and freedom; whereas, that urged upon the world by Mr. Cobden—having for its object an increase in the necessity for the services of the trader—tends towards centralization, which is always the road towards slavery and death.

§ 8. Sweden is naturally a very poor country, much of its surface being hilly, and even mountainous, and the soil and climate but little favorable to agriculture. In her commercial policy she has followed the lead of France, her system having been based upon the idea of bringing the consumer and the producer together, and thus diminishing the tax of transportation. Thirty years since,* her tariff was slightly modified in the direction of free trade, but six years later that step was retraced, protection having been then restored. Let us now examine what have been the effects.

The manufacture of cotton goods in 1831 was about 2,000,000 ells; but ten years later it had risen to 6,000,000. In the former the import of raw cotton was 800,000 pounds; in the latter it had reached 1,800,000, and in 1852 was one half more. The import of hemp, hides, and wool, had also steadily increased. The manufacture of woollen cloth is found everywhere throughout the country, in the houses of the peasants, giving employment to time and mind that would otherwise be wasted; and yet the cloth annually made in larger establishments exceeded, ten years since, 1,200,000 yards. In the short space of thirteen years the iron manufacture had nearly doubled. In the single year 1853 no fewer than 327 new mines were opened, and double that number of old works re-opened.

The movement of population has been as follows:—

1751.........1,795,000 1805.........2,414,000 1853.........3,482,000

We have here a constantly accelerated movement, giving increased power of association and combination, and facilitating the further growth of wealth.

The quantity of physical and mental effort given to the work of conversion has, as the reader has seen, greatly increased, yet so far has this been from producing a diminution in the power to devote time and mind to the work of cultivation, that it has wonderfully increased, as is shown by the following facts:—In the ten years ending 1787, the average import of grain was 196,000,000 pounds, or 100 pounds per head. In the decade ending 1853 it was but 34,000,000, while the population had almost doubled. That the people were far better fed in the latter period than in the former is proved by their greatly increased purchase of cloth, food being the first of man's animal wants requiring to be satisfied. The amount of coffee, sugar, and other foreign articles consumed has greatly increased, showing that the growth of commerce at home had been attended with the increase of commerce abroad, *the power to buy the products of other nations being dependent on the power to sell one's own.*

§ 9. As commerce grows, land grows in price, and becomes divided. The peasant proprietors in Sweden were reckoned, twenty years since, at 147,974; and that the tendency is toward further division is shown in the fact, that from 1822 to 1837 the sales by noble proprietors amounted to 10,000,000 of Swedish dollars, the land thus sold being purchased in almost equal quantities by the middle and the peasant classes.

What is the condition of the small proprietors, and how manufactures and agriculture are combined throughout the larger portion of the kingdom, will be seen from a perusal of the following passages from a distinguished British traveler:

"Angermanland, in which I now am, is like a manufacturing district in England. The loom is heard in every room of every house. Every burn-side has its webs of linen on its green banks. This manufacture is entirely domestic, being carried on upon the little farm on which the flax grows, and the whole by the females of the house, except the ploughing and sowing. It is not, however, confined to linen for household use, or for family clothing. The linen is sold all over the kingdom; and at one little inn, Horsta, there was a table laid out, as we sometimes see in manufacturing districts in England, with products of the place." "These people seem to unite, on a small scale, all the advantages of a manufacturing and agricultural population more fully than in any district I have ever seen. The men do the farm business, while the women drive a not less profitable branch of industry. There is full employment at the loom, or in spinning, for the old and young of the female sex. Servants are no burden. About the houses there is all the neatness of a thriving manufacturing, and the abundance of an agricultural, population. The table linen laid down even for your glass of milk and piece of bread is always clean; the beds and sheets are always nice and white. Everybody is well clad, for their manufacturing, like their farming, is for their own use first, and the surplus only, as a secondary object, for sale; and from the number of little nick-nacks in their households, the good tables and chairs, window-curtains and blinds, (which no hut is without,) clocks, fine bedding, papered rooms, and a few books, it is evident that they lay out their winnings on their own comfort, and that these are not on a low scale of social well-being."*

The more perfect the power to maintain commerce, the greater is always the tendency towards mental development.

* *Laing, Tour in Sweden*, pp. 191–192.

It is, therefore, no matter of surprise, that here, as in Denmark, we find a rapidly growing literature developing itself in the capital, while exhibiting itself in the smaller towns in the form of well-provided book-shops. "I am here," says Mr. Laing, writing from a village in Lapland, "in a cleaner and more comfortable house than in any of our smaller towns in the north of Scotland, excepting, perhaps, Inverness, can boast of. In this little town of 1100 inhabitants, at a distance of 470 miles from the capital, there are two good booksellers' shops, in which I found a good stock of modern books, among others, the Life of Columbus, by Washington Irving, in English."

Such was the state of things nearly thirty years since, and so far as we may judge by the import of paper, the course has been steadily onward, the quantity imported having risen to 400,000 pounds in the three years ending in 1853, against 150,000 in those ending in 1846.

§ 10. The tendency to equality grows with the growth of wealth; and therefore is it that we find in Sweden a slow and gradual correction of the evils of political centralization. Thirty years since two-thirds of the land paid all the taxes, while its owners were excluded from representation in the legislative body. Now, "all who belong to the peasant class are entitled to represent and be represented in the Chamber of the Peasantry." Freedom here, as everywhere, grows with the diversification of employments, doing so despite the existence of a political centralization of the most oppressive kind. Functionaries abound to such an extent that, according to Mr. Laing, "it may truly be said that they are not made for the public business, but the public business for them." For their maintenance taxes are required amounting to no less than one-fifth of the total produce of the land, and one-nineteenth of its actual value. Much of it being exempt from taxation, the weight presses still more heavily on the small proprietors, most of whom pay to the government, in addition to their local taxes, no less than a third of the total product of land and labor.

So far as regards intercourse with foreign nations, Sweden has followed the lead of Colbert, but she yet needs a Turgot for the removal of obstacles to commerce at home.

§ 11. We have now studied the operations of six communities, differing in race, habits, manners, and religion, and agreeing only in the adoption of a system tending to increase in the power of association, and in the development of the various faculties of their members; and in the results thereby obtained. In all of them we see :—

A steady increase in the *proportion* of the labor of the community given to developing the powers of the land, and diminution in that required to be given to trade and transportation;

A great increase in the power to maintain commerce at home, with large increase in the value of land and the reward of labor;

A large increase in the power to maintain foreign commerce;

A steady increase of population and wealth;

And a growing individuality, enabling them more and more to occupy an independent position among the various nations of the earth.

Man seeks association with his fellow-man. To have association, there must be diversity of employment and development of individuality. As these are obtained, and as the consumers and producers more and more take their places by each other's side, the prices of raw materials and of finished products steadily approach each other, with constant decline in the value of all, and increase in the wealth, the power, and the value, of man; and with constant tendency to have society assume the form of greatest stability, that of a true pyramid, as here is shown :—

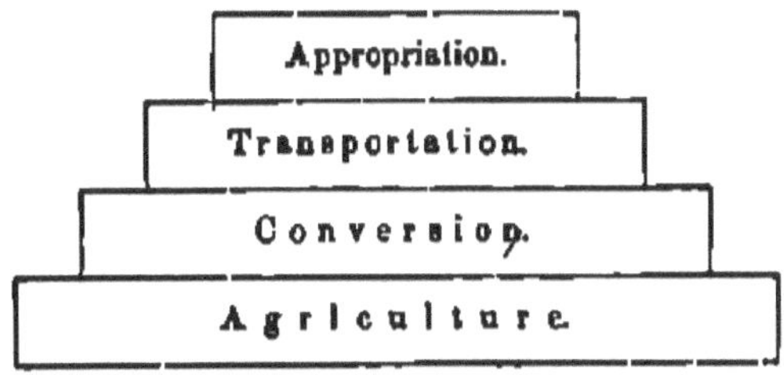

Such is the tendency in all the countries that follow in the lead of France, and in France herself.*

* The recent commercial treaty between France and England is commonly spoken of as a great free-trade measure, and yet the French tariff is, at this moment, more intelligently protective than that of these United States.

When, on the contrary, they are not obtained, and when, consequently, the prices of raw materials and of finished products recede from each other, the reverse is seen, society then assuming the form here exhibited :—

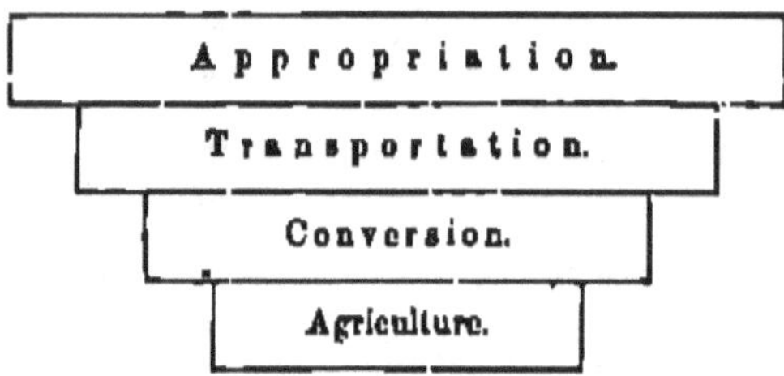

Such is the tendency in all the countries that follow in the lead of England, and in England herself. Instability is, therefore, the characteristic of all those countries.

American policy has been in harmony with neither. While recognizing generally the expediency of protection, and the propriety of creating a domestic market for the planter's and the farmer's products, powerful parties have held that it was to be regarded, not as a measure of national policy promotive of the good of all, but as a special favor to certain classes whose interests were to be promoted at the cost of all; and for that reason to be granted only so far as was consistent with the raising of the greatest public revenue. Instability has, therefore, been the especial characteristic of American policy, protection having been resorted to whenever the public treasury was empty, and abandoned whenever it had again been filled. As a consequence of this it is that we are now afforded the opportunity of studying, on the same ground, the working of both the systems already examined in reference to so many, so different, and so widely-scattered nations; and to that examination it is proposed that we now address ourselves.

CHAPTER XXI.

OF VITAL CHANGES IN THE FORMS OF MATTER—CONTINUED.

§ 1. The American Union a country of contrasts—its social system tending towards centralization and slavery, while its political one is based upon the idea of decentralization and freedom. Natural tendency towards association and combination. Counteracted by a national policy tending towards dispersion.

§ 2. Early tendencies towards the adoption of the system which looked towards bringing together the producer and the consumer. Variable character of American policy since the close of the great European war.

§ 3. Policy of Colbert and Cromwell adopted in regard to shipping. Freedom of trade obtained by means of protective measures.

§ 4. American policy, generally, in full accordance with the doctrines of the British school. Consequent decline in the prices of the rude products of the farm. The man who must go to any market, must pay the tax of transportation. Heavy taxation of American farmers.

§ 5. Civilization grows in the direct ratio of the removal of obstacles standing between the producers and the consumers.

§ 6. The planter steadily giving more of his raw materials, and receiving less in exchange for them. Consequent exhaustion of the soil, and weakness of the State.

§ 7. Barbarism grows, everywhere, in the direct ratio of the export of the rude products of the soil, and consequent decline in the powers of the land.

§ 1. France, as has been shown, is a country of "contrasts," resulting from the fact that its social and political systems are not in harmony with each other, the former tending regularly towards increase in the value of land and of man, the creation of local centres, and the establishment of freedom; the latter as certainly towards decrease in the value of land, centralization of wealth and power in the capital, and reduction of men to the condition of mere machines, to be used by men whose trade is politics.

In the American Union, too, we find "contrasts," whose existence is due to the fact, that it has a social system which looks towards centralization and slavery, standing in the presence of a political one based on the idea of local activity and perfect self-government. In France, a sound social system is slowly, but certainly, correcting the errors of the political one, with constant tendency towards increase of freedom; whereas, in these United States, social error is gradually triumphing over political truth, with growing tendency toward the further dispersion of man, the absorption of local centres of action, the centralization of power in great cities, and the increasing subjection of those who labor to the will of those who live by the exercise of their powers of appropriation. First among the nations of the earth to declare that "all men are born equal," they now stand alone among civilized communities in having among them teachers who assert that "free society has proved an utter failure;" that "slavery, whether for the white man or the black, is a legitimate, useful, and expedient institution;" and that it is a duty to strive "not merely to retain it where it is, but to extend it to regions where it is yet unknown."*

* The reader is here requested to bear in mind that the picture of the American Union now about to be presented is the one that was furnished by Mr. Carey several years prior to the breaking out of the pro-slavery rebellion in 1860–61. With the exception of the short period from 1842 to 1847 the country had been then for more than a quarter of a century wholly subjected to that system which looked towards having but a single workshop for the world—towards compelling all the raw materials of the world to travel thousands and tens of thousands of miles in search of the little spindle, the little loom, and other little and inexpensive machinery of conversion—and towards a constantly increasing subjection of the producers of the earth to the will of those who controlled and directed the machinery of exchange. In all other countries such subjection had been attended by constant increase in the tax of transportation, by decline in the powers of the land, and by diminution in the laborer's power to control his own actions, and it would have been fair to presume that the same results would certainly here be realized. That they had then been so, was proved by the facts, that exhaustion of the soil had been constant in all those portions of the country in which employments had not been much diversified—that the dispersion of the American people had been greater than had ever before been known—that the tax of transportation had therefore borne a constantly increasing proportion to the selling prices of the farmer's and planter's products—that the laborer had become more and more a mere instrument in the trader's hands—that absenteeism had steadily grown—and that the tyrant Southern overseer had become more and more the master of both land and laborer.

So far as regarded the nation at large, these results had then exhibited themselves in a constant increase of the Slave Power, and in a tendency towards disunion that has since culminated in a civil war the like of which has no existence in the annals of the world. Had the people of these United States followed the example of France instead of traveling in the direction indicated by English traders—had they steadily maintained that system of policy which tended towards bringing the consumer and the producer together, and towards increasing the diversity of their own pursuits—Northern and Southern land would both have grown in their money value as Southern laborers had been becoming more free, and Federal power would have grown as local institutions had become more and more developed. To the fact that such a system was not maintained, and to that alone, are we now indebted for the waste of life and property, and for the destruction of human happiness, that

In no part of the world does the political system, based as it is on the idea of local centres counteracting the great central attraction, so nearly correspond with that wonderfully beautiful one established for the regulation of the universe. In none, therefore, are the natural tendencies of man towards combination with his fellow-man so fully exhibited. The type of the system is seen in the "bee," or union of the older members of a settlement for the purpose of providing accommodation for their newly arrived neighbors. The logs are to be rolled, the roof is to be raised, or the corn to be husked. Each of these operations would require severe exertion on the part of the lonely settler; but all are rendered light by means of combination among those around him. The new-comer has, probably, neither horse nor plough; one neighbor lends him the former, while another supplies the latter, and thus is he enabled soon to obtain both horse and plough of his own. A place of worship being required, all, whether Methodists, Episcopalians, Baptists, or Presbyterians, unite to build it; its pulpit to be occupied by the itinerant preachers of the wilderness. On one day we find them associating for the making of roads, and holding meetings to determine who shall superintend their construction and assess the taxes required for that purpose. On another, they meet to select persons to represent them at the county board, in the State Assembly, or in the Congress of the nation. Next they settle where the new school-house shall be built, who shall collect the funds required, or select the little library that is to aid their children in applying the knowledge acquired from their teachers. Again, they form associations for mutual insurance against fire; or little savings' funds, called banks, at which the man who wishes to buy a plough may borrow the little money that he needs. Little mills grow up, and expand into large ones, in which the capitalists of the neighborhood, shoemakers and sempstresses, farmers and lawyers, widows and orphans, are interested; little towns appear, in which every resident owns his own house and lot, and is therefore directly interested in the advancement of all, each feeling that the first of the objects needed to be attained is

have attended the three past years. That waste and that destruction, great as they have been, and the debt that has been created, large as it is, constitute but portions of the price that the country is now required to pay for the abandonment, in 1832, of the policy that had been instituted by the passage of the protective tariffs of 1824 and 1828

an entire security in the enjoyment of the rights of person and of property. The power to associate steadily increases, and with it the habit of combination, which is most seen where wealth and population most abound, in the New England States. There we see a network of association so far exceeding any thing elsewhere known, as to be entirely beyond comparison. Nevertheless, look to what quarter we may, we find a state of things in striking "contrast" with all this, as will here be shown.

The population of the Union is now (1856) 27 millions, and the surface comprised between the Mississippi and the Atlantic is 640,000,000 of acres, each of which could support a full-grown man; yet are men flying to Kansas and Nebraska, Utah and Oregon, there to commence their labors far from market and under circumstances the most disadvantageous.

The natural tendency of man is to combine his labors with those of his fellow-men; yet here, men fly from their fellows, wasting their labor on the road, and employing it unprofitably at their journey's end.

His natural tendency is to combine his axe with his neighbor's spade, lending the one and borrowing the other; yet here, the man who owns the axe flies from him who has the spade.

His natural tendency is to commence on the thin soil of the hill-side, and to work down towards the rich soil at its foot, gathering manure on the one to enrich the other; yet here, he flies from the rich soils near him to seek poor ones at a distance.

His natural tendency is to combine with his neighbors to improve old roads; yet here he flies to a distance and opens new ones, so that two are to be maintained instead of one.

His natural tendency is to combine with his neighbors for improving the character of education in old schools; but here, he flies to places where no schools exist.

His natural tendency is to hold in regard old places and old houses, mellowed by time and sanctified by the recollections of those who had before inhabited them; but here, he flies from them to cut out new places in the woods, whose rudeness is enhanced by the recollection of those he has left.

Why is this so? Why do men fly from rich lands to seek poor ones in the West? Why, in rich countries with canals and railroads, towns and telegraphs, does population cease to grow, and land become from day to day more consolidated, always an evidence of declining civilization?

Because the policy of the country has opposed the development of COMMERCE, *while favoring the supremacy of* TRADE, *and compelling constant increase in the necessity for, and in the tax of*, TRANSPORTATION.

§ 2. The Revolutionary War having originated in the determination of the colonists to release themselves from the system under which Ireland and the Indies have since been so entirely exhausted, it might have been expected that they would follow in the direction indicated by Colbert, adopting measures to bring the consumer to the side of the producer, and thus relieving themselves from the most oppressive of all taxes, that of transportation. That such were the early tendencies of the government is shown in an elaborate Report of Alexander Hamilton, Washington's Secretary of the Treasury, one of the ablest economical papers ever written. Therein it is shown that "not only the wealth, but the independence and security, of a country appear to be materially connected with the prosperity of manufactures. Every nation," as he continues, "with a view to these great objects, ought to endeavor to possess within itself all the essentials of national supply. These comprise the means of subsistence, clothing, and defence; and, though it were true that the immediate and certain effect of regulations controlling the competition of foreign with domestic fabrics was an increase of price, it is universally true that the contrary is the ultimate effect with every successful manufacture. When a domestic manufacture has attained to perfection, and has engaged in the prosecution of it a competent number of persons, it invariably becomes cheaper. Being free from the heavy charges which attend the importation of foreign commodities, it can be afforded cheaper, and accordingly seldom or never fails to be sold cheaper, in process of time, than was the foreign article for which it is a substitute. The internal competition which takes place soon does away every thing like monopoly, and by degrees reduces the price of the article to the minimum of a reasonable profit on the capital employed." This accorded, as he thought, "with the reason of the thing, and with experience."

The great war of Europe had then begun, and its effects came soon to be felt in the increased demand for food, furnishing the farmer with a temporary market, and preventing him from reflecting on the fact, that the price of his land wholly depended on its subjection or exemption, from the tax of transportation. Time, however, brought the correction of his delusions, in the form of Orders in Council, and Berlin and Milan Decrees, by which were annihilated the rights of neutral nations. The American flag being driven from the ocean, it became necessary, in self-defence, to prohibit intercourse with either of the belligerents. Pressing need of cloth and iron then compelled resort to domestic manufactures. It being, however, always the first step that is the most costly and the least productive, the progress was necessarily slow, and the war of 1812 found the country so entirely unprovided, that the government was driven to the expedient of taking possession of Amelia Island, belonging to Spain, for the sole purpose of enabling its citizens to evade its own laws, by introducing cargoes of woollens whose regular importation had been forbidden, but which had been collected there in anticipation of a repeal of the non-intercourse laws.

That war produced effects similar to those witnessed in Continental Europe, causing the erection of furnaces and factories, and the opening of mines, and thus furnishing so extensive a market for food, that the price of flour was higher than it ever before had been, although the export trade had almost wholly ceased. With the return of peace and the re-establishment of free trade, however, manufactures disappeared and manufacturers were ruined, and thus was lost to the nation all the skill and experience accumulated in the decade through which it then had passed.

Commerce declined, labor ceased to be in demand, and land sold for one-third of the prices it had before commanded. Peace had brought with it ruin, and not prosperity. Universal distress, however, led to the semi-protective tariff of 1824, followed by the really protective one of 1828, by which the policy of Colbert and Hamilton was, for the first time, installed as that of the American Union. Threatened resistance on the part of the cotton-growing States, however, caused the abandonment of that policy before it had even five years trial, and in 1833 it was suspended by the Compromise tariff, in virtue of which protection was gradually to be withdrawn, wholly ceasing in 1842. Before that time, however, commerce had died away, and poverty and ruin had taken the place of the prosperity that had before existed. The necessity for a change of policy became once again obvious, and protection was again in 1842 adopted as the law of the land.

Again, however, in 1846, the system was changed, and protection was withdrawn. The gradual tendency towards its ultimate complete adoption then, however, exhibited itself in the fact that as the rate of duty to be raised was fixed as high as 30 per cent.

The expediency of protection has, to a greater or less extent, been recognized in every tariff passed since the formation of the Federal Constitution, but it has only twice been made adequate to the attainment of the object—in the four years ending in 1833, and the four ending in 1846—and in both cases the laws were repealed almost at the moment when they had begun to operate.*

§ 3. Such is the history of these United States as regards protection to the farmer and planter in their efforts to draw the consumer to their side. When, however, we come to the question of the transportation of their products, we find a policy widely different. There, following the lead of Colbert and of Cromwell, the policy of the British Navigation Laws was adopted, and has been since steadily maintained. Home-built shipping in the foreign trade was adequately protected, and in the domestic market foreign shipping was absolutely prohibited; and the effect is seen in the establishment of a mercantile marine unequalled in the world.

Nor has that been the sole result. The object of Cromwell's laws was that of giving to British ships advantages in the trade of Britain with the world at large, and thus excluding other ships from competition even for the trade of their respective countries. The object of America was that of establishing equality of rights on the ocean, and in the ports of Britain. In this she fully succeeded; and, her example being followed by Prussia, freedom of *trade* was thus conquered by means of that same protection by which Germany and France are now acquiring for themselves freedom of domestic and foreign *commerce*. By both of those countries it is clearly seen that the nearer the market can be brought to the farmer, the higher must be the prices of labor and land, and the lower those of cloth and iron.

§ 4. The average export prices, and the average exports, of

* Since the above was written protection has been again reinstated by means of the Morrill Tariff of 1861.

flour since the beginning of the present century, have been as follows:—

	Price.	Exports.		Price	Exports.
1810–15	11 60	uncertain	1841,45	$5 10	$16,800,000
1821,25	6 20	$13,000,000	1846,50	5 44	39,000,000
1826,30	6 20	12,000,000	1850	5 00	26,000,000
1831,35	5 95	14,000,000	1851	4 73	22,000,000
1836,40	8 00	12,500,000	1852	4 24	26,000,000*

The facts here presented are worthy of most careful attention. The highest average was from 1810 to 1815, at a time when foreign trade scarcely existed. The extent of the domestic market then created may be judged from the fact that the cotton manufacture, which in 1805 had required only 1000 bales, absorbed in 1815 no less than 90,000.

The policy of the country having changed with the return of peace, the price of flour declined, until it reached, in 1852, just before the Crimean War, a lower point than had been touched since the peace of 1783. Directly the reverse of this is what is seen in France, Russia, and all those other countries

* The very trivial effect of short European crops upon American prices is clearly proved by the fact, that in the period of the great Irish famine, 1846,50, the average price of flour was but one-third of a dollar higher than it had been in that from 1841 to 1845, in which the great financial crisis had closed a large portion of the European workshops, and deprived those who had previously worked in them of the means to purchase bread. It is further shown by the following figures, exhibiting the export of breadstuffs to Europe, in the three past years, and the prices of flour at a period when short crops had rendered necessary a large import of food into nearly all of Eastern Europe:

	1860.	1861.	1862.
To Great Britain and Ireland	$44,000,000	$70,000,000	$17,000,000
To France	2,300,000	12,700,000	720,000
Prices of flour	$5 44	$5 60	$6 15

Estimated in gold, the prices of the two latter years are less than was that of the first, and yet the needs of Europe for foreign food were then greater than they had ever before been known to be.

Comparing now the recent prices, when gold so much abounded, with those of the past, we see that the country obtained far less for a barrel of flour than it did in the period from 1830 to 1840, when the existence of the gold deposits of California and Australia remained yet unthought of—the farmers of the country having thus failed to profit in any manner by the remarkable auriferous discoveries of the period that had intervened. The cause of this is to be found in the fact, that the policy of the country had tended to render them daily more and more dependent upon the use of British ships and mills, and more and more the slaves of those who controlled the machinery of trade and transportation.

which are engaged in *bringing the market to the farmer*, instead of placing the farmer under the necessity *of going to the market*. In all such, the price of food has tended, and still does tend, steadily to rise.

No truth is more susceptible of demonstration than this: *that the man who must go to market pays the cost of getting there*. It is one which sad experience teaches every farmer; and one, too, that the student may find demonstrated by Adam Smith. The corn that is twenty or thirty miles distant from market sells for as many cents less per bushel than that which is at market; and potatoes one hundred miles from market are almost worthless, while those raised close to it command a liberal price, the difference between the two being the cost of transportation.

Another important truth is: *That the price of the whole crop depends on that which can be obtained for the small surplus that must go abroad; or which must be paid for the small quantity required to be brought from a distance.* Give to any certain district 20,000 bushels of wheat more than are required, and the *whole crop* will fall to the level that can be obtained abroad for those few bushels. Let the same district in another year require as many additional bushels, and the *whole* will rise to the price at which they can be obtained from abroad—the difference being perhaps as follows:—

300,000 bushels at the medium price of $1	$300,000
320,000 bushels at the lowest price, 75 cents	240,000
The crop being small, and 20,000 being required, the price will rise to $1 25, giving for 280,000 bushels	350,000

The question here between a high and a low price, differing to the extent of nearly one-half, depends altogether on the existence of a demand slightly below or above the quantity produced at home and needing to be sold.

Looking now to the quantity exported, we see a growing necessity for resorting to a distant market, accompanied by a decline of 30 per cent. in prices; but if we compare 1850–52 with the period from 1810 to 1815, when the home consumption was equal to the whole supply, the reduction is no less than 63 per cent. Admitting, however, that the prices of the first of the above periods would, in the event of the creation of a domestic market, be the standard, we obtain as the result, that the same crops which now sell for $1,500,000,000, would then command $2,200,000,000, making a difference of $700,000,000. These prices are those at the port of shipment; but were we to add to this the saving of inland transportation resulting from the creation of local markets, the difference would reach $1000,000,000—*which may be regarded as the actual price paid by the agricultural body for the privilege of almost giving away food to the extent of less than $30,000,000.*

§ 5. It may be said, however, that the food consumers would suffer from the adoption of such a policy as would correct this waste. Directly the reverse, however, has been the case in all other countries. At no period of England's history has the condition of the people so much improved as in the thirty years preceding the wars of the French Revolution, when the prices of raw materials and of finished products were most steadily approximating. Circulation becoming from year to year more rapid, labor became more and more economized, with large increase of wealth. Land and man almost doubled in their money value; and all because of the relief from the tax of transportation then resulting from the growth of domestic commerce. So, too, in France. For centuries the price of corn had not been so low as it was in the days of Louis XV.; and yet, at none had the people so severely suffered from want of food. Commerce had then scarcely an existence. Since then the price has greatly increased, enabling the farmer to gain on both hands: first, by obtaining more money for his corn; and second, by obtaining more cloth for his money. Farm wages rise, and with them those of every other department of labor, the former being the standard by which all others are regulated.

As in England and France, so would it be in these United States. Labor being in demand its price would rise, and the greater would be the power of accumulation; the more abundant would be the machinery applied to utilizing the forces of nature; the larger would be the proportion of the mental and physical force of the community given to developing the resources of the earth; and every step in that direction would furnish further evidence of the existence of a perfect harmony in the true and permanent interests of farmer and artisan, laborer and capitalist.

The proposition, that *civilization grows in the direct ratio of the removal of obstacles standing between the producer and the consumer, and the consequent approximation of the prices of the products of the earth in their rude and their finished forms*, is a great and universal law, to which no exception can be found. Thus far, as we have seen, the policy of the

Union has tended steadily towards lessening the price of food; and as this tends inevitably towards barbarism, it is here we must look for an explanation of the extraordinary contrasts above referred to.

§ 6. Looking now to the other great staple of America, cotton, we find the crop of 1814 to have been 70,000,000 pounds, of which the domestic consumption was nearly 30,000,000. The crop increasing while the manufacture declined, there arose an increased necessity for pressing it on foreign markets, with the result that is here exhibited:

Export 1815 and 1816	average	80,000,000	price	$20,500,000
" 1821 and 1822	"	134,000,000	"	21,500,000
" 1827 to 1829	"	256,000,000	"	26,000,000

The quantity had now more than trebled, while the receipt had increased little more than 25 per cent. The prices here given being those of the shipping ports, and the quantity to be transported having so greatly increased, and having required so great an extension of cultivation, it is, we think, reasonable to assume that the planter gave 256,000,000 of pounds for no more money than six years previously he had received for one-third of that quantity.

1830 to 1832	average	280,000,000	$29,000,000
1840 " 1842	"	619,000,000	55,000,000
1843 " 1845	"	719,000,000	51,000,000
1849	"	1,020,000,000	66,000,000

We have here nearly 940,000,000 of pounds to be transported, additional to the quantity of 1815–16, and from an area that, because of the unceasing exhaustion of the soil, had been enormously extended.* Such being the case, it may be doubted whether the price received by the planter

* The following paragraph is from a speech of a distinguished citizen of Alabama, and exhibits the action of the system in a State that but forty years since had no existence:—

"I can show you, with sorrow, in the older portions of Alabama, and in my native county of Madison, the sad memorials of the artless and exhausting culture of cotton. Our small planters, after taking the cream off their lands, unable to restore them by rest, manure, or otherwise, are going further west and south in search of other virgin lands which they may and will despoil and impoverish in like manner. Our wealthier planters, with greater means and no more skill, are buying out their poorer neighbors, extending their plantations, and adding to their slave force. The wealthy few, who are able to live on smaller profits, and to give their blasted fields some rest, are thus pushing off the many who are merely independent. Of the $20,000,000 annually realized from

was more than twice as great as had been received for 80,000,000.

1850–1851 ....pounds 781,000,000..............$92,000,000

The great fact is here presented to us that the *less* cotton the planter sends to market, the *more* he obtains for it, while saving largely of the cost of internal transportation.

1852.........................pounds 1,093,000,000..............$88,000,000

Here is an increase of 312,000,000 of pounds requiring to be transported, accompanied with a diminution of gross receipt of $4,000,000; and of net receipt that cannot be estimated at less than $10,000,000. As compared with 1815–16 *the planter must have been giving five pounds for the price before received for one.*

Such a course of things is without a parallel in the world. In the natural order of things the cultivator profits by improvements in manufacture; yet here, although each successive year had brought with it increased facilities for the conversion of cotton, we find the planter to have been steadily giving more of it for less money. The cause, as we are told, is, that too much cotton is produced, and the planters hold meetings with a view to reduce the quantity; yet still the cultivation extends, with constant decline of price. Struggle as they may, the case is still the same, they being required from year to year to give more cotton for less money, and that in spite of a great natural law in virtue of which he should have more money for less cotton.*

the sale of the cotton crop in Alabama, nearly all not expended in supporting the producers is re-invested in land and negroes. Thus the white population has decreased, and the slave increased almost *pari passu*, in several counties of our State. In 1825 Madison county cast about 3000 votes; now, she cannot exceed 2300. In traversing that county one will discover numerous farm-houses, once the abode of industrious and intelligent freemen, now occupied by slaves, or tenantless, deserted, and dilapidated; he will observe fields, once fertile, now unfenced, abandoned, and covered with those evil harbingers, foxtail and broomsedge; he will see the moss growing on the mouldering walls of once thrifty villages; and will find 'one only master grasps the whole domain' that once furnished happy homes for a dozen white families. Indeed, a country in its infancy, where fifty years ago scarce a forest tree had been felled by the axe of the pioneer, is already exhibiting the painful signs of senility and decay apparent in Virginia and the Carolinas." —C. C. Clay.

* During the whole of the period above referred to, the British people were steadily engaged in stimulating the competition of

§ 7. We are thus presented with the remarkable fact that the two chief products of the Union have been, under the free trade system, steadily declining in their power to command the precious metals in exchange.

The larger the price of corn the greater must be the power of the farmer to purchase cloth, and the higher the price the planter will obtain for his cotton. The tendency of American policy, however, is towards reducing the price of corn throughout the world, and as a necessary consequence, towards destroying the power of the people of France and Germany, Russia and Austria, England and Ireland, to purchase cloth. Were it possible now to say that no more food should go hence to any part of the world, the European market would be relieved from the pressure by which it is kept down, the prices of food would rapidly advance, affording inducement to the extension of cultivation and causing a demand for labor, with large increase of wages, and consequent increase in the power to purchase cloth. Agricultural wages would rise in price, rendering indispensable an increase in the wages of factory labor.

Such, too, would be the home effect of protection fully adopted and permanently maintained. The measures required for making a domestic market for food, and for thus relieving the farmers of Europe from American competition, would produce rapid domestic circulation, and the American farmer would soon obtain as much for his corn as now is paid in France or England. Agricultural labor would rise in price, followed by rise in that which was otherwise employed; and at the close of a few years the domestic consumption of

India with America for permission to pass their cotton through the very narrow passage offered by British ships and mills, and with every step in that direction there was increase of friction, decline in the rapidity of movement, increase of profit to the owners of machinery of trade and transportation, and diminution of price to the producer. The latter were assured that any rise of price would stop consumption, and with a view to prove that such must necessarily be the case, the mill-owner diminished his working hours, with a view to increase the "stock on hand," and thus to check the tendency towards rise of price. Happily, the events of the three past years have furnished evidence that low prices are not needed for producing large consumption. What it is that really is required, is rapidity of circulation resulting from closer proximity of producers and consumers. Had the planter twenty years since followed the advice of Adam Smith, in combining his food and wool in the form of cloth, his people would have been becoming from day to day more free, his land would have been steadily acquiring

cotton would be thrice as great as now, enabling the planter to receive for large crops a higher price per pound than he now receives for it when crops are small.

Adam Smith denounced the British system of his day, because it was based on the idea of cheapening the raw materials of manufacture. That of the present day looks to the same results; and therefore is it that it has been resisted by all the civilized nations of the world—America alone excepted. In all of them, consequently, raw produce rises in price; while here alone is found a civilized community in which raw produce has during half a century steadily declined in price—the farming and planting interests, strange to say, having been most consistent in the pursuit of a policy tending to diminish the quantity of money to be received in exchange for a bale of cotton or a barrel of flour.

The history of the Union for the last forty years is an enigma of which the solution is found in the following proposition:—Barbarism grows in the ratio of the export of the rude products of the land, and the consequent exhaustion of the soil—the raising of such products for distant markets being the proper work of the barbarian and the slave, and of them alone.

a larger money value, and his successors would be now enjoying a degree of prosperity equal to any thing the world had ever known. To this fact that the planters of the past did not do this those of the present stand indebted for the ruin they now experience. The greater the variety of pursuits, the greater must ever be the tendency towards union, peace, happiness, wealth, and strength.

CHAPTER XXII.

OF VITAL CHANGES IN THE FORMS OF MATTER—CONTINUED.

§ 1. Wealth consists in the power to command the services of nature. Great increase of British wealth, resulting from the command of steam. Extraordinary amount of undeveloped power in the United States. Combination of action required for its development. National policy adverse to association and combination.

§ 2. Waste of power resulting from the exhaustion of the soil, and consequent dispersion of men. Gradual consolidation of the land.

§ 3. Trader's power steadily increases, while that of the farmer and planter as steadily declines. Consequent instability and irregularity of the societary movement. Trader profits by instability. Remarkable steadiness and regularity of the societary movement in all those periods in which the protective policy has been maintained.

§ 4. Growing commerce enables the farmer to pass from the cultivation of the poorer to the richer soils. American policy restricts him to the former. Growing commerce tends to increase the power of labor over capital. American policy gives to capital greater power over labor. Growing commerce tends towards peace, and an economical administration of the affairs of government. American policy looks to extension of the trader's power at the expense of commerce. Increasing tendency towards war and waste. Growing commerce tends towards development of the latent powers of earth and man. American policy tends towards exhaustion of the one and enslavement of the other.

§ 5. Speculative and gambling spirit engendered by a growing dependence upon the trader and transporter. Decline in the feeling of responsibility resulting from irregularity in the societary movement. Political and judicial corruption resulting from the growth of centralization.

§ 6. The higher the societary organization the more rapid is the movement and the more instant the exhibition of the effects of a sound, or unsound, course of policy. Frequency and rapidity of changes in these United States.

§ 7. Phenomena of declining civilization now (1856) exhibited throughout the Union.

§ 8. Human progress manifests itself in decline in the trader's power, and the attendant creation of a scientific agriculture. Opposite tendency of the American policy, and consequent decline of civilization.

§ 9. As agriculture becomes a science the land becomes more productive, and its products tend to rise in price. Consequent double profit to the farmer. As raw materials rise in price finished products fall, with further profit to the farmer. Man and land at one end of the scale of prices, and the most highly finished products at the other. The more rapid the societary circulation, the greater is their tendency towards approximation. Agricultural improvement waits upon, and never precedes, industrial development.

§ 10. As raw materials and finished products approximate in price, commerce grows, with constant increase in the steadiness of the societary movement. As they become more widely separated, trade acquires power, and the movement becomes, from year to year, more fitful and irregular. With the one, the real MAN becomes daily more developed. With the other, man becomes from day to day more thoroughly enslaved.

§ 1. CIVILIZATION grows with the growth of wealth. Wealth itself consists in the ability to command the always gratuitous services of nature. The power of steam employed in Britain is equal to the united forces of 600,000,000 of men, and yet the number of persons employed in British coal mines but little exceeds 100,000. Her entire population being but little more than 20,000,000, it follows that, were the power equally divided, each individual would have the equivalent of nearly thirty willing slaves, employed in doing his work; slaves, too, requiring neither lodging, food, nor raiment. Such is the wonderful effect of combination in increasing human force.

Of all the communities of the world, no one has within its reach so great an amount of material force as have these United States. Their soil, enriched through ages, is a great reservoir of wealth, requiring for its development only the magic power of ASSOCIATION. Nevertheless, there is in no country so great a *voluntary* waste of both material and mental force. In Ireland and India, Turkey and Portugal, similar waste takes place, but in none of these is there even a pretence that the people direct their own course of action. Here, the reverse is the case, every man being supposed to constitute a part of the government, and to aid in directing its action so as to enable him and his neighbors to profit most by the gifts of Providence;. yet here it is that men are most disposed to exhaust the soil and thus compel themselves to fly apart from each other, thereby depriving themselves of the power to substitute the great natural forces for the unaided strength of the human arm.

§ 2. To enable men to come nearer together the land must have returned to it the refuse of its products. Of all the raw material required for human purposes manure is the most important, and yet of all it is the one that is least susceptible of being carried to a distance. The waste of fertilizing matter in our cities is so great as to be almost beyond calculation. The city of New York and its vicinity, alone, calculated at only two cents a day for each person, and making but a small allowance for the animals, would amount to $10,000,000 per annum. The potash and phosphoric acid contained in the corn and wheat crops of 1850 were estimated at nearly $30,000,000; nearly all of which was lost. Add to this the large export of breadstuffs, of ashes, and of the bones of cattle, and "it would be improper," says a distinguished agriculturist, "to estimate the *annual waste* of the country at less than an amount *equal to the mineral constituents of* 1,500,000,000 *bushels of corn!*" This was said ten years since. Such an estimate now made would carry the figures up to 2,000,000,000 of bushels.

Such being the facts, it is no cause for surprise that every intelligent foreigner is forced to remark on the low condition of American agriculture generally, and on the steady diminution of the powers of the soil. In New York, the average product of wheat is but half of what it was estimated at 80 years since. In Ohio it is but eleven bushels to the acre, and in Virginia less than seven. Tobacco has been raised in the Border States until the land has been utterly exhausted; while throughout the cotton growing country there is exhibited a scene of destruction unparalleled in the world to have been accomplished in so brief a period. The people there are living on their capital, selling their soil at prices so low that they do not obtain one dollar for every five destroyed; and hence it has been that the laborer has been becoming more and more enslaved. As the power of the land declines, it becomes more and more consolidated in the lands of large proprietors who grow poorer from year to year. All this, we are sometimes told, is a natural consequence of the fact, that slavery is not adapted to the operations of scientific agriculture; but here, as usual, modern political economy puts effect in the place of cause—*the continued existence of slavery being a consequence of the absence of that combination which is needed for the advancement of agriculture.*

§ 3. The trader profits of changes in the prices of his commodities. He desires to buy cheaply and sell dearly; and the more frequent the vicissitudes of trade, the more numerous are his chances for accumulating fortune. The farmer, the planter, and the miner, on the contrary, desire steadiness, needing, as they do, to make their arrangements for years ahead. The cotton mill requires much time for its construction, and for the collection and organization of the people who are therein to work. The preparation of the mine, the furnace, and the rolling-mill, requires long periods of exertion and large expenditure before their owners can begin to reap reward. The trader, on the contrary, buys and sells from hour to hour; and the greater his power to produce changes in the prices of wheat, cloth, and iron, the greater is the probability that he will ultimately enter upon the possession of the land of the farmer, the mill of the cloth manufacturer, the furnace of the maker of railroad bars, or the road of the man who has invested his fortune in a great improvement—and at half the cost at which this machinery has been constructed. Trade and commerce thus look always in opposite directions, the one desiring and producing frequent and rapid changes, the other seeking and promoting regularity of movement.

Steadiness is an essential characteristic of civilization;

unsteadiness, of barbarism. In savage life there is no stability, man being there the slave of nature. With growing wealth he becomes her master, and society then assumes a regular form, the movements of each day being distinguished from those of the one preceding only by a steady and gentle increase in the rapidity of exchanges. This is advancing civilization. The reverse is seen in all countries of advancing barbarism, crisis following crisis, each more severe than the last, until the societary machine falls to pieces, and chaos once more reigns. Tried by this standard, the American Union tends towards barbarism, the crisis of 1842, which preceded the tariff of that year, having been more fearful than that of 1821, which prepared the way for the tariff of 1824; and that now (1856) in preparation being likely as far to surpass that of 1842, in severity, as that had exceeded the one by which it had been preceded.*

§ 4. Commerce enables the farmer to reclaim the rich soils. Growing supremacy of trade drives men to the poorer ones.

Commerce tends to elevate the laborer and the small capitalist towards the level of the great one. Growth of power in the trader tends to sink the small capitalist to a level with the day laborer.

Commerce gives to the labors of the present increased power over the accumulations of the past. The growing power of trade produces the reverse effect, raising the rate of interest, and destroying the power to obtain reward for labor.

Commerce creates local centres, thus relieving the farmer from the tax of transportation, and enabling him to vary his cultivation. Trade, by crushing local centres, compels the farmer to confine himself to those products that will bear transportation to the distant city, while compelling him to constant exhaustion of the soil.

Commerce promotes the development of the treasures of the earth, and enables men to live nearer to one another. Growing supremacy of trade travels hand in hand with the increasing dispersion of men.

Commerce, making no wars, looks to peace, wealth, and

* In a note of Mr. Carey, written in 1858, he here informs his readers, that the above sketch of the movements of the American Union was written in 1856, in the midst of a glare of fancied prosperity, such as never before had been known, and which proved to be but the herald of the terrible crisis of 1857.

happiness. Trade, always dispersive and warlike, thirsts for the acquisition of Cuba and Central America, sends fleets to Japan, and fits out filibustering expeditions, thus seeking outlets for population abroad while closing the markets for labor at home.

Commerce enriches the people while producing economy in the administration of government. Increase of the trader's power tends to impoverish the people, while enriching those connected with the expenditure of public revenue. Thirty years since, $10,000,000 supplied all the means required. Ten years later, under the system of dispersion and exhaustion, the expenditure was quadrupled. Commerce being reinstated in the direction of affairs, the amount was reduced one-third. Trade, however, again obtaining the direction of affairs, the expenditure grew to $60,000,000. Moving steadily forward in the same false direction, the country has since reached a state of war which makes now (1864) an annual demand for $600,000,000.

Commerce diminishes the necessity for the transporter's services, and lessens his power. Trade tends to make of him the master of men who drive the plough and swing the flail.

Commerce opens mines and builds furnaces, and thus creates the power to make local roads. Trade destroys the power to support them when they have been made, but it creates great thoroughfares, whose management is so directed as to tax the local commerce for the support of that with distant people.

Commerce looks homeward, promoting domestic intercourse by means of the improvement of rivers, the construction of harbors, and the opening of mines. Trade, looking outward, measures the prosperity of a country by the extent of its intercourse with people who are distant, and with whom exchanges can be but few in number.

Commerce tends to increase the power of self-government, lessening the dependence on foreign markets, while increasing the power to go to them. Trade increases the necessities of man while diminishing his powers. General comfort, happiness, and prosperity, follow in the train of the one, while poverty and over-population are the invariable attendants of increase in the power of the other.

Commerce tends to produce harmony among men. Five-and-twenty years since, the stranger was always welcomed, but with the abandonment of the protective policy in 1833, there was for the first time exhibited that feeling of jealousy which was indicated by the creation of a political party having for its object the exclusion of foreigners from the rights of citizenship. With the re-establishment of that policy the demand for labor grew, and the party died away, to spring again into existence on a larger scale under the free trade system of 1846. Look where we may, we see discord following in the trader's wake.

§ 5. With the growth of commerce the necessity for transporting commodities declines with diminution in the risks from the dangers of the sea, while stone and iron take the place of wood, and risks from fire diminish. In no civilized country do fires so much abound as in these United States, and in none is so large an amount required to pay for the loss that thence results. That the *proportion* increases is evident from the fact that the rates of insurance steadily rise, whereas they should as steadily decline. The loss resulting from the waste of property and labor thus produced, is *more than the total value of the merchandize received in the Union from every quarter of the world;* and yet it is with a view to foster the distant trade that the country pursues a policy which forbids the development of the mineral and metallic riches that so much abound, and by means of which structures could be built of materials that would almost set at defiance the risk of fire.

Neither is it here alone that the wasteful effects of the system may be seen. The necessity for roads grows with the dispersion of the population, while the power to make them diminishes as men are forced to fly apart from each other. The country is therefore covered with half-finished roads, requiring unceasing and large repairs. So, too, with the steamboats of the Western rivers, constructed of inflammable materials, where otherwise they would be made of iron, the ores of which abound to an extent elsewhere unknown. Property and life are wasted, and reckless habits are everywhere generated as the feeling of responsibility declines, and that decline is in the direct ratio of the dispersion of population.

As the domestic commerce declines, steadiness diminishes and a reckless and gambling spirit appears, speculation taking the place of honest labor. Never in the history of the United States did this spirit so little show itself, as in those periods of quiet prosperity which followed establishment of the pro tective system by the Acts of 1828 and 1842. Never before had it been so rife as in the period which followed the repeal of the first of these Acts in 1833; yet even that is now (1856) exceeded, the whole country having become one great gaming house, in which men of every degree are stocking the cards with a view to plunder of their neighbors. The crime that so abounded in that period is now thrice exceeded—robbery, riot, swindling, arson, and murder, having become so common as scarcely to attract the attention of the readers of the journals in which they are recorded.

"The ruin or prosperity of a State," says Junius, "depends so much on the administration of the government, that to be acquainted with the merit of a ministry we need only observe the condition of the people. If we see them obedient to the laws, prosperous in their industry, united at home, and respected abroad, we may reasonably presume that their affairs are conducted by men of experience, ability and virtue. If, on the contrary, we see a universal spirit of distrust and dissatisfaction, a rapid decay of trade, dissensions in all parts of the empire, and a total loss of respect in the eyes of foreign powers, we may pronounce, without hesitation, that the government of that country is weak, distracted, and corrupt."

The first of the pictures here presented exhibits the state of the American Union at the close of the war in 1815; again in 1834, at the date of the repeal of the protective tariff of 1828; and again in 1847, when the highly protective Act of 1842 had just ceased to be the law of the land. The second is found on an examination of the condition of the country in the period from 1818 to 1824, when protection had ceased, and when the legislatures of numerous States had found themselves compelled to stay the action of the laws for the collection of debts; in 1841–2, when "stay laws" were again resorted to, and when the Federal government was nearly bankrupt; and, lastly, at the present period, (1856,) when there reigns "a universal spirit of distrust and dissatisfaction;" when there are "dissensions in every part of the empire;" when slavery and free trade grow in strength together; and when the "respect of other powers" has ceased to exist.

§ 6. The more perfect the form of the ship, the more rapid will be her passage, under proper guidance, to her destined port; but the more rapid, also, will be her destruction should the pilot run her on the shoals. So it is with nations. The higher their organization, the more rapid is the societary movement, and the more instant the shock that attends a stoppage in the circulation. The passage of an invading army through Peru or Mexico produces little effect beyond a small destruction of life and property; but in England it would cause the closing of factories, the stoppage of mills and furnaces, the dispersion of the people, and the suspension of all the machinery of local government. The power of recuperation, however, exists in the same degree, and the recovery from the effects of war in countries like France and England is much more rapid than it can be in countries of languid circulation.

In none, however, are the effects of change so speedily felt as in these United States; because, the political organization being more natural, the rapidity of circulation tends to be so very great. Universal instruction throughout the northern portion of the Union tends to produce great mental activity; and whatever may be the direction in which the Ship of State is guided, the movement is there most rapid. Such being the case, it is easy to account for those extraordinary changes, those sudden transitions from adversity to prosperity, from solvency to bankruptcy, that so much surprise the people of other lands.

§ 7. He would have been regarded as a false prophet who, ten years since, (in 1848,) should have predicted—

That, at the close of a single decade, the regular expenditure of the Federal government, in a time of peace, would reach sixty millions of dollars, or five times as much as it had been thirty years before:

That the recipients of this large amount, whether contractors, clerks, or postmasters, would be held liable for the payment of a formal and regular assessment, to be applied to the maintenance in office of the men by whom they had been appointed, or by whom the contracts had been made:

That payment of these assessments would be made the condition upon which their own continuance in office should depend:

That, coincident with these demands upon the *employés* of the government, all salaries would be largely raised; and that thus the treasury would be largely taxed for purely party purposes, and for the promotion of private interests:

That centralization would have become so far perfected as to enable those in office to dictate to a body of officials, sixty or eighty thousand in number, all their modes of thought in reference to public questions:

That a constantly growing difficulty of obtaining the means of support, and constant increase in the rewards of public service, would be attended with corresponding increase in the number of claimants for offices and in their subservience to those at whose pleasure offices were held:

That the Executive authority would dictate to the members of the legislature what should be their course, and publicly advertise the offices that were to be given to those whose votes should be in accordance with its desires:

That the growing mental slavery thus indicated would be attended by corresponding growth in the belief that "one of the chief bulwarks of our institutions" was to be found in the physical enslavement of the laborer:

That the extension of the area of human slavery would have become the primary object of the government, and that with that view the great Ordinance of 1787, as carried out in the Missouri Compromise, would have been repealed:

That, for the attainment of this object, the treaties with the poor remnant of the native tribes would have all been violated:

That, with the same end in view, wars would be made, piracy encouraged, and territories purchased:

That the Executive power would have so far grown, as to enable those charged with the administration of the government to adopt measures provocative of war, with a view to the spoliation of weaker neighbors:

That it would have been officially declared that might made right, and that, if a neighboring power refused to sell the territory desired, the Union would then be justified in taking possession of it:

That the re-opening of the slave trade would be publicly advocated, and that the first step towards its accomplishment would have been taken by a citizen of the United States, in rescinding all the prohibitions of the Central American government:

That the substitution, throughout all the minor employments of society, of slave labor for that of the freeman, would be publicly recommended by the Executive of a leading State of the Union:

That, while thus acquiring territory in the South, the rights and interests of the people would be bartered away, for the sole purpose of preventing annexation in the North:

That it would have been declared, that the free navigation of the South-American rivers must be obtained, "amicably, if it could, forcibly, if it must:"

That the effect of these measures would have been the entire alienation of the other communities of the Western world:

That the legislation of the country would have fallen almost entirely under the control of navigation, railroad, and other transportation companies, and that legislators would largely partake with their managers in the profits of enormous grants of money and of public lands:

That centralization would so far have grown as to cause the expenditure of a single city to become nearly equal to that of the Federal government thirty years since:

That the expenditure of city revenues, and the maintenance of public order, would have fallen into the hands of magistrates, many of whom would be regarded as worthy only of the penitentiary:

That the contest for the distribution of those revenues would have become so fierce as to cause the purchase of votes to an extent, and at a price, before unknown; and that elections would be carried on by means of bowie-knives, pistols, and even cannon:

That Lynch law would have found its way into the Senate Chamber: that it would have superseded the provisions of the Constitution throughout the Southern States: that it would have wholly superseded the civil authority in one of the States of the Union: that the right of the States to prohibit slavery within their limits would have become so seriously questioned as to warrant the belief that the day was at hand when it would be altogether denied: that the doctrine of constructive treason would have been adopted in the Federal courts: and that the rights of the citizen would thus have become equally imperilled by the extension of legal authority on the one hand, and the substitution of the law of force on the other:

That polygamy and slavery would have gone hand in hand with the extension of the trader's power, and that the doctrine of a plurality of wives would be publicly proclaimed by men holding highly important offices under the Federal government:

That religious discord would so far have grown, that the question of the private opinions of a candidate for the presidency, in regard to matters of religious faith, would be discussed throughout the Union: and finally,

That the discord between the Northern and Southern portions of the Union would have nearly reached the point of civil war, attended with growing disposition to look complacently upon the idea of dissolution of the connection.

This is a gloomy picture, but it is a true one. Not one of these things would have been deemed possible ten years ago, yet they are, one and all, now matters of history.*

§ 8. The form of society in barbaric ages may thus be represented :—

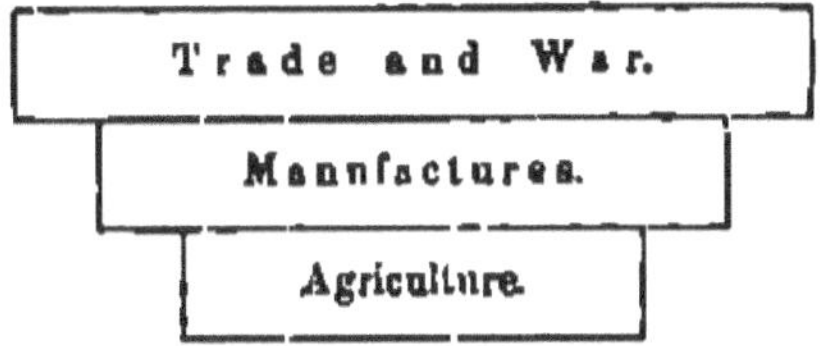

Instability is, of course, its essential characteristic.

With the increase of numbers, and the growth of the power of association, it assumes the form of highest stability, as is here shown :—

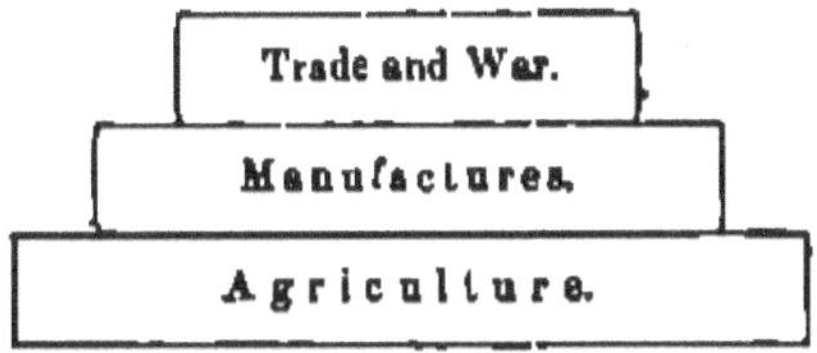

Throughout the British Empire and in this Union, the tendency is *towards* the former; and that because the policy pursued gives to trade the mastery over domestic commerce. We are thus presented with the remarkable fact, that in those countries which have been hitherto regarded as the especial friends to freedom, there exists a growing tendency towards centralization and slavery; and that in both we meet the phenomena that elsewhere have attended decline of civiliza-

* This picture dates back to 1856, and it has been deemed well to preserve it here, as showing what were then the tendencies of the country under the free trade policy, and what was the preparation then being made for the rebellion of 1860, and the civil war which since has followed. At that time there had been already a speck of civil war in Kansas, and on the border of Missouri.

tion. In both, the producer and consumer are receding from each other. In both there is a diminution in the power of association, and in the development of individuality. In both, the feeling of responsibility declines. In both, the power of progress diminishes from year to year. In both, property in land tends to become more and more consolidated. In both, the accumulations of the past are obtaining increased control over the labors of the present. In both, the proportion of the population engaged in the work of production tends to decrease, and that engaged in transportation to increase. In both, stability and regularity diminish. In both, the trader acquires increased control over the legislative action. In the foreign policy of both, the end is held to sanctify the means. In both, there is an unceasing thirst for territory, to be acquired by any means, however foul. In both, there is a steady growth of pauperism on the one hand, and of luxury on the other. In both, strength declines. Both are gradually losing the power to influence the movements of the world; yet both imagine themselves to be increasing in strength and power. The greater the difficulties resulting from the existing system, the more determined are both to find in it the road that leads to slavery, the route towards freedom.

§ 9. The greater the improvement in agriculture, the greater is the tendency to a *rise* in the price of the commodities produced; and to a *decline* in the price of manufactured goods.

The reader may, however, ask: Must not improved cultivation tend to cheapen corn, as improvements in the mode of conversion tend to cheapen cloth? That such is the case is certain, the discovery of new manures, and the invention of more powerful instruments, having a tendency towards reducing the quantity of labor required, and lessening its price. Here, however, as everywhere, the harmony of interests is maintained by means of balancing attractions, this downward movement being more than counteracted by an upward and opposing force.

Improvements in the mode of cultivation tend to raise the price of land, while depressing that of corn. Improved methods of grinding raise the price of corn while lowering that of flour. Improved culinary processes raise the price of flour while depressing that of bread. Improvement in the mode of converting food into iron, gold, lead, or any other of the commodities required by the food producers, tends to raise the price of bread while depressing that of the commodities whose production is thus facilitated. At each and every stage of progress, the land approximates more nearly to the corn, the corn to the flour, the flour to the bread, and the bread to the iron—the ultimate effect of all these changes being an ever growing approximation of that first of all raw materials, the land, to the last and most remote of the finished commodities which the earth and its products can be made to yield.

Man and land thus stand at one extremity of the scale, and the commodities of highest finish at the other, the former steadily increasing as the latter decline in value. The earth, as man's throne, thus rises with its sovereign, its services and those of all its parts descending, until they bow to his feet. His needs and his powers together constitute a constant quantity—growth in the latter being attended by steady diminution of the former. In other words, as wealth increases, value tends steadily to pass away.

It may, however, be asked: Might not ameliorations of cultivation take place, unaccompanied by improvement in the conversion of its products; and would they not, in that case, be attended by reduction in the prices of the raw material of human food? Were that possible, such would certainly be the case. It is, however, no more possible, than it would be, that the attractive power of the sun should increase, leaving unaffected the motions of the various bodies by which he is attended in his course. *Agricultural improvement waits upon, and never precedes, industrial development*—the application of new manures, the discovery of improved modes of applying power, and the invention of machines, being consequent upon that diversification of pursuits by means of which the various human faculties are stimulated into action, and men are fitted for that association with their fellow-men required for enabling them to direct the forces of nature to their service.

§ 10. We thus arrive at the following conclusions:—

That, with the development of agricultural science, consequent upon increased diversification of employment, the farmer obtains more from his land, while the prices of his products rise:

That, simultaneously therewith, the prices of manufactured commodities tend to fall; so that he not only has more corn to sell, but he obtains more in exchange for every bushel of corn:

That, at every step in this direction, commerce increases, with daily diminution in the power of the trader, and constant increase in the facility of association, in the development of individuality, in the feeling of responsibility, and in the power of further progress:

That, on the other hand, as agriculture ceases to be a science the farmer obtains less from his land, while prices tend to fall:

That, simultaneously therewith, the prices of manufactured commodities tend to rise; and that thus, the farmer obtains less in exchange for a bushel of corn, while having fewer bushels to sell:

That every step in that direction is attended with decline of commerce, increase in the power of the trader, and constant decline in the facility of association, in the individuality of the people, in the feeling of responsibility, in the power of further progress, and in the freedom of man.

Social science and the political economy of the schools are the precise antipodes of each other. Such being the case, it has been deemed necessary to study the phenomena presented by the various communities of ancient and modern times, with a view to show, that, while the facts of every country are in exact accordance with the doctrines that have been here propounded, all are equally opposed to those which commonly are taught. One of these systems must be absolutely true, the other as absolutely false. On which side lies the truth the reader will decide for himself.

We now proceed to the consideration of *the great instrument* provided by the Creator for facilitating that process of combination without which the various human faculties must remain for ever undeveloped.

CHAPTER XXIII.

OF THE INSTRUMENT OF ASSOCIATION.

I.—*Of Money and Price.*

§ 1. Difficulty, in the early periods of society, of making exchanges of service. General adoption of some certain commodity as a standard for the comparison of values. Recommendations, for this purpose, of the precious metals.

§ 2. Facility of association and combination resulting from the use of money. Of all the machinery in use among men it is the one which most economizes human effort. To the social body it is what atmospheric air is to the physical one—both supplying the machinery of circulation.

§ 3. Definition of price. Prices of raw materials rise as we approach the centres of civilization, while those of finished commodities as regularly decline. Double loss to the farmer who is distant from market, resulting from the low prices of the one, and the high prices of the other. The more highly finished a commodity, the greater is its tendency to fall of price.

§ 4. Land and labor, the ultimate raw material of all commodities, rise in price as men are more enabled to associate, and combine their efforts. Money the great instrument furnished by Providence for facilitating association and combination. The more perfect the supply thereof, the greater is the tendency towards freedom.

§ 1. The power of man over matter is limited to the effectuation of changes of place and of form. For the first, he needs wagons, ships, railroads; for the second, spades, ploughs, mills, furnaces, steam-engines. To effect exchanges among themselves, and thus to combine their efforts, men seek to obtain the aid of some general medium of circulation. The machinery of exchange is, therefore, of three kinds: first, that required for producing changes of place; second, for effecting changes of form; and, lastly, for facilitating exchanges of service.

In the early periods of society there is but little to exchange; and the few exchanges that are made are by direct barter skins being given for knives, clothing, fish, or meat. With the progress of population and wealth, however, all communities have gradually adopted some standard by means of which to measure the value of the commodities to be exchanged. Cattle were so used by the early Greeks; slaves and cattle by the Anglo-Saxons; wampum by the Aborigines of America; codfish by the people of New England; and tobacco by those of Virginia.

Such exchanges being inconvenient, we find man everywhere seeking to remove the difficulty by adopting iron, copper, and bronze, preparatory to obtaining gold and silver, to be employed in aiding circulation.

Of all the substances of which the earth is composed, the precious metals are those best fitted for that purpose. Scantily diffused throughout the globe, and requiring much labor for their collection, they represent a large amount of value. Being of small bulk, they may readily be stored, or carried from place to place. Not being liable to rust, they can be preserved uninjured for any length of time, and their quantity is consequently less liable to variation than that of wheat or corn. Capable of the most minute subdivision, they can be used for effecting the smallest as well as the largest exchanges—those of a single cent, or those of hundreds of millions of dollars.

To facilitate their use the various nations are accustomed to have them cut into small pieces and weighed, after which they are so stamped as to enable every one to discern how much is offered him in exchange for the commodity he has to sell; but the value of the piece is but in a very slight degree due to this process of coinage. In the early periods of society all the metals passed in lumps, requiring to be weighed; and such is now the case with much of the gold that passes between the Western and Eastern continents. Gold dust has also to be weighed, and allowance made for impurities; but with this exception its value before and after its passage through the Mint is almost precisely the same.

§ 2. A proper supply of gold and silver having been obtained, and divided, weighed, and marked, the various members of society are now enabled to effect exchanges, even to purchasing for a single cent a share in the product of the labors of tens of thousands of men employed in making railroads, engines, and cars, and carrying upon them millions of letters; or in that of hundreds of men who have contributed to the production of a penny newspaper. The mass of small coin thus becomes a *labor-saving machine*, facilitating combination, and giving utility to countless billions of minutes that would be wasted were there not a demand for them at the moment when the power to labor had been produced. Labor being the first price paid for every thing we value, the progress of communities is in the direct ratio of the presence or absence of the *instant* demand for the forces, mental and physical, of each individual, resulting from the power to offer in exchange for it something equivalent in value. It is the only commodity that perishes at the instant of production, and that, if not then put to use, is lost forever; and in order that it may be so used, there must exist that incessant division, subdivision, and recomposition, which attends an active commerce. This is seen in the case above referred to, where coal, iron, and lead-miners, furnace-men, machine-makers, rag-gatherers, carters, bleachers and makers of bleaching-powders, railroad and canal men, type-makers, compositors, pressmen, authors, editors, publishers, news-boys, and hosts of others, combine their efforts for the production of a heap of newspapers that is to be at once divided among its hundreds of thousands of consumers. Each of these latter pays a single cent, and then perhaps subdivides it so that the cost to each reader may be no more than a cent a week, yet each obtains his share of the labor of all the persons by whom it had been produced.

Of all the phenomena of society, this process of division, subdivision, composition, and recomposition, is the most remarkable; and yet, being a thing of such common occurrence, it scarcely attracts the slightest notice. Were the newspaper referred to divided into squares, each of which should represent the labor of one of the persons who had contributed to it, it would be found to be resolved into very many thousand pieces of various sizes, each representing a little scrap of human effort. Numerous as are these latter, they are all combined in every single sheet; and each member of the community may, for the most trifling piece of money, enjoy the advantage of the information therein contained, as fully as if it had been collected for himself alone.

Improvements in the modes of transportation are highly important, yet do they render but little service to man when compared with their cost. Those of a ship worth $50,000, employed in effecting exchanges between men on the opposite sides of the Atlantic, cannot exceed five or six thousand tons per annum; whereas a furnace of the same cost will effect the transmutation of 30,000 tons weight of coal, ore, limestone, food, and clothing, into iron. Nevertheless, the labor exchanged by means of this latter, will not exceed in its money value a quarter of a million of dollars. Let this be compared with the commerce effected in a year by the help of $50,000 worth of little white pieces representing labor to the extent of three or five cents, and it will be found that the service rendered by each dollar is greater than is rendered by hundreds, if not thousands, employed in manufactures, or tens of thousands in ships or railroads; and yet there are able writers who tell us, and with the utmost gravity, that money is "an important portion of the capital of the country that produces nothing."

"Money, as money," says Mr. J. S. Mill, "satisfies no want, answers no purpose." The difference between a country with, and one without it, would, as he thinks, be only one of convenience, like grinding by water instead of by hand. In like manner, however, a ship, as a ship, a road, as a road, a cotton-mill, as a cotton-mill, "satisfies no want, answers no purpose." They can be neither eaten, drunk, nor worn. All, however, are instruments for facilitating the work of association. To what extent they do so, as compared with money, we may now inquire.

Let us suppose that by some sudden convulsion of nature all the ships of the world were annihilated, and try to imagine what would be the effect? Ship-owners would lose heavily; sailors and porters would be thrown out of employment; the price of wheat would temporarily fall, while that of cloth would, for the moment, rise. At the close of a single year most of the operations of society would be moving as before, commerce at home having taken the place of that abroad Cotton and tropical productions would be less easily obtained in northern climes, and cloth less easily in southern ones; but in the chief exchanges of a society like that of France, Germany, or these United States, there would be, even for the moment, scarcely any suspension. So far otherwise, indeed, would it be, that in many countries commerce would have become far more active, the loss of ships producing a demand for the opening of mines, for the construction of furnaces and mills, that would make a market for labor such as had never before been known.

Let us next suppose that the ships had been spared, and all the gold and silver annihilated, and look at the effect. The reader of newspapers, unable to pay for them in beef, cloth, or iron, would be compelled to dispense with his usual supply of intelligence, and the journal would no longer be printed. Omnibuses would cease to run for want of sixpences, and places of amusement would be closed for want of shillings. Commerce would be at an end, except so far as it might be possible to effect direct exchanges, food being given for labor, or wool for cloth. These, however, could be few in number, and men, women, and children would perish by millions because of the inability to obtain food and clothing in exchange for service. Large cities would soon exhibit blocks of unoccupied buildings, and the grass would grow in their streets. Men might, it is true, return to the usages of those primitive times when wheat or iron, tobacco or copper, constituted the medium of exchange; but society, as at present constituted, could have no existence. Tons of such commodities would be needed to pay for the food consumed in a single eating-house, or the amusement furnished in a single theatre; and how the wheat, iron, or copper, could be fairly divided among the people who had contributed to the production of the food or the amusement, would be a question entirely incapable of solution.*

The precious metals are to the social body what atmospheric air is to the physical one; both supply the machinery of circulation, and the resolution of the physical body into its elements when deprived of the one, is not more certain than that of the social body when deprived of the other. Of all the labor-saving machinery in use among men, there is none that so much economizes human power and facilitates combination as that known by the name of money. Wealth, or the power to command nature's services, grows with every increase in the facility of combination; and this latter grows with the ability to command the aid of the precious metals. Wealth, then, should increase most rapidly where that ability is most complete.

§ 3. The power of a commodity to command money in exchange is called its PRICE. Prices fluctuate, much food and wool being sometimes, or at some places, given for little money, while at others much money is given for little of either wool or food. What are the circumstances which tend to affect prices generally, we may now consider.

A thousand tons of rags, or wool, at the Rocky Mountains, would not exchange for the smallest piece of money; whereas, a quire of paper would command, perhaps, an ounce of silver. Passing eastward to the plains of Kansas, their relative values would have so much changed, that the price of the rags would pay for many reams of paper Coming to St. Louis, a further change would be experienced, rags having again risen, and paper again fallen. So, too, at every stage of the progress eastward, until in Massachusetts, three pounds of rags would command more silver than would purchase a

* The legal tender notes now in use throughout these United States are substitutes for the precious metals, and their value in exchange for commodities varies with the variation in their value in exchanges for gold.

pound of the paper made from them. The following diagram exhibits these changes:—

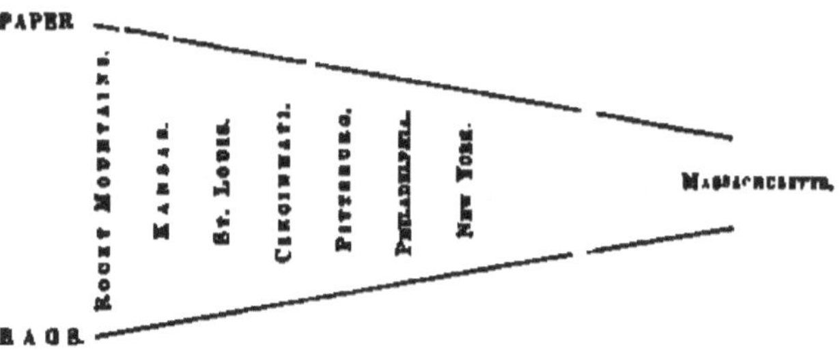

The price of raw materials tends to rise as we approach those places at which men are most enabled to combine for obtaining power to command the services of the great forces of nature. That of finished commodities moves in an opposite direction, both tending thus to more close approximation. Cotton is low on the plantation, but high in Manchester or Lowell. Corn in Illinois is often so cheap that a bushel does not even pay for a yard of coarse cotton cloth, whereas in Manchester it pays for a dozen yards.

Raw materials tend to rise in price with the progress of men in wealth and civilization. What, however, is raw material? In answer to this question, we may say, that all the products of the earth are, in turn, finished commodity and raw material. Coal and ore are the finished commodity of the miner, but the raw material of pig iron. The latter is the finished commodity of the smelter, yet only the raw material of the puddler, and of him who rolls the bar. The bar is again the raw material of sheet iron, and that, in turn, becomes the raw material of the nail and the spike. These, in time, become the raw material of the house, in the diminished cost of which are concentrated all the changes in the various stages of passage from the rude ore, lying useless in the earth, to the nail and spike, the hammer and saw, used in the construction of a dwelling.

In the early and barbarous ages of society land and labor are very low in price, and the richest deposits of coal and ore are worthless. Houses are then obtained with such exceeding difficulty, that men are forced to depend for shelter against wind and rain upon holes and caves they find existing in the earth. In time, they are enabled to combine their efforts;

and with every step in the course of progress, land and labor acquire power to command money in exchange, while houses lose it. As the services of fuel are more readily commanded, pig iron is more easily obtained. Both, in turn, facilitate the making of bars and sheets, nails and spikes, all of these in turn facilitating the creation of boats, ships, and houses; but each and every of these improvements tends to augment the prices of the original raw materials—land and labor. At no period in the history of the world has the general price of these latter been so high as in the present one; at none would the same quantity of money have purchased so staunch a boat, so fleet a ship, or so comfortable a house.

The more finished a commodity, the greater is the tendency to a fall of price; and for the same reason, that all the economies of labor of the earlier processes are accumulated together in the later ones. Houses, thus, profit by all improvements in the making of bricks, in the quarrying of stone, in the conversion of lumber, and in the working of the metals. So, too, is it with articles of clothing—every improvement in the various processes of spinning, weaving, and dyeing, and in the conversion of clothing into garments, being found gathered together in the coat. The more numerous those improvements, the lower will be its price, while the higher will be that of the land and labor to which the wool is due.

§ 4. The views now presented may be embodied in the following propositions:—

Man seeks association with his fellow-man. It is his first and greatest need:

That he may associate, there must be that development of individuality which results from diversity of employments, the artisan taking his place by the side of the planter and the farmer, and exchanging services with them:

That such exchanges may be readily made, there is needed an instrument which shall be small in bulk, easily preserved, capable of almost infinite division and subdivision, readily convertible into various commodities required for the purposes of man, and for all these reasons universally acceptable:

That this instrument is furnished by Providence in the two metals, gold and silver, each of them possessing all the qualities above described:

That the more abundant the supply of these metals, the more *instant* become the exchanges of society, the more rapid the societary circulation, the greater the economy of mental and physical force, and the greater the power to produce commodities to be offered in exchange:

That the countries which furnish them to the world are distant from those which produce cotton and corn, lead and iron:

That the obstacles to exchanges between the countries that do, and those that do not, produce them, result from the necessity for effecting changes of place; and that they exist in the ratio of the difficulty of transferring the things required to be exchanged:

That land and labor are the things least susceptible of being changed in place; and that they are always in the early stages of society very low in price:

That the most highly finished commodities, as more susceptible of being transported, are, in those ages, very high in price:

That with the growth of wealth and of diversity of employments, the bulk of commodities tends steadily towards diminution, corn and wool becoming combined in the form of cloth, and being thus enabled readily to travel to the gold-and-silver producing countries of the world:

That with every such change in the form of the rude products of the earth international exchange is facilitated; and that with the growth of domestic and foreign commerce there is a tendency towards equality of price, that of highly finished commodities falling, and that of rude products rising—the rise being greatest as we approach most nearly to the ultimate raw material of all commodities, land and labor:

That this approximation of prices is a consequence of increased facility of combination, which is, itself, a consequence of increased ability to command the services of the great instrument of association; and that with every stage of progress in this direction there is a tendency to equality, among the various members of a community, in the power to obtain the commodities and things required for the maintenance and improvement of their physical, moral, and mental forces, with daily augmentation of their ability to command the aid of the natural forces placed at their service by a bounteous Providence:

That the greater that ability the greater must be the tendency towards increase in the price of land and labor and of the rude products of both, towards an equality in the prices of the more and the less finished commodities, and towards an approximation in the character of the books, clothing, furniture, and dwellings of the various portions of society; and the greater the power to maintain commerce between those countries which do, and those which do not, yield the metals which constitute the raw material of money.

For proof of the truth of these propositions the reader may look to any of the advancing communities of the world. In the days when the French peasant was required to give an ox for a ream and a half of paper, wine was much higher than at present, peaches were unattainable, the finer vegetables were unknown, and an ell of Dutch linen exchanged for the equivalent of 60 francs ($11 25). Now, the price of meat has wonderfully increased and the farm laborer is better paid; so that with the price of an ox the farmer can purchase better wine than then was drunk by kings, can obtain not only paper but books and newspapers, can consume apricots and peaches, tea, sugar, and coffee, and can have a supply of linen that would, in earlier times, have almost sufficed for the entire household of a duke. Such are some of the results of an increase in the facility of combination among men; and the instrument to which they are most indebted for the power of combination, is that to which we give the name of *money*.

Let us now inquire what are the circumstances under which the power to command the use of this instrument tends towards increase or diminution.

CHAPTER XXIV.

OF THE INSTRUMENT OF ASSOCIATION—CONTINUED.

II.—*Of the Supply of Money.*

§ 1. Commodities tend to leave those places at which they have the least utility and greatest value, and to seek those at which their value is least and their utility greatest. The raw material of money flows, therefore, from those places at which food and wool are cheap and cloth and iron dear, towards those at which the former are dear and the latter cheap.*

§ 2. Flowing always towards those countries in which raw materials and finished commodities approximate most in price, the power to command their services is proof conclusive of advancing civilization.

§ 3. Central and Northern Europe now becoming the great reservoirs of those metals. The more the rude products of their soil rise in price the greater must be the tendency of gold and silver in that direction. Raw materials tend to leave the countries in which employments are not diversified, and to go to those in which diversification most exists. The precious metals follow in their train.

§ 4. Results of American experience. Excess export of those metals in all the free trade periods, and excess import of them in all the protected ones. Stoppage of the societary circulation in the former, and increased rapidity of movement in the latter. General tendency of American policy that of reducing the prices of rude products and increasing those of finished commodities.

§ 5. Money the indispensable instrument of society. Of all the instruments in use among men, the one that performs the largest amount of service in proportion to its cost. Economists assert that the only effect of an influx of the precious metals is that of rendering a country a good place to sell in, but a bad one in which to buy. That theory contradicted by all the facts of history, the direct tendency of such influx having, and that invariably, been that of reducing the prices of the finished commodities required by the producers of gold and silver. With every step in this direction agriculture tends to become a science, and the supply of food becomes more abundant.

§ 6. The use of circulating notes tends to diminish the value of the precious metals, while increasing their utility. All commodities going to those places at which their utility is greatest, the use of such notes should promote the influx of those metals. Error of Great Britain and the United States in seeking to promote that influx by means of a war against circulating notes.

§ 1. UTILITY *is the measure of man's power over nature.* The more complete the development of the utility of any commodity, the larger is the demand for it, and the greater the tendency towards increase in the supply and decline of

* The reader may be disposed here to ask: Can it be, that wheat has greater value in Ohio where it is produced, than in England to which it is sent? It has, and for the reason that less labor is required in the latter for the production of 40 bushels to the acre than is given in the former for obtaining 10 or 12. Value is the measure of nature's resistance to the gratification of man's desires. That resistance diminishes as the market is brought nearer to the farmer, and as agriculture becomes more and more a science. It increases with every increase in the necessity for sending to a distance the produce of the farm, and thus annihilating the power to return to the soil the refuse of its products.

its value. Raw materials always tend towards those places in which their utility is greatest, and there the value of the finished article is always least. Wheat tends towards the grist-mill, and there flour is cheapest. Cotton tends towards the mills at which it is to be spun and woven, and cloth is there very cheap, while always high on the plantation on which the wool had been produced.

Such precisely is the case with the precious metals which are always tending towards the places where their utility is greatest—where men most combine their efforts—and *where the charge for the use of money is lowest;* leaving those at which their utility is small and in which combination of action least exists, a state of affairs always attended by a high rate of interest.

§ 2. For more than a century Britain was the reservoir into which was discharged the major part of the gold and silver produced throughout the world. There, the artisan and the farmer were most nearly brought together, land and labor were most utilized, and the consumption of the precious metals greatest. Now, all is different. Great Britain having passed from being a place at which commodities are produced to be given in exchange for the produce of other lands, to being a mere place of exchange for the people of those lands, the power to retain the precious metals has correspondingly diminished.

The gold of California does not, to any material extent, remain in these United States. Touching the Atlantic coast, it is thence transferred to Britain, where it meets the product of Australia, the two amounting annually to more than $100,000,000. Both come there, however, merely in transit, being destined ultimately to pay the people of the Continent for raw products that have been converted and exported, or finished ones that have been consumed. Much of it goes to France, and there remains, because *French exports are almost wholly composed of the direct products of French labor, while England does little but buy foreign food and other raw materials, change their forms, and then re-export them.* The position of the former is that of the enlightened farmer, who sells his productions in their highest form and is therefore free to apply to the support of his family, the education of his children, and the improvement of his land, *the whole of the commodities he receives in exchange.* That of the latter is the position of the trader, who passes through his hands a large amount of property of which he is entitled to retain *the amount of his commission and nothing more.* The one has an immense and growing *commerce;* the other performs a vast amount of *trade.*

§ 3. The precious metals are steadily flowing towards the north and centre of Europe, to Denmark and Sweden, Austria and Belgium, but especially to Northern Germany, now so rapidly advancing in civilization. These countries, as well as France, are large importers of raw materials, and *gold and silver always follow in their train.* Directly the reverse of this, there has been an unceasing drain of the precious metals from Ireland, Turkey, and Portugal, followed by a decline in the productiveness and price of land, and in the freedom, happiness, and power of man. The poverty of Spain increased from the hour when, by expelling her manufacture, she made herself dependent on the workshops of other countries. Mistress of Mexico and Peru, she acted merely as the conduit through which their wealth passed to the advancing countries of the earth, as is now the case with Great Britain and these United States.

Raw materials and the precious metals tend, thus, *toward* those countries in which, employments being most diversified, land and labor tend most to rise.

They tend *from* those in which, employments being least diversified, the power of combination least exists.

The portions of the world *from* which the precious metals flow, in which agriculture declines and men become less free, are those which follow in the lead of England, preferring *trade* to *commerce*—Ireland, Turkey, Portugal, India, Carolina, and other exclusively agricultural countries.*

The portions *toward* which they flow are those which follow in the lead of France, preferring the extension of commerce to the enlargement of the trader's power. Germany, Denmark, Sweden, and New England, are in this position. In all of them agriculture becomes more a science as employments become more diversified, the returns to agricultural labor increasing as raw materials rise in price.

* Recent stoppage in the supply of American cotton has caused a great demand upon India for that most necessary commodity, with large increase of price, and consequent increase in the necessity for exporting to the East the produce of the mines of Mexico, the Indian government having persisted in maintaining silver as the standard by which the value of all other commodities must be measured.

In the countries *to* which they flow, the prices of raw materials and of finished commodities tend steadily to approximate, the farmer giving smaller quantities of wool and corn for larger quantities of iron and of cloth.

In all those *from* which they flow, those prices become more widely separated, the planter giving more of wool or corn, for less of cloth or iron.

§ 4. Inquiring now how far the views above presented are in accordance with the experience of these United States, we find that whenever their policy has tended towards bringing the artisan to the side of the farmer, they have been importers of the precious metals; and that the contrary effect has been produced whenever the opposite policy has been pursued; limited, however, for the period immediately following the change, by the existence of a credit that has enabled them to run in debt to Europe, and thus for a time to arrest the export of the precious metals. The course of trade in reference to those metals during the thirty years preceding the discovery of the California gold deposits was as follows:—

	Excess exports.	Excess imports.
1821–1825	$12,500,000	....
1826–1829		$4,000,000
1830–1834		20,000,000
1835–1838		34,000,000
1839–1842	9,000,000	....
1843–1847		30,000,000
1848–1850	14,000,000	....

We see here, that in the closing years of the free-trade system of 1817 the average annual excess of specie export was about $12,500,000. If to this be added only a similar amount for consumption in the arts, and waste, we obtain a diminution of $25,000,000, while the population had increased ten per cent. That those years should have been marked by calamity, affords, therefore, no cause for surprise. At Pittsburg, flour sold at $1 25 per barrel; wheat, in Ohio, for 20 cents a bushel; while a ton of bar iron required nearly 80 barrels of flour to pay for it. Such was the state of affairs that produced the tariff of 1824, by means of which, imperfectly protective as it was, an inward current was soon established. The total *net* import under it was $4,000,000. In 1828 was enacted the first tariff tending directly to the promotion of association throughout the country; and its effects are seen in an excess import of the precious metals, averaging as much annually, notwithstanding the discharge of the whole of the national debt that had been held in Europe, amounting to many millions. Putting together the discharge of debt and the import of coin, the balance of trade must have been in favor of the country to the extent of more than $10,000,000 a year. As a consequence, prosperity then existed to an extent never before known, and the list of free commodities was greatly enlarged, tea, sugar, and many others being added to it. *Thus did efficient protection carry the country one great step forward in the direction of freedom of international commerce.*

The first few years of the Compromise tariff of 1833 profited largely of the prosperity produced by the Act of 1828. Five years of protection had raised American credit to a point that until then had not been thought of, with the effect of facilitating the contraction of foreign debt to an immense amount, thereby stopping the export of specie, and producing an excess import averaging more than $8,000,000. Prosperity seemed to exist, but it was of the same description that marks the present period (1856), when the value of all property so entirely depends on the power to obtain foreign cloth and foreign iron in exchange for bonds.

As the free-trade tariff became more fully operative furnaces and factories were closed, with constantly increasing necessity for remittances of specie. The annual export, nevertheless, but little exceeded $2,000,000; but if we add to this $3,000,000 for consumption, we have in four years a reduction of $20,000,000, accompanied by an almost total suspension of the societary circulation. The whole country was in a state of ruin, laborers were thrown out of employment, and the power of accumulation ceased to have existence.

The change in the value of labor consequent upon this trivial reduction, cannot be placed at less than $500,000,000 a year; and yet the difference in regard to money, between the two periods ending in 1833 and 1842, was only that between an excess import of $5,000,000 and an excess export of $2,500.000, giving a total of $7,500,000 a year. No one who studies these facts can fail to be struck with the wonderful power over the conditions of men exerted by the metals provided by the Creator for furthering the work of association among mankind. Of all the machinery furnished for man's use, there is none so equalizing in its tendency as money; and yet men claiming to be regarded as economists would have us believe that the satisfaction felt in the knowledge that it is flowing in, is evidence of ignorance, and that any reference to the balance of trade is beneath the dignity of men who tread in the footsteps of Hume and Adam Smith.

The condition of the nation in 1842 was humiliating in the extreme. The Treasury was unable to negotiate a loan at 6 per cent. in the same foreign markets in which it had recently paid off at par a debt bearing an interest of only 3 per cent. Some even of the oldest States had been forced to suspend the payment of interest on their debts. The banks were, to a great extent, in a state of suspension, while those which professed to redeem their notes were fettered by the demand for coin to go abroad. Throughout a large portion of the country the use of the precious metals had wholly ceased. The Federal government, lately so rich, was driven to the use of inconvertible paper money in its transactions with the people. Of the merchants, a large portion had become bankrupt. Commerce, whether domestic or foreign, had scarcely an existence. Nevertheless, so magical was the effect of a measure calculated to turn the balance of trade, that scarcely had the Act of August, 1842, become a law, when the government found that all its wants could be supplied at home. Labor became again in demand, and before the close of the third year of protection, prosperity almost universal reigned. States recommenced payment of interest on their debts, railroads and canals again paid dividends, and real estate doubled in value; and yet the average net import of specie during the first four years was but $4,250,000. The last year was marked by the Irish famine, when the demand for food caused an import of no less than $22,000,000, making a total in five years of $39,000,000. Deducting $4,000,000 a year for consumption, we have an annual increase for circulation of less than $5,000,000; yet the differences in the prices of labor and land, as compared with 1842, would be moderately estimated at $2000,000,000.

With 1847, however, there came another change of policy, the nation having then again been called upon to try the system under which it had so lately been prostrated. In compliance with the orders of foreign traders and pro-slavery dictators, protection was again repudiated; and within three years factories and furnaces were once more closed, labor was again everywhere seeking demand, and gold again flowed out even more rapidly than it had come in under the protective tariff of 1842. The excess export of these three years amounted, as shown above, to $14,000,000, and if to this be added as much for consumption, it follows that the reduction in those years must have been fully equal to the increase under the protective system. Circulation was everywhere being suspended, and a crisis was close at hand, when fortunately for the advocates of the free trade policy, the gold deposits of California were brought to light.

In the year 1850–51, the quantity received from that source was more than $40,000,000, of which one-half was retained at home. The consequence was a reduction in the rate of interest, and the re-establishment of commerce. In 1851–2, $36,000,000 were exported, leaving perhaps eight or ten millions, which, added to that retained in 1851, made an addition to the currency of probably $30,000,000, with great increase of the societary circulation. The following years gave still a slight increase, but in '54 and '55 the export rose to $97,000,000. Adding to this a domestic consumption of probably $25,000,000, we obtain a total amount withdrawn exceeding the receipts from all the world. As a consequence of this there is now good reason for doubting if the *effective* addition to the coin much exceeds a dollar a head. It may possibly amount in all to thirty or thirty-five millions; and small as is that sum it would have produced a great effect in promoting the rapidity of circulation, had it not been that the indebtedness to foreign countries had so much increased as to need, for the payment of interest alone, an annual remittance equal to the whole export of food to all the world, thereby palsying the movements of commerce. As a consequence, the country now (1856) presents the extraordinary spectacle of a community owning one of the great sources of supply for money, in which the price paid for its use is thrice, and in some parts six or eight times, as great as in those countries which find their gold mines in their furnaces and factories.

The power to command the services of the precious metals grows with the growth of association. The policy of the United States is hostile to association, and hence it is that cotton, flour, and tobacco decline in price, while money remains so dear.

§ 5. "In every kingdom into which money begins to flow in greater abundance than formerly, every thing," says Mr. Hume, "takes a new face: labor and industry gain life; the merchant becomes more enterprising, the manufacturer more diligent and skillful; and even the farmer follows his plough with more alacrity and attention."

That this is so, is well known. Why should it be so? Because the societary circulation then becomes more rapid, and all power, whether in the physical or social world, results from motion. Of all the machinery in use among men, there is none that exercises over their actions so great an influence as that which gathers up, divides, and subdivides, the minutes of which the time of a community is composed. It is the *indispensable* machinery of progress; and therefore do we see in all poor communities so constant an effort to obtain something to be used in place of it. In the Western States, a currency of some description is felt to be among the prime necessities of life. Many of the Eastern banks supply notes expressly for Western circulation, and the people there receive and pass them from hand to hand, because any money is better than none, and good they cannot get because metallic money flows *from* the place where the charge for its use is high, *to* that at which it is low. Money thus obeys the same law as water—*seeking always the lowest level.*

We are told by Mr. Hume—and in that he is followed by most teachers of the modern political economy—that an increase in the supply of gold and silver can have no other effect than that of "heightening the price of commodities, and obliging every one to pay more of these little yellow or white pieces for every thing he purchases." Were such the case, it would be little short of a miracle that we should see money always passing in the same direction—*to* the countries that are rich and *from* those that are poor, so poor that they cannot keep the little needed for their few exchanges. The gold of Siberia leaves a land where labor is at the lowest price, to seek St. Petersburg, where it will purchase less than it would do at home; and that of Virginia and Carolina goes year after year to the countries to which they send their cotton and their wheat. The silver of Mexico and its cochineal travel together to the same market; and the same steamer carries to Britain the gold of Australia and the wool of its flocks.

Every addition to the stock of money, as we are assured by the ingenious men of modern days engaged in compiling treasury tables and financial reports, renders a country a good place to sell in, but a bad place to buy in; and as the trader's object is to attract customers, he is led by this theory to believe, that the less the supply of money, the greater will be his trade. To what countries, however, have men resorted when they have desired to purchase? Have they not gone, until recently, almost exclusively to Britain? Why? Because it has been there that finished commodities were cheapest. Where have they gone to sell? Has it not been to Britain? Certainly, because there gold, wheat, cotton, and other rude products were dearest. Where do they now go to purchase silk or cloth? To France or Germany, because there raw materials are highest, and finished ones cheapest. Gold follows raw materials generally; and such being the case, it would seem that increase in the supply of money, so far from having the effect of causing men to give two pieces for an article that could before have been had for one, has, on the contrary, that of enabling them *to obtain for one piece the commodity that had before cost two.*

Money tends to diminish the obstacles interposed between the producer and the consumer, precisely as do railroads and mills. Every diminution in the competition of railroads, or in the number of mills and furnaces, tends to lessen the price of labor and land; and so does, in a still higher degree, every diminution in the supply of money. Why such is the case is, that with every improvement in the machinery of exchange, the *proportion* of the transporter, the miller, and the owner of money, is diminished, leaving more to be divided between the producers and the consumers. Both obtain larger wages and are enabled to apply more capital to the improvement of land or the conversion of its products, thus cheapening the products of the garden and the factory. Manufactures, and the higher products of a skillful agriculture, fruits, garden vegetables, and flowers, steadily decline in price in all countries into which money is flowing: because *agricultural improvement always accompanies manufactures, and manufactures always attract the precious metals.* Food thus becomes more abundant in those countries into which gold flows, and less so in those from which it goes. In all the latter, land and labor are low in price. Give them manufactures, enabling their people to combine their efforts, and they will obtain and retain gold; then they will make roads, and the supplies of food will increase as cloth and iron become cheaper and land and labor rise in price. The most necessary part of the machinery of exchange being that which facilitates the passage of labor and its products from hand to hand, any diminution of its quantity is felt with tenfold more severity than is a diminution in the quantity of railroad cars or steamboats. Nevertheless, writers who congratulate the nation on the building of new ships, look with indifference on a drain of the precious metals that must always be attended by a diminution of that societary motion to which alone we can safely look for increase of force.

§ 6. The use of bank-notes tends, we are told, to promote the expulsion of gold. Were this so, it would be in opposition to the great general law in virtue of which all commodities tend *to*, and not *from*, the places where their utility is greatest. A bank is a machine for utilizing money, by enabling A, B, or C, to obtain the use of it at the time when D, E, and F—its owners—do not need its services. The effect of the establishment of such institutions in the cities of Italy, Holland, and other countries, was always that of causing money to flow towards those cities, because it was in and around them that its utilities were most developed. Even then, there were difficulties attendant on its exchange, the owner having been required to go to the banking-house, and write it off to other parties. Later, they were permitted to draw checks, by means of which they could transfer their property without stirring from their houses.

The difficulty, however, still existed, that private individuals not being generally known, such checks could, in general, effect but a single transfer; and thus the recipient of money found himself obliged to go through the operation of taking possession of that which had been transferred to him, after which he had in his turn to draw a check when he, himself, desired to effect another change of ownership. To obviate this circulating notes were invented, and by their help property in money is now transferred with such rapidity that a single hundred dollars passes from hand to hand fifty times a day, effecting exchanges, perhaps, to the extent of many thousands, and without the parties being required to devote a single instant to the work of counting, or carrying, the coin. This was a great invention, for by it the utility of money was so much increased as to enable a thousand pieces to do the work that without it would have required hundreds of thousands.

This, we are told, supersedes gold and silver, and causes them to be exported. Money, however, promotes the societary circulation, and the more rapid that circulation the greater will always be the demand for the precious metals. The check and the bank-note, therefore, stimulate their import, as is proved by the fact, that for a century past, they have flowed towards Britain, where such notes were most in use. Their use increases rapidly in France, with constant increase in the inward flow of gold. So, too, does it in Germany, towards which the precious metals flow so steadily that notes which are the representatives of money are rapidly taking the place of those irredeemable pieces of paper by which the use of coin has so long been superseded.

Bank-notes increase the utility of gold and silver, and should, therefore, attract, not repel them. Nevertheless, the two nations of the world which claim best to understand the principles of commerce, are now (1856) engaged in a crusade against such notes, in the vain hope of thereby attracting the precious metals. England in this follows America, Sir Robert Peel's restrictions being several years later in date than the declaration of war fulminated against circulating notes by the Federal government. It is a pure absurdity; and its adoption here is due to the fact that our system tends to that expulsion of the precious metals which always follows persistence in that barbarous policy which looks to export to distant countries of the raw products yielded by the earth. The precious metals are great civilizers, and they fly from all those communities which give their powers to the proper work of the barbarian and the slave. At one time only, within the last twenty years, has there been any excess import of them, and that was under the highly protective tariff of 1842. Then, money became abundant and cheap, because the policy of the country looked to the promotion of association and the extension of domestic commerce as the foundation on which to build a great international commerce. Now, notwithstanding the vast additions made by California and Australia to the stock of the precious metals, it is scarce and dear, because that policy limits the power of association, and establishes the supremacy of trade. What are the circumstances which tend to influence the charge for the use of money, we may now examine.

CHAPTER XXV.

OF THE INSTRUMENT OF ASSOCIATION—CONTINUED.

III.—*Of the Charge for the Use of Money.*

§ 1. The charge for the use of land, houses, ships, and all other commodities and things, declines with every diminution in the cost of reproduction. So, too, with money, the rate of interest tending downwards, as man acquires greater power for the direction of the natural forces—that power constituting wealth. Interest, therefore, tends to fall in all those countries which follow in the lead of Colbert and of France, while rising in all those that follow in the lead of England. Phenomena presented for consideration by the United States.

§ 2. Money is capital, but capital is not necessarily money. Interest paid for the use of money alone. Various modes in which compensation is made for the use of capital in its various forms. Error of distinguished economists in supposing that interest is paid for the use of capital in other forms than that of money. Tendency of interest to fall as the societary motion becomes more rapid.

§ 3. The utility of money increases as its circulation becomes more rapid. Its value increases as its movement becomes retarded.

§ 4. Increase in the supply of money tends to promote equality among men. Phenomena observed in India, France, and Holland.

§ 5. Communities increase in strength as the rate of interest declines—raw products then rising, and finished commodities falling, and thus presenting evidence of advancing civilization. Teachings of economists generally in regard to money directly opposed to the lessons taught by the common sense of mankind. Gold and silver properly denominated the precious metals—being, of all commodities, those which most contribute to the development of individuality, and to the promotion of the power of association.

§ 1. WITH every increase in the facility of reproduction, there is a decline in the value of all existing things of a similar kind, attended by a diminution in the price paid for their use. The charge for the use of the existing money tends, therefore, to decline as man acquires control over the great forces provided by the Creator for his service; as is shown by the gradual diminution of the rate of interest in every advancing country. So, too, is it as we pass from the sparsely-peopled regions beyond the Mississippi toward the more thickly settled New England States, interest varying in the first from 15 to 60 per cent., while in the last its greatest variation is from 5 to 20 per cent. Look, too, where we may, we shall find that the tendency towards diminution of the charge for the use of money is in the ratio of the approximation of the prices of finished commodities to those of raw materials, land and labor included.

The power to purchase money and consequent decline in the rate of interest, exists in every community in the precise ratio of the activity of the societary circulation. In the free-trade period that followed the close of the great European war, circulation in these United States almost ceased, labor was everywhere being wasted, and money was almost unattainable at any price. After the passage of the Act of 1828, every thing was different: the circulation became rapid, labor was in demand, and money became cheap. With the Compromise tariff of 1833 the scene once more changed; production declined, while money rose with such rapidity that banks suspended, States defaulted, and the Federal government became absolutely bankrupt.* Once more, in 1842, the protective policy was adopted; and production rapidly increased, while the rate of interest fell. It is now (1856) high, because *production is steadily declining in its ratio to the population.* The facts of the present time, therefore, correspond with those observed in 1836, and there is every reason to expect a crisis as severe as that which then occurred.†

§ 2. Money is often spoken of as the exclusive *capital;* and we are told that interest is high because "capital is scarce." There would, however, be as much propriety in saying that rents, tolls, or freights, are high because of the scarcity of capital. Houses, roads, ships, money, equally constitute portions of the capital of a community. Interest is always high when this last, from whatsoever cause, is scarce; and the high price then paid for its use constitutes a deduction from the rents of the first, and freights of the others. The owner of money then profits at the expense of all other capitalists. Interest is the compensation paid for the use of the *instrument* called money, *and for that alone.* In countries in which that is high, the rate of profit is necessarily so, because the charge for the use of his money enters so largely into the trader's profits.

The mistake of confounding *money* with *capital* appears in a recent work by a leading French economist, who regards it as an error to say that "money is plenty, or money is scarce, to indicate the state of things that exists when the artisan seeking for capital obtains it with facility or finds it difficult to be obtained." In his opinion, the English expression, "money market," should be changed to "capital market;" and when the farmer complains that "money is scarce," he

* In the closing years of the protective policy of 1828, the Federal government paid off a large amount of debt bearing interest at *three* per cent. In the free-trade period of 1841–2, it was totally unable to borrow money even at *six* per cent.

† This prediction was realized in the following year, 1857.

regards him as being "the dupe of a metaphor, in virtue of which, in ordinary speech, capital is termed money, because money is the measure of capital."*

The error would seem here to be on the side of the economist, and not on that of the farmer, whose daily experience teaches him that when money circulates freely, he is prosperous, and that when it is scarce his prosperity disappears. It is *not* capital that is then needed, but money, and that alone. The capital of the United States, in houses, factories, mines, ships, and other property, has (1856) within ten years increased by thousands of millions, yet are there on all sides visible roads half finished, laborers unemployed, mills stopped, and men of business compelled to curtail their operations. Why? Because the drain of money has produced an extreme sluggishness of the societary motion. Were it possible now to announce, that by reason of a change of policy the export of gold would henceforth cease and the produce of California be here retained, money would at once become abundant and cheap, circulation would recommence, and prosperity would reign throughout the land; and yet, the difference in the ensuing year in the quantity of the machinery of circulation, would not amount to *a fourth of one per cent. of the value of the land, and labor, and other capital of the country.*

§ 3. It is not, however, in the *quantity* of money held by a country that we are to find the test of its prosperity, but in the rapidity of its circulation. The gold held by the banks, the people, and the government of these United States, is said to exceed by $100,000,000 what was held a few years since; but, there being no regularity in the societary motion, credit is much impaired, circulation is sluggish, and interest is high. The monied capitalist profits by this, but it is the cause of ruin to the cloth-maker and the miner.

France has a large stock of the precious metals; but frequent revolutions have so impaired confidence that much of it is hoarded, and performs no part of the societary service. The rate of interest is therefore high, while wages are low because of frequent intermissions in the demand for labor. The manner in which all this would be terminated by a small increase of the machinery of circulation is thus shown by a distinguished French economist in the following passage:—

* CHEVALIER: *De la Monnaie*, p. 380.

"On one side we see a machinist, a blacksmith, and a wheelwright, whose shops are closed, not because of any want of raw materials, but because of the absence of demand for their products. Elsewhere are manufacturers in want of machinery, and farmers in need of agricultural implements. Why do not the latter give to the former the orders for want of which they continue idle? Because they must be paid in money, which the others have not to give; and yet they have, in shops or barns, abundance of commodities that they desire to sell, and by the possession of which many of their neighbors would be greatly served. Why do they not exchange? Because, direct exchange being impossible, they must begin by selling, and as they, in their turn, must demand money, they cannot find purchasers. Here we have a suspension of labor on both sides; and in cases like this, production is languid and society vegetates, though surrounded by all the elements of activity and prosperity. Means might, however, be found for removing this difficulty. If the machinist, the blacksmith, and the wheelwright, refuse to deliver their products except for ready money, it is not because they entertain any doubt of the future solvency of the farmer or the manufacturer; but because it is not convenient to them to make credit sales that would diminish their active capital, and perhaps prevent them from continuing their operations. Let each one, then, in delivering his articles, as he has confidence in the future ability of those who now demand them, require only, in place of money, a note that he can use in his turn with those who furnish him. On this condition, circulation will be re-established, and labor resumed. True, but we must first be sure that these notes, when accepted, will be received elsewhere, or otherwise it becomes at once a simple sale on credit. This certainty, however, cannot be obtained, therefore they refuse the notes; not because of any suspicion of their ultimate value, but because of doubts of the possibility of disposing of them. At this moment, a bank intervenes, and says:—'You, machinist, deliver your machinery; you, blacksmith, your instruments; you, ploughman, your raw materials; you, manufacturer, your manufactures; accept freely notes payable at a future time, provided you have confidence in the goodness of those who will then become your debtors. I will take charge of all those notes, and hold them until they shall become due, giving you in exchange other notes, issued by me, that you will be certain to find of universal acceptation.' Forthwith all difficulty is at end;

sales are made, goods circulate, and production becomes animated. There are no longer raw materials, instruments, nor products of any description, remaining, even for a moment, unemployed."*

There is here no change whatsoever in the quantity of capital owned by the community; and yet its members are seen passing at once from a state of inactivity to one of productiveness. But what was it that gave value to these notes, making them circulate so much more freely than those of the blacksmith and the farmer? It was the confidence that existed in the community that *behind them stood a pile of money sufficient to redeem each and every one of them, whensoever and by whomsoever presented.* Without that belief they could not have circulated, as would soon be seen were there established a drain of gold, producing a steady diminution of the quantity in the bank, until even a single one of the notes failed to be paid on presentation. Instantly their circulation would be stopped, suspension of movement would again take place, and the exchanges they had facilitated would be at an end. *Money is to society what fuel is to the locomotive and food to the man: the cause of motion, whence results power.* Withdrawal of food from the man is followed by paralysis and death; and such is, precisely, the effect of a failure of the necessary supply of the machinery of circulation.

When, therefore, men complain that money is scarce, they are right; it *is* money that is needed. *Money is capital, but capital is not necessarily money;* and there is strict propriety in the use of the term "money market" in preference to that of "capital market," which it is proposed to substitute for it.

§ 4. With increase in the supply of money, there is a steady tendency towards an equalization of the price paid for the services of this great instrument of association. When money is scarce, the rich man borrows at ten or twelve per cent., while the small manufacturer can scarcely do so at any price: so soon as it becomes abundant, the prices charged for its use tend towards a level—the small operator of good character obtaining loans at nearly as low a rate as his opulent neighbor.

With increase of the supply of money, there is, too, a diminution of the burden imposed by pre-existing capital.

* Coquelin: *Du Crédit, et des Banques.*

Mortgages become more oppressive as money becomes scarce; but as the supply increases, there is a diminution of the weight of the mortgage, both as regards the interest and the repayment of the capital In the former case, if the movement be long continued, it results in the forced sale of the encumbered property, as has been seen in this country at the close of every free-trade period, and as is now to be seen in every one that fails to appreciate the great fact that the raising of raw produce for the supply of distant markets is the proper work of the slave and the barbarian. The rich are thus made richer, but the poor are ruined.

Again, with every increase in the abundance of money, taxes become less oppressive to those who pay, and less beneficial to those who receive them, except in so far as the consequent reduction in the prices of finished commodities makes amends for diminution in the quantity of money received.

§ 5. The strength of a nation grows with that decline in the rate of interest which is always a consequence of that *influx* of the precious metals, and that increase of their utility which is observed in all those countries which place the consumer by the side of the producer. In such countries credit grows, commerce becomes rapid, mind is developed, land acquires value, and man becomes more civilized, more happy, and more free.

The strength of a nation declines with the increase in the rate of interest resulting from the *efflux* of the precious metals, or from diminution of the rapidity of their passage from hand to hand. This takes place in all those nations in which the tendency towards exportation of their produce in its rudest form is a growing one. In all such, credit declines, commerce decays, the societary circulation becomes more sluggish, and man becomes more and more the slave of nature and of his fellow-man.

Of all the machinery in use among men, there is none whose yield is so great in proportion to its cost as that employed in effecting exchanges from hand to hand, none whose movements are so strong an evidence of increase or decrease of the productive power of the community,—none, therefore, that affords the statesman so excellent a barometer by which to judge of the working of his measures. It is, nevertheless, the one whose movements are generally regarded by modern economists as being least worthy of their consideration. All their teachings on this subject are in direct opposition to the common sense of mankind; and, as is usually the case, that to which men are prompted by a sense of their own interests, is far more nearly right than that which is taught by philosophers who look inward to their own minds for the laws which govern man and matter—refusing to study the movements of the people by whom they are surrounded.

The uninstructed savage finds in the waterspout and the earthquake the most conclusive proof of the wonderful power of nature. The man of science finds it in the magnificent, but unseen, machinery by means of which the waters of the ocean are daily raised, to descend again in refreshing dews and summer showers. He finds it, too, in that insensible perspiration which carries off so nearly the whole amount of food absorbed by men and animals. Again, he sees it in the workings of the little animals, invisible to the naked eye, to whom we are indebted for the creation of islands elaborated out of earth that has been carried from the mountains to the sea, and there deposited. Studying these facts, he is led to the conclusion, that it is in the minute and almost insensible operation of the physical laws he is to find the highest proof of the power of nature, and the largest amount of force. So, too, is it in the social world. To the uninstructed savage, the ship presents most forcibly the idea of commerce. The mere trader finds it in the transport of large cargoes composed of cotton, wheat, or lumber; and in the making of bills of exchange for tens of thousands of dollars, or of pounds. The student of social science, on the contrary, sees it in the exercise of a power of association and combination resulting from development of the various human faculties, and enabling each and every member of society to exchange his days, his hours, and his minutes, for commodities and things to whose production have been applied the days, the hours, and the minutes of the various persons with whom he is associated. For that commerce pence, sixpences, and shillings are required; and in them he finds willing slaves, whose operation bears to those of the ship the same relation that is elsewhere borne by the little coral insect to the elephant.

It is by means of combination of effort that man advances in civilization. Association brings into activity all the various powers, mental and physical, of the beings of whom society is composed, and individuality thus grows with the growth of the power of combination. That power it is which enables the many who are poor and weak to triumph over the few who are rich and strong; and therefore do men become more free with every advance in wealth and population. To enable them to associate there is required an instrument by help of which the process of composition, decomposition, and recomposition, of the various forces may readily be effected; so that while *all* unite to produce the effect desired, *each* may have his share of the benefits thence resulting. That instrument was furnished in those metals which stand almost alone in the fact, that, as Minerva sprang fully armed from the head of Jove, they, wherever found, come forth ready, requiring no elaboration, no alteration to fit them for the great work for which they were intended, that of enabling men to combine their efforts for fitting themselves worthily to fill the post at the head of creation for which they had been designed. Of all the instruments at the command of man, there are none that tend, in so large a degree, to promote individuality on the one hand, and association on the other, as do gold and silver—properly, therefore, denominated the PRECIOUS METALS.*

* Recent American experience furnishes, as we think, proof conclusive of the accuracy of Mr. Carey's views above presented. Notwithstanding the gigantic character of the existing civil war, the rate of interest is low, the societary circulation is great beyond all precedent, the people are, to an extent never before known, free from debt, and the reward of labor is large. Why is it so? Because, for the first time in its history the country has been supplied with machinery of circulation in quantity adequate to the performance of the work that needed to be done. The government has furnished this, and the people pay for the use of this machinery precisely as they would do were it composed of the precious metals; doing so for the reason that all have perfect confidence in the responsibility of the party by whom it has been supplied.

CHAPTER XXVI.

OF THE INSTRUMENT OF ASSOCIATION—CONTINUED.

IV.—*Of the Trade in Money.*

§ 1. The precious metals the only commodities of universal acceptance, being the indispensable instruments of commerce.

§ 2. Proportion borne by money to the amount of commerce increases in declining countries and decreases in advancing ones.

§ 3. Centralization, retarding the societary motion, increases that proportion. Decentralization diminishes it. Man then becomes more valuable and more free.

§ 4. Money being the one indispensable instrument of society, governments have always assumed to control its management, as supplying the most productive of all the machinery of taxation. Falsification of money by European sovereigns.

§ 5. Banks established with a view to the emancipation of the currency from the control of governments. Deposit banks of Italy, Germany, and Holland. Institution of banks of discount.

§ 6. Enlargement of the operations of discount banks.

§ 7. Banks of circulation commence with the Bank of England.

§ 8. How the expansions and contractions of banks affect the societary movement.

§ 9. Great power of banks for good or evil. Banking monopolies, like those of France and England, give to a few individuals a power over the societary movement compared with which that exercised by the sovereigns of old sinks into insignificance.

§ 1. The single commodity that is of universal demand is money. Go where we may, we find hosts of people seeking commodities required for the satisfaction of their wants, yet widely differing in the nature of their demands. One needs food; a second, clothing; a third, books, newspapers, silks, houses, cattle, horses, or ships. Many desire food, yet while one would have fish, another rejects the fish and seeks for meat. Offer clothing to him who sought for ships, and he would prove to have been supplied. Place before the seeker after silks the finest lot of cattle, and he could not be induced to purchase. Among all of these, nevertheless, there would not be found even a single one unwilling to give labor, skill, bonds, lands, horses, or whatsoever other commodity might be within his reach, in exchange for money—provided, only, that the quantity offered in exchange were deemed sufficient.

So, again, if we look throughout the world. The poor African searches anxiously in the sands for gold, while the yet poorer Lapp and the wretched Patagonian—almost the antipodes of each other—are alike in the fact, that they are ready, at any moment, to exchange their labor and its products for either of the precious metals. So, too, has it been in every age. The Midianite merchants paid for Joseph with so many pieces of silver. Rome was sold to Brennus for gold. That of Macedon bought the services of Demosthenes; and it was thirty pieces of silver that paid for the treason of Judas. Sovereigns in the East heap up gold as provision against future accidents, and finance ministers in the West rejoice when their accounts enable them to exhibit a full supply of the precious metals. When it is otherwise—when, because of war, or of other circumstances, the revenue proves deficient—the highest dignitaries are seen paying obsequious court to the controllers of the supply of money. So, too, when roads are to be made, or steamers built. Farmers, contractors, and stock-holders, then go, cap in hand, to the Crœsuses of the great cities, anxious to obtain a favorable hearing, and desiring to propitiate the men of power by making whatsoever sacrifice may seem to be required.

Of all the materials of which the earth is composed, there are none so universally acceptable as gold and silver. Why should it be so? Because of their having distinctive qualities that bring them into direct connection with the distinctive qualities of man—facilitating the growth of association, and promoting the development of individuality. They are the *indispensable* instruments of society, or commerce. Therefore it is, that we see them to have been seized upon by the class that lives by virtue of the exercise of their powers of appropriation, as furnishing the most efficient of all the machinery of taxation.

§ 2. In the infancy of society, when poor and scattered men are compelled to limit themselves to the cultivation of the least fruitful soils, the quantity of money in use, trivial as it is, bears a large *proportion* to the commerce that is maintained. Among the Altai mountains, an ounce of silver purchases 250 pounds of beef, while on the Pampas of Buenos Ayres a pound of gold exchanges for horses that count by thousands. The recipients of these precious metals wrap them up with care, hoping never to have occasion to cause them again to see the light. In such cases, the utility of money is very small, but its value is very great. With increase in the power of association the former rises, but the latter falls; and with every stage of progress the quantity of money bears a diminishing *proportion* to the exchanges performed, as is proved by comparing the amount used in the great centres of trade for effecting operations that count by almost hundreds of millions daily, with that required in

India or Peru, where, society being torpid, each exchange must be accompanied by delivery of the coin needed for its accomplishment. Here, as everywhere throughout nature, increase in the rapidity of motion is attended by decline in the proportion borne by the material that is used to the effect that is produced.

§ 3. Centralization, whether political or trading, tends to retard motion and thus to increase the quantity of money required for carrying on any given amount of commerce. The heavier the taxation the larger will be the quantity of coin always on the road to the treasury, and the longer the time that must elapse before, if ever, it returns to the place whence it had been sent. The greater the distance between the farmer and the artisan the heavier are the charges, the slower are the exchanges, and the greater the need of the banker's services. Every increase of taxation, and every increase in the necessity for transportation, tends, therefore, to diminish the power to cultivate the richer soils, while increasing the proportion borne by money to the amount of commerce.

Decentralization, or the establishment of local centres of action, tends, on the contrary, to increase the amount of commerce while diminishing the quantity of money required, and to *diminish its value while increasing its utility.* With every step in this direction there is an increasing tendency to steadiness in the value of the precious metals. . The fluctuations of new settlements are, as is well known, exceedingly great. At one moment, money may be hired at 8 or 10 per cent.; at the next it commands 40, 50, or 60 per cent. At the one, produce is high in price; at the other, it falls so low that the farmer and planter find themselves reduced to bankruptcy.

§ 4. The tendency of gold and silver towards steadiness in value constitutes their principal recommendation for use as standards with which other commodities may be compared; and were the trade in money free from interference, they would be almost as perfect in that respect as are the yard-stick and the bushel as measures of length and of capacity. The corn and sugar in market in any year being consumed within the year, a failure of crop may make a change of even a hundred per cent. in the price; whereas, the quantity of gold and silver always in market being hundreds of times more than is required for a year's consumption, a total failure of the year's crop should not affect it even to the extent of one per cent. So numerous, however, have been the interferences with the commerce in money, that of all things it is the most subject to sudden variations. It is a yardstick of perpetually changing length—a gallon that contains sometimes three quarts, and at others, six or eight. Why this is so, we may now inquire.

Centralization giving power to the class that lives by appropriation, the soldier and the trader, every increase therein produces a demand for increased taxation, and the subjects selected are always those of positive necessity, such as salt and sugar. There being none, however, so indispensable as money, it is for that reason that we find its management to have been so universally assumed by governments, to be exercised for public or private profit.

With the growing centralization of power in the State of Athens we mark a constant increase in the rapacity of money dealers. In many of the subject cities the precious metals became so scarce as to compel recourse to coins of copper and of iron, circulated at rates far exceeding their real value. At a later period money almost disappeared, the land being then cultivated by slaves, to whom all use of the great instrument of association was utterly denied.

As centralization grew in Rome coins were diminished in weight, while the charge for the use of money as steadily increased. That Brutus received four per cent. per month is matter of history; but even this must have been thrice exceeded in the minor operations of the imperial city. The poorer a people the larger is always the rate of interest, and therefore it is that we see such colossal fortunes accumulated where pauperism most abounds.

It is, however, in history of a later date that we find this system carried to its highest point. Philip the Fair, of France, changed the coinage thirteen times in a year, and more than a hundred times in the course of his reign. His successors followed his example, calling in heavy pieces and issuing lighter ones in their stead, and to such extent that at the date of the Revolution it required 66 livres to give the quantity of silver that had formerly been contained in one. France has always been distinguished for the exactions of money-dealers; hence it is that credit has had so slight an existence, and that such squalid wretchedness has accompanied so great magnificence. That centralization, splendor, poverty, and weakness, are close companions, is proved by every page of history; but nowhere is it more fully shown than in those which record the histories of France and Spain, in which latter fraudulent debasement of the coin was continued until so late as 1786.

Such, too, was the case in Scotland, the present Scottish pound representing but a thirty-sixth part of its original weight, owing to long continued falsification of the coin.

Down to the days of Edward III. the English pound contained a full pound of silver, of a certain fineness. Incessant wars for the pursuit of glory, however, forced that monarch to the adoption of frauds similar to those then so common beyond the Channel, and the practice continued until the pound had lost two-thirds of its weight. The English monarchs, however, less warlike than those of France, were less frequently forced to plunder their subjects by tampering with the currency; while these latter, being more free, were less disposed to submit to such exactions.

§ 5. The state of things above described it was that led to the formation of the Bank of Amsterdam, the first institution of any importance established exclusively for the promotion of commerce, its predecessors of Venice and Genoa having been chiefly devoted to the management of affairs of state. It, on the contrary, looked wholly to the faithful guardianship of the moneys deposited with it for safe keeping, guaranteeing to its owners that equivalent amounts of coin should always be at their command. For the faithful performance of its duties the States-General of Holland became security, as a consequence of which the bank became at once the centre of the moneyed world, and the city in which it was established the chief European market for the precious metals. Hamburg, Nuremburg, and Rotterdam, speedily followed the good example, thus providing for the countries watered by the Rhine, the Weser, and the Elbe, places of secure deposit for money, and facilities for exchanging it free from the taxation of French or German sovereigns. The whole proceeding was a measure of resistance to arbitrary power; and for it the world is indebted to the action of small communities in which had been largely developed that spirit of association which always accompanies diversification of employments and increased demand for human service.

As yet, however, these being simple deposit banks, any augmentation of the currency thence resulting was merely that which was consequent on increased security and greater facility of transfer. At the next stage, however, we meet with banks of discount. To understand the effect of this upon the currency, let us suppose all the owners of the money in the vaults to have had the will to use it profitably to themselves, and with this view to have accepted certificates of stock—being thus at once changed from mere creditors of the institution into actual proprietors of it. The instant effect of this would be that of diminishing the currency by the whole amount of capital, as all the depositors would have parted with the power to transfer their money, or to use it themselves in any manner whatsoever. The bank, however, having acquired all the power they had lost, the volume of currency would be restored so soon as it had accepted from other persons their notes or bills to an equal amount, in exchange for similar sums placed to their credit on its books.

The apparent amount of currency would now be restored, but the real one would be materially increased; and for the reason, that the whole had passed into the hands of men of business paying interest for its use, and anxious not only to earn that interest but also a profit thereon, as compensation for their services. Previous to this, much of it must have been owned by small and distant capitalists, who, unable to judge of the character of the securities in market, preferred that it should remain idle in the vaults. They now obtain security, each of the managers being required to take his share of any loss that may be suffered, and being therefore directly interested in seeing the money safely placed. Another stage of progress having been thus accomplished, its effects soon manifest themselves in the increased utility of money, and the diminished rate of interest.

§ 6. Thus far the bank has traded upon its capital only, merely passing to the credit of individuals the gold that had been placed by its proprietors in its vaults. Were it to stop here, the dividend on its stock would be less than the ordinary rate of interest, its only source of revenue being the discount received from those to whom its capital had been loaned, and the expense of management being large. Experience, however, would soon teach the directors, that although all the persons who borrowed their money desired to use it, the occasion for so doing did not simultaneously exist; and that, in point of fact, although all their capital was drawing interest, much of it remained in their vaults entirely unused

This having been observed, they could scarcely fail further to see that they might with perfect safety lend a portion of the sum usually in their hands, extending their business to a fourth, or a third beyond the actual capital, and thus obtaining an excess of interest sufficient for paying the expenses of the institution, and providing against losses that might occasionally be incurred. To their customers this would be advantageous, because it would enable the bank to dispense with the accustomed charge for keeping their money, transferring it, or paying it out. To the community it would be beneficial, because it would quicken the societary motion and cause a decline in the rate of interest.

Of what, now, would the currency consist? Every man would have it who had money in his desk; and so, too, would every one who had a credit on the books of the bank, the power of purchase with the one being as complete as it could be with the other. The currency would then consist of the money in circulation, and the debts of the bank to its customers, the latter generally known by the name of deposits—its amount having been increased by the operation here described, to the precise extent that those debts exceeded the coin that it had been accustomed to retain in its vaults with a view to be prepared for the demands that might be made upon it by those to whom it held itself indebted.

§ 7. The close of the seventeenth century witnessed the origin of the most influential moneyed institution the world has yet seen, the Bank of England,—authorized to receive deposits, make discounts, and issue circulating notes by means of which the property of individuals in its hands could be at once transferred. Here was a further improvement, tending to increase the utility of money and lessen the rate of interest. Scarcely yet established, however, we find its proprietors obtaining the enactment of a law by which it was provided, that all who desired to place their money on deposit should be limited to a choice between mere private individuals on the one hand, and their own great bank on the other. Centralization being thus established in regard to the trade in money, as it had already been in reference to so much of the foreign trade, a single corporation now assumed the entire control of a currency that was to be managed for the benefit of the few persons who were interested in its stock.

The larger the amount of its debts, the greater being its

power to make loans, and the larger becoming its dividends, there was thus at once produced an interest antagonistic to that of the society in which it operated. Whatever tended to diminish security elsewhere increased the necessity for resorting to the one great institution that allowed no interest on its debts. Further, whatever lessened the facility of association also increased the difficulty of finding satisfactory modes of investment, thus increasing the quantity of money lying unproductive to its owners, in the vaults of the bank, to be used for augmentation of its dividends. If the directors willed to use it they could thus augment the volume of the currency, having done which they could again withdraw it, thus producing those changes with which in modern times we have become so well acquainted.

§ 8. For the benefit of those who have not traced the operation of an expansion, it may be proper here to show the manner of its action. Let us suppose, first, a state of affairs in which every thing is at par, money being easily obtained for good notes at a fair rate of discount, and for mortgages at the usual rate of interest, while those who have disposable means can readily obtain good securities that will yield them the common rate of profit, the daily supply of money and of securities being precisely equal to each other. In this state of affairs the directors of the bank, knowing that it would be profitable to increase their investments to the extent of another million, purchase that amount of exchequer bills, or other securities. At once the equilibrium is disturbed, a demand for securities having been produced in excess of the ordinary supply. Prices rising, some unfortunate holder is tempted to sell, hoping that there may to-morrow be less demand, and that prices will then fall, permitting him to buy in again at a lower price. At the close of the day his bills or notes have become the property of the bank—he and others who have united to furnish the desired million having become creditors on its books for the whole amount. His money being now uninvested he appears in the market next day as a purchaser; but, unfortunately for him, the bank, too, makes its appearance again in the same capacity. The first experiment has been attended with vastly fortunate results, its "deposits" having grown with the increase of its investments. Success now emboldens it to repeat the operation, and another million is purchased, with similar results. The bank obtains the bills, and the owners receive credit on its books; and the more the debts it is thus enabled to contract, the more means it supposes itself to have at its command. With the second million, prices have further risen; with a third, they rise still higher; and so on, with each successive million. *Money* appears to be superabundant, because the former owners of the securities are seeking for profitable investments; whereas the real superabundance consists only in *debts* incurred by the bank. Prices advancing from day to day, and speculation being excited by the rapid growth of fortune, new stocks are created for the employment of the apparently great amount of uninvested capital. New roads are projected, and vast contracts are made, boundless prosperity being full in view. Men who should be planting corn are set to breaking up old roads that they may be replaced with new ones; or to building palaces for lucky speculators. Imports increase, exports decrease, and there arises a demand for gold for exportation. Bullion going abroad, the bank is forced to sell securities. Prices fall, and trade becomes paralyzed. Roads, half made, cannot be now completed. Tens of thousands of people find themselves ruined, while the bank, with difficulty escaping from the ruin it has made, rejoices at the result of its operations, and prepares to repeat them at the first convenient opportunity.

Such is the history of the inflations and consequent crises of 1815, '25, '36, '39, and '47, on all of which occasions the bank, having manufactured "deposits" by monopolizing securities, allowed itself to be misled into the belief that the increase of its own debts indicated an actual surplus of money. Whenever the bank purchases a security—always the representative of some already existing investment—the seller will certainly desire to place the proceeds in some new species of investment, no one willingly allowing his capital to remain unproductive. If this purchase be made with the money of others, the inevitable effect must be to raise prices, and stimulate the late owner of the security to increased activity in providing for himself a new one. That done, he will, either directly or indirectly, demand payment in gold, and then the security must be parted with by the bank to enable it to provide the means of payment. Prices must then fall, because the creditor has been laboring to find employment for capital which had no real existence in any other form than that of a road, canal, or other public work or debt, already created, and not susceptible of being used for the formation of other canals or roads; and thus, while the party outside of the bank has been trying to invest his funds, the bank has itself been holding the evidence of their having been already invested, and drawing interest for their use. A double action has thus been produced; and inflation and speculation, to be followed by panic and ruin, follow necessarily in its train.

§ 9. The above sketch illustrates the effects that must inevitably result from granting to private individuals an exclusive control of the great instrument of association. Tampering with the coin is now greatly censured; yet are its evil effects utterly insignificant when compared with those of the expansions and contractions above referred to. A bank is an instrument of great power either for good or evil. Well directed, it produces regularity; but ill-directed, it stimulates the gambling propensities of men. That this latter is the case has long been seen; and some economists having found its cause in the power to issue circulating notes, a remedy has been attempted in the form of restrictions thereupon. Instability, however, has grown with restriction, as is proved by the experience of Great Britain and the United States; the changes in the value of money since the passage of Sir Robert Peel's law, and the adoption of General Jackson's policy, having been greater than had ever before occurred in a time of peace.*

* "The evil of the Bank Act is, that by the provisions which it makes to arrest an external drain on the Bank, it produces an internal one also. In order to prevent the efflux of a million or two of gold, the Bank, by raising its rate of discount, and curtailing its usual advances, gives a shock to credit. And this increasing tightness of the money-market, joined to the spectacle of the Bank rapidly approaching the limit at which it must stop discounting altogether, tends to suspend the ordinary relations of credit throughout the country, producing numerous failures, and ultimately panic and a run upon the banks. Under the present system, therefore, *an external drain inevitably produces an internal drain also*—which is like lighting a candle at both ends. * * * Since 1844, there have been fluctuations in the amount, and consequent alterations in the value, of the currency—and variations still more striking in the value of loanable capital, as expressed by the rate of discount—such as were unknown under the Act of 1819. In fact, the Act of 1844 has failed in the object which it was designed to achieve, and has subjected the country to new evils, of which its framers never dreamt. * * * Left free and unfettered in Scotland, banking assumed a form as near perfection as could be devised. In England it has been so swaddled and cramped by legislation that its natural growth was arrested and all symmetry made unat-

Such should be the case; and for the reason, that the policy of both is directly opposed to all that, reasoning *à priori*, we should expect *would* be true, and to all that, reasoning *à posteriori*, we find to *have been* true. *All commodities tend to move towards those places at which they are most utilized.* Here is a simple proposition whose truth is proved by all experience. The circulating note gives to its holder a right of property in a certain quantity of money lying in the vaults of a bank, while placing it in his power to change at will the ownership therein, and without the smallest expenditure of labor. So is it, too, with the establishment of a place of secure deposit for money, the property in which can be changed by means of checks. The note and the check increase the utility of the precious metals; and therefore is it, that money tends to flow towards those places at which notes and checks are most in use—passing, in America, from the Southern and Western States towards the Northern and Eastern ones, and from America towards England, the country in which the facility of transfer has always been most complete.

It would be better that the explosive force of gunpowder and the mighty power of steam had remained unknown, than that their exclusive use should have been secured to any nation of the world; and better, far, would it be that the art and mystery of banking had remained unknown, than that its powers should longer be monopolized by any particular set of men. More than any other, the trade in money requires freedom; yet, more than any other, has it been hedged around with restrictions designed for the benefit of a favored few, whose movements have always been directed towards giving to the accumulations of the past increased control over the labors of the present. That way lies barbarism; and it is because English banking tends in that direction that British journalists, in common with Carolina owners of negro slaves, have been led to find in measures looking to the protection of the capitalist against the laborer the surest road to civilization.

tainable. First Monopoly, and now Restriction, have exercised their baneful influence upon English banking. Both are pernicious in principle, injurious to the community, and incompatible with the due use and economy of capital."—*Blackwood's Magazine* March, 1864.

CHAPTER XXVII.

OF THE INSTRUMENT OF ASSOCIATION—CONTINUED.

V.—*Of Banking in England.*

§ 1. Great power exercised by the Bank of England.

§ 2. No banking business in England at the date of the Restoration. Under Charles II. jewellers become bankers. Consequent increase in the utility of money. Establishment of the Bank of England.

§ 3. Movements of the bank from 1797 to 1815.

§ 4. Change therein, subsequent to the close of the war. Resumption of specie payments. Productive of wide-spread ruin. Producing classes impoverished, while the merely consuming ones are enriched.

§ 5. Effect of those measures that of giving to the moneyed capitalist increased command over land and labor, always an evidence of declining civilization.

§ 6. Constant succession of expansions, contractions, and financial crises, each in succession tending to increase the power of money over land-owner and laborer.

§ 7. Bank Act of Sir Robert Peel. Its object, that of producing steadiness in the monetary movement. Its effect, that of increasing the power of the bank to control the societary movement. Its total failure.

§ 8. Cause of its failure to be found in the fact that it sought to regulate the currency in use, leaving wholly out of view the action of the bank in affecting the currency seeking to be employed.

§ 9. Currency in use almost a constant quantity. Essential error of the Bank Act. Under it monetary changes become more frequent and more severe.

§ 1. THE tendency to stability in the material world is in the direct ratio of the approach to the pyramidal form. So, too, is it in the trading world—the man whose liabilities are small while his capital is large standing secure amid gales that wreck by thousands those of his fellow-merchants whose operations are based upon the capital of others, and whose liabilities bear, therefore, a large proportion to their claims upon those with whom they trade. So, also, is it in the financial world, the bank which trades chiefly upon its own capital passing safely through the storm which wrecks those of its neighbors whose debts bear large proportion to their credits.

The New England States present the most remarkable cases of banks, such as are first above described. For the most striking example of the latter class we must look to the Bank of England, based as was that institution upon a mere annuity payable by the government, and trading, as it has always done, almost entirely on the capital of others, and not upon its own. As a consequence of this it is, that the course of this great institution has, beyond that of any other in the world, been distinguished by instability and rapidity of change.

To reduce the intrinsic value of a pound from 20s. to 6s. 8d., by means of governmental action, was a movement always in the same direction, all remaining quiet from the date of one reduction until another came to be required. With the bank it has been very different, money values having been raised at one moment and depressed at another, to an extent, and with a rapidity, that have defied all calculation. In common with all other traders the bank and its managers profit by changes, ruinous as they are to all who are in any manner dependent upon it for accommodation. The interests of the two are therefore not in harmony with each other, and yet to the bank has been confided the control and direction of that great instrument upon whose proper management as entirely depends the continuity and rapidity of the societary circulation as does the circulation of the blood upon a proper supply of air and food.

§ 2. "In the reign of William," says Mr. Macaulay, "old men were still living who could remember that there was not a single banking-house in the city of London. So late as the Restoration every trader had his strong box in his own house, and, when an acceptance was presented to him, told down the crowns and Caroluses on his own counter. But the increase of wealth had produced its natural effect, the subdivision of labor. Before the end of the reign of Charles II., a new mode of paying and receiving money had come into fashion among the merchants of the capital. A class of agents arose, whose office was to keep the cash of the commercial houses. This new branch of business naturally fell into the hands of the goldsmiths, who were accustomed to traffic largely in the precious metals, and who had vaults in which great masses of bullion could lie secure from fire and robbers. It was at the shops of the goldsmiths of Lombard street that all payments in coin were made. Other traders gave and received nothing but paper.

"This great change did not take place without much opposition and clamor. Old-fashioned merchants complained bitterly that a class of men who, thirty years before, had confined themselves to their proper functions, and had made a fair profit by embossing silver bowls and chargers, by setting jewels for fine ladies, and by selling pistoles and dollars to gentlemen setting out for the continent, had become the treasurers, and were fast becoming the masters, of the whole city. These usurers, it was said, played at hazard with what had been earned by the industry and hoarded by the thrift of other men. If the dice turned up well, the knave who kept the cash became an alderman: if they turned up ill, the dupe who had furnished the cash became a bankrupt. On the other side, the conveniences of the modern practice were set forth in animated language. Two clerks, seated in one counting-house, did what, under the old system, must have been done by twenty clerks in twenty different establishments. A goldsmith's note might be transferred ten times in a morning; and thus a hundred guineas, locked in his safe close to the Exchange, did what would formerly have required a thousand guineas, dispersed through many tills, some on Ludgate Hill, some in Austin Friars, and some in Tower street."

Money having been thus utilized, and circulation quickened, the greater step was soon taken of establishing an institution somewhat similar to those existing on the continent. The last decade of the eighteenth century witnessed, therefore, the creation of the Bank of England, differing from its predecessors, however, in the fact that, while they had been instituted in the public interests alone, with a view to maintaining an unvarying standard with which to compare all other commodities, this was a mere trading corporation having for its sole object the advantage of those interested in its management. The former gave certificates in exchange for the gold and silver deposited with them; and the parties holding these certificates felt certain that the metals thus represented were actually in their vaults. The quantity of money *apparently* at the command of the community, was therefore precisely that which was *really* subject to its orders, no difference having been produced by the granting of the certificate. The latter, in like manner, gave certificates in exchange for the precious metals; but, instead of retaining the coins in its vaults it lent them out again. The power of the depositor over his money remaining undiminished, while a new and additional power had been created, the apparent quantity of money in circulation had been thereby doubled, while the real one remained unchanged. The English system, tending, as it did, to a greater utilization of money, was much the more perfect; more powerful for good, it was also greatly more so in the opposite direction.

At the outset, the bank enjoyed no exclusive privileges.

By degrees, however, its nominal capital was enlarged, until, in 1708, it had trebled, its influence meanwhile having so increased as to enable it to obtain an Act of Parliament prohibiting the application of the associative principle to the trade in money, in any case in which the partners should be more than six in number. Power was thus centralized for the benefit of a few stockholders; but to the great loss of the English people, who were thus deprived of the right to determine their own mode of action in regard to the most important of all the machinery in use among mankind. By means of the control of the currency thus secured, the dividends, notwithstanding the sinking of its nominal capital in an annuity at the rate of three per cent., were gradually carried up to no less than ten per cent., the whole difference being obtained by such a use of credit as made the apparent amount of money at the command of the community greatly larger than was the real one.

§ 3. Trading thus altogether on its liabilities, and, with the exception of its surplus profits, employing no capital of its own, the movements of the bank will be made more clear by the following sketch of its operations in the last sixty years, placing under the head of debt the amount of its circulation and of the credits on its books, and opposite thereto the quantity of bullion in its vaults, the latter representing the whole amount of capital it had borrowed and had not lent out.

At the close of August, 1796, the amount of its debts was £15,903,110, all of which, with the exception of £2,122,950, had been invested for its own advantage. Soon after, various circumstances occurred tending to diminish confidence in the institution, and in the following February, when the stock of bullion but little exceeded a million, an Order of Council was obtained, authorizing the bank to discontinue payment of its debts. Thenceforward, during nearly a quarter of a century, its paper constituted the sole legal currency of the country; and how that currency was managed is shown by the following figures:—

		Debts.	Bullion.
August	1797	£18,879,470	£4,089,620
"	1804	26,869,420	5,879,190
"	1812	34,875,790	3,099,270
"	1814	42,218,230	2,097,680
"	1815	39,944,670	3,409,040

The circulation having, in this last year, amounted to

£26,000,000, it follows, that of the notes and bills then held, no less than £10,000,000 represented the property of individuals deposited in its vaults. Charging interest for its use while allowing none, the bank was enabled to give to its stockholders double the usual rate of interest—always a sign of error in the system. The real owners felt themselves to be as fully possessed of the power of purchase as if they had the gold in their hands; and yet, it was neither in their possession nor in that of the bank, but in that of a third set of persons, to whom the latter had granted the use of it. These £10,000,000 had the same effect on prices as if their number had been doubled, having become, for the moment, to all intents and purposes, £20,000,000.

§ 4. The year 1815 brought with it the close of the great war. Two years later the bullion had increased to £11,688,000, while the liabilities had fallen to £38,600,000. Its loans of borrowed capital were therefore only £27,000,000, or less by £2,000,000 than the amount of its circulation, which had increased to £29,000,000. By the very simple operation of calling in its claims on the one hand, and reducing its liabilities on the other, the apparent quantity of money at the command of the community had been reduced to the extent of no less than £12,000,000, or little short of $60,000,000. So far as regarded the societary circulation, this was equivalent to the entire annihilation of that large sum. As compared with the money value of the property of the British people it was utterly insignificant, yet did its abstraction cause an arrest of the circulation almost as complete as would be produced in the physical body by stoppage of the supply of food. "Thousands upon thousands," says Mr. McCulloch, "who had, in 1812, considered themselves affluent, found that they were destitute of all real property; and sunk, as if by enchantment, and without any fault of their own, into the abyss of poverty." In the midst of all this ruin, however, the bank prospered more than ever, for the destruction of private credit rendered its vaults and its notes more necessary to the community, none other being regarded as entitled to the public confidence.

The ground-work having thus been laid by the bank, Parliament passed, in 1819, an Act for the resumption of specie payments, and thus re-established as the law of the land the standard that had been abandoned in 1797—among the most remarkable measures of confiscation to be found in the annals of legislation. For more than twenty years, all the transactions of the United Kingdom had been based upon a currency less in value than that which previously had existed. In the course of that period land had been sold, mortgages granted, settlements made, and other contracts of a permanent nature entered into, to the extent of thousands of millions of pounds, the terms of all of which were now to be changed for the benefit of the receivers of fixed incomes, and to the loss of those who had land, labor, or the produce of either, to part with. As a consequence, land fell exceedingly in price, and mortgagees everywhere entered into possession. Labor became superabundant, and the laborer suffered for want of food. Machinery of every kind was thrown idle, and manufacturers were ruined. Manufactures, being in excess of the demand, were forced upon foreign markets to the ruin of the capitalists and workmen, miners and machinists, of all the other countries of the world that had failed to persevere in the protective system.

Peace had thus brought with it wide-spread ruin, but it enriched the money-lender, his single commodity rising, while land became so cheap that he could purchase at less than half the previous price. The annuitant and office-holder profited, their dividends and salaries having become payable in coin, that would purchase double the quantity of food and clothing for which they had at first contracted. Farmers and laborers, machinists and merchants, were impoverished, their taxes remaining unchanged, while their labor and its products commanded less than half the money at which they would before have sold.

§ 5. The series of measures above described has been greatly lauded by some British writers, and as much condemned by others. Which of these is right the reader will decide for himself, after reflecting:—

That the progress of man towards civilization is *invariably* attended by an increase of the power of the labor of the present over the accumulations of the past:

That his progress towards barbarism is in the reverse direction; the capital accumulated in the past then *invariably* obtaining more power over the labor of the present.

Which of these was the effect produced? Did the course of the government tend to lighten the burden of rent, taxes, or interest? If it did, then did it tend towards civilization. That it did not is shown in the facts, that farmers were everywhere throughout the kingdom ruined by demands for the enormous rents whose payment had previously been agreed for; that the taxes remained unchanged, while the prices of food and labor declined; and that interest upon mortgages continued as great, when required to be paid in coin, as when it had been contracted for in the days of paper. Hence it was, that the return to peace, which should have been hailed as a blessing, was generally regarded as a curse.

§ 6. Scarcely had the effect of this destructive measure commenced to pass away, when the bank was found repeating the experiment of augmenting the *apparent* quantity of money, and thus shortening the standard for the measurement of values, preparatory to a similar return to the *real* quantity, by which the standard should again be lengthened. With the substitution of gold for one-pound notes, and with the gradual re-establishment of credit among the country banks, its circulation had fallen from £29,000,000 in 1817 to £17,000,000 in 1822. Then commenced a system of expansion by which that portion of its debts called "deposits" was nearly doubled in the period between 1821 and 1824. There was, therefore, a general appearance of prosperity; and this continued until the holders of the capital thus rendered unproductive had provided for themselves new investments—when, all at once, the scene changed, prosperity being succeeded by adversity, property falling in value while labor was unemployed, and the bank itself being saved from stoppage only by the lucky discovery of a parcel of one-pound notes that could be used in place of gold.

A few years later we meet with another repetition of the operation, the amount of the bank debts, called deposits, being once more doubled in the period between 1832 and 1835. Now came another crisis, the bank again forcing securities on the market, and thereby destroying the value of property to such an extent as to enable it in the following year to reduce, by more than £7,000,000, the credits on its books.

Two years later the performance was again repeated. In this case but a single year was required for bringing about the change, the institution having been saved from bankruptcy in October, 1837, only by means of aid granted by the Bank of France. Commerce almost ceased, and distress was universal, but the bank made its usual dividends, and money-lenders and annuitants were enriched. Such having been the uniform effect of all its movements, the reader may, as we think, find in them a key to those extraordinary changes in the ownership of real estate which have resulted in the reduction of the number of the landowners to one-sixth of that at which it stood in the days of Adam Smith.

§ 7. The frequency and extraordinary extent of these changes aroused a desire to ascertain by what laws, if any there were, the movement of the bank was governed; and a commission was instituted which, however, after examining numerous witnesses, failed to discover the laws they sought. The only conclusions at which it could arrive were, that it was administered without reference to any principle whatsoever, that its movements were invariably those of momentary expediency, and that the dangers and difficulties which had just occurred were likely to be reproduced on the first occasion. Such having been clearly shown to be the case, it was deemed necessary, on the renewal of the charter, to endeavor to subject its action to some certain law, thus fitting it to become the regulator of that of others. Hence we have now the Bank Restriction Act of Sir Robert Peel, of 1844, whose name is thus associated with two of the most remarkable acts in the history of the British monetary system, neither of which, however, can be regarded as indicating that he had given to the subject the attention demanded by its importance.

Less than three years later, in 1847, came another crisis, a spirit of the wildest speculation, promoted by the bank, having yielded to an universal panic. Consols declined to 80, while railroad stocks fell to half their previous value. The rate of interest rose to ten per cent., the government itself being forced to borrow at five for the supply of its daily wants. Dealers in corn, cotton, and bullion, were again proscribed; and thus were repeated the phenomena of 1816, '25, and '37. Deputations from the various cities claimed of the Minister a suspension of his law; assuring him that large orders remained unfilled for want of the means required for their execution, while operatives, by thousands, were standing idle because of inability to sell their labor. The bank itself, with bankruptcy staring it in the face, was compelled to enlarge its loans when it desired to contract them; and thus was exhibited, for the third time in a single decade, the spectacle of a great institution aspiring to regulate the trade of the world, yet totally unable to save itself. An order of council finally repealed the law for the time being, thus furnishing conclusive evidence of the want of knowledge of the persons to whose influence the new system had been due.

Such is the condition of the people of England under the control of its great monopoly institution. They are dependent on the chance measures of a body of gentlemen no one of whom has ever yet been able to explain the principles by which he is governed in the administration of the powerful instrument in the management of which he is placed. All of them, in their capacity of stockholders and directors, have a direct interest in producing changes in the currency; because, by so doing, they lessen public confidence and thus increase the necessity for looking to their vaults as the only place of secure deposit.

§ 8. The new system had failed to produce the effect desired—having given no steadiness in the supply of money or in its value. By some, the fault was found in the law itself; but its author, of course, asserted, that if the bank had acted "in the spirit of the law of 1844," such difficulties could never have occurred. Ready to find the cause in "the extraordinary spirit of speculation," he was well disposed to close his eyes to the real cause—the radical defect of his own measure, which professed to regulate the action of the great machine, but failed to do so. Had it so done, the directors would have found themselves compelled to act in accordance with both its spirit and its letter, and there could have been no such operation as that which had just then been witnessed; the difficulties attendant upon short crops would not have been aggravated by the total prostration of trade, the discharge of workmen, and the impossibility of obtaining wages to be used in the purchase, at any price, of the necessaries of life.

The trade in money requires no more law than that in shoes. It demands, on the contrary, perfect freedom, being so vastly greater in amount that interference to the extent of half of one per cent., is productive of more injury than could result from an interference that should affect the price of shoes to an extent of a hundred per cent.

Nevertheless, such are the penalties, prohibitions, and liabilities imposed upon all who desire to associate for the purpose of utilizing the precious metals, and so numerous are the monopolies invested with the control of the money trade, that of all commodities theirs is the most subject to sudden alteration in its value. The regulation of the currency is held to be one of the functions of government, because it affords the most simple and convenient mode of taxation. That of Great Britain has transferred it to the bank, by which the duty is so performed that at one time money is cheapened, and the State is enabled to reduce the rate of interest on its debts; while at another it becomes dear, and those who have accepted new stock in exchange find they have parted with a considerable portion of their property, receiving nothing in return. Lose who may, however, the stockholders of the bank are always secure of receiving large dividends, while its directors are ever ready to furnish what they think should be received as good and efficient reasons for such destructive changes. At one time it is an enormous import of stocks from the continent; at another, the influx of South American shares and stocks; at a third, vast loans to the United States; and at a fourth, a deficiency of crops. Stocks, however, would not come if the bank did not paralyze the action of the private capitalist by lending out his money and raising prices; and corn might be deficient without producing any material change in the value of money except in relation to corn itself.

The true cause of the difficulty is, that the task of regulation is committed to one great institution, whose movements are wholly unregulated. It is a great fly-wheel in the midst of a vast number of little wheels, all of which are compelled to go faster or slower as the great one may propel. These latter are the bankers, merchants, and manufacturers of Great Britain, all of whom have, more or less, for half a century past, been engaged in studying the law which governs the motion of the master wheel, but as yet with such indifferent success, that we hazard little in asserting that no man in England would commit that law to writing, and stake his fortune on proving that it had been operative during any single year of the century. In despair of arriving at any comprehension of the laws of its action, all resign themselves blindly to its influence, joint-stock and private banks expanding when it expands and contracting when it contracts, an error of a single million thus producing error to the extent of hundreds of millions in the money transactions of the kingdom. Hence the necessity for subjecting it to fixed and positive rules.

The currency needs no such regulator; but if there be one, its action should be rendered perfectly automatic, leaving it to the proprietors of the little wheels to use the gearing needed for enabling them to obtain as much speed as they might require. *It should be acted upon by the community, instead of acting upon them*, and then it might be consulted with the same confidence as the thermometer. The law that would effect this would not be that of 1844, which, with its cumbrous, and really ridiculous, machinery of banking department and department of issue, was totally unfitted to answer the end proposed. It was framed with a view to changes in the amount of circulation, or, *currency in use*, which are ever slow, and small in quantity; while it contained no reference to changes in the deposits, or *currency seeking employment*, always rapid and great in amount. The one is in constant use among the great body of the people, and cannot be materially increased or decreased without a great change in the state of trade, or in the feelings of the community. The other represents unemployed capital, the property of the few, liable to increase or decrease with every speck that appears in the political or commercial horizon.

§ 9. By the last charter, a sovereign, or, to a certain extent, its equivalent in silver, is required to lie in the vaults of the bank for every pound of its notes in the hands of the public, beyond £14,000,000. The circulation being an almost constant quantity, amounting to £20,000,000, £6,000,000 of bullion must, therefore, remain in the bank, not to be used under any circumstances whatsoever; and as useless to the community, while so remaining, as would be an equal weight of pebble-stones. How far the circulation can, as a rule, claim to be treated as a constant quantity, the reader may determine after examining the following table, in which is given that of the bank for the years from 1832 to 1840:—

1832	£18,449,000	1837	£18,366,000
1833	17,912,000	1838	18,872,000
1834	18,007,000	1839	16,326,000
1835	18,507,000	1840	16,818,000
1836	17,985,000		

The year 1840 was one of utter prostration. In that and the following year commerce was at an end, so far as the ruin of the customers of England, abroad and at home, consequent upon the extraordinary movements of the bank, could accomplish its extinction. Nevertheless, under these most untoward circumstances, the circulation remained above £16,000,000;

and we now find it gradually attaining a point higher than it had reached in many years:—

1841	£16,533,700	1845	£20,099,000
1842	16,952,000	1846	19,865,000
1843	20,239,000	1847	19,854,000
1844	21,246,000		

In the first period, embracing the nine years from 1832 to 1840, both inclusive—and including the crisis of 1836–7—the variation above and below the medium of £18,500,000, is under three per cent. In the second, the circulation attains a higher point than in the first. Private and joint-stock banks having been ruined by the extraordinary revulsion of 1839, and confidence in their notes having been impaired, the bank now profits by the ruin of which it has been itself the cause. The total circulation of the kingdom remained almost entirely unchanged.

Such being the facts, it would seem to be quite clear that the difficulty of the English monetary system finds its cause in the bank monopoly, and not in that paper circulation by means of which the precious metals are so greatly utilized, and the societary circulation so much promoted. Failing to see this, Sir Robert Peel enlarged the former while greatly restricting the latter, and the consequences now exhibit themselves in the fact that, notwithstanding the great increase in the supply of these metals, the changes of the British money market became more frequent, while the range of the vibration has been much enlarged.

Under this most unstable system the annual losses by failures are stated at the enormous sum of £50,000,000. Great as it is, it is yet trivial when compared with the loss inflicted upon foreign nations by the unceasing changes to which they are subjected. The crash of 1815, and those of 1825, 1836, 1839, and 1847, had there their origin; and their effect was that of injuring the farmers and planters of the world to the extent of thousands of millions of pounds. Of all the monetary institutions that now exist, that of England contains within itself least of the elements required for the production of stability and regularity; and therefore it is, that nations prosper least whose dependence upon it is greatest. Trading centralization, nevertheless, seeks, by means of British free trade measures, to render the English currency—ever varying as it is—the measure of values for the world at large.

CHAPTER XXVIII.

OF THE INSTRUMENT OF ASSOCIATION—CONTINUED.

VI.—*Of Banking in France.*

§ 1. Taxation of the French people by means of regulation of the currency.

§ 2. Private banks established at the close of the Revolution. Consolidated in the Bank of France. Monopoly powers of that institution. Directly interested in producing changes in the currency.

§ 3. Steadiness in the amount of currency in use. Financial crises have their origin in changes in the amount of currency unemployed.

§ 4. These changes due to the irregularity in the movements of the one great bank. Their result seen in the augmentation of its dividends.

§ 5. Political and monetary centralization tends to enfeeble the societary action and to diminish the amount of commerce. Counteracted, in some degree, by the maintenance of a policy having for its object the emancipation of the land from the tax of transportation.

§ 1. In the natural world the real power exerted is always in the inverse ratio of the apparent one—the rumbling earthquake limiting itself to the shattering of city walls, while the silent frost, by disintegrating rocks and levelling hills, is enabled to supply to a microscopic world the material by means of which to build up islands, out of which, eventually, continents will probably be formed. So, too, is it in the moneyed world, the skilful financier always finding his most productive taxes in those exchanges for whose performance pence and halfpence are required, and not in those which need the aid of gold. Tobacco, salt, and beer, therefore, pay heavily, while silks and velvets, pearls and diamonds, contribute little to any public revenue. Chief, however, among the subjects of taxation, is the instrument which enters into all exchanges—money. The laborer needs its aid when he requires salt, tobacco, beer, or cloth. The capitalist must have it if he would add to his lands, and without it the woman of fashion would be compelled to forego the indulgence of her tastes. Nowhere has this been more thoroughly understood than in France. Nowhere has the policy of a country more tended to the expulsion of the precious metals than was there the case throughout those dreary centuries which intervened between the accession of the House of Valois and that of the Bourbons. Nowhere, consequently, has centralization been more complete, the poverty of the government more uniform, or its necessities more urgent. Nowhere, therefore, has the fraud involved in the falsification of the coin of the realm been more systematically or more enduringly practised—the last appearance of such frauds being found in the reign of Louis XVI. Scarcely, however, had it disappeared from the proceedings of the mint, before we meet with it in another form, that of the *assignats*, or paper money of the Revolution—so freely issued that they gradually declined in value until the sum of six hundred francs, or the equivalent of more than a hundred dollars, would pay for only a single pound of butter.

Of all the instruments of taxation, that afforded by the regulation of the currency is the most searching in its effects—the most productive in time of need—the most demoralizing in its action—and the most ruinous in the end. By means of the *assignats* it was, that the early revolutionary government of France was enabled to collect the taxes by help of which its armies repelled the invasion of 1792. By similar means it has been, that the Austrian government has added hundreds of millions to its revenue during the present century—calling in depreciated paper money and replacing it with that which was promised to be good, and then repeating the operation so many times, that the original holder of dollars now holds little more than pence.

§ 2. With the growth of wealth and population power over the currency has passed gradually from the hands of government to those of traders in money, seeking to exercise it for their own benefit, and that of those with whom they are connected. So has it been in England, and so is it now in France.

At the close of the Revolution, credit having no existence, money was scarce, and the rate of interest was very high. This, of course, furnished strong inducement for the opening of shops at which money could be bought and sold; or, in other words, banks. Several were, therefore, opened; and had the government abstained from interference, no doubt can now be entertained that competition among themselves would gradually have furnished a remedy for the then existing monetary evils. Napoleon had, however, a strong belief in the necessity for the maintenance and extension of that same centralization to which his predecessor had owed the forfeiture of his throne; and it furnishes, therefore, no cause for surprise, that we find him in 1804 decreeing their consolidation into the single Bank of France, and securing to that institution a monopoly of the power of issuing circulating notes. The soldier and the trader are thus ever found in close alliance with each other, both seeking to be enriched at the expense of commerce. Scarcely, however, had the alliance been completed, when it proved that the former had used the latter for his own purposes alone, the bank having little more than come into existence before it was required to grant to the State so large a portion of its capital as to involve it in difficulty so serious as to render necessary a total change of system. Then (1806) came the definitive organization of the institution on the footing it now maintains, with a capital of 90,000,000 francs, or about $17,000,000.

While thus centralizing the monetary power in the capital, the government retained the right of authorizing the creation of local banks, and thus producing counter-attraction among the provinces. So little, however, was this power exercised, that the ensuing forty years witnessed the formation of only ten such institutions; all of them, too, of a character so entirely insignificant, that their joint capital was but 24,000,000 francs=$4,500,000—and the whole amount of their loans less than 80,000,000=$15,000,000. Such was the machinery of exchange provided for a country with a population far more numerous than that of either Great Britain or the United States.

"'There is not, probably,'" says M. Coquelin, in his excellent little work, *Du Crédit et des Banques*, "a single town of any consideration in France that has not, at one time or another, desired to have a bank. To comprehend why they have found themselves compelled to rest content, deprived of the advantage of such institutions, it is required only that the reader should understand the endless and inextricable formalities through which it is required to pass—the obstacles that are to be overcome—the measures to be pursued—the delays that are to be submitted to—before such a privilege is granted. To obtain an authorization to establish a bank was, even for the largest and best-situated towns or cities, a Herculean labor. Except the two or three departmental banks formed spontaneously at the close of the Revolution, like those of Rouen and Bordeaux, all the others were founded only after laborious effort and long and expensive proceedings, well calculated to produce disgust among others who might have felt disposed to look in the same direction. I may, for example, cite the Bank of Toulouse, which was established after years of solicitations, in which were united the council-general of the department, the municipal authorities of the city, and most of the distinguished men of the country; all of whom were compelled to harass the Minister and the Council of State, and that, too, for a series of years, before they could obtain that most simple thing, the formation of a banking company with a capital of 1,200,000 francs=$240,000. The city of Dijon, after similar efforts, was compelled, by the resistance it encountered, to abandon the idea."

§ 3. The power of the bank was to be derived, first, from the exclusive privilege accorded to it of furnishing circulation; or, second, from its capacity to afford to the owners of money a place of secure deposit. Credit being almost extinct, and its notes being of large amount—500 francs—little was, in the outset, to be expected from the first. That very little was thence obtained is proved by the facts, that in the first two years the circulation fluctuated between 10,000,000 and 45,000,000 francs; and that, in the first year of the final establishment of the bank as now constituted, (1806,) it rose to 76,000,000 and fell to 54,000.000, while in the following year it ranged between 74,000,000 and 107,000,000. The period was one of great disturbance in the political world, not well calculated for producing confidence in the minds of those who had seen cartloads of *assignats* whose value was but little greater than that of the paper that had been used to print them. Under the government of the Restoration, however, there came a change. Peace prevailing at home and abroad, there gradually arose a feeling of confidence, manifesting itself in the gradual increase of circulation, that is here exhibited:—

	Maximum.	Minimum.	Mean.
1819	135,000,000	79,000,000	107,000,000
1820	172,000,000	122,000,000	147,000,000
1833	228,000,000	193,000,000	210,500,000
1834	222,000,000	192,000,000	207,000,000
1843	247,000,000	216,000,000	231,500,000
1845	289,000,000	247,000,000	268,000,000
1846	311,000,000	243,000,000	277,000,000

Steadiness is here shown to grow with the growing utilization of money that has been accomplished by means of circulating notes. In the first of the above periods, the minimum of 1819 is less than half the maximum of the following year. In the second, the variation is less than a sixth. The third embraces four years, in the closing months of which commenced a crisis of intensity so fearful that it was with difficulty the bank could weather the storm; and yet, at the moment of severest pressure, the amount of circulation remained almost precisely where it had stood three years before.

These figures can scarcely be studied without bringing us to the conclusion, that the circulation—governed, as it is, by the wants of the people—has really nothing to do with financial crises, whose true and only cause is to be found in that other element of power, the amount of credits standing on the books of the bank, and denominated deposits. The more *they* can be swelled, the larger is the power of the bank to over-trade, and the greater must be the intensity of distress resulting from revulsion; but the greater must also be that injury to credit which forces all to look to the one great and controlling institution, the greater must be its power to charge high interest, and the larger must be its dividends. This bank, as well as that of England, has, therefore, *a direct interest in so using the enormous power conferred upon it as to produce frequent and severe revulsions.*

§ 4. The power of the bank over the currency, and over the value of property as measured by money, is, as we see, wholly, uncontrolled—it being, in this respect, omnipotent. How it has been exercised is shown by the following facts:—Between 1815 and 1818, the bills discounted were carried up from 203,000,000 to 615,000,000, and this was followed by a crisis, resulting in a reduction to 389,000,000. Scarcely escaped therefrom, the bank repeats the operation, carrying up its loans from 384,000,000 in 1821 to 489,000,000 in 1824, and 638,000,000 in the year of crisis, 1825. So was it again in the period of excitement closing in 1837. In 1847 the movements of the bank amounted to 2714,000,000. In 1850 they were but 1470,000,000, thus exhibiting a reduction of nearly one-half in the standard measure with which money values were to be compared. Such a change as this tended, of course, to the ruin of all who had labor, lands, or property of any description, that they required to sell. Two years later, in 1852, they were 2514,000,000; and then those who desired to purchase found themselves in the position which had before been occupied by those who needed to sell. One class, however, profited by all these changes—the already rich, who dealt in money. Like the Bank of England, that of France prospers always—its dividends growing steadily, and the tendency towards increase of growth being in the direct ratio of the destruction of private credit. In 1844 its stockholders had 9 per cent. The next year they received 12·4; but in 1846, preliminary to the crisis which then soon after occurred, they had no less than 14·4 per cent., or nearly thrice the ordinary rate of interest.

§ 5. In both the physical and social world increase of force results from increased rapidity of motion. The use of the circulating note tending to produce that effect, its effect is seen in the rapid growth of both the commerce and the power of France. Both, however, are small, when compared with what they might attain to be, under a system calculated to give to the movement of the societary machine that steadiness which is required for obtaining a constantly accelerating force.

"Not a man in France," says M. Coquelin, "produces as much as he could"—a fact whose cause is to be found in languid circulation. The real difficulty, as he continues, is not that of production, but that of finding a purchaser for the things produced. Why does this difficulty exist? Because of the existence of a political and financial centralization unexcelled in Europe.

France is, however, a country of "contrasts." A centralization that is unmatched tends towards slavery and death; but, on the other hand, she profits by the advice of Colbert—seeking always to bring the consumer and the producer close together, and thus to give value to the produce of the farm. The consequences are seen in the fact, that she exports a larger quantity of home-grown products in a finished form than any other country of the world—that she obtains for them a higher price than any other—that her power to attract the precious metals is steadily increasing—that she prospers in despite of a taxation for governmental purposes that is most oppressive, and a taxation for the maintenance of the stockholders of the Bank of France compared with which that required for the support of her fleets and armies sinks into insignificance.

CHAPTER XXIX.

OF THE INSTRUMENT OF ASSOCIATION—CONTINUED.

VII.—*Of Banking in the United States.*

§ 1. Gradual development of the American banking system. How it stood at the close of the half century which followed the Revolution. Its progress since that time. Large proportion borne by capital to the amount of investments.

§ 2. Steadiness in the action of banks is in the direct ratio of their dependence upon the power of affording means of circulation, and in the inverse ratio of their dependence upon deposits. American banks possess more of the elements of stability than those of France and England.

§ 3. Small proportion borne by the currency to production when compared with either of the above-named countries.

§ 4. Superior economy of the American system.

§ 5. Steadiness in its own value the great desideratum in a currency. Tendencies of the American system in that direction.

§ 6. Trivial amount of losses by American banks under the system of local action prior to 1837. Heavy losses of the people of England from the failures of private banks.

§ 7. Growth of centralization in the last twenty years, and consequent diminution in the steadiness of the currency. Maintenance of a sound and stable currency incompatible with the existence of an unfavorable balance of trade. That balance unfavorable in relation to all purely agricultural countries.

§ 8. Instability of American policy. Periods of protection and free trade alternating with each other. Prosperity the invariable attendant of the former, and bankruptcy of the people and the State that of the latter.

§ 9. The money-shop, or bank, one of the most necessary portions of the societary machinery. More than any other, the American banking system tends to promote the habit of association, the development of individuality, and the growth of wealth.

§ 1. Tue political system of these United States tends towards decentralization. So, too, does their financial ohe; but here, as elsewhere, a policy that seeks to build up foreign trade on the ruins of domestic commerce, produces disturbance, whose result is already seen in the establishment of a centralization that but a few years since would have been regarded as beyond the possibility of occurrence.

The gradual development of the banking system in the half century which followed the peace of 1783, is here exhibited:

	No. of banks.	Capital.
1811	88	$42,000,000
1815	216	89,000,000
1820	307	101,000,000
1830	328	110,000,000

The loans and investments of all kinds at the last of these dates, as nearly as can be ascertained, were $170,000,000, giving an excess beyond the capital of little more than fifty per cent.

For later periods the amounts are thus given, the item investments including not only loans and discounts, but stocks, real estate, and all other property, except specie, the mode of statement least favorable to the institutions:—

	1837.	1843.	1848.	1851.	1854.	1856.
Number	634	691	751	879	1208	1306
Capital—in millions	290	228	204	226	301	332
Investments—in millions	567	319	398	464	630	711
Excess investments	279	91	189	238	329	379

With the exception of the period immediately succeeding the great financial crisis of 1841–2, the amount of investments appears in all these cases to have been, as nearly as may be, about twice the capital; whereas, as has been seen, the loans of the banks, public and private, of England and France, are three, four, five, and even as much as ten times their capitals.

Adding the profits on hand to the nominal amount of capital, we obtain for the last of these years a total of	$345,000,000
While the investments would scarcely exceed	655,000,000
Giving as the excess of investments	$310,000,000

or about ninety per cent. That excess represents the total amount of circulation and of credits on the books, for the redemption of which the institutions have not specie in their vaults.

§ 2. The amount of the currency of a country dependent upon the movements of its banks, is to be found in the circulation and the deposits, *minus* the quantity of specie retained on hand. The first, as has been shown in the examination of English banking, is an almost constant quantity; whereas, the last tends to change with every rise and fall of the political or financial barometer. The first, while increasing the utility of gold and silver by giving greater facility for the transfer of property therein, is regulated strictly by the wants of the people themselves; as, whatever the extent to which a bank may see fit to extend its loans, it has no power to compel the persons to whose credit the securities are placed, to convert them into notes. He *may* do so if he will, but he will not do so unless it pleases him; and so long as the option rests with him, and others like himself, the amount of the circulation rests with him and them, and not with the bank. Hence it is that the tendency to steadiness in the circulation is so very great.

In the case of "deposits" directly the reverse of this occurs, increase in their amount being dependent upon the will of bank directors, who may, or may not, add to the credits on their books. Every such addition swells the amount of private capital in their hands, unproductive to its owners; and hence it is that the tendency to instability in the loans dependent upon deposits is so great. Again, the bank-note simply facilitates the transfer of an *existing* piece of money, enabling a single piece to do as much work as without its help could be done by five or ten. The loan that is based upon a deposit doubles the *apparent* amount of currency, the power of purchase remaining with the real owner of the money, while being exercised, and to the same extent precisely, by him to whom the bank has lent it.

Such being the case, the tendency to stability and regularity should be found existing in the precise ratio in which the excess of loans is based upon the circulation; and, *vice versâ*, the tendency to instability should be in the ratio in which that excess is based upon the deposits. Assuming this to be the case—and that so it is cannot be questioned by any one who has carefully examined the facts already laid before him—we may now compare the extent to which American banks are possessed of the qualities required for giving stability and regularity, as compared with those of England.

The loans of the first, not based upon actual capital, amount to about	$310,000,000
Their actual circulation is probably about	160,000,000
Leaving, as the amount of loans based upon deposits	$150,000,000

The dependence upon the variable quantity—that one which, to its whole extent, *duplicates* the money at the command of individuals—amounts, therefore, to only $160,000,000, being less than the amount of such loans made by ten joint-stock banks in London, whose whole capital is but $18,000,000. Adding to this the similar loans made by the Bank of England, the country banks of all kinds, and the Scottish ones, we should find the element of instability in the British institutions to an amount five times greater than in the American ones. Even this, however, does not truly represent the facts; and for the reason, that while the amount increases in an arithmetical ratio only, the risk of change does so in a geometrical one. A bank with a capital of $1,000,000 may safely calculate that the credit on its books can never fall below $200,000; and when the amount of its loans based upon such credits is limited within that sum, no change can ever be required. Let it, however, extend this to $400,000, and a probable necessity for considerable change will have been produced. Extending them to $600,000, a necessity for future change will have become certain. Carrying them up to $1,000,000, there will arise a high degree of probability that the change required will be so great as to bankrupt the customers, and annihilate the bank itself, with all its powers. The quantity of the excess has only quintupled, but the danger of instability has grown a thousand times. Instability and insecurity thus grow with the growth of the power of banks to trade upon the capital of individuals left temporarily in their hands; while it declines as the loans of those institutions become more and more limited to their power to furnish circulation.' Such being the case, the perfection of instability should be found in England, while the nearest approach to stability should be presented by the banks of New England, the one furnishing almost the nearest known approach to the highest centralization, and the other exhibiting a decentralization that is almost perfect.

§ 3. Centralization and slavery travel always in the same direction. So is it, too, with decentralization and freedom.

The more perfect the local action, the more *instantly* will the demand for capital follow its production, and the less will be the power of banks to trade upon deposits lying unproductive to their owners. The more perfect that action, too, the greater will be the power of association, and the less will be the proportion borne by all the instruments of circulation —whether gold and silver coins, or circulating notes—to the operations of the community and the amount of commerce Such being the case, the currency of the United States should be found representing a smaller number of days of labor than that of England or France; and that it does so is proved by the following facts:—

The specie of France is estimated at.......................................francs	3,500,000,000
The circulation and deposits of the bank—minus the specie actually in its vaults—may be taken at..	400,000,000
Giving a total of..	3,900,000,000

or about 110 francs per head—a sum representing probably 80 days of agricultural labor.

The quantity of specie in Great Britain is probably	£40,000,000
The circulation is	31,000,000
The deposits, liable to be demanded at any instant, are probably	60,000,000
	£131,000,000
From which deduct, for the specie usually held by the bank, say	11,000,000
And we have for the currency	£120,000,000

being about £4 10s. per head, or the equivalent of 45 days of labor, at 12s. per week.

The specie in the United States, in and out of banks, hoarded and in circulation, is probably	$160,000,000
Adding to this, for the amount of loans by banks, based upon their circulation and deposits	270,000,000
We have a total of	$430,000,000

giving about $20 per head, or the equivalent of 30 days of agricultural labor.

The capital of all the banks of New England, 491 in number, is	$112,000,000
Allowing to each, for surplus profits, only $6000, it would be....	115,000,000
Their investments of all descriptions, bills, notes, stocks, banking-houses, etc., are	181,000,000
The excess is 57 per cent., and amounts to	66,000,000
Deducting from this the specie in their vaults	7,000,000
We obtain, as the addition to the currency resulting from the existence of banks	$59,000,000
The gross circulation is $46,000,000, but the net amount is probably not more than	42,000,000
Leaving as the quantity of currency resulting from the duplication of the capital deposited by individuals, only	$17,000,000
The amount of circulation, and of deposits payable on demand, may be taken at about	60,000,000
To this may be added for the coin in circulation among the people	3,000,000
Giving a total of	$63,000,000

as the currency in use among a community of 3,200,000 persons. The amount per head is under $20—representing about 25 days of agricultural labor.

The currency of France thus represents the labor of			80	days.
That of England	"	"	45	"
That of the United States at large	"	"	30	"
That of New England	"	"	25	"

and in this latter it is that we find most of the elements of stability.

§ 4. The amount of the precious metals supposed to exist in France, in the form of coin, is about 100 francs per head—

Representing the labor of more than .... 70 days.
In Great Britain, about £2—representing .... 20 "
In the United States at large, $5 50—equal to .... 8½ "
In New England, $3—representing less than .... 4 "

The currency of France is the most costly. There it is that money is least utilized by means of circulating notes—that the need of improved machinery of exchange is most experienced—and that the proportion borne by the currency to production is the largest. The hoards of that country are, however, very numerous. Frequent revolutions, and the absence of local institutions in which to make small and temporary investments, tend, both, to the production of this effect. It may well be doubted if the quantity of money in actual use is even one-half of the sum at which it is usually estimated, and at which it is above put down.

The currency of England is very costly, but less so than that of France, money being there far more utilized by the means of notes. The proportion in which it stands to labor is large. Its tendency to instability is therefore very great.

Far less costly than either of the above, and with far superior claims to stability, is the highly-localized system of the American banks in general; but when we reach New England, we find the least expensive, the most useful, and the most stable of all the currencies of the world. The more perfect the freedom, the greater is the tendency to stability and the less the cost, as is proved in the passage from the Southern and Western States towards those of the North and East.

§ 5. The great desideratum of a system of currency is *steadiness in its own value*, fitting it to be a measure of changes in the value of other things. That such is the case with measures of weight and length is abundantly proved by the exceeding care with which it is sought to provide a standard with which to compare all yardsticks, all pound weights, and all other of the instruments used for determining the quantities of cloth, iron, sugar, cotton, and other commodities, that pass from hand to hand. Infinitely greater, however, is the need for steadiness in the instrument by means of which we compare the values of land, labor, houses, ships, sugar, cotton, tobacco, and other commodities and things. It is the one essential quality of a currency; and the advantage to the community resulting from the use of this great instrument of association must be in the precise ratio of its existence.

Steadiness being found in the physical world in the ratio of the width of the base to the height of the superstructure, so should it be in the financial one, there being but a single system of laws for the government of all matter, let it take what form it may. In proof of this we may take Rhode Island, which had, in 1852, 71 banks, or one for every two thousand of its population, with a total capital of $14,816,000; while all the property held by them amounted to only $19,486,000. The foundation being there very broad, and the building but of little height, the effects are seen in the fact, that changes in the value of property resulting from the action of Rhode Island banks have been too trivial to merit even the slightest notice.

The reverse of all this is seen in Pennsylvania—a State in which the security of banking is supposed to be promoted by the centralization of power in the hands of the managers of a few highly-favored institutions. The number of banks in 1850 was 63, or but one to every forty thousand of the population. Their capitals were $20,357,000, giving $8 per head; whereas those of Rhode Island gave nearly $100 per head. Their loans and discounts amounted to $44,000,000, but the total investments were nearly $50,000,000, giving an excess of no less than a hundred and fifty per cent.; with corresponding decrease of steadiness. In the one case, no circumstances could occur to render necessary a change of action amounting to even five per cent.; whereas, in the other, a change of almost fifty per cent would be required for reducing them to the point of safety at which the Rhode Island banks habitually stand.

Steadiness in the currency grows thus, as we see, in the ratio of the freedom with which men indulge their natural desire for association; and with its growth we witness everywhere a decline in the power of that portion of the community which live at the cost of their fellow-men. The stockholders of the Bank of France obtain thrice the usual rate of interest, while the men whose capital they use are compelled to be content with mere security for the return of their capital, without interest. The proprietors of joint-stock banks in England receive enormous dividends, while their creditors are required to be content with three per cent. The Bank of England divides eight per cent., while giving nothing to its depositors. Pennsylvania banks divide ten and twelve per cent.; or double the legal rate. Those of Massachusetts give seven; while Rhode Island stockholders receive an average of six, being precisely the rate of interest paid by those to whom loans are made. The more perfect the freedom of association for banking purposes, and the fewer the liabilities imposed, the greater is the tendency to equality of rights, the more secure the currency, and the less its cost.

§ 6. The average number of banks in New England from 1811 to 1830 was 97, and the failures in twenty-five years were 16, giving two-thirds of one per cent. per annum. The average capital was about $22,000,000. Those of the institutions that failed were $2,000,000, giving thirty-six-hundredths of one per cent. per annum. The loss sustained by the community cannot much have exceeded $500,000, giving an annual average of $20,000, or one-eleventh of one per cent. of the capitals of the banks, and not even the ten-thousandth of one per cent. of the operations facilitated by those institutions. The risk attendant upon transactions with the banks in New England, for the period of above a quarter of a century, cannot be estimated at even a single dollar in a million.

Taking the whole Union together, the average number of banks in existence during this period had been 242, and the total failures 167, three-fourths of which were south and west of New York, the proportion increasing with the diminution of population and of wealth. The annual average of failures was two and three-fourths per cent.; whereas the failures of private banks in England, in the period from 1814 to 1816, were 240 in number, and more than twenty-five per cent. of the whole. Even between 1821 and 1826, a period in which there was no extraordinary occurrence, the English average was nearly as high as the American one during a quarter of a century in which there had been changes from peace to war, and from war to peace—the whole world having been agitated by the extraordinary events attendant upon the great war in Europe, and the peace which followed it. It is a fact strikingly illustrative of the advantage attendant upon freedom in the exercise of the power of association, as compared with the monopoly system of England, that from the first institution of banks in America to the year 1837, the failures were less in number, by almost a third, than those of England in the three years from 1814 to 1816.

§ 7. The American system provides for the localization of capital, for the benefit of its owner and those in whom he is interested; while both the British and the French systems provide for its centralization in London and Paris, there to be used by middlemen styled bankers, who borrow money at a low price and lend it at a high one. Under the one, fully carried out, small institutions, acting as savings banks, would be everywhere found, as is now the case in the New England States. Under the other, the savings of the poor laborer of Cork, or Limerick, are required to be invested in government stocks; as are, in France, those of the workman of Sedan or Rouen, the laborer of Provence or of Languedoc. Decentralization tends towards steadiness; and yet the last half century has witnessed no less than two suspensions of all the American banks, while on another occasion more than half of them were compelled to adopt that course. Great institutions have been entirely annihilated, while many smaller ones have sunk nearly all their capital; yet, examining the general banking movement where we may, we find the loans to be so small when compared with their actual capital, as to warrant us in looking for a steadiness that would ensure to the people a regularity in the currency greater than could be found in any other country; and to the stockholders an almost entire security against serious danger. The cause of all these apparent contradictions may be found in the following proposition:—

Money cannot have that stability of value which is required for constituting it a proper standard for the comparison of values in any country in whose favor there is not a steady and regular balance of trade payable in the precious metals.

That this *must* be so the reader will readily perceive. Those metals are required for various purposes in the arts. They are liable to be lost, while, of all others, they are most subjected to the hoarding propensity; and, while hoarded, they are wholly useless to the community. For the moment, they are annihilated. Further, coin is liable to loss of weight by abrasion, as is so obvious to all who still need to use the smaller silver coins of earlier days. For meeting these demands, an inward flow of the precious metals is as much required as is such a flow of corn or oil, silk or cotton, in the countries in which those commodities are not produced.

Such being the case, it is clear that *no country can continue permanently to use gold and silver coin as currency, against which there is a steady balance of trade.* Whatever may be the quantity held, and how small soever may be the excess of export, that, combined with the consumption, must gradually so reduce the quantity as to cause distrust and hoarding, each and every step in that direction being one of constant acceleration. Rich as is Brazil, she uses paper certificates in place of coin. Abounding in gold as California does, the price of money is there enormous, and has led to repudiation of her debts. The value of Russian paper money was well maintained during many years of war, but it so declined in value after the peace of 1815, and the establishment of comparative freedom of trade, that a note for four roubles would exchange for only one in silver. With natural advantages exceeded by those of no country in the world, Turkey collects her revenue in kind, while the government debases the coin from year to year. Portugal was bankrupted by the Methuen treaty, which made provision for that export of raw produce which was to lead, inevitably, to the export of her stock of the precious metals. Spain exported raw materials, sending with them the produce of the mines of Mexico and Peru. France did the same under the treaty of 1786, and thus produced a revolution. The balance of trade, to an extent unknown in any other country of the world, having always been in favor of England, she has been enabled to use gold and silver coin. France now does the same, and so do Belgium, Northern Germany, and Russia, all of which are following in the line of policy indicated by Colbert, and so long pursued by England. All experience proves that the balance of trade *must* be against the countries which export raw produce, that the precious metals *must* flow from those countries, and that they must, while continuing in that course of policy, abandon the idea of using gold and silver coin as a standard of value.

Reasoning now *à priori*, we arrive, and that inevitably, at the same results A country that does not produce the precious metals must dispense with their use, or it must import them. To enable it to do this latter, it must establish in its favor a balance of trade payable in those metals. If it fail to do this, it must cease to use them in the arts, and must at length dispense with their use as standards for the comparison of values. To attempt to maintain the reverse of this is a pure absurdity; and yet, such is the tendency of all those teachers of modern political economy who follow in the train of Hume and Adam Smith in reference to this important question.

§ 8. The policy of these United States has been very variable, tending occasionally, and for short periods, to the arrest of the export of raw materials, and of gold. As a rule, however, the tendency has been in the opposite direction, the consequences having exhibited themselves in the stoppage and failure of banks above referred to. They are found, for the first time, in the period from 1817 to 1824, when manufactures came freely in, and coin went freely out. For the second, in the calamitous years which preceded the passage of the Protective Tariff Act of 1842. Excluding these two periods, it may be doubted if all the failures of banks throughout the Union, in the thirty years from 1816 to 1846, amounted to the thousandth part of one per cent; or, if the losses of the people by the banks amounted to even the millionth part of one per cent. upon the business which they so much facilitated. The losses resulting from the use of ships in a single year would pay a hundred times over the losses by all the banks of the country for a century, with the exception of the six years ending in 1824, and the five which closed in 1842.

Then, as now, the country was strained in the effort to produce an export of raw materials by which the soil was to be exhausted; and then, as now, the precious metals followed in their train. That policy forbade the use of gold and silver coin. It forbade the existence of credit; and hence it was, that hoarding became so general in the years from 1837 to 1840, that the large export of coin to this country by the Bank of England, in 1838, had not even the slightest effect in restoring the confidence that had been lost. So is it now (1856). The quantity of gold in the country is greater far than it has ever been, but it is shut up in treasury vaults, because of want of confidence in banks; it is being transported from South to North, or from West to East; or it is shut up in private hoards; but—and for the simple and obvious reason that confidence has no existence—it is not in circulation. All are now (1856) looking for an explosion similar to those of the periods of 1817 to 1820, and of 1837 to 1842; and all, who can, prepare for it.

Directly the reverse of this is what we meet with whenever the policy of the country tends to raise the prices of home-grown raw materials, and thus to arrest their export. Under the tariff of 1828, so perfect had become the stability of the price of flour, that it remained entirely unaffected here, notwithstanding the extraordinary changes of foreign markets. Under that tariff the precious metals flowed in, and confidence was complete. The policy was changed, and mines ceased to be opened, while furnaces ceased to be built; and then confidence disappeared. Under the tariff of 1842, money became abundant, not because of a large increase of import, but because of the almost instant re-establishment of public and private credit. The gold and silver that had been hoarded and thus for the time annihilated, then came forth, to become available for the purposes for which they had been intended.

All the facts presented by the history of the United States may be adduced in proof of the assertion, that *a country which maintains a policy tending to promote the export of raw materials must have against it a balance of trade requiring the export of the precious metals, and must dispense with their services as measures of value.*

Those facts may briefly thus be stated :—

Protection ceased in 1818, bequeathing to free trade a commerce that gave an excess *import* of specie, a people among whom there existed great prosperity, a large public revenue, and a rapidly diminishing public debt.

Free trade ceased in 1824, bequeathing to protection a commerce that gave an excess *export* of specie, an impoverished people, a declining public revenue, and an increasing public debt.

Protection ceased in 1834–35, bequeathing to free trade a commerce that gave an excess *import* of specie, a people more prosperous than any that had ever then been known, a revenue so great that it had been rendered necessary to emancipate tea, coffee, and many other commodities from duty, and a treasury free from all charge on account of public debt.

Free trade ceased in 1842, bequeathing to protection a commerce that gave an excess *export* of specie, a people ruined, and their governments in a state of repudiation, a public treasury bankrupt, and begging everywhere for loans at the highest rate of interest, a revenue collected and disbursed in irredeemable paper money, and a very large foreign debt.

Protection ceased in 1847, bequeathing to free trade a commerce that gave an excess *import* of specie, a highly prosperous people, State governments restored to credit, a rapidly growing commerce, a large public revenue, and a declining foreign debt.

Since that time California has supplied hundreds of millions of dollars in gold, nearly all of which have been exported, or (1856) locked up in public and private hoards; the consequences of which are seen in the facts that commerce is paralyzed, that the price of money in the commercial cities has ranged for years between ten and thirty per cent. per annum, and that the indebtedness to foreign nations has increased to such an amount as to require, for the payment of interest alone, a sum equal to the average export of food to all the countries of the world.

§ 9. Of all the institutions of a community none are capable of rendering a greater amount of service, and yet none are less understood or more calumniated, none in general more dreaded, than banks. Every community needs a money-shop, or place for facilitating intercourse between those who have money, and those who, having it not, desire to obtain it. One man seeks to have his little stock securely kept. Another requires an order for money to be paid at another place. A third would have a circulating note, and thus be relieved of the necessity for carrying gold or silver, both of which are far more bulky than the note. The owner of thousands, or of millions, places them in the bank, which latter pays them out in ten, twenty, fifty, or a hundred smaller sums of the precise amount desired, thus saving to its customer much labor and all the risk of loss. In the early periods of society these services are paid for by a commission upon the sums deposited and thus withdrawn; but in the later ones, banks furnish even the greater facility of circulating notes for the use of which they make no charge, the machinery of commerce thus becoming less costly as it becomes more perfect.

In the various small communities now growing up throughout the Western States, there are many little capitalists, some of whom are preparing for the purchase of houses or lots, or that of little farms; while others seek to open shops. To all of these, while thus waiting, it is desirable that their money should itself be earning something, thus adding to their little stock. To the community itself it is desirable that the accumulations of the tailor and the carpenter, the little fortunes of the widow and the orphan, and the savings of the doctor and the clergyman, should be kept in active operation. Combining their efforts, these little capitalists open a shop for the purpose of lending out their money, and for affording to the people of the neighborhood a place of secure deposit for such portions of their respective capitals as may from time to time become unemployed. The stock therein being held in shares, is readily transferable, the shoemaker, when ready to buy his house, selling out to the tailor; the clerk, when ready to open a shop, parting with his interest to the clergyman. The joint capital being security to those who trade with it for the safe return of their money, no one now finds it necessary to hide or bury his little stock. The bank, thus organized, aids the farmer in his purchases of manure, the shopkeeper in obtaining a larger supply of goods, and the builder in obtaining bricks and timber, the little savings of the neighborhood being thus actively employed on the spot on which they have been made. To pay the expenses of management the bankers must make a charge for the accommodation they afford in receiving, guarding, and paying out again, at the pleasure of their owners, the moneys deposited with them; or, they must pay themselves with the interest derived from their use. The advantage derived from the existence of the bank is the facility with which small sums may be temporarily invested and recalled, the community meanwhile profiting by the fact that all its wealth is actively employed. Were the laborer not to *lend* his fellow-laborer his horse, he could not *borrow* his cart; and were the owners of little sums of money to keep them in old stockings, they might find it difficult to borrow when they, themselves, required so to do.

The money-shop thus formed now constitutes a little savings bank for disengaged capital; as lands, houses, and lots, constitute similar banks in which is invested what would otherwise be the waste labor of their proprietors. In time, employments becoming more and more diversified, there is, with every stage of progress in that direction, a diminution in the quantity of currency required, the farmer now exchanging directly with the tanner and the shoemaker, and the hatter with the dealer in sugar and coffee, the balance alone being paid in money. Less capital being now required for maintaining the machinery of exchange from hand to hand, more of capital and labor may be given to production, and the return to both is much increased—a result towards the accomplishment of which the little money-shop contributes largely.

The owner of money, or currency, now retains some of it in his pocket-book, while other portions of it are in the bank.

In the one case he is the proprietor of what is called "circulation," and in the other he is the owner of a "deposit," the proportion borne by the former to the latter depending upon the proximity, or remoteness, of the bank. If near to him, he will keep very few notes on hand, because he can have more at any moment, his check always answering in their stead; but if it be remote, he must always have with him as many notes as will serve his purposes for a week or month. Increase in the facility of obtaining the description of currency that is needed tends, therefore, to diminish the quantity kept on hand, while facilitating exchanges, and increasing the power of combination. With the growth of wealth and population, there is a tendency to increase in the number of banks; to increase in the facility of obtaining the machinery of exchange; and to diminution in the proportion which money—whether gold, silver, or bank-notes, or in any form other than that of credits transferable by checks or drafts—bears to the amount of commerce.

More nearly than in any other portion of the world, the American banking system tends to bring together all the advantages above described, perfect power of association, accompanied by great development of individuality, to be followed by rapid growth of wealth. The system of its government is, however, directly opposed to this; and hence it is, that from year to year, those characteristics tend to disappear, and centralization, with all its vices, to take their place. Examine them where we may, these United States present the most extraordinary "contrasts" that can anywhere be found; and for the reason, that while local action is in accordance with true social science, the central government adopts the doctrine of that modern school which, in regard to money, has followed in the footsteps of Hume and Smith, whose teachings we may now examine.*

* The editor desires again to impress upon the reader's mind that the state of things above described is that which existed at a time when great imaginary prosperity was preparing the country for the severe financial crisis of 1857, and the extraordinary political one that has since occurred. This, however, was but a natural consequence of the steady pursuit of a free trade policy which built up great trading cities on the ruins of domestic commerce.

In proof of the assertion that it is the people, and not the makers of notes, who control the circulation, she gives the fact, just now made public, that with all its power the Federal Government has never been able to keep in circulation more than $20,000,000 of notes of less denomination than a dollar.

CHAPTER XXX.

OF THE INSTRUMENT OF ASSOCIATION—CONTINUED.

VIII.—*Of Hume, Smith, and other Writers on Money.*

§ 1. Theories of Mr. Hume in regard to money. Directly opposed to all the facts of history.

§ 2. His failure to observe, that while increase in the supply of money raises the prices of raw materials, it reduces those of finished products. Throughout inconsistent with himself. Accuracy of his views when asserting that no country need fear an unfavorable balance of trade that "preserved with care its people and its manufactures."

§ 3. General accordance of the views of Hume and Adam Smith. Inconsistencies of the latter. A medium of circulation the one great need of society. Hence the desire of all communities to establish in their favor a balance of trade. Inconsistencies of the opponents of this idea.

§ 4. Doctrines of the Ricardo-Malthusian school in regard to money. Mr. J. S. Mill. His views in regard to the inefficiency of money. Failure of the British economists to appreciate the services of the precious metals.

§ 5. M. Bastiat. Correspondence of his views with those of Hume and Smith. His doctrines being received as true, there can be no harmony of international interests.

§ 6. M. Chevalier holds that money is indispensable to man, and yet, that disadvantage may result from increase in its supply. The precious metals, the great instruments furnished by the Creator for the production of societary motion. The more rapid that motion, the greater must be, everywhere, the power of the individual to obtain supplies of food, and of the community to command the services of those metals.

§ 1. "MONEY is not," says HUME, "properly speaking, one of the subjects of commerce, but only the instrument which all have agreed upon to facilitate the exchange of one commodity for another. It is none of the wheels of trade: it is the oil which renders the motion of the wheels more smooth and easy."

Had he, however, found it asserted that corn, wine, and the flesh of sheep and oxen, had been "agreed upon" by men as the food they were to use, he would certainly have asked for some evidence that they really had come to such an agreement; and had not been led to act as they do, by the fact that such commodities had been *provided* by the Creator for man, while creating food of other descriptions for the nourishment of cows, horses, sheep, and other animals. He would naturally have asked the question—"Suppose they did not eat these things, what others could they eat?" and when the answer had been made, that they must either eat of them or perish, he would have regarded it as evidence that their course had been determined by a great law of nature, and had not been "agreed upon" by themselves.

So, too, with regard to the precious metals. Had he been

asked to designate any other known materials possessing the qualities required for gathering together, then dividing and distributing, and then again recombining all the minute portions of mental and physical force resulting from the daily consumption of food; any other so calculated to maintain the power of association among men; any other fitted so largely to augment the power of production, consumption, and accumulation; he would have been compelled to admit that there were none, and that gold and silver had been *provided* by the Creator for the accomplishment of those great objects.

If now it were certainly true that they had been so *provided*, not a doubt could exist that with increased facility in obtaining them there must be improvement in man's condition. Had they, on the contrary, only been "agreed upon," then it might be questioned whether or not increase would be beneficial; and that Mr. Hume thought it would not, is shown by the following passage:—

"The greater or less plenty of money is of no consequence * * * When coin is in greater plenty, as a greater quantity of it is required to represent the same quantity of goods, it can have no effect, good or bad, taking a nation within itself, any more than it would make an alteration in a merchant's books if, instead of the Arabian method of notation, which requires few characters, he should make use of the Roman, which requires a great many."

Unfortunately for our author and for those who since have followed him, the facts are directly the reverse of what they are here assumed to be, the prices of finished commodities having steadily declined as money has become more and more abundant. The amount of the precious metals circulating in France has more than doubled within the last half century, with corresponding *increase* in the quantity of the necessaries and conveniences of life obtainable in exchange for them. Wheat has risen, and so have other raw materials; but the improvement in agriculture has been so great, that almost all the products of a higher cultivation have been made more accessible to the laborer. Land and labor have risen in price, while cloth and iron have greatly fallen. Such, too, has been the course of things in every country of the world into which money has flowed; whereas, directly the reverse is observed in Ireland, Turkey, India, and those other countries in which the supply of money has diminished. The theory and the facts are thus directly at war with each other.

§ 2. Increase in the supply of the precious metals, as we are assured by Mr. Hume, causes "losses to the nation in its commerce with foreigners," because it raises the price of labor, and heightens those of commodities, thus "obliging every one to pay a greater number of those little white and yellow pieces than they had been accustomed to do."

It is, nevertheless, in those countries in which the supply increases, that the prices of raw materials and finished commodities tend most to approximate. Finished commodities being cheap, the gold, the sugar, the coffee, and the cotton, come there to purchase them; and hence it is, that commerce with distant lands increases in the gold-importing countries, while diminishing in the gold-exporting ones. For more than a century, Great Britain has had the largest foreign commerce; and for the reason, that she has exported cloth and iron with which to pay for gold. The foreign commerce of France and Germany, now probably the largest recipients of the gold of California and Australia, has rapidly increased. Where, however, the supply of the precious metals declines, as in Turkey, Portugal, Ireland, and India, we find the reverse of this, the power of maintaining commerce, whether at home or abroad, being there a steadily declining one. Here, again, we find the actual facts and the theory to be the antipodes of each other.

Strangely contradicting himself, he elsewhere assures his readers that whenever money flows into a country, "every thing takes a new face, and labor and industry gain life," it being "easy to trace the money in its progress through the commonwealth," quickening "the diligence of every individual before it increases the price of labor;" all of which is most true. Nevertheless, a moment later we find him asserting, "that it is of no manner of consequence to the domestic happiness of a state whether money be in greater or less quantity." Contradicting himself once again, he assures us, that when money decreases the people suffer, and "poverty, beggary, and sloth ensue;" and that those countries which have but little money, as was then the case with Austria, have not "a proportionable weight in the balance of Europe." The facts being thus opposed to the theory, he inquires, how do they "agree with that principle of reason, that the quantity of gold and silver is in itself altogether indifferent?" The pieces into which those metals were divided would still, as he thinks, "serve the same purposes of exchange, whatever their number might be, or whatever color they might have."

"To these difficulties," as he says, "I answer, that the effect here supposed to flow from scarcity of money, really arises from the manners and customs of the people, and that we mistake, as is too usual, a collateral effect for a cause. The contradiction is only apparent. * * It seems a maxim almost self-evident, that the prices of every thing depend on the proportion between commodities and money. * * Increase the commodities, they become cheaper; increase the money, they rise in value;" and thus it is that he reconciles reason with experience.

This is what is styled the metaphysical mode of investigation, in which men seek in their own minds for the natural laws that govern men. It is as if the chemist, leaving his laboratory, should shut himself up in his closet to study in his own mind what *ought* to be the composition of the air, the water, or the metals. Mr. Ricardo, pursuing the same course, was led to place his early settlers on the swamps and river bottoms, when daily observation shows that they commence on the poorer soils, and that it is only as wealth and population increase that they obtain power to cultivate the richer ones; while history proves that such has been the case from the earliest period to the present time. Equally natural was it, that Mr. Hume should imagine that the larger the quantity of money, the higher would be the prices of all the commodities for which money was to be given. Had he, however, reflected, that it was but a great instrument furnished by nature for producing circulation among men and their products, and that the beneficial effects he himself so well describes were but the natural consequence of an increase of the power of association resulting from increased facility in obtaining command of that instrument, he would have found the facts and "the principles of reason" in perfect harmony with each other.

In one respect, however, he was right. No government need, according to him, fear the existence of an unfavorable balance of trade, that "preserved with care its people and its manufactures." Doing that, it might, as regarded its money, "safely trust to the course of human affairs, without fear or jealousy." That such is the case, is proved by the example of England for a century past; by that of France; by those of all the countries of Northern Europe in the present day; and by that of these United States, whenever their policy has tended to the promotion of association among their people, to the diversification of employments, to the development of the powers of the land and of the men by whom it was cultivated, to the creation of a domestic market, and to the relief of the farmer from that most oppressive of all taxes, the tax of transportation. Caring "for their people and their manufactures," they have then, and only then, had in their favor a steadily-growing balance of trade, accompanied by a prosperity such as had never before been known.

§ 3. In regard to money, ADAM SMITH followed closely in the footsteps of Mr. Hume, holding with him that money makes but a small part of the capital of a nation, "and always the most unprofitable part of it." It is, nevertheless, the commodity that all men seek to obtain, that all nations rejoice in receiving, and that all regret should leave them—the common sense of mankind, and the theories of economists, being thus the poles of each other. Which is right? Seeking an answer to this question, let the reader calculate the amount of exchanges facilitated by a fleet of ships that may have cost ten or twenty millions, and then compare it with those effected by means of a single hundred thousand dollars' worth of three, five, or ten cent pieces, and he will find that the latter do more work in a month than the others could do in a year, if not in years. In the estimate of Dr. Smith, nevertheless, "the gold and silver money which circulates in any country, and by means of which the produce of its land and labor is annually circulated and distributed to the proper consumers, is all dead stock." Increase of their cheapness, in his opinion, rendered them "rather less fit for the purposes of money than they were before. In order to make the same purchases, we must," as he thought, "load ourselves with a greater quantity of them, and carry about a shilling in our pockets where we carried a groat before."

Diminution in the value of these metals in any particular country tended, according to Dr. Smith, to make "everybody really poorer;" that is, increased facility in obtaining the great instrument provided by the Creator for facilitating association among men was to be regarded as an evidence of poverty, and not of wealth! The man who wrote these words can scarcely be regarded as having studied the subject in reference to which he undertook to instruct the world.

Why it is, that the idea, so universal among men, that wealth, happiness, and progress are associated with increase in the supplies of money, is so very erroneous, is, as we are told, that—

"The rise in the money prices of commodities, which is, in this case, peculiar to that country, tends to discourage more or less every sort of industry which is carried on within it, and to enable foreign nations, by furnishing all sorts of goods for a smaller quantity of silver than its own workmen can afford to do, to undersell them, not only in the foreign, but in the domestic, market."

The answer to these assertions is found in the fact, that in all countries towards which the precious metals flow there is a constant tendency towards the approximation of prices, those of rude products of the earth rising, and those of finished commodities falling, the countries, themselves, becoming the best market in which *to sell and to buy;* as is proved by the case of England in the past, and France and Germany in the present. The theory and the facts are not in harmony with each other; and yet upon this assumption of facts that never have existed, and never can exist, is based the whole of the celebrated argument in reference to "the balance of trade."

The theory of Dr. Smith being thus, like that of Mr. Hume, unsound, it is no matter for surprise that we find the one as inconsistent with himself as we have already found the other. Believing in the advantage resulting from the use of bank-notes, he tells his readers that "every saving in the expense of collecting and supporting that part of the capital which consists in money is an improvement;" that "the substitution of paper in the room of gold and silver money replaces a very expensive instrument with one less costly and equally convenient;" that "by this operation £20,000 in gold and silver perform all the functions which £100,000 could otherwise have performed;" that "the whole value of the great wheel of circulation," the use of which is thus economized, "is added to the goods which are circulated and distributed;" and that thus is made "a very considerable addition to the quantity of that industry, and consequently to the value of the amount produced by land and labor." It is certainly difficult to reconcile these statements with the idea that the cheapening of the precious metals renders "men really poorer than before."

Foreign trade tends, however, as we are informed, to produce a correction of the difficulty, the use of notes causing an "overflow" of the metals "to the whole extent of the paper supplied," and "gold and silver to that amount" being "sent abroad," "the total amount of the circulation" remaining "as it did before."

The experience of the world is directly opposed to this, yet is it constantly assumed that prohibitions of notes are necessary for the maintenance of a sound currency, the tendency being always, as we are assured, towards using that which is bad in preference to that which is good. Everywhere else, however, the reverse of this is true, no prohibitions of bad roads, or of inferior mills, being required to secure demand for the services of good roads, or of superior mills and engines. The currency is necessarily bad in countries against which there is a balance of trade, the state of things existing in all those which find themselves compelled to export their produce in its rudest form.

In order that it may be good, and that a sound currency may be maintained, there *must*, in all countries that do not produce them, be an inward flow of the precious metals, consequent upon the existence of a favorable balance of trade. Nevertheless, on turning to Hume or Smith we find that the question of such balance is wholly unworthy to occupy the attention of those charged with the duties of government; and their doctrine has been repeated, with little change, by all the writers on money from their day to the present time. None can now study the writings of either without arriving at the conclusion that they had a most inadequate appreciation of the importance of the functions performed by money, and that, having studied in their closets the laws of nature, they forgot to verify their conclusions by studying the operations of the world around them.

§ 4. In thus examining the doctrines of the earlier English writers on money, we have, in effect, examined those of the Ricardo-Malthusian school of the present day, Messrs. McCulloch and Mill differing little from Messrs. Hume and Smith. Mr. Mill quotes, approvingly, the ideas of Hume as to the effect that would result from having every person in a nation to "wake and find a gold coin in his pocket," suggesting, however, that we might better suppose "that to every pound, or shilling, or penny in the possession of any one, another pound, shilling, or penny were suddenly added. There would," as he continues, "be an increased money demand, and consequently an increased money value, or price, for things of all sorts. This increased value would do no good to any one; would make no difference, except that of having to reckon pounds, shillings, and pence in higher numbers."

The experience of the world, however, shows, that in all countries the societary circulation becomes more rapid as the machinery of circulation is improved; that human power, mental and physical, is then economized; that consumption then more instantly follows production; that land and labor, and the rude products of both, then rise in price; that the higher products of a scientific agriculture, and finished commodities of every kind, then fall in price; and that men then grow in wealth, power, morals, intellect, and all the other characteristics of an advancing civilization.

Further in common with Hume, Mr. Mill has a slight opinion of the efficacy of money in the economy of society, it being, as he thinks, "intrinsically" most "insignificant," "except in the character of a contrivance for sparing time or labor." In that character, precisely, it is, that it is important, more being done in that way by a single hundred thousand dollars' worth of money than by tens of millions' worth of ships, canals, and railroads. "Insignificant," as it is, it has a value in the eyes of man, resulting, as he thinks, from an erroneous habit of regarding money "as a synonym of wealth;" and "more especially when borrowing is spoken of." This, in his opinion, is a grievous error, that which "one person lends to another," as well as "the wages, or rent, he pays to another," not being mere money, "but a right to a certain value of the produce of the country, to be selected at his pleasure; the lender having first bought this right, by giving for it a portion of his capital." Hence, as he says, "the loan market is called the money market;" and the equivalent given for the use of capital, or, in other words, interest, is not only called the interest of money, but, by a grosser perversion of terms, "the value of money." Here, as the reader will perceive, he is in perfect accordance with a distinguished French economist to whom reference has before been made.

The correction of the error of this passage is, as we think, to be found within itself. The borrower, or the rent-receiver, can "select at his pleasure of the produce of the country," being thus enabled to command cloth, iron, books, and the service of men of every rank in life, from the pauper to the peer. What gives him that wonderful power? Money, and nothing else. However numerous might be his hats or coats, his engines or his acres, they would give him no such power, unless the facility of converting them into money were such as to warrant him in promising to deliver to the persons around him the various quantities of the precious metals to which they might become entitled. The difficulty here, as almost everywhere, consists in the fact, that the power of money to promote the circulation of service is so wonderful as to cause them to imagine that it is the services and commodities that pass, and not the money. As well, however, might they imagine that it was the words that passed over the wires of the telegraph, and not the electric spark itself. At each and every payment, whether by delivery of the coin, by transfer of a circulating note that will be paid on presentation, or by draft upon a bank, it is the money itself that passes; and that such is the case is proved by the stoppages that occur on every occasion of diminished confidence.

All force is the result of motion, and the quantity of force obtained is dependent upon the quantity of motion *within a given time*—a body moving at the rate of a hundred feet in a minute giving a thousand times the force that would be obtained from it if moving at the rate of ten feet only. Such being the case, one of two things must be true—either there is no universality in the laws of nature, or Mr. Mill is in error. That the latter is the case, would seem to be proved by the fact, that the movement of all advancing countries is in direct opposition to the theories of that school in which originated the doctrines of over-population, and of the ultimate subjection of the laborer to the arbitrary will of those by whom the land might happen to be owned.

§ 5. Distinguished among the economists produced by France, stands the late M. Bastiat, by whom we are assured that "it is quite unimportant whether there is much or little money in the world. If there is much, much is used; if there is little, little is required: that is all."

This is but a repetition of the ideas of Hume and Smith, and, as in their case, it is opposed to the common sense of mankind. It was, indeed, the object of the tract from which the above passage has been derived, to prove the universal error of men in supposing that money was wealth, "real wealth" being to be found "in the abundance of things calculated to satisfy our wants and our tastes;" and not in the possession of the machinery by aid of which those things were to be exchanged. Money would, however, seem to be quite as well fitted to satisfy both "our wants and our tastes" as is a ship, a railroad, a wagon, or a mill, which latter are certainly, even in the estimation of M. Bastiat himself, quite as much wealth as is the bale of cotton carried in the ship, the load of wheat raised on the farm, or the package of cloth sent from the mill. The ship, the road, the mill, and money, are all portions of the machinery of exchange required by man; and among them all there is none that performs so much service at so little cost as the last; none whose possession is so essential to that combination of effort which distinguishes civilization from barbarism; and hence it was that our author had occasion to discover, as he supposed, so much error in the common mode of thought in reference thereto. Among the whole community for which he wrote, he could not have found even a single man who did not connect the idea of increased life, activity, and motion with increase in the facility of obtaining money; and motion is the cause of force, or power. Every farmer in France knows well that, when money is abundant, his produce moves rapidly from his hands, enabling him promptly to purchase clothing, manure, and instruments of cultivation calculated to increase his powers and those of his land. Equally well does he know, and feel, that when it is scarce he has to wait for purchasers, and that then the clothier, the collector of manures, and the maker of ploughs have to wait for him. Every laborer knows that when money circulates freely, he can readily sell his time, and be a good customer to the farmer; whereas, when it is scarce, he is forced to waste much time, his family then suffering for want of food, while the farmer suffers for want of a market. Men, as well as animals, have instincts; and when philosophers are led to teach what is opposed to all that those around them are led naturally to believe, it is because they study nature in their closets, and not in her own great laboratory.

M. Bastiat did not believe that the then recent discoveries of the Californian gold deposits would "add much to the comforts, conveniences, or enjoyments of the world at large." By augmenting the mass, they would, as he thought, "depreciate the whole." "The gold-seekers" would "become richer" at the expense of "those who were already in possession of gold;" all of which latter would "obtain a smaller amount of conveniences and comforts for an equal sum," the general result being a "displacement," and "not an augmentation, of wealth."

It is thus distinctly denied that increase of wealth results from increase in the facility of obtaining the precious metals.

In the ordinary and common-sense modes of thought, wealth is power. Of all the things yielded by the earth, money is that one whose possession confers most power; and yet we are here required to forswear the belief in a fact the evidence of whose truth meets us at every instant. Had M. Bastiat given the subject more careful attention, he could scarcely, with his brilliant intellect, have failed to discover that, throughout the world nations were suffering great inconvenience for want of the very instrument he so little valued; that men were constantly being forced to resort to the primitive form of barter because of the want of a proper supply of the medium of exchange; that labor was everywhere being wasted because of that deficiency in the societary motion so well described by M. Coquelin as existing in France; that everywhere the man who had money was enabled to make much larger profits than he could do were it more abundant; that he did this at the cost of the real parties to all exchanges, the producer and the consumer; and that all these difficulties were to be, in part at least, removed by the increased facility of obtaining the machine by means of which, alone, rapidity of circulation could be produced.

§ 6. In his recent work, M. Chevalier says, that "money is indispensable to man from the moment of his living in society;" and that "gold and silver have, from the earliest period, been chosen for the performance of its functions," as satisfying, more perfectly than any other commodity, the conditions required for a medium of exchange. He therefore lays it down as a principle, that, as in the case of all other commodities and things useful to man, "the diminution in the cost of producing the precious metals tends to the advancement of civilization." The only form, however, in which its benefits would be exhibited, would, as he thinks, be "in an increased facility for obtaining ornaments or utensils of gold and silver, or plated with those metals."

In all the transactions of life, a larger quantity of money would have to be given for the same commodity, prices of all things having increased in a corresponding ratio; and this, so far from being an advantage, would prove, as regarded foreign commerce, a disadvantage. The foreigner would, as he thinks, "deliver his merchandize at the price of the country, while continuing to take that of the country at its price in the general market of the world; and, under these circumstances, a nation would transact its business in the style of the great lord who, for a wager, sold on the Pont Neuf a piece of six francs for twenty-four sous."

We have here again the doctrine of Hume, Smith, and of almost all other writers on this subject; yet the world presents no single country in which such results have been produced, nor is it possible that there should be such an one. The people who produce money sell it, and they desire to sell as dearly as possible; those who get it doing so, only by supplying cheaply the commodities required by those who have it to sell; and more cheaply than any other country is able or willing to do.

The whole question, and all the philosophy of money is, however, settled by the simple proposition, of universal truth, that *in the natural course of human affairs, the prices of raw and finished commodities tend to approximate, the former rising as the latter fall, and the rapidity of the change increasing with every increase in the supply of those metals which constitute the standard with which prices need to be compared.*

Money is to society what food is to the body, the producer of motion. That food may give motion and produce power, it must be digested, and pass gradually through the very many miles of vessels by whose help it is gradually assimilated and made to yield support to the whole system—having done which, it passes gradually off, and chiefly in perspiration. So is it with the precious metals. That they may be the cause of motion and of power, it is required that they, too, be digested and passed gradually through the system—some portions being absorbed and retained, and others passing gradually and almost insensibly off, to be applied to the purchase of other commodities. In default of this, the supplies of California are, and can be, of no more service to these United States than would be supplies of food to a man suffering under dysentery, or cholera. The more the latter ate, the more certain would be the approach of death; and the more gold that comes from California the poorer do they become, under a system that closes the mills and furnaces of the country, that destroys the power of association, and that causes an export demand for all the gold that they receive, every step in that direction being accompanied by *an increase in the rapidity with which consumption follows production in other countries, and a diminution therein among themselves.*

CHAPTER XXXI.

OF PRODUCTION AND CONSUMPTION.

§ 1. Man the ultimate object of all production. Production consists in the direction of natural forces to human service. Every act of consumption an act of production. Demand the cause of supply.

§ 2. Labor-power the most perishable of all commodities. Perishes, unless the demand follows *instantly* upon its production. Waste of labor one of the conditions of early society and scattered population. Errors of Mr. Malthus and his disciples.

§ 3. Wages and productive power of England at various periods.

§ 4. The more continuous and steady the societary motion the more instant the demand for, and the economy of, labor. That continuity the test of real civilization. Diversity of employments indispensable to its existence. Waste of power in, and consequent poverty of, all purely agricultural countries.

§ 5. Errors of modern economists in regard to productive and unproductive labor. All labor productive which tends to enable man more thoroughly to direct the forces of nature to his service, wealth consisting in the existence of that power of direction. The greater the power of man over nature the more rapid the progress of accumulation.

§ 1. The ultimate object of all production is MAN, the being made in the likeness of his Creator, and endowed with faculties fitting him to obtain power over the material world.

Production consists in *the direction of the natural forces to the service of man*. The earth gives back many grains in return for the single one given to her. This grain, however, being not yet the proper food of man, he converts it into meal, calling to his aid for that purpose the force of gravitation. Being not yet food, he seeks the assistance of friction, kindling a fire, and by the aid of chemical forces producing bread. The ultimate object of all this labor is that of producing in himself muscular power, to do which he must subject to decomposition the matter that nature had before composed. Passing it now through his stomach, it is subjected to the action of other natural forces, and is thus prepared to enter again into the composition of wheat, potatoes, or any other class of food. We have here a never-ending round; but where does production end, or consumption begin?

Throughout the material world production and consumption are but parts of the same operation, oxygen and hydrogen being consumed in producing water, and water being consumed in the reproduction of its elements. In both cases *motion* is produced, giving *force*, the measure of which latter is to be found in the rapidity of the former. So it is in the physiological world, life being a constant round of production and consumption, and health and vigor being, throughout, attendant upon rapidity of digestion. So, too, in the social world, the power there existing being dependent, altogether, upon the *circulation* of the physical and mental efforts of the persons of whom it is composed. When this is rapid, the force is great; when it is sluggish, the force is small.

Association with his fellow-men, or commerce, is the indispensable condition of the development of human powers. Commerce consists in the exchange of physical or intellectual effort, each man with every other. The greater the number of men, the greater is the power of association and the more rapid the development of individual faculty, and the more does man acquire power over nature. That, in its turn, is attended with increased facility of combination, and increased capacity for reducing to his service the wonderful natural forces. We have here the same unending round seen in the material world, by which production and consumption are merged in each other, the employment, or consumption, of physical and intellectual effort producing new and larger development of material and mental powers. Here, as everywhere throughout the world, supply is consequent on the existence of demand.

§ 2. The one commodity at the disposal of all men, is muscular and mental effort, or *labor-power*. It is of all the most perishable, being lost forever if not profitably consumed at *the very instant* of production. It is, too, the one that least bears transportation, perishing in the act of being removed. The man who is a mile from his farm loses ten or twenty per cent. of his powers on the way to and from the scene of his daily labor. The quantity of human effort being dependent altogether on the demand for its production, demand is in like manner dependent on the power, on the part of others, to produce things to be given in exchange for it. The whole constituting but a single circle, the more rapid the motion the greater must be the inducement to the production of effort, and the greater the power of all to consume the commodities produced.

Unceasing waste of labor is one of the conditions of an early society and a scattered people. Where a whole population is limited to scratching the earth in quest of food, large numbers are required in harvest, for whose labor there is no demand at other seasons. In England, at the close of the fourteenth century, we read of 212 persons having been employed in harvesting 168 bushels of grain, an operation that could now with ease be accomplished by a single individual.

The wages paid to reapers were 2d. and 3d. per day, without food, while weeders and haymakers had but a single penny. Were we, however, to estimate the wages during the year at this latter rate, we should even then greatly err, because employment was only occasional, leaving a large portion of the labor-power wholly without demand through the remainder of the year. In proof of this, we may take Ireland as she now stands, occupying a position analogous to that of England when this latter was accustomed to export wool and import cloth. Tenpence per day, without food, is there the highest rate of wages, but 6d. is often willingly accepted. The ordinary rate is, however, 6d., with food.

Small as is this latter, it would yet give 3s. a week with board; and to him who, centuries hence, may study such subjects, it will appear difficult to reconcile even this with the picture of a nation "starving by millions." Examining the question, however, more closely, he would find that employment, as a rule, had been only occasional; and that, so great had been the waste of labor that the actual rate of wages had not exceeded 4d. a day, out of which the laborer had been required to purchase food for his family and himself.

In this fact, the temporary nature of employment, we find the key to that which has so misled economists in reference to English wages of the fourteenth and fifteenth centuries. In 1444, when the common laborer is said to have received two pecks of wheat per day, his allowance was 15s. per annum, with clothing of the value of 3s. 4d., and meat and drink. The cloth of russet, then used by laborers, sold at 2s. per yard; so that the whole wages of the laborer did not exceed nine yards of cloth, and his own food. Where, then, could he obtain the means of support for a family, if so unfortunate as to have one?

§ 3. In the period that followed the Norman conquest, so many English slaves were exported, that the Irish market was glutted with them; and as late as the reign of King John they might be found in almost every cottage in Scotland. At the close of the thirteenth century, a slave and his family were sold for 13s. 4d. In England, a few herrings, a loaf of bread, and some beer, constituted the allowance in harvest. Meat and cheese were delicacies not then used by laborers. A valuation of the personal property at Colchester, then the tenth city of England, exhibits the condition of the tradesmen and artificers of that period, and enables us to form some idea of the situation of the common laborer. In most houses a brass pot seems to have been the only ordinary utensil. A cobbler's stock in trade was valued at 7s.; a butcher's stock of salt meat at £1 18s. Almost every family had a small store of barley or oats, rye being little used, and wheat scarcely at all. Some families possessed a cow or two, but more had two or three hogs. In 1301 the valuation of household articles rarely exceeded 20s. Bread, beer, and milk, constituted the usual diet of the townsmen. In 1357 appeared the Statute of Laborers, by which the wages of haymakers and weeders were fixed at 2d. per day, payable either in money or in wheat at 10d. per bushel, at the option of their employers. The effect of this option may be imagined, when it is known that in the fourteenth century wheat varied between 2s. and £4 per quarter. When it was high, the laborers would be paid in money, which would not procure them food; when low, they would receive corn, which would not purchase clothing. No person was to quit his village in search of work in summer, if he could obtain employment at the above wages, except the people of Staffordshire, Lancashire, and a few other counties. Laborers were to be sworn twice a year to observe these regulations, offenders being punishable with imprisonment in the stocks. In 1360 this statute was confirmed by Parliament, and the observance of it enforced under penalty of imprisonment and burning on the forehead with a red hot iron. It was optional with the master to hire by the day or year, but the laborer was compelled to work for the statute wages by either the one or the other, at the pleasure of the employers.

How far the latter availed themselves of this option may be seen from the fact that 250 reapers were employed to cut 200 acres of corn. Harvest time over, no employment being obtainable, "many became staff-strikers, and wandered in parties of two, three, or four, from village to village;" while great numbers "turned out sturdy rogues, and infested the kingdom with frequent robberies." In 1388 the wages of labor were again regulated, a plough-driver being allowed "9s. per annum, with food, but without clothing, or other perquisite." Eden, in his *History of the Poor*, from whose work these facts are drawn, says that we may form an idea of the bad husbandry of the period, and the "consequent misery of the laborers," from the fact that five or six bushels per acre was the usual yield of wheat. The population having been then less than two and a-half millions, the power of association could have existed in but very slight degree. Towns and cities, however, were growing and employment was by slow degrees becoming more diversified, and these regulations merely prove the necessity felt by the great landlords for legal aid in compelling the laborers to accept from them a smaller remuneration than could be obtained elsewhere. The insurrection of Wat Tyler followed close on the regulation last referred to. Half a century later, Parliament fixed the annual wages of a laborer at 15s., with meat and drink, and 3s. 4d. for clothing; but that, in its turn, was followed by the insurrection of Jack Cade. In the Wars of the Roses, the people generally sided with the House of York as opposed to the great landed proprietors, authors of these laws.

In 1486 a new statute fixed the year's wages at 16s. 8d., with 4s. for clothing. So ineffectual, however, did this also prove, that twenty years later it was ordained that persons refusing to work were to be imprisoned, and every vagabond, "whole and mighty in body," was to be tied to the cart's tail, and whipped "till his body was bloody by means of such whipping." How numerous were these vagabonds, and how great the difficulty of obtaining employment, is evident from the fact, that out of a population of only three millions, there were executed in the reign of Henry VIII. no less than 72,000 "great and petty thieves."

Early in the reign of Edward VI. laws were passed by which it was enacted that "if any man or woman, able to work, should refuse to labor, and live idle for three days, he or she should be branded with a red hot iron on the breast, with the letter V, and should be adjudged to be a slave, for two years, of any person who should inform against such idler." Further, the master was to "feed his slave with bread and water, or small drink, and such refuse meat as he should think proper," compelling "his slave to work, by beating, chaining, or otherwise, in such work and labor (how vile soever it be) as he should put him to;" adding thereto, that "if he runs away from his master for the space of fourteen days, he shall become his slave for life, after being branded on the forehead or cheek with the letter S. The punishment for running away a second time was death. The same statute provides that even "although there be no man which shall demand such loiterers, yet justices of the peace shall be bound to inquire after such idle persons; and if it shall appear that any such shall have been vagrant for three days, he shall be branded on the breast with a V, made with a hot iron." A master was also authorized to "put a ring of iron round the neck, arms, and leg of a slave, for more surety in the keeping of him." Such was the condition of the people at a time when they are supposed by the advocates of the Ricardo-Malthusian doctrine "to have lived much in the same manner as husbandmen in the north of England did in the last century, or as the Scottish peasantry do in the present."

A writer in the reign of Elizabeth, when the population could not have exceeded three and a half millions, says: "the gentilitie commonly provide themselves sufficiently of wheaten bread for their own tables, whilst their household and poor neighbors, in some shires, are forced to content themselves with rie or barleie; yea, and in time of dearth, manie with bread made either of beans, peason, otes, or of altogether, and some acorns among." An eminent justice of Somersetshire says, in 1596, that 40 persons had there been executed in a year, for robberies, thefts, and other felonies; 35 burnt in the hand; 37 whipped; 183 discharged;" and yet that "the fifth part of the felonies committed in the country were not brought to trial," the magistrates having been awed by the threats of confederates, from executing justice on the offenders. Eden says truly, that "it is probable that these disorders were, in a great measure, due to the difficulty of finding regular employment for the surplus hands not required in agriculture."

Such was indeed the real cause of difficulty. England was still merely an agricultural country, exporting food, and importing manufactures from the wealthy countries bordering on the Rhine; and in the absence of manufactures, agriculture could make but little progress.

With the growth of population and wealth, cultivation has extended over the richer soils, with steady increase in the diversity of employments, and in the rapidity with which consumption and production have followed upon each other. Hence the product of agricultural labor has increased in a ratio greatly exceeding that of the growth of numbers.

§ 4. Society, or commerce, consists in an exchange of services. Continuity in the demand for labor, rapidity in the circulation of services, growing commerce, are all but different modes of expression for the same idea.

The power to perform services is the consequence of a

consumption of capital in the form of food. If that power be not applied on *the instant* that it is produced, it is lost forever. The less promptly the demand follows the supply the greater, therefore, must be the waste. The more instant the demand the greater must be the economy of power, and the amount of force.

Highest, therefore, amongst the tests of civilization, is *that continuity in the societary motion which enables all to find demand for their whole physical and mental powers; and that this may be produced, diversity of employments is the one indispensable condition.*

Comparing the various nations of the present day with each other, we obtain results similar to those obtained in reviewing the various stages of English history. India exhibits no demand for labor, and her people, therefore, sell themselves to slavery in the Mauritius. Ireland presents a scene of constant waste of labor-power; and her unhappy people, in search of harvest wages, abandon their native land where famine and pestilence reign supreme. In Portugal and Turkey mental and physical power abound, for which there is no demand. So is it in Jamaica, Mexico, Brazil, and Buenos Ayres; in all of which we find a state of facts corresponding with that observed in the earlier ages of English history, the laborer, even when nominally free, being there the mere slave of the man who owns the land, or who supplies food and clothing to those by whom it is tilled.

Turning now to France, and Northern Europe generally, we find a state of things widely different, the circulation growing daily more continuous, the demand for labor-power following more rapidly upon its production, physical and mental faculty becoming more developed as it is more and more economized, and force increasing from hour to hour.

To what cause may these great differences be ascribed? To this and this alone: the first named of these countries follow in the lead of England, adopting for their guides those economists who hold that the return to agricultural labor tends naturally to decline; that agriculture is therefore the least profitable of human pursuits; that the proportion of the land-owner tends naturally to increase, and that of the laborer to diminish; the tendency in these directions increasing as matter tends more and more to take upon itself the highest form of which it is capable—that of man. The others follow in the lead of France, adopting the policy of Colbert, which looks to placing agriculture at the head of all pursuits, and seeking the attainment of that object by means of measures tending to raise the price of labor and land, while reducing that of all the commodities required for the consumption of the land-owner and the laborer. *The first place trade at the head of the pursuits of man, while the last seek the extension of commerce.*

England herself is the birth-place of the theory of over-population, invented to account for the enormous waste resulting from the want of continuous demand for human force. At one time, the mill-owner closes his doors in order to reduce the price of labor and its ruder products; at another, long-continued strikes ruin both workman and employer. Trading centralization is there almost perfect; and centralization and stability are totally inconsistent with each other.*

§ 5. Modern political economy has sought to limit the signification of the word *wealth* to those material commodities which may be bought and sold; limiting, too, the science itself to the determination of the laws which govern man in trading operations. This has arisen from the fact, that its professors have never properly discriminated between the two very distinct classes into which society is so much divided: the one desiring to effect exchanges *with* their fellow-men, and thus to maintain *commerce;* the other seeking to effect exchanges *for* them, and thus to exercise *trade.*

Extension of the first, as has been seen, brings with it continuity of motion; whereas, increase in the power of the last tends to produce what are called "gluts," the trader seeking

* "Between our Black West Indies and our White Ireland, between these two extremes of lazy refusal to work, and of famishing inability to find any work, what a world have we made of it, with our fierce Mammon-worships, and our benevolent philanderings, and idle, godless nonsenses of one kind and another! Supply-and-demand, Leave-it-alone, Voluntary-principle, Time will mend it: till British industrial existence seems fast becoming one huge poison-swamp of reeking pestilence, physical and moral; a hideous *living* Golgotha of souls and bodies buried alive; such a Curtius' gulf, communicating with the Nether Deep, as the sun never saw till now. . . . Thirty thousand outcast needlewomen working themselves swiftly to death; three million paupers rotting in forced idleness, helping said needlewomen to die! these are but items in the sad ledger of despair. Thirty thousand wretched women, sunk in that putrifying well of abominations; they have oozed in upon London from the universal Stygian quagmire of British industrial life; are accumulated in the *well* of the concern to that extent."—CARLYLE: *Latter-Day Pamphlets.*

to cause those changes of prices which enable him to buy at low prices and sell at high ones. Some economists have imagined this difficulty of selling to be a consequence of *over-production*, when the real cause was to be found in obstacles in the way of circulation. Over-population and over-production thus combine for the formation of that which is most appropriately termed "the dismal science."

From the same omission has resulted considerable difference as to the meaning of the word *production*, of which no clear definition has ever yet been given. By nearly all economists it is limited to the consideration of those material things which may be made the subject of purchase and sale. Much diversity of opinion has, therefore, existed as to the division of society into productive and unproductive classes. Among the latest exponents of the modern school is Mr. J. S. Mill, whose views are given in the following passage:—

"All labor is, in the language of political economy, unproductive, which ends in immediate enjoyment, without any increase of the accumulated stock of permanent means of enjoyment. And all labor, according to our present definition, must be classed as unproductive which terminates in a permanent benefit, however important, provided that an increase of material products forms no part of that benefit. The labor of saving a friend's life is not productive, unless the friend is a productive laborer, and produces more than he consumes. To a religious person, the saving of a soul must appear a far more important service than the saving of a life; but he will not, therefore, call a missionary or a clergyman productive laborers, unless they teach, as the South Sea missionaries have in some cases done, the arts of civilization in addition to the doctrines of religion. It is, on the contrary, evident that the greater number of missionaries or clergymen a nation maintains, the less it has to expend on other things; while the more it expends judiciously in keeping agriculturists and manufacturers at work, the more it will have for every other purpose. By the former, it diminishes, *cœteris paribus*, its stock of material products; by the latter, it increases them."

Truth being simple, simple ideas are generally true. Complex ideas, therefore, may generally be regarded as the reverse, the progress of man in knowledge being always in the direction of obtaining expressions that, by reason of their perfect simplicity, suffice for covering all the facts. Such is not here the case. The missionary is productive, *if* "he add the arts of civilization to the doctrines of religion," that is, if he carry to the people of the South Sea Islands ploughs and harrows, and other instruments calculated to enable them to increase their stock of material products. Contenting himself, on the contrary, with laboring to produce in his flock a higher feeling of their responsibility towards their fellow-men, and towards their Creator, he is to be regarded as unproductive, even though the effort result in making sobriety, industry, and economy, the normal condition of a little community in which there had before reigned turbulence, idleness, and waste. Again, the labor of saving the life of a man is unproductive; whereas, that devoted to increasing the supply of hogs is productive. The painter is productive when he paints a picture; but unproductive when he teaches hundreds of others to make pictures equal to his own. Fourcroy and Chaptal, Davy and Berzelius, creators of science, were unproductive; but the apothecary, who by means of their discoveries is enabled to make a paper of seidlitz powders, is productive. Watt, who taught us how to avail ourselves of steam, and Fulton, from whom we learned to make it available for the purposes of transportation, were unproductive; while the man who makes steam-engines and steamships is productive. The more missionaries, the more Fourcroys, Chaptals, Watts, or Fultons, a nation maintains, "the less," we are here assured, "it will have to expend on other things;" whereas, the more it converts its people into mere agriculturists and manufacturers, "the more it will have for every other purpose!" Such is the strange result to which the grossly material character of the doctrines of the Ricardo-Malthusian school has led a writer so deservedly occupying one of the highest positions among the economists of Europe.

That labor is productive which tends to enable man more thoroughly to direct the forces of nature to his service, the power so to do constituting wealth. Such is the effect of the efforts of the missionary, of the man who saves his neighbor's life, of Fulton and Watt, Fourcroy and Berzelius; and the more such men a nation maintains the more it will certainly have "to expend on other things," the more rapidly will consumption follow production, and the greater will be the power of *accumulation*.

CHAPTER XXXII.

OF ACCUMULATION.

§ 1. Power of accumulation exists in the ratio of the rapidity of the circulation. Capital the instrument by means of which man is enabled to direct the natural forces to his service. Power of association grows as he obtains increased command over the instrument.

§ 2. Movable capital declines in its proportions as compared with that which is fixed, that decline being an evidence of advancing civilization. Centralization produces the reverse effect. Increase of movable capital in all the present free-trade countries.

§ 3. Errors of modern economists in regarding *saving* as the cause of the growth of capital.

§ 4. That growth due to the economy of human effort. That economy a consequence of diversification of employments, and consequent combination of action.

§ 5. Errors of Adam Smith in regard to the origin of capital.

§ 6. Chief difficulty of social science. Summary of the definitions thus far given in the present work.

§ 1. Consumption and production being always equal, how, it may be asked, can there be accumulation? To this it may be answered, that the power of accumulation depends entirely on the rapidity with which consumption follows upon production.

The food consumed by Crusoe was capital, obtained by means of human effort. Did it then cease to be capital? Certainly not. On the contrary, it had assumed a higher form, that of mental and physical force. Next, it reappeared in the form of a bow, to the construction of which such force had been applied. Reappearing once again in the form of increased supplies and higher quality of food, and thus enabling him to devote more time and mind to the study of nature and her powers, it promotes the further accumulation of capital in the form of that higher Intelligence by means of which he compels wind and water to do his work, thus obtaining that mastery over nature which constitutes wealth. *Capital is the instrument by means of which that mastery is acquired*, whether existing in the form of food, of physical or mental force, of bows, canoes, ships, lands, houses, mills, or furnaces. Every increase of command over the instrument is attended by corresponding increase in the power of association, in the development of individual faculties, and in the power of further *accumulation*.

§ 2. The tendency towards improvement is in the ratio of the increase of *fixed*, as compared with *circulating*, capital.

With every swamp drained, every new mine opened, every bed of marl worked, every new water power made to labor in the service of man, every new development of the wonderful forces of nature, the home has greater attractions, the family is more enabled to revolve around its own centre, the township acquires greater individuality, and the revolution of the various societary bodies becomes more continuous, with constant increase of the societary force.

Centralization, on the contrary, tends to increase the *proportion* of movable, while diminishing that of fixed, property. The great landholder compels the weak to labor for him, holding men and women as mere chattels, to be bought and sold in open market. Land is then, as now in India and Carolina, nearly valueless. The products of labor then pass through the hands of the traders in men's services on their way towards distribution. In this state of things nearly all property is purely personal, as we see to be the case in the cotton States.

The warrior-chief imposes heavy taxes on his subjects, applying to the support of armies what his people would otherwise have fixed in the form of improvements on their little farms.

The trader opposes all exchanges not made through himself, knowing that the more he can separate the producer from the consumer the greater will be the quantity of goods waiting demand, the larger his proportion of their price, and the greater his power to purchase ships and cannon with which to enforce submission to his demands.

The western settler obtains land for little money, but his horses, cattle, wagon, and furniture, cost him much. Obliged to send his produce to a distant market, he pays for the use of wagons, horses, cars, and ships; and the cost of all this circulating capital prevents increase in the value of his land.

The capital of England, in the days of the Plantagenets, consisted in large proportion of its flocks and herds. The markets being distant, produce accumulated in one part of the kingdom, while in another men perished for want of food. Land and man were cheap, but cloth was dear. Now, the value of fixed property certainly thrice exceeds that of floating capital; and this in despite of a policy based on the idea that ships, wagons, and other machinery of *trade*, are more profitable than land, the machinery of production.

Looking to Ireland, India, Portugal, or Turkey, countries whose policy tends towards giving power to the trader, we see a growing dependence on floating capital, attended by a decline in the value of labor and land; while in Belgium and Germany we see the proportion of movable capital diminishing, the value of labor and land meanwhile growing with great rapidity.

The policy of these United States having usually tended to the exhaustion of the land and the dispersion of their people, it has, as a rule, been adverse to the creation of fixed property. Again and again have mills and furnaces been built, and mines been sunk; but only to produce the ruin of those by whom such works have been created. Nowhere is so much capital applied to education; but nowhere has there been exhibited a more pertinacious determination to prevent the application of the faculties thus developed to any pursuit other than those of law, medicine, speculation, and trade. As a consequence, the unfixed property is to the fixed as 8 to 6; being a larger proportion than in any other community claiming to rank as civilized.

§ 3. We are told, however, that "it is only by means of saving that fortunes are created or increased."

Were this so, we should look for the most rapid increase of capital to those countries in which saving is most practised; yet is it precisely there that it grows most slowly. The Irish laborer is noted for his saving habits, as are the Laplander and the Hindoo. In early English and Scotch history we see families saving a supply of food, because of the uncertainty of getting more. In India, sovereigns save large sums of money by way of providing against any deficiency of revenue. The Castilian saves his food in a *silo;* and the savage of the West in a *cache.* The mistress of the house saves water in a cistern, when the supply is uncertain; but ceases to do so when the river is made to find the way to the ocean through her own and her neighbor's dwellings.

It is where there is least circulation that saving is most resorted to, and *there the waste is greatest.* Societary motion then scarcely at all exists, the faculties remain latent for want of demand for their employment, and all must seek to save if they would continue to live. Circulation being established, capital rapidly accumulates, the demand for physical or mental power stimulates the faculties that had been latent, and every increase in that demand causes an increase in the value of man, and in the rapidity of the growth of wealth.

The construction of a railroad increases capital, because, by diminishing the waste attendant on effecting changes of place, it gives a money value to land. The woollens-mill does the same, because it enables the farmers to send their wool and corn to market in the form of cloth. The opening of a mine, and the erection of a furnace, give value to land and labor by creating that diversity of employment which causes rapidity of circulation, this rapidity, in its turn, causing still more rapid increase of capital.

§ 4. To acquire power over nature being the great object of man, the more it is attained, the less is the value of the commodities he needs, and the greater is his own. To obtain power there must be association. The great obstacle to association being the necessity for effecting changes of place, the more this is removed the greater is not only man's present power, but his capacity for further progress.

The spring being distant, he calls to his aid the jug, the cask, the wagon, each diminishing the value of water; until with the growth of population he is enabled, *once for all*, to construct an aqueduct and make water cheap as air.

The Indian path being bad, he determines, *once for all*, to make a road; this is followed by the turnpike, the canal, the railroad; each in turn facilitating the construction of its more perfect successor, until merchandise is at length transported at so small a cost that land and labor are immensely increased in value.

The school-house being distant, his children must either dispense with education or waste much time upon the road. He proposes, therefore, to his neighbors, that they shall, *once for all*, give their time to the construction of a school-house; and now instruction declines so much in value that ten times as many children can profit by it.

The market being distant, he is taxed daily for the cost of sending his wool and corn to be exchanged for iron. He therefore proposes to his neighbors that they shall, *once for all*, unite to build a furnace, the laborers in which may eat the corn which they now carry to a distant market, thus terminating, *at once and forever*, the necessity for transportation.

Iron being obtained, he next suggests that steam can as well be made to spin and weave cotton in their own neighborhood as elsewhere; all that is required being that they should, *once for all*, join to put up a house, and to bring from abroad a little machinery, and the skill required for working it. Further, he says to them: "We are ourselves unemployed for more than half our time, and our children are almost entirely so. Though unfit for the labors of the field, they could perform the lighter work of tending the operations of a mill. Again, the minds of our people remain undeveloped; let us have them taught, and we shall soon obtain machinists of our own. We waste, daily, the powers of earth and air for want of little machines that would enable us to use them; we waste the faculties of our people, because there is no demand for them; we waste great part of our produce in feeding the horses and men who carry the rest to market, exhausting the soil, because that market is so distant. Let us then, *once for all*, combine to stop this waste. With every step we make in this direction we shall offer new inducements for carpenters and masons, printers and teachers, to come and eat the food which we now carry to a distant market, and we shall be enabled to improve our machinery. Commerce thus will increase among us, with increase in the societary motion, and in the value and the happiness of man."

The object here sought is, in the words of an eminent French economist, M. de Fontenay, that of "*suppressing, by means of a certain quantity of labor once performed, a certain portion of current labor and annual expense that would otherwise re-appear periodically, and for an indefinite period of time.*"

Such was the object sought by Colbert, to whom France has been indebted for the system which has increased to an enormous extent her collieries, furnaces, and workshops, raised so greatly the value of her land, and doubled, or even trebled, the power of her laborers to command supplies of food.

Directly the reverse of this, as the reader sees, is the doctrine lying at the foundation of the system that would make of Britain the workshop of the world; that, for the maintenance of which we are taught that man begins everywhere on the rich soils, old communities being forced to resort to poorer ones, with daily diminution in the demand for labor. To the farmers and planters of Brazil and the United States it says: "Cultivate your rich soils, and leave us to our poor ones. Labor being cheap with us, we can manufacture more cheaply than you can do. Do not, therefore, once for all, build mills and furnaces; continue year after year to expend your labors in carrying produce back and forth; continue to exhaust your land; continue to have no combination of effort among yourselves; and you will grow rich. The time, however, will arrive when you will be forced to cultivate the poor soils, and then you will be troubled with over-population. Wages falling, *you may then be enabled to accumulate the capital required for entering into competition with us; that is, the poorer you become, the greater will be your power.*"

Such is the doctrine that is based upon the idea of trade being the first pursuit of man. Under this system, Ireland wastes, *weekly*, more labor than would, if applied *once for all*, give her the machinery that would enable her to make a domestic market for all her food and all her labor; Portugal and Turkey waste *daily* more muscular and intellectual power than would, if applied *once for all*, give their people machinery for making all the cloth they now consume. Under it, India has seen her children condemned to remain idle when they would desire to work; to relinquish their rich soils, and permit their cities to go to ruin; to forego the advantages of domestic commerce, and become dependent altogether on the chances of trade with a people distant from them and seeking only to live at their expense.

§ 5. The error above referred to, in regard to the source to which we must look for the power of accumulation, presents itself in this *Wealth of Nations*, in which we find ourselves assured by Dr. Smith that "parsimony, and not industry, is the immediate cause of increase of capital." It is, however, merely the reduction into words of the general idea prevailing among the much degraded portions of the human race.

Man seeks to obtain power over nature, and as that end is more and more attained fortunes augment, and parsimony tends to pass away. Arkwright and Watt obtained power, by means of which they accumulated fortunes while doubling the value of the land of Britain. Was this the result of "saving?" Chaptal, Fourcroy, and Berthollet, by mastering great natural forces, contributed largely to the vast increase in the landed capital of France. Morse, seizing the power to direct electricity, acquired fortune. Fulton taught mankind to apply steam to transportation, thus adding countless millions to the price of land. Scott and Goethe found wealth in the power to amuse their countrymen. What, in all these cases, savors of parsimony? Wealth consisting in the power to direct the forces of nature, the more rapid its growth the more does "parsimony," the feeling of the slave, tend to disappear from among the qualities of the being made in the image of his Creator,—MAN.

§ 6. The chief difficulty with which social science has had to contend, has been the want of clear definitions of the terms in use. Those furnished in the present work being, as it is believed, universally true, should cover the whole ground, removing the obstacles to a clear understanding of what was really meant by any writer who used the various terms. The whole may now thus be stated:—

Utility is the measure of man's power over nature.

Value is the measure of nature's power over man, of the resistance she offers to the gratification of his desires.

Wealth consists in the power of man to command the always gratuitous service of nature.

Production consists in directing those forces to the service of man.

Capital is the instrument by help of which the work is done, whether existing in the form of land, ships, wagons, houses, mental or physical force.

Trade consists in the performance of exchanges *for* other persons, being the instrument used by—

Commerce, which consists in the exchange of services, products, or ideas, *by* men, and *with* their fellow-men.

As the power of association grows utility increases, while values decline.

As the value of commodities declines, that of man increases, with increase in the development of individuality, and in the security of person and of property.

As person and property become more secure, men and capital tend to become more fixed, and a smaller proportion of both remains in the floating state.

As men and capital become fixed, and the powers of nature are more and more developed, there is increased tendency towards the creation of local centres, and towards the establishment of the same beautiful system by means of which the harmony of the universe is maintained.

As local centres increase in number and attraction the power of association steadily augments, with diminution in the necessity for the services of the trader, increase in the power of production, in the growth of capital, and in the rapidity of its circulation—with corresponding increase of commerce.

CHAPTER XXXIII.

OF CIRCULATION.

§ 1. Little circulation of either land or man, in the earlier stages of society. Large proportion then borne by movable to fixed capital.

§ 2. Circulation increases in its rapidity in the direct ratio of the tendency of capital to become fixed and immovable.

§ 3. The more rapid the circulation the greater the tendency towards the creation of local centres, towards the development of individuality, and towards having society assume its natural form.

§ 4. Circulation becomes more rapid as employments become diversified, and land becomes divided. Social phenomena exhibited by France.

§ 5. Tendency of British policy to promote increase in the proportions of movable capital at the expense of that which is fixed. Consequent sluggishness of circulation in all the countries subject to it.

§ 6. Circulation becomes more rapid in the ratio of the tendency towards approximation in the prices of rude products and finished commodities.

§ 7. Tendency of the British colonial system to produce stoppage of the circulation. Its effects, as exhibited in the past and present of these United States.

§ 8. The more rapid the circulation the more equitable the distribution. Identity of the physical and social laws.

§ 1. In the early ages of society land is wholly valueless. Men then hunt and fish, their only property consisting of bows and arrows, skins, and the little food they may have saved in summer as provision against the wants of winter. Later, in the shepherd state, flocks constitute their only wealth. Land being superabundant, it is unhesitatingly abandoned when the pasture becomes exhausted. The community being still but nature's slave, of voluntary circulation there is none, each of its members finding himself compelled to move when others desire a change of place.

In this condition of society it is that centralization most exists, the few who are strong of arm, or intellect, controlling the floating mass who, being poor, and often suffering for want of food, are always ready to follow in the train of men like Brennus, Tamerlane, or Genghis Khan, gladly aiding in stopping the societary circulation among others more advanced in wealth and power than themselves.

Later, they obtain by means of a rude cultivation increased supplies of food, small communities then appropriating land to be temporarily divided among its occupants, as was the case in Gaul in the days of Cæsar, and is now in Russia. As a rule, however, the strong have seized upon extensive tracts of land, compelling the weak to labor for them, and giving to the slave only such portion of the product as has seemed required for preserving him in working order. This being the barbarous condition of society, wealth consists in movables, and is reckoned by the number of beasts of burden called men, women, and children, as is now the case in Carolina, Brazil, and Cuba. Land being held in vast tracts it finds no circulation, and has little value. Man being then held as property, he has no right of circulation among his fellow-men.

Population and wealth further increasing, the blacksmith, the carpenter, the miller, and the trader, come together to form the nucleus of the future town; and now land becomes divided, and is held in absolute ownership, or on payment of yearly compensation for its use.

The town increasing, land becomes divided, exchangeable property and person become more secure, land acquiring value, and men becoming more free. Towns now become places of refuge, men who have been held as slaves seeking, in association with their fellow-men, the free exercise of the faculties by which they are distinguished from the brute.

With every stage of progress, individuality becomes more and more developed—men who had been limited to the single pursuit of tillage, now becoming carpenters and blacksmiths, masons or millers, and circulating freely among each other. The various products of the earth becoming gradually utilized, the value of commodities declines while that of land and man still further rises, the slave becoming free, his late master becoming rich, and the beautiful harmony of natural laws being thus established.

§ 2. Circulation becomes more rapid as men become more free. Men become more free as land becomes more and more divided. Land becomes divided as wealth accumulates, and land, itself, acquires value. *The rapidity of circulation is, therefore, in the direct ratio of the tendency in capital to become fixed and immovable.*

In England, in the days of the Plantagenets, the descendants of Norman knights held serfs who counted by thousands, and the Church was chief proprietor; whereas, in the days of Adam Smith, the proprietors were 200,000 in number. Landed property now circulated, with constant increase in the rapidity of the circulation of service. While land continued locked up, but few exchanges could be made without the intervention of its proprietors, owners of the soil, and of the serf who occupied it. As it became divided, the class of free proprietors increased in number and in power, gradually freeing themselves from the obligation to pay rent, as well as from the limitation to the master's mill and oven when desiring to convert the product into bread. The workman of the towns, too, exchanged directly with his brother-workmen, and the restraints upon the circulation of land, labor, and its products, thus steadily diminishing, the societary motion became from year to year more rapid, with growing tendency to the development of the treasures of the earth, and to the creation of local centres of activity by means of which the centralizing effects of great landed estates, and of great trading cities, were to be further neutralized.

From age to age we mark a growing tendency towards increasing the divisibility, and thus quickening the circulation of fixed property. The stockholders of the East India Company are, in effect, proprietors of all the land of Hindostan, the right to a share in which is transferred by a simple entry on the books, and the delivery of a new certificate. Turnpikes and railroads are as fixed property as is the land on which they are laid; yet are they divisible into the smallest shares, the ownership of which is as readily transferred as is that of a horse. Mines are opened at vast expense, the property in which is held in transferable shares. Till now, the English circulation has been retarded by the maintenance of a system of barbarous liabilities handed down from olden time; but the general sentiment has recently found expression in the passage of an act of Parliament, in virtue of which mills, factories, and furnaces, may be built, and other descriptions of fixed property created, the ownership of which may be divided among thousands of persons, circulating through society with a facility equal to that which attends the bag of cotton and the circulating note. Each step in this course of progress is attended, necessarily, with an increase in the proportion of fixed property, and in the facilities of commerce.

§ 3. The conclusions at which we now arrive may be thus stated:—

That, in the early period of society all property is movable, land being wholly destitute of exchangeable value:

That, of what is then regarded as property the larger portion consists of men, women, and children, who are denied the power to determine for themselves for whom they will work or what shall be their reward:

That, as wealth augments and numbers increase employments become diversified, with constant increase in the power to reduce to cultivation the richer soils:

That land acquires a money value and becomes divided, its power of circulation increasing geometrically as the division proceeds arithmetically:

That man acquires value as the products of his labor lose it, increase in the proportion of fixed to movable property thus keeping steady pace with the growing freedom of man, and with the increase in the rapidity of the societary circulation:

That thus, the more that capital becomes fixed, the more rapid is the *circulation* of property of every description; the greater the power of association; the more rapid the development of individuality; and the greater the power of further progress:

That, with every increase in the rapidity of circulation, local attraction becomes more and more complete; with increased development of individuality in families, townships, and cities, and steady diminution of the centralizing forces by which societary action had previously been disturbed: and

That, with every such increase, the community tends more and more to take upon itself that natural form in which strength and beauty are most combined, with constant increase in its own individuality, and in its power to associate with other communities on terms of strict equality.

§ 4. Of all the countries of Europe, France has most labored to prevent the existence of that security, abroad or at home, without which there can be little growth of fixed capital. From the days of Charlemagne, her armies have been in turn invading Spain, the Netherlands, Holland, Italy, and Germany; and her waste of wealth in Asia, in the Middle Ages, has been almost paralleled in the present one by her campaigns in Russia, Egypt, and Algeria.

To her was Europe mainly indebted for that perfection of anarchy, denominated the Feudal System, whose tendencies were towards consolidation of the land, enslavement of the people, and suppression of the societary circulation. Land having then but little value, money-changers, royal and plebeian, reigned supreme, and nearly all the property of the kingdom was movable. At the close of the seventeenth century, nearly the whole of the land was held by the Church and a few great nobles, paying no taxes, yet monopolizing all places of emolument and thus absorbing the contributions of that portion of the population which cultivated their own property; while constant wars abroad required incessant contributions of men, and a taxation so severe that it absorbed more than half the product of the soil. Under such circumstances there could be little circulation, and land remained uncultivated, while the people died of hunger.

As the system of Colbert, however, came fairly into operation, employment became more and more diversified, and with the increase of commerce, the division of land commenced, and agriculture steadily improved.*

The Revolution sweeping away the Church and the nobility, their property, covering two-thirds of the kingdom, was now divided. The exclusive privileges of manufacturing corporations following next, the obstacles to circulation were, thus, to a great extent, removed, the beneficial effects of the change exhibiting themselves in the facts, that, notwithstanding an enormous drain of money and men, the agricultural population increased one-third in the succeeding twenty years, the return to labor meantime so much increasing, that its members could now have bread every day in the year, and have a surplus for other purposes equal to two-thirds of the whole wages of 1788.

Manufactures, during this period, steadily increased. The war, preventing all intercourse with England, operated as a protection to both farmer and artisan. Since then, statute law has continued the system, and the result is seen in the fact, that the price of land and labor is now increasing at a rate more rapid, probably, than that of any other country of Europe.

The free circulation of either is still, however, impeded by an excessive political centralization, which requires heavy taxation for the maintenance of fleets and armies. Land can neither be sold nor mortgaged without paying to the government an important portion of the proceeds. The *octroi* obstructs the circulation between the cities and the country, while city traders enjoy monopolies tending to fill their purses at the expense of both producer and consumer. Hence the difficulty of finding consumers for the things produced.

Division of property among children being provided for

* The recent work of M. de. Tocqueville, *The Ancient Regime*, furnishes abundant correction of the erroneous impression, so generally prevalent, that the division of the land of France is attributable to the Revolution.

by law, it has been hence inferred that the population would multiply with such rapidity as effectually to repress all power of accumulation. On the contrary, however, numbers increase but slowly, the process of division moving but little faster.

The rapidity of circulation increases steadily, with extraordinary increase in the productiveness of agricultural labor. The first and most oppressive of all taxes being that of transportation, the tendency of agriculture towards improvement is always in the direct ratio of the emancipation of the land from its payment, that emancipation being to be effected only by the creation of a market near at hand.

§ 5. In the days of Alfred, landed property was equally divided among the children of the English landholder. The Norman conquest bringing with it the law of primogeniture, before the lapse of half a century the circulation of property in the soil had almost ceased. Wealth and population, however, growing, we find a constant tendency towards its re-establishment, the result of which exhibits itself in the number of small proprietors living in the days of Adam Smith.

Up to his time, the tendency had been towards removal of restrictions upon the domestic circulation, the right of citizens to leave the kingdom having remained almost untouched. Thenceforward, however, the tendency was in an opposite direction, the prohibition of emigration having been followed up by various laws prohibiting the export of either machinery or mechanics.

The war of 1756, which established the British power in India, had raised the national debt from 72 to 146 millions. The class of annuitants had, therefore, increased in due proportion to the growth of admirals, generals, and traders, all of whom desired that labor might be cheap, and man of little value. This new debt made a great addition to the amount required to be seized on its passage from the producer to the consumer, thus augmenting the proportion borne by floating to fixed capital, to the disadvantage of both land and labor. The war of 1793 now following, the debt was again doubled, and now it was that the effect of a sluggish circulation of labor and its products became obvious in the vast increase of pauperism, the scarcity of food, the consolidation of the land, and the invention of the monstrous, unchristian, and unphilosophical doctrine of over-population.

From that time to the present, British history is a constant record of efforts at increasing the proportion borne by floating to fixed capital. The more ships needed, the larger the quantity of merchandize kept passing on the road, the longer the time elapsing between production and consumption, and the slower, consequently, the circulation between the man who raises the food and him who requires to eat it, the greater, as it is held, must be the prosperity of all. As a necessary consequence, the little proprietor disappears and the hired laborer takes his place, the trader and the annuitant becoming more and more masters of those who need to sell their labor. Inequality grows daily, the separation between the highest and lowest portions of society becoming more complete as land becomes more and more consolidated, and more and more burthened with mortgages, entails, and settlements. The policy of the country being based upon the cheapening of raw materials, and those materials being always low in price in barbarous countries, the reader will readily see that every step in that direction leads towards barbarism. Therefore it is that it has given rise to the unchristian and unphilosophical doctrines of the Ricardo-Malthusian school.

§ 6. The road to civilization lies in the direction of the approximation of the prices of raw materials and finished pro-

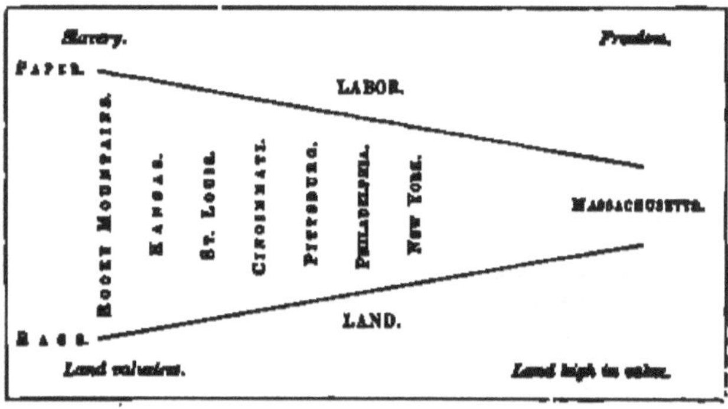

ducts, that being always accompanied by a rise in the prices of labor and land, an increase in the proportion borne by fixed to floating capital, and an increase in the rapidity of circulation. Such being the case, a policy based upon cheapening the raw materials of manufactures—food, wool, and labor—*should* tend towards barbarism and slavery: that it does so, the reader will be satisfied in an examination of the preceding diagram:—

Passing from left to right we find a steady rise in the prices of land and labor, a diminished necessity for the services of the trader, an extension of cultivation over the richer soils, an incessant activity of circulation, and an increase in the power of man, the free proprietor taking the place that first was occupied by the wretched being who had been slave to both nature and his fellow-man. This is the *forward* motion of the being made in the image of his Creator, and endowed with the distinctive faculties of MAN.

Passing now from right to left we obtain the reverse of this, land declining in price and becoming consolidated, circulation declining and man becoming more and more enslaved, the free population gradually disappearing, as fixed property declines in the proportion borne by it to that floating capital with which the trader works. This is the *backward* motion of the human animal treated of by the Ricardo-Malthusian schools; the one that must be fed, that will procreate, and that needs the whip of the tax-gatherer to stimulate him to the proper exercise of the faculties with which he has been endowed.

§ 7. The phenomena presented to view by these United States are those of consolidation of the land, extension of slavery, and decline of all their raw products, when compared with finished commodities. Why this is so we may now inquire.

The colonial system had for its object a stoppage of circulation among the colonists, with a view to compel the export of raw materials, and their importation in the forms of cloth and iron. That such a policy tended towards the destruction of the value of both land and man was well understood by Franklin, according to whom it was "well known and understood that whenever a manufacture is established which employs a number of hands, it raises the value of lands in the neighboring country all around it, partly by the greater demand near at hand for the produce of the land, and partly from the plenty of money drawn by the manufactures to that part of the country. It seems, therefore," as he continues, "the interest of all our farmers and owners of lands to encourage our young manufactures in preference to foreign ones imported among us from distant countries." Such was, then, the almost universal feeling of the country, and to this, far more than to the tax on tea, or the stamp act, the revolutionary movement was due.

With the establishment of their independence, the necessity for submission to the system disappeared. The habit of submission continuing, however, its effects are felt in the fact, that, with slight exceptions, the policy of the country has been directed towards securing markets for raw products, a proceeding resulting necessarily in exhaustion of the land, dispersion of the population, and stoppage of societary circulation.* In despite of this, certain descriptions of manufactures have, at the North, grown slowly up; but, in the Southern States, failure has attended almost every effort in that direction, and they exhibit, everywhere, scattered populations unable to combine their labors, and exhausting all their energies in the effort to reach a market. The power to combine having no existence, coal cannot be mined, nor can wool be spun. The smaller the bulk of the commodity, the less being the charge for transportation, the Virginia planter has found himself limited to the most exhausting of all crops—tobacco. He has lived, in fact, by the sale of the soil itself, and not by the product of his labor.

Allowing Virginia, at the close of the Revolution, 600,000 people, she should now have, excluding all allowance for immigration, 4,000,000, or one to every ten acres; and no one at all familiar with the vast advantages of the State, can doubt her capability of supporting more than thrice that number. Nevertheless, the total population, in 1850, was but 1,424,000—the increase in twenty years having been but 200,000, when it should have been 1,200,000. Seeking to know what has become of all these people, the reader may find them among the millions now inhabiting Alabama and Mississippi, Louisiana, Texas, and Arkansas. Desiring next to know why they are there, the answer to the question may be given in the words: "They borrowed from the earth but they did not repay, and she expelled them."

North Carolina is rich in lands, undrained and uncultivated, while coal and iron ore abound. Her area is greater than that of Ireland, and yet her population is but 868,000, having increased but 130,000 in twenty years. In South Carolina the course of things has been precisely the same with that described in reference to Virginia; yet the State, says

Governor Seabrook, has "millions of uncleared acres of unsurpassed fertility, which seem to solicit a trial of their powers from the people of the plantation States." * * * "In her borders," as he continues, "there is scarcely a vegetable product essential to the human race that cannot be furnished." Marl and lime abound, millions of acres of rich meadow-land remain in a state of nature, and "the sea-shore parishes," he adds, "possess unfailing supplies of salt mud, salt grass, and shell-lime." So great, nevertheless, has been the tendency to abandonment of the land, that, in the decade from 1830 to 1840, the white population increased but 1000 and the black but 12,000; whereas the natural increase alone would have given at least 150,000.

When men come together and combine their efforts, they are enabled to bring into activity all the vast and various powers of the earth, and they become free. When, on the contrary, they fly apart, the less becomes the value of labor and the freedom of man. British writers assure their readers that "the mode of agriculture usually coincident with the employment of slave labor is essentially exhaustive"—slavery thus being given as the cause of declining agriculture. As usual, however, cause and effect are here inverted, an exhaustive agriculture being the real cause of slavery extension.

The slower the circulation, the more is the tendency towards slavery; and hence it is that slavery so much advances. That it may become otherwise, the planter must be compelled to pay his debts to the land; and that he cannot be while obliged to resort to the distant market. Obvious as is this truth, distinguished Englishmen congratulate their countrymen on the working of the free-trade system in destroying the domestic manufactures of Southern States, and thus compelling the export of cotton in its rudest form. But a few years since, Georgia promised to become a principal seat of the cotton manufacture for the world. Now, she exports her people so rapidly, that, with every natural advantage, her population has grown, in the last five years, but three per cent. Hence the existence of a domestic slave-trade that shocks the feelings of Christian men; and hence, too, the discord between the Northern and Southern portions of the Union.

§ 8. In the physical world motion is indispensable to the existence of force. Motion, itself, is a consequence of heat. So, too, the physical and social laws being one and the same, should it be in the societary world. Whence, however, comes the heat to which its motion and its force are due? The answer to this question is found in the important principle, recently so well established, that motion is the cause of heat, as heat, in turn, is the cause of motion. The more the motion, the greater is the heat; and the greater the heat, the greater is the tendency towards acceleration of motion and of force. Desiring, now, to see the application of this simple principle to social science, the reader will do well to refer once more to the foregoing diagram. Doing this, he finds, on the left, a total absence of societary motion, of heat, and of force. Passing thence, gradually, towards the right, he finds a steady increase of all, until, at length, reaching the New England States, he finds more motion, and more heat, than in any other portion of the Western continent, and a larger amount of force.

Throughout the world, human energy is developed in the ratio of the existence of differences among the people of whom the society is composed. "The more perfect a being, the more dissimilar," says Goëthe, "are the parts." In Ireland, India, Turkey, Portugal, Jamaica, and Carolina, all the parts are alike; and hence it is, that the potential energy of their people remains latent, that the circulation is sluggish, and that their men remain enslaved. In France, Germany, and Massachusetts, differences are numerous; and hence it is, that the powers of their people become more developed from day to day, that the circulation becomes more rapid, and that men become more free.

The more rapid the circulation throughout the physical body, the more perfect is the *distribution* of force among its various parts, the higher is the health, and the greater is the force exerted. So, too, as we shall have occasion to see, is it in the social body—the distribution of the proceeds of labor becoming more equitable, and societary action more healthy, in the precise ratio of increase in the circulation. Look where we may, we find evidence of the universality of those great laws instituted for the government of matter in all its forms—heat, motion, and force, being everywhere found in the precise ratio of the development of individuality, and of the power of association and combination.

Turning, however, to Messrs. Malthus and Ricardo we find the reverse of this, man becoming more and more the slave of nature, as he grows in the power of combination with his fellow-men, and the distribution becoming more unequal and unjust as communities more abound in wealth.

CHAPTER XXXIV.

OF DISTRIBUTION.

I.—*Of Wages, Profits, and Interest.*

§ 1. Of wages, profits, and interest. Large proportion, in the early stages of society, assigned to capital.

§ 2. Capitalist's proportion diminishes as the cost of reproduction declines.

§ 3. General law of distribution. Laborer's share increases in both its proportion and amount. That of the capitalist increases in amount, while diminishing in its proportion. Tendency of this law to produce equality in the condition of mankind. Its harmony and beauty.

§ 4. Universal application of the law that is here propounded.

§ 5. Labor's proportion increases as the prices of rude products and those of finished commodities tend to approximate to each other. That tendency found in all the countries in which employments become more diversified. The reverse of this found in all the countries that adopt the doctrines of the British school.

§ 6. Erroneous views of Adam Smith in regard to the natural law regulating the charge for the use of money. Absence of consistency in the doctrines of the Ricardo-Malthusian school. The value of man rises as the rate of profit, interest, and rent, declines.

§ 1. Capital, the instrument by means of which man acquires power over the forces of nature, is a result of the accumulated mental and physical efforts of the past. The fibre of the wood which Crusoe required for his bow had been at all times equally capable of rendering him service; but without an exercise of mental effort the bow would have remained unmade. Once made, its value was great, having been obtained at the cost of serious labor; but its utility was small, for it was capable of little work.

Friday had no canoe. Had he desired to borrow that of Crusoe, the latter might have said: "Fish abound at a little distance from the shore. Without the help of my machine you will scarcely obtain food enough for yourself; whereas with it you will, in little time, take enough to supply us both. Give me three-fourths of all you take, and the remainder shall be your own."

Hard as this might seem, Friday would have accepted the offer, profiting of Crusoe's capital though paying dearly for its use. Reflecting, however, that if he can become owner of a boat he will then retain the entire product, he next makes terms with Crusoe for the use of his knife, and by its aid succeeds in making one. Both being now capitalists their conditions have much approximated, notwithstanding the advances that Crusoe may himself have made. At first his wealth stood at 10, while that of Friday was at 0. The former has now reached 40, but the latter has attained to 10. Tendency towards equality is thus the certain result of that growth of wealth by means of which man is enabled to substitute mental for merely physical force. Every increase in his power over nature is but the preparation for greater progress in the same direction; therefore, here as everywhere, it is the first step which is the most costly yet the least productive. Look where we may we find man passing from the weaker to the more powerful instruments of production, the poor settler using wood in the production of iron, though surrounded by mineral coal capable of performing thrice the service with half the labor. The more the capability of rendering service the greater is the resistance to be overcome, whether we desire to command the aid of things or of men. The laws of nature are thus, as we see, of universal truth.

§ 2. The bow and the canoe enabling Friday to economize time, he gives his leisure to the construction of a knife and a sail; and all combine to give him power to construct a house, the quantity of labor required for *reproducing* and increasing capital diminishing with every stage of progress. The first stone-knife had been the fruit of far more effort than is now required for making one of bronze, and yet the latter is by very far the more efficient instrument. The axe of stone has now no value, though its services had at first been held as equal to three-fourths of those of the man who used it. The still more efficient axes of iron and steel coming into use, the bronze axe, in turn, declines in value. Mind obtaining command over matter the great natural forces become centred in man, who now discards the earlier instruments, preserving specimens only as curious evidences of the inferiority of his predecessors.

Measuring himself against his products, man attributes to himself every increase of utility in the materials by which he is everywhere surrounded. The greater that utility the higher is his own value, and the less that of the things he needs. The cost of reproduction steadily declining, he himself as steadily rises, every reduction in the value of existing capital being so much added to the value of the MAN.

§ 3. Little as was the work that could be done with the axe of stone its value to the owner was very great; and therefore the man to whom he lent it should pay largely for its use. The latter, cutting with it more wood in a day than without it he could have done in a month, though paying three-fourths of his product, finds his wages largely increased notwithstanding the large *proportion* claimed by its proprietor, his neighbor capitalist.

The bronze axe being next obtained and proving far more useful, its owner, being asked to grant its use, is required to recollect that not only has the productiveness of labor greatly increased, but the quantity required to be given for the production of an axe has greatly decreased. He therefore demands but two-thirds of the product of the far more useful instrument. The distribution may now thus be stated :—

	Total product.	Laborer's share.	Capitalist's share.
Axe of stone	4	1	3
Axe of bronze	8	2.66	5.33

The reward of labor has more than doubled; being an *increased proportion* of an increased quantity. The capitalist's share has not quite doubled, he receiving a *diminished proportion* of the same increased quantity. The position of the laborer which had been, at first, as 1 to 3, is now as 1 to 2, with great increase of power to become himself a capitalist.

The axe of iron coming next, the cost of reproduction again diminishes while labor again increases in its proportion as compared with capital. The new instrument cuts twice as much as had done that of bronze, yet is its owner compelled to be content with claiming half the product. The new distribution will be as follows :—

	Total.	Laborer.	Capitalist.
Axe of stone	4	1	3
Axe of bronze	8	2.66	5.33
Axe of iron	16	8	8

The axe of steel now coming, the product is again doubled, with further diminution in the cost of reproduction; and now the capitalist must content himself with a less proportion, the distribution being as follows :—

	Total.	Laborer.	Capitalist.
Axe of steel	32	19.20	12.80

The laborer's share has increased; and, the product having largely increased, the augmentation of his quantity is very great. That of the capitalist has diminished in proportion;

but, the product having so much increased, *this reduction of proportion has been accompanied by a large increase in quantity*, both thus profiting by the improvements that have been effected.

Such is the great law governing the distribution of labor's products. Of all recorded in the book of science it is perhaps the most beautiful, being that one in virtue of which there is established a perfect harmony of real and true interests among the various classes of mankind. Still further, it establishes the fact that, however great may have been the oppressions of the many at the hands of the few, however large the accumulations resulting from the exercise of the power of appropriation, however striking the existing distinctions among men, all that is required for establishing everywhere perfect equality before the law, and for promoting a general equality of social condition, is the pursuit of a system tending to establish in the highest degree the power of association and the development of individuality, thereby maintaining peace and promoting the growth of wealth and population both at home and abroad.

§ 4. The law here given is true in reference to all descriptions of capital. The house, long since built, cost much more labor than now suffices to reproduce a very superior one, but it has so fallen in value as not to command in price, or rent, one half of what it did at first, and will ultimately be destroyed as wholly worthless.

So, too, with money. Brutus charged almost one half for its yearly use, and in the days of Henry VIII. the legal interest was 10 per cent. It has now so much declined, that 4 per cent. is the established British rate. A decline like this furnishes the surest evidence that the labors of the present are becoming daily more productive, that the value of all commodities as measured by labor is steadily declining, that the laborer is rising towards equality with the capitalist, and that the real MAN is becoming more and more developed.

Interest is always high in agricultural countries, money tending thence outwards. The few who possess this most powerful instrument expect a large remuneration for its use. The trader, too, must have large profits, being compelled to forego the high interest he might receive from lending out his money, even when not himself obliged to pay interest for the use of that of others. Large, however, as are the *proportions*, the *quantities* to be received are very small, the capital to be lent being trivial in amount, and the quantity of commodities sold, very small. With the increase of population and wealth the proportion declines, interest falling to five or six per cent.; but the trader finds his business so much increased, that, whereas he could scarcely live when he had 50 per cent., he now grows rich upon 10, while his neighbor, transacting business on a larger scale, accumulates a fortune from charges of but one per cent.—all thus obtaining a *constantly increasing quantity*, though retaining a *constantly diminishing proportion* of the property passing through their hands.

So, too, in manufactures. The weaver with his single loom can barely exist on half the product of his labor. Thousands of looms being brought together and driven by steam labor becomes so much more productive, that a tenth or even a twentieth part gives large return for the capital employed. The poorer the machinery the smaller is always the product of labor, and the larger must be its owner's proportion of the trivial quantity of things produced.

§ 5. The phenomena of distribution presented by all advancing societies, *passing forwards*, correspond precisely with those observed in passing *inward* from the mountains of the West towards Massachusetts, as here is shown:—

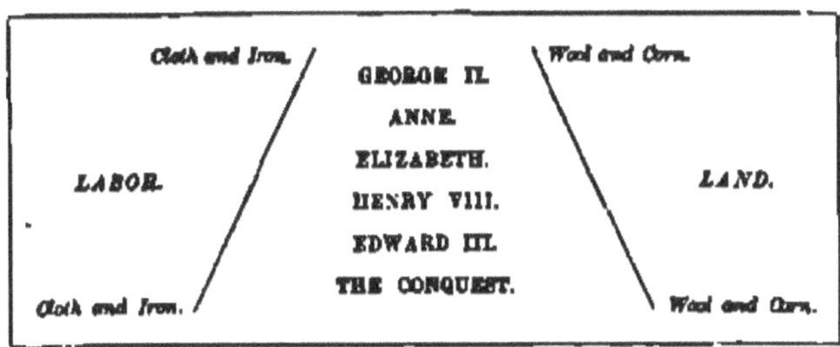

Land and labor, as we see, steadily increase in their dimensions as the proportion assigned to the trader, money-dealer, and landlord, diminishes; the prices of raw materials and of finished commodities steadily approximating, and man becoming more free as the circulation becomes more rapid.

In full accordance with this is what is now observed in

France, Germany, Denmark, Sweden, and Russia; while the reverse is seen in India and Ireland, Jamaica, Portugal, and Turkey—land there declining in value while rent increases; the trader's profits, too, increasing as money disappears, and as the charge for its use is raised. Such, too, is the course of affairs in England, agricultural labor having remained stationary while rents have nearly doubled. So, again, is it in the United States, the growth of pauperism, and the belief in the Divine origin of slavery, there steadily gaining ground, and keeping pace with the consolidation of land in the Slave States. Such are the consequences of a system tending to increase the quantity of wheat, cotton, or tobacco, required to be given in exchange for gold, silver, iron, copper, lead, or other of the metallic products of the earth.

Capital being the instrument used by man in his efforts to obtain power over nature, whatever tends to increase his power over the instrument tends equally towards equality and freedom, and towards the elevation of the labor of the present at the expense of the accumulations of the past. Whatever, on the contrary, tends to increase the power of the instrument over him, tends to elevate those accumulations at his expense—to produce inequality—and to re-establish slavery. His power over the instrument growing with the growth of association, and that growing with the growth of diversity in the modes of employment, it follows, necessarily, that the road towards freedom for man is found in the direction leading to the development of the various faculties of the individuals of whom society is composed.

§ 6. Adam Smith's doctrines on the subject of interest have for their base the erroneous theory of the Ricardo-Malthusian school. "When," he says, "the most fertile and best situated lands have all been occupied, less profit can be made by the cultivation of what is inferior both in soil and situation, and less interest can be afforded for the stock which is so employed."

Unfortunately for the view thus presented the facts are the very reverse, the first poor colonist commencing, invariably, with the poorer lands; and it being only as he obtains improved machinery that he is enabled to cultivate the richer soils. Precisely as he does this, the rate of interest falls. The larger the return to labor the greater is the facility for obtaining money, the charge for its use tending to decline with every increase in the power to command the commodity for whose use *alone* interest is ever paid.

This erroneous idea of Dr. Smith led him into many contradictions. Thus, after assuring his readers that interest falls in countries growing in wealth and population because of the increasing necessity for applying labor to the poorer soils, he tells them that it is in countries in which the wages of labor are low that interest is high. To look, however, to either Hume or Smith for consistency when they treat of money, would be as vain as to seek in the works of Ricardo and Malthus for truth in regard to the progress of wealth and population.

Mr. Mill says that "there is at every time and place some particular rate of profit, which is the lowest that will induce the people to accumulate savings, and to employ those savings productively." Saving, however, implies stoppage of circulation; whereas, the profitable employment of capital involves increase in its rapidity, the two being wholly inconsistent with each other. Four per cent. is the point at which people are willing to save in England, that rate being now, in Mr. Mill's opinion, as much productive of hoarding as was 40 per cent. in the reign of John, or now in the Burmese empire. The want of consistency in the doctrines of the British school is here most clearly obvious. Having first subjected men to a law in virtue of which labor becomes from year to year less productive and accumulation less possible, we are next told that they are *willing* to save at a certain rate of interest, thus having the power to choose for themselves whether capital shall or shall not increase, although living under a law which should render accumulation daily more difficult!

Mr. McCulloch tells us that laborers neither will nor can "be brought to market unless the rate of wages be such as may suffice to bring them up, and maintain them. From whatever point of the political compass we may set out, the cost of production," as he thinks, "is the grand principle to which we must always come at last." Laborers are "brought to market" in Ireland to work at 4d. a day, for the reason, as he thinks, that the peasantry of that country "live in miserable mud cabins, without a window or a chimney, or any thing that can be called furniture; while in England the cottages of the peasantry have glass windows and chimneys, are well furnished, and are as much distinguished for cleanliness and comfort, as those of the Irish for filth and misery."

This is certainly a convenient mode of accounting for the

wretchedness of the people under the system that first annihilated their manufactures, and then annihilated the nation so far as regarded its position among nations—though scarcely very philosophical. Following out this principle, the cause of the large wages of the lawyer, the merchant, the general, and the admiral, must be found in the facts, that they live in large houses instead of small cottages, drink wine instead of water, and wear fine clothes instead of going in rags! A better reason for the low wages of the one, and the high wages of the other, might perhaps be, that both exist under a system which looks to cheapening labor and raw material for the benefit of traders in men and merchandise.

The value of man, like that of all other commodities and things, is measured by the cost of reproduction, and *not* by that of production. In the days of the Plantagenets, "benefit of clergy" was the privilege of the man whose knowledge of letters enabled him to read. Wealth having largely grown, almost everybody now reads, the laborers of the present thus profiting by the accumulations of the past. The more rapid the growth of wealth, and the more perfect the societary circulation, the greater is the tendency towards the production of minds of higher power, with corresponding decline in the value of those which previously had been produced.

The more the prices of labor, and of the rude produce of the land, tend to rise, and the more the prices of finished products tend to fall—the two thus approximating—the smaller will be the space occupied by profits, interest, and rent, and the larger the proportions of the MAN and of the land he cultivates.*

* "We may regard the rate of interest as a sort of level, below which all labor, all cultivation, all manufactures, and all commerce, cease. It is like a sea spread over a great country, of which the mountain summits rise above the waters, forming fertile and cultivated islands. The sea flowing out, the hill-slopes, and then the plains and valleys, gradually appear, covering themselves with products of every kind. To inundate the land and destroy the cultivation, or to restore to agriculture extensive territories, it is sufficient that the water should rise or fall a single foot. It is the abundance of capital that animates to effort; and the low rate of interest is at once the effect, and the indication of that abundance." —TURGOT: *De la Distribution des Richesses*, § 89.

CHAPTER XXXV.

OF DISTRIBUTION—CONTINUED.

II.—*Of the Rent of Land.*

§ 1. Of the rent of land. Large proportion of the landlord in the days of early cultivation. That proportion diminishes as labor becomes more productive, but the amount of rent increases. The laborer's share increases with large increase in its amount, both thus profiting by increase in the power to command the services of nature.

§ 2. Ricardo's theory of rent. Teaches the reverse of this, the landlord's proportion increasing as agricultural labor becomes less productive.

§ 3. That theory based upon the false assumption that cultivation commences on the rich soils, and that labor becomes less productive as men increase in number and in power.

§ 4. No such rent as that indicated by Ricardo has ever been, or ever can be paid.

§ 5. The ultimate slavery of man the natural tendency of the Ricardo-Malthusian theory, rent rising as labor becomes less productive.

§ 6. Simplicity and universal truth of natural laws. Complexity and error of the Ricardo theory.

§ 7. Growth of rent supposed by Mr. Ricardo to be retarded by improvements in cultivation. Interests of the landlord supposed to be promoted by diminution in the supply of food, and increasing poverty of the laborer.

§ 8. The Ricardo theory one of universal discords. Harmony and beauty of the real laws.

§ 9. The more rapid the circulation, the greater the tendency towards equality and freedom among the people, and strength in the State.

§ 10. War among nations, and discord among individuals, grow with the growth of monopoly of the land. That monopoly a necessary consequence of the British policy. With every stage of its progress the more must the people suffer in the distribution between themselves and the State.

§ 1. THUS far, in our examination of the great natural laws to which man and matter are subjected, they have proved equally true whether considered in relation to the earth itself, or to the axes, canoes, or clothing, into which man converts the material by which he is surrounded. His course, in all communities that increase in wealth and population, is ever onward, the first step being always the most costly and the least productive. At each succeeding stage less effort is demanded; and as the cost of reproduction declines, so, too, does the value of all the instruments he has thus far had in use.

Rent, too, declines, the owner of land receiving a diminished proportion of its products. Had the owner of the first little farm been asked for permission to cultivate it, he would have answered: "As you can obtain by its aid as much food in a day as you could in a week without it, if you give me three-fourths of the product, your wages will be one-half increased."

The contract made, both parties can devote more time and mind to the improvement of the machinery of production. The farm, although it has cost many years of labor, yields but 100 bushels. Mental force now combining with physical, one of twice the power is produced at diminished cost. Others yet better follow, each in succession the produce of diminished effort. With each, present labor acquires power at the expense of past accumulations, and rent diminishes in proportion, though increasing in quantity. The proprietor of the first allowed to the laborer but one-fourth of the product; but that of the second finds the relative positions of capital and labor to be greatly changed. His powers have increased, but so have theirs. Instead, therefore, of three-fourths, he exacts but three-fifths, receiving 120 bushels, instead of the 75 of his predecessor, and leaving to the laborer 80, more than thrice his first allowance At each such stage the same phenomena are repeated, but with ever-increasing force, the progress being as here represented:

	Total.	Share of Capital.	Share of Labor.
First	100	75	25
Second	200	120	80
Third	300	150	150
Fourth	400	180	220
Fifth	600	240	360
Sixth	1000	333	667

The power of capital has, thus, little more than quadrupled; while that of labor has more than 20 times increased. With the growth of human force, there is, therefore, a steady tendency towards decline in the power of man over his fellow-man, and towards the establishment of equality among the various portions of the human race. That the weak may find themselves on a level with the strong, and that woman may take her place by the side of the being who everywhere has been her master, all, therefore, that is required is that wealth be permitted to grow, and that individuality be developed by means of that diversification of employments which is indispensable to rapidity in the societary circulation, and to the power of further progress.

§ 2. The views here given differ totally from those commonly received. The laws which govern the payment of rent had for more than a century occupied the attention of economists, when Mr. Ricardo, in 1817, reduced to form ideas that had been suggested by Adam Smith, Dr. Anderson, and others, giving to the world a theory of rent that has since been treated as the great discovery of the age.

Compensation for the use of land being, in his view, paid for the command of certain "original and indestructible powers of the soil," it tends to increase in its proportions as, with the growth of population and of wealth, there arises a necessity for resorting to soils of "constantly diminishing fertility," yielding a less and less return to labor, the power of nature over man steadily increasing, and he becoming more and more her slave and that of his fellow-man. Starting thus from a point directly opposite, it is not surprising that we find him arriving at a distribution directly the reverse of that above submitted for consideration, and equally opposed to all the facts that history records. His doctrines, in their simplest form, are contained in the following propositions:

First. That, at the commencement of cultivation, population being small and land abundant, those soils alone are cultivated whose properties fit them for yielding the largest return to labor—a given quantity of effort being then rewarded with a hundred quarters of corn:

Second. That, land becoming less abundant as population increases in density, there arises a necessity for cultivating less fertile soils—resort being then had to those of second, third, and fourth quality, yielding respectively ninety, eighty, and seventy quarters in return to a similar amount of effort:

Third. That, with the growing necessity for thus applying labor less productively, rent arises—the owner of No. 1 being enabled to demand and obtain ten quarters when resort is had to No. 2, twenty when No. 3 is brought into use, and thirty when it becomes necessary to cultivate No. 4:

Fourth. That the proportion of the landlord tends, thus, steadily to increase as the productiveness of labor decreases; the division being as follows:

			Total.	Labor.	Rent.
At the first period,	when	No. 1 alone is cultivated	100	100	00
" second,	"	No. 1 and 2 are cultivated	190	180	10
" third,	"	No. 1 to 3 "	270	240	30
" fourth,	"	No. 1 to "	340	280	60
" fifth,	"	No. 1 to 5 "	400	300	100
" sixth,	"	No. 1 to 6 "	450	320	130
" seventh,	"	No. 1 to 7 "	490	250	240

—there being, thus, a tendency towards the ultimate absorption of the whole produce by the owner of the land, and towards a steadily-increasing inequality of condition, the power of the laborer to consume the commodities he produces steadily diminishing, and that of the land-owner to claim them as rent steadily increasing:

Fifth. That this tendency towards a diminution in the return to labor, and towards an increase in the landlord's proportions, is found in the ratio of the growth of population, and most existing where population increases with most rapidity, counteracted in a certain degree, however, by increase of wealth, producing improvement of cultivation:

Sixth. That every such improvement tends to retard the growth of rent; while every obstacle to improvement tends to increase that growth; and that, as a necessary consequence, the interests of the land-owner and the laborer are always in opposition, rent rising as labor falls, and labor falling as rent increases in its proportions.

§ 3. The whole system thus placed before the reader rests on the assumption that cultivation commences on the richest soils, an idea that would never have been suggested had its author ever had the opportunity to study the movements of early settlers, who are always poor; or had he reflected, even in his closet, upon the fact, that rich soils are found in the river-bottoms, requiring great effort to clear, drain, and prepare them for man's service. That cultivation has always commenced on the poorer soils, and that it is only with the growth of wealth and population that the richer ones have been reclaimed, has been already shown, and the foundation of the theory having been thus proved false, it might be allowed to pass into the oblivion it merits, but that the hold it has obtained over the public mind renders it necessary to expose its many fallacies.

First among them is the assertion, that, with increase of numbers, there arises a necessity for resorting to machinery of inferior power, yielding less and less in return to labor. Were it so that man did really commence on the richer soil, then would this proposition be true, increasing numbers bringing with them a steady decline of human power, and man becoming from age to age more and more the slave of nature. The contrary proposition, however, being true, then with increasing power he must rise gradually until he attains the level of the true MAN, feeding, clothing, and lodging himself better; acting and thinking better; and exercising a volition increasing with his increased control over the material world. Which of these two classes of phenomena has been presented in all advancing countries, we may now examine

The population of England and Wales, in the fourteenth century, did not exceed 2,500,000. Fertile lands abounded, yet those in cultivation were so poor that six to eight bushels of wheat to the acre were regarded as an average crop. The people are now seven times more numerous, and the land in cultivation is at least ten times more, yet the average yield per acre has almost equally increased. Famines, now unknown, were then frequent and severe. Maids of honor luxuriated on bacon, and laborers banqueted upon "the strength of water-gruel," a piece of fat pork being to them a luxury rarely to be enjoyed. Even so late as within a century, the bread most generally consumed was made of barley, rye, and oats, the use of wheat being limited to the rich. Now it is in universal use, while beef and mutton have succeeded the salt herring on the table of the artisan and the laborer, and the mast-fed bacon that of the landlord. Within a century, the average weight of cattle has risen from 370 to 800 pounds, and that of sheep from 28 to 80, their numbers having meantime increased even more rapidly than their weight. The return to labor has thus largely augmented, as, with increased numbers, man has acquired power to subject to cultivation the richer soils.

The history of France in the Middle Ages, when land abounded and men were few, is the record of a constant succession of famines. So recently as the beginning of the last century, the people wanted bread half of their time, and went clothed in skins for want of power to obtain cloth. A century since, only 7,000,000 ate wheaten bread; now 20,000,000 do so, and the improvement in the character of the food is still greater than the increase in the numbers requiring to be fed.

The people of Russia are now much better clothed and fed than in the days of Peter the Great, notwithstanding a great increase of numbers. So, too, has it been with those of Germany and Belgium, Denmark and Sweden, all of whom are incomparably better fed than were their ancestors in the days when land was most abundant. Looking next to the early settlements of what are now the United States, we find their history but a record of severe privations, resulting from a paucity of numbers that forbade the existence of that power of combination to which alone is the man of the present day indebted for his greatly-increased control of the great forces of nature.

Every fact presented in the history of the world is in strict accordance with the following proposition:

That, as wealth and population increase, men are more and more enabled to associate together and to combine their efforts, with constantly increasing power to compel the services of nature, each and every step being marked by constant increase in the returns to labor, in the rapidity of circulation, and in the facility of production and accumulation.

§ 4. Mr. Ricardo's next proposition is, that, with the necessity for applying labor less productively, rent arises—the owner of No. 1, yielding 100 quarters, being enabled to demand 10 quarters when resort is had to those of the second quality, yielding 90 quarters; and 20, when No. 3, yielding only 80, is brought into use.

Were all land of precisely equal productive power, no such necessity could be supposed; yet compensation would still be paid for the use of a farm provided with buildings and enclosures, that would be refused for one remaining in a state of nature. *That* compensation he considers as interest upon capital, and as distinct from what is paid for the use of the powers of the soil. When lands of different capabilities are in use, all equally improved, he supposes the owner of No. 1 to receive interest upon his capital, *plus* the difference between the 100 quarters it yields, and the 90, 80, or 70 yielded by the soil of lowest power to the cultivation of which man's necessities have forced him. This *difference* he holds to be *the true rent.*

The real course of proceeding, however, is directly the reverse of this. The first little clearing with its miserable cabin cost twice as much labor as would afterwards be required for clearing a larger quantity of better land, and placing upon it a tolerable log-house. The first settler, desiring to let his little farm, finds himself forced to accept, not profits *plus* difference, but profits *minus* difference, thus obeying the same law that governs all other things. The old house, ship, or engine cost more than the better one which replaces it, and not only declines in value, but is ultimately condemned as worthless. The value of every commodity being everywhere limited to the *cost of reproduction*, and *that* declining with the growth of wealth, the owner finds himself forced to accept a diminished *proportion* of its products. No such rent as that imagined by Mr. Ricardo has ever been paid. As well might the owner of the early engine, or the early mill, expect to be paid for the use of the "original and indestructible properties" of the iron, as the owner of the early occupied land.

§ 5. The third proposition is, that, with the increase of wealth and population, and the consequent necessity for re sorting to the poorer soils, the landlord's *proportion* tends to increase, rent rising as labor becomes less productive. If cultivation *does* really commence with the richer soils then is this proposition true, the necessary result of an increase in the numbers of mankind being that of more and more subjecting the many who labor to the will of the few who own the land. The ultimate slavery of man is thus the natural termination of the Ricardo-Malthusian doctrine. If, however, the contrary be true, then must the landlord's proportion steadily diminish, leaving a *larger proportion of an increased quantity* for the laborer, whose ultimate lot is freedom.

Adam Smith tells his readers that the landlord's share in his day was but a fourth or a fifth of the product; and Mr. Malthus acknowledges that it did not in his own time exceed a fifth. This, however, he considers as a proof of increasing difficulty in obtaining food, asserting that whereas in the fifteenth century a laborer could have 122 pints of wheat as a week's wages, in 1810 he could have but 80.

In 1389, a plough-driver had 7s. and a carter, 10s. a year, without clothing, and it is doubtful if, in addition, he had even his wretched food. On an average, those wages would not command more than eight bushels of wheat, yet are we now assured that a laborer could then earn three bushels per week. The average yield having been but about six bushels per acre, it follows that the annual wages of a single laborer required the whole product of 26 acres, and that at a period when, because of the imperfection of machinery, more than ten days labor were required for harvesting the wretched product of a single acre. Such are the extraordinary statements that are now put forth by writers who know that the land and its representative then took at least two-thirds of the whole product of land and labor.

In France, as has been already shown, the number of agricultural families nearly doubled in the period from 1700 to 1840, the average wages of agricultural labor having, in that same time, quadrupled. In the first period, the proportion allotted to the laborer was 35 per cent.; in the latter, it was 60 per cent. In the first, the land-owner retained 65 per cent., or almost twice as much as the laborer's share; whereas, in the latter, he retained but 40 per cent., or only two-thirds as much. Nevertheless, so great had been the increase of product, that the smaller proportion of the latter period gave to the capitalists 2,000,000,000 of francs, in place of 850,000,000 received in the earlier one.

Such is the course of things in every country in which wealth and population are permitted to increase and commerce is allowed to extend itself, all existing commodities then necessarily declining in their value as compared with labor, and labor rising as compared with them, because of constant diminution in the cost of reproduction. In Prussia, forty years since, a third of the product was regarded as the share to which the tenant might equitably be entitled. Since then—labor having become greatly more productive—the laborer's proportion has rapidly increased.

Wealth *should* grow more rapidly than population, and every increase in the ratio of the former to the latter is attended with an augmentation of the power of the laborer, as compared with that of landed or other capital. We all see, that when ships are more numerous than cargoes, freights are low; and, *vice versâ*, that when cargoes are more abundant than ships, freights are high. When ploughs and horses more abound than ploughmen, the latter fix the wages; but when ploughmen are more abundant than ploughs, the owners of the latter determine the distribution of the product. Wealth increasing rapidly, new soils are brought into cultivation and more ploughmen are required. The demand for ploughs producing a demand for more men to mine the coal and smelt the ore, the iron-master becomes a competitor for the laborer, who obtains a larger proportion of the constantly-increasing return to labor. He, in turn, becoming a better purchaser of cloth, the manufacturer becomes a competitor with the iron-master and the farmer for his services. His proportion being again increased he now requires sugar, and tea, and coffee; and next, the ship-master competes with the manufacturer, the iron-master, and the farmer. With the growth of wealth and population, there is thus a constant increase in the demand for mental and physical effort—the increased productiveness of which, and the consequently-increased facility of accumulating wealth, are followed necessarily, and certainly, by an increase of the laborer's proportion. His wages rising, the *proportion* of the capitalist falls; yet now the latter accumulates fortune more rapidly than ever, his and the laborer's interests being in perfect harmony with each other. The highest evidence of increasing wealth is to be found in the reduction of that proportion; and yet, the cardinal principle of the Ricardo-Malthusian doctrine is found in the assertion, that with the growth of wealth and population it must increase.

The following table of the results of the two systems may be compared by the reader with what passes before his eyes:

	RICARDO'S DOCTRINE.			OBSERVATION.		
		Power of Land.	Power of Labor.		Power Land.	Power Labor.
First period	100	00	100	30	20	10
Second period	190	10	180	70	42	28
Third "	270	30	240	120	60	60
Fourth "	340	60	280	180	80	100
Fifth "	400	100	300	250	100	150
Sixth "	450	150	300	330	120	210
Seventh "	490	210	280	420	140	280
Eighth "	520	280	240	510	155	355
Ninth "	540	360	180	620	170	450
Tenth "	550	450	100	740	180	560
Eleventh "	560	550	00	870	190	680

§ 6. The next proposition is, that wealth tends to counteract those laws preventing the necessity for resorting to less productive soils, by producing improvements in cultivation.

This proposition was interpolated into the system because of the absolute necessity for leaving a place of escape for some of the thousand exceptions to its laws, and its presence is a direct admission of the unsoundness of the doctrine. Admitting its validity, wealth should grow most abundantly when and where land is most abundant. So far the reverse, however, has it been, that wealth has grown most slowly in those countries in which rich and unoccupied soils have most abounded; because there, men being few and scattered, the power of association has least existed.

The laws of nature are simple and universally true. That of Mr. Ricardo is complex and universally false. Had it been otherwise, there would have been no necessity for thus providing escape-valves for troublesome facts.

§ 7. The last proposition is, that every such improvement tends to retard the increase of rent, every obstacle to improvement tending, on the contrary, to accelerate it. The interests of the landlord and the laborer are thus always in opposition to each other.

Were it so that men did really commence on the most fertile soils, such must inevitably be the case. The landlord would take a constantly-increasing proportion, the laborer becoming his slave, thankful to be allowed to live and work, though fed on acorn-bread. The doctrine being here carried out to its legitimate result, if correct, that point must certainly, at some future day, be reached. It signifies nothing to say that the downward progress may be arrested. "How slow soever the increase of population," says one of the most eminent of the teachers of the Ricardo-Malthusian school, "if that of capital be still slower," as must certainly be the case if men do really commence on the richest soils, "wages will be reduced so low, that a portion of the population will regularly die from the consequences of want." The experience of Europe for thousands of years, and that of America for several centuries, leads us to opposite conclusions; yet are we constantly assured that *such is the law*. If so, when is it to become effective? We know of no other of nature's laws hung up, *in terrorem*, over man; none, the action of which is thus suspended, to fall, at some future period, with a force immeasurably increased. Population increases daily, and yet is man permitted to go on increasing his species in blissful ignorance of the great fact, that his descendants have been foredoomed to suffer all the pangs of hunger while landowners are to revel in abundance, the one class becoming masters, the other becoming with each succeeding century more thoroughly enslaved

§ 8. The harmony of all the permanent interests of man being perfect, it would seem to be required only that men should be persuaded of its existence, to appreciate fully the advantages of co-operation over antagonism, and to induce all honest and enlightened men to unite in an effort for enabling their fellow-men, everywhere, to indulge their natural desire for association and combination, the husbandman and the artisan taking their places by each other's side. The necessity for this, and the advantages to be derived from it by all—whether Gaul or Briton, Turk or Christian—being more fully understood, peace and commerce would take the place of trading jealousy and universal discord. The harmony of classes thus begetting a harmony of nations, the love of peace would diffuse itself throughout the earth. All would then become satisfied that in the laws which govern the relations of man with his fellow-man, there reign the same beautiful simplicity and harmony everywhere else so abundantly evident; all, by degrees, would learn that their own interests would be best promoted by respecting, in others, those rights of person and property they desired to have respected in themselves; and all become at length convinced that the whole of social science is embraced in the brief words of the great founder of Christianity: "Do unto others as ye would that others should do unto you."

Mr. Ricardo's system is one of discords, and tends to the production of war among both classes and nations. Professing an admiration for freedom of commerce, he teaches that a monopoly of the land is in accordance with a great law of nature. Believing in freedom of action, he teaches that if men and women *will* unite in marriage—thus doing that which stimulates to exertion, and tends most to improve both head and heart—starvation is their probable reward. Thoroughly approving sound morality he enforces the advantages of celibacy, thus affording countenance to the many restrictions by which marriage is prevented and profligacy promoted. Professing a desire for free-trade in corn, he teaches the landlord that his interests will be injuriously affected by it. Anxious to improve the condition of the people, he assures the land-owner that improvement in the modes of cultivation must diminish rent. Desiring that the rights of property may be respected, he instructs the laborer that the interests of the land-owner are to be promoted by every measure tending to produce a scarcity of food, rent being paid because of the monopoly, by a few, of that which a beneficent Deity had intended for the good of all. His book is the true manual of the demagogue, seeking power by means of agrarianism, war, and plunder. Its lessons being inconsistent with those afforded by the study of all well-observed facts, and inconsistent even with themselves, the sooner they shall be discarded the better for the interests of landlord and tenant, manufacturer and mechanic, and mankind at large.

§ 9. All the facts thus laid before the reader, in relation to wages, profits, and rents, and those presented by the history of the world, now range themselves under the following propositions:

That, in the early periods of society, population being small and scattered, the possession of a small amount of capital gives to its owner a great amount of power, enabling him to hold the laborer dependent on his will, as serf or slave:

That, with the growth of wealth and numbers, the power of combination increases, with great increase in the productiveness of labor, and in the power of accumulation, every step in that direction being attended by decline in the power of the already-existing capital to command the services of the laborer, and by increase of power on the part of the latter to command the aid of capital:

That the laborer's *proportion* of the increased product tends thus steadily to increase, while that of the capitalist tends as regularly to decline:

That the *quantity* assigned to both increases, that of the laborer growing, however, far more rapidly than that retained by the capitalist, the latter having a *smaller proportion* of the *augmented quantity*, while the former has a constantly-*increasing proportion* of the *increasing quantity:*

That the tendency to equality is, therefore, in the direct ratio of the growth of wealth, and consequent productiveness of labor:

That wealth grows in the ratio of the rapidity of circulation:

That the circulation increases in rapidity as individuality is more and more developed, with growing power for the diversification of employments among those who labor:

That the more rapid the circulation the larger must be the proportion of the laborer, and the greater must be the tendency towards equality, elevation, and freedom among the people, and the greater the strength of the State.

§ 10. The law of distribution above presented for the reader's consideration was first announced more than twenty years since by the author of the present volume.*

Reappearing since in the work of a distinguished French economist,† its harmony and beauty are recognized by him in the following words, whose truth will be acknowledged by all who study the subject with the attention it so well deserves:

"Such is the great, admirable, consoling, necessary, and *inflexible* law of capital. To demonstrate it is, as it appears to me, to strike with discredit the declamation with which our ears have so long been dinned, against the avarice and tyranny of the most powerful instrument of civilization and of *equalization* that results from the exercise of human powers. * * * * Thus, the great law of capital and labor, as regards the distribution of the product of their joint labor, is settled; the *absolute quantity* is greater, but the *proportional part* of capital constantly diminishes, as compared with that of labor.

* *Principles of Political Economy*, Part I. Phila., 1837.

† BASTIAT; *Harmonies Economiques*. Paris, 1850.

"Cease, then, ye capitalists and laborers, to look upon each other with eyes of suspicion and envy. Close your ears to those absurd declaimers, of whom nothing equals the pride if it be not the ignorance, who, under the promise of future harmony begin by exciting present discord. Recollect that, say what they may, your interests are one and the same; that they cannot be separated; that they tend together towards the realization of the general good; that the labors of the present generation combine themselves with those of the generations which have passed; that it is right that each who has united in the work should have a portion of the remuneration; and that the most ingenious as well as the most equitable division takes place between you by virtue of providential laws, and by means of free and voluntary arrangements, without requiring the aid of a parasitic sentimentalism to impose upon you its decrees, at the expense of your well-being, your liberty, your security, and your *dignity*."

Widely different from this are the tendencies of the doctrine which teaches that "the landlord is doubly benefited by difficulty of production," obtaining "a greater share," and being paid "in a commodity of higher value." That system, opposing, as it does, the interests of the landlord to those of the other classes of society, tends necessarily to disturbance of the right to property in land, as thus shown by one of its most distinguished advocates, Mr. J. S. Mill:

"When the 'sacredness of property' is talked of, it should always be remembered, that this sacredness does not belong in the same degree to landed property. No man made the land. It is the original inheritance of the whole species. * * * If the State is at liberty to treat the possessors of land as public functionaries, it is only going one step farther to say, it is at liberty to discard them. The claim of the landowners is altogether subordinate to the general policy of the State."

War among nations, and discord among individuals, grow with the growth of monopoly in land. Land becomes consolidated as the farmer becomes more thoroughly subjected to that policy which has for its object the limitation of the world to a single and distant workshop, and as producer and consumer become more widely separated. The more perfect its consolidation the greater must be the inequalities of society, and the more must those who labor be made to suffer in the distribution effected between the people and the State.

CHAPTER XXXVI.

OF DISTRIBUTION—CONTINUED.

III.—*The People and the State.*

§ 1. Of distribution between the people and the State. Small security obtained at the cost of heavy contributions in the early stages of society. As employments become diversified security increases and is obtained at diminished cost.

§ 2. Necessity for indirect taxation in the early period. Diminishes as fixed property increases in the proportions borne by it to that which is movable.

§ 3. Commerce tends to become more free as the proportion of movable to fixed property declines.

§ 4. Tendency towards increase of indirect taxation an evidence of declining civilization. Phenomena presented for consideration by Greece and Rome. Indirect taxation of Holland, Turkey, and other countries that are becoming more subject to the dominion of the trader.

§ 5. Substitution of indirect for direct taxation in Great Britain. Taxation of India and Carolina. The real payers of British taxes the land and labor of the various countries which furnish the raw materials consumed in British workshops.

§ 6. Revenue system of the United States. The countries in which direct taxation tends to supersede those which are indirect, are those which have protected themselves against the British system.

§ 7. The more direct the taxation the less will be its proportion to production.

§ 8. The more rapid the circulation the less the power for interference with commerce, and the greater the tendency towards improvement in the condition of man. Why not, then, at once abolish all indirect taxation? Because the power of direct taxation—being an evidence of that high civilization which is marked by the near approach of the prices of rude products and finished commodities—cannot be exercised in any country that has not prepared for it by placing consumers and producers in close proximity to each other.

§ 9. The more perfect the power to apply directly to the land and labor of the country, the greater the competition for the purchase of both, and the greater the strength of the State.

§ 1. From the moment when Crusoe discovered that he had neighbors poorer even than himself, he lived in constant fear of his life. Friday, however, having joined him, security was increased, the one watching while the other slept or labored. So has it been, and so is it now, in all the early settlements of the world. Seeking security the early people of Greece and Italy placed all their towns on the tops of hills, a course of proceeding to which they would have thus been led, even had they possessed the power to cultivate the fertile soils of the valleys capable of yielding thrice the return to labor. So was it in Southern England, almost every hill-top there presenting, even now, evidence of early occupation. So is it, now, in Kansas and Oregon, every man being compelled to prepare himself for self-defence. The regular application of labor to the work of obtaining command over the great natural forces, having, therefore, no existence, the potential energy of man remains latent, he, himself, continuing poor, because of the absence of power for combination with his fellow-men.

Friday's arrival exercised upon Crusoe's condition a double influence, greatly increasing its effectiveness when applied, and enabling him more continuously to apply it. His wants and his powers being here, as everywhere, a constant quantity, every increase of the latter was attended with an enlargement of his proportions, the resistance of nature to his further efforts diminishing as his powers of attack increased. So is it in all new settlements, security growing in a ratio far exceeding that of numbers, and being obtained in return for contributions of time and mind, or the produce of both, constantly diminishing in the proportion borne by them to the quantity of things produced. Look where the reader may, he will find evidence that the course of man towards civilization is represented by the diagram already more than once submitted for his consideration: here again reproduced, in evidence of the universality of the law under which freedom grows as the prices of raw materials and finished commodities come nearer to each other.

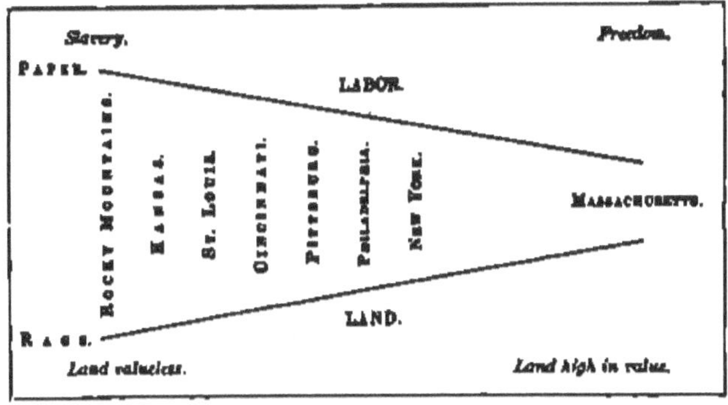

On the left there is no security, the law of force alone being recognized. The weak are there the slaves of the strong, to be taxed at pleasure. Passing towards the right employments become diversified, and individuality more and more developed. The power of association steadily increases, until, at length, in Massachusetts, we find a community enjoying a higher degree of security, and giving in exchange for it a smaller proportion of the products of labor than in any other country of the world.

Passing upwards through English history we obtain results exactly similar. The men of early England, harassed by Danes and Saxons, enjoyed even less security than those of the days of the Plantagenets. Thenceforward, to the accession of the Stuarts, there was no security in the northern and western counties. Elsewhere, the wars of the Roses, and the execution of 72,000 persons in a single reign, bear testimony to the almost total absence of security as to individual rights. The reign of Elizabeth exhibits a series of depredations on the people of the coast by Algerine and other pirates. The close of border wars is followed by civil war; yet amidst all this waste of human energies we trace a growing steadiness in the societary movement, and a constant increase in the tendency towards equity in the distribution of the societary burthens.

§ 2. In the early ages of society the contributions required for the maintenance of security bear a large proportion to the property of the community. Whence, however, can they come? Of fixed property there is none, the little capital that exists consisting of cattle, hogs, corn, or slaves. Hence it is that at this period we find the lord arresting the societary circulation, that he may claim the lion's share of labor's products. At times he demands personal service on the farm; at others on the road, or in the field. He stops the corn on its road to the mill; the meal on its way to the oven; the wool on its way to the clothier; the cloth on its way to the people who need to use it. At one time he calls in heavy gold and silver coins, paying for them in others that are light; at another, he repudiates the light, compelling his subjects to purchase of him those which are heavy, and thus pilfering that which openly he dares not take.

Wealth and population, however, increasing, land and labor acquire value as commodities lose it; and men become free as their masters become enriched. The power of interference now declines, the mill and oven monopolies passing away, and lords and masters being required to look to fixed property as a source of revenue. The slave now becomes a tenant, contracting with the land-owner for a certain rent, and being released from personal service. The tenant, too, becomes a freeman, contracting with his sovereign for the payment of a fixed amount of money, and thereby freeing himself from interference in his exchanges with his fellow-men.

§ 3. That the course of affairs *should*, in all advancing communities, be such as is above described, will be obvious to the reader on an examination of the foregoing diagram, the space occupied by property in motion being a constantly contracting one, and that of the land and the man by whom it is cultivated, being a constantly enlarging one. With the contraction of the first, the power of interference steadily diminishes, the quantity of things liable to be arrested on their passage from the producer to the consumer bearing a constantly diminishing proportion to that produced. With the enlargement of the last, the power of the producer to treat directly with those who perform the duties of government, grows steadily and rapidly, its growth manifesting itself in a steady and regular effort for removing the difficulties standing in the way of commerce.

That such *has been* the course of things in advancing countries may be seen by those who study the course of England from the time when the Plantagenets bought and sold wool, and debased the currency; when almost the only mode of taxing the land was to arrest its passage from hand to hand by means of purveyance, wardship, or taxes on alienation; down to the passage, in 1692, of a specific tax on the rental. In France, in the feudal times, we find the land exempt from taxation, while the slave by whom it was cultivated was liable to contributions of personal service in every form, and his products were taxed at every step of their passage towards those by whom they were to be consumed. Passing thence to the Revolution, we find the Constitutional Assembly abolishing numerous taxes tending to arrest of the circulation, and substituting direct contributions by lands and houses, now the most important items of the revenue. Spain, too, has done the same, a general land-tax having superseded the *alcavala* which had affected every transfer of movables, and with it numerous minor taxes which had impeded circulation. In all parts of Germany, too, we find a growing tendency to the substitution of fixed money-rents for personal service; and of taxes on fixed property for those heretofore paid on movables.

Coming next to these United States, we find a corresponding state of things on passing from the Southern States, where land is held in large plantations, and cultivated by slaves, to those of the North and East, where land is divided and men are free. In South Carolina nearly the whole expenses of the State are paid by taxes on professions, slaves, free negroes, and other movable property. In Massachusetts, on the contrary, seven-eighths of the revenue are derived from fixed property. A tax on auction sales, yielding but a small amount, is the only portion of it not derived from direct and honest application to the parties by whom it is paid.

Boston raises thrice as much as the State, the whole, except a poll-tax of $1 50 per head, being derived from taxes on property that is fixed.

Reviewing the communities above referred to, we find that commerce grows as we pass from those in which taxation is indirect, towards those in which it is direct: the circulation becoming more rapid; consumption following more instantly upon production; production itself increasing because of the economy of human force; and wealth augmenting because of a growing power of association consequent upon the removal of governmental interference with the free exchange of physical and mental service.

§ 4. The substitution of direct for indirect taxation being thus an evidence of progress, the opposite movement should be evidence of decline. That it has been so is shown in every page of history.

In Attica we see it in passing from the days of Solon, when taxation addressed itself to fixed property alone and slaves were daily becoming free, to those of Demosthenes, when men were being rapidly re-enslaved, and taxation had been so extended as to embrace "all money and money's worth."

In Italy the reader may contrast the days of Ancus Martius when the towns of the Campagna paid an unvarying tax on fixed property, with that aristocratic period when small proprietors were liable to have their farms plundered if they failed to answer the call to the field, where they served at their own expense while the booty passed into patrician chests. Returning home and finding their fields untilled, they became, of course, dependent upon their masters for the means of supporting life; and hence it is that the Roman history of this period presents to view a constant series of contests between plebeian debtors and patrician creditors.* Still more striking is the contrast with the days of the

* Every patrician house was a jail for debtors; and in seasons of great distress, after every sitting of the courts, hordes of sentenced slaves were led away in chains to the houses of the noblesse."—NIEBUHR: *History of Rome.*

Empire, when taxes had been laid on almost every possible transfer of property, and the land had become almost valueless because of the disappearance of the free population.

In Holland land became early divided, and commerce increased rapidly. Later, the thirst for trade producing a necessity for ships and colonies, constant wars caused such a taxation that commodities were said to be thrice paid for—once to the producer, and twice to the State.

In Turkey we see reproduced the system of the Middle Ages of France, taxation referring only to the quantity of his products that can be squeezed from the cultivator; while adulteration of the coin and grinding taxes on transfers of movables render land too worthless to be made the subject of direct contribution.

In India, with a population of more than 100,000,000, the revenue is wholly derived from taxes on labor and its application. To taxes on all the tools in use, from the fisherman's boat to the goldsmith's tools, are added enormous taxes on salt and opium, giving us a system of taxation the most grinding the world has yet seen,—purely personal from beginning to end. As a consequence, the price of land rarely exceeds thrice the taxes, and men perish for want of power to sell their labor.

§ 5. In Great Britain the land and house-taxes originated in the reign of William III. The first was variable, but being at length, in 1798, fixed at one-fifth of the rental, an act was at the same time passed enabling the owners to buy off the tax, thus freeing their land forever from all contributions to the public service. Almost simultaneously appeared a new theory of population having for its object that of proving that the supply of food diminished in its ratio to numbers, as numbers increased, doing so because of a great natural law in virtue of which the relation of master and slave must ultimately be re-established.

The poor-houses were filled, and pauperism became almost the habitual condition of the laboring classes, while every movement tended to arrest the wheels of commerce and to fill the pockets of those who derived their means of support from the public treasury. "Taxes were piled on taxes, until they reached," says Sidney Smith "every article which enters into the mouth, or covers the back, or is placed under foot; taxes on every thing which it is pleasant to see, hear, feel, smell, or taste; taxes upon warmth, light, and locomotion; taxes on every thing on earth, and in the waters under the earth; on every thing that comes from abroad or is grown at home; taxes on the raw material, taxes on every fresh value that is added to it by the industry of man; taxes on the sauce which pampers man's appetite and the drug which restores him to health; on the ermine which decorates the judge, and the rope which hangs the criminal; on the poor man's salt, and the rich man's spice; on the brass nails of the coffin and the ribbons of the bride; at bed or board, couchant or levant, we must pay.

"The school-boy whips his taxed top; the beardless youth manages his taxed horse with a taxed bridle, on a taxed road; and the dying Englishman, pouring his medicine, which has paid seven per cent., into a spoon that has paid fifteen per cent., flings himself back upon the chintz-bed which has paid twenty-two per cent., makes his will on an eight-pound stamp, and expires in the arms of an apothecary, who has paid a license of a hundred pounds for the privilege of putting him to death. His whole property is then immediately taxed from two to ten per cent. Besides the probate, large fees are demanded for burying him in the chancel; his virtues are handed down to posterity on taxed marble, and he is then gathered to his fathers, to be taxed no more."

Thus far, as we see, the recent progress has been from taxation on fixed property towards taxes on property in motion, being the state of things which existed in the semi-barbarous countries of the East, and which prevailed in France and England of the feudal period.

The history of direct taxation nearly closes with the repeal, in 1835, of the tax on houses. The result is that, in 1854, there were collected £21,000,000 as duties on imports; £16,000,000 from excise; £7,000,000 from stamps; £3,000,000 from horses, carriages, and railroad passengers; £7,500,000 from taxes on profits; and £1,500,000 from taxes on epistolary intercourse and other minor sources of income; making a total of £56,000,000,=$270,000,000, being $10 per head of the whole population, almost nine-tenths of which had been derived from the stoppage of property, or ideas, on their way from the place of production to that of consumption. Such is the form in which what is called freedom of trade presents itself under the British system.

The people of India sell cotton at 1d. per pound, buying it back in the shape of cloth at 20 to 40 pence. The cotton pays the dividends of the East India Company, the salary of officers, the freight of ships, hire of sailors, rent of warehouses, tolls on railroads, commission of brokers, stamps on notes—passing through thousands of hands, and contributing at every step towards the support of government. As a consequence of this, the Hindoo is too poor to buy cloth, while the Manchester operative perishes for want of bread.

So, too, is it in Carolina. Cotton leaves the plantation at six cents per pound, returning in the form of cloth at 60 cents. In its course it has paid taxes in every shape, so large a portion having been absorbed on the road that the man who raised it remains a slave, while he who converted it can scarcely obtain a shirt.

The real payers of English taxes are the people of all the countries that supply the raw materials of manufacture, buying them back in a finished form. Counting, as they do, by hundreds of millions, evidence of the exhaustive character of the system is to be found in the trivial amount that is raised when compared with the number of the persons upon whom the taxes are assessed.

§ 6. The Government of these United States has usually been misled by the erroneous idea that indirect taxation is the legitimate mode of raising the public revenue. At brief intervals, as in 1828 and 1842, tariffs were arranged with special reference to protection. As a rule, however, revenue has been regarded as the special object of interference with foreign intercourse, protection having been granted to such extent only as was thought consistent with obtaining the largest receipts for the public service. Such was the policy adopted in 1816, 1834, and 1846. In all cases the results have been great apparent prosperity, large receipts at the treasury, large profit to capitalists at the cost of land and labor, followed by financial crises which have almost entirely stopped the societary circulation.

The effects of this are seen in the facts already stated; the experience of forty years having exhibited a steady increase in the quantity of wheat, flour, rice, tobacco, and cotton, required to be given in exchange for smaller quantities of lead, tin, iron, copper, gold, and silver. That being the road towards barbarism, we have an explanation of the fact that, in the land where all men were once declared to be free and equal, "free society" is now declared to have proved "a failure."

Desiring to understand the cause of this, the reader is required only to turn to the diagram given above and to satisfy himself of the fact that the road towards civilization and freedom lies through the more close approximation of the prices of raw and finished products, while the British free-trade policy, so steadily here pursued, tends always towards the production of wider separation. The greater the space by which they are divided, the less must be the money value of land and labor, and the greater the necessity for dependence on indirect taxation.

The countries in which that necessity least exists, are those in which commerce is gradually acquiring power over trade, in which the circulation is becoming more rapid, and in which land and labor are gradually acquiring value—Belgium, Denmark, Sweden, Germany, Spain, and Russia; all of which follow in the lead of France in adopting the policy of Colbert. Those in which it most exists, are Turkey, Portugal, India, the United States, being those that follow the lead of England in preferring the supremacy of trade to the extension of commerce. In all of them the prices of raw products and finished commodities recede from each other, land and labor decline in value, and men become less free.

§ 7. The more perfect the power of self-protection the more continuous becomes the demand for human effort, the more regular is its application, the larger is the quantity of production, and the greater the facility of accumulation. Every step in this direction is attended by a diminution in the necessity for dependence on governmental aid, and diminution in the *proportion* of the products of labor required for the support of persons charged with the performance of governmental duties.

The greater the power of accumulation the greater is the tendency towards subjugation of the richer soils, towards division of land, towards diversification in the demands for human faculties, towards increase in the proportion borne by fixed to movable capital, towards increase in the rapidity of circulation, and towards the substitution of fixed and well-understood rents and taxes for the indirect taxation levied by means of claims for personal service, or interference with the movements of commerce.

The greater the tendency towards direct taxation, the less, therefore, will always be the proportion borne by taxation for the support of government to the amount of production by the people.

That such are the facts, is shown by the history of all advancing communities of ancient and modern times. More especially is it shown in the recent history of France and Northern Europe. Enormous as is the political centralization of France, and burdensome as is her taxation in the forms of personal service and pecuniary contribution, her history for the last and present centuries presents a steady increase in the proportion of the product retained by the laborer, and diminution in that taken by the government. A century since, the company of Farmers General was the real ruler of the kingdom, paying the sovereign for the privilege of taxing his people at their pleasure. Their fortunes growing with the growth of taxes, they of course omitted no contrivance by means of which the contributions might be augmented. Taxation is still most oppressively heavy; but so far as regards land while remaining in the hands of its owner, is a fixed and certain quantity, the payment of which is a guarantee against arbitrary demands by hosts of government agents, such as were of daily occurrence in the days of the early Bourbons. Although the price of landed property, as the reader has already seen, has more than doubled, the amount of tax has remained almost unchanged since the period of its first imposition, fifty years since—thus proving the diminution in the proportion taken for governmental support that accompanies a gradual substitution of direct for indirect taxation.

§ 8. The more rapid the circulation the greater is the tendency in the direction above described, the value of land and man increasing in the direct ratio of increase in the rapidity with which consumption follows production. The slower the circulation the larger is the proportion taken by governments and the greater is the tendency towards indirect taxation. The first looks towards the MAN, recognized by Adam Smith as the subject of social science; the last towards the slave—the subject treated of in Ricardo-Malthusian books—required, as he is, to give to his various masters a constantly-increasing proportion of a constantly-diminishing quantity yielded by the earth.

Why not, then, it may be asked, at once abolish all the duties of excise, duties of customs, and other interferences with commerce, establishing perfect and entire freedom of intercourse between man and man throughout the world? Such is the idea at times suggested by men who hold that the happiness and prosperity of men are to be advanced by extending the dominion of trade, and who see in the growth of the number and size of ships the most conclusive evidence of that advance. As well, however, might they ask, Why not give to each and every man a farm? Why not make all men proprietors? Why not at once quadruple the wealth of the community, and thus enable every member of it to feel himself enriched? In the natural course of things land tends to become divided; men's faculties tend to become developed; wealth tends to increase; the division between the few and the many tends towards the production of equality; and taxation tends to become more direct. All these phenomena, however, are evidences of civilization, appearing invariably in all communities in which the circulation increases in rapidity and disappearing as the circulation dies away. The more the demand for human force tends to become *instant* upon the existence of the power to produce it, the greater is the tendency towards that state of things in which direct taxation becomes *possible*. The longer the interval elapsing between production and consumption, the larger are the proportions borne by movable to immovable capital, and the greater must be the tendency towards seeking to obtain by indirect and deceptive means the supplies that cannot be directly asked for. Seeking proof of this the reader may now turn again to the diagram in the previous pages, with a view to see where on the left he can find the means of direct taxation. Man is there a mere slave, and land is so utterly valueless that hundreds of square miles would be given in exchange for a single dollar. Where, then, are the subjects of direct taxation?

Passing further east, the margin for profits decreases with constant diminution in the power of indirect taxation. Land and labor steadily assume larger proportions, the slave of the earlier period being replaced by the freeman of the later one, and the wretched owners of vast bodies of land being replaced by tens of thousands of wealthy farmers, owners of the soil they cultivate. The man and his land may now be taxed; but before they are so, the freeman must be consulted as to the mode of taxation to be adopted, the extent to which it may be carried, and the purposes to which the proceeds are to be applied.

Taxation tends to become direct as men become free; and the greater that tendency, the more rapid is the diminution borne by the claims of government to the power of the community to meet them. Men become free as the prices of raw materials tend more and more to approximate, the former rising and the latter falling. That approximation takes place in the ratio of the existence of the power of association and combination—that, in turn, being found in the ratio of the diversity in the demand for labor. The more perfect the society, the more various the demands for mental and physical faculties, the more rapid must be the circulation, the greater the power of accumulation, the larger the proportion borne by fixed to movable capital, and the greater the power to obtain through direct taxation the means of meeting those expenditures required for maintaining order, and thus securing all in the peaceful enjoyment of the rights of persons and of property.

Commerce becomes free as indirect taxation ceases to exist. The power of indirect taxation diminishes as the farmer is more and more freed from the oppressive tax of transportation. That tax diminishes as the faculties of man are more and more developed, and as the power of association more and more arises. That it may arise and may extend itself, diversity in the modes of employment is an indispensable requisite. The production of such effects having been the intent and meaning of the protective tariffs of 1828 and 1842, and those effects having been realized not only in this country, but also in all of those which follow the lead of France in adopting the policy of Colbert, the experience of the world may be adduced in proof of the assertion, that the road to perfect freedom of commerce is to be found in the adoption of measures tending to the creation of a domestic market, and to the consequent relief of the farmer from that first and most oppressive of all taxes—the one resulting from the necessity for effecting change of place. Such precisely was the idea of Adam Smith when enlarging upon the advantages to commerce resulting from combining tons of food with hundreds of pounds of wool, in the form of pieces of cloth, that could so readily be transported to the most distant quarters of the world.

§ 9. The more perfect the commerce among its people, the greater is the value of land and labor, the less is the tax of transportation, the greater is the power for honest and direct taxation, and the greater the strength of the State. Commerce grows as employments become diversified, as individuality becomes developed, and as agriculture becomes a science. That the countries which follow in the school of Colbert are becoming stronger, has been proved by the facts, that Russia maintained her credit during her recent exhausting war, while Prussia maintained neutrality in despite of every effort of the Western Powers. That those which follow in the train of the economists of England are becoming weaker, is proved by the cases of Turkey, Portugal, Ireland, and the Indies of both the West and East. It is further proved by all the experience of these United States—comparing the States of the South and West with those of the North and East, or the Union with itself, at different periods. Florida and Mississippi follow in the train of England, and stand at the present moment in a state of repudiation. California now does the same, while Massachusetts enjoys a credit equal with that of any country of the world. The Federal Government extinguished its debt in 1835 by help of the protective tariff of 1828; whereas, in 1842, with no war upon its hands, it was unable to borrow at any rate of interest. The strength of the State grows with growth in the value of land and labor, and with increase in the proportion borne by fixed to movable capital. American policy tends towards increasing the movable capital at the expense of that which is fixed, and hence the growing weakness of the State.

Every stage of progress towards increase in the proportion borne by capital that is fixed and that can be made the subject of direct taxation, brings with increase of competition for the *purchase* of labor with constantly growing freedom of the laborer; whereas, every step in the opposite direction is attended by increase of competition for the *sale* of labor and increase in the power of the capitalist to dictate the terms upon which his property may be used. With few and brief exceptions American policy has tended in this latter direction, and hence it is that the rate of interest has been so high, and that the belief in the divine origin of slavery has been a constantly growing one.

CHAPTER XXXVII.

OF COMPETITION.

§ 1. In the absence of competition for the purchase of labor-power, the laborer becomes enslaved. That power the only commodity that cannot be preserved, even for an instant, beyond the moment of its production.

§ 2. The more the competition for the purchase of labor the more rapid the circulation, the larger the production, and the greater the power of accumulation.

§ 3. Competition for the *purchase* of labor tends toward freedom. The trader desires to produce competition for its *sale*.

§ 4. Trading centralisation seeks to produce competition for the sale of raw materials and labor. Therefore adverse to the growth of value in land or man.

§ 5. Effect of trading centralization upon the condition of the British people.

§ 6. Trading centralization deteriorates the condition of the laborers of the world. Necessity for resistance thereto.

§ 7. Competition for the control of nature's services raises the value of both land and man.

§ 8. Competition for the purchase of labor tends to strengthen custom into law, in favor of the laborer. Competition for its sale tends to the annihilation of customary rights in favor of the capitalist. Where this last is found, the societary circulation becomes more sluggish, with constant growth of the disease of over-population.

§ 1. FINDING no competition for the purchase of his services Friday was glad to sell himself for food and clothing, becoming Crusoe's slave. Had the island contained other Crusoes, their competition would have enabled him to make his selection among them all, exercising thus that power of self-government by which the freeman is distinguished from the slave.

Will you buy? Will you sell? The man who has a commodity, and must sell, is forced to ask the first of these questions; obtaining, for that reason, ten, twenty, or thirty per cent less than what might otherwise be regarded as the fair market price. His neighbor, not being forced to sell, waits for the second, thereby obtaining more, perhaps, than the ordinary price. Such being the case with commodities that can be kept on hand waiting for a purchaser, to how much greater extent must it not be so in reference to that potential energy which results from the consumption of food, and which cannot be held over for even a single instant. The trader takes the market-price for his oranges, great as may be his loss; he stores his iron, waiting for a better market. The farmer sells his peaches on the instant, low as may be the price; but he holds his wheat and potatoes, waiting for an advance. The laborer's commodity being yet more perishable than oranges or peaches, the necessity for its *instant* sale is still more urgent.

The farmer and the merchant having stored their sugar, or their wheat, can obtain advances, to be returned when their commodities are sold. The laborer can obtain no advance upon his present hour, his commodity perishing at the instant of production. It must be at once either sold or wasted.

Further, the merchant may continue to eat, drink, and wear clothing, his stock meanwhile perishing on his hands. The farmer may eat his potatoes, after failing to sell his peaches. The laborer must sell his potential energies, be they what they may, or perish for want of food. In regard to no commodity, therefore, is the effect resulting from the presence or absence of competition so great, as in relation to human force. Two men competing for its purchase, its owner becomes a freeman. The two competing for its sale, become enslaved. *The whole question of freedom or slavery for man is, therefore, embraced in that of competition.*

§ 2. The man who can sell his own labor can purchase that of others. The more instant the demand for his services the more instant are his demands for those of others, the more rapid becomes the circulation, the larger the production, and the greater the tendency towards accumulation. Every man who has physical or mental effort to sell is thus interested in promoting the rapidity of the societary circulation.

This is equally true in regard to communities, those whose members find instant demand for all their powers having much to offer in exchange, and being enabled to consume much of the produce of the labor of others. Every nation is thus directly interested in promoting rapidity of circulation in every other. The harmony of all real international interests is, therefore, perfect, all the laws of nature tending towards the establishment of freedom, peace, and happiness throughout the world.

Such being the case, it follows that a course of proceeding in any one community, tending to lessen, anywhere, the power of production, is an offence against mankind at large, and should be so regarded.

§ 3. The Alabama planter tolerates no competition for the purchase of the labor of the persons who till his land. Requiring all to bring to him the products of their toil, he makes the division to suit himself. His share is large but the total product is very small, most of the labor-power that has been produced having been wasted because of the absence of competition for its purchase. As a consequence, he and his people have very little to sell, and have therefore little power to compete for the purchase of the labor of others. Slavery in any one community tends, therefore, towards the production of slavery in all.

The trader, likewise, is most intolerant of competition. History is a record of efforts to maintain monopolies; from the secret expeditions of the Phoenicians down to the annihilation of the cotton manufacture in India, and the extension over that vast country of patent laws in virtue of which machinery is forbidden to be improved without the consent of a people thousands of miles distant. It is, too, a record of wars for the same purpose: the Carthagenians having been as fully determined to prevent, at any cost, competition for the purchase of the potential energies of Central Africa, as were the Venetians and Genoese for those of Eastern and Western Europe, the Dutch for those of the Asiatic Islands, or the English for those of Jamaica or of India.

In France in the days of the Valois, as in England in those of the Plantagenets, competition for the purchase of labor scarcely existed; production was therefore small, and the power to make demand for the products of other countries was entirely insignificant. In both there has been a great increase in the competition for the purchase of service, accompanied by a corresponding one in the prices of the rude products of the soil, and in both the freedom of man has kept pace with the growth of value in the land. The higher the wages and the greater the *amount* of rent, the greater becomes the power of competition for the purchase of the produce of other lands, and the greater the tendency towards freedom abroad—that, in turn, tending to increase of freedom at home. *Every community is therefore directly interested in the resistance, by all, of every measure tending to lower the value of land and labor.*

§ 4. Centralization being of two kinds, political and trading, it is essential that they be here carefully distinguished from each other.

The sovereign, desiring to centre power in himself, imposes heavy taxes; but beyond the interference required for their collection or expenditure, he derives no advantage from any measure tending to lessen the power of association among his subjects. His people may combine for peaceful purposes, their power to contribute to the public revenue growing with the consequent increase of production. His interests and those of his subjects are one and the same; and hence it is that some of the most despotic countries of Europe have presented to view the most vigorous efforts in favor of movements tending to increase the competition for the purchase of the laborer's services, and of the earth's rude products.

Directly the reverse of this is trading centralization, its *primary object* being that stoppage of circulation which in political centralization is but an incidental result. The trader desires to keep men apart from one another, and thus to produce a necessity for numerous changes of place and of ownership, at each of which their produce may be taxed.

The power of the sovereign grows with growing diversity of employment, with the development of human faculties, with increase in the proportion of fixed property, and with the growth of wealth. That of the trader grows with circumscription of the range of employment, with increase in the proportion of movable property, with the dwarfing of human faculties, and with the growth of poverty and wretchedness among those who are compelled to contribute to his revenue. *Of all forms of slavery the most searching and exhaustive is that of trading centralization.*

Half a century since India exported cotton cloth to all the world, having first clothed the hundred millions of a population described by Sir Thomas Munro, as "not inferior in civilization to the people of Europe." Political centralization then existed in its fullest force, but the sovereign power stood between the trader and those engaged in the production, conversion, and consumption of cotton wool. Trade, however, subsequently carried the day, compelling its unhappy subjects to submit to the free importation of cloth from Europe, while deprived of all power to import machinery, or artisans who could make it. The domestic manufacture almost disappeared; and then was wasted a large portion of the potential energies of a tenth of the human race, to the essential injury of the world at large.

Half a century since these United States had established among themselves competition with Europe for the purchase of cotton. Had this continued onward and undisturbed, it would have grown to such an extent as to have produced throughout the planting States that competition for the purchase of labor which leads inevitably to freedom. Obliged, however, on repeated occasions, to succumb to the assaults of distant traders, the result has been that the American people, as well as those of India, have, during the whole of this period, been competing for the *sale* of their products, to the exaggeration of the evils of slavery where it exists, and its production where, as yet, it is not found. Exporting the rude produce of the soil, in both are seen exhaustion of the land, with growing tendency towards commercial and moral death, and political dissolution. In the one the government depends on monopolies of salt and opium for its support; while in the other we witness (1857) a frantic determination to extend throughout the continent a system that, seventy years since, was regarded by the most eminent men of the Southern States as a blight and a curse, requiring to be removed.

Half a century since there yet existed competition for the purchase of Irish labor. Political centralization had long existed; but it remained for that of the trader to annihilate all competition for the purchase of human energies at home, and all Irish competition for the purchase of those abroad. The consequence is that the many millions of Irish people do not make a market for the chief product of India and Carolina to so great an extent as a single million in Massachusetts.

Competition by A for the purchase of the labor of B tends to produce competition by B for that of C; and so on to the end of the alphabet. All the communities whose policy tends in that direction, are therefore moving towards freedom for themselves and the world; while those whose tendencies are opposite must be moving towards the establishment of slavery, both at home and abroad. Such is the fact; and yet, strangely enough, while the first embrace many of the despotisms of Europe, the last are found in the two especial traders of the world, Great Britain and these United States, the self-styled friends of freedom, and patrons of the revolutionists of the world.

§ 5. Cheap raw materials are, we are told, indispensable to the prosperity of the British people. If so, there can be no harmony of interests, cheapness of such materials being the accompaniment of barbarism, slavery, and valueless land. That it is not so, is evident from the pictures of vice, crime, and degradation, not exceeded in the world, which are presented to us by eminent Englishmen. *Cheap labor and cheap raw materials mean simply barbarism.* Reading the works of Dickens, Thackeray, or Kingsley, we are ever presented with pictures of an incessant struggle for the means of sustaining life; while public documents confirm the sad truth, that as power has been obtained for commanding nature's services the condition of the people has not improved.

Action and reaction are equal and opposite; the community that devotes its energies to the stoppage of motion elsewhere, is stopped in its own. Had India, Portugal, Turkey, and Jamaica, been encouraged to avail themselves of the powers of steam, and to develop the resources of the earth, they would have had much to sell, and would have become better customers to England; as it is, producing little, they can buy but very little. England herself, as has been shown, no longer produces *things* to be given in exchange for those she needs; her whole consumption of tea, sugar, coffee, and other commodities, being supplied by *profits* derived from standing between the people who labor to produce, and those who need to consume. As a consequence, the competition for the purchase of human service diminishes when it should steadily increase.

§ 6. We are told, however, that all nations may now manufacture if they wish, that machinery may be exported, that artisans are free to go abroad, and that the people of England rejoice in the extension of manufactures. All people, too, are free to read, but before they read, they must be taught. The growth of the habit of association comes with wealth; but wealth can never grow under a system that tends to exhaustion of the soil. That man may acquire wealth, he must have a scientific agriculture, which *always follows*, and *never precedes*, manufactures. By forbidding the existence of the latter centralization forbids the creation of the former, and hence it is that the decline in the value of land and labor becomes more rapid from year to year in all the countries of the world whose people are subjected to the British free-trade system.

Freedom of commerce has, we are told, much advanced. What, however, have been the causes of that advance? Forty years since the British navigation laws were in full force. They have now ceased to exist. Why? Because of the determined resistance of these United States, Prussia, and other countries. Forty years since, Germany exported wool, and imported it in the form of cloth paying twelve cents per pound for the privilege of passing it through English looms. That charge is no longer made. Why? Because Germany established competition with England for the purchase of wool. At that time cotton, and all other raw materials, were taxed on their entrance into British ports; but step by step, as France, Germany, Russia, and other countries, became competitors for their purchase, the duties disappeared. Every advance towards freedom of international commerce, and freedom among men, during the last forty years, has resulted from a resistance on the part of other nations to British trading centralization. The road to perfect freedom of commerce is to be found in the adoption of the system advocated by Colbert, that one by means of which men are enabled to combine their efforts for developing the powers of the earth, and for producing that state of things in which competition for the purchase of labor will be universal, while competition for its sale will cease to have existence.

§ 7. The more the competition for nature's services the more rapid is the advance in the value of land and labor, her power being limitless in its extent, and her disposition to render service being equal to all demands that can be made. A century since steam power was scarcely known in England: now it does the work of 600,000,000 men. Like England, Turkey and India have coal; and yet the people of those countries scarcely know the use of steam. Why it is so, is, that English policy has invariably sought the annihilation of competition for obtaining control over a great natural force provided by the Creator for the use of all mankind. A century since, the command of the services of iron was trivial, that used in England having been chiefly obtained from Russia: now it is produced by millions of tons. India and Turkey, too, have coal and iron ore, but they cannot mine them. Why? Because great capitals are now regarded as the true "instruments of warfare" upon the industry of other countries. The American people have coal and iron to an extent unknown in any other portion of the world, and capable of furnishing power equal to that of thousands of millions of men; yet are they busily engaged in exhausting themselves and their land in the effort to obtain a quantity of iron so very trivial, that the average consumption might be more than supplied by means of the proper application of the waste labor of a single city. Why is it so? Because they follow in the train of teachers from whom they learn that the road to prosperity lies in the direction of cheap raw materials and cheap labor. Slavery, therefore, grows, gradually taking the place of freedom.

France, Germany, and Northern Europe generally, are becoming competitors for nature's services; and therefore it is, that, in all those countries the prices of raw materials steadily approximate, the land acquires value, and the true MAN tends, more and more, to make his appearance on the stage.

§ 8. "Competition," says Mr. Mill, "has only become in any considerable degree the governing principle of contracts at a comparatively modern period. The farther we look back into history, the more we see all transactions and engagements under the influence of fixed customs. The reason is evident. Custom is the most powerful protector of the weak against the strong; their sole protector, where there are no laws or government adequate for the purpose. Custom is a barrier which, even in the most oppressed condition of mankind, tyranny is forced in some degree to respect. To the industrious population in a turbulent military community, freedom of competition is a vain phrase; they are never in a condition to make terms for themselves by it; there is always a master who throws his sword into the scale, and the terms are such as he imposes. But though the law of the strongest decides, it is not the interest, nor in general the practice, of the strongest to strain that law to the utmost; and every relaxation of it has a tendency to become a custom, and every custom to become a right. Rights thus originating, and not competition in any shape, determine, in a rude state of society, the share of the produce enjoyed by those who produce it. The relations, more especially, between the landowner and the cultivator, and the payments made by the latter to the former, are, in all states of society, but the most modern, determined by the usage of the country. Never, until late times, have the conditions of the occupancy of land been, as a general rule, an affair of competition. The occupier for the time has very commonly been considered to have a right to retain his holding while he fulfills the customary requirements; and has thus become, in a certain sense, a coproprietor of the soil. Even when the holder has not acquired this fixity of tenure, the terms of occupation have often been fixed and invariable."

Custom is "a powerful protector;" and whether man shall advance towards freedom or decline towards slavery depends on the decision of the question, whether custom shall be strengthened into law, or shall pass away, leaving the weak wholly at the mercy of the strong.

In France, the laborer retained his customary rights and gradually acquired more, until at length the land became divided among a mass of free proprietors, holding their little properties free from all claims but those of the State. In Germany, Denmark, and Northern Europe generally, such has been, everywhere, the tendency, custom having become law, and the prosperous small proprietor having taken the place of the wretched serf. In all these countries competition for the purchase of labor increases yearly, their policy being based upon the idea of approximating the prices of raw materials and finished commodities, and thus lessening the trader's power.

Turning now to the countries which follow in the train of England, we find in Scotland a total abolition of customary rights, hundreds of thousands of people, whose title to the land was equal with that of their lords, having been expelled from their little holdings with a savage cruelty that has rarely elsewhere been exceeded.

In Ireland we see custom gradually giving way until the whole people become enslaved by a middleman class who live by the plunder of the men who own the land, and the wretched people by whom it is occupied.

Looking next to India, once the home of thousands of prosperous communities, we see customary rights disappearing, and with them millions of small proprietors.

Turning now to the centre of this system, and tracing the history of the poorer classes, we find a custom early prevailing, of providing for the poor widow and her fatherless children, for the lame and the blind, for the diseased of body and mind. With the growth of commerce, custom passes gradually into a law, and the statute of Elizabeth establishes the right of such persons to claim support from those around them, honest poverty being held to be a misfortune, and not a crime. Modern science, however, having proved that matter tends to take its highest form, that of man, more rapidly than the lower ones of cabbages and potatoes, poverty has become a crime to be visited by the severest punishment, it being, as we are told, "an indubitable truth that if," by any exercise of Christian charity, "we stand between the error" which leads to over-population "and its consequences," which are poverty, wretchedness, and death, "we become participants in the crime!"

In all these latter countries trade increases in power from year to year; in all, consequently, there is a growing competition for the sale of labor.

Coming now to the United States, we find, during the half century that followed the peace of 1783, a slow, but certain tendency towards the establishment of domestic commerce. During all that period, consequently, the custom of freedom was gradually ripening into law, the right of the laborer, black or white, to profit of competition for the purchase of his services having been, in that period, fully established in all the States north of Mason and Dixon's line. South of it, too, the tendency was in the same direction, the Virginia Convention of 1832 having fully entertained the question of the right of man to sell his services in open market.

Simultaneously, however, free-trade was adopted, at the cost of domestic commerce, by the generally dominant political party, as being the high road to prosperity; and since that time, with the exception of the period from 1843 to 1847, the whole energies of the country have been turned in that direction. The result is seen in the gradual disappearance of the custom of freedom, each successive year producing local laws in virtue of which both master and slave are deprived of the exercise of customary rights, the one being prohibited from receiving either freedom or instruction, the other, from granting either.

Five-and-twenty years since, freedom was regarded as the custom of the country, slavery existing only in consequence of local laws. Now, the courts decide, that slavery is the custom, freedom holding its existence under local laws.

Look where we may, we see competition for the *sale* of labor increasing in the countries that follow the lead of England; while competition for its *purchase* increases in those which follow in the lead of France. In the latter it is that the soil becomes improved, and the supply of food and clothing increases more rapidly than population.

CHAPTER XXXVIII.

OF POPULATION.

§ 1. That the earth may be subdued, man must multiply and increase. Fecundity and development in the inverse ratio of each other. Man should therefore increase but very slowly. However long the period of duplication, if the procreative tendency is a fixed and positive quantity, the time must arrive when there will be but standing-room for the population. Can the Creator have subjected man to laws, in virtue of which he must become the slave of nature and of his fellow-man?

§ 2. Physical science testifies that order, harmony, and reciprocal adjustment, reign throughout all the realms it has yet explored. Modern economists have mistaken facts for laws. Laws are rules, permanent, uniform, and universal in their action. Theory of Mr. Malthus deficient in all these characteristics. The procreative function, in common with all others, placed under the law of circumstances and conditions. Are war and pestilence required for correcting errors of the Creator, or has the Creator so adjusted the procreative tendency as to provide the means of correcting human error?

§ 3. Power of progress in the ratio of the perfection of organization. Man, the being most susceptible of change—passing from the mere animal and becoming the real MAN, responsible to his family, his fellow-men, and his Creator. Responsibility grows with the growing power of association, and with division of the land.

§ 4. Growth of population modified by the development of that feeling of responsibility which comes with the ownership of land.

§ 5. Recklessness and poverty consequent upon absence of diversity in the modes of employment and consolidation of the land. Adaptability of the procreative power to the circumstances in which a community is placed.

§ 6. Consolidation of the land, and the disease of over-population, necessary consequences of a policy which looks to the cheapening of labor, and of the rude products of the earth. British system tends to the production of these effects. Its results, as exhibited in the condition of the English people.

§ 7. Pioneer life favorable to increase of numbers. Effects of American policy as exhibited in the duration of life.

8. Reproductive function not a constant quantity. General predominance of the nutritive and sexual functions. Antagonism of the animal propensities and higher sentiments. Fertility of the drudges of an imperfect civilization. Infertility of the hunter tribes. Activity of the intellect checks procreation. Cerebral and generative powers of man mature together. Fecundity in the inverse ratio of organization. A self-acting law of population secures harmony in the growth of numbers and of food.

§ 1. "Be fruitful and multiply," said the Lord, "and replenish the earth and subdue it." That it may be subdued men must increase in number, it being only by means of combination with his fellow-men that man acquires power to direct the forces of nature to his service.

The tendency to assume the various forms of life is greatest at the lowest point of organization, the progeny of microscopic beings counting by millions at the close of a single week; whereas the period of gestation in the whale and the elephant is long, and the product rarely exceeds a single individual. Such are the extremes, but the rule holds good at every stage; thus furnishing the law:—*that fecundity and development are in the inverse ratio of each other.* In virtue of that fixed and certain law man, the head of creation, should increase least rapidly, and, carrying out the same idea, the fecundity of the human race should itself diminish as the peculiarly human faculties are stimulated to action, and as MAN becomes more developed.*

The periods within which the population of the principal nations doubles itself varies greatly, France requiring more than a century, and Great Britain more than half a century, while the duplication of American numbers is accomplished in little more than thirty years.†

So far as regards the ultimate destiny of the human race, it is, however, of small importance whether, in obedience to fixed and immutable laws, a certain duplication is to take place in 30 or 100 years, the only difference being, that under the first, there must be some 700 years hence a million of persons on the earth for one that now exists, whereas, in the other, thrice the time will be required for producing the same effect.

What would be the effect of such increase? Obviously so to crowd the earth, as eventually to leave but standing room for the population, food growing constantly more scarce,

* "The plant and the animal are not required to become a different thing from what they already are at the moment of their birth. Their *idea*, as the philosophers would say, is realised in its fulness by the fact alone of their material appearance, and of their physical organisation. The end of their existence is attained, for they are only of a physical nature. But with man it is quite otherwise. Man, created in the image of God, is of a free and moral nature. The physical man, however admirable may be his organisation, is not the true man; he is not an aim, but a means; he is not an end, like the animal, but a beginning. There is another, new-born, but destined to grow up in him, and to unfold the moral and religious nature, until he attain the perfect stature of his master and pattern, who is Christ. It is the intellectual, the moral, the spiritual man."—GUYOT, *Earth and Man*.

† The extent to which American population has been affected by immigration has never until now been properly appreciated. The National Almanac for the present year, 1864, gives us a series of carefully-prepared tables by which it is shown, that since 1790 the number of immigrants and their descendants has exceeded 21,000,000—that the annual percentage of increase resulting from the excess of births over deaths is only 1.38—and that the time required for duplication from domestic sources alone exceeds 50 years.

Admitting the accuracy of the views now thus presented, we should find in the much more rapid increase of the negro race, from domestic sources alone, strong confirmation of the accuracy of the theory of population given in the present chapter.

and the land-owner becoming constantly more the absolute and uncontrolled master of the laborer.

Having once admitted that the procreative tendency is a positive quantity, insuring a duplication in any certain period, then it cannot be denied that slavery is the ultimate lot of the great mass of the race; nor, that the tendency in that direction is greater now than at any former period, history presenting no instance of increase as great as that exhibited in the last half century, in England, Ireland, and America.

Can such things be? Can it be that the Creator has been thus inconsistent with himself? Can it be, that after having instituted throughout the material world a system the harmony of whose parts is absolutely perfect, He has, of design, subjected man, the master of all, to laws which *must* produce universal discord? Can it be, that after having given to man all the faculties required for assuming the mastery of nature, it has been a part of His design to subject him to laws in virtue of which he must become nature's slave? Let us inquire.

§ 2. Physical science, in all those departments of knowledge in which it can demonstrate the truth of its discoveries, testifies that order, harmony, and reciprocal adjustment, reign throughout the elements, and in all the movements it has yet explored. In all the realms of natural history thus far successfully cultivated, fitness of conditions, coherence of parts, unity of design, afford logical evidence that the universe is one in system, one in action, and one in aim. Arriving, however, at the natural history of man, we find theorists violating the analogies of reason, and imagining discords in the very place where, of all others, the harmonies of creation should meet together, and where the wisdom and beneficence of the Creator should vindicate themselves in the highest perfection of orderly arrangement.

The gross error that here so obviously exists is traceable to the one common source of all false philosophy: the mistaking of facts and their apparent dependencies for the *laws* which govern them. The dispersion of ancient populations, and their frequent invasions of the lands of other nations, the constant flow of emigrants from older countries in modern times, and the death of half the inhabitants of densely-peopled regions before their arrival at half the allotted period of humanity, such are the phenomena chiefly relied upon by those who seek to demonstrate the existence of an original discord between the law of human fertility and the earth's capacity for the accommodation of the human race.

That the people of early communities suffered from want of food is an established fact. That the laboring population of many modern communities are in a situation nearly similar, cannot be doubted. These facts have been made the subject of a scientific formula which may thus be stated: Man tends to increase in a geometrical ratio, whereas, food cannot, under the most favorable circumstances, be made to increase in a ratio greater than the arithmetical one. Population, therefore, increases 128 times while food can be increased but 8 times, poverty and wretchedness being the necessary results.

These results being clear as figures can make them the waste of life recorded by history has been inevitable, the earth being incapable of affording food, or even standing-room, for the myriads of her noblest offspring, were they permitted to attain maturity. A catastrophe is, therefore, always imminent, the exposure of the Creator's blunder being prevented only by the "positive checks" of war, famine, and pestilence, operating from time to time as they are required!

Philosophy so frightful as this should not be suffered to pass unchallenged. Can it be true? *Is* the fertility of the species thus observed at its highest rate the *law* of the subject?

A law, for the purpose of our argument, may be defined as—*a rule, permanent, uniform, and universal, in its action;* enabling us in all cases to reason from effects to causes, or from causes to effects. Has this theory such universality? For an answer the reader need only look around the world, finding in some portions of it a slow rate of increase; in others a rapid one; while in a third, population steadily declines. For a further answer let him turn to the statement given by Mr. Malthus himself in reference to the absence of fertility among the aborigines of the American continent, and its abundance among those of the Pacific islands. Look where he may he will find no evidence of the general existence of any such fertility as has been assumed by the advocates of the over-population theory. It would, indeed, be contrary to the very nature of things, the reproductive function having been, in common with every portion of the human organization, placed under the law of circumstances and related conditions. Climate, health, education, occupation, and habits of life, affect it as much as they affect any other organic function. It can be pushed to excess, or reduced to deficiency, being affected by all the causes which act upon body, mind, or morals; and for this simple reason, that it is a vital function, dependent upon the organism of which it is a part.

Procreation must not, in contradistinction to every other animal function, be assumed to be a fixed, invariable action, ruled, as is inorganic matter, with mechanical rigor. Nutrition is not commensurate with the quantity of food consumed, being greatly modified by the power of digestion, the vigor of the general health, and the degree of exercise taken. The fluids elaborated by the secreting organs, as saliva and milk, are familiarly known to be liable to the greatest changes, being increased or diminished in quantity in proportion to the excitement of the glands. In like manner every action of the living body is modified by the distribution of the vital force amongst the organs which compose the complicated system of the human frame.

That the earthly fortunes of the human race must have been in the contemplation of the Creator; that the changes of condition to which it should be subjected in its passage from a state of isolation and barbarism to one of combination and civilization, must have been legislated for; that the laws fitting it to those changes must have been wrought into its constitution; are suppositions whose truth must be admitted unless we are prepared to hold that human nature forms an exception, and the sole exception, to the order and harmony everywhere else existing throughout the universe. Can it then be presumed that the working of the vital mechanism requires to be protected against its own inherent mischief, by a corrective waste of its proper products? Is it not far more probable that the high rate of human fertility occasionally observed is the one which necessarily attends that stage of society in which security is so far increased as to free its members from any efforts at self-protection, and yet to make but small demands on any of their faculties but those required for the rude labors of the field?

Take the case of England. Already peopled in the days of Cæsar, its population at the close of the fourteenth century was but about 2,400,000, and yet a single family could, at the rate supposed by the Malthusian school to be the law of growth, have risen in that time to thousands of millions. Three centuries later the number had little more than doubled. Sixty years later (1760) it was but 6,500,000, the increase having been less than 30 per cent.; and yet by 1830 that number had doubled. During all this time the procreative power had obviously been a very variable quantity. It may be said that these great differences had their cause in the increased duration of life resulting from improvement in the quantity and quality of food, clothing, and lodging, the number of children born having been the same. Admitting this, we are led to the remarkable conclusion, that increase in the duration of life resulting from increased command of the necessaries and comforts of life, leads inevitably to the establishment of pauperism and slavery as the normal condition of the masses of the human race.

At times, after war or pestilence, fertility is much increased, and the question arises—which is cause, and which effect? Is war required to correct an error of the Creator, or has He himself supplied the corrective required by human error? Does natural health require the establishment of an ulcer by the drainage of which plethora is to be relieved? or, is the large supply of fluids escaping from a suppurating surface provided to meet an accidental drainage? The human frame, threatened with exhaustion by an accidental waste of its vital fluids, can, in self-defence, double, treble, or quadruple its productive power; but is this rate of vital activity, in one direction, the *law* of the structure, demanding the correction and restraints of disease?*

Vegetable life exhibits similar phenomena. A sugar-tree, in full vigor, tapped for the first time, will yield but half a pound of sugar in the season. Let it, however, be tapped for several seasons, and it will yield three pounds, without the health of the tree being affected. Need the question be asked, whether the tree, full of life and vigor, required the drainage to relieve the plethora, or whether the drainage induced a surplus flow of sap to supply the waste? It may with equal propriety be asked—Has the drainage of population from Ireland produced a tendency of vital force in the direction of procreation; or, has the drainage been required to correct an excess of the procreative tendency?

* The wars of Louis XIV. and XV. caused a great deficiency in the supply of men as compared with women; yet at the opening of the Revolution the proportions had been restored. The wars of the Revolution and the Empire caused such waste of men, that in the year IX. the excess of females was 725,225. Later, that excess increased, and in 1820 amounted to 868,325. In 1850 it had, however, declined to 193,252.

It has been intended here to show: first, that none of the functions of the human body has any such fixed and determined rule of action as permits of its being made the basis of arithmetical formulæ; next, that they vary under varying conditions, from deficiency up to excess; third, that they vary in their form, under self-adjusting laws, in obedience to the final cause of the being's existence; and lastly, that there is no instance, throughout the whole of nature's realm, in which the known laws of the subject thwart their own object, or break the harmony of the general scheme of creation.

It may be said that the germs of life perish in a thousand seeds for one that finds root and bears fruit. The answer, however, is simple, they being the proper food of beasts, birds, and men, to that end appointed. Having performed that work their office is fulfilled. Beasts, birds, and fishes, prey upon each other, man, in turn, subsisting upon them all. Here, again, we find no violation of the order of creation, these inferior animals being plainly destined to violent death, and thus mercifully relieved from the incapacities of age. As they are furnished with those instincts which are called into action by the necessity of providing for their young, the continuance of the races is thus secured. Having no filial affection impelling them to provide aid for the aged, they have no hospitality, no family economy, no capabilities either for social service or for such self-development as would make prolonged life a blessing to them. Consequently, we find nothing in their constitution which predicts life extended beyond an average maturity.

The inferior animals subserve the purposes of man. His existence, however, has no such reference to a higher class of beings here as to warrant the idea that his life may be crippled or abridged without a violation of the harmony of that system of which he is the head. It is not the divine order, but man's disorder, that limits his earthly life so far within the period beyond which he ceases to be useful to his fellows, or to find enjoyment for himself.

§ 3. In the inorganic world the compounds are constants; the composition of coal, clay, and granite, being the same now that it was a thousand years since. In the organic world we find a susceptibility of change, the fruits and flowers developed by cultivation being greatly superior to the wild ones; and the dog and horse showing themselves capable of receiving instruction. Look where we may, we see evidence of this great law: *That the power of progress is in the direct ratio of the dissimilarity of the parts and the consequent perfection of organization.*

In man we find the highest physical organization combined with a power for intellectual development that places him far above all other creatures, and here we find *no constants*; all portions of the MAN being in a constant course of change: individuality becoming more developed in one portion of society, and less so in others; the feeling of responsibility augmenting in one man while decaying in others; one community becoming more provident while another becomes more reckless; one nation progressing towards civilization while another declines with equal rapidity towards barbarism. In one, freedom increases daily and hope in the future prompts to self-respect and forethought; while in another, slavery advances and recklessness exhibits itself as the offspring of despair.

The savage is nature's slave, driven by want to the commission of acts that, abstractly considered, are highly criminal. How far, however, is he responsible, disposed, perhaps, as he would be, to be humane and honest, if he could be so and still preserve his life? Wandering over extensive surfaces he seeks a small supply of food. Little prompted to sexual intercourse, he values little either his child or its mother. In the Spartan institutions we see Lycurgus deeming it necessary to stimulate the sexual appetite, while seeking to relieve the parent from all responsibility for his children. In the Pacific Islands sexual intercourse is the chief enjoyment of life, infanticide relieving the parent from all responsibility for his offspring.

Man becomes a responsible being, a real MAN, as land is divided and he becomes free. The societary motion then becomes rapid and regular, commerce increases, agriculture rises into a science, and rude products and finished commodities steadily approximate in their prices. He loses responsibility as land becomes consolidated; the societary motion then becoming fitful and irregular, commerce declining and trade acquiring power, agriculture becoming less a science, and the prices of raw materials and finished products becoming more widely separated. In the first, men and women become more thoughtful, the matrimonial tie being chiefly sought for the comforts of home and family. In the second, both become more reckless, sexual intercourse being sought as a means of the indulgence of passion, and as being, indeed, almost the only gratification in which the poor may legally indulge.

§ 4. "The division of land," says one of the most observant and philosophical of recent British travellers,* after a careful examination of the principal nations of Europe, "carries within itself a check upon over-population, and the consequent deterioration of the social condition, which is totally wanting in the other social system." In proof of this proposition he furnishes a lively picture of the elevated standard of comfort and of morals prevailing among the present proprietors in certain portions of Switzerland, where he had spent much time; and of the thoughtful prudence which there presides over all that concerns the contraction of marriage.

"In France," as he tells his readers, "property is widely diffused, population is increasing, yet the number of births is diminishing. Of those born many more live to be added to the population, although the actual births are in proportion almost one-third fewer in numbers than in countries in which property is not diffused as it is in France. Have we not here," he asks, "a most satisfactory proof of the right working of the great social experiment now in progress in that great country?"

It is, however, "a country of contrasts." Division of the land tends to make of each man a self-governing and responsible being, political centralization, meanwhile, tending to make him a mere instrument in the hands of the State. Taxation is terrific in amount; but thereto is added compulsory military service, for a long period of years, at merely nominal wages. Centralization causes enormous expenditures in and around Paris, the attractions of the capital counteracting those of the provinces, and lessening the power of association in the rural districts, as a consequence of which there is great suffering whenever the demand for labor, or the supply of food, is much diminished. The law of the composition of forces requires careful study from all who would become proficient in social science, there being no machine whatsoever that is subject to the action of so many and so various forces as the societary one. Modern political economy, on the contrary, teaches, that all the evils of society are the results of one great force constantly impelling man

* LAING: *Notes of a Traveller.*

in a wrong direction, increasing the number of mouths as the means of feeding them diminish.

The reader has seen evidence of the extraordinary extent to which the land of Denmark has been divided; and that the condition of the people furnishes "living evidence of the falsity of the theory that population increases more rapidly than subsistence, when the country is held by small working proprietors."

In Germany land is constantly changing hands, all classes finding themselves enabled to purchase it. The consciousness that they are not debarred from rising in the social scale, and that they can purchase a house and farm of their own, gives, says an English writer of high authority, "to the laborer of those countries where the land is not tied up in the hands of a few, an elasticity of feeling, a hopefulness, an energy, a pleasure in economy and labor, a distaste for expenditure upon gross sensual enjoyments, and an independence of character which the dependent and helpless laborers of England can never experience."

Hope is the mother of industry, and industry of temperance and self-respect. "In the German and Swiss towns," says Mr. Kay, "there are no places to be compared to those sources of the demoralization of our town-poor, the gin-palaces." Temperance is general, its existence being ascribed by this intelligent traveller to the civilizing effects of their education, and to the careful habits which the hope of purchasing land nourishes in their minds.

§ 5. Turning now to Turkey, Portugal, and Jamacia, countries in which the power of association has almost passed away, we find population slowly but steadily diminishing as land becomes more consolidated. In India, a country in which local centres once abounded, with admirable provision for instruction of the young, those centres have disappeared, and the population becomes more and more divided into the two great classes of the enormously rich and miserably poor.

In Ireland, the closing portion of the last century was spent under a regime of protection analagous to that which now exists throughout central and northern Europe. Commerce then grew steadily, the demand for labor increasing, and the community at large advancing with a rapidity not then excelled in any portion of continental Europe.

By the act of union all was changed. Manufacture

having been banished from the land, the demand for human powers was limited to the mere brute force required for the lowest order of the labors of the field. Land at any rent, or starvation, being the only choice left the people, need we wonder that hope fled, or that education, books, and libraries disappeared, leaving in their place the recklessness and improvidence that have since led to so great an increase of population? Famine and pestilence followed, but still the numbers grew, and for the reason, that the real MAN was gradually disappearing and the mere human animal taking his place.

The Irish cotter-tenant has no property in land; and all that he can save goes into his landlord's pocket in the shape of rent. He is not, as were cotter-tenants formerly in Scotland, allowed to pay his rent in kind; that is, by giving a certain proportion of his crop, retaining the rest for the maintenance of his family. It is in gold that it must be paid. "It would be just as reasonable," says Mr. Laing, "to make them pay in French wines for the squire, or Parisian dresses for the lady. Their land produces neither gold, silver, nor Irish bank-notes. It is not reasonable to make the peasant, the ignorant man, pay in those commodities, (they are but commodities like wines and silks), and to make simple men, inexperienced in trade, a prey to market-jobbers, running the double risk of selling their own commodities, and buying those in which their landlords choose to be paid their rents."

How this system tends to produce improvidence is well exhibited in the following passage:—

"Money rent deteriorates the condition of a small tenant in two ways: The more honestly he is inclined, the more poorly and meanly he must live. He must sell all his best produce, his grain, his butter, his flax, his pig, and subsist upon the meanest food, his worst potatoes and water, to make sure of money for his rent. It thus deteriorates his standard of living. He is also tempted by money-rent out of the path of certainty into that of chance. It thus deteriorates his moral condition. Ask him six barrels of oats or barley, or six stone of butter or flax, for a piece of land which never produced four, and his common sense and experience guide him. He sees and comprehends the simple data before him, knows from experience that such a crop cannot be raised, such a rent afforded, and he is off to England or America to seek a living. But ask him six guineas per acre for a piece of land proportionally as much over-rented as the other, and he trusts to chance, to accident, to high market prices, to odd jobs of work turning up, to summer or harvest labor out of the country,—in short, to he knows not what; for he is placed in a false position, made to depend upon the chance of markets, and on mercantile success and profits, as much as upon industry and skill in working his little farm."

The documents published at various times in regard to this country bear testimony to the fact, that those who have property, even to the small extent of ten pounds, exercise a prudent foresight in reference to marriage; whereas, those who have nothing marry without hesitation. Nevertheless, modern economists assert, that "the low and degraded condition into which the people of Ireland are now sunk, is the condition to which every people must be reduced whose numbers increase faster than the means of providing for their comfortable subsistence."

The proposition might, however, be differently stated. Across the Channel, Mr. McCulloch, to whom we are indebted for the passage here given, had in full view a country, that of Belgium, in which a much more crowded population, on a less fertile soil, was advancing rapidly in civilization. Why this difference? Why should the people of Ireland perish, while those of Belgium prosper? Because the system of the one has looked to the reduction of a whole people to the condition of mere beasts of burden; while that of the other has tended to their elevation to the condition of the true MAN, the being of power.

When men most resemble animals they look most to sexual intercourse as their only means of enjoyment; and they will have most children, provided the women continue chaste. The chastity of Irish women is proverbial; and to this cause, combined with the low condition of the people, we must attribute much of the rapidity of Irish increase; those very qualities which, under a sound system, would produce the greatest good, having here a most injurious effect.

In several of the countries above referred to, the effect of the stoppage of the societary circulation has been a diminution of the population; whereas, in Ireland, the reverse has been produced, furnishing evidence of the adaptibility of the human animal to circumstances. Unlike the people of those communities, the Irishman was placed between two other populations speaking the same language with himself. Among them there was found an outlet for surplus numbers; and this increased the recklessness of both sexes in contracting the marriage tie, the feeling of duty to themselves or their children disappearing in the gulf which had swallowed up all their hopes for the present or the future.*

Centralization—especially trading centralization—tends to produce inequality of condition; hence it is that the annihilation of Irish and Indian manufactures has contributed so largely to produce consolidation of British land.

§ 6. Coming now to the home of the over-population theory, we have already seen that in England the small proprietors have almost disappeared, the 200,000 land-owners of eighty years since being now represented by little more than 30,000. At that time the population was 7,500,000, having increased but 10 per cent. in seventy-five years. Now it is estimated, for 1855, at 19,786,914, having increased 150 per cent. in a period but little longer. Growth of numbers has, therefore, kept pace with a consolidation of the land that places one class above and another below the reach of hope—a state of things tending more than any other to cause development of the merely animal passions.

Consolidation driving the laborers from the soil while improved machinery expelled them from the factory, the poor were thus made poorer as the rich grew richer. As the Act of Union closed the factories of Ireland, her people were forced to emigrate to the place at which the taxes were distributed, their competition of course throwing the English laborer still more upon the "tender mercies" of the capitalist. From year to year the small proprietor was seen to pass into the condition of a day laborer, and the small employer, mechanic, or tradesman, into that of a mere receiver of wages—the whole people thus tending to become divided into two great classes, the very rich and the very poor, the master and the slave.

* "For a whole generation *man has been a drug in this country, and population a nuisance.* It has scarcely entered into the heads of economists that they would ever have to deal with a deficiency of labor. The inexhaustible Irish supply has kept down the price of English labor, whether in the field, the railway, the factory, the army or the navy; whether at the sickle, the spade, the hod, or the desk. We believe that for fifty years at least, *labor, taking its quality into account, has been cheaper in this country than in any part of Europe;* and that this cheapness of labor has contributed vastly to the improvement and power of the country, to the success of all mercantile pursuits, and to *the enjoyment of those who have money to spend.*"—*London Times.*

As England became flooded with the wretched people from the sister isle, driven from home in search of employment, the wealthy found it easier to accomplish the "great works" for which the country has been indebted to the "cheap labor" of Ireland, and the greater the influx of such labor the more rapid was the decline in the power of both Ireland and Britain to furnish a market for English manufactures. Hence arose a necessity for looking abroad for new markets to take the place of those before existing at home; and thus cheap labor, a *consequence* of the system, became, in its turn, a *cause* of new efforts for still further cheapening labor. As the Irishman could no longer buy, it became necessary to expel the Hindoo from his own market. As the Highlander was expelled, it became necessary to underwork the spinners and weavers of China. As the Bengalese are impoverished, there arises a necessity for filling Burmah and Borneo with British goods. Pauperism and recklessness lie necessarily at the root of such a system, based, as it is, upon the idea of a perpetual antagonism of interests. The result is seen in the facts, that the condition of the agricultural population is steadily deteriorating; that in despair of any improvement in their condition they marry early, and under circumstances so totally destructive of morality, that infanticide prevails to a frightful extent; and that demoralization is progressing with a rapidity scarcely elsewhere to be exceeded.*

* "The accounts we receive from all parts of the country show that these miserable cottages are crowded to an extreme, and that the crowding is progressively increasing. People of both sexes and of all ages, married and unmarried, parents, brothers, sisters and strangers, sleep in the same rooms, and often in the same beds. One gentleman tells us of six people, two of whom were man and wife, sleeping in the same bed, three with their heads to the top, and three at the foot of the bed. . . . . Nor are these solitary instances, but similar reports are given by gentlemen visiting in ALL parts of the country."—KAY, *Social Condition of England.* Vol. I. p. 472.

"It was declared by the coroner of Leeds, and assented to as probable by the surgeon, that there were, as near as could be calculated, about three hundred children put to death yearly in Leeds alone, that were not registered by the law. In other words, three hundred infants were murdered to avoid the consequences of their living, and these murders, as the coroner said, were never detected."—LEADER.

"It has been clearly ascertained, that it is a common practice among the more degraded classes of poor in many of our towns, to enter their infants in these (burial) clubs, and then to cause their

§ 7. Pioneer life, where person and property are reasonably secure, is favorable to increase of numbers, isolated men being little stimulated to the exercise of any but the merely physical faculties. Therefore it is that in the new States of North America we find the most rapid increase of numbers. In the order of nature, however, this should change as the real MAN becomes stimulated to action, economy, thoughtfulness, and a desire for higher enjoyments, becoming the characteristics of the people. Such, too, *would be* the changes observed under a system of policy which tended towards increasing the power of combination and developing a scientific agriculture. The one pursued has, however, been merely a continuation of that colonial state the essential object of which was that of stimulating the dispersion of the people subject to it, and compelling them to limit themselves to the raising of rude products for distant markets, the proper work of the barbarian and the slave.

Of vital statistics for the Union, there are none. The census returns of 1850 gave 2,555 persons over 100 years of age; while in France, out of nearly 36,000,000 there were but 102. Beyond this fact we have little of general application. Massachusetts is the only State that presents us with reliable statistics. From them we learn how excessive is the proportion borne by foreign marriages, births, and deaths, to the entire number. Of 2,536 men married in Boston in 1856, 1,503 were foreigners, and more than half the women were also foreign. Here, too, we find an extraordinary destruction of infant life, more than a fifth of all the deaths in the State occurring in the first year, those of the first five years being more than 40 per cent. of the whole. How far these facts apply to the whole Union there is no means of knowing; but in New York city we find that, whereas in 1817 the deaths under five were but one-third of the whole, in 1857 they were *seven-tenths!* Of the colored population of that city, the deaths were to the births more than 2 to 1.

In no other country do we meet with such remarkable contrasts; great length of life seen side by side with so extraordinary an infant mortality. In the 8 years ending with 1855 the average age, at death, of males of all professions, in Massachusetts, who had survived 20 years, was nearly 63½

death, either by starvation, ill-usage, or poison! What more horrible symptom of moral degradation can be conceived? One's mind revolts against it, and would fain reject it as a monstrous fiction. But, alas! it seems to be but too true."—KAY, Vol. I. p. 433.

years. On the other hand; whereas, in the city of Baltimore, from 1831 to 1840, the deaths were as 1 to 43, they are now 1 in 40; while, in New York, the proportion has increased as follows:—

1810..................1 in 46
1815..................1 in 41
1820..................1 in 37
1825..................1 in 34
1855..................1 in 28½

For the new States we have no statistics; but the general fact presents itself, that those who are driven by an unwise policy prematurely to commence the work of settlement are constantly endeavoring to cultivate rich soils in the absence of the conditions required for the preservation of health and life. Disease and death are the necessary consequences, the system which crowds the cities at the cost of life thus producing the same effects throughout the West.

§ 8. The human body consists of a multitude of parts, with an equal variety of offices and endowments—the heart, arteries, and veins, being the organs of circulation; the muscles, those of motion; the glands, of secretion. The abdominal viscera are concerned with digestion; the thoracic, with respiration; the sexual organs having the charge of reproduction. To the brain and nerves are committed sensation, perception, volition, intellection, and emotion; and especially, the supreme function of co-ordinating the actions of all the other organs and thus securing that concert and unity needed for perfect organization.

To the aggregate of those various organisms there must be a limit of vital force, some certain point at which it reaches its ultimatum. It is a consequence of such limitation, that upon an equal or unequal distribution of this vital power among the several organs will depend the respective efficiencies of each and all. The total vital force is liable to great inequality of distribution; not only in those diversions of energy from one set of organs to another that we see to occur on every change of occupation, but steadily and habitually throughout the whole of life. In some persons the muscular system is far more occupied than the mental. In others, the nutritive organs absorb much of the general vigor which it is their destination to support. In a smaller number, the intellectual and moral powers are exerted to the injury of the nutritive and muscular systems; while in women, the reproductive system, in some one or other form, trenches largely upon the intellectual faculties.

All these irregularities are found within the limits of what is called health. In disease, the disturbance of the balance of the various functions becomes much more marked. A strong man struck down with fever has his nervous sensibility excited and his circulation exaggerated, while the secreting and muscular system are nearly powerless. With every nerve tingling with excitement, with the brain in delirium, and the blood-vessels in a state of rude commotion, the patient is prostrate with muscular debility, and the action of the skin and viscera is almost entirely suspended.

Thus both in health and disease the various offices of the living body may undergo great modifications of activity. It may be said, generally, that the vital force cannot be habitually concentrated upon any one part of the structure except at the expense of other portions. It is, however, almost universally true, that those functions which minister to the animal life, and those which serve for the continuance of the race, prompted, as they are, by instinctive forces, absorb the largest share of the system's strength to the detriment of those nobler faculties which require education and discipline for their full development.

While such antagonism of the functions is thus a general result of the vital organization, it is curious to observe that a special relation of this kind obtains between the nervous and reproductive powers. Mere physical effort does not seem to be unfavorable to fecundity, the slaves of our Southern plantations and the laborers of Ireland being amongst the most prolific of mankind. The drudges of our imperfect civilization employ their muscular strength under very little nervous excitement, the action of their mental powers being at the lowest rate possible to rational creatures. The well-known chastity and infertility of the hunter tribes, on the contrary, is in striking adjustment with their circumstances. Like the beast of prey, the hunter requires a hundred-fold larger territory for his support than do men of pacific habits. His life is one of excessive toil, requiring not only severe muscular exertion, but the exercise of agility, cunning, vigilance, fortitude, and moral resolution, qualities whose exertion makes heavy drafts upon the cerebral apparatus, and tends, proportionably, to withdraw the vital power from the function of reproduction.

Another fact affords confirmation of the views now suggested. In the order of nature the power of reproduction appears in the individual about the time that the intellectual and moral powers attain a force sufficient to control the instincts, the brain thereafter losing none of its balancing power, but rather gaining upon the propensities with advance in age. This correspondence of development and continence marks a closely fitting relation of combination between them. Only in man is the sexual impulse equally active, equally responsive to restraint at all seasons. Unlike the lower animals, he has no annual season of love, irrepressible and irresistible. The propensity beginning with the dawning vigor of his intellect, is thus placed under the control of reason and sentiment, functions of the cerebral system whose efficiency is in direct proportion to the healthy development of the system of which they are a part.

It is not, however, by *moral* resistance, alone, that the admirable ends of providential order are secured, *the law being woven into the very texture of the reproductive organs.* A *physical* law here adjusts the balance, maintains the harmony, and achieves the beneficent results desired.

The law of the balance between the nervous and sexual functions is corroborated by the facts of comparative physiology. The queen ant of the African territories lays 60,000 eggs, and the hair-worm as many as 8,000,000 in a single day. Above a million of eggs are produced at once by the codfish, whereas in the strong and sagacious shark few are found. The higher ranks of reptiles are still less fertile; and among the mammalia, those which quickly reach maturity produce numerous litters, while those that are better provided with brain produce annually but a single litter. Higher in rank are those which produce singly, the series terminating with the elephant, who, in virtue of his nobler nervous system, and its accompanying reasoning powers, presents himself as the least prolific of them all.

The general law of life may be thus stated:—

The nervous system varies directly as the power to maintain life:

The degree of fertility varies inversely as the development of the nervous system, animals with larger brains being the least, and those with smaller the most, prolific:

The power to maintain life, and that of procreation, antagonize each other, that antagonism tending perpetually towards the establishment of an equilibrium.

Chemical analysis, though less accurately ascertained than might be wished, presents itself in aid of the views thus suggested; exhibiting the fact that the sperm cells of the fecundating fluid, and the neurine, or essential portion of the cerebral substance, possess in common one element, unoxydized phosphorus, by which they are specially characterized. Of this substance no less than 6½ per cent. enters into the solid contents of the adult brain. In advanced age it falls to 3¾, and in idiots it is less than 3. The evidence afforded by experience and by physiological laws is, however, more conclusive than that obtained by examination of the structure. Nothing connected with the question is more fully recognized than the general antagonism of the nervous and generative systems. Intense mental application, involving great consumption of the nervous element, is accompanied by diminished production of sperm-cells, the excessive production of these latter being, in like manner, followed by defective cerebral energy frequently amounting to imbecility.

How this antagonism affects the female system is less known; but it appears highly probable that the provision of nervous matter, as well as of nutriment to the embryo, limits the supply of nervous matter to the maternal system. It is, too, highly probable that the uterine function, beginning with puberty and continuing until the commencement of old age, is the more efficient counteractive of cerebral force in the sex.

Further, there is abundant reason for believing that certain kinds of nervous action are more efficient than others in counteracting the activity of the instincts, although the physiology of the brain is not yet sufficiently advanced to render us adequate service here. We know that the employment of the mind in passional, imaginative, scientific, moral, or devotional applications has widely different effects upon the propensities, some ministering to their growth while others counteract it.

That men of great mental activity are generally unprolific, has frequently been remarked. Occasionally it becomes possible to trace the movements, in this respect, of large bodies of men, and whenever it is so we meet with facts tending to establish the idea that the extinction of families follows closely upon high development of the mental faculties.

Twenty years since, the number of British peers was 394, of whom no less than 272 were the result of creations subsequent to 1760. From 1611 to 1819 no less than 753 baronetcies had become extinct; and yet the total number created had been less than 1400. Precisely similar facts are found in the noble families of Europe. So was it, too, in ancient Rome, Tacitus telling us that, "about the time that Claudius enrolled in the patrician order such of the senators as were recommended by their illustrious birth and the merits of their ancestors, the line of those families styled by Romulus 'the first class of nobility,' was almost extinct." Even those of more recent date, created in the times of Cæsar and Augustus, were well nigh then exhausted.

Coming to more recent times we find that of the fifteen occupants of the Presidential chair in this country, seven have been childless, while the total number of their children has been little more than twenty. The same fact meets us almost everywhere, Napoleon, Wellington, the Foxes, Pitts, and other distinguished men, not having, as a rule, left behind them the children required to fill the void created by their decease. How it has been with Chaptal, Fourcroy, Berzelius, Berthollet, Davy, and the thousand other distinguished names, scientific, literary, and military, we have little means of knowing with any certainty; but what we do know leads to the conclusion that their existing representatives do not number more than half as many as they did themselves.

In the town of Berne, from the year 1583 to 1654, the sovereign council had admitted into the Bourgeoisie 487 families, of which in 1783 only 108 remained. Similar facts are given in relation to the freemen of various towns and cities in England, all tending to prove that the excitement of trade is as unfavorable to reproduction as is that of science or of politics.

Look where we may we find that the reproductive power in man is no more a constant quantity than is any other of his powers. It may be stimulated to excessive activity by such a course of action as tends to reduce him to the condition of a mere animal, annihilating the feeling of pride in himself, and of responsibility to his Creator or to his fellow-man. It diminishes as his various faculties are stimulated to action, as employments become diversified, as the societary action becomes more rapid, as land becomes divided, and as he himself becomes more free. Such, we believe, is the self-adjusting law of population.

The nearer the consumer to the producer the greater must be the development of the real MAN, and the greater the tendency towards perfect harmony in the demands upon the earth for food, and in her power to meet the drafts that men require to make.

CHAPTER XXXIX.

OF FOOD AND POPULATION.

§ 1. Population makes the food come from the rich soils of the earth, depopulation driving men back to the poorer ones. Increased regularity in the supply of food consequent upon the increased demands of a population that is growing in numbers and in power. Diminution in the waste of human force that attends increase in the supply of food.

§ 2. Substitution of vegetable for animal food. Causes the action of man upon nature to become more direct, thereby diminishing friction and increasing power.

§ 3. The mineral world co-operates in diminishing man's dependence on the animal one. Diminution in the demand upon man's physical powers, and in the quantity of food required to supply the daily waste.

§ 4. Tendency of the lower animals to disappear. Consequent diminution in the supply of carbonic acid. Increased demand for supplies of that acid which attends the extension of cultivation. Consequent necessity for increase in the number of men. Wonderful beauty of all natural arrangements.

§ 5. That man may profit by these arrangements he is required to conform to that law of nature which demands that the consumer and producer take their places by each other. Population pressing upon subsistence in all communities by which it is violated.

§ 6. Destructive effects of British policy in causing the exhaustion of the countries that follow in the lead of her economists. Tendency in all of them towards centralization, slavery, and death.

7. Simplicity and beauty of the laws which regulate the demand for food, and its supply. Perfect harmony, throughout nature, in the adaptation of means to ends.

§ 1. That man may increase there must be increase in the supply of food. That the latter may increase men must grow in numbers, it being only by means of the power of combination that man is enabled to control and direct the earth's forces, and to pass from the condition of nature's slave to that of nature's master. Population makes the food come from the richer soils, with constant increase in the return to labor; whereas, depopulation drives men back to the poorer ones, with constant decline in the ability to obtain the necessary supplies of food and clothing.

Crusoe, at first dependent entirely on his powers of appropriation, could obtain no food but that which nature was content to offer. In time, however, acquiring a slight degree of power, he was enabled to compel her to labor for him, the supply of food then becoming much more regular, he himself becoming more independent of changes of the weather, and the demand upon his powers being much diminished. The wild man of the West needs no less than eight pounds of meat per day, yet does he often find at the close of days expended in the chase, that he has scarcely obtained as much as would fully suffice for even a single one.

Even when successful he finds a growing difficulty of transportation, the distance between his lodge and the place at which he finds his food tending steadily to increase. Gorging himself for the moment, he leaves for the crows and wolves the larger portion of the product of his labors. Gluttony and starvation go, thus, hand and hand together throughout that portion of societary history in which man is found existing as the slave of nature. Famines and pestilences, too, alternate with one another, the result being found in the fact, that numbers increase but slowly even where population does not tend entirely to disappear, as is the case throughout the extreme West.

In the shepherd state, supplies become more regular, evidence of growing human power then exhibiting itself in a diminution of the food required for meeting the daily waste, and in the growing reproductive force of the animals that man has tamed, the power of procreation being here, as everywhere, a variable quantity. In time, however, machinery is obtained, by means of which the earth is compelled to give forth products which can be used for human food without being first converted into meat, the rude agriculture of early days then making its appearance among the poorer soils of the hills, and oats, rye, or even wheat being cultivated. Irregularity of supply is, however, the characteristic of the period, grain being greatly in excess of the demand at one time or place, and famine decimating the population at others. Progress, nevertheless, has been made, a pound of flour, made from either rye or wheat, furnishing a larger amount of nutritive matter than is contained in thrice as many pounds of beef or pork, even when free from bone.

Further power is now obtained, every step of man's progress being but the preparation for a new and greater one. Richer soils being cultivated the return to labor steadily increases, the six bushels to the acre of the earlier period being replaced by the thirty bushels of the later one. Improved machinery of conversion, too, economizes various portions of the product that had at first been wasted. Cultivation becoming more and more productive, the pea, the bean, the cabbage, the turnip, and the potato, of which the earth yields by tons, take the place of wheat of which the yield is counted by bushels, and of grass that must be changed in form to fit it for human food; every step in that direction being attended by an increase in the number of persons who can draw support from any given surface, and by growth in the power of combination for obtaining the means of further progress. Each half acre thus cultivated yields more food than can be obtained from a thousand acres, when roamed over by the wretched savage of the West.

Gradual improvement in the machinery instituted by the Creator for proportioning the supply of food to the demand of a constantly-growing population, here exhibits itself in the facts:—

That the waste of human powers in the search for food, and the quantity of food required to supply that waste, are constantly decreasing quantities; that man is gradually substituting vegetable for animal food; that the quantity of food produced increases in the direct ratio of that substitution; that the various utilities of the things produced become more and more developed; that human effort is daily more economized; and that with every stage of progress there is an increase of power for directing and controlling the forces of nature, manifesting itself in the clearing, drainage, and cultivation of soils whose very wealth had rendered them inaccessible to the early cultivator.

§ 2. What, however, is the effect of this substitution of vegetable for animal food? The answer to this question is found in the fact, that rapacious animals, the shark, the lion, the tiger, and the bear, increase but slowly, even when at all; whereas, American Pampas afford conclusive proof of the rapidity with which the ox and the horse, consumers of vegetable food, may be increased. So, too, it is with man, the rapacious savage, a prey to hunger on one day and a glutton on the next, being little capable of reproduction when compared with the civilized man, whose dependence on the vegetable kingdom is large, even where not exclusive.*

The more direct the action of man upon nature the less is the necessity for animal food, and the less is the friction, but the greater is his power to please his appetite. The more he is enabled to subdue the richer soils to cultivation the

* "Fruits, roots, and the succulent parts of vegetables, appear to be the natural food of man; his hands afford him a facility in gathering them; and his short and comparatively weak jaws, his short canine teeth not passing beyond the common line of the others, and his tuberculous teeth, not permitting him either to feed on the herbage or devour flesh, unless those aliments be previously prepared by the culinary process."—Cuvier.

greater is the tendency towards placing sheep upon the poorer lands, and thus insuring a full supply of mutton. The larger the yield of turnips and potatoes the greater is his ability to obtain efficient machinery for taking the cod and the herring. The more perfect the power of association the more is he enabled to cultivate the oyster and to people the ponds and rivers with fish, every stage of progress in that direction giving increase of regularity in the supply of food, while developing the various individualities of the man who is thus engaged in placing himself in the position of master of nature, of his passions, and of himself.

§ 3. Is it, however, in relation to food alone that we observe this tendency to the substitution of the vegetable for the animal world? It is not, the same tendency being everywhere observable, and constituting one of the strongest evidences of advancing civilization. Wool is superseded by the cotton plant, of which a single acre furnishes more pounds than could be obtained from a hundred employed in raising sheep. Flax and cotton supersede the silk-worm, as furnisher of clothing. Gutta percha and muslin take the place of leather. Caoutchouc lessens the demand for both hides and wool, paper, meanwhile, furnishing a cheap substitute for parchment.

So, too, is it with the mineral kingdom, the steel pen superseding the quill, mineral manures superseding animal excrement, and the horse of iron rapidly taking the place of the one composed of muscle, bone, and sinew. Every new development of mineral treasures tends, in turn, towards increase in the number of local centres of action, towards the growth of commerce, towards decline in the taxes of trade and transportation, towards increase in the facility of obtaining improved machinery, and towards increased rapidity in the societary circulation; with constant increase in the proportion of the societary powers that may be given to augmentation in the supplies of the raw materials of clothing and of food.

This, however, is not all. The better his clothing the less is the waste of his body, and the less his need for food. The more perfect the machinery of transportation the less is his need for clothing, travelling by railroad involving less expenditure of animal heat than that performed on the horse's back. The nearer the place of consumption to that of production the less is the demand for soldiers, sailors, and wagoners, always large consumers of stimulating food. The more perfect the power of association the less is the necessity for going from home, and the less is the need for either food or clothing, the attractive and counter-attractive forces thus exhibiting themselves, here as everywhere, constantly increasing in their intensity, as the societary circulation becomes more rapid. Look, therefore, where we may, we find a constant tendency towards the perfect adaptation of the earth to the wants of a growing population; every increase in the power of combination being accompanied by *diminution in the quantity of raw material required* for the maintenance of human life, and *increase in that which may be obtained* in return to any given amount of labor.

§ 4. With increase in the numbers of mankind, the lower animals tend to diminish in their numbers, and gradually to disappear, vegetable products tending, as steadily, to increase in quantity. Were it otherwise, the world must become less and less fitted for man's residence, carbonic acid being more and more produced, and the air declining in its powers for the maintenance of human life. Increase of vegetable life tends, on the contrary, to promote the decomposition of that acid, thereby increasing the supply of the oxygen required for maintenance of animal life, while diminution in the consumption of animal food is attended by decrease in the quantity of oxygen required for human purposes.

The extension of cultivation is indispensable to increase in the supply of food. That extension involves, of course, a gradual extirpation of animal races that now consume so largely of the products of the earth, and were they not to be replaced by men the production of carbonic acid would speedily diminish, with corresponding diminution in the reproductive powers of the vegetable world. The more numerous the men and women the greater is the store of force required for the production of vegetable matter, the more rapid is the circulation, the greater is the production of carbonic acid, and the greater the power for vegetable reproduction. The more complete the power of association the more perfect becomes the cultivation, the greater is the development of the powers of the land, and the more admirably does the beauty of all natural arrangements exhibit itself in the perfect adjustment of all the portions of the wonderful system of which we are a part.

Nevertheless, although the annual product of a single acre

of land, employed in raising wheat, is capable of sustaining "animal warmth, and animal motive-power, in a vigorous man, during a period of more than two and a half years," and although each such man is capable of cultivating many acres, we can look in no direction without seeing that men are suffering for want of food. So, too, it is with regard to fuel, and to the materials of clothing, as well as houses, and all other of the commodities required for the maintenance of health and life. The questions, therefore, naturally arise—Why is not more food produced? Why is the supply of cotton and wool so small? Why is not more clothing made? Why is not more coal mined? Why are not more houses built? The reply to these questions may now be given.

§ 5. The nearer the place of production to that of consumption, and the closer the approximation of prices of raw materials and finished products, the smaller must be the proportion of time and mind required for the labors of trade and transportation; the larger that which may be given to developing the powers of the earth; the greater the ability to maintain the powers of the land; the larger the return to labor; the greater the tendency towards increase in the power to obtain supplies of food, clothing, and fuel; and the greater the ability to command the use of houses, mills, farms, and machinery of every kind.

For proof that such have been and are the facts we need but look to the Moorish Empire in Spain; to the Netherlands of the days of the Burgundian princes, and thence to the present time; to France of the present, and to all the countries now following in her lead in maintaining the policy initiated by Colbert. In all of these agriculture tends to become more a science, with constant increase in the yield of the land, in the development of human powers, in the rapidity of circulation, in the power to maintain commerce at home and abroad, in the creation of local centres of action, and in the freedom and power of man. For further proof we need but look to Ireland, India, Jamaica, Turkey, and Portugal, countries that follow in the lead of England—all of them pursuing a policy that widens the distance between the consumer and the producer, and all finding its effects in decay of agriculture, in exhaustion of the soil, in decline of human intellect, in sluggishness of societary movement, in centralization of power, and in growing subjection of those who labor to produce to the direction of those who perform the works of trade and transportation. In the first of these, the over-population theory finds less and less support with each succeeding day. In the last, we find "population always pressing upon subsistence," and requiring the aid of famine and pestilence for maintenance of equilibrium, the doctrine of Mr. Malthus being merely *descriptive* of the state of things that has arisen in every country of the world that has been subjected to that British policy so warmly denounced by Adam Smith, which has for its object the centralization on a single spot of earth of all the machinery of conversion for the world.

All the phenomena of American history tend to prove, that the more the people are limited to the labors of the field and thus subjected to that system, the less food they have to spare, and the lower are the prices; whereas, the more they are protected in the effort at diversifying their employments, the larger is the return to the work of cultivation, and the greater is the tendency towards a rise of prices In the one case we see them gradually, but certainly, receding towards the position occupied by England a century since, and in the other, as regularly advancing towards that now occupied by Germany and France.

§ 6. Coming now to England, we find a country whose people are becoming, with each succeeding year, more dependent upon distant lands for supplies of rude products, while gradually exhausting all of those from which supplies have thus far been derived. Ireland can now do little more than feed herself. Portugal and Turkey are almost blotted from the list of nations. India produces less and less with each succeeding year. Jamaica and Demarara have wholly lost the importance they once possessed. The work of destruction is proceeding rapidly in Brazil. Virginia and Carolina decline from year to year. Wheat and tobacco, as objects of cultivation, are steadily leaving the Atlantic States. The cotton-growing region of America, of half a century since, is now exhausted, while that of a later period is rapidly following in its train and furnishing proof that the close of the present century must witness the near exhaustion of the field of cotton cultivation.

The policy being thus exhaustive, its effects upon the people to whom the world is debtor for it exhibit themselves in a perpetual effort fraudulently to increase the apparent quantities even at the cost of health and life, almost every thing that is eaten being more or less adulterated. Vinegar is water and sulphuric acid. Tea is a compound of gypsum and Prussian blue. Pepper is debased with linseed cakes. Sausages are made of meat that is diseased, while red lead forms the chief ingredient of curry powder, the miller and the baker, meanwhile, adulterating the bread. Verdigris poisons the pickles and preserves. Vermillion colors the cheese. Little, therefore, as the laborer is enabled to purchase of these commodities, that little is rendered less, and often destructive, by the intermixture of substances incapable of affording nourishment, great as is their power for producing disease, to be followed by death.

Why, now, is it that such things are needed? Why is it, that with a world as yet almost unoccupied, men should suffer, even where they do not perish, for want of food, clothing, and fuel? Why are not more houses built? Why is not more fuel mined? Why is not more food produced? The answer to these questions is found in the simple propositions, that production increases with that approximation of the prices of rude products and finished commodities which always follows the near approach of the consumer to the producer; that it diminishes with their recession from each other; and that the latter is the tendency in all the countries which follow in the lead of England, embracing, as they do, nearly all, except the few in northern and central Europe to which we have referred. In all these latter the supply of food goes in advance of the demands of a growing population. In the others we find the phenomena required for maintaining the Malthusian doctrine of over-population, the tendency in all of them being in the direction of centralization, slavery, and death.

§ 7. The simple and beautiful laws by the action of which the supply of food and other raw materials is adjusted to meet the wants and gratify the tastes of an increasing population, would seem now to be contained in the following propositions:—

That in the infancy of society men, being few in number, poor and weak, are little capable of making demands upon nature, who, therefore, gives them small and uncertain supplies of food:

That as numbers grow they are enabled to combine together, thus obtaining a large increase of force:

That the more perfect the facility of association the greater is their power to make demands upon nature's treasury, and the greater the quantity of food and other raw materials obtained in return to any given quantity of labor:

That the larger the supplies yielded by the earth the greater becomes the ability to utilize the various portions of the commodities obtained, the power of accumulation thus increasing with constantly accelerating force, and facilitating the construction of new and improved machinery by aid of which further to increase the command over nature's services:

That the more perfect the machinery the less is the need for the exertion of muscular force, the smaller is the waste of human power, and the less the quantity of food required to replace the waste:

That the less the quantity needed the greater is the tendency towards substitution of the products of the vegetable and mineral kingdom for those of the animal one, the power to obtain supplies thus growing as the need declines:

That the greater the tendency towards such substitution the greater is that which leads to creation of local centres, and the larger is the proportion of the force obtained that may be given to further development of the latent treasures of the earth; the more rapid is the increase in the power of combination; and the greater is the tendency towards the production of the real MAN, capable of becoming absolute master over nature, and over himself:

That the greater the tendency towards the development of the earth's latent powers, the greater is the competition for the purchase of labor, the greater is the value of man, the more equitable the distribution of labor's products, and the greater the tendency towards development of the feeling of hope in the future, and of responsibility for the exercise of power obtained by means of action in the past:

That the higher the feeling of hope the greater is the tendency towards seeking matrimony as affording the means of indulging the kindly feelings towards wife and children, and the love of home; and the less the tendency towards seeking it as affording the means of mere animal indulgence:

That nature here co-operates with man, vital force tending more and more in the direction of further strengthening the reasoning powers, and less in that of procreation:

That, consequently, every stage of progress towards real civilization is attended with increase in the power to demand supplies of food, while diminishing the proportion borne by the demand for food to the mouths that are to be fed; and slowly but certainly diminishing the tendency towards increase in the number of mouths themselves; the ultimate effect exhibiting itself in large increase in the proportion borne by food to population.

Such are the various forces to whose combined operation we are required to look for proper adjustment of the supply of food and other raw materials to the demand for them, those forces operating within and without the human system, and tending always to establish among its several functions an orderly balance, while displaying their power in bringing up subsistence to a level with a demand that is itself constantly diminishing in the ratio borne by it to the numbers requiring to be supplied. The sciences and the arts subservient to the production of raw materials must grow with even pace as the morality and intelligence of the race become more and more developed. The forces which war upon human life, and those to which that life must look for maintenance, tend towards an equal balance, and the preponderance of the one or the other must rest with man himself, the over-ruling law of the process tending towards an exact equilibrium. In him, and him alone, the exercise of the procreative power was placed under the guidance of intellect, that intellect having been given to him that he might be enabled to place himself in the control and direction of all the wonderful forces of nature, his own included.

Even in the discord of accidental disproportion the harmony of means adapted to the production of desired ends may everywhere be seen, and when this providential order shall finally be obtained by full development of the various powers of the earth, all apparent disproportion must disappear, the law then standing vindicated against all attempts at misconstruction. Error and abuse diminishing in their proportions, the harmony and beauty of eternal truth must become more clearly visible, and the ways of Providence be justified to man.

CHAPTER XL.

OF COLONIZATION.

§ 1. Early colonization. Nature goes on adding perfection to perfection, from the poles to the tropics. Richer soils of the world as yet unoccupied, nature being there all-powerful. With the growth of wealth and population man is enabled to turn against her such of her forces as he has mastered—passing steadily from triumph to triumph and subjugating more fertile soils.

§ 2. Manufactures always precede, and never follow, the creation of a real agriculture. The country that exports its soil in the form of rude products, must end in the export of men. Trading centralization tends to annihilation of local centres, exhaustion of the soil, and destruction of the value of land and man. Errors of Ricardo-Malthusian teachers. Declining power of association throughout the American Union.

§ 3. Error in one community tends to the production of error in all. British warfare on the manufactures of other nations tends to the production of slavery abroad and at home.

§ 4. Tendency towards over-population in the direct ratio of the separation of the prices of raw materials and finished commodities. Countries which follow in the lead of England are those which furnish the facts required for demonstrating the truth of Malthusian doctrines.

§ 1. Look to the great Asiatic plateau from what quarter we may, we see vast bodies of men passing from it, north, south, east, and west, towards the lower and richer lands of the world, the soils first occupied having been those possessed in the least degree of the food-producing properties. From that point it is that the European races have passed to occupy the lands created for their use. At every stage of progress we see them stopping in their course and giving themselves to the cultivation of the higher and poorer soils—the dry Arcadia and the rocky Attica—the Etrurian and Samnite hills—the Alpine slopes—the sterile Brittany—the Scottish highlands—the Scandinavian mountain-sides—or the rock-bound Cornwall. With the growth of wealth and population, however, we find them everywhere spreading themselves over the lower slopes, and finally descending into the valleys, the facilities for combination increasing with every year; the latent powers of the earth becoming more developed; commodities steadily declining, and man as steadily rising, in value; with corresponding development of the various individualities of the persons of whom the society is composed.

"Nature," as we are told, and as we have reason to know, "goes on, adding perfection to perfection, from the poles to the tropics, except in man." So however, does she, as she passes downwards from the snowy peaks of the Himalaya to the richer soils by which they are surrounded, whether her route be towards Siberian plains, or Gangetic valleys—towards Chinese swamps, or Ægean shores—the world at large being little more than a repetition, on a grander scale, of what is seen in each of its divisions, great and small.

The whole was given for man's use—to be by him subdued; and yet how small is the proportion he has, as yet, subjected to his use! Look almost where we may, the richer soils remain unoccupied—Switzerland abounding in population while the rich lands of the lower Danube are lying waste—men gathering together on the slopes of the Andes while the rich soils of the Orinoco and the Amazon remain in a state of nature—France and Germany, Italy and Ireland, presenting on a smaller scale a state of things precisely similar. Seeing these facts, we are led necessarily to the belief that man has made but little progress in the execution of the divine command; and yet, turn in what direction we may, we are met by the assertion that all the poverty and wretchedness of mankind is due to that one great error in the divine laws in virtue of which population tends to increase more rapidly than the food and other raw materials required for the satisfaction of his wants and the maintenance of his powers.

"America," says a distinguished writer of our day, "lies glutted with its vegetable wealth, unworked, solitary. Its immense forests, its savannas, every year cover its soil with their remains, which, accumulated during the long years of the world, form that deep bed of vegetable mould, that precious soil, awaiting only the hand of man to work out all the wealth of its inexhaustible fertility." Looking to the tropics everywhere, we see so rank a luxuriance of growth that the works of man are scarcely abandoned before they commence to disappear under trees and foliage. A space of 100 square metres, containing 100 banana plants, gives according to Humboldt more than 2000 kilogrammes of nourishing substance—the quantity of nutritive matter obtained being as 133 to 1, when compared with land employed in raising wheat, and as 44 to 1, when compared with potatoes. In Ecuador, this wonderful vegetation never ceases, both the plough and the sickle being required at every season of the year. So is it in Venezuela and in the Peruvian valleys, barley, rice, and sugar, growing in the highest perfection, and the climate permitting both planting and reaping throughout the year. The valley of the Orinoco, alone, has been stated to be capable of furnishing subsistence for the whole human race. Of bread-fruit trees but three are required for furnishing abundant food for a full-grown man. Rice yields an hundred fold, and maize no less than three hundred fold.

Nevertheless, these rich lands, being almost entirely unoccupied, are scarcely at all available for human purposes. Why? Because nature is there all-powerful, it being there we find the greatest amount of heat, motion, and force. Are they forever to remain so useless? In answer, it may be said, that the obstacles to their occupation are little greater than, but two centuries since, stood in the way of the reclamation of the now rich meadows of Lancashire; or those which, even now, are presented to the Western emigrant, when seeking to reduce to cultivation the richest prairie lands. In all these cases the early man is weak for attack, nature being strong for resistance. From year to year he becomes more fitted for combination with his neighbor man, with constant growth in his powers, and constant decline in her's—each and every step in his progress, from the day on which he subjugates the horse to that on which he tames the electric force, enabling him more thoroughly *to turn against nature such of her own great powers as he has qualified himself to master.* He is constantly battering at her gates and overthrowing her walls; she, on her part, finding them crumbling to atoms about her ears, and with a rapidity that increases with each successive hour.

With every step in this direction there is a diminution in the quantity of muscular force required for the labors of the field, the mind gradually superseding the unassisted arm that had been at first employed. With each there is an increase of power to cultivate the richer soils, whether of the tropical or the temperate regions of the earth. Where is this to stop? Will it stop? Can it be that the richest portion of the earth is to remain forever in its present condition of utter uselessness? That it can be so may well be doubted by those who believe that nothing has been made in vain; and who find in the constantly-increasing utilization of the materials of which the earth is composed, evidence that such is certainly the case.*

* "Tropical nature cannot be conquered and subdued, save by civilized men, armed with all the might of discipline, intelligence, and of skilful industry. It is, then, from the northern continents

It is not, however, to the richer soils alone we are to look for extension of the fields of human operations, all experience proving the existence of a tendency towards the gradual equalization of the various soils of which the earth has been composed. In France, as has been shown, it exhibits itself in a most striking manner; and France is but the world at large in miniature. The railroad, by facilitating access to them, has already brought into activity large bodies of land that had before remained unused; and it is destined, ultimately, to do for whole provinces, states, kingdoms, and the world at large, what it has already done for portions of the soils of England, France, and the United States. Looking at all these facts, it is safe to say, that the power of the earth to afford subsistence to man is practically unlimited.

§ 2. How are all these lands to be ultimately rendered available for human purposes? The answer to this question is found in the fact, that *manufactures always precede and never follow the creation of a real agriculture.* In the absence of the former, all attempts at cultivation are limited to the work of tearing out and exporting the soil in the form of rude products, the country that pursues this policy *always ending in the exportation or annihilation of men.* Give to Turkey the power to develop her vast natural resources, enable her to make her own cloth, and a real agriculture will then arise, that will render the plains of Thrace and Macedonia once more productive. Place in Brazil the machinery required for utilizing her various ores, for making her own iron, and for converting her raw materials into clothing, and she, too, will soon exhibit to the world a state of things widely different from that which now exists. Let Carolina have the means of converting her cotton into cloth, and her millions of acres of rich meadow land will soon be made productive. Enable Illinois to mine her coal, her lead, and her iron ore, and her people will cease to see the product of the soil diminishing from year to year as now it does. Local centres of attraction being thus created in all those countries, each will then become a competitor with France and England, Belgium and Germany, for the *purchase* of labor, skill, and

that those of the south await their deliverance; it is by the help of the civilized man of the temperate continents, that it shall be vouchsafed to the man of the tropical lands to enter into the movement of universal progress and improvement, wherein mankind should share."—Guyot: *Earth and Man*, p. 330.

talent of all descriptions; and the greater that competition the greater will be the tendency towards absorbing the laborers of all those countries, the centrifugal and centripetal forces then tending daily towards a more perfect balance, with growing power, on the part of all, to make their own election whether to go abroad or remain at home. Whatever tends to *invite* emigration, is a measure that looks towards freedom. Whatever it may be that tends to *compel* emigration, its tendency is towards slavery.

Early Grecian colonization, as the reader has already seen, was a result of a counter-attraction, and therefore altogether voluntary. Later, when trade and war had become the sole occupation of the people, and when poverty and wretchedness were gradually extending themselves throughout the various classes of the state, colonization wholly lost its voluntary character, the form it then assumed being that of expeditions fitted out at the public cost for supplying the places, and taking possession of the lands, of earlier colonists who were now in course of being ruined by means of measures adopted for the maintenance of the ever-grasping central power.

Under the first of these, local centres, teeming with activity and life, were everywhere created. Directly the reverse of this has been, and is, the tendency of that modern colonization which is based upon the idea of cheapening labor, land, and raw materials of every kind, thus extending slavery throughout the earth. Under it, all local centres tend to disappear; the land declines in its power; production diminishes; the landholder acquires power; competition for the *purchase* of labor diminishes, while competition for its *sale* increases from year to year; and man becomes less free —with constantly-growing necessity for fleeing to other lands, if he would not perish of famine at home. Under it, Irishmen have been forced to fly their country, seeking in England and America the food and clothing that could no longer be obtained in their native land. Under it, the world has witnessed the annihilation of the local centres of India, attended with an amount of ruin to which there can be found "no parallel in the annals of commerce." Under it, Asiatic industry, "from Smyrna to Canton, from Madras to Samarcand," has received, as we are told by Mr. McCulloch, a shock from which it is unlikely ever to recover, the result being seen in the large export of Hindoo laborers to the Mauritius, and Chinese coolies to Cuba and Demarara. Under it, little short of two millions of blacks were carried to the British

West Indies, two-thirds of whom had disappeared before the passage of the act of Emancipation, leaving behind them no descendants. Under it, the people of Turkey and Portugal gradually decline in numbers, local centres disappearing, land declining in value, and the power of production diminishing from year to year. Under it, Canada has been deprived of all power to diversify her industry, and now presents to view vast bodies of people who are wholly unable to sell their labor—her power of attraction, as a corrector of the evils attendant upon transatlantic centralization, having, therefore, wholly ceased. Under it, China has been inundated with opium to such an extent as to have paved the way for a repetition, in that country, of the exhaustive process that has been pursued in India. Under it, the people of these United States have already exhausted many of the older States, and are now repeating the operation throughout the valley of the Mississippi. Look where we may, among the countries subjected to the British system, we find the results the same, the necessity for colonization growing steadily, with constant decline in the productiveness of the soil, and in the value of land and man.

By all the advocates of the Ricardo-Malthusian doctrine the past prosperity of the American people has been uniformly attributed to the abundance of fertile soils at their command. They have been supposed to be receiving wages for their services, *plus* the amount that elsewhere would be absorbed as rent. It being, however, the poorer soils that are first appropriated, and the richer ones remaining always unproductive until wealth and population have greatly grown, it is obvious that they have been wasting upon the former a vast amount of labor, while subjecting themselves to a tax of transportation greater than would have been required for the support of armies ten times larger than those of assembled Europe. Rich meadow lands in the Atlantic States have remained in a state of nature while millions of people have sought the West, there to obtain from an acre of land some 30 or 40 bushels of corn, three-fourths of which have been absorbed on their route to the distant markets. Acres of turnips or potatoes yield 12 or 14 tons, whereas the average yield of all the wheat land of the young Ohio is not as many bushels. The refuse of an acre of one would fertilize the poorer acres round it; whereas, the refuse of the other, sent to the distant market, finds its place on the soil of England. Bring the consumer to the side of the producer, and the latter may then raise those commodities of which the earth yields by tons. Separate the two, and the farmer finds himself limited to those of which the quantity is counted by bushels or by pounds.

Look where we may, we see that where local centres are created, where mines are opened, furnaces built, or mills established, land grows in price. Why it does so is, that where consumers and producers are brought together it becomes freed from the exhausting tax of transportation, and its owner is enabled to devote his time, mind, and means, towards compelling the rich soils to give forth the vast supplies of food of which they are capable, paying them back the refuse and thus maintaining his credit with the great bank upon which his drafts have become so large. To render meadow land worth the cost of clearing, the farmer *must* have a market in his neighborhood for his milk and cream, his veal and beef. To enable him to vary his culture, and thus improve his land, he must have facilities for the sale of potatoes and cabbages, as well as for that of rye and wheat. In the absence of that power—his rich lands not being worth the cost of clearing—he flies to the West, there to appropriate more land, to be in its turn exhausted. As a consequence of this it is, that a few millions of people are now scattered over so many millions of square miles, and are forced to devote so large a portion of their time and mind to the effort to obtain roads by aid of which they may economize a portion of that tax of transportation by the payment of which they are now impoverished.

The tendency of the American system is, as a rule, towards abstracting from nature's great bank all that it can be made to pay, giving it nothing in return—that tendency being a direct consequence of its failure to protect the people against that British system which has for its object the cheapening of land, labor, and the rude products of the earth. Such prosperity as has been attained by the people of the United States has *not* been due to the abundance of the land over which they have been dispersed. In all other countries men have been most poor when land was most abundant, and when the inhabitants had, apparently, most the choice between the poorer and the richer soils. Fertile land, uncultivated, abounded in the days of the Edwards, yet food was then obtained with far more difficulty than now. It is more abundant in Russia, Ceylon, Buenos Ayres, and Brazil, than in these United States, and yet they make but little progress. It was more abundant in France, in the days of Louis XV., than it now is, and yet men perished then "like flies in the autumn;" whereas, they are now well fed and clothed.

Prosperity comes with diversity in the demand for human effort—with development of human powers—with growing power of association—with division of the land—with competition for the purchase of labor—every step in that direction being accompanied by an increase in the power of the laborer to *determine for himself* whether to go abroad, or stay at home. Throughout the Union, emigration now (1857) increases, the power of association tending steadily to decrease. Hence it is, that the history of the past few years exhibits so rapid a growth of belief in the divine origin of human slavery, and of demoralization in the people and the State.

§ 3. There being in all the real and permanent interests of mankind a perfect harmony, error in one community tends necessarily to the production of error everywhere. The annihilation of the power of association throughout Ireland tended to compel the emigration of Irishmen to England, there, of course, cheapening labor to the great disadvantage of the English laborer.

The long-continued "warfare" upon the industry of other nations, described in a former chapter, carried on under the mistaken idea that the prosperity of the British people was to be promoted by "stifling in the cradle" all the manufactures of the world outside of Britain, was attended necessarily by the destruction of the smaller manufacturers of Britain herself, the result being seen in the facts, that there is now no place for the little capitalist in any department of manufacture, and that the proportion of society engaged in trade—obtaining a living by "snatching the bread out of other people's mouths"—is a constantly-increasing one. The necessity for emigration, among this class, grows, therefore, daily, the higher and lower classes becoming divided by a constantly-deepening and widening gulf.

Consolidation of the land driving the laborer to the cities, and consolidation of capital diminishing the competition for the *purchase* of labor in towns and cities, the power of the laborer to determine for whom he would work, and at what he would work, necessarily declined—the effect being seen in a growing increase in that competition for the *sale* of labor, now regarded as so indispensable to the progress of British manufactures, but which is only another name for slavery.

The wider the gulf which divides the great proprietors from the laborer on the land the greater is the space to be occupied by middlemen, and the smaller is the proportion retained by those who own the land, or those who do the work. The larger the space between the great manufacturer and the regiment of hands employed in his mill, the more numerous will be the intermediate agents, each and all anxious to obtain the largest prices for having the work done, while paying the smallest to those who do it.*

The system tends, everywhere, to the elevation of trade, at the expense of agriculture—looking, as it did in the days of Adam Smith, and as it now does, to the cheapening of all the raw materials of manufacture. Such being the facts, we need scarcely feel surprised at the expression, by one of the most enlightened of modern British writers, of the opinion, that it is neither an imaginary nor a distant evil, that the middle classes should "sink into nothing"—England then becoming "a Genoa in large, with one small class living in almost royal splendor and luxury, and the great mass of the community in rags and hunger."†

Under such circumstances it is, that the last few years have witnessed an amount of *involuntary* emigration from the British Islands, that is wholly without a parallel, except in the history of the African slave-trade. Australia has been peopled by convicts. Emigration commissioners have been employed in exporting the women who were required for pairing with the men who had been shipped abroad. Scotchmen have been expelled from their little holdings, and sent to Canada. Cottages, by tens of thousands, have been levelled

* "The feudalisation going on in our manufacturing social economy is very conspicuous in some of the great cotton factories. The master-manufacturer in some districts, who employs eight hundred or a thousand hands, deals in reality with only fifty or sixty sub-vassals, or operative cotton-spinners, as they are technically called, who undertake the working of so many looms, or spinning-jennies. They hire and pay the men, women, and children, who are the real operatives, grinding their wages down to the lowest rate, and getting the highest they can out of the master-manufacturer. A strike is often the operation of these middle-men, and productive of little benefit to, and even against the will of, the actual workmen. They are, in the little imperium of the factory, the equivalent to the feudal barons."—LAING: *Notes of a Traveller*, p. 177.

† *Ibid*, p. 188.

in Ireland, with a view to compel the exportation of the wretched people who had occupied them. Under such circumstances it was, that 2,144,802 persons left the United Kingdom in the short period of seven years, ending in 1854. Of these, it is probable that more than 100,000 perished on the road to their new homes, victims to the system which finds in buying in the cheapest market and selling in the dearest one the chief incentive to action, and sees in man a mere instrument to be used by trade.

§ 4. Man seeks to obtain power over nature. That he may obtain it, he must learn to utilize the various faculties by which he is distinguished from the lower animals. The more they are utilized, the more perfect becomes his power of combination with his fellow-man; the more are the various utilities of the earth developed; the more rapid is the societary circulation; the greater is the power of accumulation; the more equitable becomes the distribution; the greater is the competition for his services among the near and the distant soils, and the greater his power to make his election between them; the closer becomes the approximation of the prices of raw materials and finished commodities; and the greater is the tendency towards increase in the powers of land and man, and strength in the State, as here is shown:—

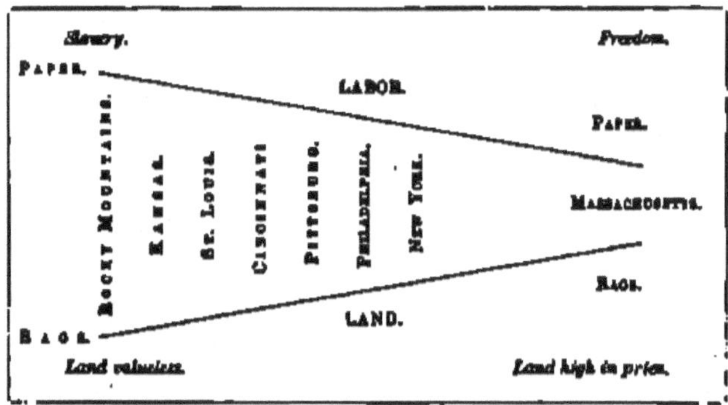

In that direction—passing from left to right—travel now all the countries that follow in the lead of Colbert and of France, and France herself. So, too, have sometimes travelled these United States, with rapid appreciation in the value of both land and man. As a rule, however, they have walked with Ireland, Turkey, Portugal, Jamaica, and other countries, under the lead of England—moving thus from right to left—and like them, have then been troubled with the disease of over-population.

The British policy is selfish and repulsive, its essential object being the separation of the consumers and the producers of the world. In that direction lie poverty and slavery; and therefore is it, that while England seeks to expel her people, no country of the world that follows in her lead, even when abounding in land that is unoccupied, offers any inducement to settlement except to those who are driven to it by poverty, if not even by actual want.*

The harmony of the world is maintained, as we have seen, by means of the perfect balance of the opposing attractive and counter-attractive forces. The more perfect the balance the more rapid is the societary motion, and the greater the tendency towards augmentation in the quantity of food obtained in return to any given quantity of labor. Throughout the realm now chiefly, even where not wholly, controlled by England, repulsion is universal; as a consequence of which the societary motion tends towards diminution, with growing tendency in all its parts to furnish, and on a larger scale, the facts required for establishing the doctrines of the Ricardo-Malthusian school.

* "One can scarcely open a newspaper from any part of the world just now in which we do not light upon a paragraph about the transfer of laborers from one country to another. The movement is so universal, in regard to intertropical colonies, and countries in near relation with them, that the question which naturally occurs to all simple-minded people is, why do not all these laborers stay where they are, and work at home? What is the use of their turning one another out, and running after or running away from each other, when each country has work to do, and people living there to do it? These simple questions appear to us perfectly rational; and no answer, we are confident, can be made which will satisfy any reasonable and honest mind. This wasteful and laborious shifting of the labor-supply—this costly effort to counteract the great natural laws of society—is a consequence of the prior violation of Nature's laws, which we call slavery, and which slaveholders describe as the beneficiary servitude of an inferior to a superior race."—*London Spectator*

CHAPTER XLI.

OF THE MALTHUSIAN THEORY.

§ 1. Constant tendency, according to Mr. Malthus, in all animated life, to increase beyond the nourishment prepared for it. Facts, however, prove that supply is, everywhere, a consequence of demand, the quantity of food prepared for beings of every kind being practically unlimited. Laws of nature vindicate the ways of God to man.

§ 2. Misery and vice attributed to deficiency in the powers of the earth to furnish food to increasing numbers. Facts of history prove the difficulty to lie with man himself, and not in errors of the Creator.

§ 3. Mr. Malthus gives facts, and calls them science. Science demands principles, asking, Why it is that such things are? Failure of Mr. Malthus to establish "the one great cause" of the various facts observed. His *Principle of Population* a mere form of words, indicating the existence of an altogether imaginary fact.

§ 4. Responsibility grows with the growth of the gifts of God to man. Poor labourer the slave of circumstances, yet held responsible for his acts. Tendency of the Malthusian doctrine to shift responsibility from the rich and strong to the poor, the weak, and the uninstructed.

§ 1. THE "one great cause" that has "hitherto impeded the progress of mankind towards happiness," that one to which are due the "vice and misery" so generally prevailing, as well as the existing inequality in the "distribution of the bounties of nature," is, as Mr. Malthus has told us, "the constant tendency in all animated life to increase beyond the nourishment prepared for it."* Before inquiring into the truth or falsehood of the idea thus propounded, it may be well to determine for ourselves the meaning of the word "prepared" as here submitted for our consideration. Were a parent to place at the command of his family the whole contents of a well-filled granary, would he, or would he not, have "prepared" for them a supply of food? Having given them, in the greatest superabundance, all the materials of fuel and clothing, and having endowed them with all the knowledge required for their conversion, could he be justly charged with not having "prepared" for them what was needed for the preservation of vital heat; that, too, for no other reason, than that he had refused to grind the corn, bake the bread, cut and transport the wood, weave the cotton, and then form the cloth into shirts and pantaloons? Having placed it in their own power to feed and clothe themselves if they would, could he be blamed if they then suffered from cold or hunger? Would the fault lie with him or them? Assuredly, not with him.

Looking now to the great family of mankind, we may in-

* *Principles of Population*, Book 1, chap. 1.

quire what is the real meaning of the word thus used, as connected with the provision made by the great Father of all for supplying its members with the food and clothing they require. Are we to conceive it as having reference only to the limited number of already organized forms, vegetable and animal, thinly scattered over the earth's surface, or as referring, far more properly, to the great stock of raw material capable of being made to assume those forms deposited in the great treasury of nature, and waiting only man's call to do him service? Have not the coal and ore now lying in the earth, and the corn and wool whose elements so much abound, been as much "prepared" for his uses, as the grass that grows upon the prairie? Has not the electricity everywhere existing been as much "prepared" for him, as that trivial quantity which manifests itself in the lightning's flash? Have not all the vast powers of earth and atmosphere, whensoever and wheresoever found, been "prepared" for his service, and has he not, himself, been endowed with all the faculties required for enabling him to compel them to minister to his wants, and aid in gratifying his desires? That such is the case is beyond all question. If, then, he perishes in the midst of this vast treasury, does the fault lie with his Creator, or with himself?

That men do so perish, and that, too, not unfrequently, we know. Why do they this? Because, as we are here told, of the insufficiency of the stock of nourishment "prepared" for their use. What evidence, however, have we of this? Have they ever found the treasury to have been exhausted? Have they not, on the contrary, found it full whenever they have complied with the conditions upon which, alone, the earth makes loans, that condition being the punctual return of the raw material after having used it? That this last has been the case is proved by the history of every advancing nation of the world, the supplies of food having increased more rapidly than the numbers of those among whom they were to be divided, in every country in which men have been enabled so to combine their efforts as to bring into activity the various powers with which they had been endowed

We are told, however, that this is an universal law, the tendency to increase beyond the subsistence that has been prepared being equally great throughout every portion of the animal world. On the other hand we learn that a single farm is capable of feeding more cattle than could find support in a whole country of forests. This being so, it is clearly obvious that more "nourishment" is, in the one case, required to be drawn from a single acre, than in the other is furnished by a hundred acres. Millions of buffaloes, as we know, could find support on prairies that now feed tens of thousands only, had man the knowledge required for enabling him to profit of the powers of the soil over which he roams. That he may anywhere obtain it he must learn to combine with his fellow-men, and divide employments with them, that being the condition upon which alone power can be obtained. Failing in this, the people of the prairies, as we may well suppose, unite with Ricardo-Malthusian writers in denouncing the "niggardliness of nature," when the real cause of difficulty is to be found in their own deficiencies.

Again, it is a well-known fact, that rapid as has been the growth of American population, that of the supply of oysters has been far more so, the consumption, per head, being greater, with thirty millions to feed, than when there was but a single million. Why is this? There has been no increase in the quantity of food "prepared" for such animals, the constituents of the water in which they grow being the same with those of the waters of the days of William Penn. Why, then, has there been so great a tendency towards this particular change in the form of matter—towards having inorganic matter take that certain organic form? Because, large as had been the store of force "prepared," it was compelled to remain latent and undeveloped, until man could qualify himself for its proper guidance and direction.

So far, then, from finding in the facts presented to us any foundation for the assertion of Mr. Malthus, even in regard to the lower animals, we meet, everywhere, with evidence that the quantity of food "prepared" for them, and for man himself, is practically unlimited, and that it rests with him alone to determine to what extent the elements shall take the form desired, the supply of sustenance tending to increase in the ratio of the demand. On the other hand, we are everywhere presented with the important facts, that just in proportion as he qualifies himself for drawing on the great bank, the absolutely necessary drafts of the individual man tend to diminish; that the growth of power in himself is attended by corresponding decrease in the quantity of food required for repairing the daily waste; that vegetable food, of which the earth yields by tons, tends to take the place of animal food, of which it yields by pounds; he himself assuming, more and more, the responsible position for which he was intended, and nature co-operating in the work by directing to the development of his brain those elements which, otherwise, would have been appropriated to the work of generation.

Study the laws of nature where we may, we find them vindicating the ways of God to man, each and every step on the road towards knowledge bringing us to a more complete perception of the perfect adaptation of the machinery to the production of the great effect desired—that of fitting the human animal for worthily occupying the place for which it from the first was destined.

§ 2. "A thousand millions of men," as we are assured by Mr. Malthus, "are just as easily doubled every twenty-five years, by the principle of population, as a thousand." Why, then, have they not increased? At the commencement of our era there were probably that number of persons on the earth, and it is doubtful if there are more at the present moment. Had they doubled in each succeeding quarter of a century, they would now count by billions of millions. Why have they not? Because in all that time, as we are told, population has been pressing upon subsistence, the tendency of matter to assume the form of highest development having been so much greater than that manifested in regard to those lower forms in which it becomes "prepared" for man's use, as to cause the existence of wide-spread "vice and misery," thus producing a necessity for the positive checks of "diseases and epidemics, wars, plague, and famine." Which, however, in these cases, is the cause, and which the consequence? Are misery and vice the cause of deficiency in the supply of food, or is this latter a necessary consequence of failure in man to exercise the faculties with which he has been endowed? This is a highly important question, deficiency in man himself being within the reach of man's correction, whereas deficiency in the powers of the great machine given for his use is entirely beyond the reach of remedy.

Seeking a reply to it, we are met by the facts, that the supply of food, in the last few centuries, has increased in its ratio to the population, in England, France, Belgium, Germany, and all other countries, in which—population and wealth having been permitted to increase—man has acquired greater power to draw upon nature's treasury; while diminishing in Turkey, Mexico, and other countries, in which, population and wealth having declined, his power to command the services of nature has steadily diminished. Look around us now where we may, we find that where the power of association is a growing one, it is accompanied by an increase in the supply of food, clothing, houses, and all other commodities and things required for man's support and comfort. Wherever, on the contrary, it is a diminishing one, the supply of all these things as steadily decreases—the value of man declining, and he himself becoming more and more the slave of nature and his fellow-man. Such being the case, the cause of present difficulty would seem to be in man himself, and not in any defect in that scheme of creation in which he had been assigned so great a part.

§ 3. Admitting, however, for the moment, that the facts have been as described by Mr. Malthus—that population has, throughout all those countries, been pressing upon subsistence—we shall still have made but little progress towards scientific truth; science always desiring to know *why it is* that such things are. For thousands of years it had been remarked that apples fell to the ground, but it was left to Newton to answer the question, why is it that apples fall? Science then asked, as it now asks, *why is it* that food cannot keep pace with population? What is the "one great cause," THE ULTIMATE CAUSE, of difficulty? Is it to be found in man's inability to make demands upon the earth, or in the incapacity of the earth to meet the drafts he makes? Is it true, can it be true, that with the growth of population and of wealth, there comes a time when "every increase of produce is obtained by a more than proportionate increase in the application of labor to the land," man thus becoming nature's slave as he grows himself in power? If he does so, why is it? Is it possible that man may, by any effort, place himself in the position for which he had been intended, that of nature's master? Is there any room for hope, or must he live on, knowing that in virtue of a great and over-ruling law the time must come when they who own the land will hold as slaves all those who need to work it? To all these latter questions, the answer is to be determined by that given to the first and greatest of them: What is the ONE great cause of the "vice and misery" now so obviously existing throughout the world? That is the question Mr. Malthus has professed to answer. How far he has done so we may now inquire.

Commencing with the American Indians, he tells his readers that the women are "far from being prolific;" that their unfruitfulness has been attributed by some to a "want of ardor in the men;" that this "is not, however, peculiar to his race," it having been remarked by Bruce and Vaillant in regard to various tribes of Africa. The causes of this are not, as he thinks, to be found in "any absolute constitutional defect, diminishing as it does nearly in proportion to the degree in which" the hardships and dangers of savage life are diminished or removed. What is, in this case, the cause of difficulty? The ONE great cause cannot here be seen, yet "vice and misery" much abound. Why is it so? Is it because of too great a tendency towards human reproduction, or is it an absence of disposition or ability in man to make the earth produce? By the admission of Mr. Malthus himself, it is the latter—"vice and misery" here resulting from the operations of the creature, and not from laws instituted by the Creator. What then becomes of his *Principle of Population?*

Turning now towards South America, we find that "in the interior of the province bordering on the Orinoco, several hundred miles may be traversed in different directions without finding a single hut, or observing the footsteps of a single creature." This is, nevertheless, one of the richest regions of the world—one in which there is perpetual summer—and in which maize yields three hundred fold. Why is it that population does not here increase?—it being, according to Mr. M., an undoubted fact that numbers are limited only by the difficulty of obtaining food, and that they tend, always and everywhere, to outrun subsistence. Where is the ONE great cause of which we are in search, and which he would here exhibit?

Looking next to Peru, we find that, having been led "by a fortunate train of circumstances to improve and extend their agriculture," its people "were enabled to increase in numbers," in spite of "the apathy of the men, or the destructive habits of the women." Nothing is here said of "population pressing on subsistence;" it being quite too obvious that the large numbers of people gathered together on the poor lands of the western slope of the Andes had been far better supplied with food than the scattered savages who wandered over the fertile soils of the eastern one, a single acre of which could furnish more food, in return to the same labor, than could be obtained from a dozen in Peru. Thus far, therefore, we have made no approach to the determination of the ONE great cause of the prevalence of "vice and misery" among mankind.

Passing now to the rich islands of the South Pacific, we find tribes of people who live on human flesh, and who, being perpetually at war with each other, "naturally wish to increase the number of their members," with a view to "greater power of attack or defence." No customs here prevail among the women unfavorable to the progress of population. Yet, admirable as is the climate, and fertile as is the soil, they are few in number. Food, nevertheless, is so scarce as to render it "not improbable that the desire of a good meal should give additional force to the desire of revenge, and that they should be perpetually destroying each other by violence as the only alternative of perishing by hunger." Does the difficulty here experienced lie with man, or with the earth? If the former, what becomes of Mr. Malthus's *one* great cause of vice and misery?

Infanticide and immorality abounding in Tahiti, Mr. Malthus was of opinion that when depopulation should have run its course, a change of habits "would soon restore the population, which could not long be kept below its natural level without the most extreme violence." That level being the supply of food, and food being here exuberantly abundant, it is clear that the "*one* great cause" cannot, on this occasion, be produced. Inequality in the distribution of the proceeds of labor being one of those phenomena of society which were to be accounted for by the constant pressure of population against subsistence, the reader of Mr. Malthus's work can scarcely fail to be surprised at finding him here asserting that "In all those countries where provisions are obtained with great facility," those of course in which the "*one* great cause" cannot be found, "a most tyrannical distinction of rank prevails," the people being "in a state of comparative degradation."

The peasants, under the Turkish rule, "desert their villages, and betake themselves to a pastoral state," hoping thereby better "to escape from the plunder of their Turkish masters, and Arab neighbors." The "one great cause" of vice and misery that Mr. Malthus desired to establish was the inability of the earth to answer the demands of man, but here he only proves the inability of man to make demands upon the earth.

Quoting from Park, Mr. Malthus describes "the wonderful fertility of the soil of Africa, and its vast herds of cattle"

—regretting "that a country so abundantly gifted by nature should remain in its present savage and neglected state." The cause of this is to be found in the fact that "they have not many opportunities of turning to account the surplus produce of their labor." Why have they not? Because they need more population—enabling them so to diversify their employments as to give them the "opportunities" they so much require—making a market on the land for all the products of their fertile soils. Absence of demand for food, however, can scarcely be adduced as proof that population tends to increase more rapidly than food. Park having attributed the dearths that frequently occurred to want of people, Mr. Malthus himself replies that what they really need is "security, and its general concomitant, industry"—and therein he is right. Population *would* then increase, and dearths *would* disappear, the great bank being prepared to answer all the drafts that can be made upon it. What, however, in this case becomes of the "one great cause?"

"The principle of increase in Egypt," as we are told, "does all that it is possible for it to do," keeping "the population fully up to the level of subsistence." A more natural explanation of the phenomena here observed would be, that insecurity and oppression keep the supply of food below the level of population. Such an one, however, would have no tendency to prove the existence of the alleged "great cause," the insufficiency of the powers of the earth to meet the demands of man.

Haunted by the idea of an imaginary fact, Mr. Malthus pressed into his service a quantity of real ones, all of them tending to prove how steadily and generally men had been engaged in preventing themselves from obtaining command of the food "prepared" for them, but none of them tending in any degree whatsoever to prove that the supply had not everywhere increased in full proportion to their power to make demand. Instead of establishing the existence of his "one great cause," he has given us an almost infinite variety of causes out of which to select the one to which we may be best disposed to attribute the "vice and misery" that are everywhere around us. In his anxiety to effect his object facts are frequently distorted, the rapid increase of population in the Western American States being first treated as a result of natural increase and without allowance for immigration, and the increase of early German tribes being then assumed as having been fully equal to that observed throughout the

United States. Where facts cannot be given, suppositions and probabilities are furnished, all of them tending, of course, to the establishment of the great facts, that the principle of increase in man is greater than in the lower forms of organized matter; that population must, therefore, outrun subsistence; and, of course, that the Creator had made a serious blunder.

Occasionally his views are accurate, as when he tells his readers that where there are no manufactures raw produce will be cheap, and finished commodities dear; that, in countries in which the agricultural system entirely predominates, "the condition of the people is subject to almost every degree of variation;" that commerce and manufactures are necessary to agriculture; and that the poverty and wretchedness of Africa, and other countries in which fertile soils so much abound, are due to that want of power to maintain commerce which always results from absence of diversity in the demand for human faculties. Rejecting these truths, while adopting all his errors, his countrymen have been most consistent in the effort to prevent the establishment of manufactures in any country outside of Britain, thereby producing, or perpetuating, throughout the world the "vice and misery" described by Mr. Malthus, and by him attributed to what he called the "Principle of Population;" that principle being a mere form of words, indicative of the existence of a great, but altogether imaginary, fact.

Few books have exercised a greater influence, yet few have had less claim to the exercise of any influence whatsoever. Few have been so prejudicial to the modes of thought, and yet no one can hesitate to believe that its author was prompted by a desire of benefiting his fellow-men.

§ 4. Responsibility grows with the growth of the gifts of God to man, he who is rich in the development of his powers, and, therefore, capable of influencing the societary action, being responsible to his fellow-men and to his Creator for the full and strict performance of his duties. The poor laborer, on the contrary, is the slave of circumstances over which he exercises no control, rising, as he so frequently does, uncertain where he shall find his daily bread, and sleeping supperless because of his having found that society did not "need his labor," and had, therefore, allowed him no place "at the table" provided for all mankind. Again and again failing to exchange his services for food, he returns to his wretched home, to encounter there the demands of a starving wife and children. Despairing, he steals a loaf, society then holding him to a strict accountability while maintaining the existence of great natural laws, in virtue of which a large proportion of every population must "regularly die of want."

That there is much of vice and misery in the world is an undoubted fact. Mr. Malthus says that it is the natural result of a divine, and therefore inevitable, law—the result, as we see, being that of relieving the governing classes of the world from any possible responsibility for the welfare of those below them. Both religion and common sense, however, teach, that the Being who made this wonderful world, in which every part is so perfectly adapted to the production of harmony, could have imposed upon man no law tending to the production of discord; that vice and misery are consequences of human error, and not of divine laws; and that the men who exercise power, and control the societary movement, are responsible for the condition of those around them. Such is the difference between Social Science, and the doctrines of the Ricardo-Malthusian school—the one holding the rich and strong to a high responsibility, while the other shifts the whole of it to the shoulders of those who, being poor and weak, are unable to defend themselves.

The one holds to a belief in the great law of Christianity, which teaches that men should do to others as they would that others should do unto them; that where there are old, blind, lame, or otherwise helpless persons, it is the duty of the strong and the rich to see that they are provided for. The other teaches, that "charity, in applying itself to the relief of the distressed, does but augment the number of the poor;" that population is superabundant, and that there is no remedy but that of "starving out the surplus;" that marriage is "a luxury" in which the poor have no right to indulge; that it is "an enjoyment" to which "the poor have no right until they have made provision for their expected family;" that "labor is a commodity," and that if poor men *will* marry and have children, and "we stand between the error and its consequences," which are poverty, wretchedness, and death, "we stand between the evil and its cure"—thus intercepting the penalty, and perpetuating "the sin." As taught by Messrs. Malthus and Ricardo, social science has been well described as being "the philosophy of despair, resting upon an arithmetic of ruin."

CHAPTER XLII.

OF COMMERCE.

I.—*Of the Relations of the Sexes.*

§ 1. Relations of the sexes. Woman a slave to man, in the early stages of society. Her condition improves as wealth and population grow, and as the real MAN is more developed. The more rapid the societary circulation, and the greater the tendency towards the creation of a scientific agriculture, the more does the sex tend towards occupying its true position.

§ 2. Condition of woman in Central and Northern Europe. Woman rises in the scale as land becomes divided, and man becomes more free.

§ 3. Saxon women sold to slavery. General improvement in the condition of the women of England. Loss of the rights of property secured to them by the early English law. Deterioration of the condition of the sex, in all the countries that follow in the train of England.

§ 4. How the condition of English women is affected by trading centralization. Growing competition for the sale of female labor. Consequent low wages, and necessity for resorting to prostitution. Protection tends to produce competition for its *purchase*, thereby benefiting the sex throughout the world.

§ 5. Extraordinary contrasts presented by the condition of the sex in the several portions of the American Union. Theory of the government favorable to the creation of local centres, and to the elevation of the sex. Its practice, tending towards centralization, adverse thereto, and hence the rapid growth of female crime and prostitution.

§ 1. THE American Indian wastes in idleness the time that is not employed in war, or in the chase, leaving to his miserable squaw the labors incident to the care of his children, and to the frequent changes of place. He shoots the deer: she carries it home. He helps himself, and if there is enough for both she may eat. If there is not, she must fast. The savage Australian marks his wife by breaking the joints of her fingers and knocking out her front teeth, thereafter treating her as a beast of burthen. The African buys his wife, and sells his daughters. The Turk fills his harem with slaves, holding their lives at their master's pleasure.—Woman is, thus, the slave of man, where man himself is nature's slave.

As he gradually becomes nature's master the distinctive qualities of the MAN become developed, and he becomes fixed at home. Cultivation takes the place of mere appropriation, domestic habits gradually replace his former wandering ones, and his wife acquires importance as the mistress of his house, the companion of his joys and his sorrows, and the mother of his children. Brain gradually taking the place of mere muscle, the weak woman passes by slow degrees from the condition of man's slave towards that of his companion and his friend.

Woman's value grows with the growth of demand for her peculiar powers, that, too, growing with the growth of wealth. Capital is, thus, the great equalizer, the demand for female faculties growing in the direct ratio of the development of man's latent powers.

Look where we may, we see that as the consumer takes his place by the producer's side the latent forces of the earth become stimulated into activity and land becomes divided, with growing tendency towards giving to every man a home of his own, to be to him a little savings' bank for all his surplus powers, and for those kindly feelings and affections which await the demands of wife and children. Improvement in woman's condition comes, thus, as man becomes more individualized and self-reliant. For proof of this, we must refer the reader once again to the diagram so often placed before him, desiring that he should trace the gradual change in the condition of the sex as he passes from the region of undivided land and homeless men, on the left, towards that of divided land and cultivated homes, on the right.

Look in what direction we may, we find new evidence that it is in the near approach of the prices of rude products and finished commodities, and consequent increase in the value of man and land, we are to find the most conclusive evidence of advancing civilization. With every stage of approximation the middlemen class, whether soldiers or sailors, traders or politicians, diminishes in its proportions, with correspondent decline in power. With each, the circulation becomes more rapid—agriculture tends more to become a science—and woman tends more towards occupying her proper place, that of man's first and nearest friend—stimulating him into activity and heightening his enjoyments, while ever ready to administer consolation in his afflictions.

§ 2. France, perpetually engaged in foreign and domestic wars, presents to view at home, during many centuries, striking contrasts in the condition of the sex, the poverty of the laboring many being in precise accordance with the magnificence of the few who live at their expense. As the feudal system was extended and the smaller proprietors disappeared, the homes of wives and daughters became less and less secure—the right of *jambage and cuissage* becoming, at length, so universally asserted, and so generally exercised, as to cause the eldest son of the tenant to be held more honorable than his brothers, because of his highly probable relation to the lord. —Abroad, her history is one of unceasing interferences with the rights of others. Towns and cities have been ruined, husbands and sons, by hundreds of thousands, slaughtered, while wives and mothers have been compelled to endure the last indignity to which their sex is liable, and daughters have been driven to prostitution as affording the only means of obtaining food. Educated abroad in the career of rape and murder her sons have practised at home what they so well had learned, the domestic history of no country of Europe exhibiting so total a disregard of female rights or honor as may there be found, from the days of Charles the Bold and his "good butchers," to those of the *noyades* and the guillotine of the Revolution.

With every stage, however, in the consolidation of the land, we find individual women become more and more the controllers of their country's destinies, the history of that country, from the days of Fredegonda and Brunechild to those of Maintenon, Pompadour, and Du Barré, exhibiting the subjection of a nation to female influence elsewhere unparalleled. With the final adoption of the system of Colbert, however, there came a change, land becoming divided, feudal rights disappearing, and the small proprietor, capable of defending the honor of his wife and daughters, gradually taking the place that theretofore had been occupied by the nobles and the Church. Further division coming, millions of people whose predecessors had been little better than mere serfs, obtain lands, houses, and homes of their own, of which the wife is chief director. "Females, both in France and Switzerland," says Mr. Laing, in his *Notes of a Traveller*, "appear to have a far more important rôle in the family, among the lower and middle classes, than with us. The female, although not exempt from out-door work, and even hard work, undertakes the thinking and managing department in the family affairs, and the husband is but the executive officer. The female is, in fact, very remarkably superior in manners, habits, tact, and intelligence, to the husband, in almost every family of the middle or lower classes in Switzerland. . . . In France, also, the female takes her full share of business with the male part of the family, in keeping accounts and books, and selling goods, and, in both countries, occupies a higher and more rational social position certainly than with us This seems to be the effect of the distribution of property, by which the female has her share and interest as well as the male, and grows up with the same personal interest and sense of property in all around her."

Throughout central and northern Europe the tendency is in the same direction, land becoming divided, men becoming more free, and woman assuming a higher place in the social scale as, with the growing power to command the use of steam and other forces, the taste and skill of the weaker sex are substituted for the muscular force of man. Such is now the tendency in Sweden and Denmark, Belgium, Northern Germany, and Russia, all of which follow in the lead of Colbert and of France. In all of these, Russia perhaps excepted, the right of the wife to the ownership of separate property, as well as her claim upon the husband's estate in case of death, is fully recognized. In none, however, does woman yet occupy her true position, the eye of the traveller being perpetually offended by the sight of women carrying burdens wholly disproportioned to their strength, and engaged in other occupations more suited to sons or husbands.

What is needed, however, to be determined is not the actual condition of any people, but the point towards which society is tending, gradual as may be the movement. In all these countries the laborer has but recently been a mere serf, and all, Germany especially, have suffered greatly from both foreign and domestic wars.

§ 3. In the days of the Plantagenets Saxon women were sold as slaves, Scotch and Irish men becoming purchasers. With the growth of wealth and population, however, their condition gradually improved; yet even so late as the days of Blackstone, the common people exercised the privilege, secured to them by the older law, of giving their wives "domestic chastisement," in "moderation."

As regards the right of property, the position of English women is far inferior to that secured to them by the early English law. So recently as the reign of Charles I., the wife retained all her own real estate, while entitled to a third of the property of her husband at his death. Now, the law gives to the husband the whole of the wife's property, while securing to her nothing whatsoever. However profligate may be the husband she can have no separate property, all her earnings being liable for his debts. In no part of the world, claiming to be held as civilized, is the wife so entirely at the mercy of the husband as in England.

In all the countries that follow in the train of Britain the societary proportions of the middlemen class are constantly increasing, when they should decrease. In all such cases it is the woman who suffers most, the man being able to change his place, while wife and children must remain at home. The annihilation of Irish manufactures having deprived Irish women of the employments to which they had been accustomed, where could they then seek to sell their labor? The whole Irish people having been reduced to the condition of mere "starvers upon potatoes and water," the men could yet roam abroad, seeking employment in England, or even beyond the ocean; but who were left to furnish food to hundreds of thousands of wives and mothers, daughters and sisters, left behind? Where "popular starvation," as we are told by a distinguished English writer, had become "the condition" of a whole people, what *could* be done with those who were weak of body or of mind? It is under such circumstances that man becomes a slave to nature, and woman a slave to man.

Passing now to Turkey, we are there presented with a picture, drawn by an English traveller, of the "hopeless competition" of industrious women and children, with the machinery of England—the latter working assiduously "from the moment their little fingers can turn the spindle," and the former giving the unremitting labor of a week for the miserable pittance of an English shilling, even where not wholly deprived of employment by reason of inability to dispose of the yarn which they have spun.

Turkey and India exhausted, we now witness a persistent effort at the demoralization of China by means of opium, *forced into that country in defiance of governmental opposition.* For the accomplishment of that object two wars have been waged, in which cities have been stormed, men have been killed, and women have been violated. How far such measures tend towards the advancement of civilization, may be judged of by American women who see in the dram-shop the greatest foe to domestic happiness and peace.

It is in the face of all this that the women of England address those of America in relation to the evils of slavery, while an English clergyman congratulates his readers on the facts, that "no civilized power" has ever been "engaged in such constant and multitudinous wars," there having been "no month or week in the history of the last two hundred years, in which it could be said" that they were "not interchanging shot or sabre stroke, somewhere or other on the surface of the globe." And this, as he further says, "is an indispensable part of the British position."

The British system gives us thus perpetual war *upon* the nations of the world by means of soldiers and sailors, and a perpetual "warfare" *within the bosom* of all those nations, this last being carried on by aid of those great capitalists who can afford to make the "sacrifices required for gaining and keeping possession of foreign markets." Against whom, however, is this double warfare chiefly carried on? It is against the weaker sex. Unfit for field labors, they find themselves driven from the light labor of conversion. And what then remains to them? In millions of cases little else than prostitution; yet are we constantly assured of the civilizing effects of that trading system, to which the term "commerce" is so erroneously applied.

§ 4. Since the days of Adam Smith more than 160,000 small proprietors have disappeared from England, so many homes having lost the husbands, wives, fathers, and mothers, who, less than a century since, stood upon their own land and among their own children. Driven from the land, the parents seek for homes in the towns and cities, wives and children seeking employment in mines and factories. Simultaneously, however, with the consolidation of the land we have the consolidation of great capitals, ever ready to crush domestic or foreign competition for the purchase of labor, or the sale of labor's products. The result is seen in the harrowing Reports of Parliamentary Committees, reports in which we are presented with females working like slaves, and perfectly naked, among boys and men, in the mines; with wives and daughters subjected to an amount of physical effort for which they were not intended by the Creator to whom they owe their miserable existence. Recently there has been an effort at improvement; the working of women in the mines having been, under certain circumstances, prohibited, and the hours for employment for children limited by law—the very necessity for such laws furnishing evidence of the absence of that competition for the purchase of labor which would enable the laborer to obtain a fair day's wages for a fair day's work. The "wasting shop," in which women are compelled to work 16 or 20 hours per day, and under a temperature so high as far to exceed the heat of the torrid zone—the shop in which their lives are "expended like those of cattle on a farm"—still exists; and all attempts at interference, with a view to the protection of these helpless women, is resisted, because of the "keenness of the competition" for the sale of cloth. What, however, is the object of this competition? That of preventing the women of India, Ireland, and America, from finding purchasers for their labor, physical or mental. The English woman is thus degraded into an instrument for crushing her fellow-women throughout the world, her own poverty, wretchedness, and recklessness, being then adduced as evidence of the truth of the doctrine of over-population. Driven to despair, hopeless of improvement in this world and careless about the future, she next is urged to the adoption of the Malthusian panacea of "moral restraint!" It is a mere mockery of words to suggest the idea under existing circumstances.

Centralization forces Irish women to seek in England purchasers for their labor, thus augmenting the competition for its sale and giving to those who need to purchase power to determine what shall be the quantity of effort given, and what the compensation paid. *That is slavery.* Centralization, in like manner, is producing the effect of making London the only place in England itself for the sale of female taste or skill, while greatly limiting the range of female employments. The effect is seen in the unhappy condition of poor girls who aspire to become milliners, compelled, as they are, to labor, for months together, no less than 20 hours out of the 24—breathing the foul air of the workshops, and receiving the poorest food in exchange for instruction of which they are perpetually defrauded. Consumption closes the career of these more delicate instruments of trade, leaving to the hardier and less-aspiring journeywomen to seek in prostitution the means of support in the intervals of seasons.

Lower, even, than these latter, are the slop-workers, the "horrors" of whose "white slavery," says a recent writer, "have not been exaggerated." "How," he continues, "could such colossal fortunes be made by Hebrew and other outfitters, if the soil from which the harvest issued were not plentifully watered and manured with blood and tears? Everybody knows that London is full of 'distressed needle-women.' But how, it may be asked, is this to be helped? There is a demand for cheap garments, and a demand for employment in the making of them, even greater than the demand for the garments themselves. Miserable as is the pittance they receive, it is better than nothing. It is better to be hungry than to die. You may see the poor creatures clustering about the doors of the slop-shops, with their sharp, eager faces, waiting for their supply of wretched work as though their very lives depended upon the issue. One wonders that it should be so—but so it is." An inquiry made some years since, showed that there were in London, of such persons, no less than 33,000, "permanently at the starvation-point—working at the wages of a few pence per day."

These poor women are all competing with each other for the sale of their only commodity, failing to dispose of which they are driven to prostitution. Need we, then, wonder that it should be now probable that 50,000 females walk the streets of that great city, at night, "*wholly because they are unable to obtain a living in any other way.*" A large proportion of these, as we are assured, have been domestic servants, needle-women, waistcoat makers, etc., "driven to dishonesty by the difficulty of obtaining honest employment; *and there is scarcely one of them who would not forsake her unhappy calling to-morrow if honorable work could be provided for her.*" "We err," says the same writer, "more barbarously than those nations among whom a plurality of wives is permitted, and who regard women purely as so much live stock; for among such people women are, at all events, provided with shelter, with food, and clothing—they are 'cared for' as cattle are. There is a completeness in such a system. But we treat women as cattle without providing for them as cattle. We take the worst part of barbarism and the worst part of civilization, and work them into a heterogeneous whole. We bring up our women to be dependent, and then leave them without any one to depend on. There is nothing for them to lean upon; and they fall to the ground."

This is slavery, and of the worst kind, and the longer the system shall be maintained the more oppressive must it become—its foundation now, as in the days of Adam Smith, being found in the idea of cheapening labor and all other raw materials of manufacture. The tendency of the modern free-trade system is towards making of woman that mere instrument to be used by trade, so well described by Hood in his admirable but melancholy "Song of a Shirt."

Colonization being, as we are told, the remedy for excess of numbers, every nerve is strained in the effort to expel the surplus population. Who are they, however, who emigrate? The men—leaving wives, daughters, and sisters behind to provide for themselves as they may. The surplus of British females already exceeds half a million, and it must increase, the tendency of the existing system being that of dispersing the men in the hope of further cheapening the rude produce of the soil, and with the effect of increasing the competition for the sale of labor.

§ 5. Here, as everywhere, the American Union is a country of contrasts, one portion exhibiting woman in the enjoyment of a degree of freedom elsewhere unknown; while in another, females, married and unmarried, are passed from hand to hand as mere chattels, being sold at the auction-block, with or without fathers, husbands, sisters, brothers, children.—Looking towards commerce, the tendency, in the former, has been towards the creation of local centres, facilitating association, and producing development of the latent powers of the earth, and of the men and women for whose use that earth was given.—Believing in the omnipotence of trade, and seeking the extension of its dominion, the latter has moved in the reverse direction—the result being seen in annihilation of local centres, diminution of the power of association, exhaustion of the soil, and limitation of demand for female powers.—In the one, the tendency is uniform in the direction of such alterations of the English law as shall give to the wife a separate right of property. In the other, it has as uniformly been in that of taking from woman the power, under any circumstances, to obtain the right of property in themselves.

Centralization, however, grows daily, and with its growth we find a tendency to the production in the first of the evils that, as we see, have been produced in England Exhaustion of the soil of the older States expels the men, while leaving helpless women behind to seek a livelihood as best they may. Manufactures decline, with constant diminution in the demand for female skill and taste, and corresponding tendency towards forcing them to seek, in distant cities, the employment no longer found at home. Competition for the *sale* of female labor, therefore, grows steadily, thousands being "crazy to work at any price." Look where we may, throughout the Union, we shall find conclusive evidence that freedom for both man and woman comes with diversity in the demand for human powers; slavery, with all its attendant evils, being a necessary consequence of limitation to the labors of the field. American policy tends in the latter direction, and therefore it is that crime and prostitution so rapidly increase. How it affects the relations of the family, we may next inquire.

CHAPTER XLIII.

OF COMMERCE—CONTINUED.

II.—*Of the Relations of the Family.*

§ 1. Relations of the Family. Weakness of the Family ties, in the early stages of society. Responsibility, in both parent and child, grows with division of the land, and with the approximation of consumers to producers.

§ 2. Education in Central and Northern Europe. Growing feeling of responsibility for proper training of youth, as manifested in all those countries in which employments are becoming more diversified.

§ 3. Reverse of this exhibited in those which follow in the train of England—employments there becoming less diversified. Condition of English children. Absence of provision for general education. Child-murder. Children regarded as mere instruments to be used by trade. Consequent necessity for a theory of over-population.

§ 4. Extraordinary contrasts here again presented by the American Union. That education given in the school may prove useful, it is needed that there be demand for the faculties there developed. That there may be such demand, it is required that there be diversity in the modes of employment. That the latter may exist, there is needed an exercise of the power of the State.

§ 1. The wretched savage, slave to nature and limited to the work of mere appropriation, sees in the birth of his child but an addition to his burthens, and, but for the affection of the mother, few, particularly of the weaker sex, would live for even a single day. Arriving at maturity, the child, in turn, sees in the parent only a useless competitor for the poor supply of food and buries him alive, or leaves him to become the prey of wolves.

The civilized man, master of nature, rejoices in each addition to his family circle. Cultivating the richer soils and finding in the neighboring markets a demand for all their products, his land and labor become, from day to day, more valuable. His leisure growing with every step in that direction, he is enabled to give his attention more fully to the formation of his children's characters, thus preparing them for becoming good and useful citizens. Combining with his neighbor, he aids in the establishment of schools and colleges, preferring the happiness and prosperity of future generations before his present appetites. The child, in turn, desires to aid his father in his age, paying the debts incurred in youth, and respecting his rights as his own had been respected.

Look where we may, we find that as employments become diversified the commerce of the family becomes more intimate, parents and children becoming more fully sensible of their responsibilities towards each other, and the holiness of home becoming more thoroughly appreciated.

§ 2. Of the European nations, one portion, as we know, follows in the lead of Colbert, seeking to place the consumer by the side of the producer, and thus relieve the farmer from the grinding tax of transportation. Chief among these is France, to which we now may turn, seeking to ascertain to what extent the pursuit of that policy has awakened any feeling of responsibility in reference to development of the youthful mind.

Always at war, abroad or at home, the tendency, throughout that country during many centuries, was in the direction of consolidation of the land, centralization of power in the nobles and the Church, and enslavement of the people. Famines and pestilences being of perpetual recurrence children were generally regarded as incumbrances, and of those that were born but a small proportion arrived at manhood. With the final adoption of Colbert's policy, however, there came a change, land becoming gradually divided, and the feeling of responsibility at length manifesting itself in a provision of the Constitution of 1791 by which it was declared, that there must be organized a system of instruction common to all, and "gratuitous, so far as regarded that instruction which was indispensable to all." Unceasing wars and revolutions, however, prevented progress in that direction, and, so recently as 1830, of all the young men subject to the conscription more than half could neither read nor write. As late as 1836, there were whole cantons, embracing fifteen or twenty communes, that were wholly destitute of schools, while, throughout the kingdom, out of nearly 23,000,000 adults, more than 14,000,000 could neither read nor write. Since then, however, the change has been very great—the law of 1833 having provided not only for gratuitous primary instruction, but, also, for a system of secondary instruction, calculated to fit the youth of the nation for employment in the arts, and in a scientific agriculture. In 1850, the total number of pupils in the primary schools was 3,784,797, having almost quadrupled in the short space of 20 years.

Turning now to Denmark, in which, but seventy years since, the peasant was liable to be flogged and imprisoned at the pleasure of his lord, we find that not only is one in every four of the population at school, but that libraries, museums, and newspapers, are to be found in all of the larger towns, while educational institutions, and other indications of intellectual tastes, are to be met with in all the smaller ones—local centres of industrial activity, meanwhile, providing for the application to the various purposes of life of the mind developed in the schools.

In Sweden, one in every six of the population being an attendant of the schools, it is rare to meet with a person who cannot read and write.

In Belgium, in 1830, the number of children attending the primary schools was 293,000. In 1856, it had risen to 1 in 8 of the total population.

In Northern Germany, every child, for the last 30 years, has been receiving a good education. "Four years since," says Mr. Kay, writing in 1850, "the Prussian Government made a general inquiry throughout the kingdom, to discover how far the school education of the people had been extended, and it was then ascertained that out of all the young men in the kingdom who had attained the age of twenty-one years, *only two in every hundred were unable to read.*

"In the towns of Germany and Switzerland," as he further says, "I was assured by Dr. Bruggeman, the Roman Catholic Counsellor in the Educational Office in Berlin, and by several teachers and other persons, that not only were the interesting works of German literature perused by the poorest people of the towns, but that translations of the works of Sir Walter Scott, and of many other foreign novelists and writers, were generally read by the poor.

"Often and often have I seen the poor cab-drivers of Berlin, while waiting for a fare, amusing themselves by reading German books, which they had brought with them in the morning expressly for the purpose of supplying amusement and occupation for their leisure hours.

"In many parts of these countries, the peasants and the workmen of the towns attend regular weekly lectures or weekly classes, where they practise singing or chanting, or learn mechanical drawing, history, or science.

"Women as well as men, girls as well as boys, enjoy in these countries the same advantages, and go through the same school education. The women of the poorer classes of these countries, in point of intelligence and knowledge, are almost equal to the men."

Half a century since, the total number of pupils in the schools of Spain was but 30,000; whereas, seven years since, it had increased to no less than 700,000—being 1 in 17 of the total population.

§ 3. Looking next to the countries that follow in the lead of England, we find that from India schools have almost disappeared; while Portugal and Turkey exhibit nothing that deserves the name of general education. Ireland, before the Union, as has been already shown, furnished so large a market for books as to warrant the republication of the principal works produced in England. With the Union that market wholly disappeared. Recently, an extensive system of instruction has been organized, and its results are highly spoken of; but of what avail is the education of the schools where there exists no demand for the faculties thereby developed? Ireland having no manufactures, and consequently no agriculture that deserves the name, there can be no power of combination; the faculties of the people must remain undeveloped; the societary circulation must remain more sluggish than that of any other country claiming to be civilized; and the great disease of over-population must continue to exist.

Arriving at the centre of this system, and the home of the over-population doctrine, it becomes essential to observe, that, while France has been the seat of civil and religious wars followed by repeated invasions of her soil by foreign armies; while Belgium has been the almost constant theatre of war for assembled Europe; and while Germany has been, for centuries, ravaged by contending armies; England has scarcely, since the Conquest, witnessed the presence of a hostile foot, and never, since the Scottish outbreak of 1745, heard the explosion of a hostile gun. Such having been the case, there exists the strongest reason for expecting to find her far in advance of Continental Europe in the manifestation of a feeling of responsibility for the proper training of her youth, and in the power to carry into effect all the measures by it suggested. So far, however, is it the reverse of this, that here it is we find a growing consolidation of the land, accompanied by a total failure on the part of the government to establish any system of education similar to those in Northern and Central Europe. As a consequence of this it is, says Mr. Kay, that, "of the children of the poor, who are yearly born in England, vast numbers never receive any education at all, while many others never enter any thing better than a dame or a Sunday-school. * * * Many town parishes," he continues, "are without any schools at all; the instruction given in most of the schools which are established is miserable in its character; infant schools are terribly needed in almost every town in England.

Efficient teachers are needed everywhere. Every child in Germany and Switzerland remains in school, or continues to receive education, from the age of six to that of fourteen, and often to that of sixteen or seventeen; while in England, even of those children who do go to school, few remain there beyond the age of nine or ten. If all this be true, is it to be wondered at that the dress of our peasants, their manners, their appearance, their amusements, their manner of speaking, their cleanliness, the character of their houses, the condition of their children, and their intelligence, should be all miserably inferior to those of the peasants of Germany, Holland, and of some parts of Switzerland and France?"

Of the males who are married in France and England, one-third make their marks when signing the parish register, the proportion in each being almost precisely the same. Of the females, rather less than half in England, and more than half in France, do so, the advantage, in this case, being on the side of the former. The question here, however, as everywhere, is not of actual condition, but of progress, and in this France takes the lead, the number of her day scholars having almost quadrupled in eighteen years, while in England it had not even doubled.*

Of the extent to which infanticide is carried we have spoken in a former chapter, but of that other species of child-murder which consists in the hiring out, by parents or

* Number of English day scholars in 1833, 1,548,890, or 1 in 11·27
" " " 1851, 2,407,409, or 1 in 8·36

The fact, however, is exhibited, says Mr. Tremenheere, in his report, that "the great bulk of the children leave the elementary schools *before they are ten years old*," that their attendance is very irregular, and that the little they may have learned "is all nearly lost after a few years."

"At the annual bindings," says Mr. Wood, Chairman of the Institute of Mining Engineers, "*there is scarcely a single man or boy who signs his own name to the bond; and yet these men and boys have gone through the schools, and we suppose that they have learned to read and write*, but they have left school at so early an age that *they lose what little they have learned*, and you find them incapable of writing their own names."

"Wherever we turn, ignorance, not always allied to poverty, stares us in the face. If we look in the *Gazette*, at the list of partnerships dissolved, not a month passes but some unhappy man, rolling perhaps in wealth, but wallowing in ignorance, is put to the *experimentum crucis* of 'his mark.' The number of petty jurors, in rural districts especially, who can only sign with a cross, is enormous."—DICKENS: *Household Words*.

guardians, of children ranging from 6 to 8, 10, and 12 years, it is proper here to speak. The persons to whom these poor creatures are transferred, and by whom they are tortured, says a recent English writer, "employ two sorts of machinery in their business: one being made of flesh, the other of wood and iron. If a wheel or strap becomes entangled," as she continues, "it is set to rights by the proper workman; if so injured as not to allow of speedy repairing, it is thrown by, and a new one substituted, to avoid any delay. Just so it is with the human department. Why should any difference be made? Why should not a child be worked as long as it can be compelled to go on, with a little occasional quick patching, and when it cannot, be thrown into the street, just as a broken wheel is thrown into the lumber-room, to fall to pieces? It is not to be expected that the master's profits of a few hundreds, or thousands, per annum, should be decreased to the amount, now and then, of one-and-sixpence, by allowing a little creature, that has worked itself ill in his service, to lie by for a week without forfeiting its eighteen pence; or to retain its claim to re-admission on recovery. But add to this the fact, that what the child earns is not at its own disposal, going to remunerate the person who has charge of it, for such food and such clothing as it gets, we may believe the little laborer to be in the position of a shuttlecock, struck alternately from one battledore to the other, until, escaping a stroke, it falls to the ground, and is trampled into kindred dust."*

That the facts are so, and that helpless little beings are thus treated as mere machines, is proved by thousands of facts that have, at various times, been brought to light by parliamentary and other investigations. No one who has studied the subject can hesitate about agreeing with this writer in her expression of the opinion, that "the misery, the wretchedness, the sufferings, the degradation of young English girls, far exceeded those of the little heathen abroad; nor is the foulest system of pagan demoralization, cruelty, and crime, second in atrocity to that which varnishes itself over with the name of Christianity, and seizes for its victims the free-born children of Britain, baptized into a faith of which they live and die in soul-destroying ignorance."

Strikingly in contrast with this is the fact, "that all the children between the ages of six and fifteen, in the German

* Charlotte Elizabeth: *Wrongs of Woman*, Part III., p. 100.

and Swiss towns, and nearly all the children in the French, Dutch, Danish, and Norwegian towns, spend *every day* in airy, roomy, clean, and well-furnished class-rooms, or in dry exercise grounds, and often in the company of children of the middle-classes, and in the society of men who are fit to be the teachers of the children of the rich."

Differing in all else—climate, soil, habits, manners, and religion—the people of the countries last above referred to are alike in the fact, that they "live, move, and have their being" under the system for which the world is indebted to Colbert—that system which looks to the promotion of the habit of association and combination, and the development of the latent powers of land and man. As a consequence, the family relation tends to become more cheering from day to day—the feeling of responsibility for the proper direction of the infant mind becoming more intense from year to year. Differing in all else, the various countries that follow in the lead of England unite with England herself in rejecting Adam Smith and adopting the principles of the Ricardo-Malthusian school, the result being seen in this, that they constitute the great treasury of facts to be used in support of the theory of over-population, the helpless child there becoming more and more a mere instrument to be used by trade.

Of all communities, past and present, there is, and has been, none so highly favored as England in respect to the power placed at its command by a beneficent Providence, to be used for promoting the happiness and prosperity of mankind at large. Of all, there is none by which the power granted has been so unscrupulously used for the destruction of happiness, morals, and life, at home and abroad; and hence it is that it has been necessary to establish a natural discord, with a view to proving that an omniscient Deity had erred in adjusting the supply of food to a growing population.

§ 4. Here, as everywhere, America is a land of contrasts, one portion of the Union prohibiting, by the most stringent laws, the education of its laboring population, while the other recognizes fully the right of all to receive instruction, and the duty of property to aid in seeing that it be obtained. In the one, teachers are imprisoned for violation of the anti-education laws, while in the other, few persons are more respected than those who most have labored to bring the means of education within the reach of all—the orphan and the criminal, the very poor as well as the very rich.

Books have been written with the intent to prove that crime and education go together; that is, that the greater the power of the man to command the services of his own faculties, the greater is his tendency to interfere with the rights of others. Were this so, it would be better to close the schools. That it is not, the reader may feel well assured. Why it sometimes so appears, is, as we think, easily explained.

That the development of human faculties may be beneficial to man, it is indispensable that there be a market for the faculties developed, the rankest weeds coming always from the richest soil, neglected by its owner. That the market may exist, there must be diversity in the modes of employment, producing competition for the *purchase* of human effort of each and every kind. Centralization tends to prevent the growth of this competition while promoting competition for its *sale*, the man who needs to sell his efforts becoming, thus, the slave of him who has means with which to purchase. The greater the tendency in this direction the more does society tend to become divided into two great classes—the very poor and the very rich—leaving no place for the proprietors of small amounts of either material or mental capital. The class of middlemen, occupying themselves as soldiers, sailors, traders, lawyers, and otherwise as non-producers, grows necessarily, the societary motion becoming slower at every stage of growth, and rendering it more difficult to obtain an honest livelihood. Crime, therefore, grows, doing this as a direct consequence of that slight excitement of human faculty produced at school, which needs the activity of social life for its full development. Under such circumstances education does little more than sharpen the human faculties for enabling man more readily to prey upon his fellow-man, that being the present tendency in England and in all the countries which follow in her train, America included.

Study the world where we may, we shall find evidence of the truth of the proposition, that the feeling of responsibility towards both God and man grows with that approximation of the prices of raw materials and finished commodities, and consequent increase in the productiveness of labor, which results from proper exercise of the powers of the State.

CHAPTER XLIV.

OF COMMERCE—CONTINUED.

III.—*Of the Commerce of the State.*

§ 1. Commerce of the State. Solidarity of the human race. Two-fold nature of man. Correspondence between the structure and functions of the individual man and the aggregate man denominated Society. Co-ordinating office of the brain. Its power limited by the necessary liberty of the individual organs. Various degrees of subordination of the parts. Necessity for exercise of the power of co-ordination grows in individuals and societies as the organisation becomes more complete. Local centres of the physical and social systems. Power and duties of the brain. Order and liberty combined and secured. Graduated and federated system of government in the human body analogous to the political organisation of that social one which constitutes these United States.

§ 2. Social science here branches into political economy—the one treating of natural laws, and the other of the *measures* required for enabling those laws to have full effect. Relation of science and art as exhibited by M. Comte. Necessity for exercise of the power of co-ordination. The more perfect the co-ordination the more complete the development of all the parts, and the more harmonious the action of the whole. Tendency to the creation of local centres. The more perfect the balance of opposing forces, the greater the tendency towards human freedom. Duty of the co-ordinating power limited to the removal of obstacles to association.

§ 3. Colbert and his policy. His full appreciation of the necessity for the exercise, by the State, of a power of co-ordination. Hume, on the necessity for preserving with care the manufactures of a nation. Adam Smith an advocate of the indiscriminate adoption of the system of *laissez faire*. Say, Rossi, Mill, and others, on the duties of a government, in reference to diversification of employments. M. Chevalier holds that within certain limits governments are but performing a positive duty when they favor the taking possession of all the branches of industry whose acquisition is authorised by the nature of things. Holds that French agriculture has ceased to be protected. Inaccuracy of the view thus presented. Heavy taxation of transportation paid by American farmers, and comparative exemption of those of France. Freedom of trade enjoyed by the latter, as compared with the restrictions on the former. Necessity for exercise of the co-ordinating power grows with the growth of wealth and numbers. The more perfect the power of association within the State, the greater the power of its people to contribute to the commerce of the world.

§ 1. THE complex organism of the human body being, by the sympathies and dependencies of its various parts, made an unit in its action and its uses, the entire race, philosophically and practically considered, may be treated as one man, the aggregate differing in degree, but not in kind, from any of the atoms of which it is composed. Politically, we have the idea embraced in our national motto, *e pluribus unum*, the same fact presenting itself in the legal ideas of joint and several obligation, and joint and several right, where each debtor is bound for the whole debt, and each creditor is entitled to look to each and all for payment. The corporation, or artificial man, is another familiar instance of the same idea, the moralist, in his turn, using the word *solidarity* for indi-

rating the liability of each and all the members of society to suffer for the errors, or profit of the judicious action, of any of its component parts. The recognition of analogy here exhibited runs through all branches of theory and practice having man for their subject, warranting the study of the many in the one, and promising helpful illustrations of the societary body to be derived from examination of the individual.

The living man, whether considered in regard to the doubling of the sexes, the union of soul and body, the individual and his race, or that aspect of his life in which he is at once an organic instrument and a being holding the relation of agent and object to the world around him, is a being of two-fold existence. He has a vegetable and an animal, or an individual and a relative life, and an appropriate set of organs for the service of each, all bound together into a happily-adjusted union, mechanical so far as regards framework and connection, but vital in all that relates to sensation, perception, consciousness and volition. The articulation of the limbs and muscles, and the collocation and distribution of the internal organs, are linked together by mechanical arrangement, the nervous system, however, presiding over and executing the co-ordination of the various parts of the body among themselves, and being, too, the sole agency by which the relative life of the individual is administered and sustained.

Man's relative life, for the purposes of our inquiry, may be comprehended in his powers of locomotion and sensation, and in his higher instincts, the sentiments, and moral and intellectual faculties of his nature. Each of these has its fitting nervous organism, and the anatomical structure of the nervous system necessarily answers to this complication and combination of offices, appropriateness of apparatus being here, as everywhere throughout creation, logically expectant upon the existence of a need for it. The nervous masses, ganglions, plexuses, and fibres, are immensely varied in form, texture, and arrangement; and those parts of the system which supply the organs of nutritive life, while so far independent of those which rule the life of relation as is needed for fitting them to maintain the economy of the frame, are yet so far subordinated to the superior portions as is required for the interests and uses of the physical organism. Over the ultimate processes of assimilation, nutrition, reproduction, and growth, the brain proper has but little conscious control.

Over those organisms which are the purveyors to the body's wants, it has an authority that is greatly larger. It has a positive control over the primary steps of the nutritive process, as in the selection, prehension, and ingestion of food. To a certain extent it modifies, suspends, or accelerates digestion, and in a considerable degree effects respiration—its power of intervention shading off towards incapacity as the actions escape from the sphere of voluntary agency into that of necessity and unconsciousness.

The external senses are still more fully subject to the brain directly as to the mental, while indirectly as to the instinctive, life of the subject. This law of gradation obtains also among them, taste and smell, which stand as sentinels over organic life, being almost entirely independent of the will. Hearing, important as it is as an inlet to the tidings of danger, is nearly as much so, while touch and vision, with their larger range of subserviency to the intellect, are proportionably obedient to its direction. High above, the brain, in its proper office of thought and emotion, is free, spontaneous, and paramount in the nervous economy of the system.

Here, to proceed no further in details, is a world of variety in unity, subordinated and co-ordinated, executive authority and independence balancing each other in a manner that fairly illustrates the various interests of the life of the human race.

The two-fold physiological division of the life of man, as an *organic* and as a *related* being, is analogous to the man as an individual and as a member of society. The physical support of the system being the primary object of nutrition, that portion of the work is not under the control of the governing brain, nor subject to its casual impulses. Nevertheless, beyond the instinctive nurture of infancy, the intellect, and its servants, the limbs, are required to act in obtaining a supply of food. Infant societies may therefore, on the same principle, supply their animal wants without the intervention of an executive intelligence. In the more mature life of the community, however, as in the developed growth of the individual, a head, with its executive ministers, becomes absolutely indispensable. The government, representing, as it does, the intelligence of the body, physical and social, has a duty and a use, and therefore a right to a place in the natural order. While ministering to the well-being of the body, it does not intervene in the central movements. *Laisser faire* is *there* the law—ruling all that has already been appropriated.

Elsewhere, we find regulative help in bringing the sustenance of the body within its reach, and guardianship in warding off all disturbing and injurious influences from without, giving liberty to the internal life, and protection to the social life—that protection, too, embracing both assistance and defence.

Further, the digestive and assimilative organs are variously related, each having its own peculiar function, though intimately interlinked with its associates. They are a corporation of converting laborers. The stomach, liver, pancreas, intestinal tube, and lacteal vessels, are principal members of the association—all, however, bound into corporate unity by the great sympathetic nerve which frees them from the control of the governing brain to the extent required for securing their due efficiency in their proper offices. Nevertheless, while supplied with power by a special and separating set of nerves, each one has a branch of direct communication with the central nervous mass. In other words, they are more closely connected with each other than are any of them with the all-governing brain, and can perform their functions for a short time, and in an inferior degree, when its agency is entirely withheld. In reptiles, the digestive apparatus continues to act long after the head has been severed from the body. In the human fœtus, the growth of the body is perfect even where the brain is absent. At birth, however, the acephalous fœtus perishes for want of the co-ordinating brain-power, the decollated tortoise doing the same after a few hours of the like deprivation. *The necessity for a co-ordinating power appears, therefore, to exist in the direct ratio of development.*

In a state of absolute isolation, or of feeble social relation, man, denied the protection resulting from combination, has but a low grade of individual existence. In the healthy maturity of society the independence of the individual cannot be entire, either in extent or in degree. Threads of common life hold him in a general dependency upon every neighbor man, while organized government stretches its lines of support, protection, and harmonizing restraint, over all the points in which his life has its relative issues.

The theory of political government of these United States is in an obvious general harmony with the vital economy as here exhibited. The individual, having rights and interests with which no one ventures to interfere, scarcely feels the rein of the ruling power, though receiving its vital impulse

The family, held together by its proper sympathetic ties, is obedient to an almost unconscious influence of the central life. The school district has powers which it exercises independently of that larger society from which it derives its powers, and to which it is responsible for the rightful exercise of its functions. The township enjoys a similar independence, feeling the corresponding control of the county. The county holds its franchises under similar conditions of freedom and limitation. The State is sovereign in all remoter and more general relations, consistent with the supremacy of the Union —that, again, being supreme only in what is essential to the harmony and well-being of the whole.

§ 2. Social science here branches into political economy—the former treating of *the laws* which govern man in his effort to secure for himself the highest individuality and the greatest power of association with his fellow-men, and the latter of *the measures* required for so co-ordinating the movements of society as to enable the laws to take effect. Careful study of the law is indispensable to success in practice, the relations of the one to the other being well expressed in the words of M. Comte: "*Science whence foresight, foresight whence action.*"

Men desire to associate, conscious that their own strength and power will thereby be increased. Met together, selfishness is found opposing itself to measures that would promote the good of all. Such being the case, some certain persons must act as umpires, empowered so to co-ordinate the societary movements as to call into activity the powers of all its members, while requiring all to respect the rights of those around them—the object sought to be obtained being the removal of obstacles standing in the way of association.

The greatest obstacle thereto being the necessity for effecting changes of place, one of the earliest wants of man is that of roads. At first, the footpath supplies the only means of intercourse; but, as numbers increase, the pack-horse takes the place of man. In time, however, better roads are needed; but now the difficulty arises, that the owner of the pack-horse, in his ignorant selfishness, opposes their construction under the belief that the demand for his services and those of his animals may thereby be lessened. The farmer, too, opposes it, because it will divide his farm, overlooking the fact that the economy of transportation must double the money-value of his property. In this state of things, society, by its head, steps in, deciding the terms upon which the land shall be yielded for societary purposes. Later, turnpikes and railroads are needed; but how, in the absence of a co-ordinating head, could such roads be made? Were each and every proprietor along the line to make his separate piece, each would be owner of his share, charging at his pleasure for its use. Here, again, society comes in, fixing the terms upon which the land may be taken, and the tolls that may be claimed, creating an artificial man, and authorizing the head of the body thus created to direct the operations.

So, too, is it with regard to various other wants of the community: as, the supply of water and gas to cities; the stamping of the precious metals for use; the establishment of weights and measures; the explorations needed for the opening of mines. In all of those, and many other cases, the central power steps in to remove the difficulties that would be created by individual selfishness and ignorance, and thus enables the community to attain the desired object.

A country embraces all the varieties of soil and climate requisite for a very varied agriculture, from the barley of the North to the sugar of the South; and yet its inhabitants are compelled to go abroad for various articles, paying many times the original cost, and losing annually more than would, if properly applied, suffice for naturalizing them at home. Society now comes to their aid, asking each and every contributor to the tax of transportation to pay into a common fund a small per centage of its amount, to be applied to the introduction of seeds and knowledge, by means of which they may in a brief period be relieved from the payment of further contributions.*

Schools develop the faculties of the younger portion of the community, but, in default of diversity in the modes of em-

* The amount paid annually for transporting tea to the United States would probably suffice for securing the successful establishment of the tea culture at home. Such a work, however, would ruin any individual, as it did beggar the enterprising man by whom, some years since, it was undertaken. The tea seed must be procured from China, whose people naturally resist the exportation of the best seed, as prejudicial to their interests. So the tea shippers, commission merchants, importers, etc., regard the establishment of the tea culture here as a deadly blow to the craft whereby they have their wealth. Then, the proper climate, soil, and culture, in this country, have all to be ascertained by patient and repeated experiments, which, however triumphant in their results, must be costly in their progress.

ployment, those who might distinguish themselves in the workshop are compelled to remain idle, if they would not follow the plow, or begin to trade. Iron ore and fuel abound, but, there being no furnaces, both remain useless, and the farmer can scarcely obtain a plough. Wool abounds, but as there is no woollens mill the farmer's daughter is idle, while he himself cannot obtain a coat. Corn abounds, but the cost of transporting it to a distant market leaves little to its producer. Building materials, and labor unemployed, abound, but those who might undertake to build the furnace or the mill would speedily find that, however much their operations might tend towards increasing the quantity of cloth and iron, their distant competitors would still so far control the market as to drive them from it, to their own entire ruin. In this state of things society says to the farmers and laborers, that the establishment of mills and furnaces would double the value of both land and labor, and that to enable them to combine their efforts for the erection of such establishments, it will require of the foreign producers of cloth and iron a certain portion of the value of all they may import—applying the proceeds to the making of new and better roads, or to paying the expenses of government; thus improving the modes of communication among themselves, while relieving them at once and forever from the oppressive tax of transportation to the distant market.

In all these cases, the political head does exactly that which is done by the physical one, co-ordinating the movements of society in such manner as to remove the obstacles to association. The more perfect that co-ordination, whether in the physical or social body, the more complete must be the development of all the parts, and the more harmonious the action of the whole.

It may, however, be said, that the exercise of these various powers tends towards centralization, yet is the reverse of this the case. Every movement above described tends towards the development of the various powers of the earth and man; towards the creation of local centres; towards increasing the rapidity of the societary circulation; towards creating a counterbalance to the attractions of the political or trading capital; and, therefore, towards concentration. The more perfect the balance of the centripetal and centrifugal forces, the greater must be the steadiness of the societary movement, and the greater the tendency towards the perfect establishment of human freedom. Are there, then, no proper limits to the sphere of action of those who guide and direct the commerce of the State? There are—*their whole duty being found in the removal of the obstacles to perfect combination.* Going beyond that point, government leaves its proper sphere, doing mischief in place of good

§ 3. Among the men who have, at any time, been placed in charge of the helm of State, Colbert stands pre-eminent for his appreciation of the fact, that the headship of a nation brought with it a necessity for the performance of great and important duties—all of them looking to the removal of the obstacles to combination. Every movement in that direction, as he clearly saw, tended towards developing the individual faculties of his countrymen, and towards fitting them for more extended intercourse with distant people. Differing widely from modern teachers, he regarded wealth only as a means, the end being found in the gradual substitution of the real MAN for the mere human animal bequeathed to him by his predecessors. That he erred occasionally in regard to the measures required for enabling him to attain the desired end, as when he prohibited the export of artisans and corn, is not extraordinary, seeing how little progress since his time has been made towards harmony among the teachers of social science, whether as regards the facts themselves, or the deductions they may be held to warrant.

Leaving Colbert we may now pass to Hume, in whose opinion, no country need fear any difficulty in commanding the services of the precious metals, provided only that it "preserved with care its people and its manufactures"—so exercising its power of co-ordination as to facilitate the near approach of producers and consumers. Of all economists, none appears more fully to have appreciated "the superior skill and industry that become developed in countries whose power of conversion have fitted them for obtaining the start of others in trade." No one has ever shown himself more sensible of the fact, that in the absence of manufactures land and labor must be low in price, and that, in countries so situated, the difficulty of regaining the ground they had lost, or gaining that which had not been previously obtained, was a great and growing one.

No economist, more than Adam Smith, has manifested his admiration of local centres of action in which agriculture and manufactures were happily combined. In his view, the course of his countrymen in seeking to centralize the machinery of manufactures for the world, and thus converting themselves into a "nation of shopkeepers," while compelling all other nations to send abroad rude produce, was not only an act of folly, but also "a manifest violation of the most sacred rights of mankind"—such a violation as, had he lived in any other country, would have led him to urge protective action. His approval of the navigation laws furnishes evidence of his disbelief in the propriety of an indiscriminate application of the idea implied by the expression, *laisser faire*.

Protection, as regarded those productions which were necessary for self-defence, he regarded as equally justifiable with that afforded by the navigation laws. The articles protected might, after a time, as he thought, "be made as cheap, or cheaper, than in the foreign country." He did not, it is true, regard it as certain that, "the sum total" of the revenue of a country could be thereby increased, yet he elsewhere proved it to be so, when he showed that the saving of the cost of transportation must enure to the farmer, giving value to both labor and land. Adding to this the commodities that before had been imported, his gain was doubled, even where not quadrupled.

Much more fully than Dr. Smith did Mr. J. B. Say appreciate the necessity for action on the part of the co-ordinating power, circumstances, in his opinion, greatly modifying the proposition that each and every individual is capable of determining the most advantageous mode of employing his capital and labor. Protection, granted with a view to promote the profitable application of labor and capital, might, as he thought, become productive of universal benefit. New modes of employment, though destined to result in great advantage when the workmen should have been trained and the preliminary obstacles surmounted, were liable, without the aid of government, to cause heavy loss to the undertaker—a result that, as he thought, was carefully to be avoided.

Following in the footsteps of his distinguished predecessor, Mons. Blanqui tells his readers, that "experience has already taught us, that a people ought never to deliver over to the chances of foreign trade the fate of its manufactures."

Turning now to one of the most eminent of recent economists, M. Rossi, we find him utterly disclaiming the idea of non-intervention by the co-ordinating power—telling his readers, that it was undeniable that there were exceptions to the free-trade principle, exceptions the reason of which were to be found in the science itself, while the foundation of others was to be found in moral and political considerations. "The sacrifice of to-day," as he further said, "might be followed by advantages that would more than compensate for it."

"Italy," says M. Moreau de Joannès, "profited of her liberty to create, in her free cities, the first manufactures that were to be found in Christendom, thereby securing to herself a monopoly of the production of silks and woollens, and of arms. Our wars having led our armies into that beautiful country, and we having thus become initiated into the secret of its prosperity, efforts were made at transplanting into our provinces the culture of the mulberry, the raising of silk, and the silk manufacture. All progress in this direction ceased, however, under the later sovereigns of the Valois family, the luxuries of France having been then exclusively supplied by the cities of Italy and the Netherlands. Manufacturing industry was, therefore, compelled to wait the appearance of Sully and Henry IV., to obtain from them the royal protection, and the aid so much required."

Mr. J. S. Mill is of opinion that "the superiority of one country over another, in a branch of production, often arises only from having begun it sooner. It cannot," as he says, "be expected that individuals should at their own risk, or rather to their certain loss, introduce a new manufacture, and bear the burthen of carrying it on until the producers have been educated up to the level of those with whom the processes have become traditional. A protecting duty, continued for a reasonable time, will sometimes be the least inconvenient mode in which a country can tax itself for the support of such an experiment."

Though generally favorable to the system commonly denominated "free trade," not one of these writers, as here is shown, has failed to see the necessity for the exercise in the social body, of that same co-ordinating and regulating power we see to be so constantly exercised in the physical man who furnishes, within himself, the type of the various societies of the world.

M. Chevalier holds that every nation owes it to itself to seek the establishment of diversification in the pursuits of its people, as Germany and England have already done in regard to cottons and woollens, and as France herself has done in reference to so many and so widely-different kinds of manufacturing industry. Within these limits, he holds that "it is not an abuse of power on the part of the Government; on the contrary, *it is the accomplishment of a positive duty so to act at each epoch in the progress of a nation, as to favor the taking possession of all the branches of industry whose acquisition is authorized by the nature of things.* Governments are, in effect, the personification of nations, and it is required that they should exercise their influence in the direction indicated by the general interest, properly studied, and fully appreciated. Therefore," he continues, "I shall carefully avoid censuring Colbert in France, or Cromwell in England, for the effort to establish in his own country a powerful commercial marine."

Nothing could be more accurate than this view of the duties of the government, yet is its author hostile to the maintenance of protection in France—assuring, as he since has done, the agricultural population of that country, that "raw materials, such as wool, and agriculture itself, incomparably the first of French pursuits, both by the number of persons engaged in it, and by the many interests dependent upon it, have ceased to enjoy the advantages of protection while bearing the charges of it wherever it seeks to obtain improved machinery of cultivation, and other articles of common use."

Is it so? *Has* French agriculture ceased to be protected? If it has then should protection be abandoned? To enable us to answer this question we must begin by inquiring why is protection needed? Because, according to M. Chevalier himself, it promotes the conversion of raw materials into finished products. In what manner, however, does that profit the farmer? Is it not by the approximation of the consumer to the producer? Is it not by diminishing the tax of transportation? The farmers of France now realize the advantages of protection in the fact that of the 2,000,000,000 francs of French products annually sent to distant countries, at least two-thirds are products of the farm that never could reach those countries unless they had been compressed together in accordance with the sound advice of the author of the *Wealth of Nations.* Such being the case, it is certainly a great mistake to say that French agriculture has ceased to be protected. *All the protection that agriculture anywhere requires is that of having the market brought to its door, and thus enabling it to maintain the powers of the land while freeing itself from the one great tax of transportation, compared with which all other taxes sink into insignificance.*

Civilized communities follow the advice of Adam Smith in

exporting wool and corn in the form of cloth, at little cost for transportation. France, in 1856, exported silks and cloths, clothing, paper, and articles of furniture, to the extent of $300,000,000; and yet the total weight was short of 50,000 tons, requiring for its transport but fifty ships of moderate size.

Semi-barbarous countries, on the contrary, export their products in their rudest state, at heavy cost. India sends the constituents of cloth—cotton, rice, and indigo—to exchange, in distant markets, for cloth itself. Brazil sends raw sugar across the ocean to exchange for that which has been refined. America sends wheat and Indian corn, pork and flour, cotton and rice, fish, lumber, and naval stores, to be exchanged for knives and forks, silks and cottons, paper and China-ware. The total value of these commodities exported in 1856—high as were then the prices—was only $230,000,000; and yet the ships engaged in the work of transport were of the capacity of 6,872,253 tons.

In the movement of all this property, there is great expense for transportation. Who pays it? Ask the farmer of Iowa, and he will answer that he sells for fifteen cents a bushel of corn that, when received in Manchester, commands a dollar, giving to the support of railroads and canals, ships and sailors, brokers and traders, *no less than eighty-five per cent.* of the intrinsic value of his products. Ask him once again, and he will reply that while his bushel of corn will command, in Manchester, eighteen or twenty yards of cotton cloth, he is obliged to content himself with little more than a single yard, eighty-five per cent. of the clothing-power of his corn having been taken, on the road, as his contribution towards the tax imposed upon the country for the maintenance of the machinery of that "free trade" which modern economists so much admire.

M. Chevalier is anxious for freedom of trade. Who has it—the French farmer, or the American farmer and planter? The one sends his food, in the form of silks and cottons, *to every part of the civilized world*, doing this directly and without the intervention of any other people. The other, having only raw products to sell, *must go to those countries and those only, which have machinery of conversion*—being as much enslaved as is the other free. Why this difference? Because France is a disciple of Colbert, while the American people follow the advice of men who teach that trade is to be promoted by cheapening labor and the raw products of the earth, finding the result in a doctrine of over-population, in virtue of which slavery is the ultimate portion assigned by the Creator to the laborers of the world. In the one, the prices of rude products and finished commodities gradually approximate, agriculture becomes a science, land grows in value, and becomes divided. In the other, those prices become more widely separated, agriculture continues in its rudest state, and land, abandoned by the small proprietors, becomes more consolidated from year to year. The one is daily furnishing evidence that protection to the people is, in fact, protection to the government itself, the other, meanwhile, proving that a government which refuses to perform the duty of protection must become daily weaker and less respected.

Look where we may, we shall find evidence that the necessity for the application of intelligence to the co-ordination of the movements of the various members of the societary body grows with the growth of wealth and numbers, and that the more wisely it is exercised the greater is the growth of production, the more rapid is the progress of accumulation, the more equitable is the distribution, the longer is the duration of life, the more perfect is the development of local centres of action, and the greater is the tendency towards the creation of a sound morality, and towards the development of the real MAN, master of nature and of himself.

We read in the *Arabian Nights* of a ship that had been carried by the current so near to a rock of adamant, that—her bolts being all drawn out—she fell to pieces. Such precisely *must* become the position of every community in which industrial development has still to be accomplished, and yet adopts the doctrine of *laisser faire*, manufactures being to the societary machine exactly what the bolts are to the ship. Turkey and Jamaica, Ireland and India, have been forced into its adoption, and the result is seen in the facts, that the power of co-ordination has ceased to exist; that land and labor are almost valueless; that the over-population theory finds there its most available material; and that they steadily decline in their power to maintain commerce with the world, that decline being attended by corresponding increase in the proportions borne by the countries which follow in the lead of Colbert and of France.

CHAPTER XLV.

OF COMMERCE—CONTINUED.

IV.—*Of the Commerce of the World.*

§ 1. Commerce of the World. In societies, as in the individual man, the power to maintain commerce is in the ratio of development—that becoming more complete as the power of co-ordination is more discreetly exercised.

§ 2. Organized bodies grow from within. Brute matter increases only by aggregation. The more perfect the development of human faculties, the higher the societary organization, and the more complete the self-dependence.

§ 3. Power for maintaining exterior commerce grows as the community becomes more self-dependent.

§ 4. Limited internal commerce of the States of the American Union. Slow growth of the power to maintain foreign commerce.

§ 5. Ultimate object of all production found in the real MAN. The higher his development, the greater the tendency towards the substitution of the commerce of taste and intellect, for that which requires for its maintenance mere brute force. Peace and harmony come with the proper exercise of the power of co-ordination. Subordination of all the parts becomes more complete as the societary organization becomes more perfect.

§ 1. THE man whose faculties remain undeveloped can maintain but little commerce. His ideas being few in number, he can have little intercourse by means of speech or correspondence. His power over nature being small, he has few commodities to offer in exchange for those he needs.—The man of high development, the real MAN, on the contrary, can have commerce with nature in all her forms, animate and inanimate. Abounding in ideas, he is fully provided with the means of maintaining commerce with his fellow-men, giving them out at one moment by means of writing or of speech, and absorbing them at another by help of eye or ear. Go where he may, he finds occasion for augmenting his stock of knowledge—the power of accumulation being here, as everywhere, in the direct ratio of the rapidity of circulation.

So, too, it is with societies, their power to maintain commerce with the world being dependent, altogether, upon the development of the various individualities of their members, and consequent development of the latent powers of the earth. Purely agricultural communities, like the pauper, maintain intercourse where they *must*, those which are highly developed doing so, on the contrary, where they *will*. Look, therefore, where we may, we shall find evidence of the truth of the great general principle, that the power to maintain commerce is in the direct ratio of the perfection of the organization—that, in turn, becoming more complete as the power of co-ordination is more discreetly exercised.

§ 2. Organized bodies grow from within, and the greater their growth the greater is their power to absorb and digest the elements by which they are surrounded, applying them to their own support, and afterwards giving them out in the form best fitted for general circulation. So it is with men, the man of high development seizing upon and digesting every new idea, and thus preparing himself for further commerce with those with whom he is connected. So, too, is it with societies, those in which trade, manufactures, and agriculture are combined, being always ready to take in the productions, mental or material, of other climes—to combine them with their own, and thus give new value to the labors of all, whether near or distant.

Brute matter, on the contrary, grows only from without, being susceptible of no increase except by aggregation.—So is it with men, those whose mental faculties are torpid being dependent upon their powers of appropriation, and the instrument they use being muscular force alone. So, too, is it with purely agricultural communities, constant exhaustion of the soil producing a necessity for appropriating other lands, to be in their turn exhausted.

Growing from within, highly organised communities find among themselves all the means required for increasing and extending their internal commerce, France, and all the countries that follow in her lead, making their own roads, creating their own local centres, and thus fitting themselves for a prosperous existence, were they even wholly debarred from intercourse with the outer world.—Purely agricultural communities, on the contrary, like Ireland, India, Portugal, Turkey, and Brazil, become from year to year, more dependent upon the foreign traders by whom their exchanges are performed.

So, too, is it with these United States. At times, their policy has looked to home development, and then they have made roads, without the need of foreign loans. As a rule, however, their policy has been adverse to the promotion of internal growth—the consequences exhibiting themselves in in a growing dependence upon foreign traders, and in a constant thirst for the annexation of distant lands.

§ 3. With growth of power for the maintenance of exterior commerce, the necessity for it declines, the love of home growing with the increase of family ties, and with the love of science and of books. So, too, is it with societies, the necessity for exterior intercourse diminishing as the power for its maintenance is increased by means of diversification of employments, and development of the latent powers of their people, and of their various soils.

Seeking proof of this, we may turn to any of the advancing communities of the world, past or present. The power of Athens grew with the development of internal intercourse. It declined as domestic commerce became less rapid, and as her dependence upon external intercourse became more complete. The great development of British external commerce followed closely upon the growth of the internal one, the latter having owed its existence to a protective system of the most stringent character. French external commerce has almost quadrupled in the last thirty years, having grown from an average of 1,000,000,000 francs, in the ten years ending in 1835, to 5.000,000,000, in 1857.

Germany, as we have seen, increased her demand for cotton from less than 400,000 cwts., in 1836, to almost 1,400,000 in 1851—her total imports, in the same period, having risen from $105,000,000 to $185,000,000. Sweden, too, followed in the same direction—exporting to the extent of more than $34,000,000 in 1853, against less than $14,000,000 in 1831.

Look where we may, we find evidence that the power to maintain commerce with the world grows with the growth of commerce at home, the power of digestion and assimilation being in the direct ratio of organization.

§ 4. Coming now homewards, we may inquire what it is that has given to the more than thirty States the power to maintain any internal commerce whatsoever? Is it not a consequence of diversity in their modes of employment resulting from the facts that, while one portion of the country is fitted for raising cotton or sugar, others are better suited to raising wheat, rice, corn, barley, or grass—that while the soil of one is underlaid with coal, that of others is underlaid with lead or copper, marl or lime? That such is the case is beyond all doubt. That without difference there can be no commerce, is shown by the facts that the cotton planter of Carolina makes no exchanges with his fellow-planter of Georgia, and that the farmer of Illinois has little intercourse with his fellow-farmer of Indiana. Ohio and Indiana are both employed in scratching out the soil, and exporting it in the form of food. Virginia and Kentucky have the same pursuits, selling their soil in the forms of tobacco and of corn. So, too, is it throughout the Union, millions of people being employed in one part of it in robbing the earth of the constituents of cotton, while in others other millions are employed in plundering the great treasury of nature of the constituents of wheat and rice, corn and tobacco, and thus destroying, for themselves and their successors, the power to maintain any commerce whatsoever, foreign or domestic.

The effect of this exhibits itself in the slow growth of American intercourse with foreign nations, as compared with that of other countries—the former having done little more than keep pace with that of population, while France and Germany have increased at a rate thrice more rapid than the growth of numbers. Examine, therefore, where we may, we meet with evidence of the great truth, that the power to maintain commerce with the world, whether by individuals or societies, grows in the ratio of the growth of their own individuality, and consequent independence of the exterior world.

§ 6. The more that a community finishes its raw products, combining its food, its wool, its fuel, and its ores, into cloth and iron, the greater, as we see, is its power for exchanges with the world. Is that, however, the highest point to which commerce may be carried? It is not; the ultimate object of all human effort being the production of the being known as MAN, capable of the highest aspirations.

The more perfect his development the greater is his desire for knowledge, the greater his love for literature and art, the greater his desire to see for himself the movements of the world, and to learn from those who are capable of affording him instruction. Every stage of advance towards diversification of employments, tends, therefore, towards development of the human faculties; towards fitting man for the higher enjoyments of life; towards elevating the character of his demands upon other communities—the products of mind, taste, and skill, gradually taking the place of those which have required for their production little more than mere brute force.

Looking now to those countries which follow in the lead of Colbert, we see them all to be engaged in increasing the attractions of their respective local centres—vieing with each other in the effort to render their various capitals, large and small, attractive of the taste, the intellect, and the wealth of the world at large.

Turning thence to those which follow in the lead of England, we find the reverse of this—Edinburgh and Dublin, Lima and Delhi, Lisbon and Constantinople, diminishing in their attractions from year to year. So, too, is it in these United States, the attractions of local centres steadily declining, with corresponding growth of absenteeism, and of belief in the divine origin of human slavery, and in the necessity for its continued existence.

Examine where we may, we shall find evidence of the perfect harmony of all real and permanent international interests, peace and commerce holding steady pace with that exercise of the power of co-ordination which looks to the removal of obstacles to combination, and to the creation of local centres of action in which trade, manufactures, and agriculture are combined in just proportions. Moving in that direction, the societary organization of the world at large becomes more and more in harmony with the arrangements of the physical world, and with the organization of man himself, the subordination of all the parts becoming more complete as the organization becomes more perfect. War and discord, with their attendant insubordination, and with the decline of commerce, follow in the train of centralization—that being the direction in which we must seek for facts to be adduced in proof of the disease of over-population.*

* All the facts of the last four years might here be cited in proof of the perfect accuracy of the views above presented, first published by Mr. Carey six years since.

CHAPTER XLVI.

OF THE SOCIETARY ORGANIZATION.

§ 1. Throughout nature, dissimilarity of the parts is evidence of the perfection of the whole, the highest organization presenting the most numerous differences. The higher the organization, the more complete the subordination of the parts. The more perfect the subordination, the more harmonious and beautiful the interdependence of the parts. The more complete that interdependence the greater the individuality of the whole, and the more perfect the power of self-direction.

§ 2. Throughout the physical and social world, harmony of movement—interdependence—a result of that local attraction which preserves a perfect independence. Subordination grows with the growth of the power of self-direction and protection. Harmony a result of the equal action of opposing forces. Its growth in all those countries in which the co-ordinating action is in accordance with the principles of Social Science.

§ 1. Throughout nature, the rank and perfection of organisms are in direct proportion to the number and dissimilarity of the parts, proof of this being found at every step from the simplest composition of inorganic matter up to the structure of MAN, in whom are reproduced all the forms and faculties of being over which, for the service of his needs, it has been given him to rule. This law not only marks the relative rank of classes of creatures, but it serves also to measure the respective positions of the individuals of whom the several classes are composed, the nearest approach to perfection being found in those men in whom the distinctive human qualities are found most developed. Following out the rule, those communities of men in which are found the largest variety of differences, and the most effective development of them into action, should present the nearest approach to perfection of societary organization. Seeking such communities we find them where the demands for human powers are most diversified, and where men are enabled most to combine their efforts, rapid societary motion there stimulating into activity all the power that, thus far, had remained latent, and enabling their members to pass from the brutifying labors of transportation, through those of the workshop, to those of a scientific agriculture.

Subordination of specialities to a general intention—diversity of functions or uses, so combined as to produce a perfect harmony of related action—is at once the mark and test of organization. The individual man is healthy and efficient within himself, in proportion to the vigor and exactness with which the bodily instruments of his will obey the governing brain—those charged with carrying on his automatic life meanwhile furnishing full support to his voluntary powers. Absolute subordination in the parts of a machine to the moving force is the constant characteristic of inanimate organizations. In a watch, steam-engine, mill, or ship, all the parts are in prompt and complete obedience, their perfection being measured by the exactness of their subordination.

In societary organizations we have the same law modified, but not repealed, by the liberty which accompanies human life—bringing with it responsibility to both God and man. The crew of a ship, the hands employed in a factory, the thousands of whom an army is composed, are organized and subordinated that they may accomplish the work for whose performance they have been brought together. So, too, is it in civil government, subordination of the subjects being essential to the well-being and the progress of the community, and to those very individual liberties which it limits, as well as to the national order for whose security it has been designed.

Throughout nature, the more perfect the organization and the more absolute the subordination, the more harmonious and beautiful is the interdependence of the parts. A rock, or a lump of coal being broken, every portion remains as perfect as it had been before. Dividing a polypus into a dozen parts, the vital force is found so existing in each and all, that each becomes again a perfect animal. Doing the same by man, he speedily passes into dust. So, too, is it with societies, the mutuality of interdependence growing with every stage of progress, from that simplest of societary forms presented to view in the history of Crusoe and his Friday, towards that high state of organization in which thousands combine to satisfy the public want for a single newspaper, hundreds of thousands then profiting by its perusal at a cost so small as scarcely to admit of calculation.

Throughout nature, the more complete the subordination and the more perfect the interdependence of the parts, the greater is the individuality of the whole, and the more absolute the power of self-direction. The rock is chained to earth, obeying but a single force; the bird, at will, rises in the air, or skims across the lake. The dog obeys his master; the master has power to direct himself and nature too. The man in perfect health determines for himself if he will go abroad or stay at home, the invalid, on the contrary, being compelled to keep his chamber. So, too, with society, its power for self-direction growing with the growth of interdependence among its various parts, and the latter becoming developed as the organization becomes more perfect, and the subordination more complete.

Organization and subordination, association and individuality, responsibility and freedom, travel thus together throughout the social world.

§ 2. The more thorough the development of differences among men, and the more perfect the power of self-direction, the more complete becomes their interdependence; the greater is the tendency towards harmony in the relations of society, and mutual respect on the part of both laborer and capitalist; the larger is the production; the more rapid is the circulation; the more equitable the distribution; the more absolute the subordination; and the greater the tendency towards freedom for all mankind. The less, however, is the tendency towards the production of those "positive checks" to population relied upon by Mr. Malthus, and known to the world as war, pestilence, and famine.

That this is so, must be obvious to all who see in the individual man the type of that grand man to which we apply the term *society*—and who appreciate the fact that this great law governs matter in all its forms, whether in that of systems of mountains, or communities of men. Throughout our solar system, harmony of movement—interdependence—is a result of that local attraction which preserves a perfect independence. So, too, is it with nations, the tendency towards peace and harmony among them being in the ratio of their interdependence—that, in its turn, being in the direct ratio of their independence. As among individuals the power of association grows with the development of individuality, and as this latter grows with the growth of the habit of combination, so does the tendency towards peaceful action among communities grow with the growth of local centres, and with that of self-dependence—subordination to the laws of right and justice among nations growing with the growth of the power of self-direction and protection. Here, as everywhere throughout nature, action and re-action are equal and contrary, harmony being the result of the perfect balance of these opposing forces.

The reverse of this, however, is what we are told in English books. From them we learn that universal peace is to follow in the train of a system that seeks a centralization of the manufacturing power of the world, thereby depriving the various nations of all ability to develop the latent powers of either earth or man—limiting them to the work of scratching out the soil and selling it in distant markets, and thus preventing the growth of agriculture. Under that system, interdependence in the bosom of the society dies away, while dependence grows, with corresponding tendency to the development of insubordination, and towards the production of the "positive checks" of the Malthusian system. The effort now being made towards the establishment of trading centralization—that policy which is advocated by the present British school—tends to the general production of a state of things similar to that exhibited in France in the days of the Jacquerie; in Germany, in those of John of Leyden and his Anabaptists; in England, in those of Henry VIII., when 72,000 criminals were hanged in a single reign; in Scotland, in the days of Fletcher; in Ireland, throughout the present century; and in India, at the present hour; that state of things in which insubordination comes as the companion of a division of society into two great forces, the very rich and the very poor, the master and the slave. Hence it is that it has given rise to the doctrine of over-population, which is simply that of slavery, anarchy, and societary ruin, as the ultimate condition of mankind—that, too, coming as a consequence of laws emanating from an all-wise and all-powerful Being, who could, if He would, have instituted laws in virtue of which freedom, order, peace, and happiness would have been their lot!

That these latter *have been* instituted, that the scheme of creation is not a failure, that it is marred by no such errors as have been indicated by Mr. Malthus, is proved by all the facts presented for consideration by the advancing communities of the world—the habit of peace, among both individuals and nations, growing with the growth of numbers and the increase in the power of self-direction. The more perfect that power, the greater is the tendency towards progress, the wretched slave to nature gradually yielding place to the MASTER OF NATURE, in whom the feeling of responsibility to his family, his country, his Creator, and himself, grows with the growth of power to guide and direct the vast and various forces placed at his command. This last grows in all those countries in which the societary energies, represented by their co-ordinating centres, are most directed to the removal of obstacles to association and combination, and therefore most in accordance with those natural laws which constitute the Social Science.

CHAPTER XLVII.

OF SOCIAL SCIENCE.

§ 1. Identity of the physical and social laws. Harmony the universal result of the unrestrained operation of natural laws. Identity of individual and national interests throughout the world.

§ 2. Agriculture the last developed of the pursuits of man. The laborer in the field the last that is emancipated. Minute machinery, by means of which nature performs her greatest operations, the last that is observed. Advantages of peace and harmony, last to meet their full appreciation. Science the interpreter of nature. Having recorded her processes it accepts them as true. Social Science treats of the laws in virtue of which man is enabled to obtain power over nature and over himself. Careful study of those laws would enable all, from the farmer and the laborer to the sovereign and the statesman, to see that advantage would result from full obedience to the great precept which requires that man should do by others as they would that others should do by them.

§ 1. THE simple laws which govern matter in all its forms and which are common to physical and social science may now briefly thus be stated:

All particles of matter gravitate towards each other, the attraction being in the direct ratio of the mass and the inverse one of the distance:

All matter is subjected to the action of the centripetal and the centrifugal forces, the one tending to the production of local centres of action, the other to the destruction of such centres and the production of a great central mass, obedient to but a single law:

The more perfect the balance of these opposing forces the more uniform and steady is the movement of the various bodies, and the more harmonious the action of the system in which they are embraced:

The more intense the action of those forces the more rapid is the motion, and the greater the power.

Such are the laws which govern masses and atoms, but there are other laws in virtue of which masses are reduced to atoms, ready to enter into chemical combination with each other, the tendency towards combination existing in the direct ratio of the perfect individualization of the particles thereby obtained. These laws are—

That heat is a cause of motion and force, motion being, in its turn, a cause of heat and force:

That the more heat and motion produced the greater is the tendency towards acceleration in the motion and the force:

That the more the heat the greater is the tendency towards

decomposition of masses, and individualization of the particles of which they are composed, thus fitting them for entering into chemical combination with each other:

That the greater the tendency towards individualization the more instant are the combinations, and the greater the force obtained:

That the more rapid the motion the greater the tendency of matter to rise in the scale of form, passing from the rude forms which characterize the inorganic world, through those of the vegetable and animal world, and ending in man:

That at every stage of progress there is an extension of the range of law to which matter is subjected, accompanied by an increase of the power of self-direction, subordination and freedom keeping steady pace with organization:

That last in the progress of development comes man, the being to whom has been given the power to guide and direct himself, and nature too, his subjection to all the laws above referred to being the most complete.

Studying him, we find—

That association with his fellow-man is a necessity of his existence, that being the condition upon which, alone, those faculties by whose possession he is distinguished from the beast of the field, can be developed:

That his powers are very various, and that the combinations of which they are susceptible are infinite in number, there being, throughout the world, no two persons who are entirely alike:

That the development of those infinitely various faculties is wholly dependent upon the power of association and combination:

That association, in its turn, is dependent upon the development of individuality:

That individuality is developed in the ratio of the diversity of the modes of employment, and consequent diversity in the demand that is made for the production of human powers:

That the greater the diversity the greater is man's power to control and direct the great forces of nature, the larger is the number of persons who can draw support from any given space, and the more perfect the development of the latent powers of both earth and man:

That the more perfect that development the more intense becomes the heat, the more rapid is the societary motion, and the greater the force exerted:

That the greater that motion and force the more does man become subjected to the great law of molecular gravitation—

local centres attracting him in one direction, while great cities, centres of the world, attract him in the other:

That the more perfect the balance of these opposing forces the greater is the tendency towards the development of local individualities, and towards the extension of the power of association throughout the interior of communities, with constant increase in the power of production, in the value and freedom of man, in the growth of capital, in the equity of distribution, and in the tendency towards harmony and peace:

That the law thus established in reference to the members of a community is equally operative among the communities themselves, the tendency towards peace and harmony among States being in the direct ratio of the development of their respective individualities, and their power of self-protection:

That there is, therefore, a perfect harmony of individual and international interests, and that, leaving out of view all higher considerations, nations and individuals would find it to their advantage to yield obedience to the great command, which requires that men should do unto others as they would that others should do unto them, that being the road in which they must travel if they would secure to themselves the most perfect individuality and freedom, the highest power of association, the largest command of nature's services, and the greatest amount of wealth and happiness.

§ 2. Of all the pursuits of man, the last developed is a scientific agriculture.—Of all equities, the last established is that between land and man—the latter then recognizing the fact, that the former is but a lender and not a donor, and that punctuality of repayment is the condition upon which, alone, the credits will be continued and extended.—Of all people, the last emancipated are the laborers in the field.—Of all knowledge, the last obtained is that of the minute machinery with which nature works when she seeks to produce her greatest effects.—In full accordance with this it is, therefore, that a full appreciation of the advantages of harmony, peace, and respect for our neighbor's rights—and of the necessity for a proper exercise of the power of co-ordination on one side, accompanied by subordination on the other—comes to man only with the growth of that real civilization which is, or should be, attendant upon increase in the number of persons occupying a given space, that increase of numbers being required for facilitating combination, and thus developing the various human powers.

Science, as we are told, is the interpreter of nature. It

reverently inquires, *what there is*, and *why it is* that such things are.* It listens that it may know. It seeks for light. It knocks that it may obtain communication, its duty being performed when it has recorded the processes of nature and accepted them as true. That department which is denominated Social Science treats of the laws which govern man in the effort for developing his own powers, and thereby obtaining entire control over the great forces of nature, at each step gained turning her batteries against herself with a view to make her subjugation more complete. The object of its teachers is that of indicating what have been the obstacles which, thus far, have prevented progress, and the means by which they may be diminished, if not removed. Careful study of those laws would satisfy—

SOVEREIGNS, that the maintenance of peace and a studious respect for the rights of others, was the surest road to power and influence for the communities in whose lead it is their fortune to be placed:

NATIONS, that every invasion of the rights of others must be attended with diminished power to protect their own:

LEGISLATORS, that their duty was limited to the removal of obstacles to association among the people with whose destinies they were charged, among the most prominent of which would be found those resulting from the failure to recognize the existence of a perfect harmony of international interests:

CAPITALISTS, that between themselves and those they employ, there was a perfect harmony of real and permanent interests:

FARMERS, that the road to prosperity for themselves and their children was to be found in the adoption of measures looking to their emancipation from the oppressive tax of transportation, and to the development of the powers of their land:

WORKINGMEN, that the more perfect their own respect for the rights of property, and the greater the tendency towards harmony and peace, the more rapid must be the growth of the productive power, with correspondent increase in their own *proportion* of the larger quantity of commodities produced:

FREEMEN, that true liberty is inconsistent with interfer-

* The questions asked by mathematicians are, *how much* there is, and *where* it may be found.

ences with the rights of others, and that in the most perfect subordination is to be found the road to harmony, peace, and freedom:

FREE-TRADE ADVOCATES, that the more varied the production of a community, the greater must be the commerce in the bosom of nations, and the greater their power to maintain commerce with the world:

ADVOCATES OF WOMEN'S RIGHTS, that the road towards elevation of the sex lies in the direction of that varied industry which makes demand for all the distinctive qualities of woman:

ANTI-SLAVERY ADVOCATES, that freedom comes with that diversification of pursuits which makes demand for all the various human powers, and that slavery is the necessary consequence of a system which looks to an exclusive agriculture:

DISCIPLES OF MR. MALTHUS, that the Creator had provided self-adjusting laws, regulating the movement of population; that the treasury of nature was unlimited in extent; that demand produced supply; and that the power to make demand increased with increase in the numbers of mankind:

PHILOSOPHERS, that war, pestilence, and famine, were the result of man's errors, and not of errors of the Creator—the Great Being, to whom we are indebted for existence, having instituted no laws tending to thwart the objects of man's creation:

REFORMERS, that nature always works slowly and gently when she desires that man shall profit by her action, and that man would do well to follow in the same direction—one of the greatest of all precepts being found in these two most simple words—*festina lente:*

STATESMEN, that power and responsibility went hand in hand together; that upon their action depended the decision of the great question, whether those whose destinies had been committed to their care, should go forward in the direction of the real MAN, master over nature and master of himself, or decline in that of the mere animal having the form of man, treated of in Ricardo-Malthusian books; and that failure to qualify themselves for the proper exercise of the powers confided to them was a crime, for the effect of which they must answer to their fellow-men, and to Him from whom that power had been derived:

CHRISTIANS, that the foundation of Christianity and of Social Science is found in the great precept—ALL THINGS WHATSOEVER YE WOULD THAT MEN SHOULD DO TO YOU, DO YE SO EVEN TO THEM.

INDEX.

A.

B.

D.

H.

I.

J.

K.

L.

M.

N.

O.

P.

Q.

R.

S.

T.

U.

V.

W.

Y.

Z.

THE END.

CATALOGUE

OF

PRACTICAL AND SCIENTIFIC BOOKS,

PUBLISHED BY

HENRY CAREY BAIRD & CO.,

Industrial Publishers and Booksellers,

NO. 810 WALNUT STREET,

PHILADELPHIA.

☞ Any of the Books comprised in this Catalogue will be sent by mail, free of postage, at the publication price.

☞ A Descriptive Catalogue, 96 pages, 8vo., will be sent, free of postage, to any one who will furnish the publisher with his address.

ARLOT.—A Complete Guide for Coach Painters.

Translated from the French of M. ARLOT, Coach Painter; for eleven years Foreman of Painting to M. Eherler, Coach Maker, Paris. By A. A. FESQUET, Chemist and Engineer. To which is added an Appendix, containing Information respecting the Materials and the Practice of Coach and Car Painting and Varnishing in the United States and Great Britain. 12mo. $1.25

ARMENGAUD, AMOROUX, and JOHNSON.—The Practical Draughtsman's Book of Industrial Design, and Machinist's and Engineer's Drawing Companion:

Forming a Complete Course of Mechanical Engineering and Architectural Drawing. From the French of M. Armengaud the elder, Prof. of Design in the Conservatoire of Arts and Industry, Paris, and MM. Armengaud the younger, and Amoroux, Civil Engineers. Rewritten and arranged with additional matter and plates, selections from and examples of the most useful and generally employed mechanism of the day. By WILLIAM JOHNSON, Assoc. Inst. C. E., Editor of "The Practical Mechanic's Journal." Illustrated by 50 folio steel plates, and 50 wood-cuts. A new edition, 4to. $10.00

ARROWSMITH.—Paper-Hanger's Companion:

A Treatise in which the Practical Operations of the Trade are Systematically laid down: with Copious Directions Preparatory to Papering; Preventives against the Effect of Damp on Walls; the Various Cements and Pastes Adapted to the Several Purposes of the Trade; Observations and Directions for the Panelling and Ornamenting of Rooms, etc. By JAMES ARROWSMITH, Author of "Analysis of Drapery," etc. 12mo., cloth. $1.25

ASHTON.—The Theory and Practice of the Art of Designing Fancy Cotton and Woollen Cloths from Sample:

Giving full Instructions for Reducing Drafts, as well as the Methods of Spooling and Making out Harness for Cross Drafts, and Finding any Required Reed, with Calculations and Tables of Yarn. By FREDERICK T. ASHTON, Designer, West Pittsfield, Mass. With 52 Illustrations. One volume, 4to. $10.00

BAIRD.—Letters on the Crisis, the Currency and the Credit System.

By HENRY CAREY BAIRD. Pamphlet. 05

BAIRD.—Protection of Home Labor and Home Productions necessary to the Prosperity of the American Farmer.

By HENRY CAREY BAIRD. 8vo., paper. 10

BAIRD.—Some of the Fallacies of British Free-Trade Revenue Reform.

Two Letters to Arthur Latham Perry, Professor of History and Political Economy in Williams College. By HENRY CAREY BAIRD. Pamphlet. 05

BAIRD.—The Rights of American Producers, and the Wrongs of British Free-Trade Revenue Reform.

By HENRY CAREY BAIRD. Pamphlet. 05

BAIRD.—Standard Wages Computing Tables:

An Improvement in all former Methods of Computation, so arranged that wages for days, hours, or fractions of hours, at a specified rate per day or hour, may be ascertained at a glance. By T. SPANGLER BAIRD. Oblong folio. $5.00

BAIRD.—The American Cotton Spinner, and Manager's and Carder's Guide:

A Practical Treatise on Cotton Spinning; giving the Dimensions and Speed of Machinery, Draught and Twist Calculations, etc.; with notices of recent Improvements: together with Rules and Examples for making changes in the sizes and numbers of Roving and Yarn. Compiled from the papers of the late ROBERT H. BAIRD. 12mo. $1.50

BAKER.—Long-Span Railway Bridges:

Comprising Investigations of the Comparative Theoretical and Practical Advantages of the various Adopted or Proposed Type Systems of Construction; with numerous Formulæ and Tables. By B. BAKER. 12mo. $2.00

BAUERMAN.—A Treatise on the Metallurgy of Iron:

Containing Outlines of the History of Iron Manufacture, Methods of Assay, and Analysis of Iron Ores, Processes of Manufacture of Iron and Steel, etc., etc. By H. BAUERMAN, F. G. S., Associate of the Royal School of Mines. First American Edition, Revised and Enlarged. With an Appendix on the Martin Process for Making Steel, from the Report of ABRAM S. HEWITT, U. S. Commissioner to the Universal Exposition at Paris, 1867. Illustrated. 12mo. . $2.00

BEANS.—A Treatise on Railway Curves and the Location of Railways.

By E. W. BEANS, C. E. Illustrated. 12mo. Tucks. . . $1.50

BELL.—Carpentry Made Easy:

Or, The Science and Art of Framing on a New and Improved System. With Specific Instructions for Building Balloon Frames, Barn Frames, Mill Frames, Warehouses, Church Spires, etc. Comprising also a System of Bridge Building, with Bills, Estimates of Cost, and valuable Tables. Illustrated by 38 plates, comprising nearly 200 figures. By WILLIAM E. BELL, Architect and Practical Builder. 8vo. . $5.00

BELL.—Chemical Phenomena of Iron Smelting:

An Experimental and Practical Examination of the Circumstances which determine the Capacity of the Blast Furnace, the Temperature of the Air, and the proper Condition of the Materials to be operated upon. By I. LOWTHIAN BELL. Illustrated. 8vo. . . . $6.00

BEMROSE.—Manual of Wood Carving:

With Practical Illustrations for Learners of the Art, and Original and Selected Designs. By WILLIAM BEMROSE, Jr. With an Introduction by LLEWELLYN JEWITT, F. S. A., etc. With 128 Illustrations. 4to., cloth. $3.00

BICKNELL.—Village Builder, and Supplement:

Elevations and Plans for Cottages, Villas, Suburban Residences, Farm Houses, Stables and Carriage Houses, Store Fronts, School Houses, Churches, Court Houses, and a model Jail; also, Exterior and Interior details for Public and Private Buildings, with approved Forms of Contracts and Specifications, including Prices of Building Materials and Labor at Boston, Mass., and St. Louis, Mo. Containing 75 plates drawn to scale; showing the style and cost of building in different sections of the country, being an original work comprising the designs of twenty leading architects, representing the New England, Middle, Western, and Southwestern States. 4to. . $12.00

BLENKARN.—Practical Specifications of Works executed in Architecture, Civil and Mechanical Engineering, and in Road Making and Sewering:

To which are added a series of practically useful Agreements and Reports. By JOHN BLENKARN. Illustrated by 15 large folding plates. 8vo. $9.00

BLINN.—A Practical Workshop Companion for Tin, Sheet-Iron, and Copperplate Workers:

Containing Rules for describing various kinds of Patterns used by Tin, Sheet-Iron, and Copper-plate Workers; Practical Geometry; Mensuration of Surfaces and Solids; Tables of the Weights of Metals, Lead Pipe, etc.; Tables of Areas and Circumferences of Circles; Japan, Varnishes, Lackers, Cements, Compositions, etc., etc. By LEROY J. BLINN, Master Mechanic. With over 100 Illustrations. 12mo. $2.50

BOOTH.—Marble Worker's Manual:

Containing Practical Information respecting Marbles in general, their Cutting, Working, and Polishing; Veneering of Marble; Mosaics; Composition and Use of Artificial Marble, Stuccos, Cements, Receipts, Secrets, etc., etc. Translated from the French by M. L. BOOTH. With an Appendix concerning American Marbles. 12mo., cloth. $1.50

BOOTH AND MORFIT.—The Encyclopedia of Chemistry, Practical and Theoretical:

Embracing its application to the Arts, Metallurgy, Mineralogy, Geology, Medicine, and Pharmacy. By JAMES C. BOOTH, Melter and Refiner in the United States Mint, Professor of Applied Chemistry in the Franklin Institute, etc., assisted by CAMPBELL MORFIT, author of "Chemical Manipulations," etc. Seventh edition. Royal 8vo., 978 pages, with numerous wood-cuts and other illustrations. . $5.00

BOX.—A Practical Treatise on Heat:

As applied to the Useful Arts; for the Use of Engineers, Architects, etc. By THOMAS BOX, author of "Practical Hydraulics." Illustrated by 14 plates containing 114 figures. 12mo. $4.25

BOX.—Practical Hydraulics:

A Series of Rules and Tables for the use of Engineers, etc. By THOMAS BOX. 12mo. $2.50

BROWN.—Five Hundred and Seven Mechanical Movements:

Embracing all those which are most important in Dynamics, Hydraulics, Hydrostatics, Pneumatics, Steam Engines, Mill and other Gearing, Presses, Horology, and Miscellaneous Machinery; and including many movements never before published, and several of which have only recently come into use. By HENRY T. BROWN, Editor of the "American Artisan." In one volume, 12mo. $1.00

BUCKMASTER.—The Elements of Mechanical Physics:

By J. C. BUCKMASTER, late Student in the Government School of Mines; Certified Teacher of Science by the Department of Science and Art; Examiner in Chemistry and Physics in the Royal College of Preceptors; and late Lecturer in Chemistry and Physics of the Royal Polytechnic Institute. Illustrated with numerous engravings. In one volume, 12mo. $1.50

BULLOCK.—The American Cottage Builder:

A Series of Designs, Plans, and Specifications, from $200 to $20,000, for Homes for the People; together with Warming, Ventilation, Drainage, Painting, and Landscape Gardening. By JOHN BULLOCK, Architect, Civil Engineer, Mechanician, and Editor of "The Rudiments of Architecture and Building," etc., etc. Illustrated by 75 engravings. In one volume, 8vo. $3.50

BULLOCK.—The Rudiments of Architecture and Building:

For the use of Architects, Builders, Draughtsmen, Machinists, Engineers, and Mechanics. Edited by JOHN BULLOCK, author of "The American Cottage Builder." Illustrated by 250 engravings. In one volume, 8vo. $3.50

BURGH.—Practical Illustrations of Land and Marine Engines:

Showing in detail the Modern Improvements of High and Low Pressure, Surface Condensation, and Super-heating, together with Land and Marine Boilers. By N. P. BURGH, Engineer. Illustrated by 20 plates, double elephant folio, with text. $21.00

BURGH.—Practical Rules for the Proportions of Modern Engines and Boilers for Land and Marine Purposes.

By N. P. BURGH, Engineer. 12mo. $1.50

BURGH.—The Slide-Valve Practically Considered.

By N. P. BURGH, Engineer. Completely illustrated. 12mo. $2.00

BYLES.—Sophisms of Free Trade and Popular Political Economy Examined.

By a BARRISTER (Sir JOHN BARNARD BYLES, Judge of Common Pleas). First American from the Ninth English Edition, as published by the Manchester Reciprocity Association. In one volume, 12mo. Paper, 75 cts. Cloth $1.25

BYRN.—The Complete Practical Brewer:

Or Plain, Accurate, and Thorough Instructions in the Art of Brewing Beer, Ale, Porter, including the Process of making Bavarian Beer, all the Small Beers, such as Root-beer, Ginger-pop, Sarsaparilla-beer, Mead, Spruce Beer, etc., etc. Adapted to the use of Public Brewers and Private Families. By M. LA FAYETTE BYRN, M. D. With illustrations. 12mo. $1.25

BYRN.—The Complete Practical Distiller:

Comprising the most perfect and exact Theoretical and Practical Description of the Art of Distillation and Rectification; including all of the most recent improvements in distilling apparatus; Instructions for preparing spirits from the numerous vegetables, fruits, etc.; directions for the distillation and preparation of all kinds of brandies and other spirits, spirituous and other compounds, etc., etc. By M. LA FAYETTE BYRN, M. D. Eighth Edition. To which are added, Practical Directions for Distilling, from the French of Th. Fling, Brewer and Distiller. 12mo. $1.50

BYRNE.—Handbook for the Artisan, Mechanic, and Engineer:

Comprising the Grinding and Sharpening of Cutting Tools, Abrasive Processes, Lapidary Work, Gem and Glass Engraving, Varnishing and Lackering, Apparatus, Materials and Processes for Grinding and Polishing, etc. By OLIVER BYRNE. Illustrated by 185 wood engravings. In one volume, 8vo. $5.00

BYRNE.—Pocket Book for Railroad and Civil Engineers:

Containing New, Exact, and Concise Methods for Laying out Railroad Curves, Switches, Frog Angles, and Crossings; the Staking out of work; Levelling; the Calculation of Cuttings; Embankments; Earth-work, etc. By OLIVER BYRNE. 18mo., full bound, pocket-book form. $1.75

BYRNE.—The Practical Model Calculator:

For the Engineer, Mechanic, Manufacturer of Engine Work, Naval Architect, Miner, and Millwright. By OLIVER BYRNE. 1 volume, 8vo., nearly 600 pages $4.50

BYRNE.—The Practical Metal-Worker's Assistant:

Comprising Metallurgic Chemistry; the Arts of Working all Metals and Alloys; Forging of Iron and Steel; Hardening and Tempering; Melting and Mixing; Casting and Founding; Works in Sheet Metal; The Processes Dependent on the Ductility of the Metals; Soldering; and the most Improved Processes and Tools employed by Metal-Workers. With the Application of the Art of Electro-Metallurgy to Manufacturing Processes; collected from Original Sources, and from the Works of Holtzapffel, Bergeron, Leupold, Plumier, Napier, Scoffern, Clay, Fairbairn, and others. By OLIVER BYRNE. A new, revised, and improved edition, to which is added An Appendix, containing THE MANUFACTURE OF RUSSIAN SHEET-IRON. By JOHN PERCY, M. D., F.R.S. THE MANUFACTURE OF MALLEABLE IRON CASTINGS, and IMPROVEMENTS IN BESSEMER STEEL. By A. A. FESQUET, Chemist and Engineer. With over 600 Engravings, illustrating every Branch of the Subject. 8vo. $7.00

Cabinet Maker's Album of Furniture:

Comprising a Collection of Designs for Furniture. Illustrated by 48 Large and Beautifully Engraved Plates. In one vol., oblong $3.00

CALLINGHAM.—Sign Writing and Glass Embossing:

A Complete Practical Illustrated Manual of the Art. By JAMES CALLINGHAM. In one volume, 12mo. $1.50

CAMPIN.—A Practical Treatise on Mechanical Engineering:

Comprising Metallurgy, Moulding, Casting, Forging, Tools, Workshop Machinery, Mechanical Manipulation, Manufacture of Steam-engines, etc., etc. With an Appendix on the Analysis of Iron and Iron Ores. By FRANCIS CAMPIN, C. E. To which are added, Observations on the Construction of Steam Boilers, and Remarks upon Furnaces used for Smoke Prevention; with a Chapter on Explosions. By R. Armstrong, C. E., and John Bourne. Rules for Calculating the Change Wheels for Screws on a Turning Lathe, and for a Wheel-cutting Machine. By J. LA NICCA. Management of Steel, Including Forging, Hardening, Tempering, Annealing, Shrinking, and Expansion. And the Case-hardening of Iron. By G. EDE. 8vo. Illustrated with 29 plates and 100 wood engravings $6.00

CAMPIN.—The Practice of Hand-Turning in Wood, Ivory, Shell, etc.:

With Instructions for Turning such works in Metal as may be required in the Practice of Turning Wood, Ivory, etc. Also, an Appendix on Ornamental Turning. By FRANCIS CAMPIN; with Numerous Illustrations. 12mo., cloth $3.00

CAREY.—The Works of Henry C. Carey:

FINANCIAL CRISES, their Causes and Effects. 8vo. paper . 25

HARMONY OF INTERESTS: Agricultural, Manufacturing, and Commercial. 8vo., cloth $1.50

MANUAL OF SOCIAL SCIENCE. Condensed from Carey's "Principles of Social Science." By KATE MCKEAN. 1 vol. 12mo. $2.25

MISCELLANEOUS WORKS: comprising "Harmony of Interests," "Money," "Letters to the President," "Financial Crises," "The Way to Outdo England Without Fighting Her," "Resources of the Union," "The Public Debt," "Contraction or Expansion?" "Review of the Decade 1857-'67," "Reconstruction," etc., etc. Two vols., 8vo., cloth $10.00

PAST, PRESENT, AND FUTURE. 8vo. $2.50

PRINCIPLES OF SOCIAL SCIENCE. 3 vols., 8vo., cloth $10.00

THE SLAVE-TRADE, DOMESTIC AND FOREIGN; Why it Exists, and How it may be Extinguished (1853). 8vo., cloth . $2.00

LETTERS ON INTERNATIONAL COPYRIGHT (1867) . 50

THE UNITY OF LAW: As Exhibited in the Relations of Physical, Social, Mental, and Moral Science (1872). In one volume, 8vo., pp. xxiii., 433. Cloth $3.50

CHAPMAN.—A Treatise on Ropemaking:

As Practised in private and public Rope yards, with a Description of the Manufacture, Rules, Tables of Weights, etc., adapted to the Trades, Shipping, Mining, Railways, Builders, etc. By ROBERT CHAPMAN. 24mo. $1.50

COLBURN.—The Locomotive Engine:

Including a Description of its Structure, Rules for Estimating its Capabilities, and Practical Observations on its Construction and Management. By ZERAH COLBURN. Illustrated. A new edition. 12mo. $1.25

CRAIK.—The Practical American Millwright and Miller.

By DAVID CRAIK, Millwright. Illustrated by numerous wood engravings, and two folding plates. 8vo. $5.00

DE GRAFF.—The Geometrical Stair Builders' Guide:

Being a Plain Practical System of Hand-Railing, embracing all its necessary Details, and Geometrically Illustrated by 22 Steel Engravings; together with the use of the most approved principles of Practical Geometry. By SIMON DE GRAFF, Architect. 4to. . $5.00

DE KONINCK.—DIETZ.—A Practical Manual of Chemical Analysis and Assaying:

As applied to the Manufacture of Iron from its Ores, and to Cast Iron, Wrought Iron, and Steel, as found in Commerce. By L. L. DE KONINCK, Dr. Sc., and E. DIETZ, Engineer. Edited with Notes, by ROBERT MALLET, F.R.S., F.S.G., M.I.C.E., etc. American Edition, Edited with Notes and an Appendix on Iron Ores, by A. A. FESQUET, Chemist and Engineer. One volume, 12mo. $2.50

DUNCAN.—Practical Surveyor's Guide:

Containing the necessary information to make any person, of common capacity, a finished land surveyor without the aid of a teacher. By ANDREW DUNCAN. Illustrated. 12mo., cloth. $1.25

DUPLAIS.—A Treatise on the Manufacture and Distillation of Alcoholic Liquors:

Comprising Accurate and Complete Details in Regard to Alcohol from Wine, Molasses, Beets, Grain, Rice, Potatoes, Sorghum, Asphodel, Fruits, etc.; with the Distillation and Rectification of Brandy, Whiskey, Rum, Gin, Swiss, Absinthe, etc., the Preparation of Aromatic Waters, Volatile Oils or Essences, Sugars, Syrups, Aromatic Tinctures, Liqueurs, Cordial Wines, Effervescing Wines, etc., the Aging of Brandy and the Improvement of Spirits, with Copious Directions and Tables for Testing and Reducing Spirituous Liquors, etc., etc. Translated and Edited from the French of MM. DUPLAIS, Ainé et Jeune. By M. MCKENNIE, M.D. To which are added the United States Internal Revenue Regulations for the Assessment and Collection of Taxes on Distilled Spirits. Illustrated by fourteen folding plates and several wood engravings. 743 pp., 8vo. $10.00

DUSSAUCE.—A General Treatise on the Manufacture of Every Description of Soap:

Comprising the Chemistry of the Art, with Remarks on Alkalies, Saponifiable Fatty Bodies, the apparatus necessary in a Soap Factory, Practical Instructions in the manufacture of the various kinds of Soap, the assay of Soaps, etc., etc. Edited from Notes of Larmé, Fontenelle, Malapeyre, Dufour, and others, with large and important additions by Prof. H. DUSSAUCE, Chemist. Illustrated. In one vol., 8vo. . $10.00

DUSSAUCE.—A General Treatise on the Manufacture of Vinegar:

Theoretical and Practical. Comprising the various Methods, by the Slow and the Quick Processes, with Alcohol, Wine, Grain, Malt, Cider, Molasses, and Beets; as well as the Fabrication of Wood Vinegar, etc., etc. By Prof. H. DUSSAUCE. In one volume, 8vo. . . $5.00

DUSSAUCE.—A New and Complete Treatise on the Arts of Tanning, Currying, and Leather Dressing:

Comprising all the Discoveries and Improvements made in France, Great Britain, and the United States. Edited from Notes and Documents of Messrs. Sallerou, Grouvelle, Duval, Dessables, Labarraque, Payen, René, De Fontenelle, Malapeyre, etc., etc. By Prof. H. DUSSAUCE, Chemist. Illustrated by 212 wood engravings. 8vo. $25.00

DUSSAUCE.—A Practical Guide for the Perfumer:

Being a New Treatise on Perfumery, the most favorable to the Beauty without being injurious to the Health, comprising a Description of the substances used in Perfumery, the Formulæ of more than 1000 Preparations, such as Cosmetics, Perfumed Oils, Tooth Powders, Waters, Extracts, Tinctures, Infusions, Spirits, Vinaigres, Essential Oils, Pastels, Creams, Soaps, and many new Hygienic Products not hitherto described. Edited from Notes and Documents of Messrs. Debay, Lunel, etc. With additions by Prof. H. DUSSAUCE, Chemist. 12mo. $3.00

DUSSAUCE.—Practical Treatise on the Fabrication of Matches, Gun Cotton, and Fulminating Powders.

By Prof. H. DUSSAUCE. 12mo. $3.00

Dyer and Color-maker's Companion:

Containing upwards of 200 Receipts for making Colors, on the most approved principles, for all the various styles and fabrics now in existence; with the Scouring Process, and plain Directions for Preparing, Washing-off, and Finishing the Goods. In one vol., 12mo. . $1.25

EASTON.—A Practical Treatise on Street or Horsepower Railways.

By ALEXANDER EASTON, C. E. Illustrated by 23 plates. 8vo., cloth. $2.00

ELDER.—Questions of the Day:

Economic and Social. By Dr. WILLIAM ELDER. 8vo. . $3.00

FAIRBAIRN.—The Principles of Mechanism and Machinery of Transmission:

Comprising the Principles of Mechanism, Wheels, and Pulleys, Strength and Proportions of Shafts, Coupling of Shafts, and Engaging and Disengaging Gear. By Sir WILLIAM FAIRBAIRN, C.E., LL.D., F.R.S., F.G.S. Beautifully illustrated by over 150 wood-cuts. In one volume, 12mo. $2.50

FORSYTH.—Book of Designs for Headstones, Mural, and other Monuments:

Containing 78 Designs. By JAMES FORSYTH. With an Introduction by CHARLES BOUTELL, M. A. 4to., cloth. $5.00

GIBSON.—The American Dyer:

A Practical Treatise on the Coloring of Wool, Cotton, Yarn and Cloth, in three parts. Part First gives a descriptive account of the Dye Stuffs; if of vegetable origin, where produced, how cultivated, and how prepared for use; if chemical, their composition, specific gravities, and general adaptability, how adulterated, and how to detect the adulterations, etc. Part Second is devoted to the Coloring of Wool, giving recipes for one hundred and twenty-nine different colors or shades, and is supplied with sixty colored samples of Wool. Part Third is devoted to the Coloring of Raw Cotton or Cotton Waste, for mixing with Wool Colors in the Manufacture of all kinds of Fabrics, gives recipes for thirty-eight different colors or shades, and is supplied with twenty-four colored samples of Cotton Waste. Also, recipes for Coloring Beavers, Doeskins, and Flannels, with remarks upon Anilines, giving recipes for fifteen different colors or shades, and nine samples of Aniline Colors that will stand both the Fulling and Scouring process. Also, recipes for Aniline Colors on Cotton Thread, and recipes for Common Colors on Cotton Yarns. Embracing in all over two hundred recipes for Colors and Shades, and ninety-four samples of Colored Wool and Cotton Waste, etc. By RICHARD H. GIBSON, Practical Dyer and Chemist. In one volume, 8vo. . . . $12.50

GILBART.—History and Principles of Banking:

A Practical Treatise. By JAMES W. GILBART, late Manager of the London and Westminster Bank. With additions. In one volume, 8vo., 600 pages, sheep $5.00

Gothic Album for Cabinet Makers:

Comprising a Collection of Designs for Gothic Furniture. Illustrated by 23 large and beautifully engraved plates. Oblong . . . $3.00

GRANT.—Beet-root Sugar and Cultivation of the Beet.

By E. B. GRANT. 12mo. $1.25

GREGORY.—Mathematics for Practical Men:

Adapted to the Pursuits of Surveyors, Architects, Mechanics, and Civil Engineers. By OLINTHUS GREGORY. 8vo., plates, cloth $3.00

GRISWOLD.—Railroad Engineer's Pocket Companion for the Field:

Comprising Rules for Calculating Deflection Distances and Angles, Tangential Distances and Angles, and all Necessary Tables for Engineers; also the art of Levelling from Preliminary Survey to the Construction of Railroads, intended Expressly for the Young Engineer, together with Numerous Valuable Rules and Examples. By W. GRISWOLD. 12mo., tucks $1.75

GRUNER.—Studies of Blast Furnace Phenomena.

By M. L. GRUNER, President of the General Council of Mines of France, and lately Professor of Metallurgy at the Ecole des Mines. Translated, with the Author's sanction, with an Appendix, by L. D. B. Gordon, F. R. S. E., F. G. S. Illustrated. 8vo. $2.50

GUETTIER.—Metallic Alloys:

Being a Practical Guide to their Chemical and Physical Properties, their Preparation, Composition, and Uses. Translated from the French of A. GUETTIER, Engineer and Director of Foundries, author of "La Fouderie en France," etc., etc. By A. A. FESQUET, Chemist and Engineer. In one volume, 12mo. $3.00

HARRIS.—Gas Superintendent's Pocket Companion.

By HARRIS & BROTHER, Gas Meter Manufacturers, 1115 and 1117 Cherry Street, Philadelphia. Full bound in pocket-book form $2.00

Hats and Felting:

A Practical Treatise on their Manufacture. By a Practical Hatter. Illustrated by Drawings of Machinery, etc. 8vo. $1.25

HOFMANN.—A Practical Treatise on the Manufacture of Paper in all its Branches.

By CARL HOFMANN. Late Superintendent of paper mills in Germany and the United States; recently manager of the Public Ledger Paper Mills, near Elkton, Md. Illustrated by 110 wood engravings, and five large folding plates. In one volume, 4to., cloth; 398 pages $15.00

HUGHES.—American Miller and Millwright's Assistant.

By WM. CARTER HUGHES. A new edition. In one vol., 12mo. $1.50

HURST.—A Hand-Book for Architectural Surveyors and others engaged in Building:

Containing Formulæ useful in Designing Builder's work, Table of Weights, of the materials used in Building, Memoranda connected with Builders' work, Mensuration, the Practice of Builders' Measurement, Contracts of Labor, Valuation of Property, Summary of the Practice in Dilapidation, etc., etc. By J. F. HURST, C. E. Second edition, pocket-book form, full bound $2.50

JERVIS.—Railway Property:

A Treatise on the Construction and Management of Railways; designed to afford useful knowledge, in the popular style, to the holders of this class of property; as well as Railway Managers, Officers, and Agents. By JOHN B. JERVIS, late Chief Engineer of the Hudson River Railroad, Croton Aqueduct, etc. In one vol., 12mo., cloth $2.00

JOHNSTON.—Instructions for the Analysis of Soils, Limestones, and Manures.

By J. F. W. JOHNSTON. 12mo. 38

KEENE.—A Hand-Book of Practical Gauging:

For the Use of Beginners, to which is added, A Chapter on Distillation, describing the process in operation at the Custom House for ascertaining the strength of wines. By JAMES B. KEENE, of H. M. Customs. 8vo. $1.25

KELLEY.—Speeches, Addresses, and Letters on Industrial and Financial Questions.

By Hon. WILLIAM D. KELLEY, M. C. In one volume, 544 pages, 8vo. $3.00

KENTISH.—A Treatise on a Box of Instruments,

And the Slide Rule; with the Theory of Trigonometry and Logarithms, including Practical Geometry, Surveying, Measuring of Timber, Cask and Malt Gauging, Heights, and Distances. By THOMAS KENTISH. In one volume. 12mo. $1.25

KOBELL.—ERNI.—Mineralogy Simplified:

A short Method of Determining and Classifying Minerals, by means of simple Chemical Experiments in the Wet Way. Translated from the last German Edition of F. VON KOBELL, with an Introduction to Blow-pipe Analysis and other additions. By HENRI ERNI, M. D., late Chief Chemist, Department of Agriculture, author of "Coal Oil and Petroleum." In one volume, 12mo. $2.50

LANDRIN.—A Treatise on Steel:

Comprising its Theory, Metallurgy, Properties, Practical Working, and Use. By M. H. C. LANDRIN, Jr., Civil Engineer. Translated from the French, with Notes, by A. A. FESQUET, Chemist and Engineer. With an Appendix on the Bessemer and the Martin Processes for Manufacturing Steel, from the Report of Abram S. Hewitt, United States Commissioner to the Universal Exposition, Paris, 1867. In one volume, 12mo. $3.00

LARKIN.—The Practical Brass and Iron Founder's Guide:

A Concise Treatise on Brass Founding, Moulding, the Metals and their Alloys, etc.: to which are added Recent Improvements in the Manufacture of Iron, Steel by the Bessemer Process, etc., etc. By JAMES LARKIN, late Conductor of the Brass Foundry Department in Reany, Neafie & Co's. Penn Works, Philadelphia. Fifth edition, revised, with Extensive additions. In one volume, 12mo. . . . $2.25

LEAVITT.—Facts about Peat as an Article of Fuel:

With Remarks upon its Origin and Composition, the Localities in which it is found, the Methods of Preparation and Manufacture, and the various Uses to which it is applicable; together with many other matters of Practical and Scientific Interest. To which is added a chapter on the Utilization of Coal Dust with Peat for the Production of an Excellent Fuel at Moderate Cost, specially adapted for Steam Service. By T. H. LEAVITT. Third edition. 12mo. $1.75

LEROUX, C.—A Practical Treatise on the Manufacture of Worsteds and Carded Yarns:

Comprising Practical Mechanics, with Rules and Calculations applied to Spinning; Sorting, Cleaning, and Scouring Wools; the English and French methods of Combing, Drawing, and Spinning Worsteds and Manufacturing Carded Yarns. Translated from the French of CHARLES LEROUX, Mechanical Engineer, and Superintendent of a Spinning Mill, by HORATIO PAINE, M. D., and A. A. FESQUET, Chemist and Engineer. Illustrated by 12 large Plates. To which is added an Appendix, containing extracts from the Reports of the International Jury, and of the Artisans selected by the Committee appointed by the Council of the Society of Arts, London, on Woollen and Worsted Machinery and Fabrics, as exhibited in the Paris Universal Exposition, 1867. 8vo., cloth. $5.00

LESLIE (Miss).—Complete Cookery:

Directions for Cookery in its Various Branches. By MISS LESLIE. 60th thousand. Thoroughly revised, with the addition of New Receipts. In one volume, 12mo., cloth. $1.50

LESLIE (Miss).—Ladies' House Book:

A Manual of Domestic Economy. 20th revised edition. 12mo., cloth.

LESLIE (Miss).—Two Hundred Receipts in French Cookery.

Cloth, 12mo.

LIEBER.—Assayer's Guide:

Or, Practical Directions to Assayers, Miners, and Smelters, for the Tests and Assays, by Heat and by Wet Processes, for the Ores of all the principal Metals, of Gold and Silver Coins and Alloys, and of Coal, etc. By OSCAR M. LIEBER. 12mo., cloth. . . . $1.25

LOTH.—The Practical Stair Builder:

A Complete Treatise on the Art of Building Stairs and Hand-Rails, Designed for Carpenters, Builders, and Stair-Builders. Illustrated with Thirty Original Plates. By C. EDWARD LOTH, Professional Stair-Builder. One large 4to. volume. $10.00

LOVE.—The Art of Dyeing, Cleaning, Scouring, and Finishing, on the Most Approved English and French Methods:

Being Practical Instructions in Dyeing Silks, Woollens, and Cottons, Feathers, Chips, Straw, etc. Scouring and Cleaning Bed and Window Curtains, Carpets, Rugs, etc. French and English Cleaning, any Color or Fabric of Silk, Satin, or Damask. By THOMAS LOVE, a Working Dyer and Scourer. Second American Edition, to which are added General Instructions for the Use of Aniline Colors. In one volume, 8vo., 343 pages. $5.00

MAIN and BROWN.—Questions on Subjects Connected with the Marine Steam-Engine:

And Examination Papers; with Hints for their Solution. By THOMAS J. MAIN, Professor of Mathematics, Royal Naval College, and THOMAS BROWN, Chief Engineer, R. N. 12mo., cloth. . . . $1.50

MAIN and BROWN.—The Indicator and Dynamometer:

With their Practical Applications to the Steam-Engine. By THOMAS J. MAIN, M. A. F. R., Assistant Professor Royal Naval College, Portsmouth, and THOMAS BROWN, Assoc. Inst. C. E., Chief Engineer, R. N., attached to the Royal Naval College. Illustrated. From the Fourth London Edition. 8vo. $1.50

MAIN and BROWN.—The Marine Steam-Engine.

By THOMAS J. MAIN, F. R.; Assistant S. Mathematical Professor at the Royal Naval College, Portsmouth, and THOMAS BROWN, Assoc. Inst. C. E., Chief Engineer R. N. Attached to the Royal Naval College. Authors of "Questions connected with the Marine Steam-Engine," and the "Indicator and Dynamometer." With numerous Illustrations. In one volume, 8vo. $5.00

MARTIN.—Screw-Cutting Tables, for the Use of Mechanical Engineers:

Showing the Proper Arrangement of Wheels for Cutting the Threads of Screws of any required Pitch; with a Table for Making the Universal Gas-Pipe Thread and Taps. By W. A. MARTIN, Engineer. 8vo. 50

Mechanics' (Amateur) Workshop:

A treatise containing plain and concise directions for the manipulation of Wood and Metals, including Casting, Forging, Brazing, Soldering, and Carpentry. By the author of the "Lathe and its Uses." Third edition. Illustrated. 8vo. $3.00

MOLESWORTH.—Pocket-Book of Useful Formulæ and Memoranda for Civil and Mechanical Engineers.

By GUILFORD L. MOLESWORTH, Member of the Institution of Civil Engineers, Chief Resident Engineer of the Ceylon Railway. Second American, from the Tenth London Edition. In one volume, full bound in pocket-book form. $2.00

NAPIER.—A System of Chemistry Applied to Dyeing.

By JAMES NAPIER, F. C. S. A New and Thoroughly Revised Edition. Completely brought up to the present state of the Science, including the Chemistry of Coal Tar Colors, by A. A. FESQUET, Chemist and Engineer. With an Appendix on Dyeing and Calico Printing, as shown at the Universal Exposition, Paris, 1867. Illustrated. In one volume, 8vo., 422 pages. $5.00

NAPIER.—Manual of Electro-Metallurgy:

Including the Application of the Art to Manufacturing Processes. By JAMES NAPIER. Fourth American, from the Fourth London edition, revised and enlarged. Illustrated by engravings. In one vol., 8vo. $2.00

NASON.—Table of Reactions for Qualitative Chemical Analysis.

By HENRY B. NASON, Professor of Chemistry in the Rensselaer Polytechnic Institute, Troy, New York. Illustrated by Colors. . 63

NEWBERY.—Gleanings from Ornamental Art of every style:

Drawn from Examples in the British, South Kensington, Indian, Crystal Palace, and other Museums, the Exhibitions of 1851 and 1862, and the best English and Foreign works. In a series of one hundred exquisitely drawn Plates, containing many hundred examples. By ROBERT NEWBERY. 4to. $15.00

NICHOLSON.—A Manual of the Art of Bookbinding:

Containing full instructions in the different Branches of Forwarding, Gilding, and Finishing. Also, the Art of Marbling Book-edges and Paper. By JAMES B. NICHOLSON. Illustrated. 12mo., cloth. $2.25

NICHOLSON.—The Carpenter's New Guide:

A Complete Book of Lines for Carpenters and Joiners. By PETER NICHOLSON. The whole carefully and thoroughly revised by H. K. DAVIS, and containing numerous new and improved and original Designs for Roofs, Domes, etc. By SAMUEL SLOAN, Architect. Illustrated by 80 plates. 4to. $4.50

NORRIS.—A Hand-book for Locomotive Engineers and Machinists:

Comprising the Proportions and Calculations for Constructing Locomotives; Manner of Setting Valves; Tables of Squares, Cubes, Areas, etc., etc. By SEPTIMUS NORRIS, Civil and Mechanical Engineer. New edition. Illustrated. 12mo., cloth. $2.00

NYSTROM.—On Technological Education, and the Construction of Ships and Screw Propellers:

For Naval and Marine Engineers. By JOHN W. NYSTROM, late Acting Chief Engineer, U. S. N. Second edition, revised with additional matter. Illustrated by seven engravings. 12mo. . . . $1.50

O'NEILL.—A Dictionary of Dyeing and Calico Printing:

Containing a brief account of all the Substances and Processes in use in the Art of Dyeing and Printing Textile Fabrics; with Practical Receipts and Scientific Information. By CHARLES O'NEILL, Analytical Chemist; Fellow of the Chemical Society of London; Member of the Literary and Philosophical Society of Manchester; Author of "Chemistry of Calico Printing and Dyeing." To which is added an Essay on Coal Tar Colors and their application to Dyeing and Calico Printing. By A. A. FESQUET, Chemist and Engineer. With an Appendix on Dyeing and Calico Printing, as shown at the Universal Exposition, Paris, 1867. In one volume, 8vo., 491 pages. . $6.00

ORTON.—Underground Treasures:

How and Where to Find Them. A Key for the Ready Determination of all the Useful Minerals within the United States. By JAMES ORTON, A. M. Illustrated, 12mo. $1.50

OSBORN.—American Mines and Mining:

Theoretically and Practically Considered. By Prof. H. S. OSBORN. Illustrated by numerous engravings. 8vo. (*In preparation.*)

OSBORN.—The Metallurgy of Iron and Steel:

Theoretical and Practical in all its Branches; with special reference to American Materials and Processes. By H. S. OSBORN, LL. D., Professor of Mining and Metallurgy in Lafayette College, Easton, Pennsylvania. Illustrated by numerous large folding plates and wood-engravings. 8vo. $15.00

OVERMAN.—The Manufacture of Steel:

Containing the Practice and Principles of Working and Making Steel. A Handbook for Blacksmiths and Workers in Steel and Iron, Wagon Makers, Die Sinkers, Cutlers, and Manufacturers of Files and Hardware, of Steel and Iron, and for Men of Science and Art. By FREDERICK OVERMAN, Mining Engineer, Author of the "Manufacture of Iron," etc. A new, enlarged, and revised Edition. By A. A. FESQUET, Chemist and Engineer. $1.50

OVERMAN.—The Moulder and Founder's Pocket Guide:

A Treatise on Moulding and Founding in Green-sand, Dry-sand, Loam, and Cement; the Moulding of Machine Frames, Mill-gear, Hollowware, Ornaments, Trinkets, Bells, and Statues; Description of Moulds for Iron, Bronze, Brass, and other Metals; Plaster of Paris, Sulphur, Wax, and other articles commonly used in Casting; the Construction of Melting Furnaces, the Melting and Founding of Metals; the Composition of Alloys and their Nature. With an Appendix containing Receipts for Alloys, Bronze, Varnishes and Colors for Castings; also, Tables on the Strength and other qualities of Cast Metals. By FREDERICK OVERMAN, Mining Engineer, Author of "The Manufacture of Iron." With 42 Illustrations. 12mo. $1.50

Painter, Gilder, and Varnisher's Companion:

Containing Rules and Regulations in everything relating to the Arts of Painting, Gilding, Varnishing, Glass-Staining, Graining, Marbling, Sign-Writing, Gilding on Glass, and Coach Painting and Varnishing; Tests for the Detection of Adulterations in Oils, Colors, etc.; and a Statement of the Diseases to which Painters are peculiarly liable, with the Simplest and Best Remedies. Sixteenth Edition. Revised, with an Appendix. Containing Colors and Coloring—Theoretical and Practical. Comprising descriptions of a great variety of Additional Pigments, their Qualities and Uses, to which are added, Dryers, and Modes and Operations of Painting, etc. Together with Chevreul's Principles of Harmony and Contrast of Colors. 12mo., cloth. $1.50

PALLETT.—The Miller's, Millwright's, and Engineer's Guide.

By HENRY PALLETT. Illustrated. In one volume, 12mo. $3.00

PERCY.—The Manufacture of Russian Sheet-Iron.

By JOHN PERCY, M.D., F.R.S., Lecturer on Metallurgy at the Royal School of Mines, and to The Advanced Class of Artillery Officers at the Royal Artillery Institution, Woolwich; Author of "Metallurgy." With Illustrations. 8vo., paper. . . . . 50 cts.

PERKINS.—Gas and Ventilation.

Practical Treatise on Gas and Ventilation. With Special Relation to Illuminating, Heating, and Cooking by Gas. Including Scientific Helps to Engineer-students and others. With Illustrated Diagrams. By E. E. PERKINS. 12mo., cloth. $1.25

PERKINS and STOWE.—A New Guide to the Sheet-iron and Boiler Plate Roller;

Containing a Series of Tables showing the Weight of Slabs and Piles to produce Boiler Plates, and of the Weight of Piles and the Sizes of Bars to produce Sheet-iron; the Thickness of the Bar Gauge in decimals; the Weight per foot, and the Thickness on the Bar or Wire Gauge of the fractional parts of an inch; the Weight per sheet, and the Thickness on the Wire Gauge of Sheet-iron of various dimensions to weigh 112 lbs. per bundle; and the conversion of Short Weight into Long Weight, and Long Weight into Short. Estimated and collected by G. H. PERKINS and J. G. STOWE. $2.50

PHILLIPS and DARLINGTON.—Records of Mining and Metallurgy;

Or Facts and Memoranda for the use of the Mine Agent and Smelter. By J. ARTHUR PHILLIPS, Mining Engineer, Graduate of the Imperial School of Mines, France, etc., and JOHN DARLINGTON. Illustrated by numerous engravings. In one volume, 12mo. . . . $2.00

PROTEAUX.—Practical Guide for the Manufacture of Paper and Boards.

By A. PROTEAUX, Civil Engineer, and Graduate of the School of Arts and Manufactures, and Director of Thiers' Paper Mill, Puy-de-Dôme. With additions, by L. S. LE NORMAND. Translated from the French, with Notes, by HORATIO PAINE, A. B., M. D. To which is added a Chapter on the Manufacture of Paper from Wood in the United States, by HENRY T. BROWN, of the "American Artisan." Illustrated by six plates, containing Drawings of Raw Materials, Machinery, Plans of Paper-Mills, etc., etc. 8vo. $10.00

REGNAULT.—Elements of Chemistry.

By M. V. REGNAULT. Translated from the French by T. FORREST BETTON, M. D., and edited, with Notes, by JAMES C. BOOTH, Melter and Refiner U. S. Mint, and WM. L. FABER, Metallurgist and Mining Engineer. Illustrated by nearly 700 wood engravings. Comprising nearly 1500 pages. In two volumes, 8vo., cloth. $7.50

REID.—A Practical Treatise on the Manufacture of Portland Cement:

By HENRY REID, C. E. To which is added a Translation of M. A. Lipowitz's Work, describing a New Method adopted in Germany for Manufacturing that Cement, by W. F. REID. Illustrated by plates and wood engravings. 8vo. $6.00

RIFFAULT, VERGNAUD, and TOUSSAINT.—A Practical Treatise on the Manufacture of Varnishes.

By MM. RIFFAULT, VERGNAUD, and TOUSSAINT. Revised and Edited by M. F. MALEPEYRE and Dr. EMIL WINCKLER. Illustrated. In one volume, 8vo. (*In preparation.*)

RIFFAULT, VERGNAUD, and TOUSSAINT.—A Practical Treatise on the Manufacture of Colors for Painting:

Containing the best Formulæ and the Processes the Newest and in most General Use. By MM. RIFFAULT, VERGNAUD, and TOUSSAINT. Revised and Edited by M. F. MALEPEYRE and Dr. EMIL WINCKLER. Translated from the French by A. A. FESQUET, Chemist and Engineer. Illustrated by Engravings. In one volume, 650 pages, 8vo. $7.50

ROBINSON.—Explosions of Steam Boilers:

How they are Caused, and how they may be Prevented. By J. R. ROBINSON, Steam Engineer. 12mo. $1.25

ROPER.—A Catechism of High Pressure or Non-Condensing Steam-Engines:

Including the Modelling, Constructing, Running, and Management of Steam Engines and Steam Boilers. With Illustrations. By STEPHEN ROPER, Engineer. Full bound tucks $2.00

ROSELEUR.—Galvanoplastic Manipulations:

A Practical Guide for the Gold and Silver Electro-plater and the Galvanoplastic Operator. Translated from the French of ALFRED ROSELEUR, Chemist, Professor of the Galvanoplastic Art, Manufacturer of Chemicals, Gold and Silver Electro-plater. By A. A. FESQUET, Chemist and Engineer. Illustrated by over 127 Engravings on wood. 8vo., 495 pages. $6.00

☞ *This Treatise is the fullest and by far the best on this subject ever published in the United States.*

SCHINZ.—Researches on the Action of the Blast Furnace.

By CHARLES SCHINZ. Translated from the German with the special permission of the Author by WILLIAM H. MAW and MORITZ MULLER. With an Appendix written by the Author expressly for this edition. Illustrated by seven plates, containing 28 figures. In one volume, 12mo. $4.25

SHAW.—Civil Architecture:

Being a Complete Theoretical and Practical System of Building, containing the Fundamental Principles of the Art. By EDWARD SHAW, Architect. To which is added a Treatise on Gothic Architecture, etc. By THOMAS W. SILLOWAY and GEORGE M. HARDING, Architects. The whole illustrated by One Hundred and Two quarto plates finely engraved on copper. Eleventh Edition. 4to., cloth. . $10.00

SHUNK.—A Practical Treatise on Railway Curves and Location, for Young Engineers.

By WILLIAM F. SHUNK, Civil Engineer. 12mo. . . $2.00

SLOAN.—American Houses:

A variety of Original Designs for Rural Buildings. Illustrated by 26 colored Engravings, with Descriptive References. By SAMUEL SLOAN, Architect, author of the "Model Architect," etc., etc. 8vo. $2.50

SMEATON.—Builder's Pocket Companion:

Containing the Elements of Building, Surveying, and Architecture; with Practical Rules and Instructions connected with the subject. By A. C. SMEATON, Civil Engineer, etc. In one volume, 12mo. $1.50

SMITH.—A Manual of Political Economy.

By E. PESHINE SMITH. A new Edition, to which is added a full Index. 12mo., cloth. $1.25

SMITH.—Parks and Pleasure Grounds:

Or Practical Notes on Country Residences, Villas, Public Parks, and Gardens. By CHARLES H. J. SMITH, Landscape Gardener and Garden Architect, etc., etc. 12mo. $2.25

SMITH.—The Dyer's Instructor:

Comprising Practical Instructions in the Art of Dyeing Silk, Cotton, Wool, and Worsted, and Woollen Goods: containing nearly 800 Receipts. To which is added a Treatise on the Art of Padding; and the Printing of Silk Warps, Skeins, and Handkerchiefs, and the various Mordants and Colors for the different styles of such work. By DAVID SMITH, Pattern Dyer. 12mo., cloth. $3.00

SMITH.—The Practical Dyer's Guide:

Comprising Practical Instructions in the Dyeing of Shot Cobourgs, Silk Striped Orleans, Colored Orleans from Black Warps, Ditto from White Warps, Colored Cobourgs from White Warps, Merinos, Yarns, Woollen Cloths, etc. Containing nearly 300 Receipts, to most of which a Dyed Pattern is annexed. Also, A Treatise on the Art of Padding. By DAVID SMITH. In one volume, 8vo. Price. . . . $25.00

STEWART.—The American System.

Speeches on the Tariff Question, and on Internal Improvements, principally delivered in the House of Representatives of the United States. By ANDREW STEWART, late M. C. from Pennsylvania. With a Portrait, and a Biographical Sketch. In one volume, 8vo., 407 pages. $3.00

STOKES.—Cabinet-maker's and Upholsterer's Companion:

Comprising the Rudiments and Principles of Cabinet-making and Upholstery, with Familiar Instructions, Illustrated by Examples for attaining a Proficiency in the Art of Drawing, as applicable to Cabinet-work; the Processes of Veneering, Inlaying, and Buhl-work; the Art of Dyeing and Staining Wood, Bone, Tortoise Shell, etc. Directions for Lackering, Japanning, and Varnishing; to make French Polish; to prepare the Best Glues, Cements, and Compositions, and a number of Receipts particularly useful for workmen generally. By J. STOKES. In one volume, 12mo. With Illustrations. . $1.25

Strength and other Properties of Metals:

Reports of Experiments on the Strength and other Properties of Metals for Cannon. With a Description of the Machines for testing Metals, and of the Classification of Cannon in service. By Officers of the Ordnance Department U. S. Army. By authority of the Secretary of War. Illustrated by 25 large steel plates. In one volume, 4to. . $10.00

SULLIVAN.—Protection to Native Industry.

By Sir EDWARD SULLIVAN, Baronet, author of "Ten Chapters on Social Reforms." In one volume, 8vo. $1.50

Tables Showing the Weight of Round, Square, and Flat Bar Iron, Steel, etc.,

By Measurement. Cloth. 63

TAYLOR.—Statistics of Coal:

Including Mineral Bituminous Substances employed in Arts and Manufactures; with their Geographical, Geological, and Commercial Distribution and Amount of Production and Consumption on the American Continent. With Incidental Statistics of the Iron Manufacture. By R. C. TAYLOR. Second edition, revised by S. S. HALDEMAN. Illustrated by five Maps and many wood engravings. 8vo., cloth. $10.00

TEMPLETON.—The Practical Examinator on Steam and the Steam-Engine:

With Instructive References relative thereto, arranged for the Use of Engineers, Students, and others. By WM. TEMPLETON, Engineer. 12mo. $1.25

THOMAS.—The Modern Practice of Photography.

By R. W. THOMAS, F. C. S. 8vo., cloth. 75

THOMSON.—Freight Charges Calculator.

By ANDREW THOMSON, Freight Agent. 24mo. $1.25

TURNING: Specimens of Fancy Turning Executed on the Hand or Foot Lathe:

With Geometric, Oval, and Eccentric Chucks, and Elliptical Cutting Frame. By an Amateur. Illustrated by 30 exquisite Photographs. 4to. $3.00

Turner's (The) Companion:

Containing Instructions in Concentric, Elliptic, and Eccentric Turning: also various Plates of Chucks, Tools, and Instruments; and Directions for using the Eccentric Cutter, Drill, Vertical Cutter, and Circular Rest; with Patterns and Instructions for working them. A new edition in one volume, 12mo. $1.50

URBIN.—BRULL.—A Practical Guide for Puddling Iron and Steel.

By ED. URBIN, Engineer of Arts and Manufactures. A Prize Essay read before the Association of Engineers, Graduate of the School of Mines, of Liege, Belgium, at the Meeting of 1865–6. To which is added A COMPARISON OF THE RESISTING PROPERTIES OF IRON AND STEEL. By A. BRULL. Translated from the French by A. A. FESQUET, Chemist and Engineer. In one volume, 8vo. $1.00

VAILE.—Galvanized Iron Cornice-Worker's Manual:

Containing Instructions in Laying out the Different Mitres, and Making Patterns for all kinds of Plain and Circular Work. Also, Tables of Weights, Areas and Circumferences of Circles, and other Matter calculated to Benefit the Trade. By CHARLES A. VAILE, Superintendent "Richmond Cornice Works," Richmond, Indiana. Illustrated by 21 Plates. In one volume, 4to. $5.00

VILLE.—The School of Chemical Manures:

Or, Elementary Principles in the Use of Fertilizing Agents. From the French of M. GEORGE VILLE, by A. A. FESQUET, Chemist and Engineer. With Illustrations. In one volume, 12 mo. . . . $1.25

VOGDES.—The Architect's and Builder's Pocket Companion and Price Book:

Consisting of a Short but Comprehensive Epitome of Decimals, Duodecimals, Geometry and Mensuration; with Tables of U. S. Measures, Sizes, Weights, Strengths, etc., of Iron, Wood, Stone, and various other Materials, Quantities of Materials in Given Sizes, and Dimensions of Wood, Brick, and Stone; and a full and complete Bill of Prices for Carpenter's Work; also, Rules for Computing and Valuing Brick and Brick Work, Stone Work, Painting, Plastering, etc. By FRANK W. VOGDES, Architect. Illustrated. Full bound in pocket-book form. $2.00
Bound in cloth. 1.50

WARN.—The Sheet-Metal Worker's Instructor:

For Zinc, Sheet-Iron, Copper, and Tin-Plate Workers, etc. Containing a selection of Geometrical Problems; also, Practical and Simple Rules for describing the various Patterns required in the different branches of the above Trades. By REUBEN H. WARN, Practical Tin-plate Worker. To which is added an Appendix, containing Instructions for Boiler Making, Mensuration of Surfaces and Solids, Rules for Calculating the Weights of different Figures of Iron and Steel, Tables of the Weights of Iron, Steel, etc. Illustrated by 32 Plates and 37 Wood Engravings. 8vo. $3.00

WARNER.—New Theorems, Tables, and Diagrams for the Computation of Earth-Work:

Designed for the use of Engineers in Preliminary and Final Estimates, of Students in Engineering, and of Contractors and other non-professional Computers. In Two Parts, with an Appendix. Part I.—A Practical Treatise; Part II.—A Theoretical Treatise; and the Appendix. Containing Notes to the Rules and Examples of Part I.; Explanations of the Construction of Scales, Tables, and Diagrams, and a Treatise upon Equivalent Square Bases and Equivalent Level Heights. The whole illustrated by numerous original Engravings, comprising Explanatory Cuts for Definitions and Problems, Stereometric Scales and Diagrams, and a Series of Lithographic Drawings from Models, showing all the Combinations of Solid Forms which occur in Railroad Excavations and Embankments. By JOHN WARNER, A. M., Mining and Mechanical Engineer. 8vo. $5.00

WATSON.—A Manual of the Hand-Lathe:

Comprising Concise Directions for working Metals of all kinds, Ivory, Bone and Precious Woods; Dyeing, Coloring, and French Polishing; Inlaying by Veneers, and various methods practised to produce Elaborate work with Dispatch, and at Small Expense. By EGBERT P. WATSON, late of "The Scientific American," Author of "The Modern Practice of American Machinists and Engineers." Illustrated by 78 Engravings. $1.50

WATSON.—The Modern Practice of American Machinists and Engineers:

Including the Construction, Application, and Use of Drills, Lathe Tools, Cutters for Boring Cylinders, and Hollow Work Generally, with the most Economical Speed for the same; the Results verified by Actual Practice at the Lathe, the Vice, and on the Floor. Together with Workshop Management, Economy of Manufacture, the Steam-Engine, Boilers, Gears, Belting, etc., etc. By EGBERT P. WATSON, late of the "Scientific American." Illustrated by 86 Engravings. In one volume, 12mo. $2.50

WATSON.—The Theory and Practice of the Art of Weaving by Hand and Power:

With Calculations and Tables for the use of those connected with the Trade. By JOHN WATSON, Manufacturer and Practical Machine Maker. Illustrated by large Drawings of the best Power Looms. 8vo. $10.00

WEATHERLY.—Treatise on the Art of Boiling Sugar, Crystallizing, Lozenge-making, Comfits, Gum Goods.

12mo. $2.00

WEDDING.—The Metallurgy of Iron;

Theoretically and Practically Considered. By Dr. HERMANN WEDDING, Professor of the Metallurgy of Iron at the Royal Mining Academy, Berlin. Translated by JULIUS DU MONT, Bethlehem, Pa. Illustrated by 207 Engravings on Wood, and three Plates. In one volume, 8vo. (*In press.*)

WILL.—Tables for Qualitative Chemical Analysis.

By Professor HEINRICH WILL, of Giessen, Germany. Seventh edition. Translated by CHARLES F. HIMES, Ph. D., Professor of Natural Science, Dickinson College, Carlisle, Pa. . . . $1.50

WILLIAMS.—On Heat and Steam:

Embracing New Views of Vaporization, Condensation, and Explosions. By CHARLES WYE WILLIAMS, A. I. C. E. Illustrated. 8vo. $3.50

WOHLER.—A Hand-Book of Mineral Analysis.

By F. WOHLER, Professor of Chemistry in the University of Göttingen. Edited by HENRY B. NASON, Professor of Chemistry in the Rensselaer Polytechnic Institute, Troy, New York. Illustrated. In one volume, 12mo. $3 00

WORSSAM.—On Mechanical Saws:

From the Transactions of the Society of Engineers, 1869. By S. W. WORSSAM, Jr. Illustrated by 18 large plates. 8vo. . . . $5.00

www.ingramcontent.com/pod-product-compliance
Lightning Source LLC
Chambersburg PA
CBHW031936290426
44108CB00011B/573

* 9 7 8 3 7 4 2 8 0 2 2 3 1 *